WITH BAYONETS FIXED

WITH BAYONETS FIXED

FIXED

12th and 13th (Service) Battalions of
the Durham Light Infantry

1914–1918

John Sheen

Pen & Sword
MILITARY

This book is dedicated to the memory of the Officers, Warrant Officers, Non Commissioned Officers and men of the

12th and 13th Battalions Durham Light Infantry 1914–1918

First published in Great Britain in 2013 by
Pen & Sword Military
an imprint of
Pen & Sword Books Ltd
47 Church Street
Barnsley
South Yorkshire
S70 2AS

Copyright © John Sheen, 2013

ISBN 9781781590324

A CIP catalogue record for this book is
available from the British Library.

Typeset in Palatino 10pt

Printed and bound in the United Kingdom by CPI

Pen & Sword Books Ltd incorporates the imprints of Pen & Sword Aviation, Pen & Sword
Maritime, Pen & Sword Military, Wharncliffe Local History, Pen and Sword Select, Pen and
Sword Military Classics and Leo Cooper.

For a complete list of Pen & Sword titles, please contact
Pen & Sword Books Limited
47 Church Street, Barnsley, South Yorkshire, S70 2AS, England
E-mail: enquiries@pen-and-sword.co.uk
Website: www.pen-and-sword.co.uk

CONTENTS

Foreword

Having completed works on the locally-raised (Pals) battalions of the regiment and then a volume on the 2nd Regular Battalion, it seemed to me that the run-of-the-mill Service Battalions were largely forgotten. Yes, they had been covered in *The Durham Forces in the Field* by Captain Wilfred Miles but that book covered ten service battalions and then skimmed over their activities. Only gallantry winners are mentioned by name and very often the deeds of individual men are not recorded unless a VC winner.

With the 12th and 13th Battalions serving together in 68 Brigade, a volume on these two battalions was a feasible project. However, true to form, while there was a lot of material about the 13th Battalion in the form of letters, diaries and photographs the same could not be said for the 12th Battalion. Where the War Diary of the 13th went into detailed dispositions, the Diary of the 12th simply recorded 'Battalion in the trenches'.

The release of the Soldiers Documents to the National Archives and these now being available online has made this book much closer to the soldiers than previously possible. The Documents for many of the dead of the 12th and 13th Durham Light Infantry have largely survived, although badly damaged by fire and water. From these I have managed to extract some very tragic stories from the records of Courts of Inquiry after cases of accidental death by shooting, drowning or traffic accident. This has added the voices of those making statements to the book, and given an insight to the day-to-day activities of an infantry battalion.

This is the story of two 'Faithful' battalions of the Durham Light Infantry that fought in France, Flanders and Italy during the Great War. The fighting spirit and determination of the two battalions comes through as part of the 23rd Division, a formation that never failed to take an objective and which once taken was very seldom lost.

John Sheen
Durham
29 November 2012

Acknowledgements

Thanks are due to many people, and this work could not have been completed without the support of the Trustees of The Durham Light Infantry Museum and Major (Retd) Chris Lawton, The Rifles Secretary, Durham Office.

Also Steve Shannon at The Durham Light Infantry Museum; his help and advice as always have been greatly appreciated. Since the work started Steve has retired, but Alastair Bowden his temporary replacement has been just as helpful.

The staff at Durham City Library, Darlington Library and Gateshead Library.

The Staff at the Durham County Record Office. In particular Gill Parkes and the County Archivist Liz Bregazzi.

The late Mr Malcolm MacGregor for assistance with Honours and Gallantry Awards to members of the 12th and 13th Battalions.

Clive Dunn, Malcolm Anderson, and Andrew Brookes who loaned material from their collections and Andrew Jukes of the Hexham Medal Centre who allowed me to copy and use material that came through his shop.

Pam and Ken Linge of the Thiepval Project who passed on photos.

Sean Godfrey of the Teesside Branch of the WFA who helped with obtaining photographs.

Last but not least those relatives who loaned photographs of individual soldiers.

Bibliography

The Regimental Archives of the Durham Light Infantry are now held at Durham County Record Office.

Local newspapers: *Durham Chronicle, Durham Advertiser, North Star, Chester le Street Chronicle, Consett and Stanley Chronicle.*

Personal photographs – from collectors, family, author's collection or Regimental Archives.

Officers Died in the Great War, 1914–1919
Soldiers Died in the Great War, 1914–1919: Part 62, The Durham Light Infantry
Becke, Major A. F., *Order of Battle of Divisions: Part 1 – The Regular British Divisions*
James, Brigadier E. A., OBE, TD, *British Regiments, 1914–18* (Samson Books Ltd, 1978)
Moore, William, *The Durham Light Infantry* (Leo Cooper Ltd, 1975)
Military Operations, France and Belgium, 1915, 1916, 1917, 1918
Military Operations, Italy 1915–1919
The British Army Review No 106

MAPS

Chapter One

The County Regiment

THE DURHAM LIGHT INFANTRY first came into being on 29 September 1756 as the Second Battalion of Lieutenant-General Huske's Regiment or the 23rd Regiment of Foot, later the Royal Welch Fusiliers. At that time fifteen regiments of infantry were authorised to raise second battalions. In 1758 these second battalions became separate regiments and were numbered between 61 and 75, thus the second battalion of the 23rd Regiment, Lieutenant-General Huske's, became the 68th Regiment. The battalion was raised in the Leicester area where it remained until the end of April 1757 when a move was made to Berkshire, followed by further moves made to Chatham and Dover. Then both battalions of the 23rd marched to the Isle of Wight in 1758, and it was here that the two regiments separated and the 2nd Battalion 23rd Regiment became the 68th Regiment of Foot.

In 1782 General John Lambton had the 68th linked to his home county of Durham.

It was on 13 May 1758 that Lieutenant-Colonel John Lambton of the Coldstream Guards was authorised to raise recruits, 'by beat of drum or otherwise in any county or part of our kingdom'. In 1782 Lambton had the 68th linked to his home county of Durham, although not many of the men were recruited from the county at that time; indeed there were probably more Irishmen than English. The regiment saw its first action in a raid on the French coast, at Cancale on the coast of Brittany. A few days were spent ashore before withdrawing to the ships and sailing back to the Isle of Wight. In July another successful raid took place but in September a third raid went wrong and the Grenadier Company of the 68th along with the grenadiers of the other regiments involved suffered casualties when covering the retreat to the ships.

The next posting for the regiment was to the West Indies; in 1764 the regiment sailed to the island of Antigua. Here they lost 150 men to fever and still more were lost to disease in St Vincent before returning to Britain. They were posted back to the West Indies in 1794, to St Lucia and then to Grenada, where fever took its toll of all ranks. By the middle of

1796 there were only sixty men fit for duty. After being sent back to England and reformed, they returned to St Lucia for a number of years and again lost many men to disease. Returning to England again the regiment was selected to train as light infantry; skirmishers who used their initiative, using the tactics of fire and manoeuvre and carrying out orders by bugle call. Armed with an improved musket, with better sights and a dull or browned barrel, the regiment was soon called to action. Its first action as a regiment of light infantry was as part of the invasion of the island of Walcheren on the Dutch coast. After taking part in the capture of Flushing the 68th joined the garrison of South Beveland. For six months they remained here losing men daily to the 'Walcheren Fever', a kind of malaria that even after the regiment returned to England was rife among the ranks. Refitted and reorganised the regiment's next posting was to General Wellington's army in Spain. Here they took part in the battles of Salamanca and Vitoria and the fighting in the Pyrenees. They didn't play any part in the final defeat of Napoleon at Waterloo and over the next forty years in postings to Canada, Jamaica and Gibraltar established a reputation as a smart regiment.

The year 1854 was the next time the regiment would see action; from their base in Malta the 68th joined the 4th Division and sailed for the Crimea to fight the Russians. Although they were present at the Battle of the Alma on 20 September, the regiment saw little action. However, on 5 November at the Battle of Inkerman, Private John Byrne won the regiment's first Victoria Cross when he rescued a wounded man under enemy fire. A second Victoria Cross was awarded to the regiment in May 1855 to Captain T. de C. Hamilton for action at Sebastopol. The force he

At the Battle of the Alma on 20 September the regiment saw little action.

Bugler M. Sherry, well covered in fur skins against the cold of the Crimean winter.

Colour Sergeant Henry Sladden DCM 68th; in 1860 he became the Regimental Quartermaster.

commanded was attacked by the Russians: at midnight, in a howling gale they managed to enter the trench held by the 68th and spike one of the regiment's guns. Captain Hamilton immediately led a counter-attack and recovered the weapon, during which time they killed two Russian officers and a number of their men. The conditions in the Crimea were miserable but the regiment remained until the end. This was the first war to have a photographer with the army in the field and the outstanding thing to emerge was the bravery of the soldiers and the conditions that they endured, while the generals displayed a total mismanagement and indifference to their suffering. It is largely due to the war correspondents that changes to the army were brought about.

There followed a few pleasant years in stations around the Mediterranean before the regiment finally arrived back in England in 1857. However, the government didn't keep the 68th sitting about at home: within three months the regiment was on its way to Burma and afterwards in 1863 to New Zealand. In one of Queen Victoria's 'little wars'

The graves of soldiers of the 68th Light Infantry who died at Te Ranga, New Zealand, in 1864.

The Maori, a brave and resourceful warrior, fought hard and was a difficult opponent. D/DLI/2/1/308(3)

a fierce conflict took place in those South Sea Islands where the Maoris, the native people of New Zealand, resented the fact that their lands were being stolen. The Maori, a brave and resourceful warrior, fought hard and was a difficult opponent. The 68th had to take them on hand-to-hand and on 21 June 1864 Sergeant John Murray won the regiment's third Victoria Cross, leading a bayonet charge, in which he saved the life of Private Byrne VC by killing a Maori who was just about to kill Byrne. The war ended and by 1866 the regiment was back in England. After six years at home it was posted to India.

In 1881 Cardwell, the Secretary of State for War in the Liberal Government, brought in some sweeping changes to the army. He linked all infantry regiments to a county, and for all those without a second battalion, he linked them to another regiment. The 68th, already with Durham in its title, became linked with the 106th Bombay Light Infantry.

The 106th started life in 1839 as the 2nd Bombay Europeans in the Honourable East India Company's forces. They saw action in Persia at the battles of Reshire and Bushire in 1856, and when taken onto the British Army establishment became the 106th Bombay European Light Infantry. From 1881 the two regiments became the 1st and 2nd Battalions of the

12

Durham Light Infantry. One of the other ideas of the reforms was that a regiment would always have one battalion overseas and one battalion stationed in the United Kingdom, the home battalion supplying drafts of men to the overseas battalion. The regiment next saw action in 1885 in the Soudan, where 2/Durham LI fought at the Battle of Ginnis against the wild Dervishers of the Mahdi's forces who had taken Khartoum and killed General Gordon and the garrison.

Throughout the 1890s 2/Durham LI served in India where they excelled on the polo field: training their own ponies, they won many cups, beating and upsetting many rich cavalry regiments along the way.

The next time the regiment went into action was in South Africa during the Boer War. Ordered out in October 1899 as part of the Army Corps under the command of Sir Redvers Buller, 1/Durham LI won fame on 5 February 1900 when they stormed the hill at Vaal Krantz. With 3/King's Royal Rifle Corps on their right, in extended line the two battalions advanced, taking casualties from enfilading rifle fire from a hill known as

Group photograph of officers of the 68th Light Infantry, and an Indian man, 'Bhickaju', taken at Poona, India, 1872. Left to right: Captain Kay, Lieutenant Spencer, Lieutenant H.J. Tollemache, Assistant Surgeon Burnett, Lieutenant Molyneux, Lieutenant Mansel, Quartermaster Sladden, Lieutenant Fulton, Lieutenant Barnard, Paymaster Heatley, Lieutenant Stewart, Lieutenant-Colonel Kirby, Lieutenant Stanley, Lieutenant Tickell, Major Blood, Captain Covey, Lieutenant Hilliard, Lieutenant Burton, Captain Boulderson, Lieutenant Woodland, Lieutenant and Adjutant Hood, Lieutenant Tyndall. D/DLI/2/1/266/1

At Colenso 1/DLI, part of Lyttelton's 4th Brigade, assisted in extracting Hart's Irish Brigade which had taken numerous casualties. D/DLI/2/1/19(10)

Men of 1/DLI receive mail from home out on the South African veldt. D/DLI/2/1/270(60)

Doorn Kloof. They pressed on up Vaal Krantz and took the crest at bayonet point; as they advanced up the steep hill, the regiment left a number of dead and wounded along the way from the rifle fire of the Boer marksmen armed with their Mauser rifles. On 6 February the Boers launched a counter-attack which retook some of the ground they had lost the previous day. However, the British troops were rallied and a brilliant bayonet charge by the Durhams and KRRC regained all the ground that the Boers had recaptured. After the Relief of Ladysmith, the regiment was employed guarding blockhouses along the railway and patrolling the countryside. They were joined by the Volunteer Company formed from the Volunteer Battalions of the Durham Light Infantry, the Territorials of their day.

The taking of the summit of Vaal Krantz is one of the regiment's famous actions.

At the Delhi Durbar in 1911 1/DLI paraded the old Colours with the Queen's Crown and the new Colours with the King's Crown. D/DLI/2/1/274(20)

In 1908, Lord Haldane brought about changes to the Volunteer movement and created the Territorial Force. All the Rifle Volunteer battalions were renumbered and became battalions in the new force; thus the 5th Stockton, 6th Bishop Auckland, 7th Sunderland, 8th Durham City and 9th Gateshead Battalions of the regiment came into being, the 3rd (Reserve) and 4th (Extra Reserve) Battalions being draft-finding units for the two regular battalions. By 1914 1/Durham LI had been back in India for several years and had seen some action on the North-West Frontier; 2/Durham LI was stationed at Lichfield in Staffordshire, with one company detached at South Shields.

Lord Haldane.

Chapter Two

The Call to Arms

O N THE BRIGHT SUNNY MORNING of Sunday 28 June 1914, the visit of the Archduke Franz Ferdinand and his wife, the Duchess Sophie, to Sarajevo, the capital of the Austrian province of Bosnia-Herzegovina was to set Europe alight. It was a National Fête Day and the streets were decked with flags and thronged with people as the royal train arrived at the station. Security arrangements began to go wrong almost immediately: when the royal cars left the railway station, the security detectives were left behind and only three local policemen were present with the royal party. The Archduke with General Oskar Potiorek, the Military Governor, travelled in an open-top sports car, which, at the Archduke's request, travelled slowly so he could have a good look at the town.

As the car drove along the Appel Quay, near the Central Police Station

The Royal Party travelled slowly along the Appel Quay in order that the Archduke could have a good view of the town.

Crowds gathered to witness the carnage caused by the bomb.

a tall young man named Cabrinovic threw a hand grenade at the car. The grenade bounced off the folded roof and exploded under the following car, wounding several officers. Despite the threat, Archduke Ferdinand ordered a halt to find out who had been injured and it was now that it was discovered that a grenade fragment had grazed the Duchess. Archduke Franz Ferdinand arrived at the town hall in an outrage and decided to

brinovic – threw bomb.

Princip – fired shots.

visit one of the wounded officers who had been taken to a nearby military hospital; he would then continue with the visit to a local museum as arranged. The cars left the town hall and went back along the Appel Quay, this time at high speed, but the drivers had not been told of the unplanned visit to the military hospital. The first two cars turned right at the corner of Appel Quay and Franz Josef Street but General Potiorek shouted at the driver of the third car that he was making a mistake. The driver, obviously confused, braked sharply and brought the car to a halt, in the worst possible place. Standing right at the spot was a young Bosnian, Gavrilo Princip, who emerged from the crowd only some three or four paces from the Archduke's vehicle. Drawing a pistol he fired two shots into the car; the first mortally wounded the Archduke and the second struck the Duchess Sophie in the abdomen. The car raced to the Governor's official residence but the bumpy ride only made matters worse and the royal couple were pronounced dead shortly after arrival.

If Austria-Hungary was to continue as a world power this outrage could not go unchallenged.

If Austria-Hungary declared war on Serbia, this would bring in the Russians, but Austria was allied to Germany and as early as the beginning of July the Kaiser, who was a personal friend of the Archduke, is reported to have said 'The Serbs must be disposed of'. Then on 23 July the Austrian Government sent a strong memorandum to the Serbs listing ten demands, the strongest of which was that Serbia allow Austria to suppress local agitation and subversion directed against her. Although the Serbs accepted most of Austria's conditions Austria deemed it inadequate and declared war. The nations of Europe rushed to mobilise: the Tsar, Nicholas II of Russia tried to maintain peace but the Russian Army mobilised on 31 July. To counter this Germany declared war on Russia, having first offered France the chance to stay out of the conflict and remain neutral. The French, however, remained true to their treaties and refused the German offer; the Germans therefore declared war on France. Having declared war on France, on 3 August the Imperial German Army crossed the border into Luxembourg and threatened to move into Belgium. Belgium had mobilised on 2 August and the Germans sent an ultimatum on the pretext that the French had crossed the border into Belgium. The French in fact had retired so that they could not give any cause for such an accusation. The note said that if the Belgian Army could not stop the French the Germans would, and if the Belgians resisted then it would be considered an act of war. The Belgian border with Germany was covered by a line of forts and the key to these was the fort at Liege on the river Meuse. The main invasion of Belgium began on 4 August, although a cavalry patrol had crossed on 3 August. The German cavalry moved quickly through the frontier towns and villages, their task

On 30 July, more by luck than planning, the majority of the Territorial Army were on their annual camp. Here men of 8/DLI take a break from the route march.

to capture the bridges over the Meuse before the defenders could blow them up. They also had the task of providing a screen in front of the advancing infantry and carrying out advance reconnaissance.

Meanwhile in England mobilisation had been ordered. On 30 July, more by luck than planning, the majority of the Territorial Army were on their

A group of German soldiers under the command of a senior NCO pose for the camera before they leave for the front.

annual camp. They were recalled to their home drill halls and the *Durham Chronicle* recorded the arrival of 8/Durham LI back in Durham City with these words:

> The 8th Durham Light Infantry under Colonel Blackett returned from their camp at Conway early this morning and headed by the regimental band marched through the streets from the station to the Market Place, where they bivouacked. The men attracted a great deal of attention during the morning and the unusual spectacle was witnessed of their meal being cooked and partaken of in the Market Place. At mid-day the men were released until evening, when they were to assemble for a route march and it is expected that tomorrow they will proceed to any station that has been allotted to them by the War Office. The Territorials had been expected about midnight and crowds of people had assembled at the station to meet them and passed away the waiting hours singing patriotic and national songs.

Most Territorial units were quickly moved to their war stations guarding vulnerable points on the coast and along railway lines and docks. The Belgians had a treaty with England and when the German Army crossed the frontier, Britain sent an ultimatum to Berlin. No reply was received so the British Empire declared war on Germany on 4 August 1914. The British Army at home in England and Ireland had been organised as an Expeditionary Force of six infantry and one cavalry divisions and at a meeting of the principal Ministers, including Lord Kitchener who became Secretary of State for War on 6 August, the decision was taken to send four infantry divisions and the cavalry division to France on 9 August. The other decision taken by Kitchener was to raise New Armies, each army of six more divisions of civilian volunteers and on 7 August, he appealed for the 100,000. He launched his poster 'Your Country Needs You' and the recruiting offices were packed with recruits, over 10,000 men enlisting in five days.

All over the county the news of Lord Kitchener's appeal appeared in the local press and this was added to by local dignitaries. On 7 August the Lord Mayor of Durham issued an appeal in the *Durham Chronicle* after he received two appeals from the Royal Family. Under the heading, 'The Mayor of Durham's appeal', the following message was printed:

> To the Citizens of Durham. I have received the following appeals:
>
> From His Royal Highness the Prince of Wales:-
> Buckingham Palace.
> All must realise that the present time of deep anxiety will

...our King and Country Need You.

A CALL TO ARMS.

...a addition of 100,000 men to his Majesty's Regular ...my is immediately necessary in the present grave ...ational Emergency.

...rd Kitchener is confident that this appeal will be ...once responded to by all those who have the ...ety of our Empire at heart.

TERMS OF SERVICE.

...neral Service for a period of 3 years or until the ...r is concluded.

...e of Enlistment between 19 and 30.

HOW TO JOIN.

...ll information can be obtained at any Post Office in the Kingdom or at any Military Depot.

God Save the King!

Kitchener's recruiting posters were displayed all over the country and also appeared in the local press.

be followed by one of considerable distress among the people of this country least able to bear it.

We most earnestly pray that their sufferings may be neither long nor bitter, but we cannot wait until the need presses heavily upon us.

The means of relief must be ready in our hands to allay anxiety and will go some way to stay distress.

A national fund has been founded and I am proud to act as its treasurer. My first duty is to ask for generous and ready support and I know I shall not ask in vain. At such a moment we all stand by one another and it is to the heart of the British people that I confidently make this most earnest appeal.

Edward R

To this a message was added from Her Majesty the Queen.

From Her Gracious Majesty The Queen:-

Buckingham Palace

A national fund has been inaugurated by my dear son for the relief of the inevitable distress which must be bravely dealt with in the coming days.

To this end I appeal to the women of our country who are ever ready to help those in need, to give their services and assist in the local administration of the fund.

Mary R

To these two appeals was added the following reply from the Lord Mayor:

I may, I am sure, rely upon a hearty response from the loyal Citizens of Durham to these Royal appeals. They are fresh proof, though proof is not needed of the deep concern of our Royal Family for the need of our people.

Persons wishing to give subscriptions should make their cheques payable to HRH the Prince of Wales and all subscriptions should be addressed to His Royal Highness at Buckingham Palace. Envelopes should be clearly marked 'National Relief Fund' and need not be stamped. I am forming a small but representative Local Committee of ladies and gentlemen to assist in the distribution of this fund and am confident that in this action I shall have the war support of Durham's Loyal Citizens.

Charles Caldecleugh, Mayor, 7 August 1914.

The news of the outbreak of war brought many from the surrounding villages into Durham, where it was reported that newsagents shops and the railway stations were besieged by people eager to read the latest news, indeed, some people were reported to be paying up to three pence for a halfpenny special edition which reported that on the night of 4 August immediately that war was declared, Major Mander assisted by Captain Harry Hare and Lieutenant Victor Yate with a detachment of men from 2/Durham LI boarded the *Albert Clement*, a German merchant ship lying in the Tyne, and arrested the crew and seized the ship. Another vessel, the German steamer *Henry Furst*, had loaded with coke at Dunston Staithes and was actually steaming down the River Tyne when she was stopped and arrested by the Naval Authorities. Handed over to H.M. Collector of Customs, the vessel was taken back up river to Dunston. Down the coast at Seaham Harbour, Inspector Morgan and Sergeant Wood of the local constabulary boarded the Flensburg-based, German steamer, *Comet*. In all these cases, no opposition was offered by any of the officers and crews of the vessels boarded.

Throughout the region the various units of the Territorial Force, which had returned from annual camp in Wales, assembled and paraded at their drill halls and prepared to move off. In North-West Durham the Consett Company of 6/Durham LI prepared to join Battalion Headquarters at Bishop Auckland. The *Consett and Stanley Chronicle* reported their send-off with these words:

> The War spirit is abroad and the absorbing topic of conversation at present is the prospects since a state of war between England and Germany was declared on Monday night. In view of the possibilities the whole volunteer force of the country is now being mobilised and territorial regiments fresh back from camp are now again all called up in readiness for service.
>
> The Consett Companies paraded on Wednesday morning at the Armoury with full equipment under orders for Bishop Auckland as the first stopping point pending further instructions. There was a scene of tremendous enthusiasm when they left Consett shortly after two o'clock in the afternoon. The whole town was agog with the excitement and the streets were densely packed with sightseers. Marching to the martial strains of a band of musicians from bands in the district the Territorials under the command of Captain Petherick with Captain Parker and Lieutenants Park and Davison and Sergeant Major Perry passed along Middle Street and Front Street to the station amid the huzzas and cheery goodbyes of inspired crowds. Every window vantage was occupied and there were even to be noticed a number of sightseers gazing down upon the moving spectacle from the tower of the Parish Church. 'God Save the King' was played before the order was given to march off and the send-off was quite in keeping with the patriotic sentiment of the moment.

As well as the Territorials, Regular troops and Regular Reservists were also on the move. The Regimental Depots of the Northumberland Fusiliers and the Durham Light Infantry at Fenham Barracks in Newcastle were extremely busy as the reservists rejoined and each man was issued their equipment and sent off to join their respective battalions. The *Newcastle Evening Chronicle* carried a small report on 6 August as these parties left the town:

> The machine of mobilisation on Tyneside worked smoothly and rapidly all through this morning and afternoon, and several hundreds of Regular and Territorial troops left Newcastle for other stations and mobilisation points. Stirring scenes were witnessed and keen interest was taken in the

Men of the Langley Park Platoon of 8/DLI leave the village for their war station.

No 2 Company of Bavarian Landwehr Regiment No 10 ready to leave for the front. In France they served in Lorraine until transferred to the Russian Front in 1917.

Adverts appeared in the local newspapers every day.

departures. *The crowds about the central station were not as large as on Wednesday but they were considerable. The draft for 1st Battalion Northumberland Fusiliers came from the barracks and swung into the station with a brisk stride. The splendid physique and bearing of the men was generally admired. The Durham Light Infantry also took their departure and the men came in for a hearty reception. Reservists left in large numbers and accompanied by their relatives were, despite their civilian garb, easily recognised by the crowd.*

Another report in the same newspaper recorded the scene at the station the day before on 5 August:

Great excitement prevailed in Newcastle last night and the crowd which had gathered during the day at the Central Station increased in numbers and traffic to and from the station was conducted with difficulty, despite the efforts of the police. The crowd was waiting to witness the troops and as the batches of men left or entered the station they were loudly cheered. About 9 o'clock a party of army reservists entered the station and their arrival was the occasion of an enthusiastic demonstration. The crowd cheered the men lustily and surged into the portico until it was packed. For some time after the men got into the station the crowd continued to cheer.

Meanwhile in Durham City the 2nd (Durham) Battery of the III Northumbrian Brigade, Royal Field Artillery TF was stationed on the racecourse which became a large military camp when they were joined by the 1st (Durham) Battery from Seaham and the 3rd (Durham) Battery from Hartlepool. A large number of horses had been requisitioned for war purposes from local tradesmen and farmers, and these were to be found tethered in long lines between the batteries of guns. For the entertainment of the men the Durham University Union Society was opened, and magazines etc were furnished for their use. It is not known how long the men were to remain in the city, but it was expected that after a very short time they would be moved to Aldershot.

With the send-off of the Regulars and Territorial units the attention of the press now turned to the recruiting of Kitchener's New Army. All over the region various offices were opened for recruiting. In Durham City the Assize Courts were opened and long lines of men waited patiently for their turn to come. The men were attested and medically examined, then sent off to the depots of their new regiments. In the Consett and Stanley district, the recruiting officer, Colour Sergeant Pensioner William Brooks was kept very busy. He was interviewed by a reporter from the *Consett and Stanley Chronicle* on 25 August, at Consett railway station, when he was seeing off another batch of men to Newcastle. He recorded that his biggest problem was a supply of attestation papers and that it was a lack of these that was holding things up as he had a large number of young men ready and willing to enlist. The Consett Iron Company assisted in the recruiting by providing clerks who handled much of the paperwork. The local magistrates were also kept busy swearing in the men as they passed the medical. The same day it was reported that there had been a busy day at the Army recruiting office at 65 Westgate Road in Newcastle. Other areas were doing equally well and some men were even going direct to Fenham Barracks to enlist.

The next day, Wednesday 26 August, a crowd of 1,500 people gathered at Consett station to see off a large batch of recruits on the 09.34 train to Newcastle. The men were sent off with rousing cheers and reported to be among them were a good number of time-expired men who had re-enlisted. It was now that a committee was assembled by the Lord High Sheriff of County Durham, Mr Francis Priestman, who called together representatives of the various political parties and organised meetings and rallies throughout the county. At each meeting there were a number of local dignitaries who addressed the crowd with stirring patriotic speeches. Also present was a recruiting officer, a magistrate and a doctor so that anyone who had possibly been inspired by the speakers and wished to enrol could do so there and then.

By far the biggest problem facing the authorities at Fenham Barracks was the question of accommodation for the men. To solve this, men were formed up into batches and sent off to training camps in the south of England. From the end of August and throughout September drafts marched out of the Depot and down to the Central Station where they were met by crowds of cheering people.

On Thursday 3 September, the *Newcastle Evening Chronicle* reported:

> *In spite of the fact that large contingents of recruits from Newcastle have been drafted to other places for training, the scene at the Newcastle Barracks this morning was of a remarkable character. Large crowds of men were waiting to be enrolled, while on the adjacent open spaces the instructors were hard at work on the raw material, which is of promising character. On Wednesday night a company of 600 recruits left Newcastle by train for the south and this morning another 500 were despatched from the Central Station. They were enthusiastically cheered as they marched through the streets of the city and they had a hearty send-off from the crowd gathered in the station.*

Over 10,000 men were sent away in this fashion and they formed the 8 to 14 Battalions of the Northumberland Fusiliers (NF) and 10 to 15 Battalions of the Durham LI (DLI). Around 4,000 of these men arrived at Bullswater near Pirbright in Surrey; here they were formed into the 10 and 11/NF and

The requirement for trained NCOs brought a number of men into the ranks of 12 and 13/DLI.

the 12 and 13/DLI. They were brigaded together and became 68 Brigade of the 23rd Division. The other two Brigades of the Division, 69 and 70 were forming at Frensham and largely comprised regiments from Yorkshire.

Bullswater was a tented camp and both Durham battalions were accommodated in long lines of bell tents, each holding thirteen men, with larger marquees providing cover for the cookhouse, dining tent and quartermaster stores, company and battalion headquarters and a guardroom. For a long time there were no tent boards available so the men had to sleep on the ground. Fortunately the missing boards were issued before the weather broke. The battalions were hampered by two main shortages. Firstly there was a lack of trained instructors. This difficulty was overcome by the War Office advertising for ex-NCOs to re-enlist to serve as drill instructors, with no liability to serve overseas if they were over 45 years of age. Secondly, there was a real shortage of equipment; khaki uniforms had rapidly run out after the formation of the first New Army. There were also shortages in equipment and weapons, all of which had to be overcome to complete the training of the New Armies. For a number of weeks the men paraded in their own civilian clothing, which owing to the nature of the training was rapidly wearing out, as were their boots. Owing to this lack of uniforms and equipment, training was somewhat limited to route marching, squad drill, physical training, running and entrenching.

If there was a shortage of NCOs, the shortage of officers was even greater: there was less than one regular officer in each battalion of the 23rd Division and in the case of 12 and 13/DLI command was given to a retired officer, commonly known as a 'Dug out'. Command of 12/DLI went to Lieutenant-Colonel Lincoln Edward Cary Elwes. Born on 10 June 1865, he had first been commissioned into the Durham LI on 29 August 1885; by 1903 he had reached the rank of major and he then retired in 1905. Likewise, command of 13/DLI went to Lieutenant-Colonel George A. Ashby: born on 26 March 1856 he had been commissioned on 29 November 1875, reaching the rank of colonel before retiring on 27 August 1908. The higher command of the 23rd Division was given to Lieutenant-General Sir James Melville

Babington and that of 68 Brigade to Brigadier General G.H. Ovens; the latter was replaced on 19 November 1914 by Brigadier General B.J.C. Doran.

Brigadier General Ovens was responsible for appointing men who had applied for commissions to posts in 68 Brigade; one group appointed to 68 Brigade came from men who had enlisted into 6/Duke of Cornwall's LI. Among them was George Butterworth, whose father Sir Alexander Butterworth was the General Manager of the North Eastern Railway (NER). George was born in London on 12 July 1885. Educated at Aysgarth School in Yorkshire and Trinity College Oxford, he had by 1910 become a music teacher at Radley but left to become a student at the Royal College of Music. When war broke out he and a group of his friends enlisted in 6/Duke of Cornwall's LI and after a few days at Bodmin found themselves sent to a camp near Aldershot. Here Butterworth and his friends applied for commissions and were appointed to battalions in 68 Brigade. He recorded the events of the time in his diary:

Command of 12/DLI went to Lieutenant-Colonel Lincoln Edward Cary Elwes. Born on 10 June 1865, he had first been commissioned into the Durham LI on 29 August 1885; by 1903 he had reached the rank of major and he then retired in 1905. Pictured here with 1/DLI in India in 1904.

D/DLI/2/1/850

> *Only yesterday I had a letter from General Ovens, of the North Command, practically offering me a commission in his Brigade, the 68th, stationed at Pirbright, near here; and also asking me to name others of our party.*

> *After some discussion, it was decided that I should follow this up, and propose the names of Morris, Brown, Woodhead and the two Ellises; as we considered it improbable that all would be accepted, I grouped the names in pairs – Morris with myself, Brown and Woodhead together, and the two Ellises together – so that no one should be left alone in the lurch.*

> *The only remaining member of our original party (Keeling) is now a corporal, and prefers in any case to remain in the DCLI N.B. – There are no commissions vacant in our battalion.*

> *General Ovens had told me to write to the Brigade Major at Pirbright, but, after consulting the Officers here, we decided that a personal interview would be simpler. Accordingly F.B. Ellis and myself were given leave to go over to Pirbright in Ellis's motor car, which he has been keeping by permission at Farnborough. We had a memorable afternoon. At Pirbright*

George Kaye Butterworth enlisted into the Duke of Cornwall's Light Infantry as a private, prior to obtaining a commission in 13/DLI.

RECRUITING WAS VERY BRISK IN THE NORTH YESTE

The Durham press made a great deal about the number of men from the North Country that had enlisted.

ENTHUSIASTIC SCENES AT BISHOP AUCKLAND.

*The **Northern Despatch** on 21 September 1914 carried this photo of men leaving Bishop Auckland to join Kitchener's Army.*

village we stopped for beer, chiefly for the sake of seeing once again the inside of a country inn, and arrived at the camp of the 68th Brigade at about 4-30. It is a much larger camp than ours, as it houses the whole brigade – 4 battalions; on the other hand, things are obviously less advanced, not a single uniform to be seen. The Brigade Major is the Officer temporarily in charge of the whole camp, and we went off to his tent rather uncertain how to approach so exalted a person. We had no need to be nervous; the sentry, whom we had first to satisfy, turned out to be a seedy Tynesider, with a two-day's beard; an intensely comic picture. The Brigade Major himself – though more respectable – was scarcely more formidable; what is familiarly called a 'dug-out'; …Like everyone else in the camp he was dressed in mufti, and appeared to be very vague on the subject of commissions. One theory of his was that all the second lieutenancies were filled up, but that we could probably become first lieutenants or even captains if we chose! Our interview was very amusing, but would not have satisfied a stickler for military etiquette. We came away with an increased respect for the organisation of the DCLI., and without arriving at any result, for the Brigade Major had no power to nominate us himself, and had received no instructions from General Ovens. He promised to let us know something more definite in a day or two.

With the men from the colliery villages moving to the south of England word was soon being sent back home about the conditions in the camp and how they were being treated. A private from C Company of an unnamed battalion, who wished to remain anonymous, had this letter published in the *Consett and Stanley Chronicle* on 11 September:

Robert Comber Woodhead, another of those commissioned from the DCLI into the battalions of 68 Brigade.

> *Sir, you will be surprised to receive this letter, but I am writing to let you know the way we are treated by the British population when at depots or travelling. As you will be aware there were about 200 Consett men in Kitchener's Army at Newcastle alone. We were all expecting to come home on Saturday but have reached Woking instead. All the way we have been travelling we have received cigarettes, cakes, etc from passengers on the platforms. Some even went to the stalls at the stations and bought whole boxes and distributed them to the troops while passing. From all the houses in Woking people are giving men apples, plums and pears, and in many cases have asked them in to have tea. Two of the chapels give teas and concerts at the price of one penny each to all soldiers in uniform every night, and all writing material is given free. So if you like you can let the young men of Consett and district know how good people are to Tommy Atkins. I had to write and let you know the kind way one and all are treating us.*

Throughout September drafts left Newcastle to join those already in the south. On 25 September, the *Consett and Stanley Chronicle* reported on another large draft which included a batch of Consett men that left Newcastle for the training grounds:

> *In the grey dawn of Monday morning another large detachment of 'our boys' for Kitchener's Army, who have been located for some time in Wingrove School, left for the Central Station, en route for one of the training camps? The spirits of the men were exuberant, and while the preliminaries were being arranged, popular songs were given lustily and with a vim that can hardly be described. 'It's a long way to Tipperary' was by far the most popular ditty. Judging by the names responded to at the roll call England, Ireland and Scotland were all well-represented.*
>
> *The residents in the near neighbourhood of the school have been extremely hospitable to the men who have so nobly responded to the call. A pleasing feature was a request from the ranks for 'Three cheers for the women over the way', a call which was responded to with a unanimity and the volume which showed their great appreciation of the many kindnesses shown by the residents of Wingrove, an encore being requested and as heartily responded to on their filing out of the school grounds.*
>
> *We may add that this contingent includes most of the Consett young fellows who have volunteered for active service. They join the 68th Regiment, Durham Light Infantry and go into camp near Woking, Surrey. The camp is known as Bullswater Camp and is situated not many miles from Guildford. The smart picturesque county town of Surrey, which*

possesses in its High Street the finest street in the south of England and one of the best in the country.

As time went on the situation gradually improved, uniforms in the shape of the blue serge that became known as 'Kitchener Blue' were issued and the situation with rations was greatly enhanced when the messing arrangements for the 23rd Division were taken over by Messrs Lyons and Co. The news reached County Durham via the local press that:

The food supply has greatly improved and that a proper erection has been prepared for the recruits to partake their meals therein. In addition to severe drilling and marching, the lads have been supplied with parts of their kits and rifles. Each recruit is supplied with three blankets and a greatcoat and they are sleeping fourteen to a tent. There are church parades and services in the YMCA marquee. All the battalion officers have been made up and they are now a line unit. This means that the young fellows are bound for the front whether the war is finished or not. If hostilities are still in progress they would have to go and relieve those who have borne the brunt of the fray. Lord Kitchener has given it out that in any case his New Army must either 'Storm Berlin' or march through the capital.

After they had been issued with their Kitchener Blue and as soon as they had some free time, those with some spare money headed into Woking

The Crown Prince of Baden speaks with men who have been involved in the recent fighting.

where the local photographer was taking portrait pictures. This was recorded in a letter sent to his family living at Usworth Colliery by Private Alex Stephenson, who was serving with C Company of 12/DLI:

Dear Mother and Brothers,

Just a few lines in answer to your letter. I was very sorry to hear about Jimmy Campbell being killed at the front, also about Barney Connolly's death, well he is better off now I think. You can send me a few things if you want but not things to wear because they will only lie about and get full of lice, but if you send anything try and get a tin biscuit box and wrap it in brown paper and fasten it with string and put my address on it and I am sure to get it, that is if you mean to send cakes or anything like that. I have not got my number yet and won't get one till we get our proper uniforms. The Teddy Carter you mean, is it the one we used to call 'Tiger Carter'?

I wrote a letter to Nellie Marshall but I haven't had a reply yet, but I am expecting one tomorrow. Ask Henry Simpson if he has sent any letters yet, because if he has I haven't got them! I got one off Jack Palmer yesterday when I got yours, I don't know how Jack managed to send one as he cannot write. Is Dick still going on all right with his putting, I hope he is. Tommy got his photo taken at Woking when we were there on Saturday. He got the loan of a hat the same shape as a khaki but it is a blue one. I think he will have taken a good photo. I would have had mine taken but for the spots on my face. I thought you said the pit would be closed in for a month. I hope it doesn't. Well I think that is all this time from your loving son and brother, Alex.

PS if you put this address on it will be sure to find me:

A Stephenson
12 Platoon
C Company
12 Durham Light Infantry
Bullswater Camp
Woking
Surrey

Very soon the photographer was allowed into the camp where many group photographs beside the tented accommodation were taken.

The issuing of the blue uniforms brought many comments and there was concern that men of the New Armies would serve overseas in the blue uniform and not in khaki. At the end of September an article in the *Northern Despatch* denied this and under the heading THE BLUE UNIFORMS OF THE NEW ARMY stated the case for the clothing contractors:

The task facing Army contractors for the forthcoming winter is a huge one. In the next six months they are expected to turn out over one million uniforms, greatcoats, boots etc. All the mills and factories are working at the highest pressure.

The men were issued with what we now know as 'Kitchener Blue' uniforms; the man standing second left has got the bugle of the regimental shoulder title as a cap badge.

In six months at the outside every man in the Regular and Territorial Armies will be supplied, one of the chief Army contractors said yesterday, all our resources are at the disposal of the Government. Scores of thousands of uniforms etc. have been supplied already and uniforms are being turned out at the rate of about 200,000 per month.

There are no extra things for a winter campaign despite the fact that the men have to fight in trenches almost filled with rain and snow. Men on active service have to travel with a minimum of material, which can hardly be equalled.

I notice that a number of newspapers have referred to the fact that the supply of khaki-coloured cloth is insufficient for present requirements and that soldiers for the front will be supplied with blue uniforms. There will be no thin blue line seen on the battlefield. This colour of uniform will be supplied for use in depots and camps in this country, but before the men are sent to the front they will have khaki and discard the blue.

You might be interested to learn that we have previously supplied the French and Greek Armies with uniforms and representatives from these Governments have been here for supplies this week. There is no doubt that they would have given any price, but we did not quote. We have enough on hand already. Nor is it likely that they will fare any better elsewhere.

Those recruits and reservists who joined the colours without overcoats are being supplied with ordinary garments of this kind until the military coats are ready. The orders were received on Wednesday and the Government are buying big stocks. There is no doubt that the men are being looked after so far as is humanly possible.

On 2 October, the *Consett and Stanley Chronicle* carried a long article about the Consett men at Bullswater and the conditions in the camp.

Some interesting items in regard to the Bullswater Camp where the local recruits for the Durham Light Infantry and the Northumberland Fusiliers are now being trained have come through to Consett. Bullswater is about four miles from Woking in Surrey and is situated in the midst of a picturesque countryside. It may interest Consettonians to know that the lads from this district are included in A Company, and being the smartest in the battalion walk in their marches immediately behind the regimental band. The young fellows find it rather cold when they have to turn out at 06.15 every morning, but it is hot enough during the day. Aldershot is within easy distance and the station for the camp is Brookwood which is the station for Bisley rifle range.

The recruits are allowed two blankets and a waterproof sheet to lie upon; twelve lads being housed in each tent. It is not expected that the recruits will stay at Bullswater very long in as such as the authorities are building wooden huts at Bisley and the probability is that they will be provided with quarters there during the winter.

Aeroplanes are flying about in all directions, at least from a dozen to twenty a day being seen. There is little fear of a visitation from a German aeroplane. The airship which guards London passes over the camp about 8.30 every night and returns at 5 in the morning. It is housed at Farnham about six miles distant from Bullswater. The recruits have eight footballs in the camp, so no doubt they will enjoy themselves in their leisure time, some of the chaps have failed to pass the medical examination in the camp and have been discharged. It appears that only those youths who are thoroughly sound and healthy are retained. The dialect of the southerners is highly amusing to the north countrymen.

Here there are guards stationed all over the place but the recruits are free to go where they like after their day's training is done. The only spot debarred is Aldershot, which they are not allowed to visit without a special passport from the Adjutant. The locality is patrolled by mounted infantry and mounted police are found on nearly all the roads. Guildford which is only five miles away is an exceedingly beautiful town.

The journey from Newcastle to Bullswater occupied ten hours. It is an entirely new camp. The supply of rations has considerably improved since the recruits first entered upon their new camp. At Brookwood a large hall has been set apart for the use of recruits to write letters, read the papers and partake of refreshments. The recruits seem very happy and contented and the new mode of life is very exciting and fascinating to them.

In 13/DLI on 6 October there was a mass promotion to lance-corporal. The surviving remnants of burnt documents reveal that around thirty men were promoted on that day: many progressed but a few reverted to private at their own request, while others blotted their copybook and were deprived of their stripe by the commanding officer.

The arrival of so many northern working men of the mining, steel-working and labouring classes was bound to cause some comment in the leafy lanes of Surrey, but most behaved themselves and brought favourable comment from the local population. Captain Harold Danvers, the officer commanding A Company of 12/DLI writing from Bullswater Camp to the *Consett and Stanley Chronicle* had this letter published on 9 October:

> *The following is an extract from a letter I received from Mr J. St Loe Strachey, High Sheriff of Surrey and editor of* The Spectator *which might interest your readers.*
>
> *Most of the men mentioned were working in the pits from a fortnight to three weeks ago:-*
>
> *I cannot tell you what a pleasure it was for me to see your camp and men. The drilling of those pitmen is a sight that will live in my memory for years. I quite fell in love with them. I thought them a splendid type. Men who will give up 12s to take 1s and the chance of getting to France from purely patriotic reasons are men to be proud of. Good Luck to the regiment and a quick flitting to the front, and especially A Company.*

It was at about this time in early October that each battalion was issued with 100 obsolete Lee Metford rifles. This allowed the training to progress from just foot drill to arms drill also. The men were taught all the various

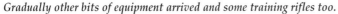

Gradually other bits of equipment arrived and some training rifles too.

drill movements from shoulder arms, port arms to trail arms and gradually they became more like soldiers than civilians. There was further improvement when there was an issue of 400 sets of the old 1888-pattern Slade Wallace buff equipment to each battalion. Gradually the companies were pulled together and as the basics of military discipline began to take effect, the two battalions of the 'Faithful Durhams' drilled and did physical training in the hope that they would soon get to France. However, that was not to happen and when it became obvious to the divisional staff, the training regime was relaxed and the men were given a day off on Sundays.

George Butterworth and his friends had now joined the Brigade as officers and he continued the story in his diary:

> General Ovens, head of the 68th Brigade, offered commissions to self and five friends. This offer was gratefully accepted, subject to the sanction of the DCLI officials. The latter, however, did not show us as much goodwill as I expected. Our company commander lodged an objection – trivial as well as inaccurate – on the ground that we had already been offered commissions in the DCLI and refused them. To this we replied that we had not previously been given the opportunity en bloc, and had not cared to risk breaking up the party by accepting offers singly.

> The situation was a curious one. General Ovens, having once made up his mind, stood by us splendidly. I kept up communications with him by means of Ellis's motor car, which carried messages to and from Bullswater [General Ovens' Headquarters] almost daily, and for a whole week a ridiculous three-cornered correspondence went on. General Ovens would send me what practically amounted to a command to join; this I passed on to the Commanding Officer, who invariably ignored it. Why he was so anxious to keep us I cannot conceive, but I fancy it was just bluff, his only object being to save the face of our company commander by making things as difficult for us as possible.

> However, to cut a long story short, one day a more than usually firm message came from the General, we were all called off parade and ordered to report ourselves as soon as possible at our new headquarters. An hour or two later the motor car, supplemented by a taxi, was conveying us and all our belongings to Bullswater Camp.

Before long, old-pattern Slade Wallace equipment was brought out of stores and issued to the men.

On the whole we were not sorry to leave the DCLI – I have already explained why. Of our original party of eight, two remained behind – Toye, who had been given a commission, and Keeling, who had been promoted to sergeant, and preferred to stay on.

On arriving at Bullswater we found that matters were far from being settled. The General received us most cordially but explained, with some embarrassment, that he really did not know what to do with us now that he had got us. Owing to the delay, some of the vacancies had been filled up, and the War Office, in fact, pretended that there were none left. This he knew to be an exaggeration, but at the same time he hesitated to take us on then and there without some kind of confirmation from headquarters. In any case it was necessary for us all to go up to London to get uniform and kit, and so it was decided that we were to remain at home until sent for. To anyone who knows how the War Office usually deals with these matters, it will not seem surprising that we were kept waiting a good many days. I found the delay most demoralizing as well as annoying. After five strenuous weeks, the feeling of being absolutely idle, while everyone else was busy, was trying in the extreme. One almost began to share the ordinary civilian anxieties from which soldiers in camp are quite free. Perhaps it was as well for one's intelligence that one's interest in the war and things in general should be revived, and I found that this interest remained with me afterwards, which shows the difference between an Officer's life and the almost purely physical life of the private – at any rate, under Watts Common conditions. While in town I read Bernhardi's 'Germany and the Next War', and came to the conclusion that Germany's crime is primarily an intellectual one – too much theory – the doctrine of the end justifying the means is wrong, because it is impossible to prophesy accurately what either will be.

Another rather depressing feature of London at this time was the darkness of the streets at night – the result, apparently, of an Admiralty order. The idea was to obliterate important landmarks in the event of a Zeppelin raid, but it is difficult to see how this would work, and it certainly did not make things any more cheerful.

Getting uniform, etc., was not difficult; Moss Brothers, Bedford Street, W.C., are wonderful people, and 'their Mr. Peter' is especially wonderful – he threw things incontinently on my back, and they just stuck there, and fitted beautifully. I need not go into details about the tedious settlement of our affairs; by the end of the second week in October we were all definitely established at Bullswater Camp. Our dispositions were as follows:-

F. B. Ellis 1st Lieutenant 10th Northumberland Fusiliers.
R. A. Ellis 1st Lieutenant 10th Northumberland Fusiliers.
Woodhead 1st Lieutenant 12th Durham Light Infantry.
Brown 2nd Lieutenant 13th Durham Light Infantry.
Morris 2nd Lieutenant 13th Durham Light Infantry.
Self 2nd Lieutenant 13th Durham Light Infantry.

136

With bayonets fixed they are now starting to look more like soldiers.

> *Originally we were all appointed 1st Lieutenants, but, as the 13th Durhams seemed to be particularly strong in junior officers, Brown, Morris and self requested to be made seconds.*

The weather started to turn wet and the ground in the camp was soon churned up into mud and quagmire, more like a ploughed field than an army camp. This made life uncomfortable to say the least for the men, who were unable to dry their clothes fully. Word soon came down from the top that they wouldn't have to put up with the conditions much longer and that by the end of November they would be quartered in barracks in Aldershot. Word of this was soon on its way to the north-east; a number of letters survive to tell the story of this time at

An unknown sergeant poses for the camera in his 'Kitchener Blue'. The white line on the front of the cap, when the size is enhanced can be seen to be the word 'Durham' embroidered into it.

38

Bullswater. The first was written by two brothers serving in 13/DLI; John (Jack) and William (Bill) Anderson, who came from the small village of Station Town near Wingate in south-east Durham:

Ptes John & William Anderson
A Company
13th Batt DLI
Bullswater Camp
Woking
Surrey
Oct 13 1914

Dear Father & Mother, Brothers and Sisters,
We received your letter & parcel together on Tuesday. We were both on guard at the guard tent looking after prisoners, which we were not supposed to leave till someone relieved us and we got them fetched to our door. There is four of us on duty from 10 o'clock on Tuesday morning till 10 o'clock on Wednesday morning, one relieving the other all the time. We have one prisoner in and he is very quiet and we got our meals brought to us. We are all right after having our arm inoculated but the elbow was a bit stiff. The General gave it out to us on Sunday that we would all be at the north camp Aldershot by the 15th of next month for the winter. We think we will be going into barracks or huts they have been building. There was some more men got their discharge and Keniry from up the street was one of them. Next time you send us anything will you send us our gloves as it is cold at mornings. There is plenty of amusement here at nights in the big tents, people coming from round about giving concerts and some teaching ambulance and others teaching the men to talk French and German.
Don't send us any more shirts or anything and don't send a lot of eatables through but we could do with four card laces and no more.
No more at present from your two sons Jack and Bill.

The second letter was one published in the *Consett and Stanley Chronicle*, sent to his parents by 17765 Private John William Shield whose wife resided at 11 Dodds Terrace, Low Fell, while his parents were living at 10 Council Street, Stanley. Published in the newspaper on 23 October, it tells a story of one soldier's time under the influence of alcohol under the heading A LIVELY NIGHT:
Private J. Shield DLI now stationed at Bullswater Camp gives a graphic account of a fellow soldier's fall from grace.
Dear Father and Mother, I got your letters today, Wednesday, and am very pleased you sent the purse, but it didn't matter about the photos, because they might have got lost. We are just beginning to get very wet now. It was raining yesterday and nearly all day today, but we have not been on parade, just in a big marquee listening to an officer giving a good

lecture. I have heard another different tale about us going away and that is not until the 15th of next month.

We had a lively night on Monday in the tent through one of our lads going bad with the horrors or the blues. Number One Platoon was playing Number Two and to celebrate the event I think Geordie went and got tight and when he came into the tent he was as sick as a dog, and soon after we had to hold him down. So the Doctor came and said he had a poisoned stomach. They took him to the camp hospital and washed his stomach out and the next day he was alright, but he didn't know anything about the night before.

We get plenty of aeroplanes down here to look at; they are as common as pigeons and not far above the camp. As they are flying over we can hear their engines going and the other day I saw an army airship. It was a great big thing like a cigar, and it was quite close to us that you could tell the men in it. It would be about the size of a big canteen. It was a sight worth seeing. We are going to be inoculated again in about ten days' time, but if it is no worse than it was before I think I will stand it alright. So keep up your heart. We are all champion just now, laughing at each other's top coats which we wear during the wet only.

Wishing you all the best of luck. Jack.

Jack Shield only served another month before he was discharged on 21 November as unlikely to become an efficient soldier.

Before the move to Aldershot took place there occurred a sad event for 12/DLI. On 13 November the battalion Adjutant, Captain W.E. Rogerson died suddenly from heart failure at Bullswater Camp. The deceased was 42 years of age and he was the brother of Mr J.E. Rogerson of Mount Oswald, Durham City and the son of Mr John Rogerson who was so prominently identified with the Consett Iron Works. Very well known in sporting circles in the north of England, Captain Rogerson enjoyed the esteem of a large circle of friends who no doubt were sad to learn of

This lad has really worked hard to clean his uniform up for the photographer. The regimental shoulder title is worn as a collar badge and he has obtained a cap badge for his side cap.

On 13 November the battalion Adjutant, Captain W.E. Rogerson died suddenly from heart failure at Bullswater Camp.

his untimely death. Well-known in the Darlington area, the late officer resided at Neasham Abbey near Darlington. His body was taken by train back to Darlington where he was interred in the West Cemetery.

The news of the death of the Adjutant and the coming move into Aldershot was relayed to Usworth Colliery in a letter from Alex Stephenson. However, at the time of writing his knowledge of army ranks was sketchy as he reports the death of 'the General':

Dear Mother and Brothers,

I write these few lines hoping to find you all in good health as it leaves me at present. I am still keeping all right here, that is for the meat we are getting. We are to move to North Camp, Aldershot next Monday; in fact we are forced to because we have had some very heavy rain this week which has washed all the big tents down. The YMCA tent washed down that is the reason I have to write this letter in pencil, I can't get ink now and I am writing in the dark so excuse if I have missed the lines on the paper. Well we had a funeral procession here today our General was getting buried and we had to march behind till we got to the station at Brookwood as he was going to be buried in Darlington, the station where we went was in Brookwood Cemetery which is the second largest cemetery in the world, it has a wall about ten miles long around it and two railway stations so it is a big one.

How are they paying Dick for his putting, I have heard he is only getting four shillings a day, if he is tell him he wants to see someone about it. Margaret Armstrong tells me their Jimmy has listed but I can't think who he is because I don't know who the McCabes are or the Quinns. I will close now with love to you all from your loving son and brother, Alex.

Malplaquet barracks Aldershot: men of 13/DLI with their platoon commander.

PS Please send me a shirt down if you have one to spare as I only have one now. Don't forget to write back soon.

One of the men serving at Bullswater Camp, known only by his first name, Bob, wrote to his parents in Consett or Stanley and the letter was published in the *Consett and Stanley Chronicle* on 23 October:

Bullswater Camp

Dear Father and Mother,

I received your parcel safe last night. Pleased with what you sent me but don't send me any more socks because we have received some today. Please ask Joe if the pits are still working up there. Tell him to come down here, he will get work. I saw Mrs Todd last night from the Moor and she told me you were sending me a parcel on. Father, I did enjoy your cigars and cigarettes; they were a treat. I would be pleased with some stamps or money because I cannot get any here. We are going to be knocking this week.

I heard that we are coming to Edinburgh to stay but I don't know whether it is true or not. I will write and tell you. I am keeping in the best of health and expect you are the same at home. Tell Lily and Sally I send my love; pleased if they would write. Don't forget to tell our Joe to send something on. It is very cold down here under canvas but we are getting used to it now.

Bob.

With the weather so wet and cold it was planned that the 23rd Division would concentrate in Aldershot. On 16 November the advance party of

Among this group of D Company 12/DLI is 19521 Sergeant John Donaldson who would be Killed in Action on 8 July 1916; sadly the family do not know which man he is.

13/DLI set off but at the last moment the orders were cancelled and they had to return to the tents at Bullswater.

During this period before they moved camp there was another issue of essential kit. Alex Stephenson told his family about it and asked about lads from the village who were enlisting in a letter written on 21 November:

Dear Mother and Brothers

I write these few lines to let you know that I received the shirt which you sent. I was going to send for one about three weeks since I was expecting another one from the army I kept putting off till I couldn't put off any longer. I have had this one on ever since I sent you my clothes and just as I got your parcel they shouted us out and gave us another one each.

Well I never thought Henry Simpson would list although he used to talk about it so much, do you think you could get his address for me? I know that his mother will set the blame on me, because she did when I was at home. I hear that there is about a foot of snow up in the north, well we haven't had any yet but the weather has turned very cold here. Poor Tommy is playing war because he cannot get home for the weekend. They have cancelled all passes because we are expecting to move any minute, as for me I can't get home till we get a furlough as I haven't got the money and I am depending on them giving us a free pass on Christmas. I am very sorry to hear about Michael Fitzpatrick being killed at the front. We are getting on all right with our drill, when we get to Aldershot we shall only be there for a fortnight for firing on the ranges then we are going to be billeted. We go to a town called Guildford every Saturday night and a lot of our men have got invitations to tea on the Sunday by old gentlemen, so I am going to try my luck this time. The people down here think a lot of Northumberland and Durham men; they say we are a lively set.

Well I think this is all this time from your loving son and brother Alex.

With the men back in the tented camp they needed some recreation and consequently they were allowed into nearby Guildford. The town was patrolled by regimental policemen from all the battalions of 68 Brigade. On Saturday 21 November a large group of soldiers were in town and there had been a little bit of trouble. That evening 21635 Sergeant John Castling of 13/DLI had three men from 10 and 11/NF under arrest on the back of a lorry. He was taking them back to Bullswater Camp and as the lorry moved off a group of men tried to climb aboard to get a lift back to camp. Most did so from the tailboard at the back, but one man, 13295 Corporal James McGrother who had enlisted in Middlesbrough on 3 September, decided to get in over the side. He either slipped or was pushed and fell off and went under the back wheel. Severely injured, he was taken to the Surrey County Hospital in the town. He survived for six days and died on 27 November. Conforming to War Office rules about accidental injuries, the Commanding Officer had ordered a Court of Inquiry which took place on 26 November.

The President of the Court was Major Nicholas Biddulph who was assisted by two Lieutenants: Arthur Austin and Joseph Downey. The first witness called was Sergeant Castling who related the story told above, but added that he did not know the man and with the noise of the men singing in the back of the truck he did not know that the man had been hurt and added that as most of the men were under the influence of drink, he allowed the lorry to drive on.

The Court called 17773 Private George Straker who had this to say:

At Guildford about 2125 hours on 21 November, I was with Corporal McGrother. He asked me to go with him in a Motor Bus. I said I would if he would wait a minute while I got a packet of cigarettes and I went into a shop. When I came out a man told me that the Corporal had been run over by a motor lorry. I went up the road about fifty yards and found Corporal McGrother lying on the road with his leg out. There was a crowd round him. I helped take him to the hospital. He was quite sober at the time.

The members of the Court then removed to the Surrey County Hospital where they interviewed two more witnesses. The first was the House Surgeon of the Surrey County Hospital, T.R. Trounce MRCS who stated:

On Saturday evening 21 November between 2100 and 2200 hours the patient Corporal McGrother was admitted to Guildford Hospital suffering from lacerations of the left leg. The two men who were in charge of him and who appeared to be under the influence of drink made statements concerning the case which were quite contradictory. The injuries are of such a nature as to incapacitate Corporal McGrother for further military service. The leg in all probability will have to be amputated.

The three officers then went to the ward where Corporal McGrother was lying and questioned him as to what had happened. He said:

On Saturday 21 November 1914 I was off duty and had gone to Guildford. I intended to return by motor wagon in which were some of my friends. The lorry moved off and I jumped up at the side to climb on the lorry. I got hold of the side but someone must have pushed me off or I slipped and fell under the wheel.

The statement was read back to him by Lieutenant Ernest Bellamy who had written the words of the dying man. Another visitor attended Corporal McGrother that day. Lieutenant William Jardine RAMC, the Battalion Medical Officer arrived and later added these words to the summary of evidence:

I went to Guildford on Wednesday 25 November 1914 and saw Corporal McGrother, he was suffering from contusions and lacerations of the soft tissue of the leg. The injuries in my opinion will necessitate the amputation of the limb and render him unfit for further service.

The evidence was typed up and presented to the Commanding Officer who added the following comment:

I am of the opinion that 19306 Corporal Joseph [13295 James, sic]

McGrother 13/Durham LI met with an accident when not on duty through his own fault in attempting to get onto a moving Motor Lorry. I am also of the opinion that his injuries will incapacitate him from further service as a soldier.

Two days later the Brigade Commander Brigadier General B.J.C. Doran simply added: 'I concur with the above opinion.'

It was obvious that the injuries were very serious and that the injured man may die, so his mother was sent for and she arrived in time to be with her son in his last hours; he passed away on 27 November and was taken home to Middlesbrough and buried in St Joseph's RC Churchyard in Ormesby.

George Butterworth wrote a long passage in his diary of his first impressions of the Battalion, the camp and the soldiers under his command:

Of the next four weeks I will only give a short summary. On the whole I have enjoyed it very much, chiefly because of the men with whom I have had to deal – in particular, those whom I have been actually commanding. The enormous difference in the rank and file between this and the DCLI is easily explained:-

(1) These men are almost all strictly local, instead of a mix-up of Birmingham, London, etc.

(2) They are almost all working men (in my platoon 90 per cent are miners).

(3) They are Northerners.

Coming here was exhilarating in much the same way as detraining at Newcastle Station – everyone seemed so very much alive.

There is no doubt that as raw material our men are wonderfully good – physically strong, mentally alert, and tremendously keen; they do not altogether understand the necessity for strict military discipline, but are very eager to learn their job as quickly as possible. They are also very good fellows indeed, and in short it is a great pleasure to be with them.

As to the Officers, it is difficult to form any estimate; except for the Colonel, very few have been in the regular army; a few have seen active service in South Africa or elsewhere, but the large majority have had merely Territorial or O.T.C. experience. This is all that could be expected in the case of the subalterns, and in the 13th we seem to have a very good lot, but the lack of real military experience among the senior officers is a serious draw-back.

In the present state of our training a still greater source of trouble is the inexperience of the NCOs, and here we are distinctly worse off than in the Cornwalls; many of them are merely recruits promoted, and practically none have any of the regular's snap and assurance. Perhaps the greatest surprise I had on arriving was to find that after five weeks' training I knew quite as much as my company sergeants; at first this was rather a relief, but now one is beginning to wish for more support; the sergeants and corporals are mostly splendid fellows, but have very little authority.

CAMP.

Bullswater Camp contains, of course, the whole of our Brigade, the lines of the four battalions being separated from each other by a small open space. This makes about 350 living tents in all, so that we cover a considerable acreage. The men sleep 10 to 15 in a tent, and I suppose are quite as uncomfortable as we were on Watts Common. On the other hand, the marquee accommodation is very good, there being several large recreation tents, besides canteens.

The Officers sleep two in a tent, at a short distance from their respective battalions. The worst thing about the camp is its extreme dirtiness, the natural surface being completely worn away. In September I believe the dust was fearful, and now, of course, it is mud.

WORK.

On arriving I was appointed to command the 11th platoon, C Company; Morris has the 10th of the same. Our company commander is Captain Walker; second in command, Lieut. Blake, and the other two subalterns are 2nd Lieutenants Clarke and Pullen. I believe we are about the only company in the brigade with a full complement of Officers, and I am glad to say that we all get on very well together.

I ought to mention that the Commanding Officer of the 13th is Colonel Ashby, a distinguished soldier who fought at Tel-el-Kebir. We are very lucky to have such a good man, as it is probably only his age which prevented his being snapped up before.

Our second in command is Major Biddulph, also a retired regular.

The daily routine is very much the same as in the Cornwalls, about six hours' work, with occasional lectures in the evening. We are progressing, however, very slowly indeed, being very badly off for equipment of all kinds. Our rifles are of an obsolete pattern, and quite useless except for drill purposes. Another serious drawback is the lack of space; there is practically no flat ground for drilling, and very little open country either. If only we could get going, I am sure we should become efficient very quickly, as the men are very keen and physically quite first-rate.

He continued the entry on 30 November, describing the weather conditions that prevailed at Bullswater at that time:

Sunday, November 30th.

The last fortnight has been extremely trying for all of us, owing to the complete break-up of the weather; one realises now how extremely lucky we have been in this respect. The autumn being exceptionally fine, we had begun to think that after all a winter camp would be quite tolerable, but we do not think so now. Our first catastrophe occurred one very squally evening, when a sudden gust of wind carried away four of the largest marquees, burying several men beneath them. The alarm was sounded, and

Here men of D Company 13/DLI pose with their dinner in Malplaquet Barracks. Only one man has a cap badge and that has a Queen Victoria's Crown on it: he could be a time-expired ex-regular; several of the others have the embroidered DURHAM on the left front of the cap. D/DLI/7/805/100

we swarmed on to the parade ground, but fortunately no one was hurt.

Soon after this we had a week's cold snap – unusually severe for the time of year, 20 degrees of frost being reported one night. Luckily we escaped snow, but of course hard frost under canvas is no joke, particularly because of there being no warm place to sit in.

All this time we were expecting almost daily to be called away to our winter quarters at Aldershot. Our move to Malplaquet Barracks was definitely fixed for November 16th, and the advance party had actually left, when suddenly we heard that the whole thing was postponed. Apparently the authorities were expecting a raid on the coast, and in order to facilitate the emergency transport arrangements, all other movements of troops were temporarily cancelled. It was even suggested that we might have to keep the camp going over Christmas, but fortunately this turned out to be an exaggeration. After several false alarms our long-overdue exodus took place on the very last day of November. This was probably just in time to prevent disaster; the last few days were desperate; after the frost broke we had a bad spell of wet, which not only swamped the camp, but penetrated everything inside the tents. For several nights there was hardly a dry blanket to be had, and it is clearly impossible to carry on with that sort of thing indefinitely.

It would be difficult to over-praise the men's behaviour through all this discomfort; I often used to go down the lines to enquire how they were getting on, and always got a cheerful answer. It is all very well to say that it is much worse in the trenches, but the men in the trenches get relieved, and there is no billeting at Bullswater. I certainly think the authorities ought to have provided extra blankets and better accommodation, and probably this would have been done, had we not been expecting to leave any day.

It is to be hoped that those who grumble at national slackness will make an exception in favour of the working people of Durham County; the large majority of these men have given up good jobs and comfortable homes for the best reasons, and are willing to stand almost anything, if only they are to be allowed to get out and finish off the war.

One other event of the last fortnight must be mentioned, namely, the retirement of General Ovens, who was reported unfit for service abroad. I think everyone was sorry to lose him, and, not least, his friends from the Cornwalls.

They remained under canvas for another week or so and then on 30 November and 1 December the whole of 68 Brigade moved into barracks in Aldershot. 12 and 13/DLI were allocated accommodation in Malplaquet Barracks: this old Victorian barracks was designed to hold one infantry battalion, not two, so things were quite tight and every spare space was taken up. The married quarters were emptied of the families left behind when the BEF left for France and some men from 12/DLI were moved in. During early December the men were issued with old-pattern water bottles and white haversacks and an ammunition pouch. The news that the men of 12/DLI were living in the married quarters was conveyed to Consett in a letter from 17788 Private Frank Eales, who was the son of a reporter on the *Consett and Stanley Chronicle* and an old boy of Consett Secondary School who was serving with 13/DLI. The letter was published in the newspaper on 26 February 1915:

Malplaquet Barracks
Aldershot

A short outline of my experience since joining the Army may interest you. I made my first acquaintance with the British Army on 1 September and after ten monotonous days 'awkward squad' drill on the Newcastle Town Moor, I was removed with the 12/ and 13/DLI to Bullswater Camp, eight miles from Aldershot, where we soon put into practice one of the principles of a good soldier, i.e. to be a good fighter at times especially on account of the shortage of food. The contractor was supplying food for 2,000 men whereas there were 4,000 men altogether in camp, with the natural result that the better the fighter the better the reward in the shape of the meal the said fighter received. However the state of things was corrected after a few days and we settled down to the really heavy work of training.

We were situated in a beautiful countryside and for the first three weeks were blessed with splendid weather, which made camping out a pleasant experience. Being only 26 miles from London week-end excursions to the metropolis were very frequent, and we also paid visits to the neighbouring towns of Aldershot, Guildford and Woking.

Towards the end of October we were visited with some heavy rainfalls and between that time and the end of November, when we struck camp, we were flooded three times, with the result that the camp ground was transformed gradually from a heather-covered moor into a sort of quagmire, making travelling a difficult and unpleasant job. However we managed to keep the tent floors pretty dry, except when the tide rose, in which case we were obliged to bale out the water with a jam tin. These experiences all provided with a certain amount of fun of course and such incidents as having the tent dropped on us on a blustering wet night by some midnight marauder from another Company, thereby causing confusion among the half-awakened inhabitants of the tent, were all taken in good part and another practical joke played upon the suspects in return.

Our training took the form of squad drill, platoon drill, company drill followed by rifle drill, musketry and bayonet practice, skirmishing and route marches with perhaps two hours' physical drill. At nights and on wet days we attended lectures on signalling, hygiene, and so on. After we had become fairly proficient in all these things we began sham fighting etc and did a certain amount of Morris tube shooting. After about three months of the joys of camping, during which time we had ample opportunity of becoming hardened to every possible variety of the English climate, we were removed to quarters at Aldershot, where we tasted for the first time since leaving home the joys of sitting in an armchair in front of a huge fire. We are in the married quarters and all the furniture has been left behind. We are very comfortable now compared to the camp and the change was very much appreciated. We are really in Farnborough and are situated on the edge of Laffan's Plain which has been converted into a military flying ground, an aircraft factory being nearby. Full route marches are the order of the day here and sham fights are very frequent, this latter makes the training very interesting.

By the time the battalion embarked for France, Frank Eales had been promoted to Corporal and then in January 1918 he was commissioned as a Second Lieutenant in 12/Rifle Brigade.

Second Lieutenant George Butterworth also recorded the move to Aldershot in his next entry in his diary on 30 November:

Monday, November 30th.

The move to Aldershot. This was rather an interesting performance, as the whole brigade marched in as a body, 100 yards separating each battalion. Appropriately enough the weather was at its worst – a gale of wind and driving rain. This did not make the job of packing and loading any easier, but by mid-day we were all ready to move off. One got some idea from this of the vast scale on which army transportation has to be worked; a brigade is, of course, a comparatively small body, and we were certainly not over-stocked in any way, but it took something like 100 traction engines and motor lorries to move our stuff. These were ranged along the road in an apparently endless line, and made us feel very important. Owing to the wet we were, of course, unable to strike camp, and a party was left behind to do this as soon as the weather allowed.

After an early dinner had been served, we marched off triumphantly in drenching rain, and so, farewell to Bullswater, and at the other end comfortable barrack rooms, and fires in each!

With the first weeks of December taken up with the route-marching and mock battles, the thoughts of the men in the ranks turned to Christmas leave. Possibly to ease the strain on the railways of moving so many men back to the north it was decided that the battalions would only allow one company to be on leave at any time. With each company granted seven days' leave it would take a whole month for every man in a battalion to get home. This was relayed to his family by Alex Stephenson in a letter dated 10 December:

Dear Mother and Brothers

Just a few lines to let you know I won't be home for Christmas as we don't get our furlough till New Year's week. We are getting away a company at a time, the first ones go away this Monday which is the 14th and come back on the 21st the next on the 21st and come back on the 29th then we go away on the 29th till the 5th of January that is seven days we get, but I don't know how we are on about the train fare yet, I have heard we get a free pass, but you haven't to believe all you hear. I had a letter from Margaret Armstrong yesterday and she says that Auty cannot get home either so she will be vexed when she gets my letter saying I cannot get because she was expecting all of us being at their house. Well we are going to be billeted on Monday for a week and I saw some of the soldiers that are in the houses now and they say it is alright, so that is not so bad. Well I think I will close now with love to you all from your loving son and brother, Alex.

It was now decided that battalion training would be carried out and to this end 23rd Division was allotted a training area north of the Basingstoke–Aldershot canal and south of the Reading–Wokingham Railway. 68 and 69 Brigades were therefore allotted billets in the training area and duly moved out of Aldershot. 68 Brigade were billeted in and around Wokingham in the villages of Swallowfield, Arborfield, Hartley and Shinfield. In these rural Berkshire villages there was little in the way of good accommodation and many men had to be content with sleeping in the barns of the farms in the district. However, the bad weather continued and there was not much training done as the men struggled with the

68 Brigade carried out training in the Wokingham–Reading area; here a company of 11/NF of 68 Brigade have their photo taken on the Wokingham–Reading road. Note how they have stained the Slade Wallace equipment a drab colour.

heaths and moors being waterlogged. Indeed, communication and the delivery of rations became a difficult matter for those supplying food to the troops.

By the middle of December they were back in barracks at Aldershot where Christmas leave was opened on 16 December, each battalion going away one company at a time, being granted seven days and a return warrant to their home. The first to go experienced trouble with the railway authorities when they reached the north-east, for although each man had been given a return railway warrant, many men had been given a warrant to the nearest big town and not to their home village. On arrival at Darlington, Newcastle or Sunderland, the men simply got on the next train to their village, bearing in mind that at that time every village in County Durham was connected to the railway because of the coal mines. This change of trains caused trouble with some of the ticket inspectors and many men had to leave number, rank, name and unit so that the North Eastern Railway Company could reclaim the extra fare.

There was some absenteeism from men of both battalions at this time as many took an extra couple of days and the surviving conduct sheets show anything from twelve hours to seven days overstaying of leave.

However, two Sunderland men, both sergeants in 12/DLI, started their journey back to Aldershot on 7 January which led to the death of 3/11487 Sergeant Joseph Rushforth. A time-expired regular of 2/DLI, he had re-enlisted on 14 September 1914 and had joined 3/DLI before being posted to 12/DLI; his previous service quickly ensured promotion in Kitchener's New Army. What happened is recorded in the *Nottingham Guardian* which carries the report of the inquest under the heading:

FELL FROM A TRAIN, SOLDIER'S DEATH AT GRANTHAM.

The Grantham Coroner, Mr A H Malim yesterday held an inquest on the body of Joseph Rushforth 34 a Sergeant in 12th (Service) Battalion Durham Light Infantry now stationed at North Camp, Aldershot.

The evidence showed that the deceased had been home at Sunderland for a week on furlough and on Wednesday at noon with Sergeant Virtue of the same regiment, left the GNR at Sunderland for the purpose of travelling to London to re-join the regiment. Travelling with them was a member of the Naval Flying Corps. After York they fell asleep, deceased being stretched at full length on the rear seat. Shortly after passing through Grantham the naval man woke in consequence of feeling a draught from the window; he got up and closed it, he then missed the deceased and waking Virtue they made a search of the corridor carriage, but failed to find him. Later deceased was found in the six foot between the main lines a little way south of Grantham Station. He was conveyed to hospital where it was found he was unconscious and suffering from a fractured skull. He died the next morning in consequence of his injuries.

The Jury returned a verdict of 'Accidental death' and expressed the opinion that when deceased awoke from his sleep it was his intention to go to the lavatory, but opened the wrong door and fell onto the line.

Like Sergeant Rushforth, 3/10865 Sergeant John Virtue had a lot of previous service, although in his case it was with the Special Reserve having enlisted into 4/DLI in 1894. When war broke out he enlisted on 6 October into 3/DLI and again like Rushforth was posted to 12/DLI in November 1914. When the battalion left for France he was posted to 16/DLI and eventually discharged in May 1916.

By the middle of January 1915 all the men had been allowed home and the vast majority returned on time, but some like 19304 Private Peter Kilburn were reported as deserters in the *Police Gazette* and did not serve overseas with the Durham Light Infantry.

After their return to Aldershot, Jack and Bill Anderson wrote again to their family in Station Town:

Jan 11/15, J and WH Anderson
A Company
13 Batt DLI
Malplaquet Barracks
North Camp, Aldershot

Dear Father & Mother, Brothers and Sister

Just a few lines hoping to find you all well, as this leaves us at present. We received the parcel on the Monday morning and your letter dated Jan 10 on the night. We were pleased with the parcel but don't send any more now till we send for them, to let the others get one or two sent. One fellow got one sent and he was acting the game saying 'parcels was no good' it was postal orders he was wanting so he could go out and drink it. You can send the washing back anytime but keep the towel back. We have not touched the Friars Balsom and other yet. We will not take harm here if we get no parcels from home, as long as we have little Tommy with us. Tommy does the shopping. If Joe has a wet cavil there is a lot here that would like to work it for him. [A mining reference to a wet work place.] *That was a good parsnip but I doubt I will not be back to put the seed in this time as all the parsnip seed should be in by the last of next month, February. But we think the war will not be long if Italy and Rumania step in as the papers say down here that they might take up arms any day. We think you will get no money from the Government till those papers of ours is found as there is some more cases here just like ours* [and they have] *lost their papers as well.*

We might have been at home since we enlisted till now and they might not have known. There was a man telling us that when they had the strike at Bullswater there was a man walked away and he is working in Newcastle now and they have never missed him, they might have lost his papers as well. So if you go to Clark tell him that you think the delay is at York as our papers are either mislaid or lost. But don't say anything about the man working in Newcastle.

From Your two loving sons J & W H Anderson

PS That other Anderson that is in our company was an officer's servant along with another lad at Minley Manor and they were working with the Officer's revolvers and the other lad shot Anderson through the neck and he is now in Hospital. So if you hear anything about it up in the north, don't be alarmed.

On 22 January the Division was inspected by M. Millerand, the French Minister of War, and Lord Kitchener. That morning snow had fallen and was lying 4 inches deep when at around noon, it turned to heavy rain. The inspecting party was supposed to arrive at 1430 hours but eventually turned up at 1530 hours. The Divisional Infantry was drawn up in line of battalions in mass. The men in their blue serge uniforms and civilian overcoats were soaked to the skin, having stood out in the pouring rain for so long. However, they appear to have suffered very few men reporting sick with colds.

In the middle of February the long-awaited khaki uniforms arrived and were quickly issued to all ranks. It is related in the divisional history that this was achieved by General Babington telling the War Office that Lord Kitchener was going to inspect the Division. This resulted in authority

In the middle of February the long-awaited khaki uniforms arrived and were quickly issued to all ranks. It is related in the divisional history that this was achieved by General Babington telling the War Office that Lord Kitchener was going to inspect the Division. Here a young lad from the Crook area of County Durham shows off his new kit.

being given for the issue of the khaki uniforms.

It was while 13/DLI was stationed in Wokingham that a 25-year-old miner by the name of Private Harry Craddock attracted the attention of his superior officers. At Bullswater he had received a punishment of seven days confined to camp and then at Aldershot a further three days' confinement. But on 24 January 1915 he was placed under arrest for striking two junior NCOs. He was tried by District Court Martial on 30 January, the charges being:

The accused No 16194 Private Harry Craddock 13th (Service) Battalion of The Durham Light Infantry, a soldier of the Regular Forces is charged with:

When on Active Service offering violence to his superior officers in the following instances in that, he, at Wokingham, on the 24th January 1915, struck with his fist on the head, No 18061 Lance Corporal T W Duncan and that he, at Wokingham on the 25th January 1915, struck with his fist on the head, No 17943 Lance Corporal M Weatherley.

The verdict was guilty and the sentence forty-two days' detention; Private Craddock's sentence was remitted by seven days for good behaviour. He would be in trouble again before the battalion embarked, but in France was among the best fighting soldiers in the battalion and was promoted and awarded the Military Medal and the Distinguished Conduct Medal.

There was a meningitis scare in early February 1915 and two men of 12/DLI were admitted to the Connaught Hospital in Aldershot and placed in the isolation ward. On 14 February both men passed away. 18264 Private John Simpson who was aged 21 and from Gateshead was buried in Aldershot Military Cemetery, while 22-year-old 19435 Lance Corporal Andrew Briggs from Nottingham who had originally

Second Lieutenant Lesingham Eden Start had served as a sergeant in 6/Somerset LI prior to being commissioned into 13/DLI in December 1914. He was only with the battalion a few weeks before he was admitted to Aldershot Military Hospital where he passed away on 23 February 1915.

enlisted into the Seaforth Highlanders but for some unknown reason had requested a transfer to the Durham Light Infantry was taken home and buried in Nottingham General Cemetery.

On 23 February Second Lieutenant Lesingham Start died in Aldershot Military Hospital. He had only been commissioned into 13/DLI on 18 December and he was buried with full military honours in Aldershot Military Cemetery. Then the following day the 23rd Division received orders that on 26 February they would move to the Shorncliffe area. On the night of 25 February a farewell concert was held in the new YMCA hut in Malplaquet Barracks for the men of 12/DLI. This was the first concert held in the hut which had been specially erected for the work of the YMCA. The *Durham Chronicle* records that the battalion Regimental Sergeant-Major, John Thomas Illingworth, presided and was ably assisted by some of the officers, and that:

A first class concert was given and refreshments, chocolates and cigarettes, provided by the regimental funds, were handed round at intervals. Lieutenant Hethrington gave six or seven items which will be long remembered by all who had the pleasure to hear so brilliant an artiste. Special mention should also be made of Sergeant Wardle, Lance Corporal Coleman and Privates Spedding and Edwards, all of whom gave excellent turns. Messrs Egleton and Perring both professional singers and now with the YMCA staff were encored again and again. Mr A Guest of Spennymoor who is in charge of the hut, on behalf of the YMCA thanked the officers, chairman, artistes and all who in any way had contributed to so enjoyable an evening. It was a brilliant send-off for the new hut and a magnificent farewell to the boys from the north.

The next morning the battalions paraded and marched out of their barracks and in three brigade columns set off towards their assembly areas. En route Lord Kitchener inspected two of the brigades on the march. When they reached their destination 12/DLI went into billets in the village of Willesborough near Ashford, while 13/DLI found they were actually billeted in the town. Here the pace of the training stepped up a gear and got harder with numerous days spent out in the field. As the battalion training was completed they moved on to training as a brigade and then with divisional field days. There were also several inspections by senior officers: on 8 and 9 April the infantry were inspected by Major General Laurence Drummond CB, MVO, the Inspector of Infantry and then on 7 May by General Sir Arthur Paget GCB, KCVO, DSO, who was at that time the Commander of Southern Command. Both these officers had served in the Scots Guards. Then four days later along came Sir Archibald

Murray GCMG, KCB, CVO, DSO, the Chief of the Imperial General Staff, who was also the Colonel of the Royal Inniskilling Fusiliers. He had been commissioned into that regiment in August 1879. Each of these senior officers expressed their satisfaction with the training of the men of the 23rd Division.

Second Lieutenant George Butterworth wrote a short entry describing Ashford and his opinion of the workers that had gone on strike:

> Ashford, March 5, 1915.
>
> We are here for an indefinite time – billets very comfortable, other prospects poor. No progress whatsoever to report, except that we are now khaki-clad.
>
> These strikes are a nuisance, and I see there is a small one on the NER. Personally I should do three things:
>
> (1) Hang (or bayonet) all employers whose profits show an increase on previous year.
>
> (2) Imprison for duration of war all who organize cessation of labour in important industries.
>
> (3) Make Lord Robert Cecil dictator for duration of war, as being the only man in Parliament who has anything useful to say.

While stationed in Ashford the mail arrangements were such that the men were not allowed to have anything sent to the house where they were billeted. The other thing worrying the Durham miners at this time was the payment of their insurance contributions; this information was relayed to their parents by the Anderson brothers in a letter of 25 April:

> Dear Father and Mother, Brothers and Sister,
>
> Just a few lines hoping to find you all well as this still leaves us in the best of health. We received your letter and are pleased you are going to settle in that new house. We are sending you ten shillings through. It is no use us asking for a week's leave as it takes some all their time to get away when they get a telegram saying some one is very ill at home, they [the army] telephone through and get all the particulars before they will let them go. There are rumours every day saying we will be getting a furlough shortly. We were all given our insurance cards to fill in the name of the society we are paying to and they will be sent on to the Bristol Lodge headquarters. Both cards had four and three pence worth of stamps on as we just pay 11/2p per week, but we could not fill in our numbers as we did not know them, so you might tell who ever has the job now of collecting the money for the lodge and he might write and give them our numbers and it will save them a lot of trouble. We are pleased you are going to get your photos took. We are sending you some more pictures. We are sending you J Carr the Irishman we told you about, don't be frightened when you look at him he was trying to look smart, but he got a little twist on his face. Bill's Insurance card at this end had W A Anderson on it and when he was at home it had W Anderson on it, so you might draw their attention to it. Please send us the number of the house if you have one.

7 Platoon, B Company, 13/DLI, photographed in Ashford in spring 1915.   D/DLI/7/165/1

While they were stationed in Ashford 13/DLI marched through the town to church parade on Sunday.
Albert Hewitson asked his aunt and uncle if they could spot him on the photograph.

Never address any letters to the house we are staying at as there is a lot here getting into trouble for it as it is against the regulations.

J & WH Anderson
No 2 Platoon, A Company
13 Batt DLI
South Ashford
Kent.

The Anderson brothers don't seem to have provided the address where they were billeted, but one who did was 15548 Private Albert Hewitson serving in C Company. He sent a photograph of the battalion marching through Ashford to his aunt and uncle:

Albert Hewitson
13 Batt DLI C Comp
62 Providence Street, South Ashford, Kent
Dear Aunt and Uncle, just a few lines hoping this card finds you in the best of health as it leaves me the same at present. Well Scopy you have fine weather up your way as we have had some fine weather up till today and it has

15548 Private Albert Hewitson served with C Company 13/DLI until transferred to the Labour Corps in 1917. He was discharged on 6 March 1919.

been snowing but it has given over now. Well how is little Harry getting on, I trust he is a big lad now. I heard we are going to France on 15 April. I only wish we were going now. Well I think that is all for present. Can you find me just coming round the bend, well good night, write soon, Albert.

17398 Private Bill Horn who was serving in A Company sent a card on 15 March on which he gave his address as A Company 13 DLI C/O Mrs Cramp, 12 Francis Road, South Ashford, to his sister in which he said:

Dear Sister,

Just a few lines hoping you are well as I am A1. It is lovely weather. I had a 28-mile ride on a bike on Saturday, good roads, best love. Bill.

17398 Private Bill Horn who managed a 28-mile bike ride one weekend while the battalion was stationed at Ashford.

The Regimental Orderly Room was kept busy in Ashford and one of those appearing on orders was Harry Craddock, who when found guilty received another twenty-one days in detention, this time for 'making a highly improper remark to an NCO and not complying with an order'.

On 7 April 15721 Private Robert Milburn was admitted to the local Voluntary Aid Detachment Hospital at 30 Church Road, Ashford. He was in an unconscious state, having been ill in his billet for some days. He was diagnosed with septic pneumonia and never fully recovered consciousness. He died on 9 April and was buried in Ashford.

The training in the Ashford and Folkestone area carried on until late

The Darlington Evening Despatch carried this photograph of the Orderly Room staff, A Company, 13/DLI, in the 9 March 1915 issue.

SEATED 18361 CQMS G HODGSON FROM COUNDON DIS TO COMMISSION, 24747 CSM A NICHOL FROM ROTHBURY BECAME RSM, STANDING 18360 SGT JOHN JOSEPH HODGSON FROM FERRYHILLTRF R ENGINEERS AS 156343 COMM 2Lt R ENGINEEERS 25/12/16 KIA 13/8/17, 18362 J A HODGSON FROM LEASINGTHORNE DIS KR 392, 15894 F O LAMB FROM ESH HILL TOP SGT MM, 18489 PTE H VIPOND Z RES, (BROTHER IN C COMPANY MM) 16708 PTE C MUIR CPL Z RES, 24809 PTE E KELLY TRF R ENGINEERS AS 360307 Z RES 28/1/19

Men of A Company 13/DLI photographed in Ashford, in spring 1915: standing second left is 17750 Pte Michael Brough who would win the DCM and the MM and Bar. D/DLI/7/75/805(3)

May and although the battalions had become proficient in field training, they had had little opportunity to carry out any shooting. To rectify this, 23rd Division was moved by train from Kent to Bramshott near Bordon in Hampshire. Here 68 and 69 Brigades went into a new hutted camp and 70 Brigade was quartered in the barracks at Bordon.

The news of the forthcoming move and the conditions at the new camp were recorded by Second Lieutenant George Butterworth in his diary for May 1915:

Above: Unidentified officers of 13/DLI on manoeuvres with a tent in the woods near Bramshott 1915. D/DLI/7/560/13(6)

Below left: Second Lieutenants Blake, Rees and Sheardown relax on the ranges at Bramshott. George Sheardown transferred to the King's Royal Rifle Corps before embarkation and was awarded the Military Cross with the KRRC. D/DLI/7/560/13(9)

Below right: Second Lieutenant James Tait from Coxhoe, County Durham embarked with 13/DLI but transferred to the Royal Flying Corps in February 1916. D/DLI/7/560/15

Above: Lieutenants Sheardown, Tate, Greenwood and Clarke relax during an exercise in the summer of 1915. D/DLI/7/560/13(8)

Above: Second Lieutenants Blake and Rees on the steps of their hut at Bramshott 1915; note the beer bottles and soda bottle for the whisky. D/DLI/7/560/13(12)

Left: Second Lieutenant Frederick Rees kept this photo of his batman Pte Kent. D/DLI/7/560/16

Below: The interior of an officer's hut at Bramshott recorded by Frederick Rees. D/DLI/7/560/14

Extract from **The War Illustrated**, *volume 2, no. 40, featuring a group photograph of the officers of the 12th Battalion, The Durham Light Infantry, 22 May 1915. Back row: Second Lieutenant J.H. Lowes; Second Lieutenant E.A.G. Stamp; Second Lieutenant A. Hare; Second Lieutenant J.F. Dodds. Second row (standing): Second Lieutenant F.A. Bristow; Lieutenant J.B. Jacques; Lieutenant M.A.B. Nelligan; Second Lieutenant M. Campbell-Jones; Second Lieutenant M.R. Pearse; Second Lieutenant T.W. Hetherington; Second Lieutenant C.T. Barclay; Second Lieutenant N.V. Smith; Lieutenant S. Holmes; Lieutenant C.S. Summerhayes; Second Lieutenant C. Powell-Smith; Second Lieutenant H.N. Grimwade; Second Lieutenant G.G. Armstrong; Second Lieutenant E.W. Lafone; Second Lieutenant P. Baylock; Second Lieutenant J. Longstaffe. Third Row (sitting): Lieutenant G.L. Wood; Captain T. Carr-Ellison; Lieutenant and Adjutant H. Carr-West; Captain H.E. Pease; Captain J.P. Day; Major E. Gales; Lieutenant-Colonel L.C. Elves, D.S.O.; Major H. Danvers; Captain C.E. Cummins; Captain A.B. Mawer; Lieutenant R.C. Woodhead; Lieutenant and Quartermaster A. Rendel. Front row: Second Lieutenant A.D. Hetherington; Second Lieutenant R.A. Lumsdale; Second Lieutenant A.T. Carr-West; Second Lieutenant R. Burns.*

Group photograph of the officers of the 13th Battalion, The Durham Light Infantry, 1915. Back row: Second Lieutenant W.A.L. Dray Cooper; Second Lieutenant Start, died 23 February 1915; Second Lieutenant H.S. Bailey; Second Lieutenant E.A. Pullen, killed in action; Second Lieutenant Geach; Second Lieutenant D.M. Clarke; Second Lieutenant W.A.O. Read; Second Lieutenant Cooper; Second Lieutenant Butterworth, killed in action 4 August 1916; Second Lieutenant J.G.M. Bell. Middle row: Lieutenant P. A. Brown, killed in action, 4 November 1914 [sic, 4 November 1915]; Second Lieutenant Oliphant; Lieutenant E.A.P. Wood, wounded 2 June 1916; Captain E.A. Bellamy; Second Lieutenant L.M. Greenwood, killed in action August 1918; Lieutenant G.M. Long, wounded, July 1916; Lieutenant S.Q.M. Snow; Second Lieutenant Saverbeck, wounded, July 1916; Lieutenant N.A. Target, killed in action, 4 August 1916; Captain W. Miles; Lieutenant Jardine, Royal Army Medical Corps; Second Lieutenant C.G. Hancock, wounded, July 1918 T.O. [sic; possibly Transport Officer]. Front row: Lieutenant H.L. Markham; Captain Blakiston, Chaplain of the Forces; Captain W.A.L. Downey; Captain U.S. Naylor, killed in action 3 September 1916; Colonel G.A. Ashby C.B.[?]; Lieutenant E. Borrow, Adjutant; Captain H. Austin, killed in action 4 August 1916; Captain Blake, killed in action September 1916; Second Lieutenant Howard. This photo must have been taken in January or very early February 1915 as Lesingham Start died on 23 February. D/DLI/7/75/26

Ashford, 20th May, 1915.

We move on Sunday to huts near Liphook. Address 13th DLI, Bramshott, Hants. Since returning I have been rather hustled – it is bad enough being transferred to a strange company, but, in addition, owing to the absence of the junior captain, I found myself temporarily second in command – then a further shock last night; the company-commander, an excellent man, is suddenly summoned to join the Expeditionary Force in France at 24 hours' notice, so now I am in charge of 240 men, scarcely one of whom I know by sight! This is likely to continue for perhaps a fortnight, and involves immensely complicated accounts and considerably more responsibility than is good for anyone at such short notice.

However, I hope to pull through!

Bramshott, 30th May, 1915.

We arrived here safely (by train) on Sunday. This camp holds two Brigades, 68th and 69th, and is situated just south of the Portsmouth Road, 11/2 miles west of Hindhead; it's a splendid position – the officers' quarters are 1/4 mile from the road and overlook the valley along which the railway runs. Mrs. B.'s cottage is about 11/2 miles off, and I have been there twice for bath and dinner. I think the huts quite a success. It is like being under canvas without some of the discomforts. The men have straw mattresses and plenty of elbow room. The whole business is more like active service than anything we have done yet. We have eschewed the caterer's mess for officers and draw the ordinary army rations; these are supplemented by groceries, etc., and cooked (very excellently) by our own soldier cooks. It seems curious that we have not done this before, because, besides saving expense, we are certainly feeding better than at Bullswater, or even Aldershot.

I am getting into the way of my new job. The business part gives me most bother, but at present the accounts are simplified by the fact that all the Company Books are in the hands of the Paymaster, so that one can't attempt to make out a balance.

No sign of rifles or ammunition yet, but there is a general feeling that the days of our training are numbered and I rather expect to make a sea voyage before arriving at my 30th birthday.

Eventually the desired rifles and ammunition arrived and every man was put through the musketry course on Longmoor ranges; by the middle of July everyone was trained in the rifle and some in the new Lewis gun, which had been issued to the infantry to increase their fire-power. In A Company of 13/DLI the Anderson brothers had been moved into the company machine-gun section and were now Lewis gunners. With the training completed embarkation leave was granted; this was divided into two periods with half the battalion away at once. By the second week of August everyone was back and the embarkation tables, mobilisation stores and all the equipment required for active service were brought up to strength. On 14 August Jack and Bill Anderson wrote once again to their parents:

J and W H Anderson

No 1 MG Sect

13 Batt DLI

The Hutments, Bramshott, Hants

Dear Father & Mother, Bro and Sister,

Just a few lines to say we have sent a parcel & we just want the socks back, but we will tell you when to send them on. We got the jersey given off a sergeant & the pants are those I fetched back when I was through. We are sending 10 shillings again & we are taking no hurt for money and grub, so don't send any parcels till we ask for them. We are still at Longmoor but we had a march on Saturday & we just halted at Bramshott for 10 minutes, we did about 15 Mile. I am sending a card of German prisoners, nothing startling here at present. We don't know how much longer we will be at Longmoor yet so don't worry if you are a few days getting a letter from us as we are generally on until 8 o-clock at night.

From your two sons J & WH.

Shortly after this letter was written the whole division was assembled on Hankley Common, where they were inspected by His Majesty King George V. Then the next day orders for embarkation were received.

Chapter Three

Flanders Fields

S O IT CAME TO PASS that at 0400 hours on 24 August 1915 the advance party of 12/DLI, consisting of the Machine Gun Section and battalion Transport left Liphook station for Southampton. They were followed at 0940 hours by the same sections of 13/DLI. At Southampton they were quickly taken on board a transport ship which sailed for the French port of Le Havre.

On 25 August at 1800 hours, half of 12/DLI entrained at Liphook for Folkstone, followed by the rest of the battalion at 1900 hours. Likewise 13/DLI travelled in two parties. The first entrained at 1955 hours and the second at 2035 hours, both being transported to Folkstone where both battalions went on board a transport bound for Boulogne.

The departure of the latter battalion was recorded in his diary by George Butterworth in this way:

Bramshott, 25th August, 1915.

We are off this evening but don't know from what port.

There had been some changes of personnel; Colonel Ashby left us some weeks ago (superannuated) and Major Biddulph is now C.O. There was also some inter-company exchange of officers, and I myself was transferred to A Company in May (after promotion to full Lieutenant). For nearly a month, in the absence of the seniors, I was Acting Company Commander, and am now the senior subaltern, in charge of No. 2 Platoon.

At the time of writing we had been stationed for three months in huts at Bramshott, near Haslemere. The first sign of possible business to come was on Thursday, August 19th, when the King came down to review the 23rd Division. Very short notice was given, and several officers who were on leave at the time had to be recalled by wire.

This inspection was rather more interesting

When the Commanding Officer Colonel Ashby was retired, Major Nicholas T. Biddulph, an ex-regular, was appointed to command 13/DLI. In this picture he is seen when he was a captain serving with 2/DLI in Ireland in 1903. D/DLI/2/2/136(64)

than most; the Division had its rendezvous in open country about half way between Guildford and Haslemere – an ideal spot for the purpose. It was certainly a fine sight, and the moment when the King, at the head of his train, galloped into sight through a defile in the hills, was quite thrilling.

However, no one suspected any immediate developments, and the interrupted leave was resumed, but it was not destined to be more than a one-day excursion, for on the evening of Friday, August 20th, orders came that we were to mobilize.

Of course everyone was very excited; one felt that a little of the real thing, after months and months of sham and boredom, must be a change for the good. The camp was in uproar most of the night – quite in the old Bullswater style.

However, the actual process of mobilizing, apart from the uncertainty of our movements and destination, was not very exciting. As far as I was concerned, it consisted chiefly in making out lists of kit deficiencies and 'pinching' as much as possible from the quartermaster. We were not able to get away, as the authorities pretended that we might be starting any moment.

Eventually we got our orders to march on Wednesday, August 25th.

We knew that we were bound for France, but our exact route was not stated, and the censor will not allow me to say anything about it. We had a perfect crossing, by night – getting on and off the boat was a matter of minutes only, and it was impossible to believe it was the work of the WD.

A single destroyer acted as escort, and no incident occurred.

The first to arrive was 12/DLI who marched straight to the rest camp where they arrived at 0100 hours; 13/DLI didn't get there until 0400 hours. Both battalions spent the day resting. At 2000 hours 12/DLI marched out of the rest camp to the railhead at Pont de Briques; here they were rejoined by the advance party, Machine Gun Section and Transport, and then at 2200 hours they entrained for Watten. They were followed in the early hours of 27 August by 13/DLI whose advance party had also by now arrived from Le Havre. Both battalions detrained at Watten and then moved by route march to the village of Moule where they went into billets.

The move was recorded by Second Lieutenant Philip Brown in a letter to his mother:

August 26 1915

My Dear Mother,

On Wednesday night we started at last after so many months of training. It was not so very hot, but very dusty, marching down to Liphook. This is the last name I may mention, as we are specially forbidden to tell the route. However we went by the route which Folk would least expect. There I must leave it. The night was lovely, moonlight, rather misty on land, but clear and calm at sea. A destroyer came alongside and steamed for a while by our side, but then left us. I was told that the French fishing fleet was

near, and I suppose that had a patrol of its own handy. We landed before dawn on cobbled quays, very slippery, and marched up to a fine rest camp, the best appointed camp I have ever seen, in a lovely situation. We leave it again tonight and I fancy that the hard work will begin then. So far it has been tiring, but not hard work. Since I began this letter I have had a regular holiday afternoon. I nearly managed a bathe but the tide was too low. I walked round the town; saw the Cathedral and some big hospitals, mine-sweepers, a jolly fish market, soldiers everywhere, in all manner of dress and colour. The men are very pleased with their move at present. Of course all the hardship is to come, but they are certainly glad to be on active service at last.

Yours always, Philip.

PS the embargo is now taken off as we are leaving. The crossing was Folkestone–Boulogne and we have been at Boulogne all day.

Second Lieutenant Philip Brown was commissioned into 13/DLI from 6/DCLI and died from wounds received on a patrol in November 1915 when he was rescued by his observer Private Thomas Kenny.

The journey of 13/DLI was also recorded by George Butterworth:

We landed in the early morning and marched a few miles to camp, where we rested for the remainder of the day. In the middle of the night we moved on again, marched a few miles to a railway and then sat down and waited for a train to take us to the front. The transport arrangements at this point were defective, as we had to wait about two hours by the side of the line, during which time some fifty trains must have passed us, mostly empty and returning to the base. At length ours turned up – three first class compartments for the officers and cattle trucks for the men, 40 in each. A rumour got about that we were going straight up to the front, but after a few hours' journey the train pulled up at a small wayside station; here we got out, a French interpreter took charge, and we marched five very hot and dusty miles to …, a village where billets were provided for us.

Here we remained for over a week – about 40 miles from the firing line – and were fairly comfortable, the officers being quartered in farm houses and the men in adjacent barns. We could hear the big guns quite distinctly most days. During this period we went on training exactly as in England, and quickly relapsed into our dull and monotonous habits; in fact things seemed much quieter than at Bramshott, and the only sense of war was provided by the heavy traffic and scorching despatch riders on the main road which led direct to the British Headquarters.

The country here is not unlike England – and the people also. It is possible that they have been unconsciously influenced by the English invasion, and they have certainly been tremendously sobered by the war.

*This was very striking, in contrast with our people at home; I never heard
a soul speak either jestingly or excitedly about future prospects; the French
people are certainly going to stand firm. As for the French soldiers, there
were none to be seen. The English army fills the whole countryside, and has
become part of the normal life – relations with the inhabitants are excellent,
but of course there is none of the enthusiasm such as would have greeted us
a year ago.*

Second Lieutenant Philip Brown wrote to his mother again on 27 August,
this time recording the events after the battalion left the rest camp up to
the arrival in Moule:

27 August 1915

My Dear Mother

*I continue my adventures while they are fresh in my mind. After my
easy day in Boulogne we began our trek. It was not far, but it took a long
time. We did not start till after midnight and then marched through
beautiful country – high woods and meadows in full moonlight – it was so
bright that the roll was called at 1 am without artificial light. We passed one
beautiful chateau behind high railings. Then we waited for hours on the rail
side, reminding me of our adventures on the road to Marlaix. The train
when it came was immense, containing all our wagons and horses as well
as the men, who were packed in cattle trucks, 40 in each. They must have
spent a miserable night. Then we got to our present destination, which is
behind the firing line, and had a blazing hot march to the little village on
the hill top, where we are in billets. I am in a pleasant enough spot a little
inn, 'At the sign of the Archers.' A dozen men are in a barn behind, and I
and another officer share a little bedroom. Feeding is rather a problem, but
we have got eggs and omelettes and good bread and butter, besides our
rations, which are chiefly bully beef, biscuit and tea.*

In Moule the two battalions started training: various courses of instruction
were set up and 12/DLI sent Second Lieutenants Noel V. Smith, H.N.
Grimwade and H. Haymer to Brigade Headquarters where the Brigade
Machine Gun officer ran a three-day course for battalion machine-gun
officers. Second Lieutenant Arthur D. Hetherington went to Hallines for a
bombing course. The training continued for over a week and the officers
quoted wrote home about the work they were doing and the conditions in
the rear area of the line. Lieutenant George Butterworth said:

*One of my daily tasks is the censoring of men's letters; I have to read
them, sign the envelope and then they are franked by the Orderly Room.
This becomes irksome after a time, but it is also of great human interest. I
don't think I ever before realised the difference between married and single!
As to what they say, of course there is very little news – they all seem
astonished at finding they can't understand the language, and they all
complain because they can't get English cigarettes. Any present of these
will be welcome, but they must be 'Woodbines' (1d. a packet).*

Second Lieutenant Philip Brown wrote the following to his mother:

My Dear Mother

We are still resting in our billets and are really very comfortable and well fed with ration meat, bread, jam and tea, besides good butter, eggs and coffee in small bowls, which reminded me of St Jean du Doigt. The road is very interesting. Long trains of wagons go past, then Generals, English and French, then a company of Engineers and some guns going into neighbouring billets. This morning we were out marching at 0630 hours and went over a sort of down ridge, but all cultivated in small plots with no hedges. We seem to be on the edges of these hills and E of us the land slopes away. I have been putting censorship stamps on the Battalion letters – a big job. There were a thousand of them, I should think in all.

He continued the story in another letter sent the next day:

31 August 1915

Last night we practised an alarm. About 10 o'clock when the battalion was in billets the word went round and our company was on parade and practically ready to move in 15 to 20 minutes. The men are supposed to put all their kit ready every night and this was to test them. Today we are not doing much, but tomorrow we start early on a big exercise and I shall not be very much surprised if we moved on without further warning. A prisoner came past this morning while we were at work with a guard of soldiers. I did not see him but was told he was a spy. The soldiers' letters are very amusing, one writes: 'Dear Mother, we are now in the land of Nod and cannot understand the twang.' They all complain of a lack of cigarettes, 'Tabs,' but otherwise they are very content to be here.

Yours always,

Philip

That day Second Lieutenant Gerald Bailey, the Battalion Signals Officer was evacuated to hospital. When the training was finished it was time to move nearer to the front line: accordingly at 0530 hours on 6 September 12/DLI left Moule and proceeded by march route via St Omer and Arques to billets in Hazebrouck. They were followed by 13/DLI who took a slightly different route marching via Tilques, St Martin and Arques to Hazebrouck. On arrival there was only room in the billets for three of the companies and one had to bivouac in the nearby fields. After a night's rest the march continued: 12/DLI went via Boure and Strazeele to billets at Maison Blanche, while 13/DLI followed the same route but were billeted in Steenwerck. The heat had a trying effect on the men who were carrying all their equipment and the war diary of 13/DLI records that thirty-seven NCOs and men were left in one of the four Casualty Clearing Stations located in Hazebrouck.

The move nearer the front was recorded by both officers who again left written descriptions of the march.

Lieutenant George Butterworth wrote:

On Monday, September 6th, we moved on – a long march of over 20 miles. For various reasons this exhausted us very much – in fact far more than anything we had ever done, the chief causes being (1) heat, (2) cobbled roads, (3) weight of packs. As regards the last, I ought to say that out here the men carry all their belongings on their backs, and as we have not yet learnt what to throw away the weight is tremendous. At least one in ten fell out, and one can hardly blame them. The weather has been very hot almost all the time so far.

On arrival at destination we put up in billets for the night.

Next day, September 7th, we marched again – only 15 miles this time, but weather hotter still. Nearly half the Brigade fell out on the way!

This march brought us within five or six miles of the front, and we could hear the rifles cracking quite distinctly.

Billets of the usual country type, i.e., farms and barns.

Second Lieutenant Philip Brown didn't write to his mother until 8 September, when he described the march and his new billet:

8 September 1915

My Dear Mother,

I got your long and very interesting letter in our latest billets, which are a good twenty miles nearer the Front than those I wrote to you from before. We started in lovely weather on Monday morning about 6 and did a march till about 6 then billeted near a small town. The day was fairly hot and the men had a fairly stiff test. We were in a pleasant farm house for the night and slept in the back parlour, clean and so much better furnished than an English farm parlour. Unfortunately the floor was of tiles, clean but cool and hard. Next day we marched on, a shorter march but in blazing sun and very glad we were to form up in a fallow field and eat our dinners. Then we marched on to billets, another farm house with fine barns, big enough to take our whole Company. We officers are in a small bare room enough for our valises. I was told off this morning, as an officer who had a working knowledge of French, to buy stores and had rather an amusing morning, bumping along the twisting roads among dykes and the thatch and plaster farms into a little town, where I bought mineral waters, candles, coffee, sauce and similar stores. I must turn in as I expect a fairly hard day tomorrow. Good night.

Yours always

Philip.

The next day the Commander of III Corps, Lieutenant-General Sir William Pulteney KCB DSO inspected both Durham battalions and explained to the assembled officers and men that they would now be attached by companies to the battalions holding the line, and that they would spend one or two days in the line before they would take over a section of it as a unit.

September 8th, we were inspected by the General Commanding our Army Corps, who kindly informed us what we were supposed to be doing,

Lieutenant-General Sir William Pulteney KCB DSO.

a subject about which we had all been very much in the dark.

He said that we were to go up into the trenches by platoons, for 'instructional purposes,' 24 hours at a stretch, being attached to the units actually on duty there. We were to do this for four days (two days in and two out), and then retire into safety for further training and finally take up our own positions in the line, in perhaps two or three weeks' time.

Thus wrote George Butterworth as he prepared to move up to the line for the first time. 13/DLI was split up between the battalions of 61 Brigade. Two platoons of each company were attached as follows: A Coy DLI attached 7/Duke of Cornwalls LI, B and C Companies DLI attached 12/King's Liverpool Regiment; the remainder were attached to 7/Somerset LI in billets at Rue de Quesne. Likewise 12/DLI left Maison Blanche and moved to Estaires and were attached to 60 Brigade. Here A and B Companies were attached to 12/King's Royal Rifle Corps for twenty-four hours and the battalion's first casualty occurred when one man was wounded during the tour of the line. On 10 September C and D Companies moved up to the line and relieved the other two companies. When their twenty-four hours was up they were moving back out of the line when they came under fire and a further six men were wounded. A similar story occurred to the men of 13/DLI; the remaining platoons went into the trenches of the battalions they were attached to and relieved the two platoons that had gone in the day before. At about 1915 hours as they were leaving the trenches the men commanded by Captain Urmston Naylor and Lieutenant George Butterworth were caught by machine-gun fire and suffered five casualties, one of whom was only slightly wounded and remained on duty.

Second Lieutenant Philip Brown continued the story of the battalion's sojourn in the line in a letter to his mother when he came out of the trenches after his platoon's turn in the line:

11 September 1915

My dear Mother,

I am actually writing to you from a fire trench within a short distance of the German lines, though I may be back in billets again when it reaches you… We rested a day, or rather we were inspected and inspected ourselves and I went to the nearest town to buy stores. Next night we started in the

73

evening and marched, first in the hot sunset with a brilliant sky of gold and purple, then in twilight, finally at night, passing through a small town full of English soldiers and out onto the road again where for the first time we came across shelled buildings, and saw the sky through broken rafters and floorings. We parted, some to go straight into the trenches, others into billets. My platoon was very tired, and fell straight down into their barn and went to sleep. I slept in the open and kept waking up to listen to the firing and watch the flares which both sides send up to see what the others are doing. Next day we woke up in real war scenery, battered cottages, white puffs of smoke almost always in the cloudless sky, whistles blowing, and sentries on the road everywhere. I went out with a working party from the RE and had the opportunity of seeing a house set on fire by shell fire a few hundred yards away. The whistling drone of the shell was so distinct that one felt puzzled at not seeing any sign of it till the roof suddenly smoked and burst into flames. In the afternoon I added to my experiences by seeing an aeroplane knocked out by shell fire. It was a pitiful thing to see it suddenly topple and collapse. That evening, yesterday, we started to come into the trenches ourselves, we were to share them with another battalion already in occupation. We marched so far, and then were met by a guide. We went along a road in file, turned at an angle and immediately felt a few stray bullets whistling. Quite close to the trenches a small house still showed a light. We passed beyond it and then through a cluster of transport and then got behind the first barrier and into a long line of communication trenches, which ended up in the actual fire trenches of the Front. As soon as the men were settled we got a cup of tea in a little dug out, which forms Officers headquarters and then started round the trenches. Everywhere there were sentries looking over the parapet and firing, continual shots thumping against the sandbags or skimming the parapet, coloured flares and occasional bursts of hammering, which means machine guns fire and of rattling, which means rapid rifle fire. The night is the busiest time and the early morning seemed nearly interminable. Now in the sunshine, we have had a most lucky week of fine weather, there is little to do. The snipers are at work and I can hear heavy guns, but they are not at work on us. I am sitting in a dug out of sand bags and look over some dry banks at a yellow cross to the memory of a soldier who died in action here last spring; there are trees on a flat sky line behind; nothing but the cross and a few soldiers crossing the doorway and some rumbles and thumps remind one of the war. It has been a great advantage to be in with officers of a regiment which had some experience of active warfare in trenches already. I think I may be out in billets again tomorrow...

Yours always

Philip

The same day as Philip Brown wrote this, the Battalion Headquarters of 12/DLI went into the line attached to 12/KRRC while the rest of the battalion was in billets in Estaires. It was here that a tragic accident occurred when 18535 Private Andrew Carrol serving in A Company from Tanfield in County Durham was drowned in the River Lys. He is buried in Estaires communal cemetery but his gravestone records he died on 7 September which conflicts with the battalion war diary.

At 0845 hours the next day A and B Companies were attached to 12/KRRC and 6/Oxfordshire and Buckinghamshire LI [OBLI] and spent twenty-four hours in the line and as they left the trenches one man was wounded. They were relieved by C and D Companies who during their time in the line had two men wounded. The battalion moved back into reserve and there began a period of rest which consisted of working parties every night. Parties of men in the hundreds were attached to the Royal Engineers for various forms of manual labour.

When they were relieved the battalion moved to L'Hallobeau where the Commanding Officer Lieutenant-Colonel Elwes gave orders for a Court of Inquiry into the death of Private Carrol. On the morning of 17 September under the presidency of Captain Thomas Carr Ellison, the members of the Inquiry, Lieutenants Cyril Powell-Smith and Maurice Pease assembled. They then proceeded to take evidence of the witnesses, who all came from B Company.

The first witness was Lieutenant Frank Golden, who after being sworn in stated:

At Estaires about 0830 hours on 11 September I saw a crowd of men on the canal bank. They said a man had fallen into the canal, a rescue had failed, they said the man had been under water ten minutes to quarter of an hour. I took my clothes off and with two other men searched the canal for him. We found the body in about three minutes and brought it to the bank.

The bridge over the canal entering Estaires from the north.

It was in about nine feet of water. Artificial respiration was at once started and the doctor sent for.

The next witness was 16524 Private Albert Howes from Gateshead who said:

At Estaires on the morning of 11 September about 0830 hours I was in my billet near the canal bank, I heard a shout that there was a man in the Canal. I ran out threw off my jacket and shirt and dived into the Canal. I reached the man who was in the middle of the Canal with only his hands showing above the water, and caught one of his hands. I then started to paddle towards the bank. As he was sinking his grip of me relaxed and as I was exhausted I had to make for the bank myself.

The third man called to give his evidence was 21210 Private John James Roberts who added this statement:

About 0830 hours on 11 September I was getting ready for parade when someone shouted that there was a man in the canal. I threw off my equipment and ran to the canal. Private Howes was in the Canal and had hold of the man. I jumped into the canal to help him but when I reached him he had lost hold of the man and I was unable to find him and returned to the bank being exhausted.

The fourth and final witness was 15474 Private George Fenwick, a resident of Hebburn New Town, who after being sworn in stated:

About 0830 hours on the morning of 11 September, I was one of the piquet on duty at the Canal bank to see that no one stripped to bathe in the Canal. I was at the far end of my beat when I hear the shout of a man in the water. I ran along to the place and when I got there Private Howes was in the water and Private Roberts followed him in in about three minutes. I saw nothing of the man except his hands. It was about ten minutes after this that Lieutenant Golden with the help of two other men succeeded in recovering the body.

Having heard the evidence the Court found that Private Carrol had died of 'Suffocation due to being immersed in water'. The evidence was duly typed up and sent to the Adjutant General's office at the base.

Meanwhile No 1 Machine Gun Section of 13/DLI under the command of Lieutenant Herbert R. Markham remained in the trenches with 12/King's Liverpool Regiment while that battalion was relieved by 7/Somerset LI. During the day the German artillery shelled a disused gun emplacement and a farmhouse.

At 1920 hours the following evening No 1 Machine Gun Section was relieved by No 2 Machine Gun Section, under Second Lieutenant G.M. Long, but No 1 left behind three NCOs and seven men.

We have been in the fire-trenches three times – twenty-four hours at a stretch. This was just a preliminary canter, and we none of us had any real responsibility, merely assisting those already in possession. Naturally enough we were not put into any of the dangerous sections, but it may be

German sniper.

of some interest to describe what a normal day on a quiet part of the front is like. The first day we started from a point some miles in rear, and timed our march so as to get up after dark. As we got nearer and twilight set in, the artillery noises grew more and more insistent; ours seemed to predominate, and every gun within miles had its turn at the evening 'hate', which is an affair of regular occurrence. As night set in the artillery fire ceased, but the rifles went on cracking continuously with every now and then a splutter of machine guns. We reached the entrance of the communication trench safely; it is about 600 yards long, and as our guide lost his way several times, we spent quite a long time in it; stray bullets were now flying all about, and the explosive sound they cause as they pass overhead was new to most of us; the depth of the trench, however, made things quite safe. At last we filed into the fire-trench, and immediately opposite the entrance I found, to my astonishment, a little wooden shanty, and the officers of the company having dinner; so just at the moment when I felt braced up for a vigorous onslaught on the Hun, I was hauled off to roast beef and beer, while a sergeant posted my men.

Later on I went along the line with the officer of the watch. Every minute or so a flare went up, and then the enemy position was plainly visible, about a quarter of a mile away (the trenches here are really breastworks, built up high with sandbags).

The sentries and snipers on either side exchange compliments pretty frequently; though there is rarely anything to fire at (I have not seen a German yet). In the trench, one is perfectly safe from them; it is the working parties behind who are worried by the stray bullets. And so it goes on all night, and every night; occasionally a machine gun gets on to a target (real or imaginary) and then there is half-a-minute's concentrated fury, after which comparative peace again.

It is extraordinary how soon one gets accustomed to all this rattle. I slept excellently each night I was in, and as I was not on any special duty I was able to get a decent amount of rest.

By day there is very little rifle fire, the sentries are fewer in number and work by periscope; the German snipers make it dangerous for anyone to expose his head above the parapet by day for more than a second or two (even at 500 yards).

In this respect they are all over us – and in fact we are still well behind the Hun in all the tricks of trench warfare; as regards machine guns we have *pretty well caught up, and our artillery distinctly has superiority.*

As far as my platoon was concerned, we had a very quiet time each day we were up; only one shell fell anywhere near us and we have not had anyone hit. Others have not been quite so lucky; one platoon was caught by a machine gun on its way home the very first night (presumably through the guide's fault), and had five wounded. Another lot narrowly escaped destruction by a mine explosion, but the battalion has lost less than twelve wounded altogether and none killed.

This was how George Butterworth recorded this period of the battalion's time in France.

Early the next morning the Germans exploded a mine under a machine-gun section of 7/Somerset LI but fortunately the men of the attached machine-gunners of 13/DLI escaped without injury. Meanwhile 12/DLI was back in the line with 12/KRRC and 6/OBLI near Levantie and during their time in the line they had two men wounded. On 15 September the two companies out of the line, A and B, supplied working parties for the Royal Engineers. They then moved back to billets in L'Hallobeau and for the next few days were employed on working parties for the Royal Engineers. While out at rest 13904 Private Charles Stephenson, a 37-year-old man from Cannon Row, Sherriff Hill, Gateshead, wrote to his wife, who had the letter published in the *Newcastle Evening Chronicle* on 4 October:

We have been in the trenches twice, but we have had a few days' rest. We are likely to be in for eight or nine days before being relieved and then we will get a week's rest as they call it; but we are always doing something to keep us in training. Where we are, we can hear the guns booming all day long. Aeroplanes are flying here and there and the guns are firing shells at them. We saw one German machine brought down at the last place we were at. I don't think the fellow would be much use after his fall. Very likely he will be flying with the angels now. The Germans are very sly and cunning and seem to be well up in warfare; but with it all we are still skinning the sausage, slowly but surely. I wish we could get fairly at the brutes; then it would not be long, but as it is we are fighting slowly, but surely, and after victory is sure to be ours in the end, but at a heavy cost. We are here to go through with it, and we must do our best to put the devils down. Although it looks like being hell we must keep a good heart and get through it. All along the road up which we came we saw a lot of wrecked buildings. Churches and big buildings of any note have been brought to the ground. Some houses have iron bedsteads flattened out in the debris, and sewing machines all broken to pieces were lying about. It makes one's blood boil to think that there are such fiends in a Christian world to cause such misery. If those at home who are shirking could but see it I think they would come forward. They just want to think what their own homes might be like if the Germans got to them. We all know that their spite and bitterness are much

Main street in Estaires during the war.

> *greater against us than against our allies, so it beholds every man medically*
> *fit to come forward to prevent such like happening in our own houses.*

It was on 2 October that they moved back into the line where in the evening they completed the relief of 8/Green Howards. This was an uneventful tour with one man wounded on 5 October. In the meantime 13/DLI were moving from their billets in Estaires to billets in Rue de Biez and Rue de Lettree; here they provided working parties. B Company sent a party to Tramway Farm where 16768 Private Frederick Pilcher, a Hartlepool man aged 23 was slightly wounded.

Lieutenant Philip Brown wrote again to his mother describing being in charge of a working party and what it was like moving through the communication trenches at night:

> *16 September 1915*
>
> *My Dear Mother,*
>
> *I wrote my last letter the first time I was up in the trenches. The second time I was only up for a night in charge of a working party carrying up stores for the RE. This time I went to different trenches by a long communication trench past the ruins of an Abbey of the Chartreuse, which has been fought for desperately during the earlier part of the war. As we came near the fire trenches we heard a great deal of shouting mixed with the firing. The Germans were calling out, 'Kitchener's Boys' and 'What about the Kaiser now,' in very good English. I believe, though I didn't hear it myself that they shouted to our people, 'Durham Donkey-drivers, have you had your breakfast.' They have a rather uncanny knowledge of our movements, much more than we have of theirs. The next night I went up to a third set of trenches, where things were quieter. The Germans were further away, and they made very little attempt at anything except sniping. It was*

curious to look round the sally port and see the whole line in daylight, not a soul stirring, and hardly a shot. But early the night before they had exploded a mine under part of the trenches from which I had wrote to you. I was in billets in the open air and was wakened up about 0500 hours by a terrific bombardment, salvoes of artillery. This was in reply to a message about the mine, and was very comforting as it was so vastly superior to anything the Germans do. The last time I came back from the trenches I found orders to get the men supper and then bring them on here, which is a small not very interesting town full of British soldiers, and is used as a rest place and a base. We enjoyed a complete day's rest here, and now expect to move off somewhere to trenches of our own. I have been foolish enough to leave the strop of my Auto strop razor on a barbed wire entanglement.

Yours always

Philip.

George Butterworth penned a few more lines in his diaries and letters:

So much for our period of instruction; we are now in divisional reserve four miles behind the front, and expect to take up duty in our own allotted section in about a week's time. There is not much excitement here, but we hear the artillery at work practically all the time; usually it is simply a gun or two trying to annoy somebody, but occasionally there is a concentrated 'strafe' for half-an-hour or so, and then we all sit up and wonder if someone is trying an attack; and of course there is always a chance that we may be shelled ourselves. But no one minds that.

Sept. 20.

And so the Zepps have been to London at last; such things seem small out here, where the sounds of destruction are audible all day and night. It is extraordinary how long one may manage to keep out of it. I have been three times up to the front line, and so far have seen only one shell burst, and have not seen a single

(a) dead man,

(b) wounded man,

(c) German,

(d) gun.

I have sent the General [his father] two instalments of news; will you please ask him to see that nothing I send home gets into print. The authorities are getting nasty about it, even when the matter is harmless.

On 26 September at 1123 hours the battalion received word from Headquarters 68 Brigade reporting that they had been placed under command of the 20th Division and would move at 1500 hours. At 1353 hours a further wire came ordering billeting parties to proceed to Estaires. The battalion paraded and left Petit Moulin at 1520 hours and marched to Estaires where they arrived at 1730 hours. By 2300 hours they had completed billeting in the Rue Bassee. They were now in support of the Meerut Division which had made a diversionary attack at Pietre in support of the main attack at Loos. Although they had had an initial success they were eventually forced to retire to the British front line.

Before they had marched Philip Brown was writing to his mother when he was called out to lead a working party up the line; in this letter he describes the difficulty of moving through the mud:

26 September 1915,

I was writing this when I was called out to take a working party of 125 men to work in the trenches. It was 1845 hours and had been raining nearly all day. I ran back to my tent, slipped and fell full length. This was unpleasant, but it did not matter much as everything was a paste of clay-mud, which daubed everyone more or less before the night was over. The lane outside the bivouac was a canal of mud and the meadows beyond it a lake of mud. Then we got on to the pavé which for once was a relief. We twisted about in the darkness, being halted by sections outside farm houses, where troops are billeted and meeting Red Cross vans and GS limbered wagons clattering over the cobbles, and mounted Orderlies galloping and spurting mud all over us. Finally we got to the appointed place, a small inn-farm house among high trees at a cross roads a thousand yards behind the firing line. We found the road packed with other working parties, which was not pleasant, as the spot is what is called 'unhealthy', that is, a regular spot for the guns and had as a matter of fact been shelled that afternoon. However, after one hour's wait we got tools and moved off down the same road as I had gone down two days before, and up a communication trench and into reserve trenches, where we set to work on earth works. Things began to improve from this point. The mud was awful, but the men were glad to get to work. We were not shelled and only had a few bullets over our heads. Standing on the parapet I could see the line of trees leading up to the fire trench and the flares and the flashes of the shells which our own guns were sending over our heads. The moon had risen, and the sky gradually cleared. When we started home about two the night was lovely, except under foot, a very bright moonlight, in which haystacks and pollarded willows took romantic shapes. We marched one and a half hours and got in about 0330 hours. They had hot tea for us, and I slept soundly as you can imagine. This morning we hear of another move and I should not be surprised if we were back tonight in our front trenches or billets just behind.

Yours always

Philip

On 27 September the danger of an enemy counter-attack was considered over and 68 Brigade were ordered to return to Petit Moulin where they arrived at 1650 hours; here they were joined by a draft of ninety-nine NCOs and men from 17/Durham LI in England.

After supplying various working parties, 12/DLI on 2 October went back into the line at L'Hallobeau where they relieved 8/Green Howards. The time in the line was very quiet and only one casualty was reported when one man was accidently wounded. Meanwhile 13/DLI were supplying large working parties for 173 Tunnelling Company Royal Engineers. Then on 7 October, 13/DLI moved up and took over the sector held by 12/DLI. Before they went in, George Butterworth wrote in his diary:

> Oct. 7, 1915.
>
> We have moved again, and are now in reserve to our own Brigade. We relieve the 12th D.L.I. shortly, and shall be in the trenches for perhaps a week. Things very quiet in fact much quieter than when we first came out. There seems to be a temporary shortage (or economy) of shell on both sides, which is probably inevitable after the deluge of September 23-25.

The relief was complete by 2210 hours and at 0130 hours an officer's patrol commanded by Lieutenant Tait went out and carried out a reconnaissance of No Man's Land. The next day was dull with a light wind and the German snipers were busy on the battalion front. They caused two casualties: in B Company 23659 Private James W. Brett, a resident of Richmond, North Yorkshire was killed in action; while in A Company 17667 Sergeant J.T. Johnson who came from Twyford in Berkshire was wounded. In 1917 he was commissioned into the Labour Corps where he served as a Captain with 509 Agricultural Labour Company. A third casualty occurred when 19014 Private William Baxter of B Company was wounded when he accidentally shot himself. He was evacuated and eventually the following June he was discharged, from the regimental depot, as unfit for further war service. A few shells fell near Burnt Farm on 10 October and then the enemy started firing rifle grenades: one that landed on A Company wounded a Gateshead man, 16300 Private George Brown, who sadly died from his wounds thirty minutes later. The following day the enemy sent six 4.2cm shells over. A patrol was sent out under Lieutenant Howard, during which two men became separated from the officer. Lieutenant Howard heard a noise behind him and on turning round and seeing someone coming towards him, he drew his revolver and fired, severely wounding 23647 Private Edward Brass of A Company who came from Stanley, County Durham. Unfortunately he died from his wounds at 0645 hours on the morning of 10 October. The Company Commander Captain Naylor held an inquiry on the spot.

During this tour Philip Brown wrote again to his mother, recording that he had met and had a quick chat with Woodhead, one of those commissioned from the DCLI into 12/DLI in late 1914:

> 8 October 1915
>
> We started up at about 1900 hours and got to the communication trench without mishap. It was extremely muddy and difficult to keep a footing in the communication trench. Two planks were put down on one side to walk on, but they were very slimy. We relieved 12/DLI and it was a pleasant piece of luck that we actually took the place of their C Company where

Woodhead is, so that I had a few minutes conversation with him… I lay down before coming on duty at 0100 hours and about 1230 hours a man came and said they could hear moaning over the parapet. I was afraid that this meant that some of my men who had just started on a listening patrol had been hit. They went out by a sallyport or slit in the trench, dropping into another trench. I went down this with my 'observer' a very nice Irishman from County Durham, [17424 Private Thomas Kenny] who goes with me everywhere and crept along a line of willows in a very shallow trench. We soon came on one man down in the bottom of the ditch. It was difficult to move him, but finally my observer got him up on his back. Poor fellow, he had a bad wound in the side. After this, the night passed quietly. My business was to visit the sentries and listening posts, and to fire a few rocket flares to see what the enemy was doing. They were not doing much.

Yours always

Philip

It is highly probable that the man carried out on the back of Private Kenny was Sergeant Johnson. Kenny would repeat the feat with another casualty in a few weeks' time. Two days later Philip Brown again sent another long detailed letter to his mother, this time trying to describe his daily routine while in the front-line trenches:

10 October 1915

My Dear Mother,

The night after I wrote to you – I posted in the afternoon – another man was hit, not I think badly. Since then no one in my platoon has been touched, though we have a few casualties. The weather is fine, though unsettled today, and we have really enjoyed ourselves up here since the mud began to dry. There is greater freedom in the line for everyone, in spite of the cramped quarters. The enemy is well away from us, and there was a sharp burst this morning, on each side of us. I wonder if I can give you any idea of what life is like. We have our turns of duty and off duty. If I am off in the middle of the night my day begins with 'stand to' at dawn. I wake up and listen for a minute to the sentries talking and mice scuttling. Everything is grey and damp in the morning mist. A few stray shots, but little more. I tramp down each narrow lane between the high banks of sandbags and past my men in a little row of three or four in each bay, standing with bayonets fixed and generally yawning. The order 'Stand down' comes, the day sentry sits down and looks up into his periscope, and the others stretch themselves and move off, to get rations, to light fires, to clean rifles. One party pushes a trolley with a load of rum bottles down to a ruined farm to get water. Soon there is a smell of frying bacon and I go round to examine rifles before breakfast. After breakfast some men are set on to clean the wooden boards in the footway, others are working at a dugout, others sleep, and they get most of their sleep in the day. I am told of an extraordinary apparition in front of one sentry's post – a black dog. I inspect through a periscope but can see nothing. Next I crawl down the trench where my man was wounded and decide it must be deepened. This covers me with mud from the waist down as I crawl all the way. Lunch or dinner as it is our chief meal, and then sleep. Tea and 'Stand to'. The trenches begin to look gloomy now, with dripping rain and darkness coming on. Mice scuttle over the path as I go my rounds and a rat hops over a sandbag on the top of the parapet. Work begins again at 'Stand down.' There are more sentries, a party for water, a working party improving the parapet and wire, and so on. We are just going to enjoy a dinner – supper of soup and sardines on toast. Then I go on night duty, visiting the sentries and the listening posts, firing an occasional flare out into the darkness and receiving all kinds of information, much of it highly imaginative. One man hears a dog 'Whinnying' as he calls it, in front, another can see a man up in a tree and a third is certain that someone is shooting from behind our line.

    (Not signed)

On 12 October 12/DLI moved forward once again to relieve 13/DLI. During the relief 13/DLI had one man, 23439 Private Robert Gott of A Company, a miner from Thornley Colliery, killed by a sniper and two men, 24513 Private J.W. Orton and 24607 Private D. Nelson, both of B Company were accidentally wounded. Private Gott, a married man with two children, had originally enlisted in the Northumberland Fusiliers but had transferred to the Durhams and was a hewer at Thornley Number 1 Pit. His platoon commander Second Lieutenant Charles T.W. Sauerbeck, who had been commissioned into the Regiment from the London Electrical Company, Royal Engineers, Territorial Force, wrote to Private Gott's wife:

    Will you please accept my deepest sympathy in the loss of your husband, killed in action on 12 October! I was standing by his side in the trenches, just before sunrise, when a sniper who had been giving us some trouble, fired a bullet which caught your husband killing him instantaneously. It will be very hard for you, but you will have the satisfaction of knowing that your husband could not have done more than give his life for his country.

Just like 13/DLI before them, 12/DLI waited a few hours and then sent an officers' patrol out into No Man's Land. This five-man patrol led by Second Lieutenant Maurice Neligan was a minor disaster for the battalion. The events in No Man's Land were relayed in a letter from the Company Commander, Captain John Day, to the parents of Second Lieutenant Neligan:

    France 14 October 1915

    I have the sorrowful duty of reporting to you that your boy is missing and believed to be a prisoner in the hands of the Germans. Two nights ago he went out in charge of a patrol which succeeded in getting quite close to the German barbed wire. Unfortunately the patrol was discovered, heavy fire was opened on them and bombs were thrown. Maurice threw a bomb in

reply, but the Germans were swarming out along a side trench and cut off the retreat of the patrol. Three of the five managed to get back; your boy and Private Wilson the bomber did not. Of the three who returned, two had been left as a covering party twenty or so yards behind Maurice and in a ditch. These men fired on the advancing Germans and did not leave until Maurice and Wilson were surrounded. I fear it is possible that one or both of the captured men may be wounded, but we hope that they are now being safely nursed behind the German Lines. Maurice has done wonderfully well. He was one of our most popular officers both with his men and his fellow officers. He had made quite a reputation for himself in patrol work and was a very gallant leader in these dangerous enterprises.

This letter was followed two days later by a letter from Lieutenant-Colonel L.E.C. Elwes, officer commanding 12/DLI:

Second Lieutenant Maurice Neligan 12/DLI was killed on a night patrol in No Man's Land, 14 October 1915.

France 16 October 1915

You will by now have been communicated with regarding your son; and I asked his Captain to write to you and say everything he knew about the actual events which led to his becoming reported missing and probably wounded, on patrol work. I have personally interviewed the three men of the patrol who succeeded in getting back; but it is impossible to state with certainty what actually did take place, owing to the darkness, and to the fact that the man in closest proximity is also missing. Captain Day's account, which I have read, appears to give a fair description as far as we are able to judge, and I see no reason for not having every hope that we shall see him again some day.

I can now only say how much I sympathise with you in your anxiety, also that I never met a boy who so easily gained the affection of every one he came in contact with or a more plucky young officer. I miss him enormously on account of his great value to us, and for the real affection I had formed for him.

This was then followed by a letter from the C of E Chaplain attached to 68 Brigade, the Reverend John N. Blakiston, who wrote to his parents as follows:

Let me add a word of sincerest sympathy. The anxiety you are in concerning your son's safety must be intense and I only hope and pray that he is all right. I have been Chaplain to the Brigade for over a year, and I *knew your boy to talk to quite well. In case he did not tell you; I thought this fact might be of interest to you: On the Sunday before he was taken we had a celebration of the Holy Communion immediately after an open air parade service. The service was held in a room in a farmhouse and your son came and made his communion with several of his brother officers.*

I have been chatting with men of his regiment this afternoon and they all speak highly of him. One Sergeant said that they considered him to be the best of all the young officers as a soldier, and that there was not a man who would not have followed him. May God bless you in your trouble and keep your son safe.

However, despite all the hopes that Second Lieutenant Neligan and Private Wilson were alive, they were in fact dead. Their bodies were recovered and today lie side by side in Ration Farm Cemetery. One strange fact is that the War Graves register shows that Maurice Neligan died on 13 October 1915 and that 25561 Private George Wilson from Primrose Hill, Willington, County Durham died on 14 October 1915.

In the reserve line Second Lieutenant Philip Brown was writing another letter to his mother:

15 October 1915,

My Dear Mother

I am writing to you about 0130 hours in a small heavily sand-bagged dug out, which is our officers' mess in the new trenches we are in. I am on night duty and just resting between my labours of visiting the sentry posts. We left the front trench on Tuesday night and came down here to reserve trenches which are ¹/₄ to ¹/₂ a mile behind. Coming in to them in the dark they seemed very tortuous and scattered. We were all consumed with desire to sleep and I could do with some more as these night duties break in on one's night 2 to 4 last night 12 to 2 tonight and Stand To at 7. We are in a line of dug outs linked up by trenches with two or three gaps where streams and paths go through and all of those have to be watched. The people here before us were great alarmists and thought there was a sniper who slunk about and fired on us at night, but I disbelieved the whole story, though of course there are a lot of bullets coming over the fire trenches to us here. Our chief business has been to strengthen the dug outs which needed it for we are near a road with guns and the Germans shell them. The first morning for instance after breakfast, we heard our guns start from behind. Then a distant report and the whizz of a coming shell; it is quite different to the noise of a going shell. You can here that it is on the downward curve and of course you don't get the concussion of firing. Whiz, bang! It went over the farm and road into a field; then another to the right, then shrapnel bursting noisily in the air; apparently clean over some men

The Battalion Padre John N. Blakiston wrote to the boy's mother.

on the road thirty yards away. Then a whizz, and no bang. A dead shell i.e.
it failed to explode. Then as I go up the line to see the men are under cover,
a bigger crash and a lot of black and yellow and black smoke mixed.
Explosive shell, probably with shrapnel mixed in it, but it came to nothing,
and I don't think we are likely to be in anything at present. Lower down
there has been another great set to and we are all hoping for great news
soon. Today or yesterday I should say I was out of the trenches on musketry
business and was glad to stretch my legs, as I think we shall be up in the
front trenches again in one or two days.

The contents of your beautiful medicine chest suffered a sad calamity
one night. We were going into billets and I was glad to put my equipment
on the ground, while I got the men settled into barns. Our field kitchen
came up and in the inky darkness one of the heavy draught horses trod on
and obliterated the medicines. Thank you by the way for the broadsheets
which I enjoyed very much.

Your always
Philip

On 15 October 12/DLI had another man wounded and then on 16 October
13/DLI, as predicted by Philip Brown, relieved them and 12/DLI sent two
companies to the reserve trenches in the Bois Grenier line and two
companies to billets in Rue de Lettres. Here they provided the normal
working parties until on 20 October they took over from 13/DLI in the
same trenches as before. During this tour in the line each day they had one
man wounded and one of them, 16941 Private George Bennett, a resident
of Albert Street, Windlestone, County Durham made it as far as the
Dressing Station at Sailly sur Lys before he died from his wounds. The
battalion held the front line until 25 October when they were relieved by
1/Sherwood Foresters and moved back to reserve billets in La Rolanderie.
Out in reserve the battalion found large working parties for work at
Tramway Farm where one man was wounded by a stray rifle or machine-
gun bullet. After four days 12/DLI relieved 1/Sherwood Foresters in the
same sector which at the time was very quiet.

When 13/DLI took over from 12/DLI on 16 October the weather was
dull, cold and damp. It wasn't long before Battalion Headquarters
received word that a German sniper had been located in a tree at I.20.d.8.5;
the battalion had one of the new catapult guns and they fired two bombs
at the sniper and a machine gun from D Company enfiladed his position
and the enemy parapet. Then two of the battalion sniper section, 18192
Lance Corporal William Clair from A Company and 19644 Private Robert
Hickson from D Company went out into No Man's Land at 0430 hours.
They had orders to return at 1930 hours. At dawn they shot and killed two
Germans who showed themselves above the parapet. However, from that
time on No Man's Land was under close observation by the enemy and
they were unable to move. They lay out there throughout the day and

night and it wasn't until 0830 hours on 18 October that they were able to return.

These events were recorded by George Butterworth in a rather long entry in his diary; at this time he described the routine and described the trenches the battalion was holding:

28 October,

Since my last communiqué (!) we have had two turns in the trenches and a short rest between; we are now in billets (fairly comfortable), and it is quite uncertain what we are going to do next, or when.

I will try and give some idea of what daily life in the trenches (i.e., ours) is like, so far as is permissible.

In the first place, there are practically no real trenches at all in this part of the country; we are here practically at sea level, and the spade finds water almost at once, hence protection has to be given with barricades of earth and sandbags. The front barricade is continuous all along the line, and behind it – for protection against shell fire – is a conglomeration of passages and cross walls; the geography of these is worthy of the maze at Hampton Court, and in striking contrast to the neat regularity of trenches built for training purposes. (Incidentally I had never seen a breastwork before coming over here.)

As these walls have now been standing for nearly a year, they are in need of constant repair; there are enough rats in them to eat up the whole British Army. One advantage of breastworks over trenches is that one can walk about behind them to a depth of about 25 yards without fear of being hit by bullets.

As to our routine – by night we have a good number of sentries watching the front; these are relieved periodically, and the spare men are kept in readiness for emergencies.

By day there are, of course, fewer sentries, and they work entirely by periscope.

Sentry duty is always taken very seriously, no matter how easy the conditions, and a sentry found asleep is automatically sent up for court-martial.

The difference between day and night conditions is very great. By night, although spasmodic firing is always going on, we have not had a single man hit, and one could quite happily eat one's supper on the parapet, provided one retired below for one's smoke!

On the other hand, by day it is usually (though not always) extremely dangerous to expose even the top part of one's head for more than two or three seconds. A German sniper, even at 400 yards, can make pretty good practice at a six inch target, and we have already lost an officer and one or two men in that way. Moreover they frequently crawl out at night and take up a position from which by day they can pot away at our parapet without fear of detection. Of course it is the telescopic rifle that does it, and it is curious that the authorities do not think it worth while to put us on an equality in this respect. But in reality this sniping business is more of a nuisance than a danger, as it is quite unnecessary for anyone to expose himself by day, and by night the sniper can do nothing much.

So much for sentry duty – and there is not much else, as far as routine goes. The rest of the men's time is divided up between (a) rest (chiefly by day); (b) carrying supplies up from the dumping ground (which can be done at any time thanks to the communication trenches); (c) repairs (chiefly by night).

As to the Officers, our duties are similar; we take it in turn to be 'officer of the watch,' which means constantly visiting the sentries, noting incidents of interest, and generally keeping a look-out; at other times there are occasional odd jobs, but otherwise one can rest, and I usually managed to get six hours' sleep out of twenty-four, which is pretty good – boots always on, when asleep. There is a fairly plentiful supply of dug-outs, and one can be quite comfortable. One dug-out serves as a mess-room for the officers of the company, and we have no difficulty in getting up provisions; the men also get their ordinary rations, and so long as the weather is fine (which, curiously enough, has been the case with us so far) all is well.

So much for daily routine. Now for a few incidents, chiefly connected with sorties into No Man's Land.

On one occasion we decided to attempt 'reprisals' against the German snipers; two men were detailed to go out before daybreak, take up a position, annoy the enemy as much as possible during the day, and return as soon as it got dark. We waited anxiously for their return, and eventually Headquarters 'phoned up that we were to send out a strong search party (of which more anon). This was not successful, and we had given the men up, but in the middle of the next morning, to our great joy, they turned up, having been in the open for 36 hours.

It appears that they crawled close up to the enemy parapet, and accounted for two men during the day; when it got dark they tried to get back, but were cut off (or thought they were) by patrols; so they lay still all night. Next morning they managed to crawl into a ditch, which fortunately led almost up to our lines. For this exploit they are probably getting a D.C.M.

With the two snipers trapped in No Man's Land the battalion decided to send out a patrol to try to rescue them. George Butterworth was put in charge and recorded the events in his diary:

The Rescue Party. – This was a very tame affair. I was put in charge, and perhaps did not take it very seriously, but it seemed to me that we had a very small chance at night time of finding men, presumably wounded, without having some definite idea of where to look for them. However, it was a novel experience, and probably did us good.

We filed out (about 16 strong) by the usual exit, myself in rear, according to instructions. When just clear of our wire everyone suddenly lay down, and at the same time I heard a noise in a tree just to our left. Feeling sure that it was a man I got hold of a bomber, and together we stalked up to the tree. I then challenged softly, and no answer being given, the bomber hurled his bomb, which went off in great style. It struck me afterwards that it was foolish to give ourselves away so early in the proceedings, but I am only narrating this as an example how not to conduct a patrol. After satisfying ourselves that there had never been anyone there, we rejoined the others, and I passed up the order to advance. After ten yards crawling everyone lay down again, and this went on for about half-an-hour. By this time I was getting tired – also wet, and as we only had a limited time at our disposal, I decided to go up to the front – instructions notwithstanding – and push on a bit faster; our procedure, moreover, was beginning to strike me as rather ludicrous, as we were strong enough to frighten away any patrol likely to be out. So we went forward about 150 yards without meeting anything, and as time was getting short, I decided to circle round and return by a different route to our starting point. By this time everyone had acquired a certain degree of confidence – seeing that not a shot had been fired in our direction – and the last part of our journey was carried out at a brisk walk, and without any attempt at concealment. And so ended my first and (at present) only attempt at night patrolling. Casualties, nil.

Results, ditto, except some experience and amusement.

I think that is all I have to say about our trench experiences to date. Next time we shall probably find out what it is like in wet weather.

P.S. – Anyone reading the above must see that none of it gets into print.

On 18 October the enemy fired three shells just beyond the support trench and then between 1020 and 1120 hours they fired a further twenty-nine rounds at Park Row near Ration Farm. During the day Second Lieutenant Gerald Bailey was wounded in the head while positioning some guns on high ground behind the front-line trench. Then in the evening the battalion sent out an offensive patrol under the command of Captain Naylor. The objective was to drive the enemy working party out of the trench found by Lance Corporal Clair. Second Lieutenant Charles Sauerbeck went ahead of the main party and threw two bombs into the trench. As the bombs exploded, the battalion machine guns opened fire and swept the enemy parapet. As the patrol withdrew Second

*Captain **Urmston Shaw Naylor** was promoted to the rank of Major and attached to 6/Royal Irish Regiment as second in command. He was Killed in Action with that unit on 3 September 1916. He has no known grave and is commemorated on the Thiepval Memorial to the Missing.*

Lieutenant Charles Sauerbeck was wounded by a bomb, 23924 Private Jacob Pearson, 20595 Private George Strong and 18721 Private Robert Gaskell were also wounded, while a 21-year-old Page Bank man, 17115 Private Henry Stringer was killed.

On 20 October 12/DLI came up and took over the front line and 13/DLI moved back to billets at Jesus Farm. At No 3 Casualty Clearing Station Second Lieutenant Gerald Bailey, the Battalion Signalling Officer, died from his wound in the head and his funeral took place in Bailleul. He had originally served as a Private in 5/Hampshire Regiment prior to gaining his commission in December 1914 in the Durham Light Infantry.

The news of his death and of the patrol was relayed by Philip Brown in a letter to his mother:

21 October 1915

My dear Mother,

Since I wrote the officer who was shot in the head has died. It was a very bad wound, clean through the head and there was very little hope of the result. Our first loss in officers, and especially sad because it really was unnecessary. He and I had fixed up a rifle battery to fire over our trenches at the back of the German line. The next morning he set to work to alter the position and rigged it up on an exposed bank in full view of the enemy's parapet, from which I have no doubt the shot came. He was young and an exceedingly capable officer, our signalling officer among other things.

The night of the day he was shot, the 19th we had a little affair of our own. A party went out in charge of an officer to surprise a German working party, they bombed them, and then our artillery and machine guns opened fire. Our party got back safely to within a few yards of our line, where they had an encounter and a bomb was thrown, and the officer slightly wounded – rather a good wound, we all say enough to send him home, but not enough to prevent him enjoying it.

My part of the story begins with the bomb which exploded near our wire. I was in the Company mess and heard a bomb quite close. I had just put out a small party to work on the outside of the parapet, and feeling sure that they were being attacked I seized my revolver and ran headlong down our lines to the sallyport with my observer after me. We crept out and no sooner were we outside than our own artillery and machine guns opened. We were perfectly safe as they were over our heads, but the cracking of the machine guns was tremendous and we could see the shells exploding and

Second Lieutenant Gerald Bailey served with 5/Hampshire Regiment and the Inns of Court OTC prior to being commissioned in 13/DLI. He Died of Wounds at Number 3 Casualty Clearing Station in Bailleul on 20 October 1915.

An artist's impression of a night patrol in No Man's Land by an officer and two men.

sheets of flame bursting up into the sky. We crept down to the new trench.
The first man I came across was a sentry who was lying down and shaking
violently as he looked out. I touched him on the shoulder and he nearly
leaped over the parapet. I found the party quite safe but nervous as no one
had told them what was coming and they thought they were in the middle
of an attack. We brought them in and I then went down to the listening post
with White my Company Commander. The men reported the bombing
party had all rushed in together except one who was missing. We had only
been there a minute when we made out someone creeping behind a post –
the listening post is at the end of our wire and White called me out to him

in a little hole where the sentry sits. 'Shall I shoot' he said. I advised him to challenge first and as soon as he did so the password came back, and we found our own Grenadier coming back after some hairbreadth escapes from bombs and our own shells.

Yesterday night we were relieved again and I saw Woodhead once more. We marched back to a big farm near the river which runs between our old centre A- and our old centre E-. It is not far from where we have been before. We got a hut between us and enjoyed our first full night midnight until 0730 with boots off for some time. I hear that we are going to be attached to a regular Line Battalion for instruction. Then I expect we shall go up into the trenches again.

Yours always

Philip

On 29 October 12/DLI took over from 1/Sherwood Foresters in the same trenches they had previously held. This was a very quiet tour with only one man of A Company being wounded. 13/DLI came up on 2 November and took over from 12/DLI. Before they left the billets in the rear, Lieutenant George Butterworth wrote a quick note home:

2 November

I hope you have got my last budget.

We have now had a full fortnight's 'rest,' and for myself it has been almost literally rest. I have done practically nothing but eat, sleep and play chess! No chess in the trenches, because one is glad to sleep all one's spare time. There is nothing else to do here – no places to go to, the most frightfully dull country imaginable, and any amount of rain.

We are shortly going to start another round of duty. I had a splendid parcel from D., rather extravagantly large. We have a Company Mess of five officers, and all contribute. We also get the ordinary soldier's ration, and are usually able to buy milk, butter, etc., so we are not badly off.

They left Jesus Farm at 1630 hours and made their way up the line and by 2030 hours they had completed the relief. The enemy was quiet but the major problem was the rain which was causing the parapets and dugouts to cave in. This was recorded in what would prove to be his last letter to his mother by Second Lieutenant Philip Brown:

3 November 1915

My Dear Mother,

The chief event of the last twenty four hours has been that we have gone back into the trenches and to such trenches. I don't think any words can adequately describe them. It has been raining nearly continuously for some time and the soil here very quickly dissolves into mud of a very fluid kind. There is not a patch of dry ground anywhere. Boards soaked in mud, sandbags bursting with mud, ponds even wells of mud, where there have been pits for shelter against shell fire. One of my men fell into one of these on the way up, soaked himself in yellow sauce and lost his rifle which had to be fished out with crooked sticks. At one place in the communication trench one had to plunge boldly in and wade in a foot or two of water. The ways out to our listening places are simply canals. All this sounds much worse than it is for myself, because after getting thoroughly wet and cold I got hold of some long trench boots and have had warm dry feet ever since. But only a few of the men get these and the condition of many is pitiable. I think we shall soon be better supplied. Meanwhile I felt quite ashamed to go round on my watch last night in my long boots and see the men standing in the rain. Things were better this morning when I woke up after an hour or two's sleep. More rain but clear intervals, when one could see lovely cloud masses on the horizon, and delicate tints of black, brown and blue trees against a pearly sky. All the water in the air made the colours divine and to look back into the trenches was a shock, yellow mud, greasy ponds, dirty clothes and heaps of mangled sandbags. A great deal of trench work is collapsing in the wet, as was to be expected and it keeps us busy reconstructing it. We had a certain amount of shell fire but very little rifle fire yet. A mild enemy in front of us I think.

Thank you for your letters. I hope Theodore was better before he went back. Now I must stop, as I am on duty and should go the rounds.

Yours always

Philip

The following day Second Lieutenant Philip Brown was ordered to take a working party out into No Man's Land. It was very misty as the men worked on the barbed-wire entanglements. Second Lieutenant Philip Brown, accompanied by his observer 17424 Private Thomas Kenny moved forward towards the enemy lines. They lost direction in the fog and found themselves near the enemy parapet. The enemy opened fire on them and Philip Brown was shot through both thighs. The enemy fire was quite heavy but Private Kenny lifted the officer on to his back and tried to carry him back to the British lines. He refused to go on alone, although ordered to by the officer. Carrying the officer became quite a struggle and Kenny resorted to crawling through the mud with the officer still on his back. Finally when he was almost exhausted he put the wounded officer in a safe place where he made him as comfortable as possible. He then set off for the British lines to get help. He found a party under the command of Captain George White who had with him Sergeant W. Calvert, Corporal R.A. Campion and Privates C. Cameron, M. Brough, T.O. Kerr, R. Watt and E. McLane. Kenny guided them back to where Philip Brown lay, but in the meantime a party of German soldiers had crept out into No Man's Land and they attacked the rescue party. Captain White ordered the party to carry the wounded officer back and he himself provided covering fire and held the Germans off. Philip Brown's last words to his 'Observer' were 'Kenny you're a Hero.' Sadly, despite the efforts of Kenny and the rest of the rescuers, Second Lieutenant Philip Brown died from his wounds.

17424 Private Thomas Kenny, a miner from Wingate, County Durham, was awarded the Victoria Cross for his rescue of Second Lieutenant Philip Brown who described Kenny as 'a very nice Irishman from County Durham'.

Two of the rescue party were hit. 16874 Private Robert Watt aged 22 from Olive Street, West Hartlepool was killed outright and was buried beside the officer in Ration Farm Cemetery. Another man, 20-year-old 16706 Private Ernest McLane who came from Carlton Street, Middlesbrough, died from his wounds at the 69th Field Ambulance in Erquinghem and is buried in Erquinghem Lys Churchyard extension, while in the trenches a third man, 24760 Private T. Fisher serving in A Company was also wounded.

For his gallant efforts 17424 Private Thomas Kenny was awarded the Victoria Cross, the first awarded to the Regiment since that won by Sergeant John Murray in New Zealand in June 1864. Second Lieutenant Philip Brown's mother wrote to him from the family home in Kent:

I am writing to express to you the deep gratitude I feel to you for your most gallant and heroic service on 4 November, when you risked your life over and over again in rescuing Lieutenant Brown when he was wounded. I am thankful to feel that he died amongst friends, and that he was able to thank you. I know you would value his last words. He had often mentioned you to me in his letters home as 'a very nice Irishman from County Durham, who goes with me everywhere.' I am glad to hear your heroism will be recognised and rewarded. You have earned our deepest gratitude, and I can never thank you enough. I pray you may be spared to see the hour of victory, which will surely come.

On 6 November 12/DLI came up and took over the trenches and 13/DLI went back to billets in the Bois Grenier Line and Rue de Lettree. The weather at this time was cold and dull but at least the rain had stopped for a short time. In the line 12/DLI had a very quiet time. The only points of note were that one man, 20841 Private Matthew Killeen, was wounded in the head on 8 November, later dying from his wounds and the enemy shelled battalion headquarters on the following day. On 10 November 13/DLI replaced 12/DLI again, the latter taking over the billets vacated in the Bois Grenier Line and Rue de Lettree.

The following day the enemy shelled the trenches which resulted in the death of 42-year-old 17744 Private Arthur Sowerby from Newbiggin near Carlisle, and wounding two other men.

On 13 November, in fire bay number six in the front line held by a section of B Company, 21032 Private Thomas Guy, a Felling man, was accidentally killed. The Commanding Officer ordered a Court of Inquiry to be held and Major Cecil Walker along with Captain Edward Borrow and Second Lieutenant Charles Handcock made up the court. The first witness to give evidence was the Officer Commanding B Company, Captain George White who said:

At about 0730 hours on the morning of 13 November, I heard a shout for stretcher bearers. On proceeding to the spot near Citadel Trench I.26.24, I found Private Guy lying on his back with a bullet wound in his stomach. After making enquiries I had Private Davison placed under arrest. It is against orders in my company for any man to have a live cartridge in the breech of the rifle unless actually going to fire it. Private Davison's rifle was brought to me by Sergeant Wilkinson, there was an empty round in the breech and the magazine was out altogether, i.e. it was not in its socket.

Adjutant, Lieutenant (later Captain) Edward Borrow was appointed to the Court of Inquiry into the death of Private Thomas Guy. D/DLI/7/75/27

The next to give evidence was 13269 Private William Reid of the Battalion Machine Gun Section, who added these comments:

Shortly before 0700 Hours on 13 November I had taken over sentry duty and I asked Private Davison for a loan of his rifle as Machine Gunners are not allowed to load their weapon without permission. Private Davison answered 'You're too late there's nothing doing', as he had started to clean his rifle. He took the magazine out and touched the trigger and the rifle went off and Private Guy gave a shout and fell down. I ran out shouting 'Stretcher Bearers'!

The Court then called another of the men who had manned Number 6 Bay that morning. 16482 Private Thomas Richardson stated:

About 0700 hours on 13 November I was in my dug out, Privates Davison and Guy were both outside cleaning their rifles. I asked Private Guy for a cigarette, he lent down to give me one and there was a shot, Guy shouted, 'Oh Tom I'm shot'. I said, 'Where'? and he answered, 'In the privates', and then looking down I saw the blood coming out of his side.

The next witness to give his evidence was the NCO in charge of the bay, 17021 Lance Corporal Alexander Hosie, who because he was away collecting the rations had not been present when the actual shooting occurred. He added:

I was NCO of the watch in number six bay and I relieved Private

Davison and placed Private Steel in his place. [This conflicts with Private Reid's evidence.] Private Davison's rifle was handed over to the new sentry. It was very wet and the idea was to keep as many rifles as dry as possible. I then went away to collect the rations for my section. On my return shortly after 0700 Hours I found Private Guy lying wounded.

22076 Private Arthur Davison then volunteered to give evidence in his own defence and had this to say to the three officers:

On the morning of 13 November, Private Guy was the last of the night sentries. He and the others had been using my rifle in order to keep our rifles dry. Guy handed me the rifle about 0700 hours. About 0705 hours Private Steel wanted to borrow my rifle for a shot but I had just started cleaning it. I told him it was empty as I thought it was and took out the magazine. I removed the only round in it. Then I took off the safety catch feeling sure the rifle was empty. It was then the rifle went off and the round hit Guy. I am one of the new men who joined the battalion on 6 October.

Second Lieutenant Charles Handcock, the battalion Transport Officer, was appointed to the Court of Inquiry into the death of Private Thomas Guy.

Both Private Davison and Lance Corporal Hosie mention Private Steel but there is no statement from a man of this name. Two men of that name served in the battalion and both died before the end of the war. 16451 Private James Steel from Wigton in Cumberland served with D Company and 22618 Private (later Lance Corporal) Stewart Steele from Cornsay Colliery served in B Company and it is possible that the latter was the man mentioned but difficult to prove.

During the day Private Arthur Leet killed a German sniper who had given away his position and then later that evening 12/DLI came back into the line. The battalion War Diary of 12/DLI is very sparse and it appears that apart from some shelling they had another quiet time in the line. During their time in the trenches, ten officer cadets were attached to the battalion from the GHQ Officers School for instruction, and spent twenty-four hours in the line with the battalion. Then on 16 November at 1915 hours they were relieved by 2/Northamptonshire Regiment and moved to La Dormoire. Over the next week they daily provided large working parties of over 100 men for several locations such as Rue Marle, Bois Grenier Line and the Corps Dump.

In the meantime 13/DLI had been replaced in reserve by 2/East Lancashire Regiment (2/East Lancs) and had moved further back to billets in L'Hallobeau. Here they spent the week training and some men like

George Butterworth were sent away on courses of instruction. He wrote to his relatives:

> *Nov. 14.*
>
> *Just a line to let you know my present movements. I have just been sent on an eight days' course of instruction in bombs – they are gradually training all men and officers. So for the present I am away from the battalion, and away from all danger, except our own clumsiness in bomb-chucking. I am billeted with two other officers in a nice farm house – with beds (!) – and our only discomfort is the MUD. This word may be said pretty well to describe our existence – it is bad enough here and everywhere, but in the trenches there is nothing else (even the water is really liquid mud). My trench coat now has an extra thickness from top to bottom. In short we are getting some idea of what a winter campaign really is.*
>
> *You will be very sorry to hear that Brown has been killed; he was out in front of the parapet one night, and seems to have lost his way and fallen into an ambuscade; the man with him managed to carry him back – a wonderful performance, as he was under fire most of the way and had to crawl – and he died on the way to the dressing station.*
>
> *P.S. – We get the daily papers regularly, but an occasional magazine (Punch, Strand, etc.) would be welcome – novels are not much used.*

When the course was finished and he had returned to the battalion he wrote again:

> *Nov. 22.*
>
> *I am afraid I have left you some time without a letter, but there has been nothing to write about. I suppose you got my letter from the Bombing School. I am now back with the Battalion (in billets). We go into trenches again some day this week – weather very cold, but we all prefer the frost to wet. By the way, we are just starting leave – you must let me know when you would like me to come – my turn will normally come about the New Year, but it will not be easy to arrange very long beforehand.*

On 24 November the battalion marched out of L'Hallobeau and took over trenches from 8/West Yorkshire Regiment. Then the next day a draft of fifteen Other Ranks led by Second Lieutenant Robert Stubbs reported to battalion headquarters; they were accompanied by Lieutenant Noel Target, who had originally been commissioned into 11/Durham LI, and Second Lieutenant Thomas Oliphant; commissioned into the battalion in December 1914, he had been left in England at the time of embarkation. Last but not least was Second Lieutenant Lewellyn Parker: a Londoner from Putney, he had originally been a Private in the 1/13/County of London Regiment, Princess Louise's Kensington Battalion and had served in France from 3 November 1914. He had been selected for a commission and became an officer in the Durham Light Infantry on 20 March 1915, then sent to 4/Durham LI prior to the battalion leaving for France. The next two days were cold but at least the enemy were quiet, that is until the British Artillery opened fire on a German working party. Very quickly the

German gunners replied in kind which resulted in two men of 13/DLI being wounded. On the night of 28 November they handed over to 12/DLI again and went to the billets in Rue Marle.

When they came out of the line George Butterworth wrote home once more:

Nov 28

We have just completed another turn in trenches – hard frost all the time, but on the whole we rather enjoyed it. I'm afraid the men found it difficult to sleep because of the cold, but we are managing to keep clear of frostbite and other trench ills. We had a very quiet time, and I think it was the first tour of duty in which the company had no casualties at all.

I hope the NER Battalion will have luck [the Battalion here referred to was a Pioneer Battalion raised by the North Eastern Railway Company 17/NF] – *it is rather thankless work* [meaning obviously the work of the Pioneer Battalions] *out here, and our Pioneer Battalion has certainly had more than its share of artillery and machine gun fire.*

Many thanks for the books, which I hope to read in time.

At the beginning of December the weather turned really nasty with high winds, and rain fell almost continuously. On 2 December 12/DLI were once again relieved by 13/DLI in the front line. The former battalion moved into support positions with one company in the Bois Grenier Line, one company at Chapelle D'Armentieres and two companies along with Battalion Headquarters at Rue Marle. As usual, when out at rest they had to find working parties for the many and varied tasks that came the way of the infantry. On 4 December C Company provided a working party forty men strong to work at 68 Brigade Headquarters. At 1615 hours they came under heavy high-explosive shellfire from enemy 4.7cm guns. Six men were killed: 21085 Private John Fowler, Lance Corporal Charles Revell, both from Sunderland; 3/11673 Private George Pearson and 16794 Private Joseph Rogers were both Hartlepool men; while 26595 Private Robert Robinson came from Pendleton in Manchester but was living at Ferryhill when he enlisted. These five all lie in Plot I of Erquinghem-Lys Churchyard extension. The sixth man, 19735 Private James McMullen from New Silksworth, was buried in Houplines Cemetery. As well as the dead, another seven men were wounded; one of whom, 19124 Private Hugh Gray of Barnard Castle died of his wounds three days later in the Casualty Clearing Station in St Omer.

Meanwhile in the front line 13/DLI were keeping up their active patrol work. At 2330 hours on the night of 5 December a two-man patrol consisting of 18513 Corporal William Hornby and 21603 Private Joseph Worton, both of A Company, left the battalion lines with the objective of examining a ruined farmhouse known as German House. Moving carefully towards their objective they were thwarted by new barbed-wire entanglements that had been erected around the building. They then crawled along the German line until at one point they heard voices behind the parapet. Here they threw bombs into the enemy trench which caused a great uproar and allowed them to make good their withdrawal to the British Lines where they arrived at 0230 hours. By way of reprisal the enemy artillery shelled the battalion positions which caused two slight casualties, both of whom remained at duty. The enemy repeated the shelling the following day, during which 13312 Corporal Mark Cawthorn from Ryton was killed in action. Then in the evening 12/DLI came up and took over the line, while 13/DLI moved back to billets in Rue Marle.

The tour in the line of 12/DLI was fairly quiet: on the first day one man was evacuated with a self-inflicted wound, and on 8 December 18948 Private Thomas Whalley from Blackhill near Consett was shot in the head and killed while on sentry duty. During the night as the orderly officer made his rounds he found the sentry 16152 Private George Bell from Spennymoor serving with C Company asleep at his post. The unlucky Private was immediately placed under arrest and taken into custody. Further casualties occurred and two more men were wounded; one shot through the cheek and the other through the arm on the following day.

Corporal Hornby (above) and Private Worton carried out a difficult and daring reconnaissance and brought back valuable information. They also bombed some enemy snipers with good results before they returned. Gateshead Library

The front line was being held by the Lincolnshire Regiment on the left, 12/DLI in the centre and 11/NF on the right when there erupted a very heavy artillery duel, during which communication was cut between 11/NF and 68 Brigade HQ. All messages between the two were passed through 12/DLI signallers who worked hard to keep the lines open. The battalion was relieved on the night of 10/11 December when 13/DLI returned and took over the line once more.

Out at rest, 12/DLI prepared a Field General Court Martial for George Bell who had spent the last five days in the care of the Provost Sergeant. The penalty for sleeping at his post could have been death but George was lucky and he received a sentence of twelve months' imprisonment with hard labour; this was remitted to 112 days' imprisonment with hard labour and the sentence was confirmed by the Brigade Commander. However, when the paperwork reached Headquarters FIRST ARMY on 14 December the GOC General Sir Douglas Haig suspended the sentence and Private George Bell was returned to duty, doubtless letting out a deep breath of relief. Five days later Sir Douglas Haig took over command of the BEF where he wasn't so lenient to other miscreants of the regiment.

13/DLI spent an uneventful few days manning the trenches before being relieved by 2/East Lancs and then moving back to billets at Fort Rompu.

About this time George Butterworth got two letters away to his family:

Dec. 9th, 1915.

I think I have been getting things pretty regularly, except perhaps the last week or so. I have been away four days, and when that happens our battalion postal arrangements are apt to break down; if anything has gone astray, I shall probably get it about Christmas. The reason for my absence is that I got a chill, and went to a convalescent home instead of the trenches. I am all right again now. I'm afraid I have not sent you any news for a long time, but our existence is pretty monotonous – in fact, it is just bare existence, and nothing besides. I never know what the day of the week is, even Sunday.

I read 'Aunt Sarah' in bed, and enjoyed it, though I don't think the author has been to the front and the chronology is poor; there was no trench warfare in August, 1914, and a new recruit would hardly be home wounded at the time of Ypres (No. 1)!

Shall be glad of literature occasionally, if not too bulky.

I didn't send you any account of the bomb school, because it was rather a farce as far as I was concerned, being really a course for men, not officers. However, I threw a few bombs with fair accuracy (20-25 yards). It is an easy subject to master, especially now that we have at last got the things standardized – there is practically only one kind used now, and it is a very neat weapon. In a battle the chief difficulty is to organize your parties, and keep them supplied the whole time; at the present stage of things, of course, we practically never use bombs.

I can probably arrange to take my leave on January 22, so that if you can fix a date in that week, all will be well.

Dec. 13 (in trenches).

Please tell the General [his father] *not to bother about the armour plating, as it is not the sort of thing which can be done privately. No special news – the wet is terrific – one wades to one's bed, and eats one's dinner with water over the ankles, but with waders and four changes of socks I keep fairly dry.*

On 15 December both battalions of the Durham LI in 68 Brigade paraded and marched to an area set aside as a parade ground. Here in the presence of men from all units in the III Corps, the Corps Commander Lieutenant-General Sir William Pulteney KCB DSO presented the ribbon of the Victoria Cross to Thomas Kenny, who since his gallant efforts to save Second Lieutenant Philip Brown had been promoted to Lance Sergeant. This was followed on 17 December when the Divisional Commander

Major General J.M. Babington CB, CMG visited 13/DLI and presented the ribbon of the Distinguished Conduct Medal to 21603 Private Joseph Worton of A Company for his part in the action on the night of 5 December. After his visit to the battalion the General moved on to the 69th Field Ambulance RAMC and presented the same decoration to 18513 Corporal W. Hornby, who was a patient at the Field Ambulance.

Out at rest both battalions were supplying working parties for various duties, digging and carrying for the Royal Engineers being the main activities. On 19 December 13/DLI reported the arrival of Second Lieutenant Samuel Tyssen to the battalion; originally commissioned into 12/DLI on 16 January 1915, he had been posted to 16/Durham LI prior to embarkation. On 22 December 12/DLI took over trenches from 9/Yorkshire Regiment and the following day during an artillery duel 22158 Private Joseph Robson, aged 22, who came from Teams in Gateshead was wounded and died from his wounds at the dressing station in the Brewery at Bois Grenier.

They spent Christmas Day in the trenches, where the ground was so wet that the sandbags were collapsing and dugouts were caving in. At 1315 hours on Christmas Day the enemy artillery opened fire on the British support positions and the barrage struck the sector held by B and C Companies of 13/DLI: this resulted in the death of 22229 Private T. Purvis and the wounding of 21152 Private G. Williamson who died from his wounds at 0250 hours on 26 December at the 26th Field Ambulance. On Boxing Day Lieutenant Frank Golden who had been commissioned into the battalion on 19 September 1914 was killed by shrapnel from an enemy shell during the enemy's barrage.

When 13/DLI took over the line the enemy was heard pumping water over their parapet, which flowed downhill into the British lines. This was mentioned in one of his first long letters home by the newly-arrived Second Lieutenant Frederick Rees:

> An Officers' Mess
> Front Line
> Somewhere in France
> The above address sounds alright, the aforesaid mess however is a wee dug out 10 feet by 4 feet where four officers of the 'Contemptible Little army' assemble for meals. Well I will go back to Sunday and tell you all that has happened since we started off for the

Christmas card commissioned specially for B Company 12/DLI sent by 15943 Lance Corporal John Thomas Caley to his family in Langley Moor, near Durham. On the original the bugle is in bright colours.

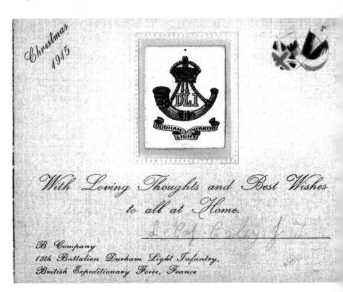

trenches. Sunday night we passed through a small town completely 'strafed' by shells all in ruins, a guide met us and led us into the trenches. I being in charge of one platoon, we were all issued with long rubber boots up to the hips and very useful they are as the water all along one part of the trench is well above the knees and if you are not careful and step into a hole, you go in up to the waist, still we go splashing and whistling along and have a tremendous roar if some poor fool suddenly sits down in it. I was on second watch, that is the second half of the night and wander about seeing the sentries are awake and occasionally sending up a flare, which is fired from a special pistol, it makes a brilliant light and we can see the German trench quite plainly, it is within easy shouting distance, still I have not seen one yet although I have heard them splashing along in their trench and pumping water out. There are hundreds of rats here, I amused myself on my rounds during the night by firing at some with a revolver but couldn't see them well enough in the dark. Things are very quiet here, the artillery keep 'strafing' but the Huns opposite us keep pretty quiet, of course snipers keep trying their luck.

Last night we had a small strafe (excuse the frequency of the word but we never call it anything else) well we woke up the Huns with a bomb or two and some rapid fire which I don't suppose hurt anyone, but gave them a bit of a start. At five this morning we fired two rifle grenades over, which we saw land just inside their trench with some explosion. I have reason to believe that they at once sang a Hymn of Hate at any rate they seemed fearfully annoyed and replied with a large bomb and a rifle grenade and fired over 20 whizz bangs – a shell so called from the noise it makes, however they never got near anyone. We can hear their shells going over all day long and see them burst right away behind us.

This Mess is some place – I don't think – as you see there is not a great deal of room but we have shelves a table and a stove, also an acetylene table lamp, we feed quite well, dine at night, soup, joint, sweet, so you see we are really doing quite well. The other fellows say it is the worst part of the line they have been in yet for discomfort. I mean we still only have a few days and then a few days in billets, huts, old houses, or anything for a rest, then in the trenches again, but we shall not come back to this particular part again. Last night I had the same watch again and strafed more rats, one fellow told me they were as big as a retriever dog, in fact they are the biggest I ever saw.

I am very warm in my dug out which I share with two others, there is just room to creep in, but it is not much used as we have not much time for sleep, except during part of the day. This morning I issued the rum to them all and did not forget myself. It is jolly good stuff and keeps you topping and warm.

It is really not a bit cold and although we live up to the knees in water except when in the dug outs or the mess I have never had my feet cold yet.

A great trick with these rats is to put a bit of cheese on the end of a bayonet and rest it on the parapet and when a rat starts nibbling pull the trigger – result no more rat.

I had a look through a periscope today. They are wonderful things, I could see all along the Hun trench, of course a sniper must have a shot at it and scatter mud over us with the bullet hitting the parapet. So I decided to rag him and left the periscope up and signalled a miss to him every time with a flag waved over the parapet, he had eight shots but failed to hit, he was a rotten shot.

We have a gramophone with us which plays ragtime. Last night I had a wee pup with me all night, it sleeps by the cook house stove. It is now tea time, my old stick is useful, you would roar to see me nearly falling down in the mud and doing Charlie Chaplin walk to save myself.

Well much love, yours in the pink.

Over the next few days the German and British Artillery continued to duel which led to several men being wounded and on 29 December 16768 Private Frederick Pilchet was killed in action.

On 30 December 12/DLI returned to the front line; while out at rest they had provided the normal working parties. What is interesting is that neither battalion records any Christmas festivities or special meals for the men. In the official War Diary, however, the Adjutant of 13/DLI noted in his volume that Christmas dinner was served to all ranks.

At around 1300 hours on 31 December an incident occurred in the trenches held by B Company 12/DLI where the men were busy repairing the sand bags. 22155 Private John Pledger and 18817 Private John Deakin were working away when a party of men went past them, a single shot rang out and three men fell wounded by the same bullet. 19339 Corporal John Everist from Seaham Harbour was the worst hit with the bullet wound to the right lung; the other two wounded men were 25476 Private John Bowerbank and 24414 Private David Lawton. All three were quickly evacuated to the Regimental Aid Post and from there to the Field Ambulance.

So 1915 came to a close: the two Durham battalions of 68 Brigade were by now fairly experienced in trench warfare but 1916 would bring far more testing times for them.

Chapter Four

1916, January to June

NEW YEAR'S DAY 1916 opened with 12/DLI in the trenches and 13/DLI in reserve. At 0130 hours the British Artillery and machine guns opened up a heavy barrage to cover a raid by 11/NF on the left of 12/DLI. The German artillery replied in kind but fortunately did little damage to the trenches held by the Durhams. This was followed the next day by a particularly heavy barrage on both Battalion Headquarters and the support line but again little damage was done.

When the firing died down a Court of Inquiry assembled in the trench at I.31.5 where an accident had occurred the previous day. The president was Captain John Day with Second Lieutenants Mervyn Campbell-Jones and Percy Blaylock as members. They interviewed a number of men from B Company and took statements from them as a report had to be made to Divisional Headquarters in the case of accidental and self-inflicted wounds.

The first witness was 22155 Private John Pledger who stated:

> *At around 1400 hours 31 December Private Deakin and I were repairing the parados near our dug out. I was in charge of a sniper scope rifle and I laid it slantingly against part of the parados with the butt towards me and a yard away. It was loaded but the safety catch was on. While I was working I heard a shot go off and looking round saw Private J R Wilson putting the rifle down. It was put down on the other side of the parados with the muzzle towards me. I saw Corporal Everist lying in the traffic trench and went to his assistance. Private Deakin was the only man near me at the time. I did not say anything to Private Wilson about his touching my rifle.*

The three officers then heard the statement of 18817 Private John Deakin who added this statement:

> *About 1400 hours I was working inside the dugout shelter with Private Pledger and heard a shot ring out and saw Corporal Everist fall. I ran towards him and heard a man say, 'Oh Lord! Have I hit Jack, is he much worse?' I could not recognise the voice and I could not identify the man as by that time several men had gathered round.*

They then took a statement from 19103 Private John Wilson who said:

> *About 1400 hours I was in my dugout with Private Lawton. He went out to start work and I followed about five or six paces behind. I was in the dugout when the shot was fired. Lawton was about six paces in front of me on the boards. I did not stumble against anything. I did not notice the rifle and saw no other men except Privates Pledger and Deakin. When I came out I saw Corporal Everist lying on the boards. I had no rifle in my hand.*

The final witness of the day was B Company Sergeant Major 25523 Henry Lockyer who had assisted the wounded men. He stated:

> About 1400 hours I met Private Bowerbank with his cheek cut. While I was dressing him he said, 'That's the fruit of playing with a strange rifle.' I went on to the help of the men. Later I examined the sniper scope rifle and found an empty cartridge case in the breech and three rounds in the magazine.

The officers found the evidence somewhat contradictory and it was decided to place Private Wilson under arrest in the guardroom and to adjourn the proceedings until at least one of the two slightly wounded men returned to duty.

On 3 January the enemy again shelled the trenches held by 12/DLI: Brewery Post came under fire and three casualties occurred. 19182 Private Michael Riley, a native of Stockton-on-Tees but resident in Chester-le-Street was killed outright. The second man, 18234 Private William Murray of A Company, who came from Brunel Street in Ferryhill, made it as far as the Dressing Station at Sailly-sur-la-Lys before he died from his wounds. The third we must presume survived for there is no further mention of him. Later that evening they were relieved by 13/DLI and moved back to billets in La Rolanderie. On the morning of 8 January the members of the Court of Inquiry reconvened at Rue du Diez to hear the evidence of 24414 Private David Lawton who had returned to duty from the Field Ambulance. His evidence was added to the report as follows:

> About 1345 Hours having finished my dinner in my dugout I went to the Sergeants dugout to report to Corporal Everist. He told me to follow him and he would show me where to work. I walked along the boards followed by Corporal Everist and Private Bowerbank in the order named. I was rather deaf and heard no shot, but felt a hit under the left arm and looking round saw Corporal Everist on the ground. Private J R Wilson was in the dugout when I left it and he did not follow me to the Sergeants dugout. I did not see him again until after Corporal Everist was hit. When I re-passed our dugout leading Everist and Bowerbank I did not meet Wilson or see him.

The Commanding Officer then added his comments to the proceedings:

> The evidence of Private Lawton [sic, should have been Bowerbank)]has not been taken and I consider that the injuries were caused by the accidental firing of a rifle by No 19103 Private J R Wilson who should be dealt with on account of his gross carelessness.
>
> Signed L C Elwes Lieut Col
> Commanding 12th Durham L.I.
> 8 Jan 1916

Although some of the soldier's documents for Private Wilson survive at The National Archives there is no record of a Court Martial or of any punishment, but before the year was over Private Wilson was killed in

HM Hospital Ship **Brighton.**

action. Corporal Everist having been treated for four weeks at No 26 Field Ambulance RAMC was still very seriously ill when on 27 January he was loaded onto a Hospital Barge and taken down to the Lahore British General Hospital in Calais, where he arrived on 29 January. On 4 February he was trans-ferred to HM Hospital Ship *Brighton* and taken home to England. After spending some time in hospitals in the south he was moved in December 1916 to the Northumberland War Hospital in Gosforth and remained there until his death in November 1917.

When 13/DLI took over they very soon came under fire and this resulted in the death of 19442 Private Samuel Byford from Leamington Spa in Warwickshire. Over the next few days the artillery of both sides was fairly active and on the morning of 5 January at 0720 hours two pigeons were seen flying in a straight line in the direction from Fleurbaix to Lille, then three hours later another three birds were seen following the same route. This gave rise to the stories of enemy spies sending information about the battalion positions to the German gunners, as scarcely had the birds disappeared from view than a heavy barrage of 77mm shells fell on Brewery Post; this enemy fire didn't let up until the British gunners retaliated. That night an enemy working party commenced work repairing a breach blown in their parapet. They worked until the battalion Lewis guns opened fire and successfully dispersed them. Although the next day was described in the War Diary as quiet, four men were wounded and 21036 Private Andrew Wood from Windy Nook near Gateshead was killed. On 7 January the Divisional Trench Mortar Battery, 109 Brigade Royal Field Artillery (RFA), A Battery 105 Brigade RFA (Howitzers) along with B Battery 102 Brigade RFA (18 Pounders) started a heavy fire on known hostile gun emplacements opposite the line held by 13/DLI. Within eight minutes the enemy gunners were replying in kind and Brewery, Emma, White City and Stanway Posts received their share of 77mm shells before the firing ceased at 1230 hours. Later in the evening 2/East Lancs came up and took over the line, while 13/DLI moved back to billets at L'Hallobeau where they relieved 1/Worcestershire Regiment.

Meanwhile out at rest, 12/DLI had done very little resting; every day they assigned parties of men for many and varied tasks. The Royal Engineers were the main beneficiary of these parties; however, these working parties were often under fire and 20937 Private Tom Hall, a farmer from Blackhill, was slightly wounded but remained at duty on the evening of 7 January when they moved to Fort Rompu where they relieved 2/Northamptonshire Regiment. In this location the work continued and at one stage over 600 men were employed carrying, digging, wiring and providing labour of one form or another. This lasted until 15 January when they took over the line in the vicinity of Rue du Bois from 10/West Riding Regiment. They spent several quiet days in the line here, but 20937 Private Tom Hall was wounded for a second time, this time with a shrapnel wound in the back. He was evacuated via 2/Casualty Clearing Station and Number 18 Ambulance Train to the 8/Red Cross Hospital, where it was found that apart from his wounds he also had a very bad case of scabies and was moved to 20/General Hospital and from there to England. It would appear that the Army lost track of Tom Hall for on 19 February, Number 1 Infantry Records Office at York wrote to his father:

Seated 20937 Private Tom Hall and two friends of 12/DLI. Tom was wounded for a second time in January 1916; with shrapnel wounds in the back he was evacuated to England. When he returned to the Front in July 1916 he was posted to 13/DLI.

> Sir,
>
> *Will you kindly inform me on the back of this letter whether you have heard from your son Tom Hall 12th Battalion Durham Light Infantry whose correct Regimental number is 20937, and if so can you give me his present location? Information received in this office to the effect that a soldier No 25218 Pte T Hall 12th DLI was admitted to No 8 Red Cross Hospital, Paris Plage, on 4/1/16 suffering from a slight wound to the back and since transferred to 20 General Hospital, Camiers.*
>
> *It is thought that some mistake has occurred in the Regimental Number of the men serving in 12th Durham Light Infantry by the name of Hall, so I shall be glad if you will please inform me in your reply which is the Regimental number of your son. The Attestation gives his name as Tom Hall enlisted at Consett on 21 October 1914 at the age of nineteeen years and three months with the occupation of Farmer.*

No reply from Mr Hall is mentioned in Tom Hall's documents.

During this last tour of the trenches only one fatality was recorded: on 17 January 13828 Sergeant William Muxlow from Guisborough, North Yorkshire was killed in action. Two days later according to the War Diary the German Air Force and the Royal Flying Corps were active over the front line and one hostile machine was brought down and fell into the German lines. That night 13/DLI returned to the line and 12/DLI moved back into support positions with one company in the support trenches and one in reserve at Chapelle d'Armentieres with Battalion Headquarters and the other two companies at Rue Marle.

At 2030 hours after 12/DLI had departed, the German heavy artillery started to fire against the British line at Laventie. They repeated the barrage at 2200 hours and again at 0230 hours: during this shelling one man of 13/DLI, 21313 Private J. Green of B Company was wounded and 18980 Private James Clarke who was born in Bensham, Gateshead and was serving with C Company was killed. Over the next few days the enemy shelled various parts of the line held by the battalion causing a number of men to be wounded but no further fatalities.

During this period Second Lieutenant Frederick Rees sent another letter home:

Wednesday afternoon I took a working party to the trenches; two of us went with about 130 men about 5 miles in motor lorries and then marched about a mile and a half into the trenches. This was just after it got dark. The men had a lot of digging to do and filling sandbags, building up the parapet, a few bullets were flying about and one of our fellows with a tone of most indignant surprise shouted across to the Huns, 'Here stop that game there, you very near hit me then'. It was such an indignant tone that everyone was tickled. We were working for four hours and then marched back, turning up here at 1130 hours quite ready for supper and bed, everyone back safely.

This morning I was on another working party myself and 60 men, but this time did not go far and were working just outside a town at some stores, not in the trenches.

Leave had opened for the battalion and the Adjutant's war diary reports Lieutenants Greenwood and Howard returning from England. Overnight on 20/21 January there was some rain and the next evening 24 Brigade opened heavy rifle fire on the enemy trenches to draw the enemy into their line; the British artillery then opened fire on the enemy line, to which the Germans replied with whizz bangs. This caused three men of 13/DLI to be wounded: 22211 Private George Greener and 17187 Private Michael Brown both of C Company, and 22699 Private James Fairless of B Company. Greener and Fairless had both joined with the first batch of reinforcements in September 1915. 17797 Private Patrick serving with D

Company, another original member of the battalion that had landed the previous August, was also wounded and subsequently discharged. Late that night as the Orderly Officer made his rounds of the front-line sentry posts he came up to a post manned by 22166 Private George Kilburn; the luckless soldier had fallen asleep at his post and he was placed under arrest.

Second Lieutenant Frederick Rees sent a number of letters home at this time. On 16 January he told of an attack on the enemy line:

> *A great joke took place in the trenches the other night, some of our men went across and hurled bombs into the Hun trenches and then rushed back. The Huns were driven out and thought our fellows had taken their trench, so organised a boming attack on their own empty trench. This they bombed and then took no doubt thinking they had won a victory until they found no dead English there.*

Then on 20 January he wrote a long letter to his mother in which he described his dugout in the line:

> *Redholme, the above is written on my dugout door, I suppose some one has named it after some place he knows. I am just having a rest in my dugout before lunch and am very comfortable. It is about eight foot long by four wide, a bedstead is built along one side, wooden framework with wire netting stretched across, my servant collected a lot of empty sandbags and spread them over this with my blankets on top I have a luxurious bed. There is a good shelf on the other side. A wooden floor, corrugated iron roof with sandbags on top. The inside walls and ceiling are lined with sacking. So now you see I am quite snug.*
>
> *I was up at 0630 hours and issued rum to the men which warms them up after the night. I have been having a look round my bit of trench to see which places want building up, ready to get the men working tonight when it is too dark for the Huns to spot us.*

On 23 January the Commander of III Corps, Lieutenant-General Sir William Pulteney KCB, KCMG, DSO visited the line and toured the sector held by 13/DLI. Then that night 12/DLI returned to the line and 13/DLI marched to billets in Rue Marle, leaving A Company and two machine guns in support of 12/DLI in the Bois Grenier Line.

Yet again the Diary of 12/DLI gives little information on its time in the line. On 25 January there is a report that aeroplanes are active over the battalion front and that the enemy are firing at the British planes with rifles and machine guns. The next day the enemy artillery are active and during a heavy barrage the battalion signals dugout was hit and five men killed. On 26 January the battalion came under heavy enemy machine-gun fire, during the night a patrol was sent out and they chanced upon two enemy patrols; these were engaged immediately with bombs and then the men of 12/DLI cut an enemy trip wire and retired to a forward listening post.

Lieutenant-Gener
Sir William Pulten

The battalion in support was tasked with finding working parties for the Royal Engineers, carrying stores up to forward dumps and digging. At this time the 34th Division had just arrived in Flanders and the various brigades were attached to different formations for training in trench warfare. 12/DLI had companies of 15/Royal Scots of 101 Brigade attached.

On 27 January the two battalions changed round again in the same trenches: 13/DLI went into the line with B Company of 15/Royal Scots attached and deployed with D Company and two platoons of Royal Scots on the right; C Company with one platoon of Royal Scots in the centre and B Company and one platoon of Royal Scots on the left; while A Company remained in the support trenches of the Bois Grenier Line. That night at 2300 hours the German Artillery opened a heavy bombardment on the front-line and support trenches; to this the gunners of the 23rd Divisional Artillery quickly replied and fired about twenty howitzer shells. One enemy shell hit a dugout in which two men of the divisional pioneers were sitting: surprisingly both were uninjured, however, the Royal Scots were not so lucky and they had two men wounded. This artillery duelling was kept up over the next few days and on 28 January the Officer Commanding D Company reported that the front line at I.23.3 was completely blown in and untenable. HQ 13/DLI then rearranged the defence so that the gap was covered by a machine gun and two bombers were posted in a listening post forward of the front line, with one platoon from A Company, taken from the Reserve Line, in support. During this period 16978 Private S. Chicken of C Company and 23472 Private W. Drinkhall of D Company were wounded and evacuated, while 18489 Private H. Byford of A Company was slightly wounded and remained at duty and 3/11603 Sergeant J. Davison of D Company was shellshocked. That afternoon B Company of 15/Royal Scots moved back to Brigade Reserve with 12/DLI and was replaced by D Company of the same battalion. They were deployed with one platoon attached D Company 13/DLI, two platoons with C Company 13/DLI and one platoon with B Company 13/DLI.

At 2113 hours on the night of 29 January Captain Joseph Downey led a patrol out from a listening post in the British front line. They were to try to penetrate the enemy-held line but when about 160 yards from the German trench they put up a covey of partridge. The noise of the birds alerted a German sentry who immediately stood his company to arms. A patrol left the enemy line and made its way into No Man's Land. They then put up Very lights but the British party were hiding in a shell hole. At 1140 hours Captain Downey tried to move forward again but they were discovered once more and the enemy attempted to surround them. The British party again went back to the shell hole. At 0024 hours Captain Downey and 19041 Sergeant W. Galley moved forward to reconnoitre and again the enemy attempted to surround them and again the British pair fell back. A little later they tried again, this time further to the right, but again they were discovered and fell back. At 0140 hours the moon rose and removed any chance of surprise so the party returned to the British lines and the operation was cancelled on the orders of GOC 68 Brigade. Only one casualty occurred during the time in No Man's Land when 24758 Private J. McCormick of A Company was wounded.

The next day B Company of 15/Royal Scots was replaced by A Company of the same battalion. In the evening 2/East Lancashire of 24 Brigade arrived and took over the line and 13/DLI moved back to Fort Rompu where they went into billets.

Second Lieutenant Rees wrote again on 1 February. In this letter he described his company sanitary man:

> One of our sanitary men is very funny, when in the trenches he gets ten rounds and a rifle just before dawn and blazes away over the parapet in the darkness, aiming at nothing. A huge idiotic grin on his face, crowds gather and cheer him on with, 'Howay Geordie thoos killing em be the thousands', after that he goes off thinking he has done his bit for the day.

This was followed the next day by a letter to his father with news of a working party:

> I have been back today in reserve trenches all day with a working party, marched about five miles away. It was misty when we started work but cleared up later and the old Hun spotted us and sent over a few whizz bangs and shrapnel which made us scuttle for shelter. But as no more came over we carried on and got back safely. I am sorry for the people here, people in England ought to be jolly thankful. I was through a village this morning about the size of Barmby, completely destroyed, the church – no roof – hardly any walls and only one side of the tower left. The only thing that seems intact is the notice board on one wall which still hangs pathetically with its notices still up.

When 13/DLI arrived in the rest billets preparations were made for the Field General Court Martial of Private George Kilburn: he was found guilty and was lucky not to be sentenced to death; instead he received two years' hard labour which on 9 February was suspended and he was returned to active duty.

In the meantime 12/DLI were in Brigade rest at L'Hallobeau where they were doing anything but rest; large working parties were supplied to the Royal Engineers of III Corps, over 500 men of the battalion being employed at several different locations each day. Now that 13/DLI were out of the line they too joined in with the work. A Company sent 150 men to work for Lieutenant Podmore of 101 Field Company, while the remainder of the company were employed by Second Lieutenant Edelstone of 102 Field Company. They set to at 1800 hours rebuilding the revetments of Queen Street and worked until 2130 hours. On 5 February an accident occurred in the billets of A Company 13/DLI when a defective bomb exploded: this led to 23446 Private W. Hedley and 16444 Private J. Irving being wounded although they remained at duty. That night D Company was ordered to work on Shaftesbury Avenue under the command of 102 Field Company, but when they were halfway there they received a message from Second Lieutenant Edelstone that the weather was too bad for work so the party marched back to billets.

On 8 February 12/DLI took over the trenches from 11/West Yorkshire Regiment (11/West Yorks) and on the way in had one man wounded. The next day they had the unusual experience of capturing an escaped Russian prisoner of war: it turned out that he had escaped from a working party in Lille and had made his way through the German lines and across No Man's Land where he was captured by men of 12/DLI. Sometime during 10 February 13714 Private John Peel from Haswell Plough was hit in the face by a German sniper: he remained alive and was quickly evacuated to 69/Field Ambulance and from there to Number 2 Casualty Clearing Station in Bailleul where he received further treatment before being placed on an Ambulance Train and sent down to Number 4 General Hospital at Camiers on the French coast. Although he remained alive he was considered to be dangerously ill and permission was given for his wife Frances to travel to France to visit him. The family was not well off and Frances had to get the local vicar to sign a statement that she couldn't afford the fare, so that she could be issued a warrant. She travelled on 2 March via Folkstone to Boulogne and spent almost two weeks with her husband. On her return she wrote to the Durham Light Infantry Records Office in York:

> Mrs J Peel
> South Cross Row
> Haswell Plough
> Co Durham
> March 21st 1916
> Dear Sirs
> You will find enclosed the certificate which I was informed must be sent after my return from France. Everyone was very kind and considerate towards me throughout my journey also during my stay in France. For which I thank you very much. Things would have been very pleasant had my journey been under different circumstances. Again thanking you for your consideration.
> Yours Truly
> Frances Peel.

The wounded soldier's mother also wrote to York begging permission to be given a warrant to visit her son and stating that another son was fighting with the Tyneside Scottish. There is no evidence that she was allowed to visit him. On 23 March John Peel died from the head wound and was buried in the British Military Cemetery at Etaples.

On 11 February they had another man wounded and then another unit of the 34th Division arrived for instruction. This time it was a company from 25/NF (2nd Tyneside Irish). They quickly received a baptism of fire, for the next day the Germans placed a heavy barrage of high explosive shells and trench mortar bombs on the sector held by 12/DLI which lasted for three hours. This resulted in the deaths of 19519 Private James Dutton from Blackburn and 10693 Private William Foster, a resident of Pelton. Further to these casualties another sixteen men were wounded, one of whom, 24717 Private Thomas Price, a Quarrington Hill man, subsequently died from his wounds, while the Tyneside Irish Company had two of their men wounded.

Out at rest 13/DLI had not escaped the attention of the enemy gunners: on the afternoon of 9 February at 1545 hours a barrage had fallen on B Company billets with the result that 21030 Lance Sergeant W. Stokoe and 21175 Private R. J. Dixon were wounded. Companies of 25/NF also joined 13/DLI for instruction. George Butterworth was one of those that had managed to get a few days' leave and on rejoining the battalion he was sent away on a signals course. He wrote home with the news:

> Feb. 5, 1916
>
> I have been sent on a course of signalling (i.e., telephone, buzzer, etc.). It promises to be interesting, and at any rate novel. To-day (the first) I have already learnt to make a clove-hitch knot, mend breaks in cable, Morse alphabet (more or less), and how to run a line across country – all of which seems very remote from the war, though of course it is part of a very important department.
>
> One result is that probably we shall be in Corps reserve by the time this is through, in which case I may see no more of the trenches until the end of March!
>
> I had an uneventful journey back, except for fog in the channel; the day in Boulogne was pleasant, but much more expensive than the Cecil.

Second Lieutenant Frederick Rees sent another letter home on 8 February in which he described the latest fashion for wear in the trenches:

> Most of the men have been given steel helmets at least they call them helmets; they are just like oval pie dishes and look terrible, however that doesn't matter they are supposed to be some protection from shrapnel.

At 1945 hours on 12 February 13/DLI accompanied by one company of 25/NF took over the line from 12/DLI. During the night 16151 Corporal George Stout and 25757 Private Joseph Pratt from Durham City were both wounded. The next morning at 0930 hours the enemy shelled Bois Grenier, which was followed at 1430 hours by a heavy barrage on the right sector held by 10/NF. Retaliation was called for from the British gunners and C Battery 103 Brigade Royal Field Artillery (RFA) fired

25757 Private Joseph Pratt died from his wounds and was buried in the Erquinghem-Lys churchyard extension.

about ten rounds. At the dressing station in Erquinghem Joseph Pratt died from his wounds and was buried in the churchyard extension. At 1500 hours the enemy turned their attention to the trenches held by 13/DLI and a heavy barrage fell on Battalion Headquarters and the right and centre companies: again retaliation was called for and A Battery 105 Brigade RFA fired eight rounds, followed some time later by C Battery 103 Brigade and the Heavy Battery who also fired a salvo. By 1630 hours the enemy fire had ceased but they had caused a fair bit of damage to the British trenches and five Other Ranks were killed and fourteen wounded.

One man died from his wounds after the entry in the Battalion War Diary was made; this was Cyril Nattress who made it as far as the Casualty Clearing Station in Bailleul. At least three of the wounded would be killed before the end of the war and five would be discharged on account of the wounds received in action. This was the first large casualty list suffered by 13/DLI.

Frederick Rees mentioned the shelling in a letter dated 13 February:

I was talking to my sergeant and another fellow and getting the men out, when one burst beside us and just about deafened me. But I was lucky as it hit my sergeant in three places and caught the other fellow in the back.

The Adjutant also recorded in his diary that 'the retaliation called for, partly due to wires being broken, was of the feeblest and quite ineffective'. In several places the enemy breached the parapet and damaged a machine-gun emplacement, as well as scoring a direct hit on a dugout. That evening the attached company of 25/NF left the line and joined 12/DLI in support and at the same time a small group of nineteen reinforcements arrived from 23 Infantry Base Depot (23/IBD). These men were ordered to remain at the transport lines until the battalion left the trenches.

The following morning the sounds of an enemy working party were heard in No Man's Land and the coordinates were quickly passed by a Forward Observation Officer to an 18 Pounder Battery in the rear. They quickly fired two salvoes at the enemy position which met with a heavy reply from the German Artillery. Battalion Headquarters at White City received the brunt of the whizz bangs and then later the enemy shelled Bois Grenier too. This retaliation resulted in four men being wounded: 13617 Lance Corporal David Young, a Middlesbrough man serving in A Company; 17171 Private Robert Angel from West Hartlepool was wounded in the right knee; 25821 Private Reginald Draper, a resident of Littletown near Durham City; and 25910 Private Ralph Mason. The last three were serving with B Company, the latter two having only arrived with a draft of reinforcements on 22 December 1915. The shelling continued on 16 February but no casualties occurred and then on 17 February the battalion snipers claimed two Germans killed during the day, and at the same time the enemy shelling wounded 23444 Private John

Fisher of A Company. That night 12/DLI came up and took over the front line and 13/DLI moved into support positions. On the way out 17807 Private Arthur C. Smith, a C Company man, was wounded and evacuated.

12/DLI started this tour quite quietly but after twenty-four hours in the line casualties started to mount; one officer and two men were wounded and 13828 Sergeant William Muxlow, a native of Guisborough, North Yorkshire, was killed in action. The next two days were very quiet and on the night of 21 February 16/Royal Scots of 101 Brigade, 34th Division came into the line to relieve 12/DLI. The Durham Battalion moved back to Fort Rompu. With both battalions out at rest a signal was received from HQ 68 Brigade to the effect that the brigade would remain under command of 34th Division for the time being. Over the next couple of days there were heavy falls of snow and out at rest a Senior NCO of 13/DLI, 11229 Sergeant Francis Burns, a Gateshead man from Southey Street serving with B Company, managed to get hold of some strong drink. This led to an act of insubordination when he refused to obey a lawful command given by a superior officer and he was taken into detention on 22 February. Sergeant Burns was subsequently tried by Field General Court Martial on two counts: 1) While on active service disobeying a lawful command given by his superior officer and 2) Drunkenness.

His court martial took place at La Rolanderie Farm on 2 March when he was found guilty and sentenced to be reduced to the rank of Private and transferred to D Company. After three days at Fort Rompu 12/DLI moved to Sailly where they were in reserve to 8th Division. They were only there one day before they marched to Morbecque where they were in Corps reserve. Here they were joined by 13/DLI on 27 February. The time had now come to go to another sector of the front and on 28 February word came through that 68 Brigade would move by train to Bruay. On the afternoon of 29 February 12/DLI left Morbecque and entrained for Bruay and reached billets there at 1800 hours. Meanwhile 13/DLI marched to Steenbecque station; they entrained at 1545 hours and were transported to Calonne and marched to billets at Auchel where they arrived at 2330 hours. They had been preceded by the battalion transport section, who moving by road had arrived at 1530 hours.

George Butterworth rejoined the battalion just before the move and sent several short letters home about the new area of operations and what the battalion was up to:

Feb. 28.

I rejoined the Battalion yesterday; at the present moment we are in Corps 'rest,' some miles behind the line. Normally we should be here a month, but from the unsettled look of things it hardly seems likely we shall get our full time. The Verdun business is tremendous; so far (Sunday's paper) results seem satisfactory.

March 4.

I hope you got my last, saying that I had rejoined the battalion – actually before posting it we got orders to move, and were hurried off by train to an entirely different part of the front – or rather not the front, but a town about 15 miles behind it. Our present function is obscure; apparently we are no longer general reserve, because we (i.e., our Division) have been definitely attached to a new Army Corps. The idea at present seems to be that we are shortly going to take over a definite section of trenches in this neighbourhood.

Whatever happens, thank goodness, we have got away from the plain. This is a hilly, mining neighbourhood, very like the north of England. We are billeted (very comfortably) in a large mining village, so the men are thoroughly at home; in fact the last few days have been about the best rest we have ever had.

I told my N.C.O.s yesterday that I thought the next two months would see a definite decision (though not the actual finish). It seems arithmetically possible for the Germans to make one more offensive on the scale of Verdun, but I think that is their limit, and when that is over we shall be through with the winter, and a combined offensive on all fronts will be practicable. At present we are having a renewal of bad weather – heavy snow to-day.

March 5.

We are moving to-morrow; the Division is taking up a new sector of line. We shall be in reserve at first, and go into trenches in about a week's time. It is supposed to be rather a hot neighbourhood, but it is certainly our turn to do something.

Lieutenant-General Sir Henry H. Wilson.

23rd Division had now joined IV Army Corps and on 2 March the Corps Commander Lieutenant-General Sir Henry H. Wilson KCB, DSO visited 13/DLI and inspected the battalion in heavy rain. The weather remained cold and dull and on the following morning a squad of fourteen reinforcements arrived from 23 Infantry Base Depot. Five days later 13/DLI moved from Auchel to billets in Hermin where they relieved a battalion of the X French Army. The pressure on the French at Verdun had led to the British extending their portion of the front and relieving French troops so they could be employed at Verdun. 13/DLI recorded that on 9 March two batteries of 20th French Artillery passed through their billets in Hermin, followed an hour later by the 268th and 290th Infantry Regiments.

Second Lieutenant Frederick Rees recorded the move to Hermin in a letter sent home on 7 March:

We marched here last Wednesday only seven miles; this is a little village like Barmby, but in hilly country with a very quaint old church. The people have never had any British troops here before. We have a nice big room for a mess in a farm house and two of us sleep in another farm, quite a comfortable little room with two beds with the usual look out over the fold yard. We have had a lot of snow but a good thaw has set in today. The men are really awfully funny when you overhear them talking, two were

117

discussing one fellow who got killed in a very casual way. 'Aye,' he said, 'A great shell came over and took his heed clean off and went on and niver bust, leastwise I don't think it did. Howiver o' course he didn't give a bugger whether it bust or not after it had taken his heed off.'

On 11 March the new commander of 68 Brigade, Brigadier General Henry Page Croft inspected the men of 13/DLI, he had arrived in France in October 1914 with 1/Hertfordshire Regiment and was a Territorial soldier not a regular. The Battalion Adjutant, Captain Edward Borrow then recorded that he went forward on a reconnaissance with Major Naylor to have a look at the sector they were about to take over.

Went to trenches with Major Naylor, South East of Souchez, occupied by 2/East Lancashire Regiment. Trenches in a bad state Souchez and Carency levelled to the ground: Ground honeycombed with disused trenches: French and German dead in No Man's Land both sides freely exposing themselves in Front Line – unofficial truce, left battalion isolated during daytime, returned to Hermin at 1800 hours.

The next day he recorded that he went to 68 Brigade Headquarters where the Field General Court Martial of Sergeant Roberts took place. What crime the sergeant had committed has not come to light, nor has the punishment.

On 16 March 13/DLI began moving back towards the line, marching via Fresnicourt and Verdrel to Coupigny where they took over billets from 21/London Regiment. Just before they moved the following day a draft of thirty-one Other Ranks arrived from 16/DLI based at Rugeley Camp on Cannock Chase in England. At 1730 hours the march continued through Bully Grenay to Calonne where they took over as left front battalion of the left Brigade on the divisional front, and by 2045 hours the relief of 17/Middlesex

An artist's impression of how the trenches were manned at night with one soldier firing a flare.

Regiment was complete. On the battalion right 10/NF held the right sector of 68 Brigade Front, while on the left the front line was held by regulars of 1st Division.

About this time both officers whose letters have survived were sending snippets of the doings of 13/DLI. Lieutenant George Butterworth wrote as follows:

March 15.

We have been billeted in a pleasant village here for the last week, and plans have slightly altered again. We are going to take over trenches (in a day or two) a few miles off where we expected to go. I hear they are very good trenches. No other news. The last of the snow has disappeared, and we are having lovely weather.

Then a few days later Second Lieutenant Frederick Rees sent this letter home:

18 March

We are now in the trenches again, moved up last night. They are trenches we have taken over from the French and they are very comfortable and a good deal safer than the last we were in. It was just a month last night since we were in the line so have had a good quiet month. These trenches run along the edge of the village, of course most of the houses are just about flat but they nearly all have cellars which we use as dug outs, quite shell proof as all the broken down house is on top. I have a fine dug out in a cellar, fire place, bedstead, book shelf, large mirror, chairs, in fact I am thinking of taking up my abode here for the duration of the war.

The men have dugouts about twenty feet down, get in there and you are as safe as if you were in bed at home.

The next couple of days were fairly quiet, the enemy shelling the battalion sector but causing no casualties until 19 March when seven men were wounded: 15093 Private George Potter, B Company; 21943 Private Thomas Campbell and 16979 Private John Curran, both of C Company; 15115 Private J. Ramsden and 25078 Private Robert Frith, both serving with D Company; and 15894 Sergeant Francis Lamb and 23630 Private James Shilling, both with A Company. The next day one of B Company scouts, Lance Corporal Robinson, discovered a party of eight Germans working in a dry ditch in No Man's Land. He returned to the battalion lines and a bombing party of five Lance Corporals, twelve bombers and bayonet men was organised. They went out into No Man's Land and drove the enemy party out of the ditch. The right company then opened fire with rifle and Lewis-gun fire in an attempt to cut off the German retreat. This was quite successful and two of the eight Germans were killed and two wounded. However, this brought heavy retaliation from the German gunners and two men, 17166 Private Joseph Allen and 25045 Private Joseph McMullen, both from Middlesbrough, were killed.

On 21 March 12/DLI took over the front line from 13/DLI; they reported that the enemy was very quiet, but the following day the German trench mortar batteries were very active even though heavy snow was falling. Word came through that 13714 Private John Peel, a 32-year-old married man who came from the colliery village of Haswell Plough in County Durham, had died from his wounds in one of the hospitals near Etaples. After only four days in the line 12/DLI were relieved by 13/DLI and moved to billets in Bully Grenay. Here they were employed by the Royal Engineers; each day 400 or more men were out carrying stores up to the forward dumps.

Out at rest with 13/DLI, George Butterworth sent this letter home:

March 22.

We have just returned from our first turn in trenches, and it was quite enjoyable – trenches dug down deep in chalk soil, and no water – much safer than what we have been accustomed to.

Things are moderately lively; we are not likely to have serious trouble here, though there is historic ground on either side. Weather has been fine and warm.

We have got a new Brigadier (our fourth). You will be interested to know his name, i.e., Page Croft, M.P.; you sent me a newspaper report of one of his speeches in the House – he seems a good man.

I have just seen in The Times *that poor old Victor Barrington-Kennett is missing.*

The last named, a family friend was a Major in the Grenadier Guards but serving with 4 Squadron Royal Flying Corps. His two younger brothers had already fallen.

Second Lieutenant Frederick Rees also wrote home when he arrived in the billets in the support line:

22 March

We are now out of the trenches for four days, only about three or four hundred yards behind it in a huge colliery village [Bully Grenay] *and when we are out of the trenches for four days we live in the cellars of the houses.*

We have not much to do except take working parties to work in the trenches.

A message was received at Battalion Headquarters of 13/DLI from Brigadier General Page Croft CMG:

The Brigadier congratulates the 13th Durham Light Infantry on the successful minor operation carried out on the night of 20/21 March – By careful organisation and determination the attackers inflicted several casualties on the enemy and suffered no losses themselves. Great credit is due to all concerned and to Lance Corporal Robinson in particular for the part he played in the previous reconnaissance and organising the attack.

They had not long been out of the line when the enemy shelled the billets where A Company were resting: this resulted in the death of Second Lieutenant Oliphant's batman, 23-year-old 21627 Private William Atkinson who came from Winlaton Mill. He was buried in the British section of Bully Grenay Communal Cemetery French Extension.

One of the parties employed by the Royal Engineers was tunnelling and there was a serious accident when 19841 Private Walter Robinson fell through into a hidden cellar, severely injuring his back and right arm. This led to a Court of Inquiry which took place at Colonne Square. The president was Major Naylor and the members Second Lieutenants Johnson and Rees who gathered evidence from other members of the working party. The news came through that 23630 Private James Shilling had died at the Casualty Clearing Station in Lillers where he had been since being evacuated wounded a few days earlier.

At 1730 hours on 25 March 13/DLI took over from 12/DLI, again the relief being completed by 1845 hours. The next day the German trench mortar batteries were active and at 0900 hours a number of whizz bangs fell in the rear of C Company; these were followed at 1145 hours by some heavier high-explosive shells, one of which hit a dugout where men of Number 8 Platoon B Company were resting. Two men, 23754 Private John Jones from West Hartlepool and 24813 Private Richard Fawcett from South Shields, were killed and 17764 Lance Sergeant John Roberts and 23768 Private Edward Thrush were wounded. Then about an hour later 11665 Private Albert Ingleby was wounded in the cheek by shrapnel; he would be transferred to the Northumberland Fusiliers with whom he was awarded the Military Medal. Brigade Headquarters now organised a retaliatory barrage all along the Brigade front: every trench mortar, machine gun, rifle grenade and artillery opened fire at 1400 hours. Immediately the firing started, all personnel not involved went down into the dugouts to avoid any enemy retaliation. Although the Germans did reply, they caused no casualties. Later that night a patrol went out at 2200 hours from the battalion and on their return reported that the enemy sap at M.15.b.8.4 was manned by five enemy soldiers who were very quiet. The next night at the same time three men set out to bomb the sap, but when they got there the enemy had left. On their way back they found a loaded German rifle beside the enemy barbed wire in No Man's Land; this was duly brought back as evidence that they had been out in No Man's Land.

During the day Lieutenant George Butterworth send a hurried letter home which briefly described the conditions in the trenches:

> *March 27.*
>
> *We are in the trenches again, and the weather is compelling us to resort to rubber boots again, though we are not likely to get water more than ankle-deep in this soil. Nothing else to report – 'situation normal,' in the words of the daily bulletin.*

On the morning of 28 March, just after breakfast a number of whizz bangs fell behind that part of the line held by C Company and more followed at around 1020 hours which led to the wounding of 17116 Private John Simpson. Preparations were being made to hand over to 12/DLI and a billeting party was making its way to the rear in order to take over the billets from the outgoing battalion when they came under shellfire and 23663 Private Gibson Snaith from Witton Gilbert near Durham was wounded in the hip by shrapnel.

12/DLI in the meantime had spent the last four days in billets behind the front in Bully Grenay: here they daily provided working parties for the Royal Engineers, digging and carrying and the other monotonous tasks assigned to the resting infantryman. Too quickly though, it was time to go back into the line and by 2045 hours on 29 March 12/DLI completed the relief of 13/DLI. The sector was now held by 1/Black Watch on the left, 12/DLI in the centre and 11/NF on the right. On 30 March the German artillery was very active and again on the following day when over 1,000 shells of various calibres fell on 12/DLI between daybreak and noon. However, casualties were light and only three men were wounded.

13/DLI out at rest found time to send a party to a *Flammenwerfer* demonstration which was held at the 23rd Divisional Bombing School at Sains-en-Gohelle. Although they were out at rest they were not safe from the enemy artillery or his aircraft, at which the British Anti Aircraft gunners opened fire. On 31 March the German Artillery shelled Fosse 10 for two hours in the morning and their aircraft were also active; this led to 23773 Private Thomas Forrest from Low Spennymoor being wounded by a fragment of shrapnel from an anti-aircraft shell. Lieutenant George Butterworth sent another short letter home to let his family know he was safe:

> March 31
>
> *We are at present in reserve, after another tour in trenches – having a pretty good time – lovely spring weather at present, different from what you seem to be getting. Future movements uncertain, but I don't fancy the present quiescence will continue long, considering what is happening in Russia and Italy. By the way, I think you are wrong about the British line; I have certainly seen it stated in the papers that it is now continuous from Ypres to the Somme, in which case it must have been pretty well doubled since Christmas.*
>
> *Have heard from Colonel B.-K. Victor's fate is uncertain but it seems probable that he was hit (or machine damaged) at a great height, and fell nose down.*

The next morning a party of men from the battalion were working at Cite Calonne when they came under fire and 24610 Private Owen Ruddy was wounded by shrapnel in the left shoulder; he was evacuated and returned to England and was discharged on 16 December. Later in the day a French aeroplane was brought down near the battalion positions, both the pilot and observer being killed when it hit the ground. On 2 April the two battalions changed over once again, with the same pattern of working parties for the support battalion and the battalion in the line being shelled occasionally. On 4 April the enemy shelled the right of A Company 13/DLI and 19-year-old 24565 Private Edwin Elliott from Bank Top, Burnhope, was killed in action. Then at 0130 hours a patrol left the battalion lines at a point known as Pit Prop Corner; their mission was to inspect a terrace in No Man's Land to see if it was occupied by the enemy. The patrol carefully approached the position but it was found unoccupied, with no evidence of any recent occupation or work. The War Diary of 12/DLI for this period simply records that they were in billets in Cite Calonne and provided the usual working parties for the Royal Engineers.

On the morning of 6 April the front was quiet until noon when the German artillery launched a heavy barrage on 13/DLI. The parapet was breached and one shell hit a dugout where men of the left platoon of C Company were sheltering and three men, 21151 Corporal William Storey, a married man who came from Consett, 21283 Corporal Thomas Robinson who although born in Durham was aged 21 and was resident at Burnhope, and 24994 William Taylor who was aged 18 and came from Cassop Colliery, were killed in action. The Adjutant's War Diary records that the body of one of the three men killed was blown into the air and over the parapet where the remains landed on the British barbed wire. However, the Company recovered the body and today the three lie close together in Bully Grenay French Cemetery Extension.

21151 Corporal William Storey, a married man who came from Consett, was killed with two comrades when their dugout was hit by a shell.

That afternoon 12/DLI returned to the line and 13/DLI moved back to the billets vacated by the incoming battalion. For the next three days the usual artillery duels carried on and it was reported that A Company Officers' Mess dugout was hit by a shell and Lieutenant Jacques and Captain A.B. Mawer were evacuated injured. On 10 April a sham attack was planned. At 1330 hours all the 23 Divisional Artillery opened a steady bombardment. Prior to the barrage the infantry had dug jumping-off positions and assembly trenches. During the early stages of the bombardment, in some places men let themselves be seen dressed in gas helmets. Then at 1600 hours phosphorous bombs and smoke candles were thrown over the parapet into No Man's Land. At this the enemy artillery increased their rate of fire. Half an hour later the British Artillery formed a barrage on the German front line and five minutes later lifted onto the support trenches. At the same time the German gunners placed a barrage in front of the Durhams' front line and shells of every calibre were fired into the British front and support lines. This led to the deaths in action of 15858 Private James Harrison from South Moor and 25791 Private William Gunn, a married man from Fencehouses. By 1730 hours the front had fallen quiet and in the evening the two battalions swapped over once again.

While they had been out at rest on 8 April 13/DLI had had one man accidentally killed: this was 13947 Private Henry Maughan from Chester- le-Street, and again the Adjutant's War Diary throws some light on the circumstances when it records that 'He was supposed to have been tampering with a dud shell.' However, on 11 April a Court of Inquiry was assembled: the president was the Battalion Adjutant Captain Edward Borrow and the members were Captain A. Fraser RAMC attached 13/DLI and Second Lieutenant Frederick Rees. The first witness called was 24818 Lance Corporal Walter Hope of B Company, who said:

> I was Corporal of the Machine Gunners Guard on 6 April 1916 and I mounted the deceased 13847 Private J B Maughan at 0600 hours. At 0700 hours I visited the sentry, at 0730 hours I heard two taps followed by an explosion and proceeded with 16817 Sergeant Stabler to investigate. On coming up out of our cellar we found Private Maughan lying on the ground in the room above the cellar and he died a few minutes later. The room bore abundant traces of the explosion, I could smell powder.

13947 Private Henry Maughan from Chester-le-Street was killed when he tampered with an unexploded shell. He was buried in Bully Grenay Cemetery. D/DLI//7/75/36

> Later I found pieces of the base of the aluminium band of the nose cap of the whizz bang. I also found a new hole in the floor of the top room where such a piece of metal might come through.

The next man to give evidence was 17805 Private Arthur Dewing, A Company Machine Gun Section, who added:

> At about 0645 hours on 8 April 1916 I spoke to the deceased Private J H Maughan. He was on sentry and mentioned that there was an unexploded shell outside his billet. He showed me where it was and then picked it up. The aluminium ring in the nose cap was loose and he turned the ring round saying that it would make a fine souvenir if he could empty it. Whereupon I took the shell away from him and laid it down telling him he ought not to meddle with it. Then we came away and the accused went back to his beat. At about 0730 hours I heard an explosion but no sound of a flying shell.

The third witness was 16817 Sergeant John Stabler also from the Machine Gun Section, who on examination added this statement:

> At 0730 Hours on 8 April 1916 I was in charge of 13/DLI Machine Gun Section in Callone, all the section except the sentry, 13847 Private Maughan were together in the cellar. At 0730 hours we heard an explosion and on proceeding upstairs to investigate we found Private Maughan lying on his back moaning in the room above the cellar. The room was in a state of great disorder and later I picked up pieces of the base of a Whizz Bang. I at once called the stretcher bearers from the South Staffordshire Regiment in the next street. When they arrived a few minutes later Private Maughan was dead. I saw an unexploded Whizz Bang the previous day in a field behind the billet. I searched for it after Private Maughan's death but could

not find it. Both Private Maughan's legs were severed above the ankle and he had a deep gash above the right eye. I heard no sound of a shell flying over before the explosion took place.

The final statement was that of the court, which concluded that:

In the opinion of the Court 13847 Private J. H. Maughan received his injuries which caused his death by meddling with an unexploded shell. The explosion was accidental but due to his own carelessness and disregard for standing orders as to the handling of unexploded shells.

On 11 April 13/DLI were relieved in support by 11/NF and made their way up to the line and took over from 12/DLI; the latter on being relieved went back to billets in Estree Cauche. Once 13/DLI was settled in, the trench routine began once more; it rained overnight and just before dawn the battalion 'stood to'. Then at 06:00 the German artillery fired on the right of Middlesex Trench: this fire lasted until 07:00 when the enemy must have stopped for breakfast, because exactly one hour later whizz bangs fell on A and B Company positions. The pattern changed at 09:00 when the enemy started using shrapnel and concentrated on A Company lines. There was a lull from 10:00 until noon when their mortars opened fire. A Company called for retaliation and the 18 Pounders of the 23rd Divisional Artillery fired two salvoes. This didn't stop the German fire and by 17:20 they were shelling A Company with heavy stuff. Again retaliation was requested, this time from D Battery 105 Brigade RFA Howitzers, but the request was declined and the battery would not open fire until the fire of the 18 Pounders was proved to be ineffective. The damage caused during the day was the destruction of two machine-gun emplacements in B Company holding the battalion right front. The parapet was badly breached and one man killed and one wounded. The dead man was 17080 Private Albert Nichol, born at Tudhoe Colliery but resident at Croxdale near Durham, and unlike many in the battalion he was not a coal miner, but had been a greengrocer when he enlisted. His wife Kate received two letters bearing the news of his death; the first came from the battalion Wesleyan Chaplain Leonard Babb who wrote:

I deeply regret having to report that tonight I conducted the funeral of your heroic husband, who heard and answered the call to higher service, when on duty in the trenches last night… It will be some comfort to know that Private Nichol did not suffer at all, his death being instantaneous, and so he was spared the pain that so many brave fellows have to pass through. Sergeant P B Smith of Spennymoor wishes me to express his sympathy and to state that he and other comrades were present at the service, under the moonlit sky, in the little cemetery, so hallowed as the resting place of many brave men.

Another letter arrived in Croxdale; this one came from Second Lieutenant E.A.P. Wood, the deceased soldier's platoon commander, who wrote:

I am writing to ask you to accept my sincerest and deepest sympathy on the loss of your husband. He was killed on the 12th by a shell dropping into an emplacement. I can assure you he suffered no pain and his death was instantaneous. We have lost a valuable machine gunner. I have known your husband for over a year now and I shall miss him greatly, as he was a splendid fellow.

One other man of B Company, 18319 Private Robert Summerson, a coal miner from Railway Cottages, Ferryhill, was evacuated with shell-shock. In A Company 13640 Lance Corporal George Barnard, a Middlesbrough man, was also affected by the shelling and evacuated too, while in C Company 24401 Private James Vicerage from Houghton-le-Spring who had joined the battalion the previous October was wounded but remained at duty. During the night Lieutenant Denzil Clarke carried out a patrol of the enemy's line in front of the battalion to examine an enemy sap at M.15.B.a.6. He had to return to the British Line but in the early hours of the following day he went out again to complete the reconnaissance. On his return he was able to report the existence of three unmarked enemy saps: this suggested that the enemy were preparing to advance their front line by joining up the sap heads.

During 14 April the regulars of 3 Brigade on the left of 13/DLI carried out the relief of 2/Munster Fusiliers by 1/South Wales Borderers in the Maroc sector, while 1/Gloucestershire Regiment relieved 1/Duke of Wellington's Regiment (1/DWR) in the left subsector, and to their left 1 Brigade took over from 2 Brigade. The enemy must have been alerted as some shelling took place and 17745 Private John Crozier of A Company became the 160th casualty of 13/DLI. He was evacuated and although he was posted to 16/DLI and was with them when they became 1/Training Reserve Battalion, he did not fully recover from his wounds and he was discharged on 22 November 1916.

On 15 April 12/DLI returned to the front line and during the relief the enemy shelled the right company and the communication trench leading up to that position. During their sojourn in the line little is reported in the Battalion War Diary, but on 16 April 26-year-old 19073 Private John Scott, a resident of Pickering Knook, was killed in action. Throughout their four-day tour the enemy artillery and aircraft were active but no significant events are recorded. After four days in the line the battalion was relieved by 13/Essex Regiment. They then marched to Fosse 10, where they daily provided working parties of 400 men for the Royal Engineers. It was on one of these working parties that Lieutenant Christopher Summerhayes was wounded and evacuated on 23 April; when he was fit again he was posted to the Gloucestershire Regiment and never rejoined the Durhams. 12/DLI remained at Fosse 10 for seven days and then on 26 April they marched to Ourton which was designated as a 'Rest Area'; however, they were required to provide 350 men to the Royal Engineers on 29 April. The working party must have come under enemy fire for 13171 Private George W. Nicholson, a 32-year-old miner resident at Wallsend and serving in A

Company, was killed in action. His death caused a few problems for the staff at GHQ 3rd Echelon, because when the battalion embarked for France the Orderly Room staff took with them the enlistment documents for 20633 Private J.W. Nicholson and this was the name that appeared on the casualty lists. It wasn't until George's brother Robert started making enquiries as to his whereabouts that the mistake came to light and the correct name and number were added to the casualty list.

Meanwhile 13/DLI had been relieved in support by 17/Middlesex Regiment and 2/Oxfordshire and Buckinghamshire Light Infantry (OBLI) and had moved to billets in Coupigny. Here the men were allowed into the local estaminet and were able to purchase strong drink. For the majority this wasn't a problem but one man, 15340 Private Henderson Brankston, a 20-year-old miner from Lanchester, got drunk. In every place the battalion had been billeted before leaving for France he had been in some form of trouble; indeed his company and regimental conduct sheets are interesting reading. On this occasion he was charged with: 'While on Active Service 1) Drunkenness; 2) resisting an escort whose duty it was to have him in their charge.' He was kept in custody until a suitable time could be found for his court martial.

A large party of 105 Other Ranks under the command of Lieutenant Noel Target and Second Lieutenant Richard Johnson moved to Bouvigny-Boyeffles where they were attached to 216 Army Troops Company Royal Engineers.

Over the next few days there was little to report, but on 22 April Second Lieutenants Charles H. Robins and H. Adams reported bringing with them twenty-two Other Ranks. Then two days later Second Lieutenant Oswald A. Kerridge arrived with twenty-three men from 23 Infantry Base Depot. On 25 April Major Shaw Naylor left the battalion to take up the appointment of Second in Command of 6/Royal Irish Rifles. Then the next afternoon 13/DLI marched to Barlin station and entrained at 1618 hours and was transported to Pernes. The next four days were spent here and presumably some training and refitting was done but the War Diary only comments on the fine weather.

On 28 April Lieutenant George Butterworth managed to get a short letter away to his family:

April 28.

Summer has descended on us in some style, and the clothing problem has suddenly taken a new turn.

We have moved further back and are now billeted in a pleasant country town in nice country – fairly complete rest, of which the M.O. has taken advantage to inoculate us all again.

It is difficult to realise that we have really come through a winter campaign; I suppose one can consider it satisfactory as a test of physical fitness, though we have certainly been lucky, the worst weather nearly always having found us in billets. We have been equally fortunate as regards the attentions of the enemy, and there must be few battalions with seven months' trench experience whose total killed amount to less than fifty.

The start of May saw both battalions training hard and for once the War Diary of 12/DLI imparts more information than that of 13/DLI. During the period 5 May until 17 May the training followed the normal army pattern. The training commenced with the company in the attack, followed by musketry and bombing practice, followed by a rearguard action. On 6 May Second Lieutenant Frederick Rees was able to send a letter home in which he mentioned that he had command of his company of 13/DLI and the training they were doing:

6 May

We are having quite a good time here, having moved again. We left the last place yesterday morning at 0500 hours, so we had an early breakfast. We thought we would make an early start as we had 16 miles to go and the weather is somewhat hot. The commander of the company has leave for about a week so the company is left to my tender mercies for the present. I rather scored as I have a horse so it saved my feet from getting sore on the march. We landed at 1130 hours and had another breakfast on the road.

Last night we went out to look round the manoeuvre ground and had a topping gallop on the hills. This morning we were out all morning and shall be out again tomorrow from 0800 until 1430 in the afternoon, doubling over the hills, dales, valleys and mountains like the good old days at Bramshott. It makes a grand change from the trenches and the weather is glorious. I think we shall be here for about a week.

By 8 May half of 12/DLI was attacking and half defending, followed by more musketry and bombing. This went on until 12 May when there was a full Brigade exercise with 12/DLI in the front line. But on 13 May the weather broke and heavy rain forced the abandonment of manoeuvres and the men were given lectures in their huts. The rain lasted for two days and it wasn't until the afternoon of 15 May that they were able to undertake a battalion route march. A further Brigade exercise took place the following day but this time 12/DLI was in reserve. Then on 17 May they marched to Pernes-en-Artois where they entrained and were transported to Barlin; here they spent the night and next morning all ranks were able to take a bath. Then in the afternoon they marched out of Barlin and relieved 15/London, The Civil Service Rifles, in the C section of the Notre Dame de Lorette sector. At the same time 13/DLI had also entrained at Pernes and on detraining at Barlin had marched to billets in Coupigny where they had arrived at 1700 hours on 19 May.

It was during this time out of the line that time was found to set up a Field General Court Martial for 15340 Private Henderson Brankston, whose story was mentioned earlier. He was found guilty on the charge of drunkenness but not guilty on the charge of resisting the escort. His punishment was three months' Field Punishment Number 1: this would be served when the battalion was out of the line, thereby leaving him free to join the battalion in action and then undergo more punishment when out of the line.

Lieutenant George Butterworth managed to write home during the time 13/DLI was on the training area:

May 9.

We are having a good long rest, i.e., away from trenches, at present in a remote country village, full of orchards, birds and streams – manoeuvres all the morning, which at least help to keep one healthy. Shall probably keep at the same sort of thing for a week or so.

The General [his father] *seems very pessimistic about the Government! I am sorry he goes so far as to support the 'Ginger' group. I would rather be governed by Harry Tate than by Carson, and L.G. seems to be playing to the gallery at least as much as at Limehouse.*

On 20 May 13/DLI moved forward and took over the front line in the Souchez sector from 1/Sherwood Foresters, the relief being complete by 1245 hours. In front of the battalion the British barbed wire was in poor condition but the line held was generally in good repair apart from two gaps where the parapet had been blown in. The weather at this time was very hot with a light wind and fortunately the enemy was quiet during the relief and no casualties occurred. On the following afternoon the enemy started a heavy barrage on the sector of the line held by 1/7/London and 1/8/London of 140 Brigade. The shelling not only covered the front line and machine-gun and observation posts, but also fell on the communication trenches and back to the Brigade and Divisional Headquarters of the 47th (London) Division. For four hours the shelling carried on, the Divisional artillery of the 47th Division suffering as much as their infantry comrades in the front line. At 1945 hours the barrage lifted and then a mine was exploded and through the smoke and dust German infantrymen could be seen advancing in line. Mixed in with the high-explosive shells the enemy used lachrymatory (tear gas) shells and the gas released drifted down the line into the sector held by 13/DLI. During the day the enemy fired onto the battalion positions and 13/DLI had five men wounded: in D Company, 11229 Private Francis Burns and 12813 Private James Finley; in C Company, 21626 Lance Sergeant George Readman and 17347 Private Harold Gill. In B Company 16491 Lance Corporal Charlie Gowland was also hit; he was evacuated and didn't return to the front. When fit again he was transferred to the Royal Defence Corps.

The enemy captured almost 1,500 yards of the 47th Divisional front and penetrated up to 300 yards before being halted by running into their own barrage. In the early hours of 22 May a hasty counter-attack was attempted by 1/15 and 1/18/London which lasted around twenty-five minutes before being repulsed by the Germans.

On 23 May the Headquarters of 13/DLI came under fire in the afternoon and in the early evening the artillery fire of both sides increased until at 23:30 things finally settled down. During the day 19055 Private James Hutchinson was wounded by shrapnel. During the shelling both the Officers' Mess and the Sergeant Majors' dugouts were destroyed by direct hits. Things got a little hotter over the next two days and the casualties began to mount. Three men, 16704 Private Frederick Murray from Hartlepool, 19697 Private John Lee from Usworth and 24781 Private John Raine of Evenwood, all of D Company, were killed in action, while a fourth man, 15330 Robert Donnison from Gateshead also serving with D Company, was wounded.

Meanwhile in support 12/DLI had stood to in battle positions ready to repel any attack if it came their way. Just behind their battalion headquarters a battery of guns was dug in and these attracted the attention of the German heavy batteries which resulted in a great deal of shells falling about the battalion headquarters, the outcome being that the Officers' Mess and Battalion Orderly Room of 12/DLI were both completely wrecked. On 25 May 12/DLI were relieved in the support line by 10/NF and moved forward to relieve 13/DLI in the front line. As 13/DLI made their way out of the line a bullet came

The original grave marker of 19697 Private John Lee from Usworth who was killed in action 24 May 1916. D/DLI/7/397/1

spinning through the night and hit and penetrated the helmet of 15340 Private Henderson Brankston. The steam was taken out of the bullet by the helmet and although he was wounded in the head, it was a superficial wound and after a few days at 69 Field Ambulance and the 23 Divisional Rest Station, he was able to rejoin the battalion. Serving in the same company was Henderson's younger brother Alex who had enlisted in December 1914: he was tall for his age and had told the recruiting sergeant that he was 19 years 11 months old when he was in fact 16 years and 11 months old. Now eighteen months later he was a qualified machine-gunner in his platoon's Lewis Gun section.

During this period as usual Lieutenant George Butterworth wrote a short letter home:

Sunday, May 28.

As you probably guessed, we have been in the trenches again – rather sooner than I expected. You may also have imagined that things have been more lively than usual; as a matter of fact, on our immediate front things have been quiet; casualties below normal, which is astonishing considering what was going on within a mile or two of us, i.e., the battle of ...., which presumably you have read about. It was a pretty intense business, as far as artillery is concerned, and a new experience for us, for we practically overlook the ground in dispute. I am expecting leave shortly, so will reserve further account.

He was lucky enough to get a second home leave from 1 to 8 June, unlike many of the Other Ranks who had been out in France just as long and had not even been home once.

Meanwhile in the line 12/DLI endured a few days of shelling without mishap and then on the night of 28 May a patrol was sent out from D Company, its mission being to reconnoitre a German sap that led back to the German front-line trench. With the information gained by this patrol, the next night a twelve-man fighting patrol went out from D Company with the objective of bombing the enemy sentry post at the head of the sap. The mission was successful and both the sentry post and the enemy trench were bombed and valuable information gained; this led to the patrol being mentioned in 68 Brigade Orders. On the next day the enemy trench mortars and rifle grenadiers were actively bombarding the line held by 12/DLI, to which the battalion replied in kind and then sent a message to the Howitzer battery in close support requesting retaliation. The battery fired several rounds, after which the Germans fell silent. In the line 1st Section 68 Light Trench Mortar Battery (68/LTMB) was actively replying to the enemy fire and 21010 Private Fred James was busy replying when suddenly his post was damaged by an enemy shell. However, he did not pause until out of ammunition and then he went to the dump and carried back more bombs, before bringing the mortar back into action.

Then that night 13/DLI returned to the line and 12/DLI marched back to the hutments at Bois de Noulette. By 2030 hours on 30 May 13/DLI was in control of the front line. 12/DLI was now under the command of Captain H.H.L. Arnot, 2/East Lancashire Regiment. Nothing is mentioned in 12/DLI War Diary but the Adjutant's War Diary of 13/DLI in the Regimental Archives gives the reason for the change in command of 12/DLI: '26 May 1916 Lt Col Elwes cracked up, 27 May 1916 Major H Danvers cracked up.'

Both these gallant officers had seen much service with the Durham Light Infantry in South Africa: Lieutenant-Colonel Elwes with 1/DLI, where he had been awarded the Distinguished Service Order and Major Danvers with 4/DLI. Lieutenant-Colonel Lincoln Elwes when fit again commanded a Training Reserve Battalion in England and in 1918 took over command of the Northern Command Musketry Camp at Whitley Bay, Northumberland. Major Harold Danvers went on to transfer to and serve at the Machine Gun Corps Training Centre.

On 31 May 13/DLI came under repeated shelling at 1000 hours. The Straight and Hun Trench were under fire from enemy trench mortars and whizz bangs. Hun Trench was blown in near Solferino and a number of casualties occurred. 25865 Sergeant William Fawcett serving with B Company, from Hetton-le-Hole, was killed in action; he had only come out to the battalion on 30 December. At the same time 16213 Private Herbert Pickford and 20620 Private John Manning were wounded. John Manning from South Shields died from his wounds the following day. During this time the fighting on Vimy Ridge on the battalion's flank was continuing and on 1 June a mine charged with 4 tons of dynamite was blown under the German front line.

Lieutenant Edwin Wood was wounded in the back by shrapnel on 1 June 1916 and had to be evacuated.

At the same time 6th (London) Brigade was pushing forward into the enemy positions. The enemy replied by shelling Rotten Row and Sebastopol, two positions held by 13/DLI; in one of these Lieutenant Edwin Wood was wounded in the back by shrapnel and had to be evacuated. Throughout 2 June there was a lot of mutual shelling and 176 Tunnelling Company, Royal Engineers blew a camouflet in Rotten Row.

Headquarters 68 Brigade was now actively planning a raid on the enemy trenches and with the issue of Brigade Operation Order No 58 the task was allotted to 13/DLI. The raid was led by Lieutenants Denzil Clarke and Noel Target and consisted of three parties: a total of two officers and twenty-three Other Ranks.

At 0100 hours on the night of 2/3 June the Divisional Artillery opened fire on the German front line and one minute later the raiders left the British trenches, making their way straight to a gap previously cut in the wire. Luck was with them and they were able to get through the enemy wire and into their front line without being detected. The attacking party then turned to the left and worked about 40 yards up the trench. In that short time seven Germans were encountered and disposed of in the trench: three of these were bayoneted and two shot, while the remaining two were pushed down dugout steps and had bombs thrown after them. After working about another 30 yards up the trench, the attacking party came across a sap on the left and a bomb was thrown into it, whereupon a German rushed out and, realising a raid was

Lieutenant Noel Target, who was awarded the Military Cross for the part he took in the raid on the night of 2/3 June 1916. He was killed in action on 4 August 1916.

132

in progress, rushed back and got hold of his rifle. He then came rushing out to attack the raiders firing his rifle as he came; he was, in the words of the report, 'disposed of'. The party then threw a dozen or so bombs into two deep dugouts.

Meanwhile the first blocking party had turned to the right and worked about 40 yards along the trench and here they attempted to erect a bomb block. As they proceeded along the trench two Germans came out of different dugouts and they too were bayoneted. Four deep dugouts were also bombed by this party. The second blocking party remained at the point of entry and ensured the safe withdrawal of the raiding party. The sergeant in charge of the party was responsible for shooting one German who tried to interfere with the withdrawal. One bomber of this party had followed the first party and assisted them in bombing the four dugouts.

Owing to the wire having been cut so effectively by the 60lb trench mortar, the party detailed for the task were of little use. After around ten minutes in the enemy trench the withdrawal was carried out without any trouble from machine-gun or rifle fire; this was largely due to the excellent traversing of the enemy parapet on either flank by the battalion Lewis gunners. The raiders had three slightly wounded, including the sergeant in charge of the first blocking party.

The artillery cover was excellent and it was largely due to this that the raiders reached the enemy line unobserved. The enemy were taken completely by surprise and apart from the man in the sap, they were all in their dugouts. Those Germans that were encountered in the trench were full of fight and were not inclined to surrender. Their trench was particularly well constructed, wide and un-revetted and the dugouts were all under the parapet, in good condition and lit by electric light.

According to the Adjutant's War Diary the first blocking party under Sergeant White deserved special mention, but as everyone had done extremely well it would have been difficult to discriminate. However, one man did receive recognition for his work in the enemy trench: 15340 Private Henderson Brankston was prominent during the raid and for his gallantry he was rewarded with the remission of his Field Punishment No 1 of which he still had a couple of months to serve. However, just over two weeks later both officers and the two senior NCOs, along with twelve men of C Company were awarded the Military Medal. Another man, 15330 Private Robert Donnison who had recently been reduced by FGCM from the rank of Corporal and awarded Field Punishment had his sentence cancelled.

At 0900 hours the enemy shelled Battalion Headquarters and then throughout the day maintained a barrage on all of the battalion positions and seriously damaged Rotten Row, Sebastopol, Solferino, Bosche Walk, Hun Trench and HQ Trench. During the day congratulatory telegrams came in from HQ 68 Brigade and HQ 23rd Division. At 1930 hours the enemy launched a very intense barrage on all of the battalion front-line and support trenches and all wires to Battalion HQ were cut in the first five minutes. Given the fact that the barrage seemed to lift onto the support line, the CO ordered that SOS flares be sent up. By 2000 hours word came in from Second Lieutenant Tyssen who was holding Solferino Sap that the enemy had not attacked, so the SOS was cancelled. Immediate steps were then taken to repair the damage caused during the day: Rotten Row which was breached in no less than six places was completely repaired, while some parts of Sebastopol, Solferino and Hun Walk were not. The shelling had caused fourteen casualties, three in A Company, one each in B and D Companies and the other nine in C Company. Twelve of the men were wounded by shrapnel, but 17194 Lance Corporal William Bowran of C Company and 28754 Private James Cruddas were evacuated with shellshock. The shelling continued through 4 June until at 2100 hours the relief of 13/DLI took place.

Meanwhile the command of 12/DLI had passed to Lieutenant-Colonel Walter W. MacGregor, Gordon Highlanders. He had retired in 1913 after service in South Africa during the Boer war and on the North-West Frontier. When the SOS went up from 13/DLI, 12/DLI immediately stood to arms and prepared to counter-attack should an enemy attack take place. However, when word came through that everything was alright the battalion stood down and began preparing to move back into the line. During the early evening of 4 June 12/DLI moved back to the trenches in the Souchez sector and relieved 13/DLI, during the takeover there was some shelling by the enemy. They kept up this shelling over the next couple of days and the trenches were badly knocked about. In May the Royal Naval Division, now numbered 63rd (Royal Naval) Division had arrived on the Western Front and after a settling-down period the infantry battalions of the division had moved up and were beginning to come into

A platoon of C Company Anson Battalion training at Blanford before embarking for France.

the line for training in trench warfare. Although there were some veterans of Antwerp and Gallipoli in the ranks, the majority were new men and needed more training. Consequently on 6 June one company of Anson Battalion was attached to 12/DLI for instruction. During the day 12/DLI had one man killed by shellfire: 19223 Private Edward Lee from Leadgate was posted missing and it must be presumed that he was completely blown to smithereens. However, the Army failed to notify the next of kin and his poor parents and wife learned from the local press that he was missing. His father wrote to No 1 Infantry Records Office at York:

39 Watling Street
Leadgate
Re Private E H Lee 19223
12 Durham Light Infantry
C Company
B.E.F.
Dear Sirs,
Can you give us any further information on the above man? I notice that the 'North Mail,' has published in their issue of Saturday 8 July the enclosed cutting that he is now believed killed. It was also in the 'Northern Echo' the same day similarly worded. It does seem wrong that the general public should know before the relatives and I will thank you to let us know that it is really the case that my son has been killed or if it is a false report, as we are naturally very anxious to know the truth about him. Thanking you in anticipation.
I remain yours respectfully
William Wallace Lee.

The news was not good and No 1 Infantry Records at York sent the soldier's widow two statements from soldiers who were close by when her husband was hit. The first was from 18606 Private William Simpson, a 24-year-old miner from Annfield Plain, who had already been wounded by a bullet in the left arm while serving with 15/DLI and had arrived in 12/DLI with a draft in April. The other statement was made by 15805 Private James Shield, a miner from Esh Winning serving with 11/Northumberland Fusiliers, probably attached to 68/LTMB. Both men confirmed that Private Lee was dead.

Another family with a son in the same battalion were also writing to No 1 Infantry Records that June. On 23 June Mr Robert Adams of 42 Salvin Street, Spennymoor wrote:

Dear Sir
I understand that you have issued instructions that boys under 19 are to be placed in the reserve.
My son Frederick William Adams 16141 C Company 12 Batt DLI, BEF France who gave a wrong age when he joined the forces, has now been 10 months in the trenches and yet he is not 19 till October next (Birth cert

enclosed which kindly return).

Would you please see that he is transferred, as I am anxious about his health, being so young and out so long without even a holiday. Trusting you will give this matter your early attention and oblige.

Yours faithfully,

Robert Adams.

After two days attached to 12/DLI the company from Anson Battalion moved back and another from the same battalion came up in their place. The enemy shelling continued and the trenches suffered accordingly. That night 10/DWR from 69 Brigade moved into the line and relieved 12/DLI, who marched back to hutments in Bouvigny Wood where they arrived at 0200 hours. They had scarcely been there for an hour when a German aeroplane flew overhead and dropped bombs on the camp. They were here for two days, after which they marched to billets at Deival where they rested for the night before moving on to billets in Heuchin. After spending two nights there the battalion moved to Reckinghem where they were complimented by the Brigade Commander on their march discipline.

At 2300 hours on 8 June 8/Green Howards relieved 13/DLI in the support line at Ablain-St-Nazaire and the Durham battalion marched through heavy rain to huts at Coupigny where they arrived at 0315 hours. While the battalion was resting and refitting here they were joined by Major Robert V. Turner who was arriving to replace Lieutenant-Colonel Biddulph who had been evacuated sick. Major Turner, a regular, had seen service in South Africa with 1/DLI and had served at the front in 1914 with 2/DLI before serving as ADC to the Inspector General of Communications; his next post had been as Brigade Major of 207 Brigade in England. After lunch on 11 June the battalion paraded and marched out of Coupigny and marched to Barlin where they entrained at 1435 hours. They were transported to Pernes where they detrained and rested for the night. At 1000 hours they left Pernes and marched via Sains-les-Pernes to Lisbourg, where they were joined by a draft of men from 17/DLI. On 13 June the Brigade Commander, Brigadier General Henry Page Croft inspected the battalion. They remained at Lisbourg cleaning up and doubtlessly refitting and reorganising until 0930 hours on 15 June when they marched via Beaumetz to Delette where they arrived at 1300 hours. Here Second Lieutenant E. Thompson reported from the 3rd Infantry Base Depot.

Lieutenant George Butterworth, having returned from another leave in England, sent a few quick letters home during this period as follows:

Major Turner, a regular who had seen service in South Africa with 1/DLI and had served at the front in 1914 with 2/DLI before serving as ADC to the Inspector General of Communications, took over command of 13/DLI. Seen here as a Lieutenant with 1/DLI in 1904 in India. D/DLI/2/1/850

June 13.

As I expected, we are now out of trenches, and are apparently going to have another spell of training – there are many rumours as to our next destination, but no one really knows anything.

My journey back took two whole days, including a night at Boulogne.

No news whatever and weather awfully bad.

June 17.

Many thanks for watch-guard, which suits excellently. I think I told you we are in rest again – that being so I have of course no news; the only interest of things lies in future movements, of which I know very little and must say less. Weather improving by degrees.

Both battalions were now actively training; the main thrust of this was the Brigade in the attack. Various combinations were practised with 68 Brigade on the left flank and 69 Brigade on the right and the next day they switched round as did the battalions; one day on the left, then in the centre or on the right. Both battalions held medal parades, obviously to reward those who had carried out acts of gallantry and to inspire the others. On 19 June Major General James Babington GOC 23rd Division presented the ribbon of the Military Cross to the two officers and the ribbon of the Military Medal to fourteen men of 13/DLI who had been involved in the trench raid on the night of 2/3 June. Then on 21 June the ribbon of the Military Cross was presented to Second Lieutenant John Jacques and that of the Distinguished Conduct Medal to 21010 Private Fred James, both of 12/DLI, the latter attached 68/LTMB. After another day of Brigade tactical schemes both battalions rested.

During this time out of the line 13/DLI recorded the arrival of a draft of five Other Ranks on 20 June, which was overshadowed by the arrival of seven officers. On 22 June the following subalterns arrived: Second Lieutenant Joseph Batty had served as a Corporal in the RAMC (TF) and had been commissioned into 17/DLI on 1 January 1916 and was posted to B Company, while Second Lieutenants George Wharton and Harold Wheatley, who had both been commissioned into 17/DLI on 8 November 1915, were sent to C Company and B Company respectively. The next day another four officers reported to Battalion Headquarters. Second Lieutenant William Oakes, commissioned into 19/DLI on 28 June 1915, reported from 23/DLI and along with him came three second lieutenants from 17/DLI: Norman Thompson had been commissioned on 30 October 1915, John Dawson was commissioned on 14 August 1915 and the last named was Charleton Brown who had been commissioned in August 1915. On the night of 23/24 June it rained all night and the battalion rose early to begin its day's march. The battalion transport left at 0700 hours and moved by road, followed by the main party at 0800 hours. They marched to the railway sidings at Aire where they entrained and the train pulled out at 1326 hours. The train travelled via St Pol, Doullens and

Amiens before arriving at Longueau at 2135 hours where they detrained and marched to billets in Picquiny. After 13/DLI arrived at the railhead they were closely followed by 12/DLI; the train carrying the battalion pulled out at 1026 hours and followed the same route to Longueau where they arrived at 0600 hours and having detrained, they too marched to billets in Picquiny. The weather over the next three days was very wet with heavy rain, but even so both battalions carried out drill parades and route marches. The Army had been preparing for the Somme Offensive and to that end troops of other divisions were passing through the area where 68 Brigade were billeted. On 25 June 18th (Eastern) Division marched by on their way to the front. This was followed on 27 June by 2nd Indian Cavalry Division who began passing at 2000 hours and took until 0600 hours on 28 June for the tail end to clear the village. Other units that are recorded as passing are the Canadian Cavalry Brigade led by the Canadian Dragoons and the Canadian Horse Artillery. It was now time for 23rd Division to begin moving forward and at 1452 hours on 30 June, 13/DLI left Picquiny and marched the 12 miles to Allonville. At 1525 hours they were followed by 12/DLI who moved to Poulainville where they arrived at 1915 hours. Three more Second Lieutenants reported to 13/DLI that day: two from 21/DLI, Second Lieutenants Noel Fausset and William Charlton; the latter had served in the Inns of Court OTC prior to being commissioned. The third officer reporting was Alfred Green who had been commissioned into 17/DLI on 27 September 1915.

To the east the guns were roaring and belching out their shells as the final hours passed before the start of the big push.

Chapter Five

Battle of the Somme
The Early Stages

GENERAL SIR DOUGLAS HAIG had given the main part of the Somme Offensive to the Fourth Army commanded by General Sir Henry Rawlinson and a smaller part, to the north, to the Third Army. The Fourth Army comprised from right to left XIII, XV, III, X and VII Corps. The III Corps was commanded by Lieutenant-General Sir W.P. Pulteney, who had under his command the 8th and 34th Divisions holding the line, with the 19th (Western) Division in reserve. Moving up behind them to continue the advance was Major General Babington's 23rd Division. The offensive opened at 0730 hours on 1 July and the leading waves of the two leading divisions were mown down by the German machine-gunners, despite the fact that the front line was taken, and then the 19th Division moved up in support.

The news from the front trickled back to Divisional Headquarters and was then relayed down to the battalions. The Adjutant of 13/DLI recorded the signals as they came in: 'XIII Corps and XV Corps have taken all first objectives, 7th Division are entering Mametz, III Corps have captured all enemy front-line trenches, X Corps are hung up opposite Thiepval, but have taken the Crucifix and St Pierre Divion, VIII Corps have taken first objective except Hawthorn Redoubt and are in Beaumont Hamel.' At 1700 hours another signal came in, '30th Division have taken Montauban'; then at 2330 hours another report arrived stating 34th Division had captured four lines of German trenches and that 19th Division had passed through and taken another 3 miles. It would soon be the turn of 23rd Division to enter the fray.

Accordingly orders were issued for the various brigades and battalions to stand by to move in fifteen minutes. Consequently billeting parties moved off to take over their allotted accommodation. At 2025 hours 12/DLI moved out of Poulainville and marched up to Franvillers where they were bedded down by 0100 hours. Likewise 13/DLI marched out of Allonville and travelled on foot along the Amiens to Albert Road and ended up in the same village of Franvillers; by the time they got there the whole of 68 Brigade had arrived including 70/Field Ambulance and 68/Brigade Machine Gun Company. Throughout the daylight hours of 2 July they rested and then in the early evening they took another step towards the front line. 12/DLI left first: moving out at 1700 hours they moved to trenches along the railway line between Albert and Dernancourt where they arrived and settled down at 1930 hours. 13/DLI didn't move until 2130 hours when they moved in column of route to billets at Millencourt where they arrived at midnight. During the day news was received that 18105 Lance Corporal William Peveller had been killed in action: at the time of his death he was many miles away from 13/DLI, for he was attached to 233 Tunnelling Company Royal Engineers who were located some kilometres north of Arras at Bully-les-Mines. Major General Babington had sent 69 Brigade forward ahead of 68 Brigade and the Yorkshire Battalions had moved up and relieved the decimated units of the 34th Division. This must have been a trying time for many in the Green Howards, Northumberland Fusiliers and Durham Light Infantry battalions of 23rd Division for many of them had fathers, brothers, cousins, in-laws and friends serving in the Tyneside Irish and Scottish Brigades and they wouldn't have known if they had survived or not.

There wasn't much time for writing but Lieutenant George Butterfield managed to get a few words away to his family:

June 26.

Not much news, except that we have moved again (and a good long way) and are now in reserve to a different part of the line. Please thank D. for sunshade.

July 2.

By the time you get this the papers will be full of what is going on here. At present we know very little, except that the much-advertised offensive has started, and made some progress.

We are at present acting as reserve at what seems about the centre of the main push. We have been moving up by easy stages – billets each night – and are at present about 12 miles from the line. Everything seems very quiet, and we can scarcely hear the guns – a phenomenon I completely fail to understand. It is impossible to say how soon we shall come into action, but we are bound to do so sooner or later, unless our plans go wrong altogether. Fortunately the weather has turned fine, and seems likely to remain so. I will try to get some field postcards to correspond with, as they will reach you quicker than letters.

July 3rd.

Last night we moved up a bit further, and are now within an easy march of the front. When we got to our destination (at about midnight) we found our billets full of prisoners. So the whole brigade was turned into a field and ordered to bivouac. This consists chiefly in lying down on a waterproof sheet. The men have no overcoats! I have my Reading mackintosh, and managed three hours' sleep not bad with the temperature little above 40 degrees. There is no mistake about the bombardment now. We get very scanty news from the front, and have seen no papers since the show began. Weather still fine, and pleasantly warm in the daytime.

On 4 July 68 Brigade began to concentrate in Becourt Wood. 12/DLI left the trenches near the railway at 1400 hours and in heavy rain made their

The Germans were well dug-in and were able to provide enfilade fire from the village of Contalmaison, seen here on a German postcard of 1915. By the summer of 1916, most of the buildings were reduced to rubble but the cellars provided good cover for the defenders.

way through Albert and bivouacked in the wood; after resting here overnight, on the following morning they were detailed off to provide carrying parties. These were ordered to resupply 69 Brigade with ammunition, stores, food and water and they took with them stretchers in order to bring out the wounded; this work went on from 0900 until 2100 hours and during these operations the battalion had fourteen Other Ranks wounded. The next morning the battalion was ordered forward to relieve 8/Green Howards. They took over trenches as follows: A Company, Birch Tree Avenue; B Company, trenches in X21.b.3.9 to 5.7; C Company, trench running from X21.b.7.4 to X22.a.4.6; and D Company went to The Triangle holding a line X21.d.5.1 to X15.d.8.1.

As soon as they were in the trenches work was commenced to improve the positions: trenches were deepened and fire steps constructed, along with a general consolidation of the positions held. That night they were relieved by 11/NF and moved back to the area of X.21.d. Here they rested before moving back to support the attack of 11/NF. Two companies, D and B, advanced across the open ground and occupied and consolidated. Both companies established bombing posts on the flanks to protect against enemy counter-attacks. The advance was made under heavy machine-gun and rifle fire, the objective being to fill the gap that had opened between the Wiltshire Regiment and 11/NF. At 1330 hours C Company tried to advance but came under heavy enfilade fire from Contalmaison. This caused the men to fall back and eventually two platoons were taken forward by way of a covered trench and began digging in; they were followed by the other two platoons about fifteen minutes later. The consolidation of all three companies was made more difficult by German snipers, but these were eventually driven off by a Lewis-gunner who opened fire every time one showed himself. At 1230 hours the Commanding Officer had been ordered to send a platoon to fill the gap between 24 Brigade and 11/NF. To do this Lieutenant Francis, who had only joined the battalion in June, and Number 3 Platoon of A Company were sent. The route they were given was via Birch Tree Avenue and through Peake Wood and then to hold the trench running from X.16.d.5.1 to X.16.d.2.4. When they got to Peake Wood they found that the road was under constant machine-gun fire and it was too dangerous to send men along it. The officer therefore halted the platoon and he and Sergeant Gillespie, his platoon sergeant, went forward to reconnoitre. Almost immediately a terrific barrage opened up on 2/East Lancs who were lying out in the open in Peake Wood. Therefore the order was given to retire and Lieutenant Francis reported back to Battalion Headquarters. While they had been away the remaining three platoons of A Company had been ordered forward. Led by the Company Commander Captain Herbert St J. Carr-West, who had been commissioned into the DLI after serving with the French Foreign Legion, they went forward and fought their way into the enemy line. They bombed several deep dugouts and captured sixteen German soldiers. They held this position until dawn on 9 July when they retired, bringing with them nine of the prisoners; the other seven being wounded were left behind. Eventually relieved by men of the Wiltshire Regiment they moved back to bivouacs in Becourt Wood via Sausage Valley. During these operations the battalion had five Officers and 156 Other Ranks killed, wounded or missing.

Meanwhile 13/DLI having moved up to Becourt Wood on 4 July had been sent back to Albert. At a conference in the ruins of Becourt Château, Major General Babington had expressed concern about the number of men bivouacked in the wood and had ordered 10/NF and 13/DLI to move back to where they had come from. They left Becourt at 1645 hours and trudged back to their start point where they arrived at 1720 hours.

Here they remained until 6 July when at 0800 hours the Adjutant, Captain Edward Borrow reported to 68 Brigade Headquarters; he joined up with the Brigade Major and they went forward to 69 Brigade Headquarters in the line. Here they had a meeting with Brigadier General Thomas S. Lambert, late East Lancashire Regiment, and arranged the relief of his brigade by troops of 68 Brigade. While this was taking place 13/DLI left Albert once more and moved back to Becourt Wood. Here they bivouacked for the night and the following morning they commenced relieving the troops in front of them. Lieutenant George Butterfield wrote to his parents again before they moved forward:

July 5
I'm afraid these letters will reach you very late – the mail is much

interrupted, and I can't get any field cards. We moved here on the 3rd, about five miles behind the line; bivouacs, but we fortunately have some tarpaulin tents. Last night we were ordered forward, but after we had marched about three miles, orders were cancelled, and we returned to our starting point. At any rate we had the satisfaction of seeing a few (!) of the British guns in action.

We still get very little news – on the whole things seem going well, if rather slowly. The French have done brilliantly as usual, but they probably had the easier job.

On the morning of 7 July two companies were ordered to relieve two companies of 12/DLI and the other two companies were to relieve two companies of 11/NF. However, the orders changed before the move commenced and the Brigadier ordered them to relieve the whole of 11/NF on the line X.16c.3.0 to X.15.d.0.0 and to consult on the spot with 11/NF as to the actual dispositions. The weather had been particularly bad over the last two days and the rain had turned the trenches into a quagmire. By the time the men reached Scots Redoubt they were moving through mud sometimes waist-high and movement was almost impossible. When the Battalion Headquarters reached that of 11/NF it was found that the line held was nowhere near the positions given prior to moving off. The other problem was that the guides had no idea where they were going and only one company of 13/DLI arrived at its correct destination, the pitch darkness proving a great hindrance to the forward movement. The one saving grace was that no casualties occurred during the relief.

On 8 July the battalion attempted to straighten its line but movement was almost impossible and owing to the conditions difficult to achieve

22653 Private William Walton 12/DLI from Burnley was killed in action 8 July 1916.

without unnecessary loss. In the late afternoon a patrol returned with the news that the enemy were still in Bailiff Wood and about half an hour later two companies started to move forward to attack the Brigade objective. As they moved up they came under a heavy artillery barrage and machine guns were turned on them. Word then came from 68 Brigade Headquarters to hold up the attack and the message was quickly sent to the leading platoons. At the same time another patrol, this one led by Lieutenant Noel Target, entered the enemy trenches and proceeded northwards and after a short distance they spotted around forty German soldiers, so they moved back and rejoined the battalion. During the day casualties had steadily mounted. Second Lieutenant Harold Wheatley had been wounded and four men, 28638 Private Wilfred Bell, a Consett man serving with A Company; 23458 Private Thomas Dale, a Birmingham man who had enlisted fraudulently into 10/NF and had been convicted by General Court Martial and then transferred to 13/DLI; 27414 Private John Green, a Yorkshire man from Castleford; and 23471 Private Fred Hollingshead, a Staffordshire man from Cannock who had also been transferred in from the

Northumberland Fusiliers, were killed in action. A further twenty-one men had been wounded, three of whom remained at duty, and another three men were reported to be missing. It is interesting to note that Private Wilfred Bell is commemorated by the CWGC on the Menin Gate Memorial and is listed as serving with 2/DLI, but his Medal Roll sheet and the Adjutant's War Diary clearly show him as being with 13/DLI.

Overnight on 8/9 July there was some rain and the positions that the battalion held were gradually improved, especially on the left flank where they had to keep in touch with the men of 58 Brigade. During 9 July 68 Brigade HQ ordered 13/DLI to bomb along the trench X.16.a.1.4

to X.15.b.8.5. However, the bombing party took the wrong direction and followed a trench leading into Bailiff Wood where they came under fire from British artillery and a German machine gun. As dusk fell in the early evening C Company 12/DLI under command of Captain Herbert Pease, less one platoon, came up and assisted 13/DLI to consolidate their positions and after they had done a considerable amount of work at about 0100 hours on 10 July they moved back to Becourt Wood; the one platoon not involved was detailed to occupy and hold Bailiff Wood. Casualties in 13/DLI during the day had amounted to Second Lieutenant Oswald Kerridge and sixty-seven men wounded, of whom seven remained at duty, with a further six men shellshocked and four killed in action. Second Lieutenant Oswald Kerridge survived being evacuated through the Regimental Aid Post, the Field Ambulance, the Casualty Clearing Station and the ride on the Hospital Train to the General Hospital on the French coast. Almost two weeks later on 23 July he died from his wounds and is buried in St Sever Cemetery, Rouen. Also mentioned in the casualty list is 14334 Lance Corporal Edward Henderson from South Shields, who it was reported had wounded himself by negligence. Evacuated to 34/CCS and from there to the Base, the paperwork followed him instructing the hospital that at the earliest opportunity he was to be returned to his unit for trial by Field General Court Martial. After some time in hospital Edward returned to 13/DLI but the CO was forced to write to the Adjutant General's Department that: 'The charges against the above named have been dismissed as all the witnesses have been killed in action.'

Herbert Pease was awarded the DSO when he set a fine example of dash and bravery when leading the battalion in the attack which led to the capture of the enemy's trench. Subsequently he did fine work in the consolidation of the positions won.

13821 Lance Corporal Thomas Henry Read 12/DLI from Middlesbrough was killed in action 8 July 1916.

The other companies of 12/DLI were also busy that night: B Company carried 1,200 bombs up to 13/DLI and then sent two platoons to assist D Company 13/DLI in holding the road that led to Contalmaison. Another platoon was told off to cover three captured field guns and an ammunition dump; another party held a detached post while the remainder of the company were held in support. D Company 12/DLI in the meantime had moved up and filled the gap between 58 Brigade and 13/DLI, their right flank being in touch with 13/DLI around X.a.1.6. This last-named company sent a party forward towards the German trenches but they were driven back by the enemy. A second attack was then made and the trench blocked, consolidated and manned by two platoons of the company. During the night all positions held by the battalion were improved and consolidated. During the operations Second Lieutenant Charles Longstaff and seven Other Ranks were wounded and 13351 Lance Corporal William Dinning of Medomsley was killed in action.

On 10 July the Yorkshire battalions of 69 Brigade were detailed to take Contalmaison and during the day 12/DLI kept up a steady fire on the German positions, and when the enemy attempted a sortie from Contalmaison Wood they were able to drive them back; twice during the afternoon the Germans tried this and both times they were driven off. Consequently at 1500 hours 8/Green Howards moved up and occupied the positions held by 12/DLI and two platoons of B Company were sent back to Becourt Wood. However, owing to the heavy machine-gun fire it

Captain George Long was wounded during the fighting towards Contalmaison. After serving with the Labour Corps and the Royal Flying Corps he joined 1/DLI as part of the Army of the Rhine in 1921.

was impossible for the rest of 12/DLI to move until after 1600 hours, when owing to the heavy barrage on Contalmaison by the British artillery the remainder of B Company and all of D Company were able to move back without loss. The platoon of C Company in Bailiff Wood was able to support 69 Brigade by providing crossfire against the enemy positions. 12/DLI less that one platoon were relieved and made their way back to billets in Albert. After being relieved at 2300 hours the remaining platoon tramped their weary way back to the billets in Albert where they arrived at 0200 hours. During the day Second Lieutenant Thomas Duffy who had joined the battalion in November 1914 and seven Other Ranks were wounded, along with the following who were killed in action: 22116 Private Charles Bamford who came from Coldstream; 15338 Private Harold Harrison, a resident of South Moor, Stanley; 7888 Sergeant Stephen Mills who was born in Langley Moor; 24504 Private William Pounder from Witton Park; and 21890 Private Albert Sutherland who hailed from the village of Thornley Colliery. All five are commemorated on the Thiepval Memorial to the Missing.

At 1630 hours the attack of the Yorkshiremen of 69 Brigade passed through 13/DLI and they went on to complete the capture of Contalmaison, taking a large number of prisoners and machine guns. This had opened a gap on the left of 13/DLI and two platoons of A Company on the left were ordered to fill this gap. Then the rest of the battalion shook out to the left to cover the original battalion frontage. Another party had been detailed to block the trench at X.16a.2.6 and form a defensive flank. However, owing to the complete success of the Green Howards they were not needed and assisted the Green Howards to consolidate their positions around Contalmaison until ordered to rejoin their own battalion. Casualties during this period amounted to Captain George Long and Second Lieutenants George Wharton and Alfred Green and forty-eight men wounded, three of whom remained at duty; among them was Tom Hall who had recently joined B Company of 13/DLI after recovering from his wounds in England. There were six dead and three missing and one man evacuated with shellshock. One of the dead was serving in B Company: 16432 Private William Alliston, a 23-year-old from Dean Bank, Ferryhill, whose brother James was a Platoon Sergeant in the same company. James wrote home to their mother: 'Poor Will was killed on Tuesday morning, he got a bat with shrapnel off a big shell.' Yet another man, 23628 Private James Cairns from Hebburn, was reported to have been evacuated to a CCS, yet he had simply disappeared; it is highly likely that he and the stretcher bearers were all blown to pieces.

Tom Hall was wounded for a third time on 10 July 1916. He rejoined 13/DLI on 8 August, only to be wounded again on 14 October when he was evacuated to the coast. Once he was fit again he was posted to 2/Duke of Wellington's Regiment and was wounded for the fifth time when his skull was fractured: this proved fatal and he died from his wounds on 14 June 1917.

At 0540 hours 1/Cameron Highlanders of 1st Division arrived and relieved 13/DLI, who then marched by companies to billets in Albert which were reached by 0830 hours. Here they came under the temporary command of 34th Division. On the way back 23198 Private Thomas Ushon, a 34-year-old Nottingham man serving in C Company was wounded and sadly died from these wounds before much could be done for him. He was buried in a small cemetery near the road just south of Fricourt at Grid 62d f.9.b.10 by the Reverend R.H. Oldfield, one of 23rd Division's Padres. Thomas Ushon had enlisted into 14/DLI in January 1915 and when that battalion went overseas he was posted to 16/DLI at Darlington, then in October 1915 he was sent as a reinforcement to 13/DLI at the front. A further casualty occurred when 17691 Private Charles Nelson was evacuated shellshocked.

On 12 July they rested in Albert and time was found by some to write letters home, among them Lieutenant George Butterworth who sent two letters at this time:

> *July 12.* [His 31st birthday]
> *In brief my news is*
> *(1) We have been up to the front line for a few days.*
> *(2) Have done no actual fighting.*
> *(3) Are back in rest for a few days.*
> *I am not going to attempt any description – of course the conditions are utterly different from anything we are accustomed to. The ordinary placid*

routine of trench warfare exists no longer; one has a general sense of confusion, and shells fly about day and night. Add to that wet weather, and mud that requires all one's energy to wade through, and you will have some idea.

All the same it is obvious that our hardships are child's play compared to what the Germans are undergoing – our guns give them no rest whatever.

Am quite well.

July 14.

Very many thanks for birthday present and letter. Also your last food parcel was very opportune, as we were just starting off for the great battle.

We were up in the line for a few days, which seemed like so many weeks – but on the whole we had extraordinary luck. We never came into actual close contact with the Hun, but on the other hand we never knew exactly where he was, and often were quite vague as to where we were ourselves. Our worst enemy was the weather, which for two days was really bad. It sounds incredible, but is true that the mud was far worse than in any of the Armentieres trenches throughout the winter. This is chiefly due to the soil.

We are now back, billeted in a certain town [Albert].

I lost practically all my portable equipment, and finally came out with

1 revolver (unused),

1 map, and

1 flask (empty!)

In the evening at 1700, 1900 and 2315 hours the enemy shelled Albert and caused a further two casualties: 17221 Private Charles Brown and 25910 Private Ralph Mason. Then a congratulations telegram arrived from the GOC Fourth Army, repeated by III Corps and 23rd Division to 68 Brigade:

From Gen Rawlinson AAA Please convey to 23rd Div my hearty congratulations on their capture of Contalmaison AAA They have acquitted themselves right well and I desire to thank them most heartily for their gallantry and the fine fighting spirit displayed by all ranks AAA ends AAA

General Sir Henry Rawlinson.

12/DLI was also billeted in Albert at this time and they too had lost men wounded during the enemy shelling. Now the Brigade was put on three hours' notice to move and this was gradually reduced until at 1600 hours on 14 July they were ordered to move at thirty minutes' notice. 12/DLI moved out at 1000 hours and marched up the Bapaume Road and took up position on the left-hand side of the road in Tara Trench. Here they remained overnight until orders were received to relieve 10/Loyal North Lancashire Regiment (10/Loyals). At 1600 hours on 14 July 13/DLI left their billets in one part of Albert and moved to new accommodation in the Rue de Peronne where they awaited further orders; these eventually came in the early hours of the next morning and by 0730 the battalion was on its way to the line. A and B Companies occupied support trenches near Bailiff Wood, while Battalion Headquarters along with C and D Companies were occupying Heligoland (Sausage) Redoubt.

Prior to 12/DLI moving into the line, one Platoon Commander from each company went forward and visited the Battalion Headquarters of 10/Loyals and obtained the details of the positions their respective companies were to take over. At 1930 hours they moved out in the following order: A Company led, followed by D Company, and then C Company with B Company bringing up the rear. At 10/Loyals Headquarters in the chalk pit each company was met by a guide who led them into their respective positions. Here 12/DLI had all four companies in the line: the two companies on the left were in trenches but the two on the right were in a series of unconnected posts and shell-holes and by 2230 hours the relief was complete. Immediately parties from A, B and D Companies went about 100 yards forward and started digging assembly trenches. C Company in the meantime started connecting the posts and shell-holes. D company then started a communication trench from the front line to the assembly trench. 13/DLI was supposed to assist with the digging but owing to heavy shelling was unable to get forward. To protect the digging parties a number of patrols went out but few enemy positions were discovered.

On 17 July 12/DLI continued with the digging and consolidation of their positions. There was some sporadic shelling but the battalion wasn't much troubled by it; then at 1030 hours they started a smoke barrage in the hope that it would get the German machine-gunners to open up and reveal their positions. However, the German gunners were cleverer than that and not one gave his position away. But their snipers were very active and among the casualties was 17979 Private Herbert Parry from Weardale Street in Tudhoe Colliery and former goalkeeper of Tudhoe United. 15949 Sergeant John Sinclair, Herbert's close friend who only lived two doors from him and a former stoneman at Tudhoe Colliery, wrote to his parents:

> Dear friends,
>
> I am very sorry to have to inform you of the death of your son Herbert, who was killed in action on the morning of 17 July. A German sniper shot one of our lads and Herbert immediately rushed to his help. He no sooner got to the lad when the same sniper hit him, and he died instantly. We had to go into action that night and his last words to me were, 'Take care of yourself.' We lost a lot of fine fellows in the attack and there are very few lads left now that came out with us. We have had some very hard fighting, as you will have seen by the papers. You will be pleased to know that Herbert was a good soldier and should have had a medal or something of the sort for his bravery, for as soon as any of our lads were hit he did not lose a second before he was there at them. I will tell you more about him when I get back, if I ever do so. We just have to chance our luck and put the whole

of our trust in the King of Kings. We are not half forgetting the Huns now, and I think it will not be long before it is all over. The Huns are a dirty lot, as when our Red Cross go out they fire on them. We have advanced a long way out here, and are taking a lot of prisoners, but all of them will have to be severely dealt with as they are behaving so dirty to our lads.

Yours Faithfully,

J Sinclair, Sergeant.

In the afternoon the shelling increased on and behind the front line and was very heavy around Battalion Headquarters in the chalk pit, so much so that at 1630 hours the CO ordered the headquarters to move nearer to the front line. Then at 1700 hours a message came in from 68 Brigade Headquarters that 12/DLI would assault the enemy-held positions at X.4.c.7.4 to X.9.d.8.3, commencing at 2000 hours. The plan was that when 12/DLI went forward 13/DLI would move into the front line and if the12/DLI attack was successful then the rest of the brigade would assault Pozieres. 12/DLI had reorganised during the day and the attack was to be made on a two-company front with A Company on the left and C Company on the right. Behind A Company in support were D Company and B Company followed behind C Company.

At 2000 hours the attack commenced and as the officers' whistles blew, the leading platoons left the comparative safety of the trenches and moved towards the enemy positions. By 2004 all the attackers were moving but at this stage the Stokes mortar barrage provided by 68 Light Trench Mortar Battery (LTMB) was falling 50 yards short of the German trenches. As the

The German machine-gunners were good at concealing themselves. Here a Machine Gun Unit poses in a hollow behind the line for a unit photograph before going into action.

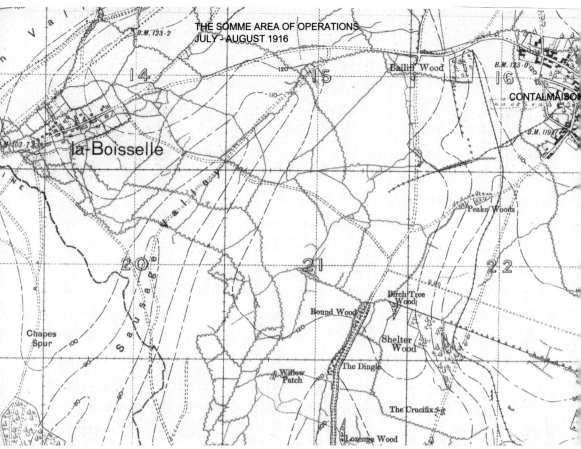

battalion went forward the German machine-gunners revealed themselves and opened an intense fire on the advancing Durhams. Although one platoon got to a point about X10.b.2.9, the cross-fire made further advance impossible. Indeed, those that survived from D Company were forced to save themselves by sheltering in shell-holes only 30 yards in front of their starting-point, otherwise they would surely have been annihilated. In C Company, Number 9 Platoon led by Second Lieutenant Leonard Harrison reached a point at X.4.d.1.1; here they were counter-attacked by German bombers and the young officer fell dead. He had originally enlisted into the 20/University and Public Schools/Royal Fusiliers, where he was numbered 4923 and he had been promoted to Corporal before they crossed to France on 14 November 1915. Selected for a commission, he had been commissioned into the Lincolnshire Regiment on 30 April 1916 but was subsequently posted to 12/DLI.

When the officer fell, his Platoon Sergeant John Hughes took over command and carried on the attack and for a further forty-five minutes he tried to press forward, carrying on a bombing fight with the enemy until the enfilade and crossfire forced him to bring the remainder of the platoon back. His skill and leadership brought him the award of the Military

Captain Robert Woodhead 12/DLI was killed in action on 17 July 1916. He has no known grave and is commemorated on the Thiepval Memorial to the Missing.

Medal. Now the machine-gun fire increased and turned on the whole of the attacking force, but on the left flank a Lewis-gun team of the battalion managed to knock out an enemy machine-gun post. C Company had managed the furthest advance, making only 100 yards before being forced to get down and crawl and they made a further 100 yards but were eventually held up by the enemy fire. The Germans sent small parties of men forward to reinforce their positions, and although C Company held on they were eventually forced to retire.

A Company on the left of the battalion had all their officers killed or wounded. The Company had gone forward at the double and although the left flank reached the enemy parapet, the right was badly held up by the barbed-wire entanglements. As with C Company the crossfire made progress impossible and at dark all companies withdrew to their original lines; they did, however, manage to bring in all the wounded. It was estimated that they had been attacking between ten and fifteen well-concealed enemy machine-gun positions. At around midnight 12/DLI less B Company were relieved by 13/DLI and made their way back to Tara Trench.

Casualties had been heavy: six officers, Captains Charles Wolstenholme and Robert Woodhead, Lieutenant Thomas Hetherington and Second Lieutenants Leonard Harrison, Richard Pearce-Brown and Theodore Warren had been killed. Richard Pearce-Brown had served as Private 13928 with the Coldstream Guards in England prior to being commissioned, and Theodore Warren had been commissioned into 17/DLI in November 1915 from the Inns of Court Officer Training Corps before landing in France on 28 June 1916.

19601 Lance Corporal Robert Hornby from Blackburn was one of those killed on 17 July 1916. He was only 17 when he died, and as he has no known grave he is commemorated on the Thiepval Memorial.

A further four officers, Captain Stanley Holmes, Lieutenant Eric Lafone and Second Lieutenants Arthur Francis and Cuthbert Haddon were wounded. Along with these officers the battalion suffered a further twenty-seven Other Ranks killed, eighty-two wounded and sixteen missing, with a further four evacuated with shellshock. Of those killed, wounded and missing, the majority were men who had landed with the battalion on 25 August 1915. Among them was the Battalion Pioneer Sergeant Peter Smith who before the war had been a miner at Page Bank Colliery; when he had enlisted he quickly rose through the ranks and

Lieutenant Eric Lafone 12/DLI was wounded on 12 July 1916. Evacuated to England, he rejoined the battalion in January 1917 and was killed in action on the Italian Front on 15 June 1918.

was eventually appointed Pioneer Sergeant in which capacity he had been badly wounded during the attack. Evacuated to 103 Field Ambulance RAMC in Albert, he passed away and is buried in Albert Communal Cemetery.

However, one of those killed, 8359 Private John Balf had landed almost two years earlier with 2/DLI. He had served in the Boer War with the 4th Yorkshire Militia (Green Howards) and in February 1903 had run away leaving a wife and child in Middlesbrough and enlisted into the Durham Light Infantry; he was posted to 2/DLI in Aldershot and was tried by a District Court Martial for leaving his family. In March 1904 he was posted to 1/DLI in India where he served until 1906. At the end of his colour service in 1906 he transferred to the Army Reserve and attended camps right through until the outbreak of war in 1914. Mobilised on 6 August 1914, he had fought on the Aisne and at Armentieres with 2/DLI until wounded in the left arm by shrapnel in July 1915. After recovering from his wound he was posted to the Regimental Depot in Newcastle from where he went absent. When he was taken by the Military Police he was tried by District Court Martial and sentenced to two years' penal servitude and sent to Wormwood Scrubs Prison. However, the Army needed men in France and the War Office remitted the sentence to three months' detention. The orders came through pretty quickly and he was transferred to the Military Detention Barracks at Knutsford in Cheshire. On his release he was posted to 3/DLI at South Shields and in March 1916 he was placed on a draft to 12/DLI in France.

The fact that he had left his wife caused some problems for Mrs Balf, as when he had rejoined the colours he had stated that he was single. Trying to get a pension after his death, she wrote to the Regimental Record Office as follows:

Dear Sir

Just a line in reply to your letter. I am sorry to hear you are unable to trace my husband under the particulars I have sent you, but the number I have sent 6343 was his number in the Boer War and he was a pension soldier and when this war broke out he was called up again to rejoin his regiment in the DLI and I am sorry to tell you I never got to know his number as I heard he had listed as a single man and I am sorry to tell you Sir that I had a nephew in France that came home on leave and he had told me he had seen my Husband and Brother in Law both killed. So I thought Sir if you was able to trace back to the Boer War you might be able to find him.

Dear Sir I am enclosing the letters I have had from him and hope you will be able to let me know something soon.

I am Sir Yours faithfully

Mrs Balf

One of those reported Missing was 18077 Private Thomas Bamborough from Grange Villa who had enlisted on 5 September 1914 in Chester-le-Street. Some time prior to the action on 17 July he had committed some act of gallantry that warranted the award of the Military Medal. The recommendation was sent through the usual channels but sadly the award didn't appear in the *London Gazette* until 23 August 1916, some five weeks after his death.

The next day as 12/DLI rested in Tara Trench the following message was received from Headquarters 68 Infantry Brigade:

> *I am of the opinion that 12/DLI which has already done such fine work in the recent attacks did all that was possible, most of the men held on in No Man's Land for upwards of 50 Minutes under a machine gun fire which was impassable. I am satisfied that not only they did their best but that their best was most gallant.*
>
> *Brig Gen H Page-Croft*

A short note was also received from Headquarters 34th Division to whom the Brigade had been attached:

> *I consider 12/DLI attacked most gallantly and did all that soldiers could have done under the circumstances.*
>
> *Major General Ingouville Williams*

It was raining when 13/DLI moved to new trenches at 1430 hours on 16 July to relieve 6/Bedfordshire Regiment. By 1630 hours Battalion Headquarters was established in Sausage Valley close to Gordon Dump, with three platoons of D Company in posts near Contalmaison Wood. C Company sent 125 men to assist 12/DLI in the consolidation of the front line. Second Lieutenant Richard Pearce-Brown and his platoon formed a bombing party and under the guidance of an NCO from 2/Royal Munster Fusiliers (2/RMF) proceeded to block and hold the trench between 68 Brigade and the troops of 1st Division. However, at 0200 hours the Officer Commanding 2/RMF ordered the platoon to rejoin its own battalion. The battalion had three men wounded: 19642 Private Richard Hughes, 11840 Private Charles Honeyman and 20959 Private Joseph Clark, the last-named self-inflicted. Also one man, 24776 Private Henry Walker was posted as missing; however, he must have turned up for he was transferred to 15/DLI with whom he was killed in 1917.

The next day was dull and overcast and as the attack had failed, the rest of the Brigade had to adjust their positions to facilitate the relief of 12/DLI. 10/NF took over the positions originally held by 12/DLI and 13/DLI sent three companies to take over the trenches on the right flank of 10/NF, while 11/NF were in support. During these operations 13/DLI had a number of men wounded; all listed by name in the Adjutant's War Diary in the Regimental Archives but too many to name here. Among them was 21603 Lance Corporal Joseph Warton who had won the DCM the previous December. Also wounded this day was 16103 Private John Moyle whose Military Medal wasn't gazetted until 10 August 1916. A third man worthy of mention was 19106 Sergeant William Freeman, who having been wounded was eventually posted to an Officer Cadet Battalion and was commissioned on 2 April 1917 into 11/DLI, with whom he was killed in action in November 1917.

At the start of another dull day, Second Lieutenant George Gray arrived from 23/DLI at Hornsea and along with him came fourteen Other Ranks from the Cheshire Regiment and eleven men from the East Yorkshire Regiment and 18/DLI. At some stage during the day A Company 13/DLI were ordered to relieve B Company 12/DLI who were then able to rejoin their own battalion in Tara Trench. In the line the shelling continued and casualties slowly mounted. During 18 July Second Lieutenant Thompson was wounded, five men were killed and twenty-four wounded, with two Privates, 18406 T. Richardson and 21165 Thomas Riddell suffering from shellshock, while 18364 Private William Jarman, although slightly wounded remained at duty. The next morning the weather cleared and C Company were moved forward to occupy a new trench, which meant that the battalion was now deployed in one long line; however, they were not in touch with the Division on the right. The shelling continued throughout the day: a further ten men were wounded and 17157 Private John Adams from Leamington in Warwickshire was killed. The enemy artillery was targeting the crossroads near Battalion Headquarters in Sausage Valley and they were mixing a lot of gas shells among the high explosive. At 0300 hours on 20 July the men of 1 ANZAC Brigade arrived and began the relief of 68 Brigade. When the Australians had taken over, 13/DLI marched back to Albert where they arrived at 0630 hours; here they rested until 1300 hours when they moved even further back and joined 12/DLI in billets in Franvillers. The latter battalion had moved there from Tara Trench at 1100 hours and had arrived at 1430. Here they were joined by Second Lieutenants Geoffrey Marks and Alexander Boyd-Smith from 21/DLI, bringing with them a small draft of twenty-four men. The next day was spent resting and General Babington visited 13/DLI and presented the ribbon of the Military Medal to 18170 Sergeant Thomas Fitzpatrick, 24775 Private William Hutchinson and 17108 Private Thomas Suddes. 15894 Sergeant Francis Lamb was also to receive the award but he had been evacuated wounded on 9 July. Later in the day a draft of fifty-six Other Ranks from the Green Howards arrived from 37 Infantry Base Depot.

During this period of rest many found time to write home and Lieutenant George Butterfield got these lines away to his family:

July 22

We are out again for a rest, and I hope a good one this time. The last was not much use, as we were still within the shell area, and the concussion of our own guns brought portions of the rickety cottages down every time.

We are now well back, and the noise of battle is only just audible.

We have now had two turns in the battle line (more or less) and the

*rgeant Thomas Smith,
/Durham Light
fantry, killed in
tion on 5 August; he
as 28 years of age and
arried, his wife
siding at Craghead,
*. Durham. Sergeant
*nith was for five years
the employment of
essrs. Isaac Poad and
*ns, agricultural
erchants, York,
*bsequent to which he
came an attendant at
*aburn Asylum. At the
*ne of enlistment in
*ptember, 1914, he was
*iployed as a miner at
ngley Park, Durham.

second was better than the first – at any rate as far as weather was concerned. I will try and write some account of our doings and post it to you at some future time, when the contents will no longer be anathema to the censor.

We have again been lucky (i.e., our battalion); twice we have been within an ace of being shoved into a desperate venture, but as a fact we have not attacked at all yet consequently practically all our casualties are from shell fire and, as you know, only a very small proportion of these are fatal, or even serious.

I have had charge of my company for the last fortnight, since the O.C. was wounded. I was standing beside him at the time, and I think the one shell laid out about a dozen (a very rare event). In fact I must have been the only man in the neighbourhood untouched, and suffered no after effects except slight deafness in one ear, which has now passed off.

I tell you this to cheer you up!!

Also getting a letter away at this time were the two Anderson brothers serving under George Butterfield in A Company; once again both signed the letter which was posted in the Green Honour envelope that allowed men to send uncensored mail home:

21 July 1916 MG Section, A Coy, 13 S Batt DLI

Dear Father, Mother, Brother and Sister,

Just a few lines hoping to find you all well as this leaves me in the best of health. We received your letter but have been unable to reply but hope to be able to write more frequent now as we are back at rest. We have been lucky and came out alright. The first time we came out there was only me and Jack left of our gun team. The second time we lost two more but no more of them were killed but we have done some good work. We are about eight miles behind the line at present & are expecting moving further back shortly for a rest. Fritz is out of his trenches altogether at the place we have been. Where the Prussian Guards were cut up, we have been in the mill this time. We are expecting having a few weeks rest now. It will have been an anxious time for you waiting for news. There is plenty souvenirs here, Mr Carr would value some very much. But we have had enough to do looking after ourselves. But a whole skin is the best souvenir here. In answer to your enquiring about sending a parcel it is no good sending them because when we come out on rest we get plenty to eat & when we are in the trenches they do not send any letters or parcels in, they just lie about in the open and spoil & it is expense for nothing. One of our mates got one today and it had to be thrown away as everything had gone mouldy. We are enclosing a PO for 14/- please mention in the next letter if you receive it. Well I think there is no more at present so now we will close hoping you are all well & in the best of health. Give our best respects to Mr & Mrs Carr.

Your two sons J & WH Anderson

If the Anderson brothers thought they were out for a long rest they were mistaken, for from midnight on 22/23 July 12 and 13/DLI were put on one hour's notice to be ready to move in support of 1st and 19th Divisions who were attacking towards Martinpuich. However, around 1000 hours news arrived that the attack had failed and they were stood down. While resting in Franvillers 13/DLI received two large drafts from battalions of the Northumberland Fusiliers that had suffered many casualties in the recent fighting. On 22 July seventy-seven men arrived from 21/NF the 3rd Tyneside Scottish and the following day a mixed batch of Newcastle Commercials, Tyneside Scottish and Tyneside Irish arrived from 31st Infantry Base Depot. The time out of the line was spent refitting and training and on 25 July at 1100 hours the III Corps Commander Lieutenant-General Sir William Pulteney inspected the whole 68 Brigade and afterwards addressed the assembled men, congratulating them on the work and fighting they had done in the previous weeks. Later in the day orders came for the move back into the line.

At 0830 12/DLI marched out of Franvillers along the Amiens–Albert road and when they arrived at Albert around 1130 hours they rested until 1530 hours when they moved up to Scots Redoubt and relieved 1/Gloucesters of 1st Division.

Likewise at 0900 hours 13/DLI moved off and followed along the same road until they too arrived at Albert around 1200 hours: they rested until 1700 hours, then continued up to Contalmaison where they relieved 2/RMF. Here they had 1st Australian Division on their left and 9/York and Lancaster Regiment (9/York & Lancs) on the right. In the early hours of the next day word was received that the Germans had retaken Munster Alley from 10/NF and at around 0500 hours the enemy artillery shelled the front line, then later another signal that 10/NF had retaken the lost trench but the shelling continued on and off all day. That evening 13/DLI took over from 10/NF. They were disposed as follows: Right Company with right flank on Martinpuich Road, Centre Company with right on junction of Gloster Alley and Old German Trench and Left Company with left flank 30 yards from junction of Sussex Trench and Old German Trench 2. A bombing post was also established in Munster Alley.

By 2200 Lieutenant Butterworth with A Company and some of 12/DLI attached dug a trench running parallel to the German Switch line and by 0330 hours this was held by two platoons of A Company. This new trench was named Butterworth Trench and although they had no men killed, Lieutenant George Butterworth and eight men were wounded, one self-inflicted accidently and one remained at duty, while two men were evacuated with shellshock.

George Butterworth wrote this to his family:

July 27 [note – this letter was not received until 4 August. On 31 July a telegram was received from the War Office reporting George as 'wounded'.]

In the trenches again, at present in support – plans uncertain. No trouble at present except intermittent shrapnel. This morning a small fragment hit me in the back, and made a slight scratch, which I had dressed. This is merely to warn you in case you should see my name in the casualty list! They have a way of reporting even the slightest cases.

At 0415 hours a report was received at Battalion Headquarters from Lieutenant Charles Sauerbeck that he had pushed up Munster Alley for a distance of 70 yards and he was consolidating and forming a bomb block. However, by 0745 hours his party had been forced back to their starting-point by a very determined German counter-attack. By 0815 hours Lieutenant Sauerbeck had been evacuated wounded and Second Lieutenant Cyril O'Callaghan took over command of the bombers of 13/DLI, gained 70 yards of the trench and formed a block When this was rushed by the enemy he rallied his men and led them with great dash until he fell severely wounded, but prevented any further loss of ground. At 0820 hours command fell to Company Sergeant-Major Morton and Sergeant Carling, who with a Lewis-gun team kept the enemy from crossing the block and drove them back. By 0825 hours the attack had collapsed and things fell quiet for a while. At 1020 hours Second Lieutenants Johnson and Robins gathered all of C Company Bombers and they were ordered to the block to assist with the defence. Then at 1500 hours Lieutenant Noel Target sent word back that he would be able to gain 100 yards of Munster Alley with artillery support. At 1725 hours he sent further word that the first enemy block to be encountered was 50 yards ahead of the British block and that as enemy soldiers had been heard talking behind the block, bombs had been thrown over and on the left the battalion's barricade had been advanced 10 yards to a better position. Support also came from one who had earlier been one of the battalion 'bad boys': Harry Craddock now promoted to Corporal asked to be allowed to take reinforcements up to the bomb block. As he led his party forward he came across some men whom he rallied and led back to the fighting, where in the words of the citation for his Distinguished Conduct Medal, he 'fought with the greatest courage'.

Harry Craddock promoted Corporal asked to be allowed to take reinforcements up to the bomb block. As he led his party forward he came across some men whom he rallied and led back to the fighting, where in the words of the citation for his Distinguished Conduct Medal, he 'fought with the greatest courage'. He was killed in action on 20 September 1917.

At 1845 hours word was received from 1st Australian Division that they were going to attack north and north-east of Pozieres and that they would endeavour to link up with 13/DLI. However, before that could happen at 2100 hours, 10/DWR of 69 Brigade came up and relieved all of 13/DLI positions except an advanced bombing post held by men of B Company which was eventually relieved by 0130 hours the following morning. However, as 13/DLI was preparing to move back, the German artillery opened a heavy barrage on O.G.1 where a number of casualties occurred. Second Lieutenants William Charlton, Charles Robins and Arthur

Dugdale were wounded and during the day casualties in the ranks amounted to seven men killed, thirty-two wounded, five shellshocked and two missing. A further two men had suffered accidental self-inflicted wounds. It took a long time for the battalion to make their way out of the line and it wasn't until 0530 hours that the battalion was quartered in billets in the Rue de Bapaume in Albert, but before the men could get their heads down and rest, General Babington visited the battalion and presented the ribbon of the Military Medal to 22611 Sergeant Smith of D Company. The next day the Commanding Officer Lieutenant Colonel Robert V. Turner was admitted to the 23rd Divisional Rest Station at Baiseux utterly exhausted, and command passed to Captain George White.

When 12/DLI had relieved 1/Gloucester at Scots Redoubt they spent the day deepening and improving the trenches and then at 2000 hours they moved up to Contalmaison and took over from 13/DLI. That evening Second Lieutenants Hughes and Sharp arrived at the Battalion Transport lines. During 28 July the enemy shelled Contalmaison between 0830 and 1030 hours and then intermittently during the day, causing two men to be wounded. At 1730 hours 11/West Yorks arrived and 12/DLI moved back to Sausage Valley: here more enemy shells arrived and one man, 25519 Corporal Arthur Barnes from Gilesgate in Durham City was badly wounded and subsequently died from these wounds, and one other man was wounded. While they were in this location seven new officers, Captain George A. Hicks and Second Lieutenants Leslie Powell-Smith, Austen Wallis, Cuthbert Vaux, William Lockett, Cecil Armstrong and Johnson Bollom reported to Battalion Headquarters. The next day was exceedingly hot and those not detailed for working parties rested and bathed where possible, but 200 men were set to carrying bombs up to the front line from Contalmaison. The following day the ground where the battalion was resting was shelled: 11884 Lance Corporal Alfred Barnes was killed and Second Lieutenant Charles Heppell and five men were wounded; one of these, 13209 Private Harry Porter died some time later. The Brigade Commander gave permission for the battalion to move further back to reduce casualties from the shelling. Once this move was completed, a party of one officer and twenty men went to the front line to complete and improve the new bomb store and two men were sent to act as guides to 11/NF. July 29 was spent resting and a few odd shells landed near the battalion. During the day Second Lieutenant Arthur T. Carr-West rejoined the battalion from Picquigny; here he had been employed as Town Major. On the last day of the month two working parties were furnished: one of 100 men carried sandbags and the other of 100 men carried grenades to the line; as they went up both parties came under shellfire and three men were evacuated with shellshock.

Out at rest, 13/DLI had begun preparing to return to the line and men

Cleaning up Contalmaison after its capture.

were packing their kit and getting ready to leave the billets when there occurred one of those awful tragedies that sometimes took place when a man's mind couldn't cope with the stress placed upon him. At 1445 hours a single shot was fired in a billet where 28909 Private Percy Howitt, an electrical engineer from Heaton in Newcastle was sitting alone. He had arrived in France with a draft from 17/DLI on 1 June and on 9 July he had been wounded slightly; however, on 1 August he took his own life with a single shot fired through the throat and exiting from the top of his head. The Officer Commanding D Company, Captain Austin and the Company Sergeant-Major, CSM Morton accompanied by the Company Quarter Master Sergeant, 21599 CQMS Roy Rudd went to view the scene. As the battalion was about to move off, the Medical Officer had already left to set up his Regimental Aid Post so the facts of the matter were relayed to the Town Major in Albert who authorised the burial of Private Howitt's remains.

The family made a request for information regarding the death, to which Second Lieutenant Charleton Brown replied:

> *Your letter asking for particulars of your brother's death, has been handed to me, as his platoon officer was severely wounded at the same time and is now in England.*
>
> *Your brother was hit by a shot when the battalion was going into action on 1 August and died before night. He was not conscious between the time*

of his being wounded and the time of his death and therefore suffered no pain.

As the battalion was not definitely in action I am glad to say it was possible for your brother's body to be buried quietly and reverently and with such rites as you and he would have wished. I am not allowed to tell you the place of his burial but a record is kept and the Department of the War Office which deals with this will inform you either now or by the time it will be possible for you to visit this country.

Your brother was in my Company in the 17th Battalion and I had some slight knowledge of him there, as being apart from the ordinary run of men one had to deal with.

Will you please convey to your sister and accept my condolences in your loss.

Lieutenant.C Brown, Second Lieutenant.

At the same time, a reply with the information that the death was due to self-inflicted wounds was sent from No 1 Infantry Record Office in York to the deceased soldier's sister, which obviously caused some upset. His brother Hugh, a solicitor, wanted some answers and wrote a number of letters and at the same time the Army started an inquiry. When the battalion came out of the line in mid-August the paperwork was waiting to be completed. One question that was asked was the opinion of the OC Unit as to the cause: 'Was it Wilful, Negligent or Accidental?' To this question the acting Commanding Officer Major George White replied: 'Impossible to say as the man was alone at the time.'

The acting Adjutant then made a statement:

There were no actual witnesses when 28909 Pte P G Howitt shot himself.

I beg to enclose statements of an officer and the Company Quarter Master Sergeant who both viewed the body.

As the Battalion was at the time moving up to the front trenches the services of the Medical Officer were not available. Death seems to have been instantaneous.

The first statement was made by Lieutenant Hugh Oldham, now Officer Commanding D Company, who said:

On 1 August at about 2.45 pm at Albert just before the regiment moved into action it was reported to Captain Austin and myself, that a man in D Company had shot himself. Captain Austin went with the Company Sergeant Major to view the body, but is since missing, believed killed, while CSM Morton has been evacuated to England wounded. I attach the statement of CQMS R Rudd who viewed the body. The matter was reported to the Town Major at Albert by the Assistant Adjutant and the former ordered the corpse to be buried. Owing to the move into action it was not, I believe, possible for the MO to view the body.

H S Oldham Lt

OC D Coy 13th D.L.I.

The statement made by 21599 CQMS Roy Rudd had this to say:

> On 1 August at about 0245 pm I was with CSM Morton when it was reported to me that 28909 Pte P G Howitt had shot himself. I went with CSM Morton to enquire and found that Howitt had a bullet wound beneath his chin and a hole in the top of his head where the bullet came out. He was quite dead. There was an empty cartridge case in the chamber and no rounds in the magazine. The man was alone at the time the shot was fired and there were no eye witnesses to the occurrence.
>
> R Rudd
> CQMS D Coy
> 13th Durham LI

With the incident over, the battalion marched out of Albert at 1500 hours, handing over the billets to 10/DWR. They marched up to Peake Wood where the relief of 8/Green Howards took place and by 1710 hours 13/DLI were settled in. Late that night the British artillery bombarded the area of Munster Alley which resulted in four men of B Company being wounded and one of them, 18061 Private Thomas Duncan from Felling, died from his wounds the following day at the Casualty Clearing Station in Warloy-Baillon. The next day was hot and fine and during the day the enemy carried out a bombardment. This was followed at 1500 hours by a British bombardment of the German Switch line. At 1700 13/DLI moved

The town of Albert with its leaning Virgin and Child.

into the front line and relieved 9/Green Howards; by 1900 hours 13/DLI was deployed with all four companies in the front line. The right company, A Company, held Gloster Avenue. The right centre company, C Company, held Butterworth Trench from its junction with Lancs Trench. The left centre was held by B Company who held from X.6.c.1.8 to X.5.d.7.8 and then to X.5.d.4.1. On the left flank D Company continued the line from X.5.d.4.1 and a post in Munster Alley and then on to X.5.d.7.8 where they linked up with 17/Australian Battalion. During the day 17788 Private Frank Eales of A Company was wounded. A party of 210 men from 10/NF arrived and overnight assisted 13/DLI. Gloster Alley and Butterworth Trench were improved and deepened and a sap was started from Butterworth Trench towards the German lines and by 0400 hours it was 70 yards long. A breach in the parapet of O.G.1 was repaired and a bomb post in Munster Alley was strengthened and wired. Then at 0900 hours a message came in from Brigade Headquarters that the Germans were expected to launch a gas attack. This was followed half an hour later by another message that two platoons of 10/NF were being sent up to hold O.G.1: by 1245 hours the first of these platoons was in position, but the second one didn't arrive until 1430 hours, having lost its way. Throughout the day the British artillery shells fell short mainly around the post in Munster Alley and at 1715 hours the Officer Commanding D Company had to report that he had been compelled to evacuate the post. At 1830 hours 10/NF came up and took over from 13/DLI and although they took over the post in Munster Alley, they too were compelled to give it up. Casualties during the day had slowly mounted: Second Lieutenant Thomas Saint was wounded and among the men six had been killed, sixteen wounded (one still at duty) and one self-inflicted accidentally, as well as six men evacuated with shellshock. This conflicts slightly with the figures in the Adjutant's War Diary where all are named and the breakdown is as follows: three men in A Company, seven in B Company, six in C Company and fourteen in D Company, who as we have seen had been holding Munster Alley. Once 10/NF had completely taken over, 13/DLI moved back to billets in Contalmaison.

12/DLI had marched out of Albert at the same time on 1 August and had marched up to Shelter Wood and that night supplied 200 men as a carrying party taking stores and ammunition up to the front line. During the morning of 2 August another 200 men went on a working party until at 1700 hours the battalion moved into the front line to the right of Pozieres where they relieved 11/Sherwood Foresters. Throughout 3 August the Germans kept up a heavy barrage on the British front line and the battalion was kept busy repairing the damage. The sniper section was very active and accounted for a number of the enemy, while patrols and bombing parties did some good work. Three men of 12/DLI fell that day: 13458 Private Thomas Arthur from Bill Quay, 19163 Private Albert

Grievson from Windy Nook and 17368 Private Harold Hodgson who came from Bedale in North Yorkshire. The same pattern continued on 4 August with the line again coming under enemy artillery fire which caused the death of 19967 Private James Sharples, a Lancashire lad from Blackburn. On that day at one of the hospitals in Etaples 15716 Lance Corporal Andrew Smith from Sunderland died from wounds he had received earlier. The next day 11/NF came up and relieved 12/DLI, who then moved back to O.G.1. The time spent here was used to improve and repair the trench which was under constant enemy fire. A large number of the battalion were employed in taking rations and water up to the front line. After two days here they were relieved by 12/Highland Light Infantry (12/HLI) and moved further back to the Becourt Road where they arrived at about 2000 hours.

On the afternoon of 4 August 13/DLI moved back into the line and relieved 10/NF. They were disposed as follows: A Company in Butterworth Trench, D Company in New Trench, B Company held from X.5.b4.1 to O.G.1 and the post in Munster Alley, C Company along with C Company 10/NF were in support in O.G.2, and B Company 10/NF held Gloster Alley to Butterworth Trench. 68 Brigade Headquarters had issued orders for an attack on Torr Trench. At 2116 hours, with bayonets fixed, the leading waves of D Company left New Trench and were immediately raked with machine-gun and rifle fire from the Germans holding Torr Trench and from a machine gun behind a barricade in Munster Alley. After crossing Munster Alley a smoke barrage put up by the Australians on the left caused some confusion. The second followed 50 yards behind the first and a few men under Captain Arthur Austin were seen to enter Torr Trench, where a bomb fight broke out and the sounds of this could be heard until 0215 hours when it must be assumed that all those who got into the enemy trench were either dead or captured. At 2132 hours a telephone message was received from Private Robinson of D Company which simply said: 'We've retired.' Then another message was received from Lieutenant Denzil Clarke which stated that: 'B Company is going forward.' When the two leading waves of D Company crumpled up Lieutenant Clarke collected the remnants and men of his company and ordered them up in support and at once ordered his bombers to work their way up Munster Alley.

Around 2145 hours the Commanding Officer instructed the Officer Commanding C Company 10/NF to send one platoon west along O.G.2 to join up with Captain Blake.

The party under the command of Lieutenant Frederick Rees that bombed up Munster Alley were stopped by a bomb block that was heavily wired and defended by a number of enemy soldiers and supported by a machine gun. They made a block of their own but were compelled to fall back and they formed another block about 18 yards from the German

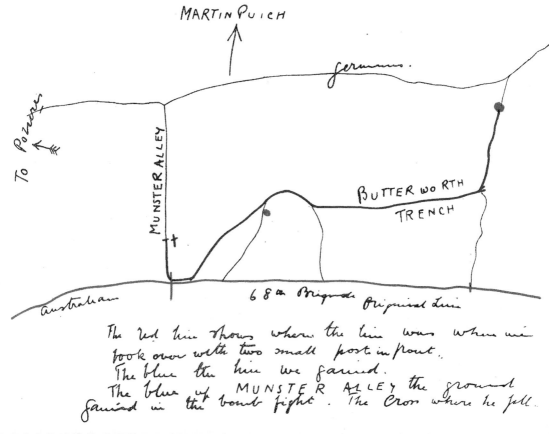

MARTIN PUICH

To Pozieres

MUNSTER ALLEY

germans.

BUTTER WORTH
TRENCH

Australian

68ᵃ Brigade Original Line

The red line shows where the line was when we took over with two small post in front.
The blue the line we gained.
The blue up MUNSTER ALLEY the ground gained in the bomb fight. The Cross where he fell.

block. The Commanding Officer went up Munster Alley himself to have a look at the situation and owing to the German machine gun decided that a further advance across Munster Alley would be unlikely to succeed, so he decided on a bombing assault around the enemy block. This assault was to be led by Lieutenant Noel Target MC; then at 2300 hours Lieutenant Clarke sent another message back saying:

> *D Company retired again so I sent B Company wave forward and instructed Bombers to work up Munster Alley. Rees reports that they have got well into the trench, so have sent bombing party from C Company to reinforce them. Why D Company retired God Knows. I got them to go forward again but without success.*

At 0005 hours Officer Commanding C Company 10/NF was ordered to move up Gloster Alley and relieve Lieutenant George Butterworth in Butterworth Trench. Then Lieutenant Butterworth was given the orders to: 'Proceed round the loop with your Company and form up there for an attack. Take bombs and tools and move as quickly as possible.' However, owing to the British bombardment he was unable to carry out this order. The situation was now very confused; reports were coming in from all parts of the battalion that they were being shelled by British artillery. Then at 0230 hours word reached Battalion Headquarters from Lieutenant Clarke that the attack led by Lieutenant Target had failed. The officer and most of his men were dead and Lieutenant Clarke had sent a party of men under Second Lieutenants Thomas Saint and Ernest Atkinson up to hold the bomb block. Within the hour most of those sent up had been killed or wounded, and another twenty men were sent up by Battalion Headquarters and held the position until relieved by an officer and twenty-five men of 10/NF.

A signal came in from 68 Brigade Headquarters stating: 'ANZACS report 13/DLI fighting in Torr Trench.' A runner was then sent off to Lieutenant Butterworth and A Company with a message saying: 'Send a strong bombing platoon up Munster Alley to hold our block.' Owing to

the shelling of the front line, Lieutenant Butterworth cannot have received this message until some time after 0345 hours. At 0330 hours Battalion Headquarters sent a message to Lieutenant Clarke with the order to: 'Send Second Lieutenant Batty with ten men to go round to west entrance to Torr Trench and try to get a trench mortar off the ANZACS.' His reply arrived at 0341 hours stating: 'We must have reinforcements up at once. The platoon of A Company has not turned up and the men I have got here are being kept here with revolvers.' Second Lieutenant Joseph Batty was given a message to pass on to Lieutenant Butterworth that he was to reinforce Munster Alley with one platoon immediately.

Lieutenant George Butterworth took his men into Munster Alley and joined in the fight and here he was visited by Brigadier General Page Croft who found him to be

Lieutenant George Butterworth had been killed just after the Brigadier left his position. A few days later he was awarded the Military Cross for his work in July. He has no known grave and is commemorated on the Thiepval Memorial to the Missing.

cheery and inspiring his men to dig in and repair the badly-damaged trench. After a few words together the Brigade Commander made his way back to Battalion Headquarters where he ordered Captain Ellis Commanding C Company 10/NF to send a party to relieve A Company 13/DLI in Munster Alley. It was then that the news came in that Lieutenant George Butterworth had been killed just after the Brigadier had left the position. Later in the early afternoon word arrived that Lieutenant Frederick Rees had been wounded and evacuated. In the evening 8/Green Howards came up and relieved 13/DLI who marched back to billets in Albert where they arrived at 2315 hours.

Casualties had been fairly heavy on 4 August: Captain Arthur Austin was posted Missing in Action; Second Lieutenants Norman

22562 Private Anthony Carr from Coxhoe joined 13/DLI in September 1915 with a draft from 17/DLI. He was killed in action on 4 August 1916, has no known grave and is commemorated on the Thiepval Memorial to the Missing.

16066 Private John H. Clark serving with C Company was one of the three men evacuated shellshocked on 4 August 1916.

Thompson, William Oakes, Ernest Atkinson and Claude Brown had been wounded, Norman Thompson dying the next day. Six men had been killed, seventy-three wounded, nine shellshocked and six missing, with one self-inflicted wound. The following day Lieutenants George Butterworth and Noel Target were killed in action and Second Lieutenants Frederick Rees and Joseph Batty wounded. Four men had been killed, eighteen wounded, three shellshocked and five missing.

On 6 August 1916 Captain Edward Borrow, Adjutant 13th Durham Light Infantry, wrote to the Butterworth family:

The Commanding Officer, Capt. G. White, has asked me to write and inform you of the very serious loss we have suffered in the death of your son. His talents as a Company Commander were undoubtedly great, and on the night of the 4/5th inst. when he was ordered to bomb up a trench and hold an important post, he personally supervised this work, so that now, as I write, the post, 20 yards from the enemy, remains in our hands. Unfortunately it was his thoroughness in supervision which indirectly led to his death. The trench had been so knocked about by bombs and shells that some places were very exposed, and a German saw him soon after dawn on the 5th. His brother officers and men dearly loved your son, and his absence from the Battalion will be greatly felt for a very long time to come.

On 8 August Captain Borrow again wrote:

The Commanding Officer wishes me to again write to you and inform you that the Commander-in-Chief has awarded your son the Military Cross. This was awarded him for the very excellent work he did during July. He again earned the Cross on the night of his death, and the great regret of the Commanding Officer and all his fellow officers is that your son did not live long enough to know that his pluck and ability as a Company Commander had received some reward.

Captain G. White himself wrote on 10 August:

The G.O.C. 23rd Division instructs me to forward you the ribbon of the Military Medal which he would have personally presented to your son to-day had Lieut. Butterworth lived. I also enclose a short account of the circumstances for which this decoration has been awarded.

On 4 August Captain Arthur Austin was posted Missing in Action. He has no known grave and is commemorated on the Thiepval Memorial to the Missing.

Enclosure

Lieutenant George S. K. Butterworth

Near Pozieres from 17th to 19th July, 1916, commanded the Company, of which his Captain had been wounded, with great ability and coolness. By his energy and total disregard of personal safety he got his men to accomplish a good piece of work in linking up the front line. I have already brought forward the officer's name for his work during the period 7th to 10th July, 1916.

Military Cross

H. Wilkinson

Lieut.-Col. A.A., Q.M.G., 23rd Division

On 13 August 1916 Brigadier General H. Page Croft, C.M.G., M.P., Commanding 68th Infantry Brigade, wrote:

I feel I must write you a note to tell you how deeply I grieve with you and yours, for the loss of your gallant son. He was one of those quiet, unassuming men whose path did not appear naturally to be a military one, and I had watched him doing his duty quietly and conscientiously. When the offensive came he seemed to throw off his reserve, and in those strenuous 35 days in which we were fighting off and on, he developed a power of leadership which we had not realised he possessed. As you know, I recommended him for an earlier action near Contalmaison for the Military Cross, which, alas! he could not wear. When in front of Pozieres he was reported to me to have done excellent work under very heavy fire in getting his men to dig a new trench right in front of the Germans, from which later, the Australians were able to successfully attack that village. Later we went into a line on the right of the Australians, S.E. of Pozieres.

Here we were about 450 yards from the Germans, and I gave orders to dig a trench within 200 yards of them so that we could attack with some chance of success.

This trench was dug in a fog, and was a very fine deep trench which saved many lives in the days to follow, and your son again superintended the work, and it was called Butterworth Trench on all the official maps.

Three days after the 13th D.L.I. attacked Munster Alley just N.W. of Butterworth Trench. They won 100 yards after a very hot fight, and I went up there at 4 a.m. in the morning to find the bomb fight still progressing, but the 13th holding their own. Your son was in charge, and the trench was very much blown in and shallow and I begged him to keep his head down. He was cheery and inspiring his tired men to secure the position which had been won earlier in the night and I felt that all was well with him there. The Germans had been bombing our wounded, and the men all round him were shooting Germans who showed themselves. Within about a minute of my leaving him he was shot, as I heard by telephone on my return. I could ill afford to lose so fine a soldier, and my deepest sympathy goes out to his relations, for I know that the loss of one so modest and yet so brave must create a gap which can never be filled.

There are a number of printed obituaries to George Butterworth and it would fill several pages to repeat them all. Suffice to quote a short passage from *The Oxford Magazine*. An Oxford friend writes of him as follows:

By the death of George Butterworth English music has been robbed of one of its most promising composers. His distinction and reveals a delicate imagination with very original utterance, and over all there is absolute sincerity of expression. It was in the year before war broke out that he added to the reputation he had already made as a song writer and folk-song expert and enthusiast by his first orchestral work, a Fantasy, 'The Land of the Lost Content,' which was produced at the Leeds Festival in 1913. This work was greeted with delight alike by a conductor (Nikisch), orchestra, audience, and music critics. It was a happy day for George's friends, and a great event in a career which would have carried him to the highest distinction. During his residence in Oxford it became more and more apparent that in George Butterworth, the rather shy, out-spoken, sometimes rude yet tender hearted undergraduate, there was the real musician with an unerring instinct for truth and beauty of expression and a wonderful ability to translate his high visions into the regions of sound. He was greatly loved by his brother musicians. His manuscript works are soon to be published and will form the most appropriate memorial to a distinguished Oxford musician.

Second Lieutenant Frederick Rees was well on his way back to England when a letter from the Adjutant caught up with him:

Lieutenant Frederick Rees: after being evacuated wounded, he learned that he had been awarded the Military Cross.

9/8/16

13th D.L.I.

My Dear Rees

I just want to write and tell you that the block you established was done so well that it resisted two counter attacks the following night from the Bosch. Poor old Butterworth received the Military Cross after his death for what he did before his death.

Yours ever

Edward Borrow.

A few weeks later he received a second letter from Captain Borrow:

7/9/16

13th D.L.I.

Dear Rees,

Babington called round today and handed me the enclosed ribbon & account of your valorous deeds on August 4/5th and these I now transmit to you with hearty congratulations of our CO Major Lindsay and all Officers who were there at the time:

We all know you jolly well deserved it and wish you the best of luck.
Yours sincerely
Edward Borrow, Captain.

While all this was going on in France, at Number 1 Infantry Record Office in York, the home of the Durham Light Infantry records, a letter was received from Mrs Brankston who resided at Oyster Shell Cottage, Lanchester, County Durham, who wrote:

Oyster Shell Cottage
Lanchester
August 4 1916,
Please Sir,
I am writing to ask you if you could get me my son Alexander out of France as he is only 18 years of age and I have nobody working at home. I have other three sons in France, one has been wounded and I would like my younger boy at home. I have no sons at home now, please oblige.
Mrs Brankston.

She neglected to say that three of her boys, Henderson, Alexander and William, were all serving in the same company of 13/DLI and that their elder brother James had already been killed in action. Originally James had enlisted into the Durham Light Infantry as 11233 but had been transferred to the Northumberland Fusiliers and posted to France on 3 May 1915; there he joined 2/NF with whom he died on 1 October 1915. Both Henderson and William were awarded the Military Medal, but only William would survive the war having served with 13th, 18th, 2nd, 13th and 19th Battalions of the Regiment.

German artillery observer in a narrow muddy trench. The Germans had a very heavy concentration of artillery on the Somme front.

Another mother, Mrs Alice Riley who resided in Accrington, Lancashire, had written a very similar letter on 25 July:

Dear Sir,
I am writing to you on behalf of my son Private Harry Riley 19859 12th Batt Durham Light Infantry, D Company, 13 Platoon, now stationed in France. I have already lost one son 20972 Private Arthur Riley 11th Batt East Lancs Regt. I am enclosing a cutting that states an act has been passed that boys under 17 had to be

discharged and boys over 17 and under the age of 19 had to be placed in the reserve. You will see by the birth certificate that my boy is not yet 18 and he has been in the Army since Sept 14 and he has been in France since Aug 1915. I would be very thankful to you if you will place my boy in the reserve. I sent a cutting and the birth certificate to his captain and he has had him sent down to the Base and told him to send the certificate home and that I must send it on to you. Thanking you in anticipation.

    I am your obedient Servant
    Alice Ann Riley
    65 East Street, Accrington.

Mrs Riley's letter did the trick and Harry Riley was sent home to the Regimental Depot on 13 August; after a few days in Newcastle he was reposted to 16/DLI and stayed with that unit when it became 1/Training Reserve Battalion. In 1917 he went AWOL for ten days and on his return was tried by District Court Martial and sentenced to forty-two days' detention. Released on 7 September, he was promoted to Lance Corporal on 14 November. On 13 February he was placed on a draft headed for 19/DLI but on arrival at the Infantry Base Depot the draft was redirected to 1/8/DLI. However, this was an unfortunate turn for Harry as he died from wounds on 27 March 1918.

Both DLI battalions moved back to the area of Albert and prepared for a move. In the billets of B Company 13/DLI, there was an accident with a revolver that led to the trial by Field General Court Martial of 18396 Company Sergeant-Major Watson Weaver Brown, who before the war had spent six years and nine months as a regular in 1/DLI and then had become a blacksmith's striker, prior to re-enlisting in September 1914. He was evacuated to 104 Field Ambulance RAMC and from there to 39 Casualty Clearing Station in Allonville where his wounds were dressed and after a time healed. After he had been discharged from the Casualty Clearing Station and returned to the battalion the CSM was tried by FGCM on 21 August. The prosecution called two witnesses: 22611 Sergeant William Smith and 18050 Sergeant Edward Wilkinson.

Sergeant Smith was called first and had this to say:

On the morning of the 6 August about 1000 hours at Albert, I went to B Company NCOs mess. While there I spoke to Sergeant Wilkinson about a revolver he had found and asked him for the case. He said I could have it and went to his pack and took out the revolver and case and handed it to me.

    I took out the revolver and saw it was loaded and remarked to Sergeant Wilkinson that he ought to unload it, laying the revolver down on his bed. At that time Company Sergeant Major Brown entered the room and said to Wilkinson, 'Are you going to give me that revolver' and Wilkinson replied, 'Yes.'

    Sergeant Major Brown picked up the revolver – I heard a report and the bullet flew over my head and I heard Sergeant Wilkinson shout, 'The bloody thing is loaded.' I turned round and saw CSM Brown with a wound in his left forearm.

Company Sergeant-Major Brown was given the chance to cross-examine the witness, but he declined to do so. The prosecution then called their second witness, Sergeant Wilkinson, who made the following statement:

At Albert on the morning of 6 August I was in my billet when Sergeant Major Brown came and asked me if I would give him the revolver which I had found in the trenches. I said, 'Yes but I have just given the case to Sergeant Smith.' He picked it up off the bed and before I had time to tell him it was loaded, I heard the report go off. Sergeant Major Brown then fell on me and I saw he was shot through the left forearm.

Once again the Company Sergeant-Major declined to cross-examine the witness.

The accused was then questioned by the prosecuting officer, who asked: 'Was your billet in B Company Sergeants Mess?', to which came the reply, 'Yes'.

Company Sergeant-Major Brown then made this statement to the court:

On the night of 5 August before leaving the trenches I saw Sergeant Wilkinson with a revolver. I asked him for the revolver and he said he would give it to me when we got out of the trenches. On the morning of 6 August about 1000 hours I got a memo from Battalion Headquarters for casualty lists to be in at once. I went over to the Company Mess to check the lists with the Platoon sergeants.

On arriving there I saw Sergeant Smith with the revolver and the case, he took the revolver out of the case and laid it on Sergeant Wilkinson's bed. I then asked Sergeant Wilkinson if he was going to give me the revolver. He replied, 'Its there if you want it.' I picked the revolver up and five or six seconds later the revolver went off. I was just passing a remark to Sergeant Smith as he was leaving the room that the revolver was no good without the case.

A character statement on behalf of the CSM was made by Captain and Adjutant Edward Borrow, who said:

Ever since the formation of the Battalion in September 1914, I have known Company Sergeant Major Brown. His character has always been excellent, more especially in the trenches and under fire.

For his conduct in the Somme battle he has been recommended for the DCM and as a Company Sergeant Major he is one of the best we have got.

The Court then retired to consider its verdict, and on considering the evidence, Company Sergeant-Major Brown was found Not Guilty. However, one wonders if this incident had any effect on the award of the DCM which he never received.

That wasn't the only case of a self-inflicted wound that occurred in the battalion. In the trenches near Contalmaison, in another case 18721 Private Robert Gaskill made this statement about the wound in his right foot:

> *I, 18721 Private R Gaskill state that I was cleaning my rifle in the support trench and the Orderly Corporal was passing. I stepped to the side to give him room, in doing so the rifle caught something and went off the bullet entering my right foot. CSM Morton was about five yards behind me at the time..*

The soldier nearest to him at the time was 24367 Private Matthew Jones, who stated:

> *I was next to Private Gaskill in the Reserve Trench by Contalmaison on the morning of 3 August. He was cleaning his rifle with the barrel pointing downwards. I turned my back then heard the rifle go off. When I turned round Private Gaskill had fallen down with a wound in his right foot.*

In this case the Courts Martial Officer, a Captain at Second Army Headquarters, decided not to bring charges as there was little chance of a conviction because all the witnesses had either been killed or evacuated wounded.

Chapter Six

Later Stages of the Somme Battles

THERE NOW CAME a quiet time as 23rd Division was pulled out of the line on the Somme Front and moved north to the Armentieres sector. Both DLI battalions moved back from the area of Albert, having been replaced by troops of 44 Brigade of the 15th (Scottish) Division. By various routes and halts they made their way to the Steenwerck area where by 1900 hours on 15 August both battalions were billeted in various farms. Replacement officers began arriving at this time. On 12 August Second Lieutenant Vere D.L. Beart, a 20-year-old South African from Durban who had volunteered in August 1914 and had eventually been commissioned into 4/DLI, reported his arrival at Battalion Headquarters. He was followed on 14 August by Second Lieutenant John Kelly who had recently been a Sergeant in the Westmorland and Cumberland Yeomanry, and then on 16 August Major Michael Lindsay 7/Dragoon Guards arrived and assumed command of the battalion; on 21 August he was appointed acting Lieutenant-Colonel. The new Commanding Officer was a New Zealander who, having enlisted into the New Zealand forces for service in South Africa in 1900 had obtained a commission into the 7/Dragoon Guards and had steadily risen through the ranks until he had been appointed as a Brigade Major in February 1916.

23rd Division now formed part of IX Corps along with 19th and 36th Divisions. At 2100 hours on 17 August 13/DLI left their billets in Armentieres and marched up to the trenches where they completed the relief of 23/Middlesex Regiment by 0010 hours on 18 August. That day a change in command took place at 68 Brigade Headquarters when Brigadier H. Page Croft handed over to Brigadier George N. Colvile DSO. The new Brigade Commander, who had been commissioned into the Oxfordshire Light Infantry had seen a lot of service in South Africa with the Mounted Infantry and had been severely wounded and awarded the Distinguished Service Order in September 1901 when serving with the 8th Battalion of Mounted Infantry.

In the rear 12/DLI were resting and refitting, new equipment was issued and a draft of eighty men arrived and was distributed among the companies. Half of the battalion paraded for drill at Pony Nieppe and the other half provided a working party of 200 men. On 20 August 12/DLI held a Church Parade and the other denominations – RC, Methodists and Non Conformists – had their own services. The next three days were spent supplying working parties, and all new officers that had not been in the front line were sent up to the line to see what it was like. In the line 13/DLI were actively patrolling No Man's Land and on the night of 22 August a three-man patrol set out from D Company to check No Man's Land: about half an hour after they left, bombing was heard from near the enemy lines. None of the three men returned and are listed in the Adjutant's War Diary, the first being 17613 Corporal William Proctor, a 37-year-old from Felling who is commemorated on the Ploegsteert Memorial to the Missing. The second man was 24793 Private Cresswell Smith, who was born in Shildon but resident at West Cornforth when he enlisted in 1914. He is buried in Marquette Communal Cemetery 3 kilometres south of Lille, so it is highly likely that he was wounded and taken prisoner and then died on his way back to a dressing station. The grave next to him contains an unidentified soldier and it is possible that it is the third member of the patrol, 20519 Private Charles Lang: the 19-year-old from Anlaby near Hull was attached to 13/DLI from 6/Green Howards and his name is also recorded on the Ploegsteert Memorial to the Missing.

Then on 24 August A and B Companies of 12/DLI moved to Le Bizet and relieved 11/NF owing to the line being extended. The other companies remained on the work detail. The next morning at 0730 hours the whole of 12/DLI took over the front line from 13/DLI. They hadn't been in the line very long before the new Brigadier came round on a tour of inspection. The next five days were fairly quiet, apart from two casualties on 27 August, and there was some sporadic shelling to which the British gunners and trench mortars replied. Then on 31 August the British released gas from the left company of 12/DLI, to which the enemy replied with considerable trench mortar and machine-gun fire. The latter was kept up for two to three hours after the release of the gas. This fire caused the deaths of three men: 18397 Sergeant William Henry Silversides who had just been awarded the Military Medal and came from Gateshead; 31897 Private George Holmes, a Yorkshire man from Shipley who had only joined the battalion fourteen days earlier; and 28367 Private John Frazer from the little colliery village of Middle Rainton near Durham, who had enlisted under the Derby Scheme in January and had joined the battalion on 10 June. As well as these three fatalities, a further six men were wounded.

Further officer replacements arrived at 13/DLI. On 27 August Second Lieutenant Edward Gray who had served in France since August 1914 as a Sergeant in 20/Hussars joined the battalion. Then on 30 August four subalterns from 23/DLI, Roderick Mitchell, Stanley Sharpe, Cyril Chapman and Arnold Candler reported their arrival. They were followed on 1 September by Second Lieutenant Arthur Hudspeth who joined from 16/DLI: although he came from Newcastle upon Tyne, Arthur had been commissioned into the South Staffordshire Regiment in 1915. That night three working parties, each consisting of one officer and forty-two men,

24796 Private William Maughan was awarded the Military Medal on 1 September 1916 for his earlier gallantry.
D/DLI/7/465/3

were organised to carry the now-empty gas cylinders out of the trenches.

Orders were now received that 23rd Division was to be relieved and consequently the various brigades and battalions were replaced by those of the 51st (Highland) Division. On 3 September 13/DLI were replaced by 1/7/Argyll and Sutherland Highlanders (7A&SH) and 12/DLI were replaced in the line by 9/Royal Scots, and on being relieved both Durham battalions moved back to camps near Bailleul. On 5 September, a dull overcast day with frequent showers, they marched to Bailluel railway station and entrained for St Omer, where on arrival they detrained and moved off to their various billeting areas, 12/DLI being located in the village of Quest Mont and 13/DLI at Norbecourt. The battalion transport sections had travelled by road attached to the Divisional Army Service Corps Supply Column and eventually rejoined their own battalions on the afternoon of 6 September. The next four days were spent training and in the afternoon various sporting competitions took place. The Divisional and Brigade Commanders both made visits to the battalions and during his visit to 13/DLI General Babington presented the ribbon of the DCM to 16194 Lance Sergeant Harry Craddock of B Company and that of the Military Medal to 12957 Sergeant James Smith from Dunston on Tyne from C Company. The latter had originally enlisted on 24 August 1914 into 11/DLI but had been discharged for misconduct; however, he had re-enlisted into 16/DLI and despite some minor disciplinary problems he rose through the ranks and then joined 13/DLI in France with the draft in early October 1915.

At 2110 hours on 9 September B Company of 13/DLI marched to the railhead at Audricque where they were to act as loading party for 68 Brigade. They were followed the next morning by each of the battalions and as they arrived they were entrained and set off for Longeau near Amiens. On arrival they quickly moved off and marched to billeting areas where they rested and waited for further orders to move. It must have been obvious to all ranks that they were on their way back to the Somme where the battle had continued in their absence. B Company caught up with the rest of the battalion at 1400 hours on 11 September in the village of Moulin-aux-Bois. The next day 13/DLI moved forward to Millencourt where they remained for two days in the rear of the rest of the brigade. 12/DLI followed the same route travelling just ahead of 13/DLI; on reaching Millencourt they went into billets and rested. The weather the next day was wet and showery but both battalions turned out for drill and training, particular emphasis being given to the training of specialists, bombers, signallers, stretcher-bearers and Lewis-gunners and special instruction was given in the consolidation of captured trenches.

At the Infantry Records Office at York another letter arrived from Mrs

Brankston in Lanchester, still unhappy that her youngest son Alexander remained in France:

Oyster Shell Cottage,
Lanchester
12/9/16
Dear Sir,
Could you do anything towards having my son Alexandra [sic] Brankston sent home from France. I may say that he is one of four sons we have out fighting for their King and Country and as my husband is a cripple having one arm and we are finding it very hard to live having all our support gone. I may also say that Alex is not nineteen years of age until 25 December 1916. Hoping you will do what you can for us seeing that all of our four sons are out in France.
Thanking you in anticipation.
Your humble servant
Mrs George Brankston..

However, her earlier letter had eventually caught up with Alexander and on 8 September he had been posted down to the 35/IBD where they were gathering all the under-age soldiers of the Durham Light Infantry and Northumberland Fusiliers. Yet, he was not sent home: because the time was close to his birthday, he was retained in France training until being returned to 13/DLI when he was aged 19.

At 0630 hours on 15 September both battalions stood to ready to move at ten minutes' notice and at 1130 hours both battalions moved off with 12/DLI in the lead. They made their way up to Becourt Wood and erected bivouacs. 13/DLI remained at one hour's notice to move and the next morning they marched via Fricourt to Bazentin-le-Grand where they arrived at 0530 hours: here they were attached to 140 Brigade of the 47th (2nd London) Division. Once they were settled they came under enemy fire, when a large number of lachrymatory shells fell on the crossroads in Bazentin-le-Grand and Battalion Headquarters. There were two casualties: 18165 Private John Murray was wounded and 17356 Sergeant Tom Garbutt shot himself. Both men (from D Company) were evacuated and the NCO was eventually tried by court martial, reduced to the ranks and returned to front-line duty. The full strength of the battalion was now employed carrying ammunition up to 140 and 141 Brigades who were attacking the enemy near Flers. At 1800 hours on 17 September, Second Lieutenants Beart and Hudspeth and a party of 100 men from B Company set off to carry bombs up to 6/London Regiment: as they made their way forward the enemy opened a barrage that split the party. Second Lieutenant Hudspeth got his men to stack their bombs in a shell-hole and brought them safely back out of the line. Second Lieutenant Beart who was leading his party on was badly wounded almost at once. The guides disappeared and Sergeants 16194 Harry Craddock and 17711 Alfred Fittes took charge and reconnoitred the route, gathered the men together and led them to their destination where they delivered their bombs to the waiting Londoners. Sadly Second Lieutenant Vere D.L. Beart, the young recently-joined South African, died from his wounds after just a month with the battalion. Two other men were killed: 22618 Lance Corporal Stewart Steele, a 34-year-old miner and father of three young daughters from Cornsay Colliery, and 25020 Private James Hart who hailed from Skinningrove in North Yorkshire. A further nine men were wounded and one man, 45934 Private Charles Collings, was posted missing and reported gassed: he had been out in France since July 1915 with the East Yorkshire Regiment and having been wounded was posted to 13/DLI as a reinforcement. The working parties continued the next day: even though it was raining hard, 432 men carried stores, ammunition and food up to the front line.

In the rear 12/DLI were having a quiet time: for two days they did some training and then on the afternoon of 18 September they relieved 11/A&SH in Gourlay Trench in front of Contalmaison Villa. When the battalion moved forward the Transport Section left Becourt Wood and moved back to Albert. On 20 September Second Lieutenant G.P.F. Thomas joined the battalion which was still in Gourlay Trench. The next day a party of officers went up to the front line to reconnoitre the trenches at Martinpuich, while the men provided carrying parties taking Stokes Mortar ammunition from Contalmaison Dump to the front line. Later in the day the battalion was shelled and this resulted in the death of Second Lieutenant Cecil Armstrong and the wounding of Captain Herbert Hayner and Lieutenant Arnold Price. It was now that a War Office photographer turned up and took some photographs and then at 1915 hours they moved off and into the front line where they relieved 11/West Yorks. As the relief was taking place the Germans must have got wind of what was going on and heavily shelled the area; this delayed the relief and it wasn't completed until 2200 hours. Three men were killed: 45890 Private Robert Charlton from Bedlington, 45898 Private Thomas Elliott from Lucker in Northumberland, and 16015 Private Robert Davision from Stanley. The first two named had recently joined as reinforcements having been transferred from the Northumberland Fusiliers, Charlton from the Tyneside Irish and Elliot from the Tyneside Scottish; both had been wounded during 34th Division's attack on 1 July. As well as these fatalities a further ten men were wounded. Another day of heavy shelling occurred on 23 September which caused the deaths of another four men, all of whom had been out with the battalion since August 1915: 16014 Private Thomas Fawcett from Stanley; 18403 Private James Kay from Gateshead; 18385 Private George Surtees from Ferryhill; and 1811 Hugh McLean from Low Fell who had only just been promoted to Corporal a couple of weeks earlier. Also a further six men were wounded. That evening at 1930 hours a patrol of one officer and two men left the battalion lines with the objective of finding out if the enemy were holding 26th Avenue. They were out crawling around No Man's Land until eventually returning to the battalion lines at 2300 hours, but the news they brought was not good for the Germans were holding 26th Avenue in some strength.

Having sent the information back at midnight, an order was received that the battalion would mount an attack on 23rd Avenue. Two platoons were detailed for the task and extra support from bombing sections was allotted. At 0800 hours on 24 September the two platoons went forward, but two German heavy machine guns opened fire. The battalion had been told these had been silenced, but that was evidently a mistake. The attacking Durhams were caught in a crossfire, were unable to make any progress and eventually were forced to return to the start point. Second Lieutenant Johnson Bollom from Ryton on Tyne and five men were killed, twenty-seven wounded and one man was evacuated with shellshock. One of the wounded, 16560 Lance Corporal Robert Whitfield, was quickly evacuated to 2/Field Ambulance RAMC and then from there to the 1/1st South Midland Casualty Clearing Station in Dernancourt; however, even though the staff tried to save him his wounds were too severe and he died on 25 September.

Second Lieutenant Johnson Bollom from Ryton on Tyne was killed in action on 24 September during the attack on 23rd Avenue

Back with 13/DLI at 1030 hours on 19 September the Staff Captain of 140 Brigade arrived at Battalion Headquarters. He reported that the enemy had counter-attacked and had driven the men of 140 Brigade from the junction of the Flers Line and Drop Alley; he requested that all the bombing sections of 13/DLI should be employed to retake the position. This request was refused by the Commanding Officer but he did lend the Staff Officer, Captain Denzil Clarke and his company. The plan was that at 0645 hours after a Stokes Mortar barrage, three attacks would be made simultaneously, covered by machine-gun fire. Two bombing sections under Second Lieutenant Hudspeth were to attack up Drop Alley and two bombing sections under Second Lieutenant Mitchell were to attack up O.G.1 with the remainder under Captain Clarke in a supporting and carrying role. The third attack was to be made by men of the New Zealand Division attacking up O.G.2. The attack up Drop Alley advanced some 70 yards and the second section fired rifle grenades over the heads of the leading section. The Germans replied very heavily with bombs and then counter-attacked over the open, driving the British bombers back to their starting-point, a trench block which they held until relieved. Most of this party, including Second Lieutenant Arthur Hudspeth, were wounded. The second attack up O.G.1 had a very stiff fight for about ten minutes and then was able to advance some 130 yards up to the junction with Drop Alley. Here they were held up owing to a shortage of bombs and they came under attack from two different directions. They then made a double trench block, but the British artillery opened fire and kept this up for four hours. Twice the block was blown down and rebuilt and finally the bombers of 13/DLI were forced to retire 20 yards down the trench and construct a new block which was held for six hours until relieved. At 1630 hours the battalion less B Company was relieved and moved via Contalmaison to Becourt Wood where they erected bivouacs. The casualties while attached to 140 Brigade had been fairly heavy: Second Lieutenant Arthur Hudspeth was missing believed killed, three men were killed in action, seven were missing and twenty wounded, and Captain Wilfred Miles [later to write *The Durham Forces in the Field*] was evacuated sick, probably with shellshock. However, of the missing, 28174 Private William Farbridge, 46045 Private Rowland Grinrod and 21413 Private George Jones eventually turned up in dressing stations. At 0500 hours the next morning B Company was relieved and rejoined the battalion in Becourt Wood where they arrived at 1100 hours. During the day Second Lieutenant P. Owen reported from 3/DLI and Second Lieutenant John Young from 17/DLI, and even though the battalion was in a back area four men were reported wounded. At 1000 hours on 22 September the Commanding Officer attended a conference at 68 Brigade Headquarters and returned with the news that the battalion would move in positions in the support line. Consequently the battalion deployed one company in Bacon Trench with one platoon in Cameron Trench. One company manned Highland Trench and one Lancs Trench, and the fourth company held Butterworth Trench and Shetland Alley. Here Second Lieutenant Henry Rudland reported to the battalion from 20/DLI;

Captain Wilfred Miles (later to write **The Durham Forces in the Field**)*, was evacuated sick.*

he had served in the South African Army Medical Corps in German South-West Africa prior to gaining a commission in the DLI. They came under some shellfire and 46008 Private Arthur Thomas, another of the Tyneside Scottish reinforcements serving in A Company, was killed and another two men of the company were wounded; as well as these casualties another three men of D Company were also wounded. The next day was hot and fine and there was a steady trickle of casualties from the enemy shelling. The Commanding Officer was wounded but remained at duty and 24505 Private James Hull from Witton Park was killed and three men wounded, among them 45966 Private George Johnson who had served with 6/Green Howards at Gallipoli prior to being transferred into the DLI.

In preparation for the next attack, Second Lieutenant George Gray was given the task of marking out a road for tanks and he was able to guide two of them up to the Factory Line where they arrived at 0200 hours on 25 September, then in the evening D Company relieved a company of 11/NF in Martin Alley and the Starfish Line, the handover being complete by 2240 hours. Then at 2335 the enemy opened fire on Battalion Headquarters

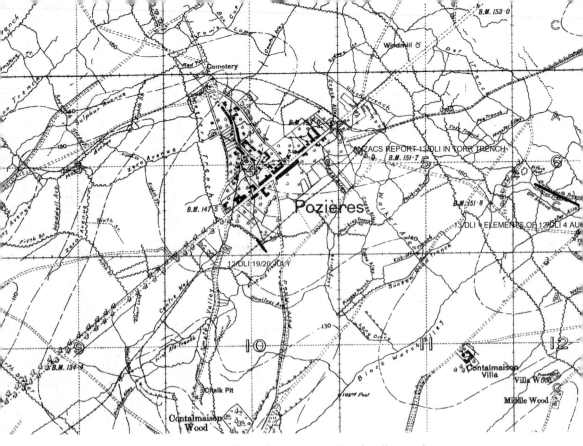

and Captain Joseph Downey, Second Lieutenant Frank Allan and six men were wounded. At 0430 hours the remainder of 13/DLI left O.G.1 and relieved 11/NF in the right battalion sector of the brigade front. Immediately they took over they sent patrols out to establish if the enemy were holding points 53 and 73. Both patrols returned unscathed and reported that the enemy were holding both positions and that below point 53 they had established a bomb block. At 1455 hours the Brigade Trench Mortar Battery was ordered to fire on point 53 and with some disdain the Battalion War Diary records they 'Succeeded in placing all their shots 100 yards to the left thereof.' At midnight the battalion was relieved by 11/Sherwood Foresters and moved back to bivouacs in Becourt Wood. However, on the way out they came under fire and 46060 Private Walter Elger was killed: he had arrived in France in May 1915 with 5 Pioneer Battalion Northamptonshire Regiment, then moved to 1/NF prior to being posted to 13/DLI. Two other men were wounded: 24747 CSM Adam Nichol and 17335 Private James Green.

At 0500 hours on 25 September 12/DLI had been relieved and returned to O.G.1; however, 10/NF suffered very heavy casualties in their attack at 1100 hours and 12/DLI received orders to send two companies back into the front line. They were followed at 1915 hours by the remaining two companies who moved up under heavy shellfire and 31631 Private James

Martin from South Shields was killed and three others wounded. The enemy shelling was not so heavy the next day but 26th Avenue was heavily shelled by the British gunners which brought retaliation on Martinpuich Factory and Gun Pit Lane, during which three men were killed and one officer and twenty-five men wounded. At 1930 hours a patrol of one officer and two men left the battalion line with the objective of reconnoitring 26th Avenue and establishing if it was held by the enemy. While the patrol was out in No Man's Land, 8/King's Own Yorkshire Light Infantry (8/KOYLI) arrived and relieved 12/DLI, and as soon as possible they moved off in small parties to the Dingle on the Fricourt–Contalmaison Road where they arrived around midnight. The patrol meanwhile had safely returned to the British lines where they were able to report that 26th Avenue was unoccupied but that two strongpoints at 2.9 and 5.3 were held and alert as flares were constantly being sent up from these two positions. The whole battalion was allowed to rest on 27 September but after that it was back to working parties. On 28 September a large party was put to work clearing roads around Contalmaison and then on the next day they were unloading RE stores at the dump in the same village. On the last day of the month fifty men went up to dig an assembly trench east of Martinpuich, while another fifty carried grenades from Contalmaison Villa dump to the new HQ dump at Martinpuich; casualties during the day amounted to four men wounded.

Although the War Diary of 13/DLI just records the endless numbers of men employed on working parties, the Adjutant recorded the names and numbers of those killed, wounded and missing during this time at rest. Second Lieutenant Charles Mann, originally commissioned into 21/DLI was killed on 30 September, as was 1711 Lance Corporal John Snowball from Spennymoor. Among those wounded were 17424 Sergeant Thomas Kenny VC of A Company and two men serving in B Company, while 21631 Private Robert Moseley, a resident of Ushaw Moor, and 22679 Private James Fairless from Trimdon Colliery were both posted as missing; the latter, however, must have turned up only to be killed in action on 6 October.

23rd Division was now tasked to assist 50th (Northumbrian) Division with the capture of the trenches known as Flers 1 and Flers 2 that ran down from the village of Le Sars to the village of Flers. Battalions of 70 Brigade were given the first task and on the morning of 1 October assembled in trenches prepared for the purpose between Destremont Farm and 26th Avenue. At 1515 hours the barrage commenced and the attack went in and secured the objective. Meanwhile the DLI battalions of 68 Brigade were placed at thirty minutes' notice to move. At 1100 hours on 2 October 12/DLI were ordered to move to Gourlay Trench: they started moving at 1630 hours and by 1830 hours they were in position. 13/DLI had moved off at 1415 hours and by 1530 hours was set up in Peake Wood.

68 Brigade was moving up in support of 151 (Durham) Brigade of 50th Division and the next morning 12/DLI moved up from Gourlay Trench at 0830 hours to Hook and Eye Trenches and then at 1200 hours continued up to Crescent Alley where they relieved 5/NF, deploying B Company into Blaydon Trench. Likewise 13/DLI moved forward and took over from 8/DLI. The Commanding Officer placed A and C Companies in Prue Trench and B and D Companies in the Starfish Line. On 4 October 46041 Private John Bell, another of the Tyneside Scottish reinforcements serving in B Company, was wounded and then the next day fifty Other Ranks under the command of Second Lieutenant Cyril Chapman carried fifty boxes of Mills bombs up to 10/NF in the front line. However, tragedy struck as they made their way forward: a box of bombs that must have been primed was accidently dropped, and it exploded wounding 16928 Private Robert Alderson and 45928 Private Joseph Johnson. The latter, who came from Crook, County Durham, was a reinforcement from the Green Howards and although evacuated to the Field Ambulance he died from his wounds.

The village of Le Sars is strung out along the Albert–Bapaume Road and it was now the job of 23rd Division to take the village. The attack was to be made by two brigades: 69 Brigade on the left and 68 Brigade on the right. It was to be made in two stages, and in each brigade the right battalion would move first. In this first phase 12/DLI would attack and take the Tangle and the Sunken Road, a series of trenches south-east of the village; while in 69 Brigade, 9/Green Howards would secure the village as far as the crossroads. In phase two, 13/DLI would move up between these two battalions and take the remainder of the village; while on the left, 11/West Yorks would take the remainder of Flers 2 north of the Bapaume Road.

On 7 October at 1300 hours Second Lieutenant William Lockett, who had joined 12/DLI from 16/DLI on 18 September and was now commanding C Company, led them forward and occupied the Tangle. Then at 1345 hours A and the remainder of C Company advanced with D and B Companies in close support. A Company were soon held up by heavy machine-gun fire but C Company, assisted by some men from two platoons of D Company led by Second Lieutenant Alan Hunt, reached the Sunken Road. Here they were joined by the remaining two platoons from D Company under the command of Second Lieutenant William Hughes. They immediately started consolidating the position and were able to inflict some casualties on the now fleeing enemy. It was about now that 22166 Private George Kilburn from Crigglestone near Wakefield carried out a daring reconnaissance and then, although wounded himself, he carried three messages back to Battalion Headquarters and tended wounded men under fire. These actions brought the award of the Distinguished Conduct Medal. Patrols were

3/10392 Private George Douthwaite from Witton Park joined 12/DLI in December 1915 and was killed in action 7 October 1916. He has no known grave and is commemorated on the Thiepval Memorial to Missing.

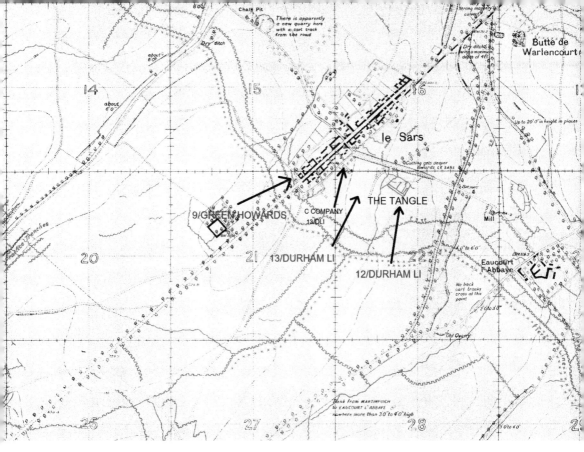

now sent out and 15874 Lance Corporal George Slasor led three patrols into No Man's Land and maintained touch with the retreating enemy for up to four hours; he too was awarded the Distinguished Conduct Medal. 12/DLI now dug new positions which were a chain of posts or strongpoints that were gradually linked up, but throughout the night they were heavily shelled by the German artillery. Casualties were fairly heavy. Second Lieutenant William Lockett was killed and the following officers were wounded: Joseph Lowes, Alan Hunt, Alfred Hales, Austen Wallis, James Hugall and William Legatt; Second Lieutenant Richard Telfer was posted as missing, later confirmed killed in action. Among the men, thirty-one were known to be killed and eighty-six were wounded. Among those listed as killed was 16512 Private George Bell from Spennymoor, who, if he had been allowed to serve his sentence for sleeping at his post the previous December, would have been serving hard labour instead of being in the line. 12/DLI had taken around seventy German prisoners during their attack and on 6 October they were relived by 8/10/Gordon Highlanders of the 15th (Scottish) Division.

On 6 October 13/DLI commenced the relief of 11/NF at 1815 hours. However, the Fusiliers were attacking the Tangle and this delayed the relief; by 2200 hours the attack was declared a failure and by 2355 hours 13/DLI had taken over the line. Battalion Headquarters was established in 26th Avenue: two companies were in O.G.2 – B Company on the left and C Company on the right – and the other two companies were in O.G.1 with A Company on the left and D Company on the right. While the battalion was moving into position they came under fire and four men from B Company, 18207 Corporal John McIntyre, a Consett man, 14876 Lance Corporal Arthur Lyons from Rowlands Gill, 17011 Private Herbert Gill who came from Witton Gilbert, and 22679 Private James Fairless who had recently been reported as missing were killed. There is now a small mystery contained in an entry in the Adjutant's War Diary. On the morning of 7 October at 0900 hours 15142 Sergeant W. Stewart of A Company was seen near a sap head by an officer of the Royal Engineers.

This officer ordered the sergeant to return to the British front line, which he did. Shortly afterwards he was seen wandering across No Man's Land towards the German lines. Sergeant James Smith MM of C Company ran out to get him but was too late and Sergeant Stewart was surrounded by enemy soldiers and taken prisoner, whereupon Sergeant Smith opened fire and shot and killed one of the captors. It was presumed that Sergeant Stewart was either drunk or mad. No 15142 Sergeant W. Stewart has been traced: the nearest man found was 19872 Sergeant W. Stewart who served with 14/DLI before joining 13/DLI.

Seated is 13921 Private Alex Stephenson 12/DLI from Usworth Colliery with his three brothers: his letters home featured in earlier chapters about Bullswater Camp. He was killed in action on 7 October 1916, has no known grave and is commemorated on the Thiepval Memorial to the Missing.

While this was going on, orders were received from 68 Brigade Headquarters that the battalion would attack and take the north-eastern portion of Le Sars after 12/DLI had taken the Sunken Road and after they had taken their objective, 13/DLI were to establish strongpoints and maintain touch with 69 Brigade on the left. These operations were discussed with all officers and NCOs. The battalion, however, was well below strength and the companies were reorganised into companies of two platoons each. Yet these platoons were

18786 Private Thomas Murphy 12/DLI from Leadgate. He was killed in action on 8 October 1916, has no known grave and is commemorated on the Thiepval Memorial to the Missing.

well below normal strength and were organised into sections of one NCO, two bayonet men and three bombers; each bomber carrying twelve bombs in his haversack. The other men were to carry two bombs and two bandoliers of ammunition each. The first company was detailed to attack the north-east portion of Le Sars with the second company in support and if not engaged to cover the northern end of the village. The task of the third company was to consolidate any position taken and start building and holding strongpoints. The fourth company and battalion details were available as a reserve with the task of assisting to clear the village. Owing to the shortage of manpower, only three men per company were to be detailed to escort prisoners back, and where possible prisoners were to be handed over to 12/DLI or 9/Yorks. One Company of 11/NF were attached to 13/DLI as a carrying party and before the operations commenced they carried a large amount of bombs, ammunition, water and other material up to a dump in O.G.1.

At 1345 hours a patrol of one officer and eighteen men went forward with the first wave of 12/DLI. The officer and five men got as far as some shell-holes close to the Sunken Road and on the left of the Tangle where they opened fire and threw bombs at the Germans in the Sunken Road. They eventually got into the Sunken Road when C Company attacked from the east. Information was slow in coming in and nothing was learned of the progress of 12/DLI until 1430 hours when it was believed that a tank had successfully attacked the Tangle. At the same time word came in from the patrol ordered to keep in touch with 9/Green Howards that the Yorkshire men would need reinforcements if they were to take their objective. On receipt of this news the CO ordered Captain Harold Blake Commanding C Company to move into the village but not to go via the Sunken Road. C Company went over in two waves and Captain Blake was killed soon after they started. The leading wave was stopped by machine-gun fire before it reached the village. Meanwhile the CO had ordered B Company under Captain Denzil Clarke to move in support of C Company, but they were to keep more to the left and if necessary were to move through the eastern side of the village. The second wave of C Company now reached their comrades in the leading wave and brought their additional fire-power to bear, engaging the enemy with rifle and Lewis-gun fire and were able to silence a German machine gun. A few minutes later and B Company arrived on the scene and together, with bayonets fixed, both companies charged into the village and the Sunken Road. On the left 9/Green Howards gained all their objectives, while C Company of 13/DLI bombed German dugouts in the Sunken Road and worked their way down the road until all enemy soldiers were dead or had surrendered. Captain Clarke, having learned that Captain Blake was

Unteroffizier Johann Eedlmaner, 5th Company Bavarian Reserve Infantry Regt No 17 was killed in action at Le Sars on 1 October 1916 just before the 23rd Division attacked.

dead took over command of all the leading troops and moved his company through Le Sars supported by one platoon of C Company and by 1545 hours it was reported that they were through the village. In the village little opposition was met and any enemy dugouts were dealt with and prisoners taken. By 1640 hours Captain Clarke was reporting that consolidation had begun 200 yards ahead of the village and patrols had been sent forward beyond the Divisional barrage to where a good view of the Butte de Warlencourt and the ground ahead could be seen. These patrols reported that they could see no sign of the enemy. During the attack at 1530 hours orders were received that the accompanying tank was to move through the village and attack the Germans holding up 69 Brigade. This message was passed to the tank commander, but he was forced to reply that his machine had been knocked out by artillery fire and he was unable to assist.

When the Commanding Officer received word that there was no sign of the enemy he ordered A Company forward to assist in the consolidation. By 1950 hours A Company reported that the strongpoints were well-established and each had a Lewis gun and that fresh patrols had been sent out and the earlier patrols had been withdrawn. Word was sent to both

186

12/DLI and 9/Green Howards asking them to move forward and link up with the posts of 13/DLI. However, owing to the failure to secure objectives on the left and right flanks it was found necessary to strengthen the defences in the northern end of Le Sars: for this purpose four Vickers guns of 68/Machine Gun Company and a company of 11/NF were placed at the disposal of 13/DLI. The Vickers guns were duly deployed, two in the northern end of the village, one in the Sunken Road and the fourth in reserve in O.G.1. The strongpoint in the Sunken Road was reinforced by the remainder of C Company, while the reserve company of 13/DLI occupied O.G.2. The company of 11/NF was deployed in O.G.1 along with a small party from the Divisional Royal Engineers and some carrying parties from 15th (Scottish) Division had brought up much-needed bombs and ammunition so that all posts had an ample supply of both.

So the attack on Le Sars had been successful but at what cost? On the plus side they had taken one machine gun, one officer and 150 unwounded men, while there was a further one officer, thirty wounded men and an estimated 130 enemy dead. On the down side Captain Harold Blake had been killed and Lieutenant Herbert Markham and Second Lieutenant Ernest Atkinson wounded, while Second Lieutenant Edward

The very wet weather had reduced the ground to porridge and trenches were falling in as the mud slipped away. Here a German soldier stands in what passed for a trench.

19192 CSM William Liddle from South Shields was awarded the DCM for his work in clearing the village of Le Sars. This photo was taken after he was commissioned into 20/DLI.

Gray was wounded at duty. In the ranks eleven men were dead, forty had been wounded, one of whom, 16978 Private Stanley Chicken from Hetton-le-Hole was wounded but remained at duty, five men were missing and 46009 Private H. Hobson was evacuated with a self-inflicted wound.

The next day was dull and overcast but it didn't prevent the German gunners from working and a very heavy bombardment fell on Le Sars. All communication was cut: the battalion signals platoon had worked hard overnight and every company had three separate telephone lines laid by different routes, but within two or three minutes of the barrage commencing all lines to the forward positions were cut and the barrage so intense that the linesmen couldn't go out to effect repairs. Later in the afternoon a patrol went out and came into contact with the enemy north-east of Le Sars. Then at 2000 hours 9/Black Watch came up and relieved the battalion. By 0400 hours the relief was complete and 13/DLI marched back to billets in Becourt Wood. Here the Adjutant recorded in his War Diary that the Battalion Doctor got drunk and that during the day the battalion had suffered more casualties, mainly in A and D Companies, with four killed, ten wounded and one shellshocked. The signals of congratulations to the 23rd Division and its infantry battalions started to come in.

On 7 October 1916 C Company 13/DLI went over in two waves and Captain Blake was killed soon after they started. He was buried after the action but the grave was lost and he is commemorated on Special Memorial No 8 in Warlencourt Cemetery.

From GOC III Corps:

Please convey to the troops of your Division engaged today my congratulations on their gallant and successful attack on Le Sars.

From III Corps G 426, from General Rawlinson:

Please convey to all ranks 23rd Division my congratulations and best thanks for their fine performance yesterday. The capture of all their objectives and 480 prisoners is a feat which they may be justly proud especially after all the fighting they have already been

19625 Sergeant Harold Hitchin was awarded a Bar to his Military Medal for action at Le Sars. He was subsequently commissioned into 18/DLI where he was awarded the Military Cross and Distinguished Service Order, and ended the war in the rank of Major.

Christliches Andenken im Gebete

an den ehrengeachteten Jüngling

Johann Sinhart

Gütlersfohn von Gendorf,

Soldat beim 16. Ref.=Regt., 1. Maschinen=
gewehr=Kompagnie,

welcher am 9. Oktober 1916 an der
Somme im 22. Lebensjahre den Helden=
tod fürs Vaterland starb.

Die Pflicht rief mich zum Krieg hinaus,
Mit Gott ging ich vom Elternhaus,
Ich dachte euer fort und fort,
Wenn ich auch weilt' am fremden Ort,
Und freute mich auf's Wiedersehen,
Wenn Krieg und Sturm zu Ende gehen.
Doch anders hats der Herr gewollt
Und hat von hier mich abgeholt.
Nun ruh' in fremder Erd' ich aus
Und bin bei Gott im Vaterhaus.
Weiß nichts von Krieg und Erdenleid
Und bin von jeder Sorg befreit;
Drum, meine Lieben, denkt stets daran:
„Was Gott tut, das ist wohlgetan."

Druck von J. Geiselberger, Altötting.

Soldat Johann Einhart No 1 Machine Gun Company of Bavarian Reserve Infantry Regt No 16 fell near Le Sars on 9 October 1916.

through during the Battle of The Somme.

From HQ 50th (Northumbrian) Division:

Congratulations from all ranks 50th Division on your excellent and subsequent capture of Le Sars.

With the relief of 68 Brigade completed the various battalions were paraded and were inspected by Lieutenant-General Sir William Pulteney KCB Commanding III Corps. Apart from the two DCM awards already recorded, the two battalions of the Durham Light Infantry were awarded the following: 12/DLI, fifteen Military Medals; 13/DLI, one Bar to the Military Cross, one Military Cross, one Bar to the Military Medal and fifteen Military Medals.

The wounded of both battalions were evacuated first to the Regimental Aid Post where they were stabilised and prepared for their onward

189

journey. They were then taken to one of the Divisional Field Ambulances and from there to a Casualty Clearing Station. Second Lieutenant Austen Wallis of 12/DLI eventually arrived in 45/Casualty Clearing Station on 8 October where he had an operation to try to save his leg. On 10 October Stanley Wickenden, a Captain in the RAMC Special Reserve from Perth, wrote to the wounded officer's father:

> *October 10 1916*
>
> *45 C.C.S*
>
> *B.E.F,*
>
> *Dear Sir,*
>
> *Your son Lt R A Wallis is at present under my care in this Casualty Clearing Station. I am therefore writing to give you particulars of his wounds.*
>
> *He was admitted on 8 October suffering from bullet wounds in the right knee and left thigh. The main artery in the right leg had been severed and an operation was performed by which we hoped to re-establish the circulation and save the leg. Gangrene however started in the foot so I regret to say the right leg had to be amputated at the knee joint. The wound in the left thigh is a severe flesh wound, but is not dangerous.*
>
> *Your son had a severe degree of shock after both operations and his condition yesterday was critical, but I am glad to be able to report that a decided improvement began last evening and has been maintained during the night. He slept well last night and his condition although still serious is much more satisfactory this morning. He is free from pain today and is very patient and cheerful.*
>
> *He wished me to give his love to all at home and to say that he will be in 'Blighty' soon and would see you. I believe the Sister I/C is writing to Mrs Wallis, but your son wished me to let you know about the amputation, so that you could break the news to his mother.*

Second Lieutenant Austen Wallis 12/DLI wounded at Le Sars had his leg amputated at 45 CCS but lived until 1963.

> *I think he has turned the corner now, and with care should progress slowly but surely although he will not be out of danger for a day or two.*
>
> *He is being well cared for by a kind and competent Sister, and has all the comforts and surgical conveniences he requires.*
>
> *Yours faithfully*
>
> *Stanley Wickenden*
>
> *Officer I/C Officers' Div*
>
> *45 C.C.S. B.E.F.*

Mr Wallis received a very similar letter from the War Office dated 20

16429 Private John E. Vipond 13/DLI had done enough to be recommended for the Military Medal, but was wounded by a shell on 7 October 1916. Evacuated to 45 CCS, he died from his wounds on 14 October. His Military Medal was gazetted on 9 December 1916.

October and a telegram dated the same day which probably arrived before the letter which stated:

War Office 20 October

Beg to inform you Second Lieutenant A B Wallis Durham Light Infantry was admitted to No 8 Gen Hosp Rouen today suffering from gunshot wound left thigh and right leg amputated, seriously ill. Further details following by letter.

Secretary War Office

Austen Wallis survived his wounds and lived until 1963, but other families were not so lucky. On 1 November Anthony and Clara Bell, the landlords of the Angel Inn in Oxford Road, Spennymoor, received word that their son 16152 Private George Bell had been posted missing on 7 October. The anxious parents waited for a letter from their son, but when no letter arrived his father wrote to the War Office on 19 January 1917:

Private George Bell 16152

12 Batt C Cmy DLI No 11 Platoon 68 Inf Brigade,

23 Division British E.Force, France.

Sir, The above was posted missing on 7 October 1916. We received the report 1 November 1916. The report stated you would communicate with us as quick as possible as to his whereabouts. We have gone through a terrible suspense expecting a letter every day yet none coming.

He was our son whom we loved when he was with us and we ask you to give us all the information abetting to our son.

Yours in anticipation

A J Bell, Angel Inn.

At 1500 hours on 11 October A and B Companies of 12/DLI left Albert by train for Longpre and were followed by the rest of the battalion some two hours later. When they arrived in the early hours of the next day they set off on foot and marched to Ergnies where they went into billets. Likewise 13/DLI moved to the railhead and boarded a later train for the same destination. On

Second Lieutenant Ernest Atkinson was wounded for the second time at Le Sars and was evacuated to England on 23 October 1916.

arrival they too took to their feet and marched to Villers-sur-Ailly where they arrived at 1000 hours on 12 October. The next day saw both battalions on the move again, this time to billets in the area of St Ricquier, where they spent the next day resting and cleaning up, and then on the morning of 15 October they entrained at St Ricquier and travelled via Frevent, St Pol and Hazebrouck to Proven, where they arrived in the late afternoon.

Once again they set off on foot and after a few hours' marching they took over billets in the rear of the Ypres Salient. They didn't rest long and by 17 October 12/DLI was back in the line in the Salient. At 1815 hours on 18 October 13/DLI marched out of Winnipeg camp bound for the Brandhoek level-crossing where they entrained and were carried up to the Asylum in Ypres. Here they left the train and took over the accommodation in the Infantry Barracks, Ypres. The Battalion transport and Lewis-gun carts travelled by road and took over the transport lines of 25/Australian Battalion. At 1700 hours on 20 October they moved to the front-line trenches where they took over from 12/DLI on a two-company front with D Company holding the right and B Company the left. A Company along with Battalion Headquarters and the Regimental Aid Post were located at Halfway House in support. In reserve were C Company but the CO ordered them forward to reinforce the front line and they took up position in Leinster Trench.

Infantry move past the ruins of the Cloth Hall in Ypres on their way to the line.

The next day the positions were adjusted and the Lewis guns were re-sited. Although the weather had turned cold there was little activity from the enemy and thankfully there were no casualties before 10/DWR came up on the night of 23 October to relieve the Durham battalion. By 0130 hours on 24 October the relief was complete and 13/DLI marched down the Menin Road into Ypres where they entrained at the Asylum and rode to Poperinghe where they went into billets. Both battalions stared sending men on working parties and time was spent cleaning up and preparing for an inspection by the Army Commander. At 1430 hours on 27 October General Sir Herbert Plumer, GCMG, KCB, General Officer Commanding Second Army arrived to inspect 68 Infantry Brigade which was drawn up on the football field in Poperinghe. The GOC was accompanied by Major General William Birdwood Commanding I ANZAC CORPS. After the parade the men went back to the working parties. Another parade took place two days later when Lieutenant-Colonel Lord Robert Manners, King's Royal Rifle Corps Commanding 68 Brigade presented the ribbon to those men who had been awarded various gallantry medals. In 13/DLI thirteen Military Medals were awarded, while 17750 Sergeant Michael Brough of A Company received a Bar to the Military Medal he had received earlier in the year. Two medals could not be presented as one recipient, 19782 Private Constantine O'Rourke of B Company was on leave at home in

General Sir Herbert Plumer.

West Hartlepool and 16429 Private John Vipond from Leadgate had died of wounds on 14 October. On the last day of October Second Lieutenant Frederick Hall reported in from 3/DLI and was posted to B Company.

12/DLI had gone back into the line and on 1 November the Commanding Officer Lieutenant-Colonel W.W. MacGregor returned from leave and took over command of the battalion. The men were employed consolidating their positions and C and D Companies provided working parties. The period in the line was quiet and uneventful and no casualties occurred. Meanwhile in the rear 13/DLI were employed on carrying parties and burying signal cable which was not without risk for Ypres was being shelled by the Germans on a regular basis. At 1700 hours on 2 November 13/DLI moved back to the line where they relieved 12/DLI in the left sector of the right brigade front. A Company took over St Peter's Street on the right of the front line and C Company held the left section of the front line. B Company in support was located in Maple Copse and Stafford Trench, while in reserve D Company was in dugouts at Zillebeke Bund, with Battalion Headquarters at Dormy House. It was reported that the trenches were generally in good condition, except Vancouver Street and Border Avenue which were very bad with practically no wire. During the day according to the Adjutant's Diary 33278 Private W. Toyn was wounded; however, no trace of this soldier has been found. The next day the battalion witnessed an unusual event when a British Observation Balloon from Number 15 Section Royal Flying Corps broke free from its moorings and was carried away towards the German lines. The British Anti-Aircraft gunners started shooting at it and the only occupant, the observer Second Lieutenant Bevan RFC destroyed his papers and jumped out, descending by parachute and landing near Elverdinghe. The balloon was last seen heading north-north-west at a great height. On 4 November the trench mortars in the trenches of the Northumberland Fusiliers on 13/DLI's right opened a barrage on the enemy; this caused the German artillery to retaliate with Minnenwerfers and field guns and a heavy barrage fell on Crab Crawl and Vancouver Street.

In A Company 20931 Private Thomas Haughey from Consett was wounded, in B Company 46065 Corporal John Alexander, originally with 16/NF, was also wounded and in A Company 24525 Private George Postle, a Leadgate man, was killed. The battalion then set to wiring and repairing the damage to the trenches. During the next day a further two casualties occurred: 36416 Private Thomas Hartley who had enlisted in December 1915 serving in B Company was wounded, and 19047 Private Henry Carson, a Felling man, was killed. The notification of his death was sent in the usual way to his mother at home in Felling and the family waited for his personal effects to be sent home. At the beginning of January they had a letter from the Company Quartermaster Sergeant of his company to say that all his personal effects had been sent down in the usual way. This prompted his youngest sister to write on the mother's behalf to the Infantry Records at York:

20 Field Street
Felling on Tyne
Co Durham
7/1/17
Sir,

Would you please oblige and inform my mother if you have any personal belongings of my brother Private Henry Carson Reg No 19047 13th DLI who was killed in action on the 6/11/16. The CQMS of my late brothers company informed my mother this morning that he had sent everything of value my late brother possessed to my mother but nothing has yet arrived. Hoping you will oblige.

yours sincerely J R Carson

It took the Records Office another two months to send the few bits and pieces home to the family.

Out at rest 12/DLI were doing anything but rest: the Royal Engineers required large carrying parties, and as well as that they were well-occupied improving their own living conditions, laying many trench boards in the reserve trenches at Zillebeke Bund. On the morning of 5 November General Babington came round and inspected the work done.

By 1930 hours on 6 November they had relieved 13/DLI in the line: they followed the same defensive pattern with two companies holding the front line, D on the right and C on the left with B Company in support at Maple Copse and A Company in reserve at the Bund with Headquarters at Dormy House. The next three days are described as very quiet with no activity from the enemy; however, the nightly work of rewiring and repairing the line was hampered by a bright moonlight. The Support Company was able to lay trench boards from Maple Copse to Sanctuary Wood and in the front line Cross Street and Vigo were drained and repaired and fire steps constructed.

On 10 November 68 Brigade was relieved and the two Durham battalions were able to move back to hutted camps in the rear of the Ypres Salient. 13/DLI, having been relieved by 10/DWR of 69 Brigade, marched back into Ypres and entrained and were carried to Vlamertinghe where they detrained and marched to Winnipeg Camp where they arrived at 2200 hours. They were followed about an hour later by 12/DLI: relieved by 8/KOYLI of 70 Brigade, they too entrained at Ypres for Vlamertinghe and on arrival marched to Montreal Camp where they took over at 2300 hours. The next day the work of cleaning and repairing equipment began and 12/DLI were inspected by their Commanding Officer with further kit inspections during the afternoon. On 12 November both battalions provided working parties: 12/DLI to assist the Royal Engineers to construct huts for an extension to Montreal Camp and 13/DLI to assist the Royal Engineers to drain Dickebusch Beck. Later that day a draft of reinforcements arrived from 35 Infantry Base Depot. Ninety men were sent to 12/DLI and seventy men were sent to 13/DLI; the latter unit recorded that they came from the 2nd, 5th, 6th, 7th, 8th and 23rd Battalions of the regiment, so all but those from the 23rd (Bantam) Battalion had served in France before. Classes of instruction were held: wiring, bombing and Lewis-gun classes, and later bayonet-fighting. On the afternoon of 14 November time off was allowed for inter-company football matches. By 16 November 12/DLI was reporting that all deficiencies had been made good and that the CO had carried out a kit inspection of the battalion. At 1700 hours that day the battalion marched out of Montreal Camp and made their way to Ypres where they relieved 8/KOYLI in the Infantry Barracks. The relief completed by 2000 hours, 12/DLI immediately started finding working parties, which carried on for the next three days. Earlier in the day 13/DLI handed over Winnipeg Camp to 8/York and Lancaster Regiment (8/York & Lancs) of 70 Brigade and entraining at Vlamertinghe, were taken up to the Asylum at Ypres where they detrained and set off for the line where they relieved 8/KOYLI, the latter battalion moving back to the Infantry Barracks to await the arrival of 12/DLI.

As usual the Adjutant of 13/DLI recorded the precise dispositions of the battalion: they were now operating on a two-company front with an extra platoon from the support company. D Company on the right with three platoons and two Lewis guns held from I.18.4 to 18.6 with a listening post at the north-west corner of Zouave Wood. This Company had one platoon and a Lewis gun in support in Rosslyn Street. The centre of the battalion front was held by one platoon of B Company from I.17.1 to I.17.2. The line was then held by C Company by a series of posts: one NCO and six men held a post at I.18.A.2.5, and there was a bombing post at I.18.a.7.6 consisting of six Other Ranks with a similar post in Regent Street. One Officer and thirty Other Ranks were established in a post at the Culvert. The remainder of the Company was at I.17.4 with one Lewis gun at Birr Crossroads. In support the remaining three platoons of B Company with two Lewis guns were in Leinster Street, one of which was a permanent garrison. A Company, with Battalion Headquarters and the Regimental Aid Post, was established at Halfway House. In the early hours of 18 November two Russian soldiers escaped from the German lines and gave themselves up to men of 13/DLI; it is not clear whether these were escaped POWs or Russians that had been pressed into German service. On 20 November Lance Corporal David Taylorson of D Company claimed that he had shot a German sniper at 500 yards. Then that night 12/DLI came up and took over the line once again.

12/DLI placed A and B Companies in the line with C Company in support in Leinster Street and D Company in reserve at Halfway House. The early hours of the morning were quite misty and this allowed a lot of wiring to be carried out by B Company who had a party quickly out into No Man's Land where they were shelled as they worked. The battalion also sent three patrols out under Captains William Arris and David Chambers and Second Lieutenant Michael O'Brien, and these brought back some very useful information. In the support line C Company commenced the construction of new dugouts and the battalion observers constructed a new observation post. There was also work carried out on a new officers' mess at Battalion Headquarters. On 24 November Regent Street came under a heavy barrage from German heavy artillery and mortars and the damage had to be repaired before 13/DLI took over that night. 13/DLI had spent the last four days providing working parties for 101 Field Company Royal Engineers and on the last working party before they moved back to the line they came under fire and 32933 Private Robert Kitchen of D Company was evacuated wounded. The German artillery was very active at this time and they shelled China Wall and Gordon Dump, where a working party from 12/DLI came under fire. The shelling continued the next day and in C Company 13/DLI 45947 Private Charles Williams, a reinforcement from the Northumberland Fusiliers was wounded. On the afternoon of 28 November two Poles, members of the 35th Landwehr Infantry Regiment, deserted their regiment and crossed No Man's Land: one entered 13/DLI lines at the Culvert and the other at I.18.4. Under interrogation these men divulged that the Germans were planning to raid the sector held by 13/DLI. An extra Lewis-gun team was ordered up to the front line from the reserve company, there was some sporadic shelling and 38303 Private William Caisley of B Company was wounded: quickly evacuated, he left France by hospital ship on 7 December and when he recovered from his wounds he was transferred to the Royal Defence Corps. The weather had turned very cold and in the early hours of 29 November a patrol was sent out to see if there was any enemy activity: in No Man's Land they came across a large working party but there was also a large covering party in place so the patrol withdrew to the British lines. Before the expected German raid took place 68 Brigade was relieved and moved back to the camps in the rear. 12/DLI moved back to Montreal Camp and 13/DLI, after being relieved in the line by 10/DWR, entrained at Ypres for Vlamertinghe, where having detrained they marched to Winnipeg Camp.

The work of refitting and drawing new clothing soon commenced, as did the inspections and parades. The GOC 68 Brigade visited 12/DLI in

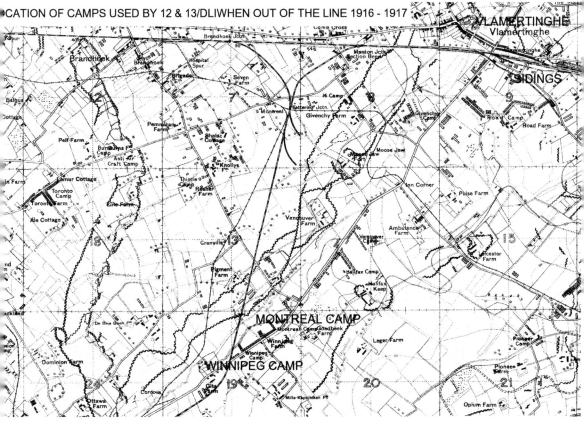

LOCATION OF CAMPS USED BY 12 & 13/DLI WHEN OUT OF THE LINE 1916 - 1917

Montreal Camp, and General Babington and the DAQMG 23rd Division, Major G. Hawes went round Winnipeg Camp when they visited 13/DLI. During the afternoon, football matches were arranged; the diarist of 12/DLI recording that the Sergeants' team beat the Officers' team 6–5. At night working parties were organised. The weather had turned colder when on 3 December Private Robert Wilson from Annfield Plain, serving with D Company 13/DLI was hit by a motor lorry and killed. The weather turned wet and this prevented much work being done on the camps as every night the men were out on working parties until very late.

On the afternoon of 7 December, led by the Battalion Bugle Band, 12/DLI marched to Vlamertinghe where they entrained and moved back to Ypres, where they relieved 8/KOYLI at Dormy House. Likewise at 1605 hours 13/DLI left Winnipeg Camp for Vlamertinghe. Here they too entrained and were taken up to Ypres, from where they made their way to the support battalion positions at the Bund where they took over from 11/Sherwood Foresters. The normal routine of battalions in the line began: in the front line 12/DLI tried to carry out wiring and took every opportunity to improve their positions, but this was made difficult by a very bright full moon each night. In support 13/DLI were supplying large working parties of over 200 men each night. On 11 December 10/NF took over the support positions and 13/DLI moved forward to Dormy House where they relieved 12/DLI. The following night Second Lieutenant George Hesleton, who had recently joined the battalion, claimed to have shot a German in the trenches opposite Cross Street, though there was no way of confirming this. The following morning Second Lieutenant Harold Buckell reported to Battalion Headquarters and was posted to A Company. He had landed in France as a Sergeant with 7/Dragoon Guards in the Secunderabad Cavalry Brigade in October 1914; promoted to Squadron Quartermaster Sergeant he had been selected for a commission and posted to 13/DLI. Later that day 32395 Private Samuel Sharp was wounded.

Then at 0900 hours on 14 December, 43423 Private Leonard Prince from Darlington of C Company 13/DLI was killed; another of those tragic accidents that seemed to happen so often. The enemy artillery kept the battalion positions under mortar fire and Lance Corporal Gowland and Private Wilson of B Company were wounded. The next morning between 0700 and 1000 hours the Germans heavily shelled the 11/NF on the right of 13/DLI and damaged Winnipeg Street and the trenches held by the Northumberland battalion. They started shelling again at 1600 hours, this time concentrating on the front line and the duckboard tracks that any supporting troops would have to use to come to the Fusiliers' aid. At 1645 hours 11/NF sent up an SOS flare as around forty German infantrymen launched a raid. The enemy managed to bomb a sap and a dugout before they retired, leaving three of their number dead in the British lines. The

German barrage caused three men in D Company 13/DLI to be wounded: 33288 Private Robert Mason, 36348 Private Robert Wilson and 46010 Private Thomas Littlewood. The last-named came from Shotton Colliery and had seen service at Gallipoli with 6/Green Howards prior to being transferred to the Durhams. Quickly evacuated, he survived the journey to No 17 Casualty Clearing Station at Remy Siding where the staff did their best for him, but sadly at 1100 hours the following morning he died from wounds to the abdomen and left thigh.

In support 12/DLI were providing the usual carrying and work parties and on 10 December they were joined by Major Robert Tyndall from 1/DLI in India, who took over command of the battalion. An Irishman from County Wexford, he had joined the regiment in 1896 and served as Signalling Officer with 1/DLI during the actions at Vaal Kranz and the Tugela Heights in South Africa, before being attached to the Staff during

the relief of Ladysmith. On 16 December they moved back up to the line and replaced 13/DLI at Dormy House. In the line 12/DLI placed A Company on the right and B Company on the left with C Company in support at Maple Copse and D Company in reserve at the Redan. During the relief they came under enemy fire and 32276 Private William Wilson from Shiney Row was killed in action. There is little activity reported in 12/DLI War Diary and it is not until 20 December that two men, one from A Company and one from C Company, are reported wounded during the shelling of the battalion positions by the German artillery. This caused Crab Crawl to be blocked and meant extra work for those in the line.

Major Robert Tyndall from 1/DLI in India, who took over command of 12/DLI.

When 13/DLI moved back to the support positions they took over the Hospice in Ypres. Here a Court of Inquiry was held into the accidental death of Private Prince, under the Presidency of Captain Joseph Downey: Second Lieutenants Cyril Chapman and John Young took the evidence from those men of C Company that were nearby when the accident occurred. The first witness was 43432 Private Albert Mole, an original Territorial who had landed with 50th Division in April 1915 and had been renumbered when posted to a service battalion. He stated:

In 60 Street off Vancouver Street [front-line trenches] *about 0945 hours on 14 December. I was standing two yards away from 43435 Private A Ramsdale who was cleaning his rifle. I looked round and saw that Private Ramsdale had his rifle in his hand, about three minutes later I heard a shot go off and Private Prince fell against my feet. There were about eight of us there at the time. A few minutes later CSM Woodruff came along and inspected Private Ramsdales rifle.*

The next witness was the NCO in charge of that section of the trench, 45948 Corporal John Holt who had originally enlisted in the Northumberland Fusiliers prior to being posted to 13/DLI. He added this statement:

In 60 Street off Vancouver Street at about 0945 hours on 14 December. I was in charge of a Lance Corporal and four men. I saw 43435 Private A Ramsdale pick up his rifle to clean it, take the magazine out and lay the rifle up against the side of the trench. Almost immediately I heard the report of a shot quite close and felt something graze my forehead and Private Prince fell to the bottom of the trench. A few minutes later CSM Woodruff came along. I saw him take up Private Ramsdale's rifle and eject an empty cartridge. Later I examined the rifle myself and found the mouth of the barrel black with powder smoke.

When I first saw the rifle it was resting with the butt on the trench boards. After I heard the shot I noticed the rifle still upright but resting with the butt on the earth but below the trench boards.

The next to give evidence was 15774 Company Sergeant-Major George Woodruff, who had this to say:

At about 0950 hours on 14 December I was sent for by the Company Stretcher Bearers to go to 60 Street. On my arrival I found Private Prince lying dead in the trench. I examined all the rifles in that part of the trench and found Private Ramsdale's rifle was leaning up against the side of the trench with the butt on the ground – not on the trench boards. I ejected an empty cartridge case from the breach. There was nothing in the breach of any other rifle. His magazine was lying on the parapet with four rounds in it.

Then Private Ramsdale volunteered to make a statement in his own defence, and he said:

At about 0800 hours on 14 December I came out of the bombing post at Lone Tree sap, my officer Second Lieutenant Heselton met us and told everybody to put a round in the breach. I had not been in the habit of having a round in the breach and I forgot to unload my rifle when I began to clean it.

The finding of the Court of Inquiry was forwarded to Brigade Headquarters and said:

It is my opinion that Private Prince was killed accidentally with a shot from Private Ramsdale's rifle. Private Ramsdale showed neglect in not withdrawing the live round from the breach. Private Prince was on duty at the time.

Dec 20 1916

Signed C E Walker Major

To this the Brigade Commander simply added: 'I concur.'

A further note was added to the documents which stated:

No 43433 Private A Ramsdale 13/DLI.

The above named was tried by FGCM on 23 December 1916 for Conduct

A large draft of junior officers reported to 13/DLI Headquarters and was posted to the various companies as follows: Second Lieutenant George W. Wood to A Company; Second Lieutenants Frank Smith and John Witherspoon to B Company; Thomas Murgatroyd to C Company; and Cecil Rollston, James Brady and William Watson to D Company. Apart from Frank Smith, the others were all commissioned from the ranks. John Witherspoon, who was born in County Durham, had enlisted into 31/Canadian Infantry at Calgary in November 1914; George Wood and Thomas Murgatroyd had served in France with 18/Royal Fusiliers; while James Brady and William Watson had landed on 14 November 1915 with the 21/Royal Fusiliers, one of the Public Schools Battalions. The remaining Subaltern Cecil Rollston was a Territorial from the 1/5 London Regiment. The weather was now very cold and on 20 December 13/DLI moved back to the line and relieved 12/DLI and that battalion moved back to the support positions at the Bund. 13/DLI meanwhile had its headquarters at Dormy House; A Company held Winnipeg Street with three platoons and the other platoon was at the Redan. B Company placed three platoons along the line from the junction of Cross Street and Vancouver Street to Crab Crawl with the fourth platoon in Sixty Street. C Company manned Cross Street with all its four platoons and D Company was located from Crab Crawl to St Peter's Street. During 21 December between 1030 and 1130 hours the Germans fired twenty whizz bangs onto the Zillebeke Road and then that evening at 2130 hours 13/DLI Headquarters at Dormy House came under shellfire; however, there were no casualties.

The next evening troops from 41st Division carried out a raid on the German lines; the resulting retaliation by the German gunners caused a number of casualties in B Company of 13/DLI. Three men, 32378 Private James Crawford from Sunderland, 36557 Private Septimus Jennings from Burnhopefield and 36562 Private Matthew Wilkins from Gateshead were killed; all three had enlisted under the Derby Scheme in December 1915 and after being called up were put on a draft from 3/DLI on 15 September. After a couple of weeks at 35/IBD they were posted to 13/DLI and joined the battalion in the Ypres Salient on 16 October. At the same time four men were wounded: 199 Lance Corporal Thomas Weatherald, a bantam, had originally enlisted into either 19 or 23/DLI, while 33255 Private George Spavin, a drayman from Brewery Cottages, West Auckland had arrived on the same draft as the three dead men. He was evacuated to No 3 Canadian Casualty Clearing Station where he died from multiple wounds to the right leg and thigh. The other two names in the Adjutant's Diary are unreadable.

On 23 December at 2145 hours 9/Green Howards relieved 12/DLI and at 2115 hours 8/Green Howards relieved 13/DLI. Both Durham battalions made their way back to the railhead at the Asylum and entrained for Vlamertinghe, where they detrained and marched to the hutted Montreal and Winnipeg camps. Here the usual cleaning-up and working parties began and they were joined by a draft from the Army Cyclist Corps, most of whom came from the East Lancashire Divisional Cyclists and the West Lancashire Divisional Cyclists who had been compulsorily transferred to the DLI. With the festive season upon them, arrangements were made for special meals for the men. At 0700 hours on Christmas Day the band of 8/KOYLI went round the camps playing Christmas carols and then at 0930 hours voluntary church services were held. At 1300 hours the Officers and Sergeants served Christmas dinner to the men; this consisted of pork, beef and trimmings with plum pudding and beer afterwards. That night the cinema was open free to all ranks. At 1900 hours the warrant officers and senior NCOs sat down to their meal and, best of all, all working parties were cancelled. During the day General Babington had visited the battalions. On Boxing Day the officers of both battalions met in a football match which 13/DLI won 3–2. Sport continued over the next few days: a boxing ring was erected in 12/DLI lines and a Brigade tug-o-war competition was won by 13/DLI, after which a Brigade boxing tournament was held although no winners were recorded. After various inspections and refitting it was time to return to the line. On 31 December 12/DLI moved first: at 1545 hours they entrained and moved up through Ypres to Halfway House where they took over from 8/KOYLI, the relief being complete by 2030 hours. They posted A Company in reserve, B Company in Leinster Street, C Company in the right front line and D Company in the left front line, with Battalion Headquarters at the Railway Cutting. They were followed at 1845 hours by 13/DLI who followed the same route and relieved 11/Sherwood Foresters in the Infantry Barracks in Ypres; they sent two platoons of B Company and two Lewis guns to man the positions known as Forts 1 and 2 at I.15.d.9.8.

So the year drew to its end. Both battalions had seen much hard fighting and had lost some gallant men who could hardly be replaced, but the coming year would bring still harder fighting for the Faithful Durhams.

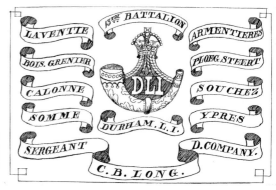

This hand-drawn card in the form of Battalion Battle Honours was sent by 14183 Sergeant Charles Long D Company 13/DLI to his girlfriend at Christmas 1916.

Chapter Seven

1917 January to June–
the Battle of Messines

SINCE 1915 PROPOSALS for an offensive in Flanders had been put forward at the various High Command conferences that took place. In November 1916 General Plumer had been asked to submit plans for a Flanders offensive that assumed there would be thirty to thirty-five divisions available for operations north of the River Lys. General Plumer's proposals were sent to GHQ on 12 December and followed more or less the plans that had been submitted earlier in 1916. The offensive would begin with a simultaneous attack to capture the Messines–Wytschaete Ridge, Hill 60 and the Pilckem Ridge. This was designed to deprive the Germans of their observation areas over the Ypres Salient. This blow would be delivered as a prelude to a further advance to the north-east of the Salient. Other preparations also began in early 1915 in the shape of mines driven under the enemy lines: these started off quite shallow at 15 feet or so below ground, but as time went on the Tunnelling Companies of

Tunnelling equipment store underground.

the Royal Engineers and 1/Canadian, 3/Canadian and 1/Australian Tunnelling Companies went deeper and deeper and constructed more mines until no less than twenty-four mines were laid under the German lines. However, it was not all offensive mining: much time was spent struggling against natural difficulties and the German miners with their counter-mines and camouflets. The experiences of the miners meant that equipment gradually improved, such as noiseless air and water pumps and better survey and listening equipment.

The Royal Engineers were not only working underground: they and the infantry were very busy constructing light railway lines and railheads to carry ammunition, engineer stores, supplies and entrainment and detrainment points for troops. They also worked on the roads and the important work of water supply was not neglected, with provision of pipelines to supply upwards of 200,000 gallons of water a day to the front line. However, these were all plans for the future. In the meantime, the battalions of 23rd Division carried on holding the Salient.

On 1 January 1917 12/DLI were positioned with two companies in the line on the right and C Company was in Zouave Wood, while on the left D Company was holding Birr Crossroads with a detachment forward at the Culvert. B Company was in support at Roslyn Street and A Company was in reserve at Halfway House. Battalion Headquarters was located much further back in a cutting near Hellfire Corner. During the morning Gordon House was heavily shelled but no casualties occurred. However, in the afternoon around 1600 hours the posts at the Culvert came under heavy shellfire and two Sergeants, 19752 Peter Mitchell MM from Front Street, Haswell and 15949 John Sinclair from Spennymoor, were killed and

A crater near Hellfire Corner.

a stretcher-bearer, 19067 Private John Tiplady from West Pelton who was going to their aid, was caught in the enemy fire and killed. Another two men were wounded and it states in the Battalion War Diary: 'otherwise it was a quiet day'. The next three days remained quiet and on the evening of 4 January 13/DLI took over the front-line positions with 12/DLI returning to the Infantry Barracks in Ypres. When 13/DLI took over they occupied more or less the same positions but Battalion Headquarters was moved forward from Hellfire Corner to Halfway House. The next day there was a great deal of enemy shelling and four whizz bangs fell on Battalion Headquarters. The enemy shelled Ypres all day and it was reported that the Yorkshire Battalions of 69 Brigade which contained a large number of Durham miners had a great number of casualties. In 13/DLI C Company, which was holding the Culvert, had only one man wounded: 15888 Private Mark Franklin.

It rained the following afternoon, but the weather got better on 7 January and this allowed a great deal of activity by aircraft over the front line: at 1145 hours the fighters wheeled above the watching Durhams and as one of the enemy planes dived down on a British plane, another British fighter swept down and drove the enemy plane off. Then at 1215 hours the German anti-aircraft gunners scored a direct hit on a British machine and it fell in flames. The rest of the day was quiet but the following morning the enemy shelled the Culvert and Leinster Street. Then in the late afternoon over 200 enemy shells fell on the area of Gordon House but no casualties were recorded. At 2045 hours the relief of 13/DLI by 12/DLI was complete and 13/DLI moved back to the Infantry Barracks in Ypres.

12/DLI reported that in the front-line area the next two days were especially quiet but that a lot of shells were going in the direction of Ypres. It was here that 45975 Private William McNay, a Wingate man serving with A Company 13/DLI was badly wounded by an incoming shell: he was hit in the left arm, left thigh and buttock. He had originally enlisted into the Green Howards and been posted to their 11(Reserve) Battalion: sent to join 6/Green Howards, his draft was diverted and on 20 July 1916 he was posted to 13/DLI. He was given first aid and evacuated to No 17 Casualty Clearing Station at Remy Siding where on 11 January he died from his wounds. The War Diary of 12/DLI sheds little light on the battalions' activities during this tour, except that on 12 January 13/DLI returned to the line and 12/DLI went back to the Infantry Barracks in Ypres. While they were out of the line 13/DLI had been joined by four new officers. Second Lieutenant Ernest Davis had been out in France since 24 January 1915 with the Queen's Westminster Rifles: selected for a commission, he was commissioned into the Special Reserve Durham Light Infantry on 16 November 1916 and on joining the battalion he was posted to A Company. Lieutenants Henry Holdsworth and Hedley Stewart were both posted to C Company and the fourth man, Lieutenant Herbert Pryse, was sent to D Company. At some stage the battalion must have received a large draft of men: no mention is made of their arrival, but at 1430 hours on 10 January the War Diary records that the Brigade Commander inspected the new draft. It was snowing when 13/DLI went back up the line and took over the same positions from 12/DLI. This time the dispositions were Headquarters at Halfway House; D Company right front; B Company left front; C Company, three platoons in Leinster Street, one platoon in Roslyn Street; A Company, three platoons at Halfway House and one platoon at Regent Street.

The next day was quiet, but on 14 January there was thick fog which allowed the battalion to do a great deal of salvage work and to repair the wire in front of the line and between the front line and the support line. Under cover of this fog, Second Lieutenant F. Hall and Sergeant Harry Craddock went out on a reconnaissance patrol to a position known as Forester Lane, but found no signs of the enemy. Using the information gathered on this patrol, the battalion planned an offensive patrol with two Lewis guns to go out on 15 January to kill any enemy working parties encountered. However, the fog wasn't as thick and the planned operation was cancelled. In the early evening of 16 January 12/DLI was relieved by 10/DWR and moved to Ypres railway station where they entrained for Vlamertinghe; here they detrained and marched to Montreal Camp.

13/DLI were not relieved until 2150 hours by 9/Green Howards and as they marched to the railway station it came under heavy fire. The result of this enemy fire was that the rails were badly damaged and this caused the cancellation of the train. This meant the battalion had to move on foot to Winnipeg Camp where they eventually arrived at 0200 hours on 17 January. During the day two Second Lieutenants reported for duty: Moses Miller and Archibald Hamilton had both been commissioned into the Highland Light Infantry but on arrival in France had been posted to 13/DLI. With snow falling heavily, little training could be carried out but the usual working parties had to carry on. The Commanding Officer and Adjutant of 12/DLI and the Commanding Officer and second in command of 13/DLI went and reconnoitred the GHQ line and met with the Brigade Commander for a conference relating to the communication between infantry and aircraft during an attack. The next day both battalions paraded and practised the attack and various methods of communicating with aircraft. Lamps and groundsheets were tried during the advance and flares were lit in the trenches when they had been consolidated. In the meantime the Adjutant of 13/DLI had visited the reinforcement camp and inspected a draft of 100 new arrivals: thirty of them were deemed to need additional musketry training and they were sent to the Divisional Musketry School. On 23 January Second Lieutenant Oswald Williams reported to Battalion Headquarters: returning to France after being wounded with 1/5/DLI he only spent three weeks with

13/DLI before being sent back to 1/5/DLI. The time had now arrived for 68 Brigade to go back into the line; 12/DLI left Winnipeg Camp and by 0100 hours on 25 January had taken over the front line in the right brigade sector from 9/Y&L. 13/DLI left Montreal Camp at 1810 hours and moved to the Bund where they took over positions from 11/Sherwood Foresters. That day the battalions were stood to, expecting a gas attack as the enemy was reported to be using gas against the brigade north of the Menin Road. During the day 21599 CQMS Roy Rudd of D Company was wounded.

On 27 January it was the Kaiser's birthday and 12/DLI celebrated by shelling the German front lines with their trench mortars. The War Diary described the enemy response as feeble; however, one man of the battalion was wounded during the counter-barrage. The next morning was quiet but at 1500 hours Zillebeke was heavily shelled; then that evening 13/DLI returned to the line, the handover being complete by 2000 hours. 12/DLI changed the dispositions of its companies in support: A Company went to the Hospice in Ypres, B Company to Kruisstraat, C Company to the Bund and D Company occupied the Cavalry Barracks in Ypres with Battalion Headquarters at the Bund. From these locations they spent the next three days providing working parties. When 13/DLI took over they located Battalion Headquarters in Rudkin House and the Companies held the trenches in front of Armargh Wood as follows: on the right A Company held I.30 1, 2 and 3; C Company in the centre manned I.30 4, 5 and 6; on the left B Company were holding I.30, 7, 8 and 9; D Company was in support in Halifax Street. On 29 January a few shells fell near Battalion Headquarters and in C Company lines 534 Private Cuthbert Colman was evacuated with a self-inflicted wound; his number indicates that he originally enlisted in either 19 or 22/DLI. The next morning just before dawn the battalion 'Stood To' as usual, awaiting any potential enemy attack. Nothing materialised and as the early morning sun rose over the section of the line held by B Company, another of those wasteful and unnecessary accidents occurred. As the order to 'Stand Down' was given, 52845 Lance Corporal Benjamin Casey gave the men in his bay the order to clean their rifles. 19982 Private Constantine O'Rourke from West Hartlepool, who had just been awarded the Military Medal, took his rifle and sat down on the fire step to clean it. Suddenly a shot rang out and he was hit in the thigh. The stretcher-bearers were sent for and he was given first aid and taken to the Regimental Aid Post and from there evacuated to No 2 Canadian Casualty Clearing Station. As was normal in these circumstances, a Court of Inquiry was held and a number of witnesses were called to give evidence. The first to make a statement was 52944 Sergeant James Ryding, who had been transferred to the Durham Light Infantry from the Army Cyclist Corps. He said:

I was visiting the sentries at the time and when I came into the bay where Private O'Rourke was wounded, I heard Lance Corporal Casey tell the men to get their rifles cleaned. As soon as Private Porteous picked up his rifle the shot was fired wounding Private O'Rourke. I immediately went for the stretcher bearers and informed the nearest officer in the trench as to what had happened.

The next to be questioned was Second Lieutenant Frederick Hall, who stated:

I was in the front trench at 'Stand down' and heard a shot fired, I proceeded along the trench and was met by Sergeant Kerr [16542 Sgt Thomas Kerr MM], who informed me that Private O'Rourke had been shot. I immediately went to the scene and found that Private O'Rouke had been shot in the left thigh. I then asked who had fired the shot in the presence of Sergeant Kerr, Private Porteous said the shot was fired from his rifle. I then examined his rifle and found four live rounds in the magazine and one empty case in the breech.

The next called to make a statement was Second Lieutenant C.F. [*sic* Oswald J.] Williams, who had only joined the company seven days earlier. He added:

I was in the front trench at 'Stand Down' when I heard a shot fired. A minute or two afterwards Sergeant Ryding came up and told me that a man had been shot. I at once proceeded along the trench and found Private O'Rourke being dressed by the stretcher bearers. Mr Hall was on the spot and he took all the necessary actions.

The fourth witness was Lance Corporal Benjamin Casey, the NCO in charge of the fire bay. He had this to say:

After 'Stand Down' was given on the morning of 30 January, I told Private Porteous to clean his rifle. Almost as soon as he picked up his rifle the shot was discharged and I heard Private O'Rourke cry out that he was hit. I immediately took the rifle from Private Porteous who said that he had not loaded the rifle. I then went for the stretcher bearers and Sergeant Ryding who was present at the time reported the matter to the nearest officer in the trench.

The last man to speak was 27256 Private Francis Porteous: a Gateshead man, he had enlisted in May 1915 and joined the Regimental Depot in June. He had spent the remainder of the year training in England and was eventually sent out to France on 2 January 1916. From the Infantry Base Depot he was put on a draft to 2/DLI. He had barely arrived in the battalion when on 12 February he was evacuated to the Field Ambulance sick. Sent down to the base on 30 March, he was on a hospital ship on his way back to England. On 17 January 1917 he was back in France and was part of the draft that had recently joined 13/DLI. He made the following statement:

After 'Stand Down' was given on the morning of 30 January Lance Corporal Casey gave the order to clean rifles. I picked up my rifle and started to clean it. When I came to the trigger guard I pulled the trigger when a shot was discharged which hit Private O'Rourke who was sitting on the fire step a few yards away. I immediately put the rifle down and went to the assistance of the wounded man. I did not know the rifle was loaded.

Private Porteous was placed under close arrest and warned for a Field General Court Martial. This took place on 17 February when the battalion was out of the line. He was sentenced to twenty-eight days' Field Punishment Number 1 and returned to duty. He would be killed in action in June 1917.

After the incident in B Company, the enemy shelled the trenches around I.30.6 held by C Company and during this barrage 45969 Private John Kirk from Helperby, North Yorkshire, one of the draft who had served at Gallipoli with 6/Green Howards, was wounded. When fit again he was posted to 18/DLI and then to 15/DLI with whom he was killed in action in 1918. The last day of the month brought more shelling and more casualties: Captain Edward Gray was wounded but remained at duty; in C Company 52906 Private Harry Nixon, a reinforcement from the Manchester Regiment, was killed; and 43715 Private J. Lintern and 19988 Private William Whitelock were both wounded. Later when shells fell on B Company, 52966 Private John Aspinall was also wounded.

February started in much the same way as the previous month's end. At 0500 hours on 1 February a very heavy bombardment was opened by the enemy and the battalion holding the sector north of the Menin Road sent up SOS flares; eventually the firing died down and the remainder of the day was spent quietly. At 1730 hours 12/DLI left the reserve positions and moved up to the front line, where by 2100 hours they had taken over from 13/DLI. Over the next three days the enemy shelling continued and on 2 February 12/DLI had 22/953 Private Antonio Geraldie from West Hartlepool killed in action. Left behind with 16/DLI when 22/DLI left for France, he had joined 12/DLI on 8 August 1916 and was slightly wounded in September but rejoined when fit. From the same battalion 31646 Private Fred Hugill, a farm labourer from Eastgate in Weardale, was evacuated to 70 Field Ambulance with acute bronchitis. He was taken to Number 10 Casualty Clearing Station at Remy Siding, but despite the attention of the nurses he died on 11 February. Out of the line 13/DLI provided the usual working parties in very cold weather and at 1730 hours on 5 February they moved off to take over from 12/DLI again. This time Battalion Headquarters moved into Rudkin House and placed B Company on the left holding I.30. 7, 8 and 9; the centre trenches I.30. 4, 5 and 6 were held by C Company; while the sector on the right, trenches I.30. 1, 2 and 3 were manned by D Company. A Company were in support in Halifax Street and the Regimental Aid Post was in Zillebeke. By 2015 hours the relief was complete and 12/DLI were on their way back to the support positions around Maple Copse with Battalion Headquarters at the Bund. Throughout 6 February there was sporadic shelling until at 1440 hours the

British Corps Artillery bombarded the enemy lines for one hour and twenty-five minutes; this was followed at 1800 hours by a barrage on the enemy front line by the 23rd Divisional Artillery which lasted for ten minutes. This brought a quick retaliation from the German trench mortars and all along the positions held by 13/DLI bombs fell on the line. These caused a few casualties: in D Company 52930 Lance Corporal Harry Foxcroft, one of the reinforcements from the draft of West Lancashire Divisional Cyclists, was killed and 15423 Private Thomas Slowther and 46017 Private Robert Johnson were both wounded. In C Company 43415 Private John Wright was wounded, while in B Company 22604 Private John Scaife was also wounded; he was evacuated to 70 Field Ambulance where he died from his wounds the following day. The next few days were much the same with some British shells falling short and landing among the trench mortar battery.

On the night of 9 February 69 Brigade came up and took over the sector held by 68 Brigade, in the support positions 11/West Yorkshire Regt took over from 12/DLI, who moved on foot to Montreal Camp. In the line 13/DLI handed over to 8/Green Howards and then marched back to Winnipeg Camp. As soon as they were settled down both battalions began

Behind the Salient.

the process of refitting and the Commanding Officers held kit inspections. In 12/DLI the Commanding Officer Lieutenant-Colonel W.W. MacGregor was ordered to report to the War Office and Major Robert Tyndall was promoted to take command of the battalion. In 13/DLI the Commanding Officer Lieutenant-Colonel Cecil E. Walker went on a course for COs and Captain Frederick Gray assumed temporary command of the battalion. 12/DLI began reforming and reorganising the platoons, referring to them as 'new fighting platoons'. On 12 February Lieutenant-Colonel Tyndall inspected all the companies and 'new fighting platoons' in full marching order. However, next day word was received from Brigade that the 'new fighting platoons' were abolished and so the battalion reverted to its original four-company organisation. The opportunity was taken by both battalions to use the Divisional baths in Poperinghe and daily parties of men were sent to bathe and get a change of underclothing; in the afternoons time was spent in inter-company football matches. Several General Officers found time to visit the battalions and the training of additional Lewis-gunners took place. The signallers carried out a scheme working with aeroplanes in preparation for the coming offensive.

After eight days out of the line 68 Brigade began moving back towards the front. On the night of 17 February 12/DLI began taking over the right subsector of the left brigade on the front held by 23rd Division where they relieved 8/KOYLI, the relief being completed by 0515 hours on 18 February. Battalion Headquarters were located at the Tuileries just north of Zillebeke. 13/DLI left Winnipeg Camp at 1730 hours on 17 February and moved on foot to the barracks in Ypres where they took over from 8/York & Lancaster Regt. In the early hours of 18 February the British artillery opened up a bombardment on the German lines which lasted for one and a half hours, then later that day the barracks came under shellfire. The enemy followed this in the evening of 19 February by using gas shells which made life uncomfortable for those there. In the front line 12/DLI were working very hard, with D Company wiring from Vince Street to Maple Copse. In the other Companies the men not actually in the line were employed in salvaging as much equipment as they could. February 20 was a very misty day during which some good work was done: at 1700 hours a very heavy preparatory bombardment took place on the right of 12/DLI where troops of the 41st Division were about to carry out a raid on the German trenches. The enemy counter-barrage fell on the front and support lines manned by 12/DLI, the only reported casualty being Captain David Chambers. A 40-year-old mining engineer, he had been commissioned into 16/DLI in September 1914, then in November 1915 he was attached to the Royal Engineers and went out to Gallipoli; at the end of that campaign he rejoined 16/DLI and was sent out to join 12/DLI in September 1916. The weather remained quite misty which allowed the salvage work to continue and also the wiring work on Vince Street before

13/DLI returned to take over this section of the front line.

By 2200 hours on 22 February 12/DLI had handed over to 13/DLI and moved back to the barracks in Ypres where they provided working parties for the next four days. When 13/DLI took over, they too had Battalion Headquarters in the Tuileries; A Company manned the front line in Warrington Avenue; B Company were behind them with one platoon in Fort Street, one platoon in Lovers Walk and the other two platoons in Maple Street. C Company were further behind in Wellington Crescent and D Company were in reserve at Ritz Street, with the battalion aid post in Zillebeke; by 2230 hours the relief was complete and the battalion settled down for the night. The next day Yeomanry Post and Wellington Crescent both received the attention of the German gunners, but despite some damage there were no casualties. The next day was quiet: 41st Division carried out another raid but little happened on the 23rd Division front. On 25 February 13/DLI sent an officers' patrol of one officer and two Other Ranks out into No Man's Land; they remained out for over an hour but neither saw nor heard any evidence of enemy activity. Whether from shelling or small-arms fire, during the day 54156 Private Frank Loat was wounded. On 26 February a shell actually hit Battalion Headquarters and later Warrington Avenue was again shelled. Two men, 52931 Private Roy Hurst and 46057 Private Norman Hall, were wounded. Later that evening they were relieved by 17/Sherwood Foresters and then moved back to D Camp west of Elverdinghe. At the same time 12/DLI were relieved by 16/Rifle Brigade and moved back to P Camp in the same area. During the day the news was received that Private Norman Hall, although he had made it to Number 17 Casualty Clearing Station at Remy Siding, had died from wounds to the abdomen. Originally a Northumberland Fusilier, he had arrived in France on a draft to the Tyneside Scottish but had wound up in 13/DLI.

Captain David Chambers, a 40-year-old mining engineer. He had been commissioned into 16/DLI in September 1914 and was killed in action with 12/DLI on 20 February 1917.

The Brigade moved even further back. 12/DLI moving via Houtkerque and Zegerscappel arrived at Merkeghem at 1530 hours on 1 March where they described the billets as 'not very good', but the march discipline had been very good and not one man had fallen out. The same day 13/DLI, having moved from D Camp to Y Camp, marched to Bollezeele where they took over billets from 10/DWR; they reported that nineteen men had fallen out on the march but all had rejoined. Both battalions immediately started cleaning up and refitting, and once that was done training started: platoon drill, handling arms, bayonet exercises and bomb-throwing. 12/DLI reported that all the employed men, that is the cooks, clerks, transport and stores personnel paraded under the second-in-command and received one hour's drill; they also reported the arrival of a small draft of twenty-one Other Ranks, recording that they were not very good and their equipment was in a very bad state. Lewis-gunners and signallers paraded under their respective officers and carried out specialist training, and musketry practice took place on a nearby range. On 4 March another small draft of twenty-three men joined 12/DLI along with Second Lieutenants John Rasche and Harold Richardson. 13/DLI were also reporting officer reinforcements: Lieutenant Herbert Markham was posted to D Company when he rejoined after recovering from the wounds he had received at Le Sars, and Second Lieutenant John P. Carrol was posted to C Company but was immediately sent on a signalling officers' course. Second Lieutenant Alexander Dunn reported to 12/DLI on 7 March. The section training continued but the cold weather and snow hampered things: the signallers were supposed to have another exercise communicating with aircraft, but owing to the mist it had to be cancelled.

On 13 March Second Lieutenant Frederick Youens joined 13/DLI and was posted to C Company. In 12/DLI both musketry and bombing practice was carried out on the ranges and Second Lieutenant Michael O'Brien was accidentally wounded in an accident on the bombing range. By the middle of March both battalions were practising Company attack in artillery formation, in accordance with instructions issued by General Headquarters. They had now been out of the line for over two weeks and it was time to start moving back.

At 0830 hours on 19 March, a very wet day, 13/DLI paraded in the Town Square at Bollezeele and at 0845 hours marched off bound for Houtkerque where they arrived at 1430 hours. Likewise 12/DLI marched to Herzeele where they were established in billets by 1400 hours. The next day's march took 12/DLI to Z Camp near Poperinghe where they arrived at 1230 hours, while 13/DLI only had a short move when they left Houtkerque at 1000 hours and had arrived at L Camp by 1140 hours. The next day they moved again, this time to E Camp where they arrived at 1200 hours: here they formed large working parties of up to 350 men each night and this work continued until the end of the month. At 0800 hours on 21 March the Commanding Officer and Company Commanders of 12/DLI moved forward to reconnoitre L Lines and at 1230 hours they were followed by the rest of the battalion. By 2100 hours the relief of 17/Royal Welsh Fusiliers was complete and 12/DLI were placed under the tactical command of the GOC 115 Infantry Brigade. They manned the defences in L Lines until relieved by 10/NF on 28 March when the battalion moved back to D Camp. Here more training was undertaken and a large number of men

Captain Samuel Rowlandson who had already been to the front with 2/DLI and wounded in January 1915 joined 12/DLI in March 1917 but left the battalion at the end of May and was posted to 1 Garrison Battalion NF in Malta.

were attached to the Royal Engineers who set them to work in Elverdinghe burying signal cables. One party of men was attached to Brigade Headquarters for the purpose of erecting tents and where possible training continued, but this was hampered by snow.

13/DLI spent the first week of April doing the same type of work as 12/DLI and then on 5 April an advance party under the command of Captain Edward Borrow set off to take over billets near the village of Millam where a training area had been established. Likewise 12/DLI moved to Bollezeele. After the usual cleaning-up and refitting, both battalions started training in attacking trenches in the mornings and in the afternoons the Brigade took part in various sporting activities. In the final of the 68 Brigade competition 10/NF beat 12/DLI by 2 goals to 1 and also took the honours in the Brigade cross-country race. 13/DLI won the rugby, and there was also a Brigade Transport competition where the transport sections of the Brigade were judged on the condition and turnout of the wagons and animals. 13/DLI won the Single Harness contest and came second in the pack animal competition. On the military training front they practised the rapid consolidation and wiring of a captured trench, all signs of a coming offensive. Down on the coast at 35 Infantry Base Depot another draft was preparing to leave for the front. This one was destined for 13/DLI and among them was a schoolteacher from Framwellgate Moor in Durham, 36054 Private William Innes; he kept a small diary and recorded a few observations:

36054 Private William Innes, a schoolteacher from Framwellgate Moor in Durham City, joined 13/DLI in April 1917.

Wed 11 Apr 1917

Parade 0615 hours for station, Leave Etaples about 1000 hours & land at Poperinghe at 2200 hours and stay at reinforcement camp.

Thur 12 Apr 1917

Left Poperinghe and changed at Hazebrouke for Esqubecq, then march to Millam, where our battalion is in billets.

Fri 13 Apr 1917

Free all day, lie in stables and then had a stroll with Bob Atkinson.

The day that the draft arrived was the last day of training and that evening a number of men from A Company 13/DLI left their billets and made their way across the canal to the far bank where there were a couple of estaminets and in one, the 'Cappellebrouk', they were served spirits, against orders. At about 2000 hours they were making their way back to the billets when one man, 22394 Private John Storey from Pallion in Sunderland, decided he was going for a swim in the canal. He had been at Loos with 15/DLI where he had been gassed and evacuated back to England. After some time with 16/DLI at Rugeley, he had been put on a draft to France and was posted to 13/DLI.

214

Private Storey swam across and turned round to swim back, but about midway he disappeared and did not surface. Immediately 21812 Private Frank Hall stripped off and went in to get him; after several attempts he reached Private Storey who was eventually got out by the use of a boat-hook and a boat.

When the battalion was in Ypres a few days later the usual Court of Inquiry was held. The president was Second Lieutenant Harold Buckell and the members were Second Lieutenants John Young and Thomas Murgatroyd. They took evidence from three witnesses, all members of A Company. The first called was 17356 Private Tom Garbutt from West Hartlepool who had this to say:

At about 1945 hours on 13 April I was returning to billets with Private Snowdon. After crossing the canal on the way to Millam we heard shouting on the bank we had just left. On looking round I saw Private Storey struggeling with Private Haw; after a few moments he broke free and jumped into the canal, attempted to swim across. Seeing Private Storey in difficulties Private Hall jumped in and endeavoured to reach Private Storey who sank before he was able to reach him. We had been in an Estaminet from about 1815 hours until 1945hours. During this time Private Storey frequently expressed a desire for a swim. Private Storey had been drinking rather freely.

The next man to make a statement was 18647 Private William Haw, the man who had tried to stop John Storey from carrying out his reckless act. He said:

On the night of 13April I was in the company of Private Storey. On reaching the canal on our way back to billets at Millam at about 1945 hours Private Storey who had been drinking rather freely, commenced to undress stating that he was going to swim. I endeavoured to prevent him entering the water but failed. In company with Private Hall who had been assisting me to restrain Private Storey I at once crossed the canal by the ferry.

The third man to speak was 21812 Private Frank Hall who added this statement:

On the night of 13 April while returning to my billet I tried to prevent Private Storey from entering the canal. Finding it useless I crossed the canal in the ferry. On reaching the opposite bank I noticed Private Storey in difficulties. I immediately stripped off and entered the water. Private Storey disappeared before I could reach him so I at once dived under to recover the body. Whilst under water I saw the body of Private Storey but was unable to grasp it owing to the strong current which carried the body towards the ferry. A Frenchman who was now in the ferry recovered the body which was brought to the bank. I attempted artificial respiration for some time but without success.

The finding of the Court was that Private Storey had drowned through being drunk and that no blame could be attached to anyone else. The

Commanding Officer Lieutenant-Colonel Cecil Walker also noted that: 'It is apparently very easy for British soldiers to obtain spirits, especially Rum and Cognac in the vicinity of Millam, more especially on the far side of the canal.' He further went on to recommend that 'the following estaminets be placed out of bounds to all troops for selling whisky, Rum and Cognac to soldiers: Mme Vve Devrce, Callelle-brouk, Mme Duhamel, A la Betterave.'

The next morning 13/DLI left Millam and proceeded on foot to Esquelbecq where they entrained at 1000 hours; arriving at Poperinghe, they alighted and moved to a camp in Brandhoek. 12/DLI followed the same route and on arrival in their camp at Brandhoek immediately sent a billeting party forward to take over the Infantry Barracks in Ypres. On 15 April it rained all day; seventy-five men were sent from 12/DLI to assist one of the Royal Engineer Tunnelling Companies at Reninghelst and another forty-eight were sent to work for the Town Major in Ypres. At 1945 hours the rest of the battalion left Brandhoek and moved up to Ypres but owing to congestion it took until after midnight for the battalion to complete the relief. Battalion Headquarters was established in the Ramparts and all four companies in the barracks. Over the next three days large working parties were supplied to the Australian Tunnelling Company working under the front line. In the meantime at 2000 hours on 15 April 13/DLI had moved from Brandhoek straight through Ypres and up to the front line where by 0200 hours on 16 April, they had taken over from 14/Hampshire Regiment. Battalion Headquarters was once again in Zillebeke, two platoons of A Company held St Peter's Street to Cross Street and the other two platoons were in Winnipeg Street. C Company placed one platoon

Poperinghe.

in Cross Street, two platoons in Vancouver Street and one platoon in Winnipeg Street. D Company placed one platoon in Sixtieth Street, one platoon in Fort Street, one platoon in Winnipeg Street and one platoon in reserve in Hill Street. B Company was in reserve with two platoons in dugouts in Crab Crawl and two platoons in Winnipeg Street and the Regimental Aid Post was located in Stafford Street. This tour in the line was quite uneventful: the enemy were quiet during the day but at night their machine-gunners and snipers were active. On 16 April 28856 Private Cornelius Howley from Byker in Newcastle who was serving in B Company must have come to the end of his tether. He took his rifle and put a bullet through his right hand. He was placed under close arrest and after treatment he was tried by Field General Court Martial and was awarded forty-two days' Field Punishment Number 1. The wound was so bad that he was evacuated to England and on 11 August 1917 was discharged as no longer fit for war service. The same day in the sector held by D Company one of the draft of cyclists, 52914 Private John Reed from Milnrow near Rochdale, was accidently wounded in the leg. The next day 22000 Private Frederick Clark, another Sunderland man was wounded. Then in the evening of 19 April, 12/DLI moved up and took over, 13/DLI moving back to the Infantry Barracks vacated by 12/DLI. This period in the line was recorded in his diary by 36054 Private William Innes:

Sun 15 Apr

Go to Church parade in morning, Go up line at night to Winnipeg Street, on a bombing post all night.

Mon 16 Apr – Wed 18 Apr

Normal trench routine all day – sandbagging at night.

Thur 19 Apr

Go back to Ypres barracks at night.

12/DLI only sent 500 men into the line on this occasion. Leaving one platoon from each company behind, they placed A Company with two platoons in Vancouver Street and one platoon in Winnipeg Street, B Company had two platoons in Crab Crawl and one platoon in Winnipeg Street. C Company manned Cross Street, Vancouver Street and Sixtieth Street with one platoon in each trench, while D Company placed one platoon in Hill Street and two platoons in Fort Street. Each night during this tour the battalion sent patrols out into No Man's Land but they all returned with nothing to report and there was no enemy activity. The shelling at this time was passing over the front line and hitting Ypres, where on 20 April 13/DLI had 24627 Private Robert Parker from Barnard Castle killed in action on a working party. By midnight on St George's Day, 23 April, 13 DLI had returned to the line and 12/DLI were back in Ypres. As usual, the Adjutant of 13/DLI recorded much more in his notebook than in the official War Diary: on 22 April Second Lieutenant James Brady was wounded in the neck by a piece of shrapnel from an anti-aircraft shell, and on the same night 54199 Private Arthur Rowley was wounded in the right knee by a stray rifle bullet while on a working party. He also recorded the actual dispositions of each platoon, and notable in the entry at this time was that B and C Company Headquarters with three Lewis-gun teams were recorded as being in 'Deep Dugouts' in Crab Crawl, one platoon of B Company was still attached to the Australian Tunnelling Company, and 11994 Private Thomas Curry from Newcastle, attached to 68/LTMB was killed in action. He had enlisted into 10/DLI in 1914 but had been sent to work on munitions at Armstrongs Works in Elswick, Newcastle. He had blotted his copybook by using foul and abusive language to his foreman and the management applied to the Army to have him returned to 3/DLI at South Shields. After a period of absence he was eventually put on a draft and joined 13/DLI in Flanders.

The next day there was an aerial dogfight over the Zillebeke sector and one British machine fell in flames and crashed near the Bund. The pilot and observer, although burned, were pulled alive from the wreckage. Later two other machines were seen to collide and fall together behind Bodmin Copse. At 0400 hours on 25 April the British artillery opened a heavy barrage on Hill 60 which continued all day: the Germans replied by shelling Battalion Headquarters in Zillebeke and the Tuileries with 4.2 and 5.9 howitzers. During the day enemy aircraft flew low over the battalion positions and the Lewis-gunners put up a stout defence. During the day 20225 Sergeant Philip Lynch and 52867 Private Thomas Carlin were wounded. The barrage on the Hill 60 sector continued at 1600 hours the next day, to which the enemy replied with a counter-barrage about twenty minutes later.

Out at rest 12/DLI started sending parties of officers, four or five at a time, to the Hill 60 sector to learn the positions of dumps, communication trenches and dugouts; they visited both the right and centre sectors that they would eventually take over. This was the beginning of the build-up to the coming offensive. Overhead, the Royal Flying Corps was very active in trying to keep the German Air Force away from the lines and seeing what was going on. The enemy were shelling Shrapnel Corner and Ypres: this forced part of 12/DLI to leave the barracks and move into dugouts in the Ramparts. On 27 April they moved back into the front line taking over from 13/DLI again; this time additional trenches on the battalion's left were taken over. A Company held the right front line, Vancouver Street from the junction of St Peter's Street to Cross Street; B Company placed one platoon in Winnipeg Street, one platoon in Hill Street and a third platoon in Fort Street. C Company had one platoon in Hill 60 Street, one platoon in Cross Street and one platoon in support in Winnipeg Street, while D Company had one platoon in Lovers Walk and two platoons in Warrington Avenue. Each company had detached one platoon to work with the Tunnelling Companies. The battalion had three men wounded the next morning when B Company Headquarters in Vigo Street was shelled.

The next day was very fine, during which a party of officers and NCOs from 9/Cheshire Regiment arrived to look round the positions they were to take over in a couple of days' time. The activity in the air continued and a British machine was hit and the observer and pilot were both wounded; the machine fell to earth and crashed behind Lovers Lane. Immediately the enemy gunners opened a heavy fire on the wreckage. Two stretcher-bearers from D Company, 19850 Private Charles Olsen and 18011 Private Charles Woodward, went out under fire; they were accompanied by Sergeant Gee and the Battalion Medical Officer, Captain Scott RAMC. The pilot had broken his leg during the crash and Private Olsen stayed out with him for over two hours and three times crossed the heavily-shelled ground to get water for the pilot. Despite the heavy shelling and some sniper fire, both the pilot and observer were eventually brought to safety. During the shelling 15419 Private Arthur Wright from Castleford was killed in action.

39861 Private Joe Nicholson joined 12/DLI from 17/DLI in the spring of 1917.

On the last day of the month 58 Brigade of 19th (Western) Division started to take over from 68 Brigade. 12/DLI was relieved by 9/Cheshire Regiment and 13/DLI was relieved by 6/Wiltshire Regiment. At 0730 hours that morning an advance party under the command of Second Lieutenant Davies left 13/DLI to take over billets in the Steenvoorde area. A similar party from 12/DLI moved to the same area by motor transport. At 1045 hours 13/DLI formed up by platoons and moved off through Vlamertinghe to where the battalion cookers were formed up. The battalion fell out on the side of the road and were fed, after which they carried on to Poperinghe and entrained. A short ride in the train took them to the Steenvoorde area where they were met by the billeting party and moved into the allotted accommodation. 12/DLI were relieved in the early hours of 1 May and marched from the front line to Ypres Sidings where they arrived at 0335 hours; here they entrained and were taken to the Steenvoorde area. Having taken over their billets, the remainder of the day was free and the battalion rested.

The billets were cleaned up and the men were marched to the baths, clean clothing was issued and refitting commenced. The next day at 1530 hours General Babington inspected 13/DLI and an hour later he moved on to where 12/DLI were drawn up in a field and inspected that battalion too. Training commenced: physical training and the training of the battalion specialists; Lewis-gunners, signallers, snipers and scouts paraded under their own officers; the platoons paraded under the Company Commanders. They began practising open warfare, establishing outposts and rapid wiring, also attacking strongpoints and defended localities. Platoon Commanders were set tasks in which they had to work out the best way to take a position with the men at their disposal, and their actions and instructions were then given critical feedback.

On 7 May a party of officers, signallers and runners took part in an exercise involving the contact of aeroplanes. During the time on the training area the Brigade ran the usual sporting competitions: 13/DLI won the tug-of-war but lost out to 11/NF in the rugby; in the boxing, Private Wilson of 13/DLI took the honours in the heavyweight final. The last day of training saw the whole brigade carry out an attack which included both 68/MG Company and 69/LTMB. They were back in billets by 1400 hours, packing up and getting ready to move.

At 0930 hours on 9 May 13/DLI set off on foot from Steenvorde and marched to the Scottish Lines south of Brandhoek where they took over the camp from 7/South Lancashire Regiment at 1300 hours. Likewise 12/DLI left their billets and marched to Montreal Camp where they arrived at 1445 hours: this was described as 'very hot and trying for the men'. Shortly after they arrived word was received that 12/DLI were to take over the Hill 60 Centre subsector from 8/Gloucestershire Regiment. Very shortly afterwards five officers and five NCOs set off for the line to begin the takeover. They were to wait there until the arrival of the main party. In Montreal Camp the rest of the battalion started preparing to go into the line: in each company five officers and four NCOs went forward to reconnoitre the positions to be taken over and later they were followed by twenty-eight men and two Lewis-gun teams under the command of Lieutenant Hill, who were to take over advanced posts. At 2115 hours 12/DLI left Montreal Camp and marched to the railhead at Vlamertinghe; however, the train was an hour late so they did not entrain until 2300 hours. Twenty minutes later they arrived in Ypres and having detrained, marched through the town to the Lille Gate where they were met by guides who led them into the line. The relief was complete by 0330 hours on 11 May with two companies in the line. D Company held the line with three posts from the Railway Cutting to I.29.c.9.5, Marshall Post, Swift Post and Allan Post, with the remainder of the company in support in Deep Support Trench to Allen Street. This sector was very badly damaged having been under an intense bombardment and had been subject to a strong raid just prior to 12/DLI taking over. The left sector was held by B Company, who also held the front with a series of three posts from I.29.c.9.5 to I.29.b.4.8; these were named Allen Crater Post, Barry Post and Glasgow Post. This sector was in a very similar condition to that held by D Company. A Company were in close support but at night sent men forward to man Lone Tree Post, Fosse Wood Post and Fosse Way Post. In reserve C Company were accommodated in Larch Wood dugouts, where Battalion Headquarters and the Regimental Aid Post were also to be found. 13/DLI had also moved back to the front line, taking over the left subsector with Battalion Headquarters at Rudkin House. The Commanding Officer placed A Company on the right and B Company on the left; D Company were placed by day in Observatory Trench and the Redan and at night they manned the sector between Glasgow Post and Gap Trench. C Company was in reserve in Maple Street and Stafford Street. As 13/DLI went back into the line, 36054 Private William Innes, the schoolteacher from Framwellgate Moor, had been found a new job. In a battalion made up mainly of miners, someone used to working with pen and paper was hard to find, so William became the Orderly Room Clerk and added these two small entries to his diary:

Wed May 9
March to Scottish Lines at Ouderdom Camp – very hot day
Thur 10 May
Working in Orderly Room all day typing.

At 0430 hours on 11 May the enemy opened fire with trench mortars against Canada Street and then later in the day Battalion Headquarters at Rudkin House was shelled intermittently. At 1700 hours the front line at I.30.3 and I.30.4 also came under fire. This shelling resulted in the death of 43698 Private William Jones from Kimblesworth, serving with A Company: originally an 8/DLI man numbered 3281, his death is recorded with 8/DLI on 10 May 1917, but the Adjutant's Diary of 13/DLI records his death with 13/DLI. A further four men were wounded. The shelling continued the next day and although the front line was blown in in several places there were no casualties. At 0330 hours on the morning of 13 May the shelling against the Mount Sorrell sector started again and then fifteen minutes later three parties of German soldiers left their trenches and advanced towards the line held by 13/DLI. The first party, about twelve-strong, headed for I.30.3; the centre party headed by an officer with about fifteen men attacked I.30.4; and the third party of about twenty men headed for Sap F at I.30.5. Parties one and three managed to enter the British lines but were very quickly thrown out, while the group commanded by the officer was pinned down and failed to get into the British trench. A second wave followed but only got about halfway over No Man's Land where they came under heavy and accurate fire from the Lewis guns of 13/DLI.

Lt Arthur Borrell had joined 12/DLI in June 1916. He was evacuated sick in May 1917, and when fit again was posted to 18/DLI.

The battalion suffered a number of casualties. Second Lieutenant E. Parr was wounded with six men killed, three from D Company and three from B Company. A further twenty-one men were wounded and one man, 43408 Private Jonathan Porritt from A Company, was reported missing. It appears that the German raid was successful in taking a prisoner as he survived the war. The following morning a patrol went out into No Man's Land where they located the bodies of two of the German raiding party. The remains of the two enemy soldiers were brought back to the British lines where they were searched for clues to identify their unit and higher formation. Later that evening 11/NF arrived and by midnight had taken over the line held by 13/DLI, who moved into support positions with Battalion Headquarters at the Bund and all four companies in Railway Dugouts.

In the meantime 12/DLI had come under some shellfire, but the work on improving and repairing their trenches was put on hold as they were ordered to provide as many men as possible to dig assembly trenches for the coming offensive. On 14 May news reached 12/DLI that from an aerial reconnaissance photograph, Intelligence had identified that the Germans had dug an assembly trench from which it was thought they would launch a raid on 12/DLI. The forward posts were all quietly withdrawn and the British heavy artillery opened fire and bombarded the enemy position for one and a half hours. When night fell three separate patrols, each consisting of an officer and two men, were sent out from different parts of the battalion front. Although they searched all along the line, no evidence of a new enemy trench was found. During 15 May the British guns continued with the work of cutting the German barbed wire, but the enemy retaliated and shelled the support trenches at Marshall Walk; this resulted in the deaths of two soldiers of 12/DLI. 31866 Private Joseph Craggs from Castleside near Consett had joined the battalion in August 1916, and 17774 Corporal Robert Anderson, although born in Widnes, Lancashire, had been brought up in Jarrow where he was employed as a miner. The next day a good deal of shelling took place all along the battalion front and they were warned that 11/NF on their right would be carrying out a raid on the German lines; however, later in the day this was cancelled.

The shelling continued on 17 May and Larchwood and the Cutting came in for a heavy barrage in retaliation for the British shelling of the German line. At 1600 hours word came that at 1900 hours a mine was to be fired under Hill 60, therefore a party was brought together under the command of Second Lieutenant Edward Tuffs: formerly a Company Sergeant-Major in the Army Cyclist Corps from Middlesbrough, he had been commissioned into the Durham Light Infantry in January 1916. Their role was to go forward and occupy the crater as soon as the mine was fired, but the time of firing was put back to 2200 hours. However, the Germans had other ideas and at 2115 hours they opened a hurricane bombardment onto the front and support lines, especially concentrating on Marshall Walk. An SOS signal was sent up by someone in 11/NF lines on the right which caused Battalion Headquarters of 12/DLI to also send up an SOS signal. This caused the Divisional artillery, who were standing by for the firing of the mine, to open fire on the German line. The mine exploded at 1014 hours and Second Lieutenant Tuffs accompanied by seven bombers went forward to establish a post in the crater. When they got there they found that no crater had formed and they moved forward into the German crater which was heavily manned. A bombing fight took place and owing to the larger numbers of enemy soldiers the men from 12/DLI were forced back, bombing all the time but closely followed by the Germans. On reaching the British line Edward Tuffs reorganised his platoon and drove the enemy back to their own line. By midnight

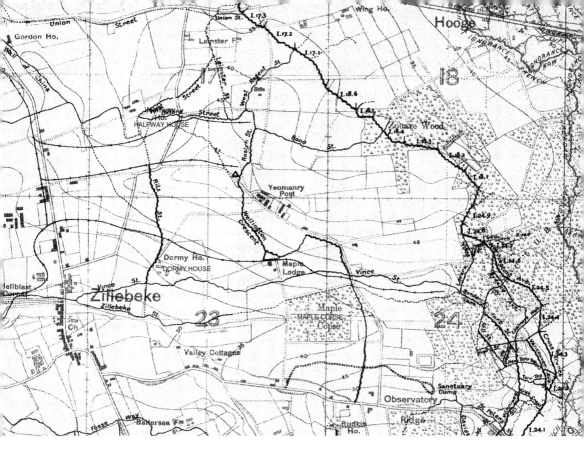

everything was quiet once more. Casualties to 12/DLI were three wounded and two men killed, the first being 27082 Private George Clough from Burdon Street, Gateshead, a married man with three children. He had originally served in France with 14/DLI and had been wounded in the thigh in August 1916. When fit again in January 1917 he was put on a draft to 19/DLI but diverted to 12/DLI in February of that year. The second fatality was a man who had been with the battalion since September 1914: 19371 Private James Garthwaite from Felling was also married but had no children. One missing man was a reinforcement who had arrived in the battalion in August 1916 to bring it up to strength after the losses during the early Somme battles. 31710 Private James Bates was single, aged 37 and an iron-dresser by trade from Huddersfield. He was initially assumed to be wounded and a Prisoner of War in German hands. However, his sister Mrs McEvoy eventually received a letter through the British Red Cross stating that Second Lieutenant Tuffs reported to Captain Duffy, commanding B Company of 12/DLI, that Private Bates was killed by a bomb before getting to the crater post in the front line. He has no known grave and is commemorated on the Ypres Menin Gate Memorial to the Missing.

The next day the enemy fire continued, at times intense especially to the right of the railway. At night the British machine guns kept up a fire on the gaps in the enemy wire. A patrol from the battalion was about to leave the front line, and just as they mounted the fire step a barrage from the British 12.9 guns fell short and 20618 Sergeant Alfred Long MM from Tow Law was killed; he had been with the battalion since September 1914. Later an officer's patrol left Swift Post with the objective of locating the body of Private Bates, but returned unsuccessful. By 0130 hours on 19 May 8/Green Howards had taken over the line and 12/DLI were marched back to Montreal Camp where they arrived at around 0400 hours. During this tour they had ten killed and thirty-two men wounded. The following day an anti-aircraft shell fell through the roof of one hut and wounded one man.

13/DLI moved A and B Companies to Halifax Camp and C and D Companies remained at the Bund where they were kept busy supplying working parties under the command of 101 and 102 Field Companies Royal Engineers. A and B Companies were employed in burying signal cables from the rear area up to the command posts in the line. During this work on 19 May one sergeant was wounded in the leg by shrapnel. The next day a large draft of 106 Other Ranks reported to Battalion Headquarters. In a working party on 22 May 38961 Private Ernest Inneard of B Company, 32650 Private Ernest Barber and 43736 Private Thomas Brown were also wounded. The last-named had landed in November 1915 and been posted to 1/5/DLI in 50th Division; numbered 4310, he had been renumbered on posting to 13/DLI. The Germans were busy shelling the British rear area and both Montreal and Halifax camps and the RE Dump came under fire. General Babington visited the battalion and presented the ribbon of the Military Medal to eight Other Ranks. Time was found to organise a soccer match against 12/DLI which 13/DLI won 2 goals to 1. The two companies at the Bund were relieved by 10/NF and rejoined the main party, and then on 28 May the battalion moved to St McAdam Cappell Camp well to the rear to begin training for the coming attack. More news of awards for gallantry came in at this time: Major J. Downey, Captain A. Howard, CSM W. Bazeley, CSM A. Nichol and Private R. Harrison were all Mentioned in Despatches, while 21812 Private F. Hall was awarded the Meritorious Service Medal. The shelling was causing a few casualties. On 28 May five men, three from A Company and two from D Company, were wounded and it was here that the Brigade bombing school was shelled with 52846 Private George Burgess, one of the West Lancs Cyclist draft, and 21029 Private Thomas Bruce being killed. Private George Burgess was the eldest son of Thomas Burgess (former Harrogate cricket professional), of 4 Primrose Terrace, Skipton Road, Harrogate. He was 27 years of age. Details of this sad occurrence are given in the following letter from the chaplain to the deceased's mother:

52846 Private G. Burgess from Harrogate was killed in action on 29 May 1917. He was one of a large draft of cyclists from the West Lancashire Division.

Dear Mrs Burgess, I am grieved to have to write to you of the sad news of your son's death. He was killed by shell as he was taking refuge in his billet. The shell came through the roof and exploded on the floor of the billet a few inches from him, and he was killed instantaneously. The funeral took place in a military cemetery in a neighbouring village, particulars of which may be obtained from the Director of Graves Registration, War Office, Winchester House, London, SW. A small cross bearing his name and regiment will be erected over his grave to mark the spot. He was much valued as a good soldier by his officers and as a good companion by his mates. Let us commend him to God's mercy, and pray God to give us courage to bear the heavy burden of sorrow that is ours just now.

The latter man came from Pelaw near Gateshead, was married with two children, and had been with the battalion since its formation in September 1914. Along with these fatalities another five men were wounded. 12/DLI also moved to the training area: they left Montreal Camp at 0300 hours on 27 May and moved to the Steenvoorde training area where they arrived at 0830 hours and came under command of 69 Brigade. The next few days were spent practising the attack and on 31 May they received orders to move back to the line. The battalion rested all day and at 2000 hours they marched to Godewaersvelde Station where at 2130 hours they entrained and were taken up to Ypres Sidings; they arrived here at 2330 hours. Under a good deal of shelling they marched up to the Bund where they took over from 9/York & Lancs. 13/DLI stayed one day longer in the training area. On the morning of 1 June, the GOC 23rd Division General Babington arrived and presented medal ribbons to Captain H.C. Buckell MC, CSM W. Bazeley DCM Croix de Guerre, Sergeant M. Brough DCM MM, Corporal R. McDonnell MM and Private H. Hall MM. Then at 2030 hours they moved out and went up to the front line where they relieved 11/Sherwood Foresters in the Mount Sorrell sector.

When they took over the front-line positions Battalion Headquarters went once again to Rudkin House; A Company took over the right sector and B Company the left, with D Company in support and C Company in reserve positions. In C Company dugouts the stress got too much for one of the reinforcements from the West Lancs Cyclists and 52875 Private Harold Orrell shot himself in the right forearm. He was evacuated to the Number 3 Canadian Casualty Clearing Station and from there to a General Hospital in Wimereux. Within days he was in hospital in England. However, in January 1918 he was back in France on a draft to 1/5/DLI and he was killed in action in April of that year. The next day a raid was planned against the enemy trenches opposite saps F and G. This was to be led by Lieutenant George Heselton and Second Lieutenant John Young: at around 1025 hours the raiding party was forming up when the German artillery opened a bombardment on the two saps where the raiders were situated. Casualties were heavy: Lieutenant Heselton, who came from Hartlepool, and eleven men were killed. Second Lieutenants Frederick Hall and George Wood along with nineteen men were wounded; this effectively stopped the raid from taking place.

The preparations for the coming battle were almost complete: the X Corps to which the 23rd Division were attached was to attack on the left of the British Second Army; three of its four divisions were in the line – from right to left, 41st, 47th and 23rd – with the 24th Division in reserve. 23rd Division on the left flank had the task of not only taking the enemy trenches in front of them but of also protecting the flank of the whole of the attack. The Divisional front was a little over 2,000 yards in length from Windy Corner to Sap H on either side of the Ypres–Comines railway. The advance was to be in three lines: the Red Line, the Blue Line and the final objective was to be known as the Black Line. The attack was to be in two phases; the first attack to go straight through to the Blue Line without stopping on the Red Line. On reaching the Blue Line the advance was to pause for three hours to allow fresh troops to move up for the final assault on the Black Line.

The 23rd Division was to attack on a two-brigade front: on the right the Yorkshiremen of 69 Brigade were reinforced by 11/NF and 12/DLI from 68 Brigade, while on the left the attack was to be carried out by two battalions of 70 Brigade. 9/York & Lancaster Regt would advance to the Blue Line, while 11/Sherwood Foresters would pivot and form the defensive flank. 69 Brigade was to attack with three of its battalions in the line – from right to left, 10/DWR, 8/Green Howards and 11/West Yorks – who were to capture the Red and the Blue Lines. Once these lines were taken 9/Green Howards and 12/DLI would move forward and at the allotted time advance and take the Black Line. 11/NF was placed in Brigade reserve. The remaining two battalions of 68 Brigade, 10/NF and 13/DLI, were held in Divisional reserve near Zillebeke. Artillery support for the operation was immense with 156 18-pounder guns and forty-two 4.5-inch howitzers allotted to the division along with 60-pounders further back. Four heavy Stokes mortars of Number 3 Special Company Royal Engineers were to fire thermite shells for ten minutes, and opposite Mount Sorrell where the German trenches were too close to the British line for safe artillery support, 68/Light Trench Mortar Battery would barrage the enemy trenches. On top of this the Divisional Machine Gun Companies assisted by Number 12 Motor Machine Gun Battery with sixty guns under command were to fire a machine-gun barrage to cover the advance. Now all along a 10-mile front things were ready: nineteen mines had been prepared under the German positions after years of labour and the ever-present danger

33075 Private John W. Marshall 12/DLI, aged 33, a miner at Emma Colliery, Ryton. KiA on 7 June 1917, he is commemorated on the Ypres Menin Gate Memorial.

Here Australians are being briefed on a large scale model of the battlefield.

from counter-mines.

In their positions at the Bund 12/DLI stared providing working parties for the Royal Engineers and on 1 June they came under heavy shellfire which caused the deaths of seven men and a further thirteen were wounded. The next day the shelling continued but there were no casualties. However, 47920 Private Herbert Fisher from Skelmanthorpe, Yorkshire who had been wounded on 1 June died from his wounds at the dressing station in Vlamertinghe and was buried in Hop Store Cemetery. On the 3rd of the month things went quiet but the German gunners did send over some gas shells which the battalion war diary records, 'caused some annoyance'. On 4 June the battalion was relieved by 10/DWR and marched back to the dugouts in the Ramparts at Ypres where they began preparations for their part in the coming attack. Final briefings took place and the men rested until at 2200 hours on 6 June they began moving forward to take up their positions for the attack and by 0030 hours on 7 June they were in position and ready to go.

On 3 June 13/DLI came under heavy shellfire and four men were killed, twelve wounded and two reported missing. Another man had been evacuated sick: 43412 Private Herbert Townend from New Seaham went to Number 3 Canadian Casualty Clearing Station where on 4 June he died from a haemorrhage of an old tuberculosis cavity in his left lung. Then that night they were relieved by 8/York & Lancs, the relief being complete by 0530 hours on 5 June. The battalion moved back to O Camp where they spent the day resting and preparing for the attack. At 2145 hours on the night of 6 June they left O Camp and marched up to their positions on the south side of Zillebeke Lake. By 2330 hours all were in position and they just had to wait for the start of the battle.

52965 Thomas Grinrod was another of the West Lancashire Cyclists. He was killed in action on 2 June 1917.

At 0100 hours word reached Battalion Headquarters of 12/DLI that Zero Hour would be at 0310 hours: by 0300 hours everything was peaceful and all the men were lying out in the open waiting for the mines to explode. Precisely on time all along the front the mines exploded and a terrific barrage from the British guns opened up. Immediately the German counter-barrage came down. The leading battalions of 69 Brigade went forward and with hardly a check at the Red Line went on towards the Blue Line; here 8/Green Howards saw the Germans running from their trenches and with much enthusiasm went beyond their objective. 12/DLI lay out in the open until 0430 when they began moving forward to their allotted second position to the left of the railway line.

They were in place and ready to go when at 0650 hours they received orders to advance. On the right 9/Green Howards attacking in the broken ground and shattered tree stumps of Battle Wood ran into well-sited machine-gun positions as well as many snipers. In the centre D Company of 8/Green Howards moved along the railway embankments where they dealt with many dugouts. 12/DLI advancing forward across the south-western slopes of the Klein Zillebeke spur met very little opposition and by 0730 hours the battalion were on their objective and starting to dig in and consolidate the position and up to this point had only taken fifteen casualties. Around 1200 hours a German spotter aeroplane flew over 12/DLI and very soon shells of all calibres were falling about the battalion positions. Casualties began to mount and by 1800 hours over 200 men were wounded or dead including around fifty who were missing. The artillery fire was reported to be coming from the

28538 Pte Herbert Rennison 12/DLI was killed in action on 4 June 1917. A reinforcement from the West Yorkshire Regiment, he came from Leeds.

left flank, from German guns in front of the British VIII Corps which had not taken part in the advance. Although this was reported to 69 Brigade Headquarters, the severe shelling never ceased. On the left flank troops of 70 Brigade had successfully wheeled to form the flank and had linked up with 12/DLI on the Black Line. This line had been occupied very quickly by a platoon of 12/DLI led by Lieutenant Cuthbert Vaux, who with great skill and coolness led his platoon to the occupation of a difficult position which he reached and reported upon, unnoticed by the enemy although in close proximity to their posts.

In the reserve positions 13/DLI had nothing to do until 0900 hours when A and B Companies were ordered forward to Battersea Farm; here they were eventually joined by Battalion Headquarters and came under command of the GOC 69 Brigade. At 2200 hours they were sent forward

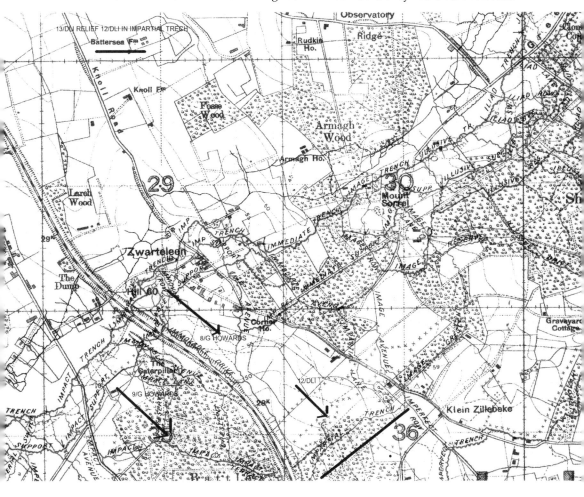

to take over from 12/DLI. By 0500 hours the relief was complete, 13/DLI were holding Impartial Trench and 12/DLI moved back to Battersea Farm. The next day was fairly quiet for 13/DLI, that is until early evening when an aeroplane flew overhead and dropped a white light; immediately the British guns opened fire with a heavy bombardment that lasted until 2200 hours. During the German counter-barrage the Battalion Headquarters of 13/DLI was heavily shelled and the battalion suffered a number of casualties: Second Lieutenant John Young from Gateshead was killed, Second Lieutenant James Brady was wounded and among the men three were killed, twenty-five wounded and one missing. At 0430 hours on 9 June C Company of 13/DLI moved forward and took over from a company of 12/DLI in the Rectangle and D Company relieved the men in Battersea Farm. During the morning the front line was shelled and two men were killed and eighteen wounded, then at 2300 hours B Company went forward and took over from two companies of 11/West Yorks. That night

The British, Australian, New Zealand and Canadian Tunnelling Companies laid mines under the German trenches prior to the Battle of Messines.

and into the early hours of 10 June C Company and one company of 9/South Staffordshire Regiment (9/South Staffs), the Divisional Pioneer Battalion, were tasked to dig a support trench about 50 yards behind Impartial Trench; this was named Durham Lane. 13/DLI were now disposed with A and D Companies in Impartial Trench, B Company in Impartial Reserve Trench and 13th Avenue, with C Company in support in Durham Lane and Battalion Headquarters at I.29.d7.4. The battalion signallers worked unceasingly and soon they were able to report that all companies were linked by telephone. At around 1700 hours a German sniper was active and he killed Second Lieutenant Archibald Hamilton and wounded Second Lieutenant Thomas Murgatroyd. Along with these officer casualties, three Other Ranks were killed and thirty wounded during the day. On 11 June the German shelling continued on and off all day and in the evening they concentrated on the front and support lines and once again the casualties mounted. Around lunch-time on 12 June a post in Railway Dugouts manned by D Company was heavily bombed and every man there became a casualty. A trench mortar barrage was organised and Lieutenant Thomas Saint and a party of bombers counter-attacked; they were at once attacked themselves and driven back as far as the junction

Another of the Cyclist draft was 52717 Pte John Harold Smith. Original from Tooting, he was resident in Colne, Lancashire when he enlisted. He was killed action on 7 June 1917.

230

Second Lieutenant Archibald Hamilton attached to 13/DLI from the Highland Light Infantry was killed by a German sniper on 10 June 1917.

43430 Pte Ernest Briggs served with 8/DLI before being posted to 13/DLI.

of Immediate Drive and Impartial Trench. Lieutenant Saint rallied his bombers, counter-attacked and regained possession of the post, during which he was wounded; a further five Other Ranks were wounded and two killed. That night 12/Royal Fusiliers from 24th Division came up and took over the line. 13/DLI marched to Vlamertinghe where they entrained and were carried to Godeswaersvelde where they detrained at 0900 hours. The rest of the day was spent resting. At the Battalion Orderly Room 36054 Private William Innes had again been left out of the battle and he recorded this period in his diary with these words:

> Wed 6 June
> Battn go up the line at night I am left behind at Transport lines
> Thur 7 June
> Very hot day, Big Mine blown under Hill 60 at 310pm. Our Div have made a big advance. Prisoners pouring in all day.
> Fri 8 June
> Battn advance as far as Battle Wood..

When they were relieved by 13/DLI at Battersea Farm 12/DLI moved back to Montreal Camp where they spent 9 June resting: here they were visited by General Babington who informed them that the rest would be very short, for on the night of 10 June they had to go back into the line. The remainder of the time was spent resting and preparing to go back. That night they moved up to Battle Wood and relieved 10/DWR. Here they found that the objective had not been gained and the position of the new line was not very clear. So as was normal for the Durhams they started to dig and improve their position. The next day was quiet but around 0400 hours an enemy aeroplane flew over the battalion and machine-gunned the men in the trenches. 12 June was quiet but 12/DLI went forward without any artillery preparation or support and managed to take the first-day objective of the Black Line. That night 3/Rifle Brigade came up and took over but refused to take over the newly-captured ground. The

The Crater of Hill 60 which was taken by 8/Green Howards of 69 Brigade 23rd Division on 7 June 1917.

relief was not completed until 0430 hours when 12/DLI marched down the railway to Vlamertinghe: on the way the Germans bombarded the route with gas shells and the battalion had to don their respirators to complete the march. When they reached the station they entrained for Godeswaersvelde where they detrained and marched to the Berthen area, arriving in camp at 0800 hours on 14 June.

The Battle of Messines had now drawn to a close and all the infantry of the 23rd Division had been relieved and was resting. Parades, inspections and church parades took place, as well as the presentation of ribbons to those who had been awarded medals for gallant conduct. However, the resting did not last long for they were put to work digging trenches for signal cable for X Corps. These working parties were not without risk and casualties occurred from enemy shelling on a frequent basis. On 23 June 12/DLI had three men killed, among them 16181 Corporal James Bonson from Spennymoor. One of the original members of the battalion, he had been evacuated in November 1915 and on returning to France in June 1916 he joined 13/DLI. He was only with them for a few weeks when on 22 July he was again wounded, this time in the leg. Evacuated via 104 Field Ambulance and 34 Casualty Clearing Station, he reached a hospital on the French coast and when he was fit again in September he was returned to the front and rejoined 12/DLI. He had not long been promoted to Corporal when he was killed. Route-marching was another feature of the rest and time was found to play a few cricket matches. At the end of the month as the first half of 1917 came to an end, the whole of 68 Brigade moved to Mic Mac Camp.

16752 Pte William P. 12/DLI deserted and w he returned to France joined 19/DLI.

Lt Herbert Hall 12/D. was born at Tickhill near Doncaster but w living on Vancouver Island when he enlis into 29/Canadian Infantry. Commissioned into 12/DLI, he was killea action on 13 June 191

German dead lie in their destroyed trench 7 June 1917.

Chapter Eight

Menin Road Ridge – Third Battle of Ypres

THE FIRST PART OF JULY was spent in Mic Mac Camp refitting and checking equipment and several drafts arrived at around this time. It was now that 23rd Division began to relieve 24th Division, and 69 and 70 Brigades had moved back into the line. Mic Mac Camp meanwhile came under the eye of the German gunners and each day the area around the camp was shelled. On the morning of 4 July the whole of 68 Brigade lined the La Clytte–Reninghelst Road and cheered as HM King George V and the Prince of Wales drove slowly along their ranks. Later that day B and C Companies of 13/DLI left the camp and moved up to the line where they relieved two companies of 8/York & Lancs; B Company manning Canada Street and C Company going into Metropolitan Left. The next morning thirty-five Other Ranks went up to Battersea Farm and joined a composite company under the command of an officer from 11/NF.

Later that morning all the battalion officers gathered at Brigade Headquarters where General Babington explained what work was to be done in the line. Then at 2030 hours the remainder of the battalion left camp and went up to the Hill 60 sector where they relieved 8/KOYLI in the front line. C Company was positioned on the right and B Company on the left with D Company in support and A Company back in reserve near Zwarteleen with Battalion Headquarters at I.29.d.6.4 just east of Zwarteleen. Having settled in, the battalion sent a patrol out but owing to enemy machine-gun fire they returned having had one man wounded. In the early hours of 7 July a patrol of three Other Ranks led by Second Lieutenant Frederick Youens left the right of the battalion trenches: their mission was to get in touch with 17/London Regt who were supposed to be on the right flank. They moved slowly along until they observed a party of about forty German soldiers carrying stores into a strongpoint. The enemy covering party tried to surround the DLI patrol and a bombing fight ensued. The British patrol was forced to retire with one man and Second Lieutenant Youens wounded. They regained the battalion lines and Frederick Youens went into a dugout to have his wounds dressed. Almost immediately the Germans put a heavy barrage onto the battalion trenches which lasted until around 0300 hours. At 0230 hours a party of around fifty enemy soldiers started a raid on the right company of 13/DLI. Although wounded, Second Lieutenant Youens left the dugout

35859 Sergeant William J. Clark 13/DLI from Mortimer near Reading, Berkshire died of wounds at one of the base hospitals in Etaples on 4 July 1917.

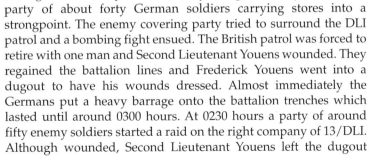

21908 Sgt John Kirkup 13/DLI was awarded the Military Medal in July 1917 for his actions at Messines. D/DLI/7/906/1

233

without tunic or shirt and rallied a Lewis-gun team that had been disorganised by a shell. As he was doing this a German soldier threw a bomb into the Lewis-gun post; Youens caught it and immediately threw it away. A second bomb came flying into the position; he picked it up and as he was throwing it away it exploded and badly wounded him and several of the Lewis-gun team. The raiders were eventually driven off by rifle and Lewis-gun fire and it is without doubt that Second Lieutenant Youens saved a number of lives in the Lewis-gun team by his actions and by his resource the raid was repulsed. Although he was quickly evacuated to the Advanced Dressing Station at Railway Dugouts he died from his wounds: his actions gained him the award of the Victoria Cross. Buried beside him is 23259 Private Robert Metcalf from Murton Colliery who was killed in the same action. The other two men to die that day, 27256 Private Francis Porteous from Gateshead and 36240 Private Charles Wright from Haughton-le-Skerne near Darlington, have no known graves and both are commemorated on the Menin Gate Memorial to the Missing. Major J.A.L. Downey wrote to Second Lieutenant Youens' mother on 12 July:

A German soldier threw a bomb into the Lewis-gun post; Youens caught it and immediately threw it away.

Dear Mrs Youens,

It is with very deep regret that I write to offer you my sincere sympathy + also that of the Officers of my Battalion, upon the death of your gallant son, Lt F Youens who died of wounds 7 July 1917.

Your son was an ideal soldier – keen, efficient and brave. Everything he did gave entire satisfaction to his senior officers + I feel that I should tell you that he was earmarked for early promotion.

On several occasions his gallant work has been noted and I sincerely hope that his last feat will be duly recognised. He was a great favourite with the Officers of the Battalion and exceedingly popular with his men, who would cheerfully follow him anywhere. I trust that the knowledge of these things may somewhat soften what must be to you a terrible blow. That God may sustain and comfort you in your great sorrow is the sincere pray of,

Yours very truly

J A Louis Downey

Major, Commanding 13th Durham L.I.

PS Your son was buried with all due rites and I am having a Cross placed over his resting place tomorrow. JALD.

Two days later another officer's patrol left the right company of 13/DLI and again a large party of German soldiers was observed. Yet again the German covering party tried to surround the DLI patrol who quickly returned to their own trenches and brought a Lewis gun to fire on the German patrol. The Germans returned to their own lines and then the whole of the battalion front line was heavily shelled. At 2230 hours 12/DLI arrived and took over the line from Davidson Street to Klein Zillebeke and 13/DLI moved back to Mic Mac Camp.

The next day was quiet but 12/DLI were determined to keep the Germans on their toes and on the night of 12 July, forty men of A Company led by Lieutenant John Weightman from Gateshead and Second Lieutenant Eric Freeman from Birmingham along with covering parties on the flank from B and C Companies raided an enemy strongpoint with complete success. Here they captured five prisoners but at some cost: Lieutenant Weightman and six men were wounded and three men were missing. Among them was 22/969 Private William Knowles: only 5 ft 3 in he should have been in 19/DLI, the Bantams, but he had not enlisted until December 1915 when 22/DLI were recruiting. When his battalion went overseas he was left behind with 16/DLI and eventually put on a draft to 12/DLI, joining that battalion on 30 August 1916. The captured men came from 8/Jäger Regiment which showed that 195th German Division was still in Flanders. The next day 12/DLI were relieved by 8/Green Howards and marched back to Mic Mac Camp. They rested for one day, only providing one working party, and on the next day they carried out musketry and gas drill and physical training in the morning and went to the baths in the afternoon.

On 11 July Lieutenant-Colonel Michael Lindsay of 7/Dragoon Guards rejoined the battalion and assumed command. The following afternoon two enemy aeroplanes flew over 13/DLI in Mic Mac Camp and dropped bombs which wounded two men; the aircraft were engaged by the battalion Lewis guns which drove them off. The next day the bombers came again and although they dropped their bombs, no damage was done. During the day Second Lieutenant Alfred Turner MC and Second Lieutenant William Hodgson reported to Battalion Headquarters. On 14 July the whole battalion paraded to see General Babington present gallantry ribbons to the following officers and men: T/Captain E. Gray MC, T/Captain L.M. Greenwood MC, T/Lieutenant C.T.W. Sauerbeck MC, 52647 CSM G. Thompson DCM, 13820 Private I. Pain MM and 20959 Private J. Clark MM. On 15 July Lieutenant Thomas Saint rejoined from hospital and was posted to D Company; at the same time Second Lieutenant George Taylor reported his arrival to the battalion and was sent to join A Company. They were followed by a small draft of Other Ranks. The battalion still had to find the odd working party and on 17 July 120 men carried ammunition up to 70/Machine Gun Company in the line. At 0700 hours on 21 July the battalion paraded and marched to the Mont des Cats area where they arrived around noon and went into billets. 12/DLI had also moved to the training area and the time until the end of the month was filled up with musketry, gas drill, sports and medal ribbon presentation parades. On 30 July both battalions left the training area and marched to Caestre where on arrival they entrained for St Omer. When they arrived they marched to billets; 12/DLI arrived in Esquerdes at 2330 hours and were quartered in very comfortable billets. Likewise, 13/DLI marched from St Omer to Wizernes where they arrived at 0100 hours but didn't record the state of the billets

On 31 July Fifth Army commenced what was to become known as the Third Battle of Ypres. That morning it started to drizzle and before night fell it had turned into a downpour but the troops of the 23rd Division remained on the training area: military training, sport and parades in various forms took place; drafts of men and new officers arrived.

In 12/DLI on 15 August Private P. Smith was tried by Field General Court Martial; however, no details of his offence have come to light. Then on 17 August 20931 Private Thomas Haughey from Consett was killed; he is shown as a member of 12/DLI. Originally he had served with 13/DLI until wounded in November 1916 and evacuated to England. Posted to 3/DLI in early 1917 he was warned for a draft to France and he deserted. He was apprehended and sentenced to a term in detention, but was released and put on a draft to France. On paper he was posted to 12/DLI but when he was given a medical before going up the line he was classified unfit and sent to join VI Corps Salvage Company. At some stage he moved to XVIII Corps Salvage Company and his documents simply state 'Killed guarding a water tank': they do not state how he was killed; by shellfire, or by bombs from an aeroplane.

The second tragedy that occurred five days later concerned the 68/LTMB. This unit was made up of men from all the battalions of 68 Brigade, so they came from 10 and 11/NF as well as 12 and 13/DLI. On 25 August a Court of Inquiry gathered at the Battery Headquarters on the orders of the battery commander Captain Alan Hetherington, to enquire into the death of 17777 Private William Ingram from Gateshead. The president of the court was Lieutenant J.B.W. Roberton 11/NF and the members Second Lieutenant John Dawson and Second Lieutenant Norman Bell 12/DLI, all three attached 68/LTMB.

The first witness called was 40256 Private Richard Newton Northumberland Fusiliers who stated:

> I saw Private Ingram at about 1615 hours on 22 August going down to the Canal bank with a towel on his arm.

The next man called was 20610 Private Thomas Alexander 11/NF who added:

> About 1630 hours on 22 August in company with Privates Reay and Bircham I was going down to bathe in the canal. We saw some clothes on the bank and not seeing anybody about we examined the clothes. They belonged to Private Ingram. Privates Reay and Bircham stayed and looked for the deceased and I went back and reported to Lance Corporal Smith who was coming along the canal. I then went on and reported the matter to Battery Sergeant Major Marshall.

The third man to give his evidence was 10432 Private Philip Reay 10/NF whose statement mirrored that of the previous witness:

About 1630 hours on 22 August in company with Privates Alexander and Bircham I was going down to bathe in the canal. We saw some clothes on the bank and not seeing anybody about we examined the clothes. They belonged to Private Ingram. Private Alexander went back to report and Private Bircham and I looked round to try and find Private Ingram, till a party came along shortly to help us.

The next witness, 202068 Private John Bircham, had originally enlisted into the East Yorkshire Regiment but had been transferred to the Northumberland Fusiliers. He made an almost identical statement to Private Reay:

About 1630 hours on 22 August in company with Privates Alexander and Reay I was going down to bathe in the canal. We saw some clothes on the bank and not seeing anybody about we examined the clothes. They belonged to Private Ingram. Private Alexander went back to report and Private Reay and I looked round to try and find Private Ingram, till a party came from the Battery to help us.

Next to speak was 19938 Lance Corporal John Smith, Northumberland Fusiliers [who would be later wounded and transferred to the Army Ordnance Corps, so the author has been unable to confirm his battalion]. He added:

About 1630 hours on 22 August I was going down along the canal bank when Private Alexander met and reported that Private Ingram's clothes were found and that Private Ingram was missing. I proceeded to the spot and found this was so. I asked some French civilians who were working fifty yards away if they could enlighten me. They had not seen anyone bathing. I called a Frenchman for a boat from between 200 and 300 yards away and brought him to the spot. After searching the bottom of the canal with poles for about five minutes the Frenchman raised Private Ingram's body to the surface. Three men were diving for the body and they got the body out onto the bank.

24757 Corporal George Slater 13/DLI was the next to be called and he said:

About 1630 hours on 22 August hearing from Private Alexander that Private Ingam was missing, I ran to the spot where his clothes had been found with Privates Howard and Chambers. We went into the water and tried to find the body. We couldn't get to the bottom on account of the long weeds and mud. In a few minutes Lance Corporal Smith came along in a boat with a Frenchman who raised the body to the surface with a pole. We got the body out onto the banks.

The court then called 7473 Private Francis Howard 11/NF who confirmed Corporal Slater's account, stating:

About 1630 hours on 22 August I went into the water with Corporal Slater to try and find Private Ingram's body. We failed owing to the thick weeds and deep mud on the bottom. We got the body out onto the bank when it was raised by a French civilian and Lance Corporal Smith a few minutes later.

The third man who went into the water was 19248 Private William Chambers, who although he was now with 11/NF had originally landed at Gallipoli with 8/NF. His statement was identical to the previous witness:

About 1630 hours on 22 August I went into the water with Corporal Slater to try and find Private Ingram's body. We failed owing to the thick weeds and deep mud on the bottom. We got the body out onto the bank when it was raised by a French civilian and Lance Corporal Smith a few minutes later.

The last witness was the Battery Sergeant-Major 24766 CQMS James Marshall 13/DLI who came from Ferryhill. He concluded the evidence with this statement:

Between 1630 and 1645 hours on 22 August hearing someone was missing I turned out the Battery to search around the canal. Three men were in the water when I arrived at the spot and they could not find the body. A few minutes later the body was brought to the surface by a civilian and Lance Corporal Smith in a boat and got out onto the bank by the men in the water. We immediately started artificial respiration and sent for a litter. We kept up the artificial respiration for about forty minutes and then being convinced that the man was dead he was carried along to the billet. The doctor arrived about 1800 hours. Private Ingram was excused duty that day.

The final two statements came from the Battery Commander and the Brigade Commander.

Captain Hetherington wrote on the record of the proceedings:

I am of the opinion after examining the papers that the deceased was accidentally drowned. He was not on duty at the time.

To this the Brigade Commander Brigadier General Colville added: 'I concur with the finding of the court.'

The last witness was the Battery Sergeant-Major 24766 CQMS James Marshall 13/DLI who came from Ferryhill.

By 24 August it was time to start moving back towards the line and so 13/DLI left Moulle and entrained at Watten at 1200 hours, detraining at Reninghelst at 1630 hours and marching to Palace Camp where they arrived at 1730 hours. Likewise, at 1800 hours on that date 12/DLI marched from the training area to Watten Station but it was not until 0130 hours that they entrained and were taken up to Reninghelst where they arrived at 0730 hours. They then set off for Cornwall Camp, arrived there at 0815 hours and spent the remainder of the day resting. The training continued: the rifle platoons had bayonet-fighting, platoon drill and gas drill, while the specialist platoons, Lewis-gunners, signallers and transport, paraded under their own arrangements. On 29 August 12/DLI Battalion Orders published a letter from Colonel J.J. Blanchard Royal Army Medical Corps which stated: 'I wish to bring to your attention the gallant conduct of 18011 Private C. Woodward D Company in giving blood to a patient in this hospital the 3rd Canadian Casualty Clearing Station on 12 July 1917.' At 1800 hours the battalion marched to huts in the Dickebusch area.

In preparation for the next stage of the offensive operations in Flanders all officers and NCOs were taken to Busseboom where a plan of the battlefield had been constructed; when they were familiar with the ground the companies were also taken to be briefed and have a look at the model. After spending time in the Dickebusch area carrying out limited training, on 2 September 13/DLI moved to billets in the Steenvoorde area where they arrived at 1630 hours. At the same time 12/DLI moved by route march to Mic Mac Camp where they spent a night being bombed by German aircraft. The next day their march continued to the Steenvoorde area. They didn't settle and on 5 September both battalions marched to Noordpeene. The weather turned very hot and in the early evening there was a thunderstorm. At Noordpeene on the afternoon of 6 September there was a conference of all battalion Commanding Officers at 68 Brigade Headquarters to discuss the coming attack. The 23rd Division was now under command of X Corps and they received a warning order from Corps Headquarters that all preparations for the coming attack had to be complete by 18 September. The time between 6 and 17 September was spent training hard; much gas instruction as well as inspections and specialist mustard-gas demonstrations took place. Between those dates there were several moves as they slowly made their way back towards the line.

The Battle of the Menin Road Ridge

The next stage of the Flanders offensive was about to take place: the attack on the Second Army front was fixed for 20 September and was to be carried out by X Corps on the right and I ANZAC Corps on the left. X Corps was to attack on a 2,500-yard front with three divisions in the line: 39th, 41st and 23rd. The three objectives were named the Red, Blue and Green Lines, the latter being between 1,500 and 2,000 yards from the start line. 23rd Division on the left of the Corps front was to attack on a two-brigade front – on the right 68 Brigade and on the left 69 Brigade – with 70 Brigade in Divisional reserve west of Zillebeke. Each of the attacking brigades allotted one battalion to each objective. Thus in 68 Brigade 11/NF was to take the Red Line, 10/NF were to pass through them and carry the assault to the Blue Line and when that was secure 13/DLI were tasked to take the final objective of the Green Line. One company of 12/DLI was allotted to each of the battalions attacking the first two lines, which left the other two companies as a brigade reserve.

The 68 Brigade front caused a number of problems for the attackers as there was a serious obstacle in the form of the Dumbarton Lakes. The banks of the lakes had been broken by British artillery fire; this had also dammed some of the streams running across the front and as a result the whole area had been turned into a swamp. For five days before the start of the battle the British gunners kept up a harassing fire on the Germans and in turn the German gunners searched for the British artillery positions with counter-battery fire.

Battle of the Menin Road Ridge: Men of the 13th Battalion, Durham Light Infantry, in trenches just prior to their attack towards Veldhoek, 20 September 1917.

On the night of 18 September A and B Companies of 12/DLI moved up to Torr Top and on 19 September, in heavy rain, they were employed as carrying parties for 10 and 11/NF and at 0230 hours on 20 September, as the rain cleared away, they moved into assembly positions in the neighbourhood of Jam Lane. At Zero Hour they moved off behind the two fusilier battalions. They were held up by a strongpoint manned by twelve German soldiers and some snipers in Dumbarton Woods and the two companies from 12/DLI were called upon to assist in clearing the position. Among those sent forward were 201352 Private John Simm from Fencehouses and a Leeds man, 302643 Private William Rollett: they entered a blown-in trench during a heavy counter-attack and assisted in rebuilding the trench, gave first aid to the wounded and buried the dead. When this work was finished they took up arms and assisted the men of 13/DLI to repulse the counter-attack.

Members of the 13th Battalion, Durham Light Infantry, prepare to advance on the village of Veldhoek, 20 September 1917.

By 0800 hours both companies were dug in about 20 yards in front of Jasper Trench in support of 10/NF. That night, command passed to 9/York & Lancs. The two DLI companies were ordered to return to Torr Top but a counter-attack developed and at 1930 hours A Company were sent forward to reinforce the York & Lancs in the Blue Line. By 2130 hours the situation had stabilised and the company returned to the area of Jasper Trench. B Company in the meantime had remained where they were to protect the right flank. At 0630 hours on 22 September the Officer Commanding 9/York & Lancs ordered the two DLI companies to return to Torr Top to comply with the previous night's order. Here they were

Men of the 13th Battalion, Durham Light Infantry, wait in trenches prior to their attack towards Veldhoek, 20 September 1917.

A signals section of the 13th Battalion, Durham Light Infantry, equipped with telescopes, field telephone and signalling lamps await news of the progress of the battalion's attack towards Veldhoek on 20 September 1917.

employed carrying bombs, ammunition and trench stores to the new dump that was being set up. There had been some casualties among the officers and senior NCOs. Showing gallantry and devotion to duty, 300920 Corporal William Littlewood from Hetton-le-Hole took over command of his platoon, and encouraging his men by his own example succeeded in getting the stores to their destination. On the first day of operations he made three separate journeys over the battlefield, which was swept by heavy shellfire, to the front line with stores and on each return journey he brought back wounded men. He received the Military Medal in 1918.

On the night of 19/20 September D Company of 12/DLI, which had the task of forming an advanced ammunition dump, formed up near Jam Lane and at Zero Hour moved behind 11/NF up to Jam Row and from there towards Jasper Drive. Between these positions they were held up by a strongpoint and were sucked into the fight; however, a Sergeant and three men attacked the pill-box and captured it, which allowed the company to move on. The company then dug in near Jasper Drive, and orders came through that they should move to the Red Line: almost immediately the orders changed and they were to reinforce 10/NF in the Blue Line. Moving forward to that line they dug in on the right of B Company 10/NF. They remained in this position until 0100 hours on 21 September when they were ordered back to the Red Line and one hour later this changed to Torr Top. C Company less the Lewis-gun sections had formed up behind 13/DLI and at Zero Hour followed 13/DLI to the Green Line.

13/DLI left the camp at Dickebusch at 1100 hours under the command of Captain, Acting Major Denzil Clarke MC on 19 September and marched to Railway Dugouts. Here they rested until 1945 hours when they moved up to the assembly positions at Torr Top; on the way up three men were wounded. At 0300 hours on 20 September Battalion Headquarters was moved to join the Advanced Brigade Headquarters. Zero Hour was set at 0540 hours and as soon as the battalion in front left their assembly trenches in the Jam area 13/DLI moved forward and took their place. Then at 0730 hours they left this area and moved up to the Blue Line where they arrived at 0850 hours. Battalion Headquarters had moved to J.20.b.7.4. At 0953 hours in conjunction with 10/DWR they com-menced the assault on the Green Line. 13/DLI had to cross the broad summit of the Tower Hamlets spur and the Menin Road which ran diagonally across the bat-talion's line of advance. Here they had a very stiff fight on their hands among the ruins of the buildings which flanked the Menin Road.

Men of the 13th Battalion, Durham Light Infantry digging out wounded from their Regimental Aid Post near Zillebeke after the position had been hit by artillery fire, 20 September 1917.

After working at a frantic pace, those digging out the Regimental Aid Post near Zillebeke have now got down near to the dugout entrance in the centre of the photo: one man appears to be trying to get inside.

The left of 13/DLI was held up by a well-sited and dug-in enemy position. Seeing this, CSM Parker of 10/DWR with his company on his battalion's right quickly assessed the situation and attacked the enemy post from the rear and front and succeeded in capturing it. This allowed the left of 13/DLI to move forward, and with their flank secure they pushed on to the Green Line. On the right of 13/DLI things were not going quite so well. The left of 41st Division had encountered a mass of concrete dugouts and pill-boxes and the attacking troops of 122 Brigade were held up by rifle and machine-gun fire from these positions. The right flank of 13/DLI was thus dangerously exposed and Captain Geoffrey Wright DCM brought up two platoons and secured the flank under heavy fire and drove the enemy back. Later during a counter-attack he behaved with great gallantry and fearlessness and though wounded, remained at his post until the counter-attack was completely defeated.

On hearing that the right flank of 13/DLI was threatened, D Company of 10/NF pushed forward from the Blue Line to cover the flank of the

Lieutenant Charles Sauerbeck was killed in action on 21 September 1917.

Durham battalion. When word of this reached Brigade Headquarters, Brigadier Colville sent a company of 11/NF to fill the gap that had opened on the Tower Hamlets Spur. Near the Battalion Headquarters of 13/DLI, the Battalion Medical Officer had established the Regimental Aid Post and this was hit by a shell during the morning. An officer, Lieutenant J.W. Blake who was nearby with a camera, took a photo as men struggled to dig out their trapped comrades. Lieutenant Blake then went on to take photos of the rifle platoons as they waited to go forward and another of the signallers watching and waiting for a signal that would confirm the success of the attack. By 1040 hours over 150 German prisoners had passed through 13/DLI Headquarters and by 1150 hours the Green Line was in Durham hands and the work of consolidating the position commenced. The carrying parties of C Company 12/DLI arrived with barbed wire, bombs and ammunition and during the day made three journeys across the battlefield under fire to bring the much-needed stores to the men digging in. Men from the Divisional Royal Engineers and the Divisional Pioneer battalion arrived and assisted with the construction of strongpoints.

At 1500 hours about 100 Germans massed in the railway cutting north of Gheluvelt and attacked the left company but they were successfully dispersed by rifle and Lewis-gun fire. Up to this time the casualties in 13/DLI had been fairly heavy: Captain Harold Buckell MC and forty-four men had been killed, Lieutenant Hubert Parker, Second Lieutenants Robert Gill, Harold Wheatley and George Orchard along with 177 Other Ranks were wounded, with a further sixteen men listed as missing. About 0800 hours the following morning the enemy again attacked the left company and were once again repulsed, this time with heavy casualties, and one officer and five men were taken prisoner.

7202 Sergeant Benjamin Cruddas was awarded the Distinguished Conduct Medal for his actions on the Menin Road Ridge.

Half an hour later the enemy attacked again, but were repulsed once more. Then at 1400 hours the German artillery started a barrage to prepare for another attack: at 1500 hours a fourth attack started, this time on the right of the line, which also broke down under the fire from the British-held line. The German barrage continued and caused some casualties to the right company of 13/DLI. At 1900 hours the enemy were observed to be massing south of the Menin Road near Gheluvelt and the right company was reinforced by Battalion Headquarters and four Lewis-gun teams from 12/DLI. An SOS signal was sent up, the attacking

Germans were caught by the barrage and dispersed before they could get their attack started. On 21 September 13/DLI had a further fourteen men killed, thirty-seven wounded and one missing.

At 0300 hours on 22 September 8/KOYLI arrived and relieved all of 13/DLI except Battalion Headquarters and two platoons of B Company who were not relieved until early evening. 13/DLI made their way to the dugouts at Torr Top where they rested: on the way they had another man killed, five wounded and 21335 Private Albert Whaley from Blackhill was reported missing. At 0730 hours the next day they made their way back to Camp Dickebusche where they again rested, and the following day they again moved and marched to York Camp at Westoutre. 12/DLI was relieved on the night of 24/25 September and made their way to Ontario Camp where they rested and then moved on foot to Aragon Camp in Westoutre. The GOC, General Babington inspected both battalions and the Commanding Officer of 13/DLI received a letter from Lieutenant-Colonel Bernard Butler Commanding 156 Brigade Royal Field Artillery of the 33rd Division. They had remained in the line to provide support for 23rd Division when the infantry of 33rd Division had been relieved. He wrote:

Men of the 13th Battalion, Durham Light Infantry, resting in trenches during their advance on Veldhoek, 20 September 1917.

> We of the 33rd Divisional Artillery cannot let you go without wishing you the best of luck and giving you our heartiest congratulations. Our FOO's [Forward Observation Officers], Battery Commanders and all are full of the 13th D.L.I. and we look on you as our own infantry. We all hope that we may again have the honour of supporting you and doing still more for you. We have had the best of good hunting together. I hope you will go off thinking half as much of the 33rd Divisional Artillery as they do of you.
>
> Bernard Butler
> Lt- Col RFA
> Cmdg 156 Bde RFA
> 33rd Divisional Artillery

Drafts arrived and were absorbed and inspections took place; working parties were sent to carry stores forward. Enemy aircraft were active and dropped bombs on the camps occupied. 13/DLI moved to the area of Mont des Cats where company training was carried out. 12/DLI meanwhile had moved to Ridge Wood Camp where they were held in Divisional reserve, providing carrying parties for Jackdaw Dump. On 2 October they were carried by motor bus to Metren and marched to billets in the Berthen Area where they arrived at around 1500 hours. The next day they marched to Thieshouck where they were quartered in tents in very wet conditions. A battalion route march took place and then that afternoon

33495 Corporal Enoch Halford, a reinforcement from the South Staffordshire Regiment who had landed in France in August 1914, was tried by Field General Court Martial: what his crime was is unknown but it would appear that he sub-sequently deserted as his medal roll sheet shows that in 1920 he was still absent.

The 23rd Division had hardly time to rest before word arrived that they must return to the line where 33rd Division was hard-pressed by German counter-attacks. 69 and 70 Brigades had gone back to the line, but 68 Brigade were not required and had continued training until they were put at two hours' notice to move on 4 October. All the Adjutants and Quartermasters gathered at Brigade Head-quarters and the move back to the front was planned. On 5 October 12/DLI moved to Caestre where they entrained and moved to Dickebusche, arriving at 2230 hours. On arrival they were told to march to a camping area but found no tents were available and the battalion bedded down with only forty half-shelters for the whole unit. Here they came under command of 21st Division for the purpose of supplying carrying parties and working for X Corps Signals burying cables. Meanwhile 13/DLI at 0900 hours on 8 October moved from the training area to Ascot Camp near Westoutre; on the next day they moved to Scottish Wood where they arrived at 2130 hours.

On 10 October they left Scottish Wood and relieved the following units: 1/HAC (Honourable Artillery Company), two companies of Royal Welsh Fusiliers and 2/Leicestershire Regiment. During the relief Second Lieutenant Albert Sebborn was wounded along with thirty-three men. Battalion Headquarters was located at the Butte J.11.a.7.8 and the next day it was shelled heavily all day: Lieutenant John Witherspoon from Shotley Bridge was killed and twenty-four men were wounded. The enemy artillery kept up its fire all through the night and into the next day, and under this shellfire Battalion Headquarters moved closer to the front line. During 12 October Second Lieutenant Cecil Hands who was from Sunderland, 19023 Private Joseph Wharton from Craghead, 31245 Private

Joseph Thompson from Gateshead, 30248 Private Charles Allen, a South Shields resident, and 203055 Private Roger Watts who hailed from Trimdon Colliery were all killed and a further fifteen men were wounded.

The dead soldiers reflect how the battalion had changed since landing in France. Private Wharton was an original Kitchener enlistment; Private Thompson had been called up under the Derby scheme in January 1916; Private Allen had also been called up under the Derby scheme but being only 4 ft 11 in tall had been sent to 23/DLI and then on a draft to 19/DLI in France. Reported wounded and missing in July 1916, the latter had rejoined the Bantams only to be rejected in January 1917; sent to a labour Company he had gone to hospital and from there to 35/IBD and got himself posted to 13/DLI. The last-named, Private Watts, was a Territorial as his number readily shows. By 0800 hours on 13 October 11/NF had taken over the line but B and D Companies of 13/DLI had to remain in support while Battalion Headquarters and A and C Companies went back to the Bund. On the way out 203853 Private George Hedley from South Church was killed and five men wounded.

At noon on 11 October 12/DLI moved up to Railway Dugouts and began preparations for going back into the line: officers and NCOs reconnoitred the route and on 13 October they moved up into the right subsector east of Polygon Wood. The shelling was extremely heavy and owing to this the relief was not completed until dawn on 14 October; on the way they had twenty casualties. Throughout the day the shelling

14534 Private Frank Harvey from Stanley, Crook. He enlisted into 15/DLI in September 1914, fought at Loos and on the Somme where he was wounded in September 1916. On his return to the Front in January 1917 he was posted to 19/DLI but the draft was diverted to 12/DLI. Frank was KiA on 15 October 1917, he has no known grave and is commemorated on the Tyne Cot Memorial at Passchendaele.

Fully-laden infantry make their way towards the line before battle.

This German soldier photographed behind the line doesn't look very happy with his lot.

was constant and a further forty casualties kept the stretcher-bearers busy. 15 October saw another twenty casualties. Then the following day nineteen German aircraft flew over the battalion trenches and strafed the men in them; as soon as the Lewis-gunners of 12/DLI opened fire the German artillery shelled the position. In the evening 10/DWR arrived and 12/DLI went back to Railway Dugouts: here they rested and cleaned uniforms and equipment. The last spell in the line had cost ninety-nine casualties, a third of them dead. Captain Cyril Powel-Smith was severely wounded and Second Lieutenant William Chapman slightly wounded. On 18 October they received a warning order that they were to go back and relieve 10/DWR on the following night. Before they left Railway Dugouts they were shelled again and 22113 Private Harry Wealleans from Guisborough was wounded and although he reached Number 2 Canadian Casualty Clearing Station, he died from his wounds. It rained all day and the ground was a quagmire through which they marched to relieve 10/DWR, but the guides got lost and it wasn't until 0700 hours that they had taken over the front line with 13/DLI on the right and 9/Green Howards on the left. 20 October was relatively quiet but a patrol from the battalion came across a German machine gun in a post in front of the battalion's position and managed to capture both the gun and its crew.

The next day the enemy aeroplanes were again over the front, strafing the trenches. Relief was due that night and the men in the front line continually sent up Very lights in order to spot any enemy movement in front of them. Again the relief was late owing to the guides losing their way and it wasn't until daybreak on 22 October that they handed over to 15/DLI. They moved initially to the Bund and from there they were carried in buses and lorries to Saint-Martin-au-Laërt where they arrived at 2000 hours.

On 14 October the two companies of 13/DLI at the Bund were relieved by 8/Green Howards and moved to a tented camp further back, and two nights later B and D Companies that had been left in position were also relieved by 8/Green Howards and went back to the Bund. The battalion held a parade and the GOC presented the ribbon of the Military Medal to thirty-seven members of the battalion. At 1300 hours on 17 October Battalion Headquarters along with A and C Companies moved up to Railway Dugouts: they must have been rejoined by the other two companies as the whole battalion went up to the front line near Reutel where they relieved 8/Green Howards. All night long the enemy shelled the line taken over with a mixture of high explosive and gas shells: Second Lieutenant J.P. Carroll was wounded and gassed, and six men were killed with another eleven being wounded. By 0630 the following morning they

The 23rd Divisional Christmas card for 1917 carried a cartoon of their doings on the Menin Road Ridge in September.

were in position and the relief complete. All day the position was under enemy fire again with a mixture of gas and high explosive: three men were killed and another three wounded.

The next day the German gunners concentrated on the area east of Polygon Wood and the Polygon Beke, but there was not a lot of fire from their snipers. Yet again enemy fighter-bombers flew over the front-line trenches and strafed the infantry holding them: the casualties mounted with five men killed and twelve wounded. On 20 October and the next day an enemy party was seen near Judge Copse: they were quickly engaged by the Lewis-gunners, to which the enemy replied with heavy shelling which killed thirteen men and wounded thirteen more. That night 9/KOYLI of 21st Division arrived and relieved 13/DLI who at 08:00 when the relief was complete withdrew to the Bund. After a quick rest they left at 1000 hours, marched to Kruisstraathoek and embussed at 1400 hours. They were carried to Tatinghem where they arrived in camp at 1900 hours. The weather was very wet so the next two days were spent cleaning uniforms and equipment and then on the morning of 25 October they were inspected by the Brigade Commander and General Babington who presented gallantry ribbons to those who had been mentioned in the *London Gazette*. Training was severely hampered by the weather, although they did manage to spend some time on the nearby rifle range.

12/DLI were also training and resting in the same area, but events far away in Italy were to affect the British Army in Flanders.

21606 Private Harold Hurworth received the Military Medal in December 1917.

A group of 12/DLI shortly after they arrived on the Italian Front. Standing in the centre of the rear ranks is 52693 Private John Newlands MM from Wylam on Tyne. John was awarded his MM in December 1917 for his work as a runner during the fighting on Tower Hamlets Ridge. He was transferred to the Labour Corps, where he served with 525 (Home Service) Employment Company.

Chapter Nine

The Italian Front

IN NORTHERN ITALY along the River Isonzo, the Italian and Austro-Hungarian Armies had been fighting since 1915. In August 1917 at the eleventh Battle of the Isonzo the Italians had forced a withdrawal of the Austrians and the Austrian High Command had decided to restore the situation by a counteroffensive against the Italian northern flank and to do so before winter set in. After various diplomatic moves, Germany agreed to make troops available to assist the Austrians, and six divisions with various army troops attached formed the German Fourteenth Army which under the command of General Otto Von Bülow was ordered to the Italian Front. Plans were made and the Germans and Austro-Hungarian troops moved up to the front. On 24 October 1917 in heavy rain and snowstorms on the heights, in poor visibility the attack commenced and took the Italians by surprise. Using a combination of high-explosive gas and smoke the attacking force, using bombs and flamethrowers, broke through almost immediately and by the end of the first day had advanced almost 25 kilometres into the Italian lines. The Italian Army was forced to withdraw, having lost thousands of men killed and more taken prisoner. The scale of the defeat and the amount of casualties incurred forced the Italian Government to request help through the British and French Military Missions. The French agreed to send four divisions and so the British Government instructed Sir Douglas Haig to select a good man and later they instructed him to select two good divisions. His choice fell on Lieutenant-General the Earl of Cavan and the XIV Corps Headquarters along with the 23rd and 41st Divisions, as well as all the support troops, supply depots, casualty clearing stations, hospitals, sanitary sections, field bakery, field butchery, pay units, veterinary hospital, mechanical workshops and a base post-office unit needed to keep them in the field.

On 28 October warning orders were sent out and advance parties of Corps and Divisional staff consisting of eight officers and thirteen Other Ranks from XIV Corps Headquarters and eight officers and fourteen Other Ranks from each division were ordered to reach Paris in time to catch the evening mail train for Italy. On 1 November units were warned that they would be

Lieutenant-General Frederick Rudolph Lambart, 10th Earl of Cavan.

moving by rail to an unknown destination shortly. The first troops of 23rd Division to leave were 68 Brigade.

Meanwhile on the training area 12 and 13/DLI were busy refitting: new clothing was drawn, men went to the baths, and frequent route marches, parades and inspections took place; also a lot of time was spent on the rifle ranges. Lieutenant-Colonel Robert Tyndall commanding 12/DLI was sent to take command of 6/DLI and Major James Longden who came from Castle Eden in County Durham assumed command of 12/DLI. Finally a medical inspection took place and any man considered unfit for campaigning in the Italian mountains was sent to hospital. At 0700 hours on 8 November the right half of 12/DLI paraded with each man carrying ten days' rations: they marched to Arques Station where they quickly entrained. By 1000 hours they were ready to leave but it wasn't until 1030 that the train pulled out and their long journey began. The train headed for St Omer then Calais, Boulogne, Abbeville, Amiens to Longeau: here they were served hot tea and the horses were watered. At 1930 hours the journey continued via Clermont and Creil arriving outside Paris at 0330 hours: here the train halted and a broken-down coach was replaced. The journey continued with stops for coffee and seeing to the horses and each day a longer stop to allow the men to wash, shave and to take some exercise. Having travelled in beautiful weather along the Riviera they eventually crossed into Italy and arrived at Vintimille: here they detrained in full marching order and went for a short route march through the town which was packed with cheering people. The train started again and carried them through San Remo and Ponto Maurizio to Albenga, arriving at Savona at 2130 hours on 11 November.

When they reached Asola at 1745 hours on 12 November they found that the Left Half Battalion who had left after them had arrived ahead of them, had detrained here and were in billets in the town. However, on they went until at 0600 hours on 13 November they eventually arrived at St Antonio: here they detrained and with the Battalion Transport marched through Mantova to billets at Gabbiana.

The next day training started: route-marching, bayonet-fighting and general skill-at-arms. There was an inspection of all the Brigade Transport in which 12/DLI came out as the best in 68 Brigade. On 15 November the Left Half battalion rejoined: commanded by Major Carr-West, they had left Saint-Martin-au-Laërt at 0645 hours on 8 November and marched to Wizernes where they had eventually entrained at 1120 hours. Their route had taken them via Aire and St Pol down past Arras and across part of the old Somme battlefield to Albert and on to Longeau, where tea was served out. They too went down to Marseilles and along the Riviera, crossing the border into Italy at around 1000 hours on 11 November. When they reached Asola at 1600 hours on 12 November they were ordered to detrain by the Italian Military Authorities and billeted in a theatre in the town.

After another day they were able to march to Gabbiana and rejoin the Right Half battalion.

At Tatinghem 13/DLI with ration strength of twenty-six officers and 854 Other Ranks were undergoing a similar training programme. They also were to travel to Italy in two half-battalion groups: on 8 November at 1000 hours the Left Half battalion marched to Arques and entrained at 1340 hours; they were followed by the Right Half battalion at 1245 hours and this party entrained at 1640 hours. Their route missed out Paris but eventually at 1230 hours on 13 November the first train arrived at St Antonio where they detrained and were quartered in the Asylum at La Pavia Mona. Later they marched to billets in Gabbiana where they arrived at 1600 hours. At 1930 hours on 13 November the second train reached Mantova where the men alighted and marched to the Asylum and the next morning they too moved on foot to billets in Gabbiana.

The journey of 12/DLI was recorded in a letter home from Lieutenant Frederick Rees, now recovered from his wounds and on arrival in France posted to 12/DLI instead of his old 13/DLI. He wrote to his mother:

> I wonder if you are thinking I have left this frail flesh or forsaken my family, however neither is true for I am very much alive and at last have a chance of getting off a letter. I had a chance a few days ago and got a letter off to Elsie and a PC to you I wonder if you got the PPC from Nice?
>
> Well we have done some travelling and in consequence I've only had one letter from England since I left home, that was from the Adjutant at Ashford, letters are beginning to come in so I may get some to-night. Well we left France + had five days in the train to start with, the most wonderful journey I ever had all along the Riviera in the most glorious weather. There was an empty open truck next to our carriage so we all travelled in that most of the time; we had a wonderful reception, flowers and fruit thrown on the train in armfuls. When we reached the end of the journey we went into billets in a small town.

Of 13/DLI's journey, little has come to light except the Battalion War Diary entries and these few lines recorded in the diary of 36054 Private William Innes who wrote:

> Sun 11 November 1917
> Pass through Toulon Pass through the Riviera a most magnificent sight, pass Cannes and Monte Carlo. Cross Italian Frontier
> Mon 12 November
> Some beautiful mountain scenery in Italy, people are very enthusiastic.
> Tue 13 November
> Landed at destination about 0200 hours and marched about 8 kilometres to Gabbiana.

Both battalions spent a few days training while higher commands sorted out what was going to be done. Eventually it was decided that the British and French Divisions would move to positions in close support of their

Italian allies and that the march should begin on 19 November. Now back with 13/DLI, before they left Gabbiana, Lieutenant Frederick Rees got a letter away in which he described the last few days:

> *I was billeted in a gentleman's house. He was a charming man and invited all the officers to tea, there was a piano so we had a sing song. He could speak French so we all got on much better as none of us know hardly a word of Italian. We were there two nights then another all night journey in the train and a three mile march, arrived in billets at 5 am very tired but good bed to sleep on, this was the morning of 15 November, we left France on 8 November. Well the next thing of interest is that I have been appointed Assistant Adjutant which is not at all a bad job out here. After a couple of days or so we started off on the march and we are now moving every day doing a good long march.*

At 0600 hours on 19 November 13/DLI marched out of Gabbiana as advanced guard of 68 Brigade and by 1300 hours had reached Castel d'Ario where they were to billet for the night. They were followed at 0715 hours by 12/DLI who arrived in the same location at 1430 hours. From then on each day they marched to a new overnight halt, were up early the next morning and on to the next halt. On the way they passed many groups of straggling Italian soldiers, many without arms and at best in rough columns, with their officers riding in carriages and their NCOs and junior officers travelling in pony carts. This left a poor impression on the men of the 23rd Division as they went up towards the line. The march went on and by 26 November 12/DLI had reached Lobia where they rested for two days; however, the British rest meant parades and drill, cleaning up and general training, so there was little actual rest. Lieutenant Frederick Rees had a few words to say about this time:

13/DLI marched out of Gabbiana as advanced guard of 68 Brigade. Italian women watch this column as they pass by.

On the way they passed many groups of Italians.

> *I'm now sitting in a farm over a good log fire. It's very interesting here, most of the Italian women seem to wash clothes in the streams. Bullocks used in waggons and for ploughing. I've just caught a glimpse of the Southern Alps. Must dry up now I'll write when I can but were on the move and only get mails out occasionally.*

On the same date 13/DLI reached San Giorgio Bosco where they too rested and the men were able to get a bath. On the evening of 26 November a concert was held in the Town Hall for the battalion. 36054 Private William Innes made one-line entries in his diary at this time. Each day's entry records the daily tramp of an infantry battalion as it approaches the fighting line: Sun 18 Mantova, Mon 19 Castel d'Ario, Tues 20 Cerea. Here he records that his feet are very sore. Then daily treks to small unnamed villages where they billet each night but the day's miles are recorded: 19 miles today, 22 miles today. By 30 November 13/DLI had reached Piombino and 12/DLI were in billets at Brusaporco. Despite being on the march, the battalion had received a draft of 110 Other Ranks and their trench strength was now thirty-one officers and 842 Other Ranks. Here Lieutenant Frederick Rees wrote to his father:

> *We are still on the move but manage to get a letter off occasionally.*

We've done a good bit of marching since we came into this country, somewhere about 120 miles, I think I'm in very good trim, in fact I am thinking of walking home when the war is over. I'm no longer Assistant Adjutant but am in command of a company but don't know how long that will be for. We had lunch and tea in the open today quite warm and sunny, but we always get a sharp frost at night.

We feed very well & all feel very fit + as yet have seen no signs of war, though we shall be in the line before very long I expect. I hear the trenches are wonderfully good, all together a great deal better than France. If only we get the old Huns on the other side on the run and chase them over the Alps all will be well, of course it will not be that easy as it sounds, but he will get a run for his money now we're here.

At the end of November orders were received that 23rd Division was to relieve the 70th Italian Division. It was decided that the front would be held by two brigades, each with two battalions in the line, one in support and the third in reserve, and the third brigade was to be in Divisional reserve but ready to move. The position to be taken over by the division was the left or western part of the high ground behind the River Piave known as the Montello. This high ground, some 7 miles long and 4 miles wide which overlooked the open plain to the south-east and west represented a very strong position, and along with this a narrow strip of the plain 1.5 to 2 kilometres wide below its western slope. Thus on the evening of 2 December 69 Brigade relieved the 135th Italian Regiment in the right sector and during the night of 3/4 December 70 Brigade took over from 136th Italian Regiment in the left sector, the Italian Regiment being the equivalent of a British brigade. 68 Brigade became the Divisional reserve situated near Montebelluna and started supplying working parties for the units in the line.

12/DLI left Brusaporco at 0845 hours on 2 December and marched via Albaredo–Vedelago–Barcon and Montebelluna to Biadene where they arrived at 1330 hours and took over billets from Italian troops. The billets were filthy and the whole of the rest of the day was spent cleaning them up. 13/DLI also moved up to Montebelluna where they relieved 1st Battalion 98th Italian Territorial Regiment. From here they deployed one officer and thirty men with a Lewis gun of A Company to Ponte di Pietra where they relieved a similar-sized Italian unit. 13/DLI also spent much time cleaning their new billets and they had to provide 250 men for working parties. At 1100 hours on 11 December the Austrian gunners fired a number of shells at 13/DLI's billets and then in the afternoon another salvo fell but fortunately no casualties occurred. For the next three weeks training was carried out in various forms, two small drafts of men joined 13/DLI, and 12/DLI even found time for extended order drill. There were a few working parties and one party of an officer and twenty-five men were attached to 101 Field Company Royal Engineers for tunnelling work.

Men of 13/DLI near their huts in the rear positions on the Montello. D/DLI//7/560/13(22)

On 19 December His Royal Highness the Prince of Wales visited both battalions and having inspected the billets, expressed his satisfaction. That evening 68 Brigade began relieving 70 Brigade and at 1830 hours 13/DLI took over from 8/KOYLI in Brigade support, the relief being complete by 2005 hours. At the same time 12/DLI took over from 11/Sherwood Foresters as the Brigade reserve battalion, but they were allowed to remain in their location where they continued with the training and route-marching with most afternoons being given over to sport. In 12/DLI the CO introduced a cup for the best platoon at soccer, and inter-platoon games took place most afternoons.

On 20 December 13/DLI sent a party of men to the Brigade School where there was an accident on the bombing range: this resulted in 18198 Corporal Joseph Spoors and 21616 Lance Corporal George Readman being wounded badly enough to be evacuated back to France. Joseph Spoors went on to hospital in England but George Readman when fit again was posted to 22/DLI. On the same day and possibly in the same incident 26342 Private James Robson, a schoolmaster from Roker in Sunderland

68 Brigade started supplying working parties for the units in the line.

serving with 12/DLI, received bomb wounds to the head; evacuated to Number 30 Casualty Clearing Station he died from his wounds. His documents which survive indicate there was a Court of Inquiry into his death, but unfortunately the records have not survived. Snow fell the next day and the weather was wet and misty and it remained like this for the next couple of days.

36054 Private William Innes recorded a tragic event in his diary at this time when he wrote:

Sun 23 December

We have our first casualties in Italy 4 killed and 6 wounded on a working party. Old Joe [his nickname for the Austrian gunners opposite] *shells the front line nearly all day.*

The four killed were 302789 Private Daniel Cooper from Chesterfield, 44984 Private Ira Greenwood from Haworth near Keighley, 204330 Private

Norman Johnson from Castle Eden, County Durham and 78491 Private John Whetton from Shipley. However, he was slightly wrong as only five men are recorded wounded in the Battalion and the Adjutant's Diary. They were 302736 Private John Mather; 302302 Private William Dart and 4495 Private Henry Woodward who had joined the battalion after serving with the Royal Berkshire Regiment and the Labour Corps; and two reinforcements who had originally enlisted into the Army Veterinary Corps, 44587 Private William Stevens and 44586 Private William Simpson. The wounded were quickly evacuated; however, William Dart, a Derby scheme enlistment in 2/8/DLI who came from near Taunton in Somerset, had been hit in the head by shrapnel and was dangerously ill. Reaching Number 24 Casualty Clearing Station, he survived until 27 December when he died from his wounds. Private William Stevens from Andover in Hampshire had shrapnel wounds to the right arm and right buttock. He too was dangerously ill, but managed to live until 15 January 1918 when he died from his wounds at 62/General Hospital which was based in Borighera on the Italian Mediterranean coast on the road to Nice in France.

13/DLI in their War Diary gave no indication of any Christmas festivities or special meals for the men, simply stating it was a very quiet day. On the other hand 12/DLI recorded that the final of the inter-platoon football cup was played on Christmas Day between Number 1 Platoon A Company and Number 13 Platoon D Company: the result was a draw after extra time with no goals on either side. There was also a guard-mounting competition, the final of which was held on the same day and judged by the Brigade Commander who decided that the smartest turned-out and best-drilled was Number 11 Section of 3 Platoon A Company. Christmas Day started with the usual Church parades for various denominations and then an inspection of the billets and cookhouses to judge the best decorated and the best Christmas dinner.

On 27 December the football final was replayed and No 1 Platoon won the cup by one goal to nil. That evening 12/DLI went up into the front line and relieved 11/NF, placing A, B and D Companies in the line with C Company in support. The Italian Aqui Brigade was on the left flank, and 13/DLI who had also moved into the line and replaced 10/NF was on the right flank of 12/DLI.

The last days of 1917 were spent improving the trenches and nightly patrols along the River Piave in front of the battalion positions.

1918

On New Year's Day 1918 His Royal Highness the Prince of Wales accompanied by several Staff Officers toured the line held by 12/DLI. The work on improving the trenches continued and the patrols from both battalions became more ambitious and daring; however, nothing of importance happened. On 2 January 12/DLI came under artillery fire from 'Old Joe' and Lieutenant Cuthbert Vaux MC was wounded by a bursting shell. The work on improving the trenches continued and that night a fighting patrol of two officers and fifteen men crossed the River Piave but were unable to hear or locate the enemy and returned safely. Also during 3 January Second Lieutenants John Agar, C.M. Watts and William Hurford reported their arrival at Battalion Headquarters. That night a patrol from 13/DLI crossed the Piave and once in position they heard enemy movements and approached the position with the objective of taking a prisoner: all of a sudden an Austrian searchlight lit up the patrol and they were forced to retire back over the river, fortunately without casualties.

Four officers of 13/DLI in the trenches on the Montello sector of the Italian Front. D/DLI//7/560/13(23)

The weather at this time was very wintry with heavy falls of snow in the evening of 4 January. 11/NF relieved 13/DLI who moved back to Pederiva where they spent time cleaning up and training. At the same time 12/DLI were relieved by 10/NF and became the Brigade support battalion. The Battalion Lewis-gunners were lectured on Anti-Aircraft fire by the Divisional Machine Gun Officer, while the men of the rifle platoons provided working parties for the Royal Engineers. On the night of 7 January the Battalion Guard Room was burnt out in a fire and word was received that Private Walton had been placed under arrest. For the next few days the working parties continued until on the night of 12 January they relieved 11/NF in the right sector of the left Brigade front with Battalion Headquarters at Ciano. 13/DLI also moved back into the line. The leading company left Pederiva at 1730 hours and by 1945 hours the relief was complete with B Company on the right, A Company holding the centre with two platoons in the line and two platoons in support, and the left flank held by C Company with only one platoon in the front line and the other three platoons in support. D Company was located further back.

Both battalions were now engaged on active patrol work, and each night officers led small groups of men out along the front held by their battalion. On 14 January a patrol from 12/DLI consisting of one officer and sixteen men crossed to the north bank of the Piave: here they were challenged by the Austrians holding the riverbank and although fire was exchanged, the patrol was unable to capture a prisoner and returned empty-handed. The same night 13/DLI reported that ice was forming on the river and it was unsafe to attempt to cross.

On 16 January a triple Courts Martial took place in 12/DLI when Privates James, Robson and Vasey were tried: unfortunately the War Diary does not record their Regimental numbers or their crimes and punishment. This was followed the next day by the trial of Private Walton who was mentioned earlier.

In the early hours of 18 January Second Lieutenant John Morrison led a fighting patrol across the river. They were accompanied by a section of 68/LTMB led by Second Lieutenant N.B. Hall, and as they crossed the last part of the river they were challenged by an alert Austrian sentry and forced to retire by the enemy's fire. That night saw 11/West Yorks arrive and take over the line, 12/DLI moving back to billets in Pederiva which had been vacated by 8/Green Howards. The last-named unit had moved up into the line and replaced 13/DLI who then moved to the reserve brigade billets in Biadene. Both battalions spent time cleaning up and then the usual parades, inspections and working parties took place. On 20 January another Court Martial was held, this time by 13/DLI: recorded in the Adjutant's Diary it simply says 'FGCM of Conscientious Objector promulgated', yet no details of the man or his punishment are given. 12/DLI regarded themselves lucky for on 24 January the whole battalion received a complete change of underclothing, luxury indeed! A small draft of six men and three officers joined 13/DLI on 28 January. Second Lieutenant Ernest Davis MC was rejoining after being wounded and was posted to A Company; Second Liuetenant John Knotts had seen service in France as a Lance Corporal with 20/DLI before being commissioned in October 1917, he was sent to join B Company. The third to join who was posted to D Company was Second Lieutenant Charles Wakeham MC, DCM, MM who had served as a Company Sergeant-Major with 10/DLI. They joined just as the battalion began training harder, outpost lines were practised and then they took part in a rehearsal for a counter-attack on the Montello. In the theatre in Montebelluna 'The Dumps', the 23rd Divisional Concert party, were giving performances of their revue 'The Babes of Polygon Wood' for the infantry battalions out of the line. On the afternoon of 31 January it was 12/DLI's turn, and then that night the Austrian Air Force bombed the battalion's billets but only wounded one man.

The enemy aeroplanes returned the following night and many bombs were dropped on Montebelluna. On 3 February it was time to move back to the line again: 12/DLI took over from 8/York & Lancs in the reserve positions of the right Brigade sector at Venegazzù, while 13/DLI relieved 8/KOYLI in the support positions in the same sector.

Behind the lines in the training area 23rd Division had organised a Divisional Rifle Meeting. 12/DLI did very well in this: the battalion team achieved first place in the rifle match, D Company Lewis-gun team won the Lewis-gun competition with C Company in fourth place and A Company in fifth place, and the B Company team finished in eighth place putting 12/DLI in the winning position. The battalion also won the officers' revolver match and the Company team match. 13/DLI reported that they were second in the battalion team event and third in the Lewis-gun competition. On the night of 10 February both battalions moved up into the front line: 13/DLI took over from 10/NF in the right subsector and 12/DLI took over from 11/NF in the left subsector.

40054 Pte Burt Chamberlain 12/DLI was wounded but remained on the Italian Front and was posted to 1/Garrison Bn The Royal Munster Fusiliers.

Work on improving the trenches continued; and nightly, both reconnaissance and fighting patrols crossed the Piave. These were mostly uneventful: 13/DLI reported that crossing the river was easy but on the other side they seldom met any enemy soldiers, even though on occasions they penetrated over 800 yards into the enemy lines. On the last patrol before they were relieved 13/DLI sent a fighting patrol of one officer and fourteen men from the right company in the direction of Casona: having crossed the river Piave they arrived at the enemy's wire, where they were challenged by an Austrian sentry. The whole of the immediate enemy front opened rapid fire and the patrol withdrew 50 yards and lay down and commenced returning fire. They remained there for around fifteen minutes and then withdrew back over the river with only one man slightly wounded. It was now time for 23rd Division to leave the line and go out for a rest, so on the night of 17 February 18/KRRC of 41st Division relieved 13/DLI. By 2130 hours the relief was complete and 13/DLI were marching back to Biadene where they spent the night. At the same time 15/Hampshire Regiment took over from 12/DLI and they too made their way back to Biadene. After an overnight stop, both battalions marched to the area of Altivole. 13/DLI described the billets here as very dirty so as usual both battalions started their rest by cleaning up the billets and preparing for kit inspections and parades.

Tragedy again struck 13/DLI when 16451 Private James Steel died in the billets: as usual a Court of Inquiry was held and witnesses called to give evidence. The Court assembled on the morning of 22 February 1918 under the presidency of Major Edward Gray DSO, MC, MM along with Second Lieutenants Ernest Davis and T. Bolton as members. The first man called was 18195 Private William Patrickson, D Company cook, who said:

Sir, I was entering the village of Altivole at 2015 hours on 20 February when I found the deceased lying on the side of the road, about 200 yards from my billet, he was drunk. Along with the assistance of Private Banks I carried him to my billet. We took off his boots and belt and loosened his shirt collar and put him to bed, three of us sleeping together, with six blankets over us. When I got up at 0530 to cook the company's breakfast I didn't notice anything wrong.

On going back to the billets to call Private Banks at Reveille, I saw that the deceased had a strange look about him and on examining him I found that he was dead. I reported at once to the MO.

The next witness was 21066 Private Tom Banks who added the following statement:

Sir, I was entering the village of Altivole at 2015 hours on 20 February in the company of Private Patrickson when we found the deceased lying on the road side about 200 yards from my billet. He was very drunk. We lifted him onto his feet but he could not walk, so we carried him to our billet, took off his boots and belt and loosened his shirt collar and put him into bed with us. Private Patrickson woke me at Reveille and asked me to look at the deceased because he looked very strange. We examined him together and found he was dead. Private Patrickson reported at once to the MO.

The Court then asked the question:

Did the deceased complain of feeling ill in the night?

The answer from Private Banks:

No Sir.

The third witness to give his evidence was the Battalion Medical Officer, Captain James Lanigan Royal Army Medical Corps from Tipperary, a Special Reservist who had been out with the BEF since 1914. He added this statement to the evidence:

About 0730 hours on 21 February at Altivole I was informed that a man had been found dead in D Company billet. On arrival there I found deceased lying on his back with legs crossed, his boots and belt were off and his shirt collar loosened. On examining him I found he was dead.

The court then asked further questions:

How long do you think he had been dead?

Rigor Mortis had set in and in my opinion he had been dead for at least two hours.

Captain Lanigan continued:

As I was unable to certify the cause of death under 23rd Divisional Orders I had him removed to the 69/Field Ambulance for conveyance to a CCS for post mortem examination.

The report from the CCS confirmed death by asphyxia due to Private Steel vomiting in his sleep.

The General Staff had realised that the Germans were withdrawing divisions from Italy and Russia and sending them to the Western Front: with this in mind they decided to withdraw some of the British and French divisions from the Italian Front and bring them back to France. At one stage 23rd Division and 7th Division were selected but this was cancelled and 5th Division and 41st Division were picked to go. In order that 41st Division could prepare for the move back to France it was necessary to

Four officers of 13/DLI in reserve positions on the Montello: holding the staff is Frederick Rees MC.
D/DLI//7/560/13(21)

replace them in the line, so after only seven days out of the line 23rd Division began to move back again.

At 1000 hours on the morning of 24 February 13/DLI marched out of Altivole and proceeded to Pederiva where they took over from 20/DLI. Likewise 12/DLI left Altivole and marched to Biadene where they spent the afternoon resting and that evening made their way into the support positions on the left Brigade front of the Montello sector where they took over from 11/Queens Regiment. They spent the next three days working under the Royal Engineers and did a small amount of training before 13/DLI arrived and took over the positions, with 12/DLI moving back to billets in Biadene. Here they did some range work and practised hill-fighting with sport in the afternoons and the men were all able to have a bath. But it was soon time to return to the front line and during the evening of 4 March 12/DLI relieved 10/NF in the left sector of the left Brigade front with Battalion Headquarters located at Zappolon. At the same time 13/DLI took over from 11/NF in the right sector of the left Brigade front: they placed A Company on the right with two platoons in the line and two in support. B Company held the centre of the battalion front and D Company held the left with C Company in support.

There had been fairly heavy rain, with the result that the Piave had risen by over 4 feet and the trenches and dugouts were full of water. This meant that a lot of energy was expended on drainage work and improving the trenches where they were collapsing. The nightly defensive patrols continued but owing to the state of the river no attempts were made to send fighting patrols across to the Austrian lines. 23rd Division was now ordered to move from the Montello sector and take over the whole of the frontage allotted to XIV Corps on the Asiago Plateau. With this in mind, Italian officers from the Italian 51st Division arrived to look round the positions held by 68 Brigade.

On 12 March 1st Battalion 46th Italian Regiment took over from 13/DLI who moved to Biadene, and on the same night 2nd Battalion 48th Italian Regiment took over from 12/DLI, who on leaving the line were billeted at Pederiva. Both Durham battalions now moved on foot to Castelfranco, 13/DLI leaving Biadene at 0845 hours on 13 March and arriving at their destination at 1615 hours. 12/DLI had a short march and arrived in billets at 1545 hours. After a night's rest they set off again: 12/DLI left at 0915 hours and eventually arrived in Lanze at 1600 hours, while 13/DLI paraded at 0720 hours and had a 22-mile hike to the village of Ruffo where they arrived at 1730 hours. The next day was spent cleaning up and erecting the usual outbuildings required by an army in the field: cookhouses and latrines were constructed and before being used had to be inspected. Training then started and on 16 March Lieutenant-Colonel Michael Lindsay rejoined 13/DLI and assumed command of the battalion.

Tragedy even managed to strike 13/DLI when they were miles behind the line. 39429 Private Walter Smith, a 22-year-old draper's assistant from Bishop Auckland, was on a course at the XIV Corps School. On the afternoon of 16 March he was given a pass and permission to go into the nearby town of Padova. He was running for a tram and tried to board the vehicle while it was moving. Walter slipped and hit his head on the road which caused a compound fracture of the skull that instantly killed him. The accident was witnessed by two officers of 69 Brigade who submitted statements to the Adjutant of XIV Corps School; both had served in the ranks of the Yorkshire Hussars and had landed in France in April 1915. Second Lieutenant Francis Flory from Great Ayton in North Yorkshire had been commissioned in September 1917 into the Duke of Wellington's Regiment but on arrival at the front had been posted to 9/York and Lancs. He stated:

> On 16 March at 1400 hours I saw Private Smith of 13/DLI attempt to board a tramcar proceeding in the direction of Padova, the tramcar was in motion, travelling at about fifteen miles per hour. The deceased missed his footing and was drawn under the car. The tramcar was made up of three carriages with a step at the front and rear of each carriage to assist with boarding and alighting, the deceased attempted to board the front section of the second carriage. Two sets of wheels passed over him and he was pinned beneath the third set of wheels when the car was brought to a standstill, fifty yards from the place where the deceased made his attempt to board it. When

Austrian troops hard at work improving their positions. D/DLI/7/75/25(59)

extricated life was found to be extinct.

The other officer present was Second Lieutenant Norman Millar from Middlesbrough who had been commissioned into the Green Howards in August 1917. He added the following statement:

> *At about 1400 hours on 16 March 1918, I saw the deceased on the Padova Road attempt to board a tramcar whilst in motion. He appeared to miss his footing and slipped underneath the car. The car travelled about fifty yards before it was brought to a standstill. He was immediately extricated and life was found to be extinct. There were three carriages to the car and he had attempted to board the front step of the centre carriage. Both sets of wheels of the centre carriage ran over him. The car was about fifty yards from a stopping place when the deceased attempted to board it and it was proceeding in the direction of Padova.*

After the accident the body of Private Smith was taken to Number 37 Casualty Clearing Station where he was buried, but in 1919 his remains were exhumed and moved to Padova. Given his height and build he should have been rejected by the Army but on his enlistment forms the Medical Board expected his physique 'Will Improve'. Called up in November 1916, he only received ten weeks' training with 4/DLI before being put on a draft on 10 February 1917 to 14/DLI. On arrival at 35/IBD he was reposted to 13/DLI and on joining them on 16 March 1917 he was posted to C Company.

In the rear area there was time for sport and a Brigade Sports and Horse Show meeting was held on 22 and 23 March. 13/DLI recorded three first prizes and three second prizes in the sports, while 12/DLI were more successful with their horses, taking first prize in the Light Draught Limber Class and winning the Transport Sergeants' Race. On the second day of the Horse Show Lieutenant-Colonel James Longden Commanding 12/DLI took first place in the flat race, the Battalion Medical Officer Captain W.H. Scott was placed second in the jumping competition, and in a special event of musical chairs Second Lieutenant Dudley Cronin was placed second. There was also a Brigade bombing competition organised in which 13/DLI took two first prizes and one second place.

A reconnaissance party consisting of Captain Lafone MC, Captain Freeman MC and Second Lieutenant T. Smithson left 12/DLI by motor lorry on 21 March to reconnoitre the new sector being taken over, but owing to the distance involved only got as far as the reserve battalion positions before being forced to rejoin the battalion. The sector to be taken over on the Asiago Plateau was unlike anything 23rd Division had held before: the eastern part of the front was concealed by dense woodland, while the western part lay on the forward slope in open ground. The positions to be taken over from the Italians comprised two strongly-built main trench lines, which ran parallel to each other and were very heavily wired. The front line was partly dug through earth but mainly blasted from the rocks. The second line, some 800 yards behind the front line but between 400 and 500 feet higher than it, was blasted from rock along its entire length. There were no communication trenches: in the east they were totally unnecessary in the thick woods, and on the western flank they were totally impossible on the steep exposed open slopes.

On 25 March 68 Brigade received orders to move up to the line and at 0700 hours 13/DLI marched out of Ruffo bound for Thiene where they arrived at 1630 hours. Likewise, 12/DLI left Lanze and arrived at Thiene about the same time as 13/DLI. The next day both battalions were transported in Fiat motor lorries of the Italian Army to Carriola. They rested in the town on 27 March and that night 12/DLI took over the right battalion sector of the left Brigade in the front line from 12th Italian Division. The battalion front was 4,400 yards in length along the Ghelpac gorge from Sculazzon to Perghele. The Quartermasters' stores and Battalion Transport remained in Carriola. 13/DLI also moved forward and took over from 3/129 Regiment of 12th Italian Division in Brigade reserve. During the relief 78472 Private John Suffill was accidentally wounded. It was very quiet along the front, but the enemy could be seen digging on a hill opposite the centre of 12/DLI.

On 28 March at 2100 hours a reconnaissance patrol under the command of Second Lieutenant William Colville from Dumbarton, who had served as a Private in the Argyll and Sutherland Highlanders, went out into No

The Traffic Control point at Tattenham Corner on the route up to the Asiago Plateau; a point well-known to the British infantrymen who marched through it.

Man's Land and looked for signs of the enemy; however, nothing was seen and the patrol returned safely to the battalion's lines. The next night another two patrols went out: one led again by William Colville and the second patrol commanded by Second Lieutenant Thomas Welford from Newcastle; he had landed in France in August 1915 as a Private with the East Yorkshire Regiment. One patrol covered the left of the battalion front and the other made its way along the centre section of the ground held. No enemy soldiers were seen but useful information was gained about the lie of the land in front of the position. 7th Division had arrived to join 23rd Division and so the following night 1/Royal Welsh Fusiliers (1/RWF) arrived and relieved 12/DLI who marched back to Carriola where they arrived at 0330 hours on 31 March. In the meantime on 29 March 13/DLI had been relieved in reserve by 2/Queens and had marched to Granezza where they spent the next day and then on the morning of 31 March they moved to Mare.

April started very wet and at Battalion Headquarters of 13/DLI in Mare word arrived that they were to march back to Granezza on the following day. Later that morning at 1145 hours their move was postponed for twenty-four hours. The next day the companies went for a route march in the rain and then at 0800 hours on 3 April they left Mare bound for Granezza where they arrived at 1500 hours. 12/DLI spent the night of 1 April in billets at Magnaboschi and the next day moved to Granezza where they became Divisional Reserve providing working parties and doing some training for the next ten days. During this time

Major James Holford DSO, Sherwood Rangers Yeomanry attached to 11/Sherwood Foresters, joined the battalion and took over command from Lieutenant-Colonel James Longden who was posted to command the 23rd Divisional Troops. One of the first things Major Holford had to order was the formation of a Court of Inquiry into the death of 44967 Private Harry Crossland, a labourer from Halifax.

The events recorded by the Court of Inquiry conflict with the Battalion War Diary in that the diary states the battalion marched to Granezza on 2 April, but all the witnesses state that the accident happened on 3 April. Also in the typed-up report the Officer Witnesses are recorded first, but in the handwritten evidence the Other Ranks are listed as witnesses 1, 2 and 3. On 7 April, three officers of 12/DLI assembled to gather information and report on the death of the above-named soldier. The president of the Court was Captain Eric Lafone MC, assisted by Lieutenant Cuthbert Vaux MC and Second Lieutenant John Hodgson. In the order of the typed-up

Frederick Rees and an unknown officer of 13/DLI outside a well-constructed dugout on the Asiago. D/DLI//7/560/13(19)

notes, the first witness called was Second Lieutenant Dudley Cronin who made this statement:

About 1340 hours on 3 April on the line of march, I was marching in the rear of D Company 12/DLI, about twenty yards behind the Lewis gun limber, when I heard some shouting. I doubled up to the limber and saw the left wheel of the rear half of the limber go over the back of 44967 Private J H Crossland of D Company. He was face down on the ground and it was not possible to stop the limber going over him. Private Crossland was unconscious when I reached him. I took off his equipment and put him on a stretcher. At this time a motor ambulance overtook us and I stopped it and gave orders that Private Crossland should be taken to the nearest Field Ambulance as quickly as possible. At the same time I stated to the RAMC exactly what had happened. Just as the Battalion was marching off about 0910 hours that same morning, Private Crossland came to the head of the column and asked Captain W L Hughes MC if he could have his pack carried, as he was not feeling very well. I saw him several times on the march and he was marching quite well and did not complain to me at all. His pack was carried all the way on the limber.

The second witness was Captain William Hughes, Officer Commanding D Company 12/DLI who said:

On the morning of 3 April 1918 about 0910 hours Private Crossland was brought up to me and complained of feeling sick. I asked him what was the matter and he said that he suffered from a rupture. I asked him why he hadn't gone sick, he replied that he felt quite well until the start of the march. He said he could march quite well if his pack was carried. I gave orders for his pack to be carried on the Lewis gun limber and for him to replace one of the men on the Lewis gun guard marching in the rear of the limber. I did not know anything about the accident until it was reported to me at about 1400 hours.

The next man to give evidence had been with the battalion since its formation and that morning was in charge of the drag rope party behind D Company Lewis-gun limber. Lance Corporal Harry Eldridge had this to say:

An unknown officer of 13/DLI outside a well-constructed dugout on the Asiago.
D/DLI//7/560/13(24)

Frederick Rees and an unknown dog outside a well-constructed dugout on the Asiago.
D/DLI//7/560/13(18)

> On the line of march on 3 April Private Crossland was on the Lewis gun guard and was marching with the same party. About 1340 hours I heard some shouting, I saw Private Crossland lying on the ground face downwards. I helped take his equipment off and called for stretcher bearers and then re-joined my party. About ten minutes before the accident I saw Private Crossland marching in the rear of the limber and I do not know how he came to be between the fore and the rear part of the limber. About ten minutes before the accident Private Crossland told me he was rather dizzy, he did not ask to fall out and his pack was being carried on the limber. I do not know what caused him to fall.

The fourth man called to speak was 45114 Private George Paling who stated:

> I was one of the drag rope party marching in the rear of D Company's limber on 3 April. Private Crossland who was one of the Lewis gun guard was marching behind me, Private Crossland then came up past me and almost immediately afterwards I saw the left wheel of the rear part of the limber on his back. I shouted to the driver to stop and went to the assistance of Private Crossland, he did not appear to be conscious. I do not know how he fell. During the march he told me that he felt bad with his breathing and chest.

Next to give evidence was 78509 Private Harold Atkinson who added the following short statement:

> I was one of the drag rope party marching in the rear of D Company Lewis gun limber on 3 April. Sometime after dinner I heard a shout and I

saw Private Crossland lying on the road face downwards and the left wheel of the limber was going over the small of his back to his shoulders. I saw him turned over by the stretcher bearers and he appeared to be unconscious.

The final witness was 46230 Private John Cawley: originally in the Northumberland Fusiliers, he had served with 1/NF and 26/NF, the 3rd Tyneside Irish, before joining 12/DLI. He only added a few additional words:

I was marching in front of D Company's Lewis gun limber on 3 April when I heard a shout and turning round I saw Private Crossland lying on the road. I went to his assistance and as a Red Cross ambulance was passing he was put straight into it.

The evidence was typed up and presented to the new Commanding Officer so he could add his observations. Major Holford wrote:

After reading the forgoing evidence I am of the opinion;

1) Private Crossland was on duty at the time of the accident.

2) That Private Crossland was solely to blame for the accident as he left his proper place in the rear of the limber.

The file was forwarded to 68 Brigade Headquarters where Brigadier General Cary Barnard wrote: 'I concur with the above stated opinion.'

Frederick Rees and an unknown officer of 13/DLI outside a well-constructed dugout on the Asiago. D/DLI//7/560/13

On the night of 11 April 12/DLI took over the right subsector of the front line from 9/York & Lancs and placed A, B and D Companies in the line with C Company in battalion reserve; immediately the relief was complete they sent patrols out to cover the area to the front, all of which returned safely. The next day passed peacefully but that night a patrol from A Company met and engaged a large body of Austrian troops in No Man's Land. The story is best told by the patrol report which is attached to the Battalion War Diary:

To 68 Infantry Brigade

A protective patrol of one officer and ten other ranks left our lines at 2015 hours accompanied by a reconnoitring patrol of one officer and one other rank whose mission was to examine the wire at Morar and endeavour to discover the gaps and routes use by the Austrian reliefs and visiting patrols. The combined parties halted for half an hour near a camouflaged road about point H.62.49 and no hostile movement having been observed moved forward to the house at Road Junction H.61.52. At this point footsteps were heard on the road near Morar.

The protective patrol halted here in a position to watch the battalion front. The reconnoitring patrol crept forward across the dry bed of the River Ghelpac and halted about fifty yards beyond the white stone bridge at H.61.0 52.5. From this point a man could be heard coughing in Morar. Later two men were seen to leave Morar and proceed along a track running from the village to Silvegnar. These men or two others returned to Morar on the same track about half an hour later. After a further wait of about thirty minutes, four men were seen to enter Morar by the same track, which was also used by four men who subsequently, after a short conversation, left the village.

The long, dry grass which surrounds the village on the south and east proved a great obstacle to quiet movement but the patrol, having completed its mission withdrew apparently unobserved. The reconnoitring patrol having re-joined the protective patrol, the combined parties moved towards our lines until challenged by an enemy party about H.620.497. Our patrol halted under cover and allowed the enemy, who were between them and our lines, to advance within fifty yards. When challenged the enemy 'bunched' offering a fine target: the result of our fire appeared most satisfactory.

The Officer in charge therefore ordered his force to move by sections in a south westerly direction, each section covering the withdrawal of the other. In this way, the withdrawal was accomplished with the loss of one man. The enemy's fire, from rifles, machine gun and trench mortars was very wild, probably owing to the good results of our first burst of fire and the subsequent steady shooting during the withdrawal. On the absence of the missing man being discovered a fresh patrol proceeded to search the ground. This patrol saw no signs of the missing man or of the enemy. The Officer in charge of our patrol estimated the strength of the Austrians at about one company.

For the next five days the front was very quiet. A few shells fell about the battalion positions and each night patrols crept about in No Man's Land trying to locate the enemy but to no avail, until on the night of 17 April they were relieved by 11/NF and moved into Brigade reserve at Kaberlaba.

13/DLI were last heard of in Granezza on 3 April. Resting in the village, the battalion spent the time cleaning up and officers and NCOs were sent

The staff of an Austrian Headquarters telephone exchange relax outside their bunker.

up to the line to reconnoitre the positions they expected to be taking over. For the first few days the weather was very wet but on 10 April there was a heavy fall of snow and in this wintry weather the following night they relieved 8/York & Lancs in the left subsector of the front line, placing D Company on the right, A Company in the centre and C Company on the left with B Company in support. Battalion Headquarters and the Regimental Aid Post were slightly further back. 13/DLI also had patrols out into No Man's Land and although they found some enemy sentries, they could not approach them to capture them owing to well-placed tripwires and obstacles.

The battalion positions were shelled intermittently over the next couple of days. On 15 April Lieutenant-Colonel Michael Lindsay DSO left the battalion and took up the post of Commanding Officer of 23/Machine Gun Corps; he was replaced by Major Denzil Clarke DSO, MC who was promoted to Lieutenant-Colonel.

That night a patrol of one officer and twenty-two men left the battalion lines at 2030 hours. They made their way through the village of Coda and from there to point H.525.495 where sounds of the enemy could be heard. The patrol was challenged and fired upon and immediately afterwards about fifty of the enemy appeared and opened fire with trench mortars, machine guns and bombs. The patrol engaged the enemy for about fifteen minutes, but finding themselves outflanked and outnumbered, withdrew to the British lines. By 2330 they were safe inside the front line with Second Lieutenant Ernest Davis MC and four men wounded.

The next few days were quiet with the usual harassing artillery fire. On 17 April reconnoitring parties from 48th (South Midland) Division came up to the line and had a look at the positions they would be taking over shortly. That evening at 2200 hours 10/NF took over the front line and 13/DLI moved back into left support; by 0015 hours 13/DLI were established in the region of Pennar, then that afternoon they were visited by a reconnoitering party from 1/6/Gloucestershire Regiment. However, 13/DLI was not allowed to rest and they had over 400 men employed on working parties, then later they practised manning the battalion battle positions. On 22 April 1/6/Gloucestershire Regiment arrived and took over the support positions and 13/DLI moved back to Granezza; the next day the march continued to Fara where they were accommodated in a hutted camp. Then at 0725 hours on the morning of 24 April they marched to Villaverla, where they arrived at 1100 hours. Here they had the unpleasant experience of being billeted in bivouacs, when the heavens opened and a heavy thunderstorm started which lasted well into the night. In very hot weather the next day's trek saw them cover 29 kilometres to the town of Costo where they arrived at 1540 hours. There was continuous rain for the next three days, so most of the time was spent cleaning up; however, one small working party of one officer and fifty men was sent to Spietro. By 30 April the weather had improved and company training started.

On 22 April 12/DLI was relieved as the Right Reserve Battalion by 8/Worcestershire Regiment and they too set off on foot for Granezza. The next day orders were issued for the battalion to move to Fara and then on 24 April the march continued to Noveledo. The instructions for these marches survive in the Battalion War Diary and the order for this last move is laid out below to give an idea of how such marches were organised:

SECRET

12th BATTALION THE DURHAM LIGHT INFANTRY

OPERATION ORDER No 112

Ref Map   BRENTA & PIAVE 1/100,000

1 The Battalion will move from FARA Area to NOVELEDO on 24th April 1919.

2 Dress :- Marching Order without blankets.

3 Order of March :- HQ, B, C, D and A.

4 Battalion will form up at the Cross-roads immediately E of Battn HQrs. B Coy will take its place in the line of march as the battalion passes.

5 Time of Starting :- 7.15 a.m.

6 O.C. A Coy will act as 2nd in Command.

7 2nd Lieut J Noble and 2 NCOs to be detailed by O.C. B Coy will remain in the rear to collect any stragglers.

8 Route of march :- Point 113, Bridge over ASTICO, SEGA – PREARA – LEVA – NOVELEDO. Intervals of 50 yards between Companies and 500 yards between Battalions.

9 L.G Limbers will move behind their companies with A.A guns ready.

10 Billeting Parties. 2nd Lieut T Smithson and 1 NCO per Coy and Battn HQrs will report to Staff Captain at 10 a.m. 24th Inst at the Church, NOVELEDO. QM will arrange bicycles.

11 Striking Camp. Camp will be struck by 6-45 a.m. and tents stacked by A, C, and D Coys on road immediately south of Camp. Any tents in possession of B Company will be stacked at starting point.

12 Kits, Mess Stores and blankets (neatly rolled in bundles of ten) will be stacked at 6-45 a.m. at nearest points on road to various Coy HQrs. 1 man per Coy will remain at Blanket Dumps as Guards.

13 Marching out states will be handed to Adjt at Starting Point. Marching in states to be forwarded to Orderly Room immediately reaching NOVELEDO.

14 Orderly Room :- 2-30 p.m.

15 Acknowledge.

Signed E E Dorman-Smith Captain

Adjt 12th Bn Durham Light Infantry

23rd April 1918

Having reached Noveledo, they were billeted for the night. However, the Orderly Room staff were kept busy as they had to type up the next Operation Order No 113 which gave details of the move to S Urbano Vigo. There were slight differences in timings and names, but it followed the pattern of the order reproduced above. In S Urbano Vigo the battalion rested for the whole of 27 April and as the weather was very inclement they spent the time cleaning uniforms and equipment. Then the following day the route continued to Lumignano which was part of the training area allotted to the British XIV Coros. Both battalions were now quartered on the training area and in very hot weather began practising hill warfare.

On 2 May 44377 Private Alexander McCaughan of 13/DLI was tried by Field General Court Martial and was awarded two years' imprisonment with hard labour which was commuted to ninety days' Field Punishment Number 1, but what he did to deserve this has not yet come to light.

The training continued and the Brigade Commander, Brigadier General Cary Barnard and then the GOC 23rd Division, General Babington visited the troops in training. Some working parties had to be carried out and C Company of 13/DLI was sent to relieve a company of 10/NF working on an RAF base near Villaverla. B Company working at San Pietro were relieved by D Company, and with two companies away there was little done in the way of larger tactical exercises. The Lewis-gunners spent a day on the ranges but soon 68 Brigade was ordered to rejoin the rest of the Division in the Tressino area and they made their way back by route march beginning on 7 May. 12/DLI Operation Order for this move survives in the Battalion War Diary and in layout is identical to the one reproduced above. There is one difference, however, in that at paragraph 6 the following is added:

A loading party of one man per company will remain as guard over kits. The following men will be detailed for this duty:

A Coy	No 45060 Pte Carter, Arthur, from Leicestershire Regt.
B Coy	No 40613 Pte Reed, G
C Coy	No 78513 Pte Bell, John
D Coy	No 44957 Pte Chicken, Sydney, Trf. to Machine Gun Corps
HQrs	No 54262 Pte Blaydon, B.T.

It is unusual to find Other Ranks named in the War Diary, hence their inclusion here.

Having moved back to S Urbano, 12/DLI spent a further five days training, while 13/DLI having moved from Rovere arrived in Lugo on 16 May. While resting here on 17 May a Field General Court Martial was assembled and two members of the battalion were tried for their crimes. The first was 44560 Lance Corporal Gordon Cresswell, a cowman from Derbyshire who had enlisted into the Army Veterinary Corps in January 1916 under a scheme to recruit men who could work with animals. Transferred to 13/DLI, he had retained his rank and rate of pay on transfer. He was tried under the Army Act for Conduct Prejudicial to Good Order and Conduct of Military Discipline in that on or about 5 April 1918 he signed the certificate on A.F.W. 3079, well knowing it to be untrue. He was found guilty and sentenced to one year's imprisonment with hard labour; on 29 May the sentence was remitted by the GOC 68 Brigade.

The second Court Martial that day was that of 45954 Corporal William Edsall who came from Middlesex. He had enlisted into 5/Northamptonshire Regiment in August 1914 and after service in France had been transferred to the Labour Corps and then to 13/DLI. His crime and trial were very straightforward: 'Drunkenness'! Found guilty and reduced to the ranks.

The next day 13/DLI marched out of Lugo and to Granezza. They did not stay there long and the next day, 19 May, they moved up into the line and relieved 1/4/Oxford and Buckinghamshire Light Infantry (1/4/OBLI) in the left battalion front of the right Brigade sector. The relief was completed by 1545 hours and no sooner were they in the line than patrols were out in No Man's Land. 12/DLI had also moved to Granezza and on 19 May they went forward and took over from 1/5/Gloucestershire Regiment; 12/DLI placed B and C Companies in the front line with D Company in support and A Company in reserve. They too sent patrols to cover the front, and in one case a whole platoon from A Company lay out all day.

Both battalions carried out raids on enemy positions but in both cases these were unoccupied. In the early hours of 23 May a patrol from 13/DLI encountered a large force of Austrians advancing from the left of the battalion front: suddenly a white Very light was fired from the Austrian lines and they opened fire with rifles and machine guns and some grenades were thrown. The patrol returned fire but being outnumbered they withdrew to the British lines. Then that afternoon a scout from the battalion discovered the body of an Austrian soldier where the patrol had been in the early morning. The body was examined but all evidence of identification had been removed. Another patrol went out in the early hours of 26 May to ascertain if the houses at S Ave were occupied. They were covered by a fighting patrol from C Company 12/DLI. The houses were unoccupied and the 13/DLI men withdrew but the patrol from 12/DLI came under heavy Austrian fire and had two men wounded. At 1050 hours on 26 May 13/DLI was relieved by 11/NF and moved into the Right Reserve positions; at the same time 10/NF took over from 12/DLI and the latter became Left Reserve Battalion.

On 2 June 12/DLI were relieved by 11/Sherwood Foresters and moved to Divisional Reserve at Monte Cavaletto where they spent the next six days training. They were followed on 3 June by 13/DLI who were relieved by 9/York and Lancs. The weather was very wet and heavy thunderstorms hampered training, so time was spent improving the camp. Late in the afternoon on 5 June a heavy snowstorm took place. Orders were received to go back into the line and at 0730 hours on 10 June 13/DLI left Granezza and relieved 8/Green Howards in the right subsector of the left Brigade front; likewise, 12/DLI took over the left subsector from 10/DWR.

There were strong rumours of an Austrian offensive against the British and French positions on the Asiago Plateau. Accordingly GOC 68 Brigade moved 11/NF into the front line on the left of 12/DLI with 10/NF in Reserve. Positioned on the right was 70 Brigade and to the left troops of 48th (South Midland) Division.

On 14 June Lord Cavan held a conference at XIV Corps Headquarters with his Divisional Commanders and confirmed that the expected assault would take place the following morning. The British Front was expected to be outside the limits of the infantry attack, but would come under artillery fire which was likely to include gas shells. The word was quickly passed from Division to Brigade and on through Battalion to Company Headquarters in the line and the defence scheme was reviewed and rehearsed. That evening an Austrian deserter came over and gave himself up and confirmed that an attack would take place at dawn. At 0300 hours just as it was breaking daylight, hundreds of Austrian guns opened fire with shells of every calibre. The barrage fell mainly on the rear area, Divisional and Brigade Headquarters and the ammunition dumps and stores dumps behind the front, but on 68 Brigade front the British barbed wire was scarcely touched. At 0320 hours the outpost line was withdrawn. The Austrian assault hit 70 Brigade first at about 0700 hours and then 68 Brigade about a quarter of an hour later. With an open field of fire, as soon as the Austrians showed themselves the infantrymen in the front line opened up a withering fire and stopped the attack dead. In spite of many gallant attempts by Austrian soldiers to press home the attack, only about ten of them reached the line held by 68 Brigade. Only on the left at the junction of 11/NF and 48th Division was there any real trouble: the enemy broke in and pushed 1/4/OBLI back which caused 11/NF to fall back and form a defensive flank. Supported by one company of 10/NF and two companies of 8/York and Lancs from 69 Brigade, the line was held. Along the front held by 12/DLI heavy casualties were inflicted on the attackers as they were pinned down in No Man's Land.

15959 Sgt Jack O'Hara 12/DLI was awarded the Military Medal for his actions during the Battle of Asiago. He was killed trying to cut the barbed wire that was holding up the advance of 12/DLI as they crossed the River Piave on 27 October 1918.

The shelling repeatedly broke the signal wires between the companies, and the Battalion Headquarters Signal Sergeant 18662 James Speed MM & Bar from Blackhill went out many times under heavy shellfire to repair the broken lines, working continuously for over twenty hours. He was awarded the Distinguished Conduct Medal. 20891 Company Sergeant-Major Thomas Martin, a Newcastle man, organised his platoon to meet the enemy advance: he maintained communication with the company on his left, continually moving over open and shell-swept ground to do so. Throughout the attack he inspired all ranks with his coolness and contempt for danger. Early on during the attack the Austrians established a machine gun in the dead ground in front of 12/DLI. 15959 Sergeant Jack O'Hara from Bishop Auckland led a party of riflemen out from the British lines and attacked the gun: they took two of the crew prisoner and killed those that stood their ground, while a few others made off rapidly towards their own lines.

All day small parties of enemy tried to return to their own front line but the majority were shot down as they retreated. A defensive patrol under the command of Second Lieutenant Rasche had remained out in No Man's Land during the bombardment and they helped in repelling the enemy before they withdrew to the front-line trench, bringing in their wounded with them. He remained at duty until ordered to the Field Ambulance at the close of the action.

Acts of gallantry were also taking place in 13/DLI. 300014 Company Sergeant-Major W. Adamson from Pelton walked up and down the trench under heavy fire, controlling the fire of his men: when the attack broke down he took a party out into No Man's Land and brought in a number of prisoners. The Machine Gun Section of A Company, led by 24803 Sergeant Jack Anderson MM from Wingate whose letters appear in an earlier chapter, accounted for a large number of the enemy. Jack Anderson handled his four guns with great skill and judgement. Taking over a Lewis gun, he himself accounted for the whole crew of an Austrian machine gun. As the action closed, he led a party out into No Man's Land and rounded up a number of prisoners.

The War Diary of 13/DLI gives a timed account of the action on their part of the front:

Second Lieutenant Rasche 20/DLI att 12/DLI had remained out in No Man's Land.

0300	*The Austrians opened a very heavy bombardment.*
0630	*Enemy reported advancing and about a dozen men in Poslen West.*
0830	*Enemy advancing in small parties and forming up on the line Poslen – Malga Cheller.*
0840	*Enemy attacking in strength. SOS sent up from front line.*
0905	*Enemy reported digging in on line Guardinalti – Poslen – Partut – Tescia – Malga Cheller.*
1055	*About fifty enemy in Poslen and numbers in Partut, Casa del Bello and Malga Cheller. Three Austrians killed on our wire and identifications brought in.*
1105	*Enemy field gun in S Ave.*
1135	*Enemy massing behind ridge right of Coda Spur.*
1200	*Back areas being shelled, Battalion Headquarters receiving special attention.*

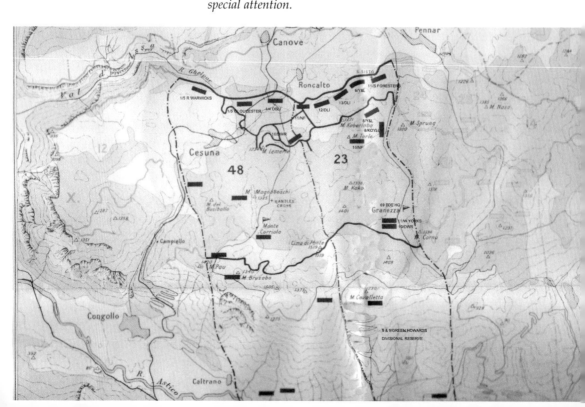

1220	*Brigade Front still intact.*
1250	*1000 enemy massing in gully behind Malga Cheller and Partut.*
1605	*Enemy shelling front line heavily.*
1615	*Fifty enemy seen in Roncalto engaged by Lewis guns.*
1710	*Two Vickers guns in position at H598.338 and H590.338.*
1745	*A Company took seven prisoners – very poor specimens of humanity.*
1750	*The battle ceased. Many of the enemy still wandering about No Man's Land, our sniping very intensive.*
2205	*Defensive patrols went out and more prisoners captured.*
2240	*Dispositions*

Front Line	*six platoons*
Thorpe Trench	*four platoons*
Redoubts	*four platoons*
Reserve	*HQ Company and two platoons.*

2240	*Enemy leave Poslem and Coldstream Trench.*
2350	*Casualties*

Wounded	*Second Lieutenant F C Smith*
Killed	*Two Other Ranks*
Wounded	*Twenty Two Other Ranks*
Wounded at Duty Three Other Ranks.	

The two dead were 19012 Corporal Robert Arnett, a miner from Felling who had been with the battalion since enlisting in October 1914, and 44623 Corporal George Payne, a Londoner who had joined as a reinforcement from the Army Veterinary Corps. Over the next three days three of the wounded died from their wounds: 21161 Private Peter Slane from Leadgate, 44392 Private Fred Palmer who was a reinforcement from the Royal Berkshire Regiment, and 18716 Private John Honey who came from Annfield Plain. 13/DLI captured three Austrian officers and forty-five Other Ranks, along with three machine guns. The casualties in 12/DLI were slightly higher:

Killed	*Captain E Lafone MC and four Other Ranks*
Wounded	*Second Lieutenant Rasche and thirty one Other Ranks*
Wounded at Duty	*Captain W Hughes and four Other Ranks*

The four dead men were all reinforcements: 78529 Private Joseph Cockcroft from Leeds and 78535 George Crossley from South Elmsall had both been called up and served with 4/Training Reserve Battalion before embarking and joining 12/DLI in November 1917. 245188 Private William Rutherford who came from Nether Whitton in Northumberland had attested under Lord Derby's scheme and joined the Reserve Territorial Battalion of the Northumberland Fusiliers in June 1916. He had not arrived in France until July 1917 when he was posted to 5/DLI and given a new Territorial number, but within a day the posting was changed to 12/DLI and he went up to the line as a replacement for the casualties at

Lieutenant William Golder 13/DLI enjoys lunch in a reserve line dugout: note the officers still manage to have plates and condiments along with a white tablecloth.
D/DLI//7/560/13

Messines. The fourth man killed that day, 52788 Lance Sergeant Albert Ward who came from Stoke Newington, had joined the battalion on 28 December 1916 with a draft from the Army Cyclist Corps. Only one of the wounded died at the Casualty Clearing Station: 78533 Private Albert Cooper from Bloxwich was another of the young lads from 4/Training Reserve Battalion.

The prisoners captured by 12/DLI amounted to two officers and nineteen men who were all wounded, plus seven un-wounded men. They had also taken four machine guns, three flame-throwers, five field telephones, nine boxes of machine-gun ammunition, one large trench mortar, three medium trench mortars, three small

RUTHERFORD, WILLIAM, Private, No. 245188, 12th (Service) Battn. The Durham Light Infantry, s. of William Telfer Rutherford, of Coldside Farm, Pauperhaugh, near Morpeth, by his wife, Jane Ann, dau. of John (and the late Isabella) Monaghan; b. Ewesley, near Morpeth, 28 Aug. 1897; educ. Fontburn Council School; was an Engine Driver, employed by the Ewesley Quarry Co., Ltd.; enlisted 30 Aug. 1916; served with the Expeditionary Force in France; saw much service at Passchendaele; went through the Battles of Polygon Wood and Tower Hamlets; subsequently proceeded to Italy, and was killed in action on the Assiago Plateau 15 June, 1918. Buried in the British Cemetery, Kabarlaba, south of Assiago. An officer wrote: "His cheery disposition and ready way to obey an order has always been admired, and been a fine example to his many comrades." Private Rutherford was a direct descendant of a family who for generations have been residents of the upper reaches of Redewater and the North Tyne; *unm.*

William Rutherford.

245188 Private William Rutherford from Nether Whitton, Northumberland had joined 12/DLI in France after serving with 4Reserve/NF. He was one of four Other Ranks of 12/DLI killed in action on 15 June 1918.

Austrian prisoners of war were made to act as stretcher-bearers and carry the British wounded back over the river.

trench mortars and a pom-pom gun, as well as ammunition for all the mortars and guns captured. Both battalions received the congratulations of the GOC 23rd Division, General Babington.

The next day saw patrols out in No Man's Land from both battalions, and a few more prisoners were brought in. A patrol from 8/York & Lancs went out through 13/DLI to occupy the enemy line at Edelweiss Spur, but met a stronger party of the enemy who opened fire on them and sent up one red and two green flares, whereupon the Austrian gunners opened fire on the British front line and the patrol made their way back to the British lines. Then at about 2100 hours an SOS flare went up from the British lines to the right of 13/DLI: the enemy artillery increased their rate of fire and the Austrian infantry joined in with rifle and machine-gun fire. The British artillery responded and opened fire on SOS lines, but as quickly as it had begun the firing died away and by 2245 hours the front was quiet again. The battlefield was gradually cleaned up and Austrian dead were given a hasty burial, the wire was checked and where needed repairs were carried out.

On 18 June 10/NF replaced 12/DLI and they moved back to Left Support where they started the work of cleaning up. This was followed on 20 June by 11/NF replacing 13/DLI who according to their War Diary moved into Left Support, but given that they were on the right of 12/DLI, it would seem that they became Right Support. The time spent in support was very quiet: although the Austrians sent over a few shells, there was little else to report. Training commenced for offensive action and B and C Companies of 12/DLI moved into battle positions, but on 26 June the action was cancelled and 68 Brigade moved back to the Granezza area where they cleaned up. On 28 June General Babington visited 13/DLI and presented medal ribbons to those who had gained them during the recent fighting. Two days later it was the turn of 12/DLI to receive their awards.

As June turned to July, both battalions were training in Divisional Reserve. On 2 July the Brigade Commander, Brigadier General Cary Barnard inspected 13/DLI in Granezza. On 4 July 13/DLI moved back into the front line in the left subsector of the right Brigade front where they took over from 8/Green Howards. 13/DLI placed B Company on the right and D Company on the left, with A Company as Right Support and C Company as Left Support. On 6 July they found

Frederick Rees having his morning shave, Asiago 1918. D/DLI//7/560/13(17)

time to send a team from each company to the 68 Brigade Assault Training competition; this was won by the team from D Company.

The next day the enemy shelled a working party from 10/NF who were working in No Man's Land. The guns then turned on 13/DLI's front line and they had a direct hit on a dugout where the Lewis-gun section of 5 Platoon B Company were resting. All of the section became casualties: five men were killed outright and two wounded. The shelling continued all day, but there was no reply from the British artillery which was having periods of extended silence.

On 10 July 12/DLI replaced 13/DLI who moved back to Right Reserve where they took over the working parties on which 12/DLI had been employed since returning to the line.

The French on the right carried out a raid on the night of 12 July supported by British artillery fire: to this the Austrians replied by shelling 12/DLI which resulted in the death of 42805 Private Herbert Hatton from Cambridge. He had joined the battalion in September 1916 and had been wounded in the hand at Messines in June 1917, but had quickly been sent back to the battalion after he had recovered from his wounds. At the same time that he was killed, another four men were wounded and evacuated. A number of advanced outposts were constructed and these were held by piquets during the day, but generally the outposts were withdrawn at night. On 17 July khaki drill summer uniforms were issued to all ranks as the weather became really hot.

23rd Division was relieved in the right sector of XIV Corps' front by 48th Division and moved back to the training areas on the plain below the mountains. Here they started cleaning up as usual and then training commenced. Special attention appears to have been given to musketry and handling of arms, while time was also found for Battalion and Brigade sporting competitions. There were a few movements between training areas but the whole Division remained out of the line until the middle of August when they started moving back to the front.

On 19 August on a winding mule track near Caltrano, tragedy once again struck 13/DLI. As they marched up the mountain tracks 15963 Private Alex Campbell, born in Kilmarnock but resident in Spennymoor, who had been with the battalion since October 1914, slipped and fell over a cliff and was instantly killed.

Having arrived at M. Brusabo the next few days were spent in further training in hill warfare, while a number of officers and NCOs carried out reconnaissances of the forward positions. They took with them the battalion runners, in order that they might learn the routes they would need to use to deliver their messages. Throughout the period there was some slight enemy shelling, and on 26 August a hut in the camp was hit and four men wounded.

On the morning of 27 August 13/DLI relieved 9/Green Howards in the right Brigade subsector as the Left Battalion: B Company were placed forward in the Outpost Line with D Company in the left front line and C Company in the right front line, with A Company in Reserve, the relief being complete by 0945 hours. At the same time 12/DLI took over as the right Brigade support battalion, all available men being employed on working parties or patrol work. 13/DLI also had a number of patrols out in No Man's Land each night. On 28 August as one group prepared to move out, the enemy artillery opened fire and three of the patrol were wounded. Nightly defensive patrols moved along the battalion front but nothing was seen or heard of the enemy except slight shelling of the British line.

On 4 September 10/NF took over from 13/DLI and the latter battalion withdrew into Brigade support at Mont Lemerle. Here they provided men for patrol work in No Man's Land and others for working parties. On the same night 12/DLI replaced 11/NF in the right Battalion sector of the right Brigade, where they spent the time improving the trenches and the barbed-wire entanglements protecting the line. Three days later 13/DLI moved into the line and replaced 12/DLI.

In France in January and February 1918, owing to shortages in manpower the establishment of the Infantry Division had been reduced from four battalions in each brigade to three, thus reducing the number of

Out at rest there was time for a little fraternisation with the locals: here officers of 13/DLI entertain two Italian ladies. D/DLI/7/75

fighting battalions in a division from twelve to nine, and at the same time the Divisional Pioneer Battalions had reduced from four companies to three. The three British Divisions in Italy – 7th, 23rd and 48th – had remained on the twelve-battalion establishment and now with the further losses in France it was decided at High Command to reduce those Divisions to nine battalions and as the battalions in Italy were up to strength, to send them to France. In each of the Divisions, one battalion from each brigade was selected to go. In 23rd Division they were 13/DLI, 9/Green Howards and 11/Sherwood Foresters.

The orders reached 13/DLI on 11 September and 8/KOYLI came up and took over the line, allowing 13/DLI to the rear. On 12 September General Babington and Brigadier General Cary Barnard inspected the battalion and wished them 'Bon voyage'. Shortly after these battalions left, it was arranged that an Italian Division would relieve 23rd Division so that it too could be sent to France.

12/DLI had spent the best part of September in and out of the line providing patrols and working parties but seeing little of the enemy except for some shelling. On the night of 26/27 September they were relieved by 3 Battalion 50th Italian Regiment and moved to a camp at Bydand Corner where they rested until motor lorries arrived and took them to Beregana Camp. The next day was spent cleaning up and during the night they moved to billets in Monteviale. Here they spent five days training and on 5 October they moved to Montecchio Maggiore, followed the next day by a move to Arzignano. Another four days' training took place and on 11 October in very wet weather a battalion kit inspection was held. It now turned out that the move of 7th and 23rd Divisions back to France had been cancelled and that both Divisions were to take part in the planned Italian offensive to re-cross the River Piave and push the Austrians out of Italy. 12/DLI continued training for this new offensive and on 14 October marched to Vicenza where they entrained at 2330 hours and were transported to Mestre; here they detrained at 1000 hours and marched to Mirano. Another five days were then spent in further training, and on 21 October they left Mirano and marched to Sambughe: this was the approach march to the coming battle.

The next day they left Sambughe, marched to Treviso and on the night of 23 October at 2300 hours they left Treviso and moved to Catena. The following day they left Catena and moved up to Assembly Point A; however, the operation was postponed and they returned to Catena and rested throughout 25 October. On 26 October they moved forward again to assembly positions on Lido Island, and this was completed successfully with few casualties.

At 0645 hours on 27 October the advance against the first objective, the Green Line,

Captain Cyril Chapman wearing the tropical uniform issued to units on the Italian Front in 1918. D/DLI/7/75

commenced. The battalion was on the northern flank of the Brigade front and the River Piave was very deep and swift; also while wading through the river they suffered heavily from enemy machine-gun fire. The leading company lost over 50 per cent of its effective strength. On reaching the far bank the companies reorganised and pressed on, only to be held up by uncut wire close to the objective. Various parties tried to move up to and cut the wire; among them Captain Charles Gibbens MC, DCM and Sergeant Jack O'Hara MM were prominent. Jack O'Hara was killed trying to cut the wire, but another man came forward. Seeing all of the party were killed except the officer, 270041 Private George Brown from Stockton-on-Tees, who had already been

Second Lieutenant John Hodgson served as Private with 7/DLI before being commissioned. He was killed in action crossing the River Piave on 27 October 1918.

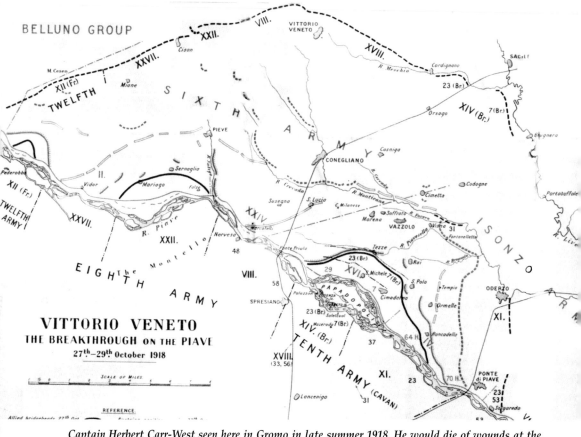

BELLUNO GROUP

VITTORIO VENETO
THE BREAKTHROUGH ON THE PIAVE
27th–29th October 1918

SCALE OF MILES

REFERENCE.

Allied bridgeheads 27th Oct.

Captain Herbert Carr-West seen here in Gromo in late summer 1918. He would die of wounds at the crossing of the Piave in October 1918. D/DLI/7/75

wounded, ran forward to help him. Although wounded again, he continued to cut the wire until a passage was effected and the battalion could advance. For his gallant conduct he was awarded the Distinguished Conduct Medal. With the wire cut, the advance went on and C Company took the first objective; D Company passed through them and moving on took the second objective, the Red Line. A Company, along with what was left of a now very weak B Company pressed steadily on and eventually reached the Blue Line. Here orders were received that as the Italians on the left of 68 Brigade had failed to cross the Piave, no further advance should be made. When his Company Sergeant-Major was wounded, 300920 Sergeant William Littlewood MM took over the duties of CSM. Showing fine courage and powers of leadership, he was of the greatest assistance to the remaining officers of his company throughout the battle, so much so that he was awarded a Bar to his Military Medal.

Behind the line 68 Brigade organised courses of instruction for potential NCOs. This appears to be the instructors: seated right is Captain Frederick Rees MC 13/DLI. Note the other officer is from one of the NF Battalions: the NF cap badge can be seen on the left side of the helmet by his foot.
D/DLI//7/560/13(20)

Another photograph of the staff on the NCOs' course: the Privates are possibly officers'
batmen and attached cooks. The two men on the left are from the NF: their circle battle-
patch is clearly seen, while the Sergeant in the centre is possibly from 12/DLI with the
rectangular patch. Frederick Rees has picked up his helmet and the DLI cap badge can
be made out on the left of it. D/DLI//7/560/13(21)

The battalion dug in with A and B Companies in the line, D Company in support and C Company along with Battalion Headquarters at C Benedetti in reserve. Here Major Edward Borrow, the second in command, was taken from the battalion to take command of 11/NF as Lieutenant-Colonel St Hill DSO had been killed during the attack. Casualties in 12/DLI were Second Lieutenants John Hodgson and Harry Fisher, along with Captain Charles Gibbens and Second Lieutenants Smith and Wade wounded. After the capture of the first objective RSM Frederick Burton DCM from Newburn on Tyne was supervising the transfer of small-arms ammunition and trench mortar shells from the battalion mule train to the company carrying parties when he was killed by a ricocheting bullet; he had originally enlisted into the 2nd Tyneside Pioneers in 1914.

Another twenty-seven men were killed, 111 wounded and eleven missing, but a lot of enemy equipment had been captured. 12/DLI had taken three guns, two heavy trench mortars and two anti-tank guns, as well as several hundred prisoners. They spent a relatively quiet night during which they reorganised and replenished their ammunition, stretcher-bearers took the wounded back across the river, and the rest prepared to continue the advance.

Next day at 1230 hours the advance continued: the barrage opened and continued until around 1300 by which time the field guns were out of range and only the Corps heavy artillery could provide support. The battalion met some opposition from the Austrian rearguard but machine-gunners moved into the upper storeys of houses and provided cover for the rifle sections to close with the enemy. Men of 68/LTMB used captured enemy machine guns to provide close support until the captured ammunition ran out. The attack had gone very well and by late afternoon the objective had been reached; casualties were relatively light with only three men killed and twenty wounded. C and D companies held an outpost line with A Company in support and B Company in reserve; however, during the night one company was sent forward to Marena a mile beyond the objective and a patrol from this company went forward to hold a bridge on the near bank of the River Monticano north-east of Marena. The battalion runners were kept busy taking messages between Battalion Headquarters and the various companies. Conspicuous among this gallant band was 302936 Lance Corporal George Nelson MM who that evening, when one of the companies became separated, crossed two streams and travelled through country swarming with Austrian snipers and machine-gun posts to locate them.

On 30 October, the Austrians had retreated so quickly that in front of 12/DLI they left behind a complete battery of 5.9 in guns. The battalion War Diary records:

> Many acts of gallantry were performed this day which will go unrecorded. A fine display of determination to succeed was given by every officer and soldier and to this alone is the success attributed.

The London Gazette of 29 August 1918 records the award of the Meritorious Service Medal for an act of gallantry to 17992 Lance Corporal John Maylia 13/DLI from Gateshead, but gives no mention of what the act was.

Gateshead Library

A further seven men were killed, nineteen wounded and two missing with Second Lieutenant W. Blenkinsop also wounded. Now 70 Brigade passed through 68 Brigade to continue the advance and at 1400 hours 68 Brigade became the Divisional Reserve. 12/DLI received orders to march to billets in Orsago. This was a long and very trying march over very bad roads. Since crossing the Piave three days earlier the men had been soaked to the skin, they had lain out in the open in frosty weather without blankets, with very little in the way of food and they had fought gallantly for three days. The march therefore was a fine performance when at 2000 hours they

The last draft to 12/DLI. Seated on the right is 96821 Private James Sewell from Hebburn: he trained as a Lewis-gunner with 3/DLI. The draft left England en route for 12/DLI in Italy on 6/11/1918 but by then the war in Italy was over.

arrived at the billets without a single man having dropped out en route. However, there was to be very little rest: at 1000 hours on 1 November the GOC called on the battalion to go to the assistance of 70 Brigade who had met stiff opposition at Sacile and needed help. Within thirty minutes the battalion had paraded, called the roll and moved off towards the sound of the guns. The march was made as quickly as possible but by the time they reached Sacile, 70 Brigade had overcome the opposition and 12/DLI went into billets for the night. The next day was spent in Sacile followed on 3 November by a march to Talponedo. Here the next morning the news arrived that an Armistice had been signed with Austria and that the war on the Italian Front was over.

In 1919 CSM Thomas Spedding 12/DLI, seen here in the 1930s, was awarded the Meritorious Service Medal for his work in Italy with the Battalion.
D/DLI/7/805/37

102341 Private Alexander Campell from Ryton joined 12/DLI on the Italian front. He was employed at the Stargate Pit Ryton where he was a Deputy Overman. He survived the war without a scratch and returned to the pit and became Under Manager.

Chapter Ten

13/DLI Back in France

HAVING MOVED BACK from the line, 13/DLI commenced their return journey to France on 14 September. The battalion formed up in two parties at Centrale: the first party marched to Thiele at 0900 hours and entrained at 1200 hours; they were followed by the second party at 1400 hours who entrained at 1700 hours. So the long journey back to France started, via Bologna, Voghera, Sampierdarena and Ventimiglia, arriving in Cannes on 16 September. They spent another three days on the train before they arrived at St Riquier where they detrained and marched to billets in Millencourt.

36054 Private William Innes made a one-line entry in his diary on this day:

> Wed 18 September
> Land at St Riquier about 1700 hours and march four kilometres to Millencourt.

13/DLI and the other two battalions from 23rd Division were now used to reform 74 Brigade of 25th Division: the battalion strength at this time was thirty-four officers and 791 men. Before they had time to get settled in, the GOC 25th Division, Major General J.R.E. Charles and the Commander of 74 Brigade, Brigadier General H.M. Craigie-Halkett carried out an inspection of the newly-arrived troops. Training started in order that they could adapt to the conditions in France, but this was hampered by heavy rain. On 24 September a warning order was received that the battalion should be ready to move either that day or the next. At noon the following day the Battalion Transport moved off by road to Henencourt. While waiting for orders, the officers played the NCOs at rugby; the NCOs taking the honours with three goals and two tries to nil.

On 26 September all the Lewis-gunners fired on a nearby range and the rest of the battalion practised deploying from column of route into battle formation. At last at 0700 hours the remainder of the transport, one Lewis-gun limber, four cookers, two water carts, two baggage wagons and an officers' mess cart under the command of Second Lieutenant J. Knott moved to Pont Remy where they entrained at 1015 hours and were carried to Edgehill where they arrived in the early hours of 27 September. As the transport left Pont Remy the rest of the battalion marched to St Riquier where they entrained for Albert; on arrival they detrained and moved on foot to Ribemont. Here the GOC 25th Division paid them a visit which was soon followed by orders to be ready to move. At 1000 hours on 29 September a convoy of motor buses, with the battalion, whose strength was given as thirty-four officers and 720 men, left Ribemont bound for Maricourt where they arrived at 1530 hours. The next day the whole of 74 Brigade practised attacking enemy positions. That night was spent in the village of Hardicourt and at 1000 hours the next morning they marched to Moislains where they spent the whole of 2 October resting. The approach march to the front line continued on 3 October when they proceeded to Ronsoy; en route orders were received to halt there for twelve hours and then proceed to Mont St Martin. Here large packs were handed in to the 2nd Echelon and the fighting troops got into battle order, while those left out of battle moved back out of enemy artillery range. The main body came under some shellfire and two men were killed and nine wounded.

36054 Private William Innes added another few lines in his diary:

Thursday 3 October

March to Rosnoy, Battalion go straight into the line, I'm left with the reinforcements in an open field a most miserable and desolate spot.

Friday

I spend most of the day making a shelter for the orderly room.

Saturday 5 October

Battalion goes over the top in the early morning a lot of men come out wounded.

At 0100 hours the battalion moved up to assembly trenches east of Prospect Hill with the object of attacking the high ground north of Beaurevoir. The initial assault was successful, but owing to heavy machine-gun fire which caused a lot of casualties they were forced to retire. The Commanding Officer Lieutenant-Colonel Denzil Clarke DSO, MC was wounded, as were Captain Cyril Chapman, Lieutenant Alfred Hales, and Second Lieutenants Edwin Forrest, Robert Robinson, Norman Willis and Ernest Callow. However, four officers were killed: Lieutenants Hylu Hart, William Golder, Cecil Dodds and Second Lieutenant Philip Smith, who had earlier been reported wounded; while Second Lieutenant F. Audas was reported missing. The casualties among the ranks were very heavy with around fifty men killed or missing, but they regrouped and advanced again and this time they managed to dig in around 400 yards in advance of the start line. The next morning the advance continued and they pressed forward as far as the Sunken Road that ran between Beaurevoir and Villers Outreaux where Second Lieutenant William Dewar 2/Border Regiment attached to 13/DLI was wounded. Here they dug in and were eventually relieved by troops of 66th Division on the morning of 8 October. The remnants of the battalion marched back to Lormisset where they were given a hearty meal and then they started cleaning up; ammunition and bombs were also issued. At 0200 hours

Lieutenant William Golder 13/DLI was killed in action 5 October 1918 attacking the high ground north of Beaurevoir.

Denzil Clarke MC had landed with 13/DLI on 25 August 1915. By October 1918 he was a Lieutenant-Colonel commanding the Battalion, and was wounded leading the attack at Beaurevoir.

D/DLI/7/75/30

Lt Col Clarke and two unidentified officers of 13/DLI. D/DLI/7/75

On the right Captain Frederick Rees MC and two other officers outside their billet in a French village October 1918. D/DLI/7/75

the following morning they marched to Serain Farm: while on the move a despatch rider caught up with orders that the battalion was to move straight into the attack.

The objective was the Central Station. For a time the battalion was held up by enemy fire along the railway embankment, but cavalry came up and assisted them to continue the advance and the objective was taken without much further opposition; however, during the attack Captain Isaac Bewley MC was killed. At 0530 hours the next morning the advance continued, the objective being to take the high ground north-east of Le Cateau. At 0930 hours the battalion was held up on the high ground south-west of St Benin: they had to wait until 1430 hours when the supporting artillery put down a barrage which covered their advance and they were then able to take the village.

Here they rested throughout 11 October until that night 2/Royal Munster Fusiliers came up and relieved 13/DLI, who on completion of the relief marched back to Honnechy. In this last seven days of heavy fighting the battalion had suffered five officers and forty-three men killed, fifteen officers and 311 men wounded, and one officer and seventy-four men listed as missing. This was over half of those that had arrived back from Italy less than a month earlier.

At 1330 hours on 12 October the battalion left Honnechy and marched to billets in Premont where the work of reorganising and refitting commenced. Initially the battalion reduced to two companies, but soon reinforcements were arriving. On 16 October Lieutenant-Colonel Percy Hone MC arrived to take command of the battalion; on the same day Lieutenants William McBay and J.B. Blyth also joined for duty. The next day a draft of 107 Other Ranks arrived, followed on 18 October by another draft of 100 men led by Lieutenant R. Skelton from 5/DLI. They began moving forward that day and spent the night at Maretz, moving the next morning back to Honnechy where three more officers reported for duty. At Honnechy the opportunity was taken to put all the Lewis-gunners through their range practice and the rifle companies trained for open warfare.

Grave-marker of Alf. Allard.

On the very wet morning of 22 October a further draft of 101 men joined the battalion and preparations were made for moving back into the line. At 2350 hours they marched out of Honnechy in the direction of Le Cateau and halted about 1 mile north-west of the town. Zero Hour was scheduled for 0120 hours and while they waited for the order to advance, tea was issued to the waiting men. Suddenly they came under enemy artillery fire and they had to quickly dig shell-scrapes as a rudimentary protection. The main attack was delivered by 7 and 75 Brigades, and 13/DLI advanced behind 75 Brigade until they reached the western edge of the Bois-l'Évêque where they passed through the battalions of 75 Brigade and continued the advance until they reached the road due west of Rue du Pont where they were held up by very heavy machine-gun fire and thick belts of barbed wire. Orders came that they were to withdraw to the Green Line for the night and dig in there. The attack was to continue on the next day and Zero Hour was set for 0400 hours, the objective for 13/DLI being the village of Rue du Pont. The attack started in bright moonlight and as soon as the battalion emerged from the wood they came under heavy machine-gun fire and ran into the uncut belts of barbed wire. However, they pressed the attack home and by 0730 hours had taken the village and commenced consolidating the position. The new Commanding Officer Lieutenant-Colonel Hone was wounded during this phase of the operation. About midday further orders were received that the attack was to be continued and Zero Hour was set for 1400 hours, the objective being the capture of the high ground east of Le Faux. Behind a creeping barrage they set off for the high ground and a stiff fire-fight developed but by 1730 hours resistance was

The original grave-marker of 46042 Private Charles Nicholl MM 13/DLI who died of wounds on 7 October 1918. He had enlisted into the 2nd Tyneside Scottish and was wounded in July 1916 prior to his transfer to the DLI. D/DLI/7/927/3

47386 Private Charle. Geldard from Bolton-by-Bowland, Yorkshi. served with the Duke of Wellington's Regiment before being wounded in October 1918 with 13/DLI. He died from his wounds on 23 October 1918.

overcome as the enemy withdrew and 13/DLI was able to begin digging in. Major Henry Faber, who came from Swainby near Northallerton and had been in France with 5/DLI since April 1915, arrived and assumed command of the battalion. During the next two days patrols from the battalion kept in touch with the enemy. Then on the morning of 27 October two posts were established in front of the line held by 13/DLI. One was in a ruined house and was used as an observation post; the other post was established at the junction of two tracks and was manned by a Lewis-gun team. During the night a platoon went forward and established themselves around the observation post already set up.

During 28 October orders were received to establish more posts on the track leading towards the enemy and Zero Hour was set for 1700 hours. However, reports from the patrols suggested that the track was strongly held, so Zero Hour was put back until 0500 hours on 29 October. At the allotted time the advance commenced with two platoons on the right flank and two on the left flank. Both parties were met by very heavy rifle and machine-gun fire. The two platoons on the left were almost surrounded and were compelled to retire back to the start line: during this advance Second Lieutenant William Walker, who had served in the ranks of 18/DLI and had been commissioned in December 1917, was wounded. After the failure of this attack 11/Sherwood Foresters arrived and took over from 13/DLI and the latter unit moved back into support positions at Rue du Pont where at 1400 hours on 31 October they were relieved by two companies of the Royal Warwickshire Regiment and moved back to a camp just outside Le Cateau.

November started with the battalion cleaning up and refitting and re-forming the companies. The Commanding Officer held a conference at Battalion Headquarters and briefed the officers on the proposals to continue the attack. The effective strength of the battalion was now twenty-eight officers and 656 Other Ranks. On 3 November the battalion marched to Pommereuil where they billeted for the night and at 0845 hours the next morning they moved along the Pommereuil–Malgarni road until they were able to dig in and consolidate for the night just east of the Sambre Canal, with Battalion Headquarters in a house on the canal bank. At 1445 hours on 5 November orders were received that 9/Green Howards and 13/DLI were to move forward and seize the crossing of the Petit Helpe River. 9/Green Howards took the lead and passed through the enemy artillery lines where they captured a number of guns. 13/DLI crossed the river by a bridge near Margoienne and took up position in a support line east of Rue des Juifs. That night they were relieved and moved back to billets in Rue des Juifs.

The following day the advance continued. At about 1200 hours orders were received to advance through Taisnieres and then south-east to Marbaix with the objective of capturing this village if it had not been evacuated by the Germans. Just as the battalion was about to enter the village, they were met with heavy shelling and suffered ten casualties but by 1700 hours the village was in the battalion's hands and they were in touch with 9/Green Howards and 11/Sherwood Foresters on the flanks. They spent the night in Marbaix and the following morning, along with the rest of the Brigade, moved to Maroilles where they were billeted for the night. They started cleaning up and in the afternoon inter-platoon football took place.

On 11 November they were put to work clearing the roads of refuse and debris and the news came in that from 1100 hours an Armistice had been signed and the war was over:

> *Monday 11 November*
>
> *Get wire at 1000 hours that hostilities cease at 1100 hours after which there is to be no movement by allied forces. The news was received very quietly.*

Thus wrote William Innes as the last entry in his small diary.

No celebrations are recorded in the War Diary and work went on as normal.

21066 Private Thomas Banks 13/DLI, who enlisted on 27 October 1914 when he was a miner at Greenside Colliery, Ryton. He was killed in action on 8 October 1918 and is buried in Beaurevoir British Cemetery, France.

This appears to be a photograph of those men who had served with one of the companies of 13/DLI from embarkation to the Armistice.

Chapter Eleven

Epilogue

WITH HOSTILITIES OVER, men were set to work cleaning up the battlefields and the thoughts of the majority turned to demobilisation. The first to be released were the miners, who were in the main released and on their way home by 3 January 1919. For those remaining in France and Italy, education classes were started with some military training included. Salvage work commenced and dumps of equipment had to be guarded.

Groups of men were sent every few days to the demobilisation camp at Le Havre and for those men of 12/DLI there was the long train ride back from Italy. In January 1919 those who remained with 13/DLI were practising 'Trooping the Colour', then on 22 January the battalion paraded and Major General J.R.E. Charles CB, DSO Commanding 25th Division presented the King's Colour to 13/DLI.

On 23 January at Veronella on the Italian Front the Corps Commander Lieutenant-General Sir J.M. Babington inspected those officers and men entitled to the 1914–15 Star; however, by then a lot of the Durham miners had already left the battalion to return to work in the coal mines. The work of demobilisation on the Italian Front was carried out fairly quickly: by 22 February 12/DLI had been reduced to one company. Meanwhile in France, theft of stores and equipment was a problem and Courts of Inquiry were held to establish how and why things like bicycles and horses were disappearing from unit lines. Some of the younger men who had only arrived in late 1918 were transferred to 20/DLI and 52/DLI serving with the Army of Occupation in Cologne.

By February 13/DLI were employed on grave registration, collecting the remains of the dead from the battlefield locations and reburying them in larger cemeteries. This work went on throughout March and in April they were employed on guard duties in the St Vaast area where, when the water supply failed, they helped the 1/Infantry Regiment of the French Army by supplying them with a water cart.

More men were sent away on 28 April when a draft was sent to join 9/DLI on the Rhine. On 22 June the orders arrived for the cadre to proceed to the dispersal camp at Cambrai, from where on 24 June the King's Colour was sent to England. On 9 July they left Cambrai for Le Havre where, under the command of Captain W. Arris MC, they had to wait until 29 July for a transport ship to take them to England. That day they embarked on HMT *Caesarea* and landed at Southampton. The battalion transport was handed over to an employee of the London and South Western Railway Company and the men dispersed to demobilisation camps, the last to leave being Captain Arris. And so ended the history of two of the New Army battalions of the Durham Light Infantry. Unlike the locally-raised battalions, there were no homecoming parades or Old Comrades Associations: the battalions simply faded away.

Honours and Gallantry Awards 12th and 13th (Service) Durham Light Infantry 1914–1919

THE VICTORIA CROSS

Kenny, Thomas, Private 11424 13th. Near la Houssoie, France 4 Nov 1915 LG 1 Dec 1915.
For most conspicuous bravery and devotion to duty on the night of 4 November, 1915, near La Houssoie. When on patrol in thick fog with Lieutenant Brown, 13 Battalion Durham Light Infantry, some Germans, who were lying out in a ditch in front of their parapet, opened fire and shot Lieutenant Brown through both thighs. Private Kenny, although heavily and repeatedly fired upon, crawled about for more than an hour with his wounded officer on his back, trying to find his way through the fog to our trenches. He refused to go on alone, although told by Lieutenant Brown to do so. At last, when utterly exhausted, he came to a ditch which he recognised, placed Lieutenant Brown in it, and went to look for help. He found an officer and a few men of his battalion at a listening post, and after guiding them back, with their assistance Lieutenant Brown was brought in, although the Germans again opened heavy fire with rifles and machine guns, and threw bombs at 30 yards distance – Private Kenny's pluck, endurance and devotion to duty were beyond praise.

Youens, Frederick, Temporary Second Lieutenant 13th. Near Hill 60, Belgium. For most conspicuous bravery and devotion to duty. While out on patrol this officer was wounded and had to return to his trenches to have his wounds dressed. Shortly afterwards a report came in that the enemy were preparing to raid our trenches. Second Lieutenant Youens, regardless of his wound, immediately set out to rally the team of a Lewis gun, which had become disorganised owing to heavy shellfire. During this process an enemy's bomb fell on the Lewis gun position without exploding. Second Lieutenant Youens immediately picked it up and hurled it over the parapet. Shortly afterwards another bomb fell near the same place; again, Second Lieutenant Youens picked it up with the intention of throwing it away, when it exploded in his hand, severely wounding him and also some of his men. There is little doubt that the prompt and gallant action of Second Lieutenant Youens saved several of his men's lives and that by his energy and resource the enemy's raid was completely repulsed. This gallant officer has since succumbed to his wounds.

ORDER OF ST. MICHAEL & ST. GEORGE
Holford, James Henry Edward, Major
(Notts Yeo) T/ Lt.Col. (DSO & Bar) CMG   1 Jan 1919   12th

DISTINGUISHED SERVICE ORDER

Borrow, Edward, T/Major   19 Nov 1917 13th att 10/DWR

For conspicuous gallantry and devotion to duty in an attack. When the leading troops were suffering severe casualties, he kept the men together by his splendid leadership. Through twice wounded, he led his men to the final objective, and stuck to his post until he collapsed from the effects of his wounds. His courage and example were an inspiration to all ranks.

Clarke, Denzil Harwood, T/Capt. (MC)   1 Jan 1918   13th

Downey, Joseph Aloysius Louis, T/Major   4 Jun 1917   13th

Gibbens, Charles, Lt. T/Capt. (MC & Bar, DCM) 2 Apr 1919   2nd att 12th

For most conspicuous gallantry and devotion to duty. At the forcing of the River Piave on 27th October, 1918, near the island of Papadopili, the battalion, after passing the most northerly stream under very heavy fire, was held up by uncut wire. He with four NCOs and men ran forward from his own company and through the leading company to cut the wire, which was swept from end to end with shellfire and by machine-gun fire from the front and in enfilade. All the party except himself were killed and he was wounded. In spite of his wound he continued until a lane had been cut, helped only by one other rank, who had already been wounded and who came up to his assistance. But for this act of devoted heroism the attack must have failed and the battalion been repulsed. Suffering from a most painful wound, he continued to lead his company until they had taken the third and final objective.

Gray, Edward, Second Lt., T/Capt. (MC)   19 Nov 1917   att 13th

For conspicuous gallantry and devotion to duty. During an attack he led his men with great initiative and determination on several enemy strongpoints, inflicting heavy casualties on the enemy and killing ten himself. During the consolidation of the captured position and subsequent enemy counter-attacks he walked up and down his line under fire with absolute disregard of danger, and kept his commanding officer well in touch with the situation. On another occasion he personally led an attack against an enemy strongpoint, capturing a machine gun and ten prisoners. Throughout the operations he set a magnificent example of courage and devotion to duty.

Greenwood, Leonard Montague, T/Capt. (MC) Jan 1919   13th

Holford, James Henry Edward, Major Nottinghamshire Yeo. Comdg 12th
T/Lt. Col. (DSO – awarded *London Gazette* 15 Jan 1901) Bar to DSO 1 Feb 1919

For conspicuous gallantry and devotion to duty in command of a battalion during the operations on the Piave front, 21 to 30 Oct 1918. Under heavy machine-gun fire he frequently reorganised his battalion and led them forward to their next objective, showing a total disregard for his own safety. His courage and able leadership were most marked.

Hone, Percy Frederick, T/Capt., A/Lt. Col. (MC) 1 Jan 1919 DSO with 21/Middx Regt.
T/Lt. Col. (DSO MC) Bar to DSO 2 Apr 1919   Comdg 13th

He commanded his battalion during the attack north-east of Le Cateau on 23 and 24 October 1918. He personally led his battalion in the attack south-east of Fontaine au Bois, having previously gone forward to reconnoitre. On 24 October 1918, when reconnoitring in advance of his battalion, he was wounded. His fine example of courage and determination contributed to the success of the operations.

Lindsay, Michael Egan, Capt. 7/Dragoon Gds T/Lt. Col. 1 Jan 1917 Comdg 13th

Pease, Herbert Ernest, T/Capt.   25 Aug 1916   12th

For conspicuous gallantry during four days of fighting. He set a fine example of dash and bravery when leading the battalion in the attack which led to the capture of the enemy's trench. Subsequently he did fine work in the consolidation of positions won.

THE MILITARY CROSS

Allison, Thomas Archibald Bates, Second Lt.   2 Apr 1919   6th att 13th
For marked gallantry during operations south-east of Fontaine au Bois. On the morning of 29 October, 1918, he led his platoon in an attack on an enemy post, and when practically surrounded refused to surrender and fought his way back to his original position, where he organised his command. He has on previous occasions done fine work.

Arris, William John, T/Second Lt.   19 Nov 1917   13th
For conspicuous gallantry and devotion to duty. He led his platoon through a heavy barrage to reinforce the front line during an enemy counter-attack. He repelled the counter-attack and dug new trenches in front of the old line, which had been badly damaged by shellfire. He showed great coolness and courage in exceptionally difficult circumstances.

Bannerman, William, T/Second Lt.   8 Mar 1919   13th
For conspicuous gallantry and devotion to duty during the advance from Beaurevoir to Le Cateau from 5 to 10 October, 1918. He took charge of his company when the company commander was wounded. He led his men through a heavy machine-gun barrage, and after being wounded in the head continued to direct operations.

Bewley, Isaac, Lt. A/Capt   15 Oct 1918   7th att 13th
For conspicuous gallantry and devotion to duty during an enemy attack. He showed great skill in the handling of his men, and kept his batlalion commander well in touch with the situation by sending back accurate reports. When the attack broke down he organised a party, and brought in several prisoners. Next morning, when the positions of the enemy were still obscure, he made a personal reconnaissance and brought back valuable information, besides accounting for two of the enemy. He has previously done fine work.

Bishop, Charles Harold, T/Second Lt.   15 Oct 1918   13th
For conspicuous gallantry and devotion to duty during an enemy attack. He worked unceasingly in driving off the enemy, and for nine hours he remained on the fire-step, personally accounting for several of the enemy. When the attack broke down he immediately organised a party, and brought in several wounded and unwounded enemy. His courage and determination were most marked.

Brandon, Thomas, T/Second Lt.   16 Aug 1917 12th att 68/LTMB
For conspicuous gallantry and devotion to duty. Aided by one of his men he captured twenty of the enemy, subsequently showing great courage and energy in taking sentry duty under heavy shellfire whilst a captured position was being consolidated. He showed great ability in maintaining touch with other units during this operation.

Buckell, Harold Claude, Second Lt.   16 Aug 1917   DLI att 13th
For conspicuous gallantry and devotion, when acting commander of a company, holding a sector in a salient. He several times visited his whole line during a violent bombardment, crawiing over many blocks, giving instructions, and it was due to his fearlessness and resource that an attack was repulsed.

Caldwell, William Thomas, T/Second Lt.   19 Nov 1917   13th
For conspicuous gallantry and devotion to duty. Owing to a heavy enemy barrage his company had become disorganised whilst assembiing for an attack. He rallied his men, led them to the fina1 objective, and assisted in the consolidation with absolute disregard for personal safety. He showed great courage and determination during an enemy counter-attack which followed, and set a magnificent example to his men throughout the operation.

Carroll, John Patrick, T/Lt.   17 Dec 1917   13th
For conspicuous gallantry and devotion to duty when in charge of Brigade Signals. He had to continually pass through heavily shelled areas to repair his line. He was blown up once, but continued to keep his communications intact.

Clarke, Denzil Harwood, T/Lt.   24 Iun 1916   13th

For conspicuous gallantry. Lieutenant Clarke, with another officer, led a successful raid on the enemy's trenches. At least 12 of the enemy were accounted for, and five deep occupied dugouts were bombed. Owing to their skill and rapidity of action there were only three slight casualties in their party.

Bar to MC   25 Nov 1916

For conspicuous gallantry in action. He led his company in the attack with great courage and determination. Later he assumed command in the front line and carried out his orders with great skill.

Colville, William Thomson, T/Second Lt.   3 Jun 1919   12th

Crooks, Joseph Edwin, T/Second Lt.   1 Jan 1919 12th, attd 68/LTMB
[*London Gazette* says James]

Davis, Ernest, Second Lt.   26 Jul 1917   SR att 13th

For conspicuous gallantry and devotion to duty (near Hill 60 18 May, 1917). He was responsible for preventing an enemy raiding party from entering our trenches. He personally shot one of the enemy with his revolver.

Dewar, William Reid, T/Second Lt.   8 Mar 1919   Border Regt att 13th

For conspicuous gallantry and devotion to duty during the advance on Beaurevoir on 6 October, 1918. When his company commander was wounded he took charge of the company and on three occasions when the battalion was held up personally took out strong patrols, outflanking the enemy machine-gun position and capturing it. He showed complete disregard for personal safety. [Gazetted as W. Dewar]

Dodd, John Freeman, T/Capt.   1 Jan 1918   12th

Dodd, William, T/Second Lt.   19 Nov 1917   12th

For conspicuous gallantry and devotion to duty when in command of a company carrying consolidating material to the front line. It was entirely due to his perseverance and disregard of danger that the material reached the front line. He afterwards remained in the front line with his Lewis gunners and materially assisted in repelling a counter-attack.

Drewery, Donovan, T/Lt., A/Capt.   3 Jun 1918   12th

Farrier, Robert Hind, T/Second Lt.   8 Mar 1919   13th

For conspicuous gallantry and devotion to duty during the advance from Beaurevoir to Le Cateau from 5 to 10 October 1918. He was commanding a company, and on several occasions he saved the situation by sending out patrols and capturing the enemy machine guns. He himself took charge of the patrols on two occasions when all the other officers and non-commissioned officers had become casualt.ies.

Ferguson, James, T/Second Lt.   15 Oct 1918   12th att 9th Y & L

He patrolled No Man's Land on several nights before an enemy attack took place, and his knowledge of the same proved of greatest value. On the morning succeeding the attack he discovered two enemy field guns and assisted in bringing them in. Later in the day he made a dangerous reconnaissance and obtained important information of enemy positions. Throughout he displayed high qualities of gallantry and initiative.

Freeman, Eric George, T/Second Lt.   17 Sep 1917   12th

For conspicuous gallantry and devotion to duty when taking part in a raid. He personally captured one of the enemy and, although badly wounded in the hand, assisted a wounded man back to our lines, carrying him part of the way. He then went back into No Man's Land and attempted to find three men who were missing. He displayed the greatest coolness and courage, it was owing to his personal example that the raid was a success.

Gardner, Harold, Second Lt.   2 Apr 1919   W Yorks Regt att 13th

For conspicuous gallantry and able leadership on 24 October 1918, during the attack at Rue du Pont. He led his company with great skill through the belts of wire in face of very heavy machine-gun fire, and finally overcame the enemy resistance. After the objective had been reached he supervised consolidation of the position.

Gibbens, Charles, Second Lt. (DCM)   17 Sep 1917   2nd att 12th

For conspicuous gallantry and devotion to duty. Despite heavy shelling he kept his men at work on a communication trench until the work was complete, rallying the men, and by his fine personal example encouraging them under very trying conditions. He also showed great judgment in keeping others in readiness to repel a counter-attack.

Capt. (MC DCM) Bar to MC   15 Oct 1918   2nd att 12th

For conspicuous gallantry and devotion to duty during an enemy attack. He handled and controlled his company so admirably that the enemy's attacks were easily beaten off by rifle fire. Throughout the battle he showed courage and powers of command.

Gray, Edward. Second Lt., T/Capt.   17 Sep 1917   DLI att 13th

For conspicuous gallantry and devotion to duty in commanding the front line for six days, during which his energy, example and absolute disregard of danger enabled the consolidation to be successfully achieved. His useful reconnaissances and initiaiive in sending out patrols and strongpoints very largely strengthened our line of defence.

Greenwood, Leonard Montague, T/Capt.   4 Jun 1917   13th

T/Capt. (MC) Bar to MC   8 Mar 1919   13th

He displayed great gallantry and devotion to duty during the operations 7 to 11 October, 1918. His commanding officer having been wounded on 5 October, he assumed command of the battalion. Before Le Cateau, on 9/10 October, when his battalion had suffered very heavy casualties he continually walked round the line under very heavy machine-gun and artillery fire encouraging his men and reorganising. In the attack on St. Benin, on 10 October, he personally led his battalion, capturing all objectives.

Grimwade, Hugh Noel T/Second Lt.   1 Jan 1917   12th

Hall, Norman Bodger, T/Second Lt.   16 Aug 1917   12th

For conspicuous gallantry and devotion to duty. He showed great coolness and skill in laying and firing his guns for several hours under heavy shellfire; later, with a small party he successfully repulsed a strong hostile counter-attack which had penetrated our line, saving a serious situation by his timely pluck and initiative.

Harris, William Henry, Second Lt.   19 Nov 1917   DLI att 12th

For conspicuous gallantry and devotion to duty. During a hostile counter-attack, he led his company forward under a very heavy barrage and helped to drive the enemy back. His coolness and absolute disregard of danger were an inspiratton to his men. He was wounded during the counter-attack, but remained with his company till the situation became normal.

Hill, William Reginald, Second Lt.   16 Aug 1917   SR att 12th

For conspicuous gallantry and devotion to duty in entering a village and capturing four enemy officers, aided by his Lewis gun section. His skilled leadership and energy were of the greatest value in consolidating the captured position, and he continually displayed great fearlessness in encouraging his men under heavy shellfire.

Lt. (MC) Bar to MC   24 Sep 1918   SR att 8th

Hughes, William Lewis, T/Second Lt.   18 Jun 1917   12th

For conspicuous gallantry and devotion to duty. He behaved in a most gallant manner when one of our aeroplanes fell in front of our lines. He went out to the assistance of the wounded observer, and under heavy fire succeeded in bringing him in to our lines.

T/Capt. (MC) Bar to MC   2 Apr 1919   12th

At the forcing of the River Piave on 27 October, 1918, and in the actions of 28/29 October 1918, he commanded his company with great skill and gallantry. When his company was held up on 28 October by an enemy strong point he personally led the final assault and captured six machine guns. He showed fine courage and leadership.

Jaques, (Jacques) John Barclay, T/Lt.   3 Jun 1916   12th

Johnston, Samuel Ferguson, T/Second Lt.   3 Jun 1918   13th
For bravery at 3rd Battle of Ypres between 20/22 September, 1917.

Kaye-Butterworth, George Sainton, T/Lt.   25 Aug 1916   13th
For conspicuous gallantry in action. He commanded his company after his Captain had been wounded with great ability and coolness. By his energy and utter disregard of danger he set a fine example in organising the defences of the front line. His name has previously been brought to notice for good and gallant work.

Lafone, Eric William, T/Capt.   17 Sep 1917   12th
For conspicuous gallantry and devotion to duty when commanding his company during an attack. He kept them well together under exceptionally trying conditions, when they were suffering heavily from our own guns, but by skilful leading was able to shift his position and lessen the casualties, afterwards gaining the final objective. His untiring efforts were mainly responsible for the ultimate success of the operations.

Mitchell, Robert Sutherland Forbes, T/Lt.   19 Nov 1917   13th
For conspicuous gallantry and devotion to duty. He carried out his duties as intelligence officer with absolute disregard of personal danger. When one of the company commanders became a casualty early in the attack, he took command of the company and led them to the final objective.

Noble, John, T/Second Lt.   19 Nov 1917   12th
For conspicuous gallantry and devotion to duty while in charge of a platoon carrying material to the front line. In spite of a heavy barrage and numerous casualties, he made three journeys from the front to rear. Throughout the operations he showed complete disregard of personal safety and was of very great assistance during the work of consolidation.

O'Callaghan, Cyril Tracey, T/Second Lt.   20 Oct 1916   13th
For conspicuous gallantry in action. He gained 70 yards of trench with his bombers and made a block. When this was rushed by the enemy he rallied his men and led them with great dash till severely wounded, preventing any further ground being lost.

Price, Arnold Thimbleby, T/Lt.   25 Aug 1916   12th
For conspicuous gallantry in action. With ten men he barricaded a road subject to heavy machine-gun fire. He then with a platoon dug himself in under fire near the captured enemy guns, and thus secured their retention.

Rasche, John Edward, T/Lt.   15 Oct 1918   20th att 12th
For conspicuous gallantry and devotion to duty during an enemy attack. He was in command of a patrol, and his retreat being cut off by the enemy barrage, he stood off the enemy until their barrage lifted, when he withdrew to his lines, bringing in his whole party, including wounded. During the withdrawal he was wounded himself but remained on duty until ordered to the ambulance at the close of the action.

Rees, Frederick Llewellyn, T/Second Lt.   26 Sep 1916   13th
With 'B' Coy 13th Bn on 4th August, 1916, Munster Alley, Somme. For conspicuous gallantry during operations. He led two bomb attacks, capturing the enemy's forward block and taking five prisoners. A further block, defended by barbed wire and two machine guns, resisted all his efforts to capture it, but he established a block only 18 yards away and held on all night in spite of desperate efforts to turn him out.

Richardson, Richard, CSM 21600   1 Jan 1917   13th

Robson, Percival Laidler, QMS 17199   3 Jun 1918   13th

Sauerbeck, Charles Theodore William, T/Lt. 1 Sep 1917   13th
For conspicuous gallantry and devotion to duty on many occasions, whilst acting as intelligence officer. He repeatedly went through heavy barrages in the performance of his duty, never once faltering though suffering severely from a wounded knee. He refused to be relieved while the battalion was in the line, and he is now in hospital in danger of losing his leg from septic poisoning. His example of steadfast courage and devotion to duty was particularly splendid to all ranks.

Shaw, George Murray, T/Capt.   1 Jan 1917   RAMC att 13th

Target, Noel Alexander, Second Lt., T/Lt.   24 Jun 1916   13th
For conspicuous gallantry. Lts. Clarke and Target led a successful raid on the enemy's trenches. At least twelve of the enemy were accounted for, and five deep occupied dugouts were bombed. Owing to the skill and rapidity of action there were only three slight casualties in their party.

Vaux, Cuthbert, Lt.   25 Aug 1917   SR att 12th
Messines, 13 June 1917. For conspicuous gallantry and devotion to duty. With great skill and coolness he led his platoon to the occupation of a difficult position, which he reached and reported upon, unnoticed by the enemy, although in close proximity to their posts. The rapidity and daring with which he carried out this operation was beyond all praise.

Wright, Geoffrey Carlton, T/Second Lt., Lt. (DCM) 19 Nov 1917 13th
For conspicuous gallantry and devotion to duty. Finding that the battalion on his right had been held up in the advance and that the flank of his own battalion was exposed, he brought up two platoons and secured the flank under heavy fire. During an enemy counter-attack he behaved with the greatest gallantry and fearlessness, and though wounded, remained at his post until the counter-attack was completely defeated.
DCM with 12/York and Lancaster Regt.   22 Sep 1916

THE DISTINGUISHED CONDUCT MEDAL

Adamson, W., CSM, 300014 13th   30 Oct 1918   Pelton
For conspicuous gallantry and devotion to duty. During an enemy attack he walked continually up and down his company front under heavy fire, encouraging his men and directing their fire. When the attack broke down he went out into No Mans Land and brought in several unwounded and many wounded prisoners. Throughout the battle he set a splendid example of courage and determination to all.

Anderson, J., Sjt. (MM) 24803 13th   30 Oct 1918   Wingate
For conspicuous gallantry and devotion to duty. During an enemy attack he handled his four Lewis guns with great skill and judgment. On one occasion he himself accounted for the entire team of an enemy machine gun. Later, he went out into No Man's Land and brought back several unwounded and wounded prisoners. Throughout the battle he set a splendid example of courage and cheerfulness to all.

Aungiers, H., CSM 13601 12th   3 Jun 1918   Grangetown
For conspicuous gallantry and excellent service at all times, and in particular during a relief under heavy shellfire. His company being left with one officer only, and the guide having lost his way, he, by his determination and skill, enabled the company to complete the relief. His cheery disposition under most trying conditions did much to keep up the fighting spirit of his company.

Bazeley, W.T., CSM 11324 13th   26 July 1917
For conspicuous gallantry and devotion to duty. He rendered invaluable assistance throughout, and was largely responsible for repelling a hostile raiding party.

Bell, R., L/Cpl. 24825 13th   3 Jun 1919   Skinningrove
For marked gallantry and devotion to duty at Beaurevoir on 5 October 1918. After reaching its objective the battalion was forced to withdraw. He refused to come back until the rest of the company had got back to a place of safety, but remained in front by himself during the withdrawal with a Lewis gun regardless of danger and although nearly surrounded, he delayed the enemy, and inflicted heavy losses in their ranks.

Brough, M., Sjt. 17750 13th   26 Jul 1917
For conspicuous gallantry and devotion to duty. He rendered invaluable assistance to his platoon officer, and throughout set a fine example to those around him.

Brown, G., Pte. 210041 12th   17 Apr 1919   Stockton-on-Tees
On the forcing of the River Piave on 27 October, 1918, a party was engaged in cutting wire which was holding the attack up. Except the officer, who was wounded, the whole party was killed. Private Brown, who had already been wounded once, then ran forward on his own initiative to help his officer. He was again wounded, but went on with the work until a passage was effected. Had the wire not been cut, the battalion could not have advanced and the attack would probably have failed.

Cowell, R., Sjt. 16101 13th   26 Nov 1917   Durham
For conspicuous gallantry and devotion to duty. When his battalion reached their objective the right flank was exposed. Although wounded, he took his platoon to cover the flank, and consolidated it under heavy fire from snipers. During an enemy counter-attack he moved his section forward out of the barrage to meet the attack, and successfully repulsed it. He showed great courage and initiative throughout the operations.

Craddock, H., Cpl. 16194 13th   26 Sep 1916
For conspicuous gallantry during operations. He asked for leave to take up reinforcements to a block 18 yards from the enemy. On his way he rallied some men who had been bombed out of our block and led them back to the block, where he fought with the greatest courage.

Cruddas, B., Sjt. 7202 12th   26 Nov 1917   Darlington
For conspicuous gallantry and devotion to duty. An enemy strongpoint which had been overlooked in the advance was causing heavy casualties to carrying parties and supporting troops. He left the carrying party of which he was in charge, and going forward alone, located the strongpoint. He then attacked it with three men, and captured it after a very stubborn fight, putting all the garrison out of action. He showed great powers of organisation, and was a splendid example to all ranks.

Dent, J.F. Cpl. 21084 12th   25 Aug 1917
For conspicuous gallantry and devotion to duty. When his officer and all NCOs were casualties, he took command of his platoon, supervised consolidation, and rallied them time after time under shellfire. He took six men forward at a favourable moment, and successfully established an advanced post in a commanding position and his conduct throughout was marked by energy, initiative, and fearlessness.

Dickinson, F.L. Pte. 22185 12th   4 Jun 1917
For conspicuous gallantry and devotion to duty. He has performed most valuable service as a runner. During operations he showed great gallantry and determination in the maintenance of communications.

Fisher, J., CSM 10194 12th   22 Sep 1916
For conspicuous gallantry and resource in successfully bringing up a platoon, under heavy fire and at a critical moment to protect an exposed flank. On two occasions he led bombing parties against superior numbers and assisted to remove wounded and dead under heavy shell and rifle fire, completely disregarding his own safety.

Gardner, J.G. Pte. 12970 12th   4 Jun 1917
For conspicuous gallantry and devotion to duty, whilst assisting to bring in a wounded officer from No Man's Land he was himself severely wounded, he placed the officer under cover and remained out with him until assistance arrived.

Hornby, W., Cpl. 18513 13th   22 Jan 1916
For conspicuous good service near Armentieres on the night of 5/6 December 1915. Corporal Hornby and Private Worton carried out a difficult and daring reconnaissance and brought back valuable information. They also bombed some enemy snipers with good results before they returned.

Jackson, G.W., L/Sjt. 36239 13th   26 Nov 1917   Doncaster
For conspicuous gallantry and devotion to duty. His advanced post was attacked by a strong patrol of the enemy. After a sharp fight he killed or wounded all the enemy, and took one officer prisoner. On two other occasions his post was surrounded but he rallied his men and drove off the enemy. He set a splendid example of courage and endurance.

James, F., Pte. 21010 12th att 68/LTMB   27 July 1916

For consistent gallantry, notably when, under very heavy shellfire, he continued to work his gun after part of the emplacement was blown in. Later he went back, brought up a fresh supply of ammunition and continued firing.

Kilburn, G.W., Pte. 22166 12th   25 Nov 1916

For conspicuous gallantry in action. He carried out a dangerous reconnaissance in daylight. Later, although himself wounded, he carried messages and tended the wounded under intense fire.

Liddle, W., CSM 19192 13th   25 Nov 1916

For conspicuous gallantry in action. He organised bombing parties and worked unceasingly in continuing the work of clearing the village. He showed marked courage and set a splendid example to his men.

Martin, T., CSM 20891 12th   26 Nov 1917   Newcastle

For conspicuous gallantry and devotion to duty. He organised his platoon to meet an enemy attack and kept up communication with the company on his left, continually rnoving over ground swept by heavy shellfire to do so. Throughout the operations he inspired all ranks by his great coolness and contempt of danger.

CSM (DCM) Bar to DCM   30 Oct 1918

For conspicuous gallantry and devotion to duty during an enemy attack. He organised and led a party which successfully bombed some enemy snipers established close to his wire. He showed great coolness and determination, and set a splendid example to his men throughout the battle.

Miller, C., CSM 20624 12th   26 Nov 1917   Spennymoor

For conspicuous gallantry and devotion to duty. When several men were buried in a dugout by an enemy barrage, he went along the top of the trench and dug them out single-handed. His prompt action undoubtedly saved their lives.

Mineards, R., Sjt. 45960 13th   26 Nov 1917   Northampton

For conspicuous gallantry and devotion to duty. When the flank of the battalion became exposed on the final objective, he consolidated his position and succeeded in silencing the enemy by rifle and Lewis gun fire. He inspired all ranks by his magnificent example of coolness and courage under heavy fire.

Nelson, G., L/Cpl. (MM) 302936 12th   17 Apr 1919   Darlington

At the forcing of the River Piave on 27 October, 1918, and during the actions of 28–29, he constantly showed the greatest gallantry and devotion to duty in carrying messages under the heaviest fire. On the evening of 29 October he carried a message to a company which had got separated across two different streams through a country swarming with snipers and machine-gun posts.

Simpson, J., Pte. 18641 12th   25 Aug 1917

For conspicuous gallantry and devotion to duty during a strong enemy attack on our flank. He dug out his gun, which had been buried, under heavy shellfire and again got it into action. It was then buried a second time and rendered useless, whereupon he and another gunner charged the enemy, who had penetrated into our trenches, and bombed them back again. He then established himself to protect a large bomb store, which he held with the greatest fearlessness and gallantry against repeated rallies of the enemy. Though wounded, he remained at duty till next day.

Slasor, G., L/Cpl. 15874 12th   25 Nov 1916

For conspicuous gallantry in action. On three occasions he led patrols, obtaining most valuable information. Later, he lay for four hours in No Man's Land, keeping touch with the attackers.

Sledge, A., Sjt. (MM) 18483 13th   12 Mar 1918   Richmond

For conspicuous gallantry and devotion to duty during the advance on St. Benin on the 30 October, 1918. Throughout the operations he set a very fine example of courage and cheerfulness. When his company commander was killed he took command of the company and led them to their objective under great difficulties. Although wounded several times he refused to leave the line. After having his wounds dressed, again he took command.

Speed, J.A., Sjt. (MM) 18662 12th   30 Oct 1918   Blackhill

For conspicuous gallantry and devotion to duty as signalling sergeant of the battalion during an enemy attack. He repaired the wires under very heavy shellfire. Although recently sick, he worked continuously for twenty hours. He set a very fine example to his signallers.

Thomson, G., CSM 52647 13th   16 Aug 1917

For conspicuous gallantry and devotion to duty. He took charge of half his company when it was in a very exposed position and subjected to heavy bombardment, by his example so encouraging the men that they were able to hold on to a series of shell holes and turn them into a good defensive line.

Woodruff, G.A., CSM 15774 13th   25 Aug 1917

For conspicuous gallantry and devotion to duty in visiting and rallying his men during an intense bombardment, which was the preliminary to an attempted hostile raid. His presence of mind in bringing up a section to the critical spot to replace a disabled Lewis gun undoubtedly was instrumental in repulsing the raid, and his constant visits to the lines, during which he fearlessly exposed himself, undoubtedly rallied and cheered the men after their ordeal of a long and heavy bombardment. He has many times distinguished himself in a similar manner.

Worton, J.C., Pte. 21603 13th   22 Jan 1916

For conspicuous good service near Armentieres on the night of 5/6 December 1915. Corporal Hornby and Private Worton carried out a difficult and dangerous reconnaissance and brought back valuable information. They also bombed some enemy snipers with good results before they returned.

THE MILITARY MEDAL

Name & Initials	Rank	Number	London Gazette No.	Battalion
Agar N R	Pte	31875	21/12/1916	12th
Anderson J	Cpl	24803	12/12/1917	13th
Anderson J	L/Cpl	21160	14/09/1916	13th
Armstrong C G	L/Cpl	13616	09/07/1917	13th
Armstrong T	Pte	24794	21/10/1918	13th
Askew J	Sjt	21256	12/03/1917	13th
Bamborough J G	Pte	21549	14/09/1916	12th
Bamborough T	Pte	18077	23/08/1916	12th
Barker C	Pte	16946	10/08/1916	13th
Barron T W	Sjt	18135	17/06/1919	13th
Beattie D	Pte	44550	17/06/1919	13th
Belcher J	L/Cpl	16185	28/07/1917	12th
Bell G	L/Sjt	24784	12/03/1917	13th
Bell R	Pte	28096	17/09/1917	12th
Bellerby T	Cpl	15384	01/09/1916	13th
Bews G	Pte	16954	17/06/1919	13th
Boagey J	L/Sjt	17190	10/08/1916	13th
Boal W	L/Cpl	22560	28/07/1917	12th
Bond W H	Pte	43392	09/07/1917	13th
Boulger J B	Pte	16947	21/12/1916	12th
Bowman J	L/Cpl	24772	12/12/1917	13th
Bowman T G	Pte	21046	09/12/1916	13th
Bowran W A	L/Cpl	17194	10/08/1916	13th
Brankston H	Pte	15340	09/07/1917	13th
Brennan T	L/Cpl	25489	06/01/1917	12th
Brough M	L/Cpl	17750	14/09/1916	13th
Brown N	Pte	18150	09/12/1916	13th
Burgess F E	Pte	52649	14/01/1918	12th

Burns H	Sjt	52840	12/12/1917	13th
Byrne F	Pte	251953	12/12/1917	13th
Campbell R	Pte	3/12646	28/07/1917	12th
Carr J	Pte	19467	28/01/1918	13th
Carter J	L/Cpl	15062	14/01/1918	12th
Cassinelli T	Cpl	35327	12/12/1917	13th
Claire W	L/Cpl	18192	14/09/1916	13th
Clark J	Pte	20959	21/08/1917	13th
Clasper J	Sjt	16980	14/01/1918	12th
Constantine A	Pte	15952	09/12/1916	13th
Cook J	Pte	18654	21/10/1918	12th
Cooper H	L/Cpl	54220	21/10/1918	12th
Cornthwaite T	Pte	52868	12/12/1917	13th
Craddock H (DCM)	Sjt	16194	09/12/1916	13th
Crossley T	Pte	52869	17/06/1919	13th
Crouch A E	Pte	302522	12/12/1917	12th
Daglish R	Pte	18240	28/01/1918	12th
Dean J O	L/Cpl	21027	12/12/1917	13th
Defty R	L/Cpl	45880	14/01/1918	12th
Dickenson H	L/Cpl	17303	14/09/1916	13th
Dobbs T H	Pte	19515	18/07/1917	12th
Dodds J T	Pte	17905	10/08/1916	13th
Donnan J	Pte	203205	12/12/1917	13th
Dyer J	Pte	17317	17/06/1919	13th
Dyson J B	Pte	18221	01/09/1916	12th
Edwards A G	Pte	54290	28/01/1918	12th
Edwards G	Pte	54224	17/09/1917	12th
Farrell J	A/RSM	4844	11/10/1916	RMLI att 13th
Fitters A	Sjt	17711	09/12/1916	13th
Fitzpatrick T	Sjt	18170	23/08/1916	13th
Fletcher T	Pte	24432	12/12/1917	12th
Galley W	Sjt	19041	14/09/1916	13th
Garvey G G	Cpl	15946	21/12/1916	12th
Gault J D	Pte	43697	21/10/1918	13th
Gerry S	Pte	54174	29/03/1919	12th
Gill W	Pte	18219	01/09/1916	12th
Gormlay T	Pte	22156	19/02/1917	12th
Gowland C	L/Cpl	16491	06/01/1917	13th
Gowland T F	Pte	15336	10/08/1916	13th
Graham D	Pte	21614	09/12/1916	13th
Gray P	Pte	21207	12/12/1917	12th
Green J G	Pte	16431	09/12/1916	13th
Halford E	Pte	33496	09/12/1916	12th
Hall W	L/Cpl	302793	21/10/1918	13th
Hammond T S	Sjt	18067	17/06/1919	13th
Harle T	Pte	17032	09/12/1916	13th
Harness J	Pte	17379	09/12/1916	12th
Harrington J	Pte	7715	01/09/1916	12th
Harrison A	L/Cpl	3/11640	09/07/1917	13th
Harrison C	Pte	17403	21/10/1918	12th
Harrison H G	Pte	20163	12/12/1917	12th
Hart W	Pte	20951	10/08/1916	13th
Hay T	Pte	15381	28/07/1917	12th
Hedley R	Pte	16121	10/08/1916	13th

Hedley R	Pte	79055	11/02/1919	12th
Henderson J J	Pte	17024	12/12/1917	13th
Hetherington E	L/Cpl	24632	10/08/1916	13th
Hetherington H	Sjt	9662	17/06/1919	13th
Hewitt G E	L/Cpl	204505	21/10/1918	13th
Hickson R	Pte	19644	14/09/1916	13th
Hitchin H E	Sjt	19625	23/08/1916	12th
Hodges E	Pte	20/582	12/12/1917	13th
Holmes R	L/Sjt	20640	17/12/1917	13th
Holt J L	Pte	45948	12/12/1917	13th
Horn W	Pte	17398	17/06/1919	13th
Horspole J W	Pte	21792	28/07/1917	12th
Howe W	Pte	45964	12/12/1917	13th
Hughes J	Sjt	19062	01/09/1916	12th
Hurworth H	Pte	21606	28/01/1918	13th
Hutchinson W	Pte	24775	23/08/1916	13th
Jackson C	Sjt	44601	23/07/1919	13th
Jackson T	Pte	18315	09/12/1916	13th
Jeffers J W	Pte	17712	10/08/1916	13th
Jefferson C W	Cpl	17417	12/12/1917	13th
Johnson F	Pte	25480	09/12/1916	12th
Jones E	Pte	54182	12/12/1917	12th
Jones E	Pte	17038	14/09/1916	12th
Jones L	Pte	45008	23/07/1919	13th
Keenan J	Pte	18491	10/08/1916	13th
Kempster S	Pte	301505	12/12/1917	13th
Kerr T O	Cpl	16542	14/09/1916	13th
Killeen J (MSM)	Sjt	13869	23/07/1919	13th
King S H	L/Cpl	53548	14/01/1918	12th
King W T	Sjt	53531	17/09/1917	12th
Kirby T R	Pte	20/386	21/10/1918	12th
Kirkup J	Cpl	21908	09/07/1917	13th
Kisby T	Pte	24980	29/03/1919	12th
Lamb E	Sjt	15894	23/08/1916	13th
Lattimer T H	Pte	23626	19/02/1917	13th
Laurie M	L/Sjt	25503	09/07/1917	13th
Leach H G	L/Cpl	52757	28/07/1917	12th
Lewins W	Pte	22046	12/12/1917	12th
Littlewood W	Sjt	300920	14/01/1918	12th
Lockey T G	Cpl	19134	09/12/1916	12th
Long A	Sjt	20618	01/09/1916	12th
Lucas A	Pte	46070	12/12/1917	13th
Luke W	Pte	17054	01/09/1916	13th
McCarthy J	Pte	15085	01/09/1916	12th
McDonnell H	L/Cpl	19/1174	21/10/1918	12th
McDonnell R	Cpl	27671	09/07/1917	13th
McKenna J	L/Cpl	21909	12/12/1917	13th
McMahon R W	Pte	17941	28/07/1917	12th
McNeal T	Pte	19085	28/07/1917	12th
McVean J J	L/Cpl	13513	29/03/1919	12th
Malloy F	Pte	45995	20/08/1919	13th
Matkin E	Sjt	1972	8/07/1917	12th
Maudlin N	Pte	18842	29/03/1919	12th
Maughan W	Pte	24796	01/09/1916	13th

Mayes F	Pte	42833	12/03/1917	12th
Middleton T W	Pte	19770	10/08/1916	13th
Milburn J	Cpl	19751	21/12/1916	12th
Mitchell A	Pte	28539	28/07/1917	12th
Mitchell P	Cpl	19752	14/09/1916	12th
Monk W	Sjt	18795	09/12/1916	12th
Moore J	Pte	18804	12/12/1917	12th
Moore J	Pte	18968	14/09/1916	12th
Morgan R C	L/Cpl	43695	17/12/1917	13th
Morrell R	L/Sgt	10125	21/10/1918	13th
Moses T	L/Cpl	45675	29/03/1919	12th
Moyle J	Pte	16103	10/08/1916	13th
Neal G W	Pte	38908	21/10/1918	13th
Nelson G	Pte	302936	12/12/1917	12th
Nessworthy W R	Pte	14246	09/12/1916	12th
Newby G E	Pte	17075	09/12/1916	13th
Newlands J	Pte	52693	12/12/1917	12th
Newman W	L/Cpl	52768	29/03/1919	12th
Nichol C	Pte	46042	09/12/1916	13th
Nichol J J	Pte	17909	29/03/1919	12th
Nixon R	Pte	20932	12/12/1917	12th
O'Hara J W	Sjt	15959	21/10/1918	12th
O'Rourke C	Pte	19782	09/12/1916	13th
Olsen C	Pte	19050	09/07/1917	12th
Orr W	Pte	19785	10/08/1916	13th
Outhwaite R	Pte	350410	12/12/1917	12th
Pain L	Pte	13820	21/08/1917	13th
Parkin S S	Cpl	13901	29/03/1919	12th
Parmley J	Sjt	25505	14/01/1918	12th
Parnaby H	Pte	78417	21/10/1918	13th
Parrett W	Pte	8777	01/09/1916	13th
Passmore G	Pte	24469	29/03/1919	12th
Patterson D	Pte	16747	12/12/1917	13th
Pattison T H	Cpl	15524	12/12/1917	13th
Pattison W	Cpl	19313	29/03/1919	12th
Pearson J	Sjt	16406	14/01/1918	12th
Peat W	Pte	16757	01/09/1916	12th
Poulter H	Pte	78424	23/07/1919	13th
Powell S	Pte	78422	17/06/1919	13th
Powell W	Sjt	19/348	12/12/1917	13th
Pull E A	Cpl	3/11907	17/12/1917	13th
Purvis R	Pte	18777	09/12/1916	13th
Pye J	Pte	16774	01/09/1916	12th
Reed J B	Pte	52910	17/12/1917	13th
Richardson A E	Sjt	18647	29/03/1919	12th
Richer W T	Pte	28527	12/03/1917	12th
Ritchie G	Sgt	13397	27/03/1919`	12th
Robinson J	L/Cpl	23447	03/06/1916	13th
Robinson J	Pte	96073	23/07/1919	13th
Robson J	Sjt	21147	12/12/1917	13th
Rollett T W	Pte	302643	12/12/1917	13th
Rowell C S	Pte	38557	12/12/1917	13th
Roy J	L/Cpl	28892	12/12/1917	13th
Russell G	Sjt	43440	17/06/1919	13th

Name	Rank	Number	Date	Battalion
Rutherford A	Pte	18377	12/03/1917	12th
Saltmarsh F	Sjt	16916	12/12/1917	13th
Saltmarsh J	Pte	40383	21/10/1918	12th
Scratcher J H	Pte	24723	06/01/1917	12th att 68/LTMB
Shanks S	Pte	16188	14/09/1916	12th
Shaw H	Pte	52914	12/12/1917	13th
Shelley A E	Pte	245250	17/06/1919	13th
Showell W F	Pte	52708	18/09/1917	12th
Silversides W H	Sjt	18397	23/08/1916	12th
Simm J	Pte	201351	12/12/1917	13th
Simms W	Pte	23767	01/09/1916	13th
Sledge A	Sjt	18483	12/12/1917	13th
Smith E C	Pte	18168	12/12/1917	13th
Smith F C	Pte	52767	18/09/1917	12th
Smith J	L/Sjt	12957	21/09/1916	13th
Smith J W	L/Cpl	24826	17/06/1919	13th
Smith W	Pte	14450	06/01/1917	12th
Smith W H	Sjt	22611	01/09/1916	13th
Snowball J	Pte	52722	28/01/1918	12th
Speed J A	Cpl	18662	23/08/1916	12th
Starkings J W	Sjt	53539	29/03/1919	12th
Stephenson A	Pte	28670	10/08/1916	13th
Stirling C A	Sjt	21618	09/12/1916	13th
Stoker W F	Pte	20382	12/12/1917	12th
Stott F	Pte	52743	12/12/1917	12th
Suddes T	Pte	17108	23/08/1916	13th
Sykes J T	Pte	20/455	28/07/1917	12th
Tait J	Pte	45887	29/08/1917	12th
Taylor F	Sjt	21075	28/07/1917	12th
Thompson W H	Cpl	18124	12/12/1917	13th
Thomson G (DCM)	CSM	52647	23/07/1919	13th
Tonkin J	Pte	13304	09/12/1916	13th
Townend G O	L/Sjt	22267	28/07/1917	13th att 68/LTMB
Umpleby J	Pte	23761	09/07/1917	13th
Vipond J E	Pte	16429	09/12/1916	13th
Waistell T	Pte	14823	01/09/1916	12th
Waldram L J	Sjt	19945	28/01/1918	13th
Walker F	Sjt	13596	28/07/1917	12th
Walton I B	Sjt	18/1488	23/07/1919	13th
Walton N	Cpl	28778	12/12/1917	13th
Watson J	Sjt	18628	14/01/1918	13th
Watson J F	L/Cpl	23752	28/07/1917	12th
Watson W B	L/Cpl	18627	14/09/1916	12th
Watson W K	Pte	25559	21/12/1916	12th
Webster W	Pte	17137	12/12/1917	13th
White R B	A/Sjt	22023	10/08/1916	13th
Wildsmith J F	Cpl	16525	21/10/1918	12th att 68/LTMB
Wilkinson E	Sjt	18050	12/12/1917	13th
Wilkinson J J	Pte	17809	01/09/1916	13th
Williams S	Pte	17148	10/08/1916	13th
Wilson G	Pte	301278	12/12/1917	12th
Wilson H	Pte	17149	09/12/1916	12th
Wilson H	L/Cpl	52763	28/01/1918	12th
Winter H W	Pte	54317	23/07/1919	13th

Name	Rank	Number	Date	Battalion
Woodhall H	L/Cpl	52796	28/07/1917	12th
Woodhead W	L/Cpl	15421	23/08/1916	12th
Woodruff J T	Pte	22/1014	14/01/1918	13th
Woodward C	Pte	18011	21/10/1918	12th
Yates J	Pte	25474	12/12/1917	12th

Bar to the Military Medal

Name	Rank	Number	Date	Battalion
Bellerby T (MM)	Cpl	15384	17/12/1917	13th
Brough M (MM)	Sjt	17750	09/12/1916	13th
Claire W (MM)	Cpl	18192	21/10/1918	13th
Clark J (MM)	Pte	20959	17/06/1919	13th
Constantine A (MM)	Pte	15952	12/12/1917	13th
Defty R (MM)	Cpl	45880	29/03/1919	12th
Hammond T S (MM)	CSM	18067	20/08/1919	13th
Harness J (MM)	Pte	17379	28/07/1917	12th
Hitchin H E (MM)	Sjt	19625	14/12/1916	12th
Lewins W (MM)	Pte	22046	29/03/1919	12th
Littlewood W (MM)	A/CSM	300920	29/03/1919	12th
Monk W (MM)	A/CSM	18795	29/03/1919	12th
Showell W F (MM)	Cpl	52708	29/03/1919	12th
Speed J A (MM)	Cpl	18662	28/07/1917	12th

MERITORIOUS SERVICE MEDAL

Name	Rank	Number	Date	Battalion
Barry J T	Cpl	13900	03/06/1919	12th
Garnett H	Sjt	43399	03/06/1919	13th
Hall F	Pte	21812	09/07/1917	13th
Hammond T S	Sgt	18067	03/06/1918	13th
Killeen J	Pte	13869	03/06/1918	13th
Lowery J B	Cpl	25538	03/06/1919	12th
Martin J W	Sjt	3/10646	03/06/1919	12th
Maylia J	L/Cpl	17992	29/08/1918	13th att 68/LTMB
Pattison W	Sjt	19313	03/06/1918	12th
Penn C W	A/L/Sjt	52719	03/06/1919	12th
Spedding T	CSM	15955	01/01/1919	12th
Telfer W	Cpl	18400	01/01/1919	12th
Walker H	Sjt	17707	03/06/1918	13th

Croix de Guerre Belgium

Name	Rank	Number	Date	Battalion
Armstrong T	Pte	24794	12/07/1918	13th
Miller T W	Pte	54187	12/07/1918	13th

Croix de Guerre France

Name	Rank	Number	Date	Battalion
Lafone E W	T/Capt		14/07/1917	12th

Medal Militaire France

Name	Rank	Number	Date	Battalion
Harness J	Pte	17379	01/05/1917	12th

Croce di Guerra Italy

Name	Rank	Number	Date	Battalion
Clements T	Maj & QM		17/05/1919	12th
Colville W T	Second Lt.		17/05/1919	12th
Constatine A	Pte	15952	29/11/1918	13th
Defty R	Sjt	45880	17/05/1919	12th
Maudlin N	Sjt	18842	17/05/1919	12th
Smithson T	Second Lt.		17/05/1919	12th
Teague E V	L/Sjt	52758	29/11/1919	12th
Wilson J	T/Capt		17/05/1919	12th
Woodhead W	CSM	15421	17/05/1919	12th

Silver Medal for Valour Italy

Borrow E	T/Maj		17/05/1919	12th
Holford J II	T/Lt. Col		17/05/1919	12th

Bronze Medal for Valour Italy

Gerry S	Pte	54174	17/05/1919	12th
Nelson G	L/Cpl	302936	17/05/1919	12th
Rasche J E	T/Lt.		29/11/1918	20th att 12th

NOTES ON THE NOMINAL ROLLS

The rolls of the officers are compiled from those handed in by battalions at the end of the war to the War Office and passed some years ago to the Regimental Museum and from there to the County Archives. I have added some small pieces of information such as home town, where it was found on a Medal Roll Index Card. I have omitted war graves information as this is easily looked up online today.

The embarkation rolls of the Other Ranks were far more difficult and it is to my regret that I must print them knowing that they are not and never can be complete. Having completed several rolls on the locally-raised battalions where it was easy to trace a soldier as his number would be prefixed by the battalion, i.e. 18/, 19/ etc I knew the service battalions of K1, K2 and K3 would be a lot harder as the numbers issued to the soldiers from 10000 to 25000 were spread across the 10th, 11th, 12th, 13th 14th, 15th, 16th and 17th Battalions. My initial thought was that the 1914/15 Star Roll would do the job but on consulting those books I found that the soldier's battalion was not given. I then decided to cross-reference the War and Victory Roll with the 1914/15 Star Roll and in that way I put together rolls of around 650 men for each battalion. I then turned my attention to those that transferred to other Corps and Regiments. The 1914/15 Star Rolls for the Labour Corps, the Tank Corps and the Machine Gun Corps all give the soldier's battalion on landing in France, as do the War and Victory Rolls for the Royal Defence Corps. On the down side, the Medal Rolls for the Royal Engineers, Royal Artillery and the majority of the other Corps do not show a transferred infantry soldier's original battalion, so even though the Medal Index card shows his date of entry into France as 25 August 1915, there is no way of knowing which battalion he landed with. That is because on that day not only were 12th and 13th Battalions arriving, but drafts to the 2nd, 10th and the DLI Infantry Base Depot.

When I first compiled rolls for the original format of Tyneside Irish it was easy to keep information in columns and record lots of information about an individual. With the move to the smaller hardback book to produce such rolls is impossible. Therefore I have abbreviated many frequently-used army unit titles and words in order to include as much information as possible.

A TRN or AMB TRN	Ambulance Train	} Preceded by a number
CCS	Casualty Clearing Station	}
FA	Field Ambulance	} thus 69/FA
S HOSP	Stationary Hospital	}
G HOSP	General Hospital	}
AUS CCS	Australian CCS	}
CAN CCS	Canadian CCS	}
S MID CCS	South Midland CCS	
NTHBN CCS	Northumbrian CCS	
ENL	Enlisted	
DIS 392	Discharged under para 392 of King's Regulations	
FGCM	Field General Court Martial	
BDE	Brigade	
LTMB	Light Trench Mortar Battery	
KIA	Kiled in Action	
DOW	Died of Wounds	
RES	Resident or Reserve	
PUO	Pyrexia of Unkown Origin	
WND	Wounded	
LAB C	Labour Corps	

Nominal Roll of Officers who served with the 12th (Service) Battalion Durham Light Infantry 1914–1918

Rank	Name	First Name	Dismbarked/Joined Bn	Left Battalion	REMARKS & REASON FOR LEAVING BATTALION	HOME TOWN OR ADDRESS ON MICARD
SECOND LIEUTENANT	AGAR	JOHN W	04/01/1918	11/03/1919	TO UK ORIGINALLY 18/1 18/DLI ENT EGYPT 22/12/1915	DARLINGTON
SECOND LIEUTENANT	ALEXANDER	H R	22/09/1914 ?		DID NOT EMBARK WITH OR REJOIN THE BATTALION	
SECOND LIEUTENANT	ARMSTRONG	CECIL	29/07/1916	21/09/1916	KILLED IN ACTION	NEWCASTLE UPON TYNE
SECOND LIEUTENANT	ARMSTRONG	G G	15/01/1915 ?		DID NOT EMBARK WITH OR REJOIN THE BATTALION	
SECOND LIEUTENANT	BARCLAY	C L T	06/01/1915 ?		DID NOT EMBARK WITH OR REJOIN THE BATTALION	
SECOND LIEUTENANT	BLAYLOCK	PERCY	31/12/1915	28/03/1916	MEDICAL BOARD	EDGEBASTON
CAPTAIN	BLEADEN	CYRIL L	12/09/1918	30/12/1918	DIED OF WOUNDS	KENSINGTON
SECOND LIEUTENANT	BLENKINSOP	WILLIAM M	29/09/1916	07/11/1918	DIED OF WOUNDS	TYNEMOUTH
SECOND LIEUTENANT	BOLLOM	JOHNSON	29/07/1916	24/09/1916	KILLED IN ACTION	RYTON ON TYNE
SECOND LIEUTENANT	BORRELL	ARTHUR	10/06/1916	27/05/1917	TO UK SICK	HETTON LE HOLE
SECOND LIEUTENANT	BORROWDALE	WILLIAM G	06/06/1917	04/03/1918	TRF TO 11/WEST YORKS	WHITBURN
SECOND LIEUTENANT	BOYD SMITH	ALEXANDER	18/07/1916	25/09/1917	WOUNDED	
SECOND LIEUTENANT	BRANDON	THOMAS	20/12/1916	15/06/1917	WOUNDED SERVED IN PUBLIC SCHOOLS BN R FUSILIERS PS/7658	TELKWA B C CANADA
SECOND LIEUTENANT	BREVERTOR	T E	12/05/1916	17/05/1916	TO UK SICK SERVED ROYAL ENGINEERS CORPORAL 32286	GOLDERS GREEN
SECOND LIEUTENANT	BRISTOW	F A	22/09/1914 ?		DID NOT EMBARK WITH OR REJOIN THE BATTALION	
CAPTAIN	CALDERWOOD	ANDREW F	15/01/1917			GLASGOW
LIEUTENANT	CAMPBELL JONES	MERVYN	25/08/1915	08/07/1916	WOUNDED	EPSOM
CAPTAIN	CARR ELLISON	THOMAS F	25/08/1915	28/02/1916	TO 16/DLI	COLCHESTER
CAPTAIN	CARR ELLISON		25/08/1916	04/06/1917	TO UK SICK	
CAPTAIN	CARR ELLISON		19/10/1917	25/10/1917	TO UK SICK	
CAPTAIN	CARR WEST	ARTHUR T	25/08/1915	25/09/1917	TO UK SICK FROM 18/8/1914 TO 1/2/1915 SERVED WITH FRENCH FOREIGN LEGION	PARIS
CAPTAIN	CARR WEST	HERBERT ST J	25/08/1915	11/07/1916	WOUNDED	BROMLEY
CAPTAIN	CARR WEST		29/09/1916	08/11/1916	WOUNDED	
CAPTAIN	CARR WEST		21/03/1917	27/10/1918	DIED OF WOUNDS	
SECOND LIEUTENANT	CASSON	J T	23/06/1916	23/07/2016	WOUNDED	
CAPTAIN	CHAMBERS	DAVID M	29/10/1916	20/02/1917	KILLED IN ACTION	
SECOND LIEUTENANT	CHAPMAN	WILLIAM R	26/07/1917	23/10/1917	WOUNDED SERVED WITH 3rd STATIONARY HOSPITAL RAMC No 73359 , MC WITH 15/DLI	WHITLEY BAY
SECOND LIEUTENANT	CHESTER	G B	30/07/1917	23/09/1917	WOUNDED	
SECOND LIEUTENANT	COLVILLE	WILLIAM T	29/10/1917	10/02/1919	SERVED AS PRIVATE S/9122 ARGYLL & SUTHERLAND HIGHLANDERS TO COMMAND DEPOT FOR D	DUMBARTON
SECOND LIEUTENANT	CORBET	NORMAN L	12/06/1916	16/11/1916	TO UK SICK TO WORCESTERSHIRE REGT LIEUTENANT	WHITLEY BAY
SECOND LIEUTENANT	COTTON	JOSEPH P	09/08/1917		POSTED TO BN BUT NEVER JOINED, SERVED ROYAL FUSILIERS GS/23020	SUNDERLAND
SECOND LIEUTENANT	CRONIN	DUDLEY S	23/10/1917		SERVED AS PRIVATE 14372 HAMPSHIRE REGIMENT	NOTTINGHAM
SECOND LIEUTENANT	CROOKS	JOSEPH E	27/12/1917	17/01/1919	TO CONVELESANTCAMP SERVED 4/ROYAL FUSILIERS 9283	NEW SHILDON
SECOND LIEUTENANT	CROWN	WS	12/07/1917			
MAJOR	CUMMINS	CHARLES E	25/08/1915	09/10/1916	TO UK	BISHOP AUCKLAND
	CUMMINS		07/01/1917	14/06/1917	LIEUTENANT COLONEL COMDG BN OF THE ROYAL SUSSEX REGT	
SECOND LIEUTENANT	DALLAS	WILLIAM	07/11/1917	14/02/1919	DID NOT RETURN FROM UK LEAVE	INVERNESS
SECOND LIEUTENANT	DALZIEL	GEORGE	26/07/1917	18/10/1917	WOUNDED, SERVED PRIVATE 7295 18/ROYAL FUSILIERS	WEST HARTLEPOOL
MAJOR	DANVERS	HAROLD	25/08/1915	30/05/1916	SICK TO MACHINE GUN CORPS	LONDON
CAPTAIN	DAVENPORT	WILLIAM N	27/05/1918	24/01/1919	SERVED PRIVATE 7/CANADIAN INFANTRY BN ENLISTED VALCARTIER WITH 13/DLI 1916/17	BORN LONDON
SECOND LIEUTENANT	DAVIS	ERNEST	15/01/1918	28/01/1918	POSTED TO BN BUT RE-JOINED 13/DLI	FARNHAM
SECOND LIEUTENANT	DAVISON	Robert	30/07/1917	21/10/1917	SERVED AS PRIVATE G/40020 MIDDLESEX REGT, WOUNDED	DURHAM CITY
CAPTAIN	DAY	J P	18/11/1914 ?		DID NOT EMBARK WITH OR REJOIN THE BATTALION	
MAJOR	DICK CLELLAND	A B	09/08/1917	17/09/1918	TO UK FROM ROYAL FUSILIERS	
SECOND LIEUTENANT	DODD	JOHN F	25/08/1915	21/08/1918	TO UK ATT NORTHUMBERLAND FUSILIERS	BOLDON COLLIERY
SECOND LIEUTENANT	DODD	WILLIAM	09/01/1917	22/11/1917	TQ UK SICK, SERVED AS PRIVATE 9/11604 B COY 9/NORTHUMBERLAND FUSILIERS	
MAJOR	DORMAN-SMITH	ERIC E	19/04/1918		LT 1/NF 13/8/1914 A/MAJOR 10/NF TO 12/DLI MAJOR 7/7/1918 REJOINED 1/NF BY 11/1919	BORDON BARRACKS WITH 1/NF
LIEUTENANT	DREWERY	DONOVAN	17/03/1916	06/01/1919	FORMERLY TROOPER 1165 NORTHUMBERLAND HUSSARS	HIGH CONISCLIFFE DARLINGTCN
LIEUTENANT	DUFFY	THOMAS B	25/08/1915	13/07/1916	WOUNDED	HEBBURN
LIEUTENANT	DUFFY	THOMAS B	29/03/1917	11/06/1917		

Rank	Surname	Forename	Date	Remarks	Birthplace
LIEUTENANT	DUFFY	THOMAS B	03/09/1917	05/04/1918 DIDN'T REJOIN POSTED TO 15/DLI DOW 16/8/1918	CLARE SUFFOLK
SECOND LIEUTENANT	DUNN	ALEXANDER	07/03/1917	09/06/1917 WOUNDED	HONITON
SECOND LIEUTENANT	DUNNE	JOHN S	25/08/1915	17/10/2017 TRF 2/GAR BN ROYAL IRISH REGT	SEAHAM HARBOUR WITH 4/DLI
LIEUTENANT COLONEL	ELWES	LINCOLN E C	09/08/1917	30/05/1917 SICK	SPENNYMOOR
SECOND LIEUTENANT	ETHERINGTON	JOHN R	22/06/1916	22/10/1917 TO UK, SERVED AS L/SGT 975 & 250021 6/DLI ENT F&F 20/4/1915	THORNABY ON TEES
SECOND LIEUTENANT	EVES	HAROLD C	25/10/1917	10/09/1916 TO UK TRF TO MGC TO 6/MGC MAJOR WOUNDED 1918	BALLIA INDIA
SECOND LIEUTENANT	FERGUSON	JAMES	09/10/1918	23/06/1918 BORDER REGT ATT DLI TRF TO 9/YORK & LANCASTER REGT SUPT OF POLICE INDIA 1920	GATESHEAD
SECOND LIEUTENANT	FISHER	HARRY L		27/10/1918 FROM 10/DLI KILLED IN ACTION	
LIEUTENANT	FLATT	W P	22/09/1914 ?	DID NOT EMBARK WITH OR REJOIN THE BATTALION	CANTERBURY
SECOND LIEUTENANT	FORD	ARTHUR	04/07/1917	15/07/1917 SERVED AS CPL 27939 2/DLI POSTED TO BN BUT NEVER JOINED RETURNED TO UK SICK	BIRTLEY
SECOND LIEUTENANT	FOSTER	GEORGE	20/11/1916	20/02/1917 SERVED AS BOMBARDIER 102 BDE RE-TRF TO 102 BDE ROYAL FIELD ARTILLERY KIA 16/5/1917	
SECOND LIEUTENANT	FRANCIES	ARTHUR G	03/06/1916	22/07/1916 FROM 15/DLI WOUNDED 17/07/1916 LT TRG RES BN	BIRMINGHAM
CAPTAIN	FREEMAN	ERIC G	09/01/1917	11/03/1919 TO UK TRF TO LABOUR CORPS	
MAJOR	GALES	E F	19/09/1914 ?	DID NOT EMBARK WITH OR REJOIN THE BATTALION	HAMMERSMITH
SECOND LIEUTENANT	GIBBONS	CHARLES	09/01/1917	12/11/1918 SERVED AS CPL 8346 2/DLI TO UK SICK	DONCASTER
Lt & QUARTERMASTER	GILL	ROLAND	13/01/1918	01/09/1921 ATT MGC	BLAYDON
SECOND LIEUTENANT	GOBEY	ALFRED J	28/12/1916	09/05/1917 SERVED AWOI 3837 2/DLI SICK DIED HOME 19/11/1920	LYMINGE KENT
LIEUTENANT	GOLDEN	FRANK C A	25/08/1915	26/12/1915 KILLED IN ACTION	WORMLEY HERTS
SECOND LIEUTENANT	GRANT	MAURICE H	02/10/1917	29/03/1918 TO UK	
SECOND LIEUTENANT	GRANT	W W	02/10/1917	02/10/1917 (POS 4280 2 A.M. ROYAL FLYING CORPS RE TRF TO RFC UNCONFIRMED)	FELIXSTOWE
SECOND LIEUTENANT	GRIMWADE	HUGH NOEL	25/08/1915	05/11/1916 POSTED TO 70 BRIGADE HEADQUARTERS MAJOR GENERAL LIST	NOTTINGHAM
SECOND LIEUTENANT	HADDON	C L	12/06/1916	28/09/1916 WOUNDED	STOKE ON TRENT
SECOND LIEUTENANT	HALES	ALFRED E	28/06/1916	21/10/1916 2 Lt 11/N STAFFS TO 17/DLI WOUNDED TO 13/DLI	BORN TICKHILL RES VANCOUVER ISLAND
LIEUTENANT	HALL	HERBERT C V	20/12/1916	13/06/1917 SERVED AS PTE 75359 29/CANADIAN INFANTRY KILLED IN ACTION	BORN GATESHEAD, RES BUXTON
SECOND LIEUTENANT	HALL	NORMAN B	06/08/1916	01/08/1918 SERVED AS L/SGT 19292 10/DLI ATT 68/LTMB	
LIEUTENANT	HAMILTON	ARTHUR D	15/01/1917	04/08/1917 SERVED AS PTE 7719 28/LONDON REGT HIGHLAND LI ATT DLI TRF 101 FLD COY RE KIA 20/10/1917	MINEHEAD
LIEUTENANT	HARDMAN	HAROLD W	25/08/1915	12/04/1916 SHELL SHOCK TRF TO ARMY SERVICE CORPS 18/12/1916	
SECOND LIEUTENANT	HARE	A H	30/11/1914 ?	DID NOT EMBARK WITH OR REJOIN THE BATTALION	
LIEUTENANT	HARRATON	JOHN R	15/03/1916	03/12/1916 SERVED AS PTE 1890 OX & BUCKS LI TO UK SICK	SLOUGH
SECOND LIEUTENANT	HARRISON	LEONARD A	24/05/1916	17/07/1916 SERVED AS PTE 4923 20/R FUSILIERS COMM LINCOLNSHIRE REGT ATT DLI KILLED IN ACTION	
SECOND LIEUTENANT	HARRISON	W H	09/05/1917	25/09/1917 WOUNDED	
SECOND LIEUTENANT	HEPPELL	CHARLES A	18/06/1916	01/08/1916 WOUNDED	JESMOND
CAPTAIN	HETHERINGTON	ALAN D	25/08/1915	23/02/1916 POSTED TO COMMAND 68 LIGHT TRENCH MORTAR BATTERY	EALING
SECOND LIEUTENANT	HETHERINGTON	THOMAS W	25/08/1915	17/07/1916 KILLED IN ACTION	
SECOND LIEUTENANT	HEYNER	HERBERT A	29/07/1916	12/10/1916 WOUNDED 21/9/1916	LONDON
CAPTAIN	HICKS	GEORGE A	29/09/1918	17/10/1916 4/DLI ATT KOYLI 1915 TO UK SICK	CHICHESTER
LIEUTENANT	HICKSON	LAWRENCE N	09/01/1917	03/02/1919 FROM 14/DLI TO UK SICK	BRADFORD
SECOND LIEUTENANT	HILL	WILLIAM R	07/11/1917	23/09/1917 WOUNDED	
MAJOR	HODGSON	JOHN	06/04/1918	27/10/1918 KILLED IN ACTION SERVED AS PRIVATE 7/1678 7/DURHAM LI	SETTLE
LIEUTENANT	HOLFORD	JAMES H E	25/08/1915	01/03/1919 MAJOR SHERWOOD RANGERS YEOMANRY ATT NOTTS & DERBY REGIMENT LT COL ATT 12/DURH, STAFF CAPTAIN HQ 4th ARMY	SHAFTESBURY
CAPTAIN	HOLMES	STANLEY	02/12/1916	19/07/1916 WOUNDED	KILLINGWORTH
LIEUTENANT	HOLMES	STANLEY	13/12/1918	DIDN'T REJOIN POSTED TO IX CORPS HQ, STAFF CAPTAIN HQ 4th ARMY	
SECOND LIEUTENANT	HOPPER	BERNARD H	06/08/1916	15/02/1919 SERVED AS PTE 24245 DLI, TO BASE FOR DEMOBILISATION	JESMOND
CAPTAIN	HUGALL	JAMES C	27/07/1916	15/10/1916 SERVED AS PTE F/16 17/MIDDLESEX REGT(FOOTBALLERS BN) TO UK WOUNDED	SUNDERLAND
SECOND LIEUTENANT	HUGHES	WILLIAM L	15/05/1916	08/02/1919 SERVED AS PTE 1448 SOUTH WALES BORDERERS TO UK	GUILDFORD
SECOND LIEUTENANT	HUNT	ALAN T	02/01/1918	10/10/1916 ATT ROYAL AIR FORCE, WOUNDED	WIMBLEDON
SECOND LIEUTENANT	HURFORD	WILLIAM E	04/07/1917	08/03/1949 SERVED AS PRIVATE 29307 NORTHUMBERLAND FUSILIERS, TO BASE FOR DEMOBILISATION	NEWCASTLE UPON TYNE
SECOND LIEUTENANT	HUTCHINSON	C R M	30/07/1917	20/07/1917 TO UK SICK	DINAS POWIS
LIEUTENANT	HYDEN	GEORGE E	25/08/1915	14/10/1918 FROM 14/DLI TO UK	BLACKHILL
LIEUTENANT	JACQUES	JOHN B	04/10/1918	10/04/1916 TO UK TRF TO 12 TRAINING DEPOT ROYAL AIR FORCE	JESMOND
LIEUTENANT	KELLY	JOHN B		25/11/1918 SERVED AS L/SGT 2023 WEST & CUMB YEO POSTED TO BN BUT NEVER JOINED TO UK SICK	DALSTON CARLISLE

Rank	Surname	Forename	Date	Notes	Place
LIEUTENANT	LAFONE	ERIC W	25/08/1915	19/07/1916 WOUNDED	GRANGE OVER SANDS LANCASHIRE
CAPTAIN	LAFONE	ERIC W	04/01/1917	15/06/1918 KILLED IN ACTION	
SECOND LIEUTENANT	LEWIS	J H	15/01/2015 ?	DID NOT EMBARK WITH OR REJOIN THE BATTALION	
SECOND LIEUTENANT	LEWIS	DAVID L	23/10/1917	25/02/1919 DID NOT RETURN FROM UK LEAVE	
SECOND LIEUTENANT	LOCKETT	ERNEST W	19/08/1918	17/09/1918 ATT 2nd ECHELON	WEYMOUTH
SECOND LIEUTENANT	LOCKETT	WILLIAM H	29/07/1916	07/10/1916 KILLED IN ACTION	CHESTERFIELD
MAJOR	LONGDON	JAMES M	08/11/1917	06/04/1918 TO 13/DLI	CASTLE EDEN
SECOND LIEUTENANT	LONGSTAFF	CHARLES C	16/12/1915	13/07/1916 WOUNDED	DARLINGTON
SECOND LIEUTENANT	LONGSTAFF	JAMES	25/11/1915	12/04/1916 SICK RELIQUISHED COMM DUE TO ILL HEALTH 4/2/1917	DARLINGTON
SECOND LIEUTENANT	LOWES	JOSEPH H	25/08/1915	12/10/1916 WOUNDED	NEWMARKET
SECOND LIEUTENANT	LUMSDALE	REGINALD A	25/08/1915	29/09/1916 SICK A/CAPTAIN NORTHUMBERLAND FUSILIERS	BANJEON POERBA SUMATRA
LIEUTENANT COLONEL	MACGREGOR	WALTER W	27/05/1916	08/02/1917 TO UK	
SECOND LIEUTENANT	MAITLAND	JAMES	19/06/1917	06/10/1917 WOUNDED	EDINBURGH
SECOND LIEUTENANT	MARKS	GODFREY D	18/07/1916	18/08/1916 TO UK SICK	ACTON HILL LONDON
SECOND LIEUTENANT	MARKS	GODFREY D	10/03/1917	17/06/1917 TRF TO ROYAL FLYING CORPS WITH 111 SQN 28/9/1917 - 21/12/1918	
SECOND LIEUTENANT	MARSH	ROBERT J	04/11/1917	17/09/1918 SERVED AS PTE R/567 K R RIFLE CORPS, ATT MACHINE GUN CORPS	TORONTO CANADA
CAPTAIN	MAYNARD	W E	22/01/1917	29/01/1917 TO UK SICK	DURHAM CITY
SECOND LIEUTENANT	MORRISON	JOHN W	25/10/1917	12/11/1917 SERVED AS PRIVATE 4/1214 GORDON HIGHLANDERS, DETACHED AS A RAIL TRPT OFF	STRATHPEFFER ROSS SHIRE
SECOND LIEUTENANT	MOSS	FRANK	27/12/1918	11/03/1919 SERVED AA PTE A CYCLIST CORPS AND YORK & LANCASTER REGT, TO BASE FOR DEMOB	REDCAR
CAPTAIN	MAWER	A B	25/08/1915	10/04/1916 SICK	HIPSWELL CAMP 52/DLI
CAPTAIN	MAWER	A B	20/06/1916	10/07/1916 SICK	
LIEUTENANT	NELIGAN	MAURICE A B	25/08/1915	14/10/1915 KILLED IN ACTION	MONKSEATON
SECOND LIEUTENANT	NICHOLSON	EDWARD ARTHUR	28/06/1916	10/07/1916 WOUNDED	
SECOND LIEUTENANT	NICHOLSON	EDWARD ARTHUR	19/06/1917	16/03/1919 TO UK	
LIEUTENANT	NOBLE	JOHN	05/10/1917	16/03/1919 SERVED AS PTE 16/354 16/NORTHUMBERLAND FUS L/CPL 86 TRG RES BN, TO UK	NEW WASHINGTON
LIEUTENANT	O'BRIEN	MICHAEL S	29/10/1916	16/08/1917 SERVED AS PTE 1644 ARMY PAY CORPS, TO UK UNFIT	NEWCASTLE STAFFORDSHIRE
SECOND LIEUTENANT	PATTISON	MILES W	07/09/1916	04/11/1916 TO UK SICK	NEWCASTLE UPON TYNE
SECOND LIEUTENANT	PEARCE BROWNE	RICHARD	17/05/1916	17/07/1916 KILLED IN ACTION	COLYFORD DEVON
CAPTAIN	PEASE	HERBERT E	25/08/1915	07/02/1917 MAJOR ATT EGYPTIAN ARMY 1920, TO UK	TUNBRIDGE WELLS
SECOND LIEUTENANT	PEASE	MAURICE R	25/08/1915	20/05/1916 TO UK SICK	SOUTHPORT LANCS
SECOND LIEUTENANT	PHILIPS	CHARLES E S	07/09/1917	25/09/1917 SERVED AS CPL 11116 2/DLI MM, WOUNDED	FRIMLEY GREEN SURREY
SECOND LIEUTENANT	PLATT	W P	22/09/1914 ?	DID NOT EMBARK WITH OR REJOIN THE BATTALION	
SECOND LIEUTENANT	POWELL SMITH	LESLIE J	25/08/1915	08/07/1916 WOUNDED RELQ COMM 19/7/1918 ILL HEALTH	LINCOLN
LIEUTENANT	POWELL SMITH	LESLIE J	29/07/1916	09/08/1916 TO UK SICK	
CAPTAIN	POWELL SMITH	LESLIE J	28/03/1917	09/12/1917 WOUNDED	CHIDINGFOLD SURREY
LIEUTENANT	PRICE	ARNOLD T	27/03/1916	04/10/1916 WOUNDED, TO 15/DLI, CAPT TRF R WARWICKSHIRE REGT	
LIEUTENANT	PRIOR	G K	18/12/1918	25/01/1919 TO BASE FOR DEMOBILISATION	CAMDEN TOWN
SECOND LIEUTENANT	PROCTOR	JOHN Mc	23/06/1916	09/12/1918 TO UK	BRADFORD
SECOND LIEUTENANT	RASCHE	JOHN E	04/03/1917	12/02/2019 TO UK SICK	LONG EATON NOTTS
LIEUTENANT	REES	FREDERICK L	28/10/1917	23/02/1918 POSTED BACK TO 13/DLI	COVENTRY
Lt & QUARTERMASTER	RENDELL	ARTHUR	25/08/1915	15/11/1915 TO UK SICK TRF TO 1/NORTHUMBERLAND FUS CAPT & QM	JESMOND
SECOND LIEUTENANT	RICHARDSON	HAROLD	04/03/1917	05/06/1917 SERVED AS PTE 6/2285 NORTHUMBERLAND FUS TRF TO 94th RUSSELL'S INF INDIAN ARMY	WEST HARTLEPOOL
SECOND LIEUTENANT	RIDLEY	JOHN M	21/06/1917	SERVED AS SGT GS/19441 ROYAL FUS	
SECOND LIEUTENANT	ROBERTSON	J		04/11/1917 POSTED TO BN BUT NEVER JOINED TO 1/5 BORDER REGT	
SECOND LIEUTENANT	ROBSON	BERTRAM B	14/12/1918	19/03/1919 SERVED PTE 2114 8/DLI TRF TO 8/YORK & LANCASTER REGT	LIVERPOOL
CAPTAIN	ROWLANDSON	SAMUEL M	29/03/1917	31/05/1917 SERVED WITH 2/DLI 1914 WOUNDED JAN 15 P B OFFICER POSTED TO MALTA	DURHAM CITY
LIEUTENANT	SCHWARTZE	HELMUTH E	20/12/1916	28/05/1918 LEAVE TO SOUTH AFRICA	
SECOND LIEUTENANT	SHARP	FREDERICK E	27/06/1916	10/08/1916 TO UK SICK	
LIEUTENANT	SHIRREFF	C R M	25/08/1915 ?	DID NOT EMBARK WITH OR REJOIN THE BATTALION	
SECOND LIEUTENANT	SMITH	NOEL V	25/08/1915	24/03/1916 WOUNDED	LEDBURY HERTS
LIEUTENANT	SMITH	NOEL V	06/09/1917	25/08/1918 TRF TO 3/34 SIKH PIONEERS INDIAN ARMY CAPTAIN	

Rank	Surname	Forename	Date	Notes	Location
SECOND LIEUTENANT	SMITH	W	07/10/1918	TO UK SICK	
SECOND LIEUTENANT	SMITHSON	THOMAS	07/11/1917	SERVED AS PTE GS/20150 ROYAL FUS TO UK	
SECOND LIEUTENANT	SPANTON	C W	26/02/1915 ?	DID NOT EMBARK WITH OR REJOIN THE BATTALION	
SECOND LIEUTENANT	STAMP	E A G	09/11/1914 ?	DID NOT EMBARK WITH OR REJOIN THE BATTALION	
LIEUTENANT	SUMMERHAYES	CHRISTOPHER H	25/08/1915	WOUNDED TRF GLOUCESTERSHIRE REGT T/CAPTAIN	BRITISH CONSULATE ALEXANDRIA
SECOND LIEUTENANT	THOMAS	GEORGE F	20/09/1916	SERVED AS SGT 300087 WEST YORKS REGT TO UK	LEEDS
SECOND LIEUTENANT	TUFFS	EDWARD W	18/02/1917	SERVED AS CSM 5117 A CYCLIST CORPS TO UK SICK	MIDDLESBROUGH
MAJOR	TYNDALL	ROBERT	11/12/1916	POSTED TO 1/6/DLI LIEUTENANT COLONEL	NEW ROSS COUNTY WEXFORD
LIEUTENANT	VAUX	CUTHBERT	29/07/1916	TO 68 BRIGADE HEADQUARTERS	DURHAM CITY
SECOND LIEUTENANT	WADE	JOHN T	15/10/1917	DETACHED AS A QUARTERMASTER ON LEAVE TRAIN	
SECOND LIEUTENANT	WAKEHAM	CHARLES	10/02/1918	SERVED AS CSM 24258 MC, DCM, MM 10/DLI JOINED FROM 13/DLI	BOURNEMOUTH
SECOND LIEUTENANT	WALLACE	JOHN	07/10/1918	TO UK	HEBBURN ON TYNE
SECOND LIEUTENANT	WALLIS	AUSTIN B	29/07/1916	WOUNDED	TYNEMOUTH
SECOND LIEUTENANT	WARREN	THEODORE S W	28/06/1916	COOMISSIONED INTO 17/DLI KILLED IN ACTION	YEOVIL
SECOND LIEUTENANT	WATSON	J	23/06/1916	TO UK SICK	
SECOND LIEUTENANT	WATTS	C M	02/01/1918	DETACHED AS A RAIL TRANSPORT OFFICER	
SECOND LIEUTENANT	WEBSTER	THOMAS	22/06/1916	SERVED AS CPL 31950 RAMC TO UK TRF ROYAL ENGINEERS	WEST HARTLEPOOL
SECOND LIEUTENANT	WELTON	THOMAS G	29/10/1917	SERVED AS PRIVATE 18557 EAST YORKSHIRE REGIMENT POSTED TO 13/DLI	
LIEUTENANT & ADJ	WEST	St J C	23/01/1915 ?	DID NOT EMBARK WITH OR REJOIN THE BATTALION	
SECOND LIEUTENANT	WHITAKER	H	07/10/1918	TO UK SICK	
SECOND LIEUTENANT	WILEY	EVELYN O S	07/10/1918	COMMISSSIONED 18/DLI DIED OF WOUNDS	
SECOND LIEUTENANT	WILKINSON	ARTHUR	27/09/1917	TO UK UNFIT	KENSINGTON
SECOND LIEUTENANT	WILSON	JOHN	04/08/1917	SERVED AS PTE R/8311 K R RIFLE CORPS TO BASE FOR DEMOBILISATION	WREXHAM
CAPTAIN	WOLSTENHOLME	CHARLES S	25/08/1915	KILLED IN ACTION	LEEDS
LIEUTENANT	WOOD	G	29/09/1914 ?	DID NOT EMBARK WITH OR REJOIN THE BATTALION	
LIEUTENANT	WOOD	G L	12/10/1914 ?	DID NOT EMBARK WITH OR REJOIN THE BATTALION	
CAPTAIN	WOODHEAD	ROBERT C	25/08/1915	KILLED IN ACTION	
SECOND LIEUTENANT	WRIGHTSON	LAWRENCE	06/06/1917	3/NORTH STAFFORDSHIRE REGT ATT, TO UK SICK	LONDON
SECOND LIEUTENANT	YOUNG	J B	19/09/1918	POSTED TO BN BUT NEVER JOINED RETURNED TO UK SICK	

Nominal Roll of Other Ranks who landed in France 25 August 1915 with the 12th (Service) Battalion Durham Light Infantry 1914–1918

19043 RQMS	BROWN	WILLIAM HENRY	CLASS Z RES
21214 CPL	BROWN	WILLIAM RENNISON	CLASS Z RES
22153 PTE	BROWN	CHARLES	TO 1/5/DLI 19/DLI CLASS Z RES
22196 PTE	BROWN	WILLIAM	ENL MIDDLESBROUGH KIA 17/7/16
18498 PTE	BRYANT	ROBERT	CLASS Z RES
15323 SGT	BULLERWELL	JOSEPH LUMLEY	INCISED WNDS BACK & NECK 5/12/15 ADM 3 CCS 5/12/15 EVAC 6/12/15 No 14 AMB TRN DIS 392 ENL 7/9/14 DIS 1/2/18
18212 LCPL	BULMER	CHARLES VICTOR	TO 3/DLI DIS 392 ENL 8/9/14 DIS 15/9/17
25584 PTE	BURGESS	THOMAS	ATT IBD 12/DLI CLASS Z RES
17216 PTE	BURN	SAMUEL	CLASS Z RES
16956 PTE	BURNHAM	THOMAS	DIS 392 TO ARMY RES CLASS P ENL 7/9/14 DIS 16/4/17
18796 SGT	BURNS	ARCHIBALD	TO LABOUR CORPS LAB C No 167119 CLASS Z RES 7/5/19
15732 PTE	BURTON	GEORGE FREDERICK	ENL SUNDERLAND 12/9/14 RES HIGH MOORSLEY TO 69/FA 11/3/16 SCABIES TO DUTY TO 4 STAT HOSP ST OMER 31/3/16 TO DUTY 5/4/16 KIA 5/4/16
25582 PTE	BUTLER	WILLIAM	ENL NORTH SHIELDS ATT IBD ATT 68/LTMB DOW 7/6/17 FORMERLY 19587 NORTHBLD FUS
15973 PTE	CALEY	JOHN THOMAS	DIS 392
18492 PTE	CALLCUTT	JOHN	ENL CONSETT 7/9/14 TO 13/DLI 17/9/14 TO 16/DLI 14/9/15 TO 12/DLI 10/12/15 KIA 7/2/16
17770 PTE	CAMPBELL	THOMAS	DIS 392 TO ARMY RES CLASS P ENL 5/9/14 DIS 28/3/19
25583 PTE	CANNON	JOHN WILLIAM	ATT 68/LTMB TO 1/9/DLI ATT E DEPOT 1/9/DLI KIA 12/09/18 FORMERLY 13760 NORTHUMBERLAND FUSILIERS
14848 CPL	CARMICHAEL	HARRY	CLASS Z RES A/SGT
22038 PTE	CARRICK	FREDERICK	TO 2/DLI, 12/DLI, DIS 392 ENL 14/11/14 DIS 22/1/19
18535 PTE	CARROLL	ANDREW CHARLTON	ENL STANLEY 12/9/14 RES TANFIELD SERVED A COMPANY ACCIDENTALLY DROWNED 11/9/15
18665 PTE	CARROLL	JOSEPH	DIS 392
15862 PTE	CARTER	JOSEPH	CLASS Z RES
18151 PTE	CARVER	GEORGE ALLAN	TO 20/DLI, CLASS Z RES
13571 PTE	CASEY	JOHN THOMAS	ATT 1st AUSTRALIAN TUNN COY, 12/DLI, CLASS Z RES
25477 PTE	CATCHESIDES	ALBERT	ENL FELLING RES GATESHEAD DIED HOME 1/3/17
17247 PTE	CAWLEY	THOMAS	TO 15/DLI, TO DEPOT DIS 392 ENL 3/9/14 DIS 8/3/18
18211 PTE	CHADWICK	FRANK	DIS 392 ENL 8/9/14 DIS 28/2/19
18244 SGT	CHARLTON	THOMAS	DIS TO COMMISSION 23/4/17
18161 PTE	CHEETHAM	WILLIAM	CLASS Z RES
19471 SGT	CHILDS	CECIL JAMES	CLASS Z RES
20876 PTE	CHIPCHASE	THOMAS	CLASS Z RES
25492 PTE	CHRISTIE	WILLIAM	ATT X CORPS HQ ATT 68 BDE HQ 12/DLI ATT 68 LTMB 11/DLI CLASS Z RES
18393 PTE	CLARK	ARTHUR	TO 2/DLI, 12/DLI, 2/DLI, CLASS Z RES
18938 PTE	CLARK	CHRISTOPHER	CLASS Z RES
21123 PTE	CLARK	FREDERICK	CLASS Z RES
18636 PTE	CLARK	JOSEPH WILLIAM	CLASS Z RES
16980 SGT	CLASPER	JOSEPH	ENL W HARTLEPOOL 2/9/14 RES SOUTH WINGATE LCPL 7/10/16 CPL 8/10/16 SGT 18/6/17 KIA 15/10/17
11445 PTE	CLOUSTON	JAMES WILLIAMSON	TO LABOUR CORPS LAB C No 184867 DIS 27/2/18
15772 CPL	COATES	JOHN ORMSTON	TO ARMY RES CLASS P DIS 392 ENL 12/9/14 DIS 25/5/17
12945 PTE	COCHRANE	JOHN URIAH	CLASS Z RES
25478 PTE	COCHRANE	JOSEPH	TO 18/DLI 14/DLI 2/DLI CLASS Z RES
22135 CPL	CONNELL	JOHN GORDON	TO 14/DLI DIS 392 ENL 17/11/14 DIS 28/3/19
15952 PTE	CONSTANTINE	ALBERT	ENL DURHAM 8/9/14 RES CORNSAY COLLIERY TO 69/FA N MID CCS, 3 CCS 12 CCS HOSP SHIP 6/11/15 - 20/11/15 TO DEPOT 13/1/16 TO 13/DLI A COY 17/3/16 MISSING 10/10/18 MM 9/12/16 BAR 12/12/17
25531 PTE	COOK	JAMES	ATT V CAMP CLASS Z RES
18654 PTE	COOK	JOSEPH	ATT 68 BDE HQ MM
17821 PTE	COONEY	THOMAS	TO 18/DLI, CLASS Z RES
25546 PTE	CORRIGAN	JOHN	TO LABOUR CORPS LAB C No 412866 DIS 7/3/19
18079 PTE	COULSON	ROBERT	TO 18/DLI, 15/DLI, 18/DLI, 20/DLI, CLASS Z RES
19084 PTE	COURTLEY	JOHN	TO 14/DLI, 20/DLI, CLASS Z RES
18320 PTE	COWAN	THOMAS	TO DEPOT DIS 392 ENL 7/9/14 DIS 7/4/17
18664 CPL	COWLEY	THOMAS SMITH	ENL GATESHEAD 14/9/14 RES GATESHEAD LCPL 14/4/16 CPL 4/8/16 WOUNDED 25/9/16 TO 13 CCS - No 4 AMB TRN 10 G HOSP 3/10/16 SMITHSOM WAR HOSP GREENOCK DOW 9/12/16
18653 PTE	CRAIG	WILLIAM	ATT 68/LTMB, 12/DLI, ATT CORPS SCHOOL, ATT 69/LTMB, 68/LTMB, CLASS Z RES
18652 PTE	CRAIGHILL	ROBERT ALFRED	ENL STANLEY 8/9/14 RES BURNHOPE GSW NECK & HAND 6/7/16 TO 58 /FA - CCS TO HOSP SHIP DIEPPE TO 20/DLI 15/6/17 KIA 21/9/17
18651 PTE	CRANNEY	JOHN	ENL STANLEY 8/9/14 RES MARLEY HILL TO 5 /FA 21/4/16 TO 70 /FA 6/5/16 WND 7/10/16 GSW BACK TO 11 STAT HOSP ROUEN 10/10/16 DOW 18/10/16
18803 LCPL	CRANNEY	WILLIAM	ENL STANLEY 8/9/14 RES MARLEY HILL TO 23 CCS 3/6/16 PYREXIA TO HOSP SHIP 16/7/16 TO DEPOT 11/7/16 CMD DEPOT RIPON 31/10/16 CMD DEPOT ALNWICK 17/11/16 3/DLI 20/2/17 2/DLI ICT L LEG 25/5/17 22/DLI 8/6/17 WND 19/7/17 55 /FA 24/7/17, 19/DLI 25/9/17 LCPL 27/4/18 KIA 1/10/18
18010 PTE	CROFT	JAMES	ENL FERRYHILL 8/9/14 RES WINGATE TO 26 /FA 2/3/16 SCABIES REJOINS BN TO 22 CCS 2/5/16 - No 15 AMB TRN 3 G HOSP LE TREPORT 3 CON DEPOT 26/5/16 REJOINS BN 77 /FA GONORRHOEA 14/7/16 12 G HOSP - 39 G HOSP INF BASE DEPOT 10/8/16 REJOIN 22/9/16 LCPL 16/11/16 CPL 14/5/17 DOW 26/5/17
17281 PTE	CROPPER	EDWIN	CLASS Z RES
13484 PTE	CROSS	JOHN	TO ROYAL DEFENCE CORPS RDC No 60305 IN FRANCE 25/8/15 TO 7/1/16
18656 PTE	CROW	ALEXANDER	CLASS Z RES
25515 PTE	CROW	RALPH	TO DEPOT DIS 392 ENL 4/9/14 DIS 2/7/17
18378 PTE	CROWTHER	OSMOND	TO 2/DLI, CLASS Z RES
7202 SGT	CRUDDAS	BENJAMIN	CLASS Z RES DCM
19185 PTE	CURRY	RICHARD	CLASS Z RES
13663 PTE	CUTCHEN	JOHN	TO MACHINE GUN CORPS MGC No 72659 DIS 392
25588 PTE	CUTHBERT	FRANKLAND	ATT 68/BDE HQ ATT IBD CLASS Z RES
17739 PTE	CUTHBERT	JAMES	TO LABOUR CORPS LAB C No 31322 CLASS Z RES 17/3/19
15857 PTE	CUTHBERT	JOSEPH	TO 10/DLI, 11/DLI, CLASS Z RES
18240 PTE	DALGLISH	ROBERT	CLASS Z RES MM
15725 PTE	DAVIDSON	THOMAS	ENL SUNDERLAND TO 20/DLI KIA 7/6/17
22110 PTE	DAVIES	EDMUND	ATT 35 IBD DIS 392
13668 CSM	DAVIS	GEORGE	BORN MIDDLESBROUGH ENL NEWCASTLE KIA 17/7/16
18815 PTE	DAVISON	JOHN	ENL BIRTLEY 8/9/14 RES WREKENTON TO 6 /FA 21/4/16 TO DUTY 24/4/16 DOW AT 70 /FA 6/7/16
16015 PTE	DAVISON	ROBERT	ENL STANLEY BORN WINLATON TO 5 LONDON /FA 22/6/16 SCABIES TO DUTY KIA 22/9/16
18800 LCPL	DAVISON	ROBERT	ENL STANLEY 8/9/14 RES MARLEY HILL LCPL 16/11/16 KIA 11/6/17
21076 PTE	DAY	CHARLES	TO DEPOT DIS 392 ENL 31/10/14 DIS 19/9/17
11432 PTE	DEBELLO	VETO	TO LABOUR CORPS LAB C No 26416 DIS 10/3/19
21084 PTE	DENT	JOHN FRANCIS	TO LABOUR CORPS LAB C No 570163 CPL DIS 17/3/19
18366 PTE	DEVINE	PATRICK	TO 20/DLI, ATT PB DIS 392
22042 PTE	DEWAR	JOHN	ATT 101 FLD COY RE, ATT 69/LTMB, 5/ARMY SCHOOL, CLASS Z RES
19132 PTE	DICK	THOMAS	DIS 392

Number	Rank	Surname	Forename(s)	Notes
17302	PTE	DICKENSON	THOMAS LOWES	TO 18/DLI, CLASS Z RES
22185	PTE	DICKINSON	FRANK LAMBERT	TO LABOUR CORPS LAB C No 117566 CLASS Z RES 1/5/19
13351	LCPL	DINNING	WILLIAM	ENL NEWCASTLE 5/9/14 LCPL 30/10/15 DOW 9/7/16 AT No 38 CCS
21506	PTE	DISS	JOHN THOMAS	DIS 392
25464	PTE	DITCHBURN	GEORGE	TO LABOUR CORPS LAB C No 377272 DIS 3/3/19
19081	CPL	DIXON	ALFRED	CLASS Z RES
18799	PTE	DIXON	ROBERT	DIS
16150	PTE	DIXON	WILLIAM	ENL DURHAM 8/9/14 RES PELTON FELL TO 26 /FA 29/2/16 - 7 CCS 7/3/16 SCABIES TO DUTY 20/3/16 WOUNDED TO 2 STAT HOSP BOULOGNE 8/7/16 HOSP SHIP ST DENIS 11/7/16 AMP THIGH 12/8/16 R HERBERT HOSP WOOLWICH DOW 12/8/16
18099	PTE	DOBSON	ANDREW RAY	ATT 68 BDE HQ, 12/DLI, CLASS Z RES
18245	PTE	DODD	CHARLES	DIS 392
14908	SGT	DODDS	ANDREW	ENL NORTH SHIELDS BORN TYNEMOUTH KIA 17/7/16
20995	PTE	DODDS	JOSEPH	TO 19/DLI, DIS 392
22114	PTE	DONACHIE	JOHN	DIS 392
25533	PTE	DONAGHY	ARTHUR	DIS 392
18303	PTE	DONAGHY	OWEN	CLASS Z RES
19521	SGT	DONALDSON	JOHN	BORN & ENLISTED SUNDERLAND 14/9/14 LCPL 29/10/14 CPL 1/12/14 SGT 4/1/15 TO 69/FA 23/CCS 22 AMB TRN 1 STATIONARY HOSP ROUEN IMPETIGO 3/5/16 REJOIN BN 1/6/16 KIA 8/7/16 THIEPVAL MEMORIAL
13124	PTE	DORAN	PHELIX	DIS 392
22138	PTE	DOWTHWAITE	GEORGE BARWISE	ENL CONSETT RES DIPTON KIA 6/8/16
3/11443	PTE	DRAKE	ROBERT	TO ARMY RES CLASS P DIS 392 ENL 7/9/14 DIS 22/4/19
22072	PTE	DRYDEN	JAMES	TO 18/DLI, ATT 257 TUNN COY RE, CLASS Z RES
19088	PTE	DUFFY	ANDREW	TO 10/DLI, 2/DLI, 10/DLI, 20/DLI, 2/DLI, CLASS Z RES
19087	PTE	DUFFY	HERBERT	TO LABOUR CORPS LAB C No 418526 CLASS Z RES 11/2/19
12688	PTE	DUFFY	JOHN	TO CLASS W RES
19300	PTE	DUFFY	THOMAS	CLASS Z RES
19519	PTE	DUTTON	JAMES	ENL ACCRINGTON KIA 12/6/16
25493	CSM	DYSON	JAMES	ENL NEWCASTLE RES CHESTER LE STREET ATT 23 IBD ATT 36 IBD 12/DLI KIA 7/6/17
18221	PTE	DYSON	JAMES BEVERLEY	ENL STANLEY 8/9/14 RES ANNFIELD PLAIN TO 70 /FA 16/6/16 BOILS TO DUTY 21/6/16 TO 70 /FA BOILS 3/8/16 TO DUTY 9/8/16 MM 1/9/16 TO 14 AMB TRN 23/9/16 BOILS LEGS 25 G HOSP TO UK HOSP SHIP ST DENIS 27/9/16 TO 2/TRG RES BN 19/11/16 TO 11/DLI 20/2/17 REPOSTED 18/DLI 11/3/17 KIA 18/5/17
17738	PTE	EASTON	ROBERT	TO LABOUR CORPS LAB C No 377207 CLASS Z RES 11/2/19
3/11422	SGT	EDWARDS	GEORGE	TO 10, 12/DLI ATT 1 AUSTRALIAN TUNN COY, CLASS Z RES
18117	PTE	ELDRIDGE	HARRY	CLASS Z RES
17931	PTE	ELLIOT	JOHN	CLASS Z RES
21078	PTE	EMMETT	BENJAMIN	CLASS Z RES
25494	LCPL	ENGLISH	WILLIAM	DIS 392 ENL 11/9/14 DIS 29/11/16
18395	PTE	EVANS	ALEXANDER	TO 11/DLI, DIS 392
13916	PTE	EVANS	ERNEST	ENL FELLING 4/9/14 IN C COMPANY KIA 27/10/18
18253	PTE	EVANS	JAMES	TO LABOUR CORPS LAB C No 451046 DIS 11/3/19
18233	PTE	EVANS	WILLIAM	CLASS Z RES
16081	PTE	EVERETT	BENJAMIN	TO 18/DLI, 15/DLI, CLASS Z RES LCPL
19530	CPL	EVERIST	JOHN JAMES	ENL DOVER 4/9/14 RES SEAHAM HARBOUR LCPL 14/10/14 CPL 10/5/15 TO 69/FA 9/10/15 IMPETIGO TO DUTY TO 26 /FA 31/12/15 GSW R LUNG ACCIDENTAL TO HOSP BARGE 21/1/16 LAHORE G HOSP CALAIS 29/1/16 TO UK HOSP SHIP BRIGHTON 4/2/16 TO DEPOT 5/2/16 ADMT 4 NORTHERN G HOSP LINCOLN DOW 15/11/17 AT NORTHUMBERLAND WAR HOSP SOUTH GOSFORTH
17004	PTE	FARTHING	JAMES	DIS 392
16014	PTE	FAWCETT	THOMAS	ENL STANLEY 28/8/14 RES WHITE LE HEAD TO 11 DLI 28/8/14 TO 12/DLI 6/2/15 TO 69/FA 10/10/15 S CCS - No 9 AMB TRN 20 G HOSP CAMIERS TO BASE DEPOT ETAPLES 18/12/15 TO 24 G HOSP DEBILITY 22/12/15 TO ISOLATION HOSP ENTERIC 25/12/15 REJOIN BN 24/3/16 KIA 22/9/16
15474	PTE	FENWICK	GEORGE	ENL JARROW 11/9/14 RES HEBBURN 11/9/14 KIA 13/5/17
25479	PTE	FITZSIMONS	WILLIAM	DIS 392 ENL 27/8/14 DIS 28/11/16
10644	SGT	FITZSIMMONS	PETER	TO LABOUR CORPS LAB C No 210715 DIS 15/4/18
18232	PTE	FLACK	THOMAS	DIS 392
3/11596	SGT	FLATTLEY	RICHARD	ENL 1/9/14 STOCKTON SPEC RES CPL 5/9/14 TO 12/DLI SGT 19/10/14 WND 31/5/16 TO No 6 CCS REJOINED 29/6/16 WND 8/6/17 GSW FACE TO No 10 CCS TO ST J A BDE HOSP ETAPLES DOW 28/6/17 PREV SERVED 4/DLI
13824	PTE	FLETCHER	JOSEPH	CLASS Z RES ASGT
17005	PTE	FLETCHER	MARK	CLASS Z RES
18551	PTE	FLYNN	MICHAEL	TO ARMY RES CLASS P DIS 392 ENL 14/9/14 DIS 31/10/16
25535	PTE	FLYNN	PATRICK	ENL NORTH SHIELDS RES DUBLIN KIA 7/6/16
3/10638	SGT	FODDEN	JOHN	TO ARMY RES CLASS P DIS 392 ENL 9/9/14 DIS 22/4/19
17757	PTE	FOGGAN	CHARLES	TO LABOUR CORPS LAB C No 167234 DIS 9/4/19
25495	LCPL	FOGGON	FRANK	CLASS Z RES
21219	PTE	FORSTER	ARTHUR	ENL SUNDERLAND 29/10/14 RES GATESHEAD KIA 17/7/16
18258	PTE	FORSYTH	ROBERT	CLASS Z RES
19548	PTE	FOSTER	ARTHUR	TO LABOUR CORPS LAB C No 438643 DIS 25/2/18
22043	PTE	FOSTER	EDWARD	ENL GATESHEAD 14/11/14 RES CHESTER LE STREET 12/DLI TO 69/FA 7/10/15 N MID CCS - 8 CCS HOSP ETAPLES TO HOSP SHIP DIEPPE 29/10/15 TO 16/DLI 30/12/15 15/DLI 7/4/16 MISSING 15/9/16
17917	SGT	FOWLER	JOHN RICHARD	CLASS Z RES
21085	PTE	FOWLER	JOHN WILLIAM	ENL SUNDERLAND 31/10/14 RES SUNDERLAND LCPL 16/1/15 AWOL REDUCED PTE 3/6/15 KIA 4/12/15
13825	PTE	FRANCIS	WILLIAM	CLASS Z RES
15888	PTE	FRANKLIN	MARK	TO DEPOT DIS 392 ENL 9/9/14 DIS 20/2/18
17330	SGT	FRASER	ARCHIBALD	ATT KING'S AFRICAN RIFLES, CLASS Z RES
18667	PTE	FRENCH	HENRY	TO 20/DLI, 11/DLI, CLASS Z RES
18224	PTE	FULLER	JAMES	TO LABOUR CORPS LAB C No 603970 CPL DIS 4/3/19
14174	PTE	GAFFREY	JOHN	TO LABOUR CORPS LAB C No 374190 DIS 19/2/19
25497	PTE	GALLAGHER	THOMAS	ENL GATESHEAD RES GATESHEAD ATT 23 DIV TUNN COY ATT 182 COY RE ATT 176 TUNN COY RE KIA 24/9/16
13359	PTE	GAMWELL	JAMES	TO 18/DLI, 15/DLI DIS 392 ENL 7/9/14 DIS 7/1/19
17340	PTE	GARBUTT	ROBERT HENRY	DIS 392
19577	PTE	GARDINER	JOHN	TO 1/7/DLI, 1/9/DLI, CLASS Z RES
15013	PTE	GARLAND	JAMES	ENL W HARTLEPOOL 25/8/14 A COMPANY KIA 7/10/16
19371	PTE	GARTHWAITE	JAMES	ENL FELLING 8/9/14 KIA 17/5/17
19576	PTE	GEE	GEORGE	CLASS Z RES
18807	PTE	GEE	MARTIN	CLASS Z RES
18257	CPL	GENT	GEORGE WILLIAM	CLASS Z RES

25498 PTE GIBSON	CHARLES		TO 1/6/DLI 11/DLI ATT IX CORPS SCHOOL CLASS Z RES
18217 PTE GIBSON	JAMES		CLASS Z RES
22123 PTE GIBSON	JOSEPH		CLASS Z RES
22271 SGT GIBSON	JOSEPH		TO 13/DLI CLASS Z RES
13155 PTE GIBSON	WILLIAM HENRY		CLASS Z RES
19587 CPL GILBERT	JAMES		TO 2/DLI, CLASS Z RES
18235 PTE GILFELLON	THOMAS JAMES		ENL STANLEY 9/9/14 WND 17/4/16 AT DUTY KIA 7/10/16
7462 SGT GILL	FREDERICK		TO LABOUR CORPS LAB C No 426983 SGT CLASS Z RES 17/4/19
18219 CPL GILL	WILLIAM		ENL STANLEY KIA 12/10/18
13437 PTE GILROY	HENRY		TO ROYAL DEFENCE CORPS RDC No 76467 IN FRANCE 25/8/15 TO 15/DLI 10/7/16 TO 18/9/16
20775 PTE GODDARD	BEN		TO LABOUR CORPS LAB C No 223030 DIS 20/1/19
21047 CPL GOFTON	FRANK		TO DEPOT DIS 392 ENL 26/10/14 DIS 21/3/17
16078 CPL GOODING	FREDERICK		TO DEPOT DIS 392 ENL 8/9/14 DIS 1/12/16
16040 PTE GOODWIN	CHARLES		ENL NEWCASTLE 5/9/14 RES CHOPWELL CPL 25/4/16 LSGT 10/7/16 KIA 17/7/16
16039 PTE GOODWIN	HENRY		TO 13/DLI, 20/DLI, 2/DLI, 19/DLI, CLASS Z RES
22183 PTE GOODY	WILFRED THOMAS		TO DEPOT DIS 392 ENL 17/11/14 DIS 9/2/17
22156 PTE GORMLAY	JAMES		ENL GATESHEAD 18/11/14 RES BOTTLEBANK DOW 18/7/16 MM
25576 PTE GRADY	JAMES		TO LABOUR CORPS LAB C No 562333 CLASS Z RES 7/4/19
25586 PTE GRAHAM	JOSEPH		TO ROYAL DEFENCE CORPS RDC No 60434 IN FRANCE 25/8/15 TO 10/7/16
18532 PTE GRAHAM	WILLIAM		CLASS Z RES
19588 PTE GRAINGER	WILLIAM		DIS 392
19557 LCPL GRAVER	DAVID		ENL SUNDERLAND 13/9/14 RES LYNN NORFOLK LCPL 10/2/15 REDUCED 15/12/15 TO 70 /FA 10/3/16 SCABIES 18 CCS TO DUTY 25/5/16 LCPL 19/6/16 KIA 17/7/16
21207 PTE GRAY	PETER		DIS 392
12107 CPL GREAVES	ARTHUR SPEIGHT	L/SGT TO DEPOT DIS 392 25/8/14 DIS 28/11/16
21201 PTE GREEN	LAWRENCE		CLASS Z RES
12822 PTE GREEN	MARK		TO LABOUR CORPS LAB C No 263543 DIS 11/3/19
19559 PTE GREEN	THOMAS		TO 18/DLI, 14/DLI, STILL SERVING 1920
21856 PTE GREENER	ROBERT RIDLEY	DIS 392
17918 PTE GREENWELL	WILLIAM		TO ARMY RES CLASSS P DIS 392 ENL 11/9/14 DIS 3/1/17
18015 PTE GREGG	WILLIAM		DIS 392 ENL 8/9/14 DIS 18/3/18
19163 PTE GREIVSON	ALBERT		ENL FELLING 9/9/14 RES WINDYKNOOK TO 5 /FA ICT LEGS 21/4/16 TO DUTY 29/4/16 KIA 8/8/16
17012 PTE GRIFFIN	JOHN EDWARD	ENL DURHAM RES HOWDEN LE WEAR TO 13/NORTHBD FUS NF No 46520 DIED 18/6/17
21088 PTE GUY	JOSEPH		TO MACHINE GUN CORPS MGC No 72661 CLASS Z RES 28/2/19
18794 PTE HALL	ISAAC		ENL GATESHEAD 8/9/14 RES GATESHEAD 24 DAYS FP No 1 16/10/15 TO 69/FA 20/10/15 PSORIAIS TO DUTY 6/11/15 TO 69/FA 11/3/16 SCABIES TO DUTY 17/3/16 KIA 7/6/17
25499 LCPL HALL	JOHN		DIS 392
20903 PTE HALL	THOMAS		ENL STANLEY 30/10/14 RES ANNFIELD PLAIN KIA 17/7/16
25218 PTE HALL	THOMAS		TO 20/DLI DIS 392 ENL 10/8/14 DIS 26/3/19
20937 PTE HALL	TOM		ENL 21/10/14 CONSETT RES BLACKHILL WND 7/1/16 AT DUTY SHRP WND BACK 13/1/16 TO 2/CCS - 18/A TRN - 8/RED CROSS HOSP SCABIES TO 20/G HOSP 25/1/16 TO UK HOSP SHIP BRIGHTON 11/3/16 TO DEPOT TO 13/DLI 1/6/16 **SEE 13/DLI ROLL**
20705 PTE HAMMAL	JOSEPH GIBSON	CLASS Z RES ASGT
25500 CPL HAMMILL	CHARLES		TO ARMY RES CLASS P DIS 392 ENL 17/8/14 DIS 31/10/16
13266 PTE HANNAWAY	PATRICK		CLASS Z RES
18671 PTE HARKNESS	GEORGE		ENL GATESHEAD 14/9/14 RES BENSHAM IN B COMPANY KIA 26/1/16
18080 PTE HARLEY	RALPH		TO ARMY RES CLASS P DIS 392ENL 5/9/14 DIS 1/5/17
17379 PTE HARNESS	JOHN		TO 29/DLI
15892 PTE HARRIS	GEORGE HENRY	ATT 23/DIV TUNN COY, 250 TUNN COY RE, 13/DLI, CLASS Z RES
17403 PTE HARRISON	CHARLES BERTIE	L/CPL DIS 392 ENL 8/9/14 DIS 25/10/19
18780 PTE HARRISON	ISAAC		CLASS Z RES
15858 PTE HARRISON	JAMES		ENL STANLEY 1/9/14 RES SOUTHMOOR KIA 9/14/16
13892 PTE HARRISON	JOHN		DESERTED 6/4/18 CLASS Z RES
15341 PTE HARRISON	JOSEPH ROBERTS	TO 1/6/DLI, 2/7/DLI, CLASS Z RES
18505 PTE HARRISON	THOMAS		TO ROYAL DEFENCE CORPS RDC No 66244 IN FRANCE 25/8/15 TO 21/8/16
21208 PTE HARRISON	WILLIAM		STILL SERVING 1920
17395 PTE HARWOOD	JAMES ROBERT	CLASS Z RES
18248 PTE HAXON	JOHN		ENL GATESHEAD 12/9/14 KIA 10/12/15
20875 PTE HAY	JOHN RICHARD	TO LABOUR CORPS LAB C No 636718 CLASS Z RES 23/4/19
15381 SGT HAY	THOMAS		MM ENL STANLEY 7/9/14 CPL 24/11/17 SGT 30/5/18 TO 69/FA 11/3/16 - 23 CCS No 5 AMB TRN 26 G HOSP SKIN DISEASE 17 CCS 10/1/17 TRENCH FEVER WOUNDED AT DUTY 7/6/17 D COMPANY KIA 27/10/18
20796 PTE HEGGIE	ALEXANDER		TO 14/DLI, 12/DLI, CLASS Z RES
19599 LCPL HELM	HENRY		CLASS Z RES
15853 PTE HENDERSON	GEORGE THORNTON	ENL CONSETT 1/9/14 KIA 25/7/16
19605 PTE HENRY	ALEXANDER		TO LABOUR CORPS LAB C No 398160 CLASS Z RES 21/2/19
16157 PTE HERBERT	THOMAS		CLASS Z RES
13971 PTE HERBERTSON	EDWARD		ENL FELLING 4/9/14 TO 69/FA 18/11/15 ECZEMA DOW 7/6/16
15382 PTE HERDMAN	SAMUEL HENRY	CLASS Z RES
13915 PTE HETHERINGTON	JAMES		ENL FELLING 4/9/14 TO No 18 CCS 28/3/16 SUSP ENTERIC TO HOSP SHIP 29/3/16 TO 3/DLI AWOL 24/9/16 D C MARTIAL 4/1/17 1YR DETENTION POSTED 19/DLI, CANCELLED TO 12/DLI 3/3/17 KIA 15/10/17
21072 PTE HEWITT	ALFRED		TO ROYAL DEFENCE CORPS RDC No 65726 IN FRANCE 25/8/15 TO 7/10/16
18227 PTE HEYWOOD	WILLIAM		TO LABOUR CORPS LAB C No 439392 DIS 5/3/19
19627 PTE HIGGINS	GEORGE		TO 18/DLI, CLASS Z RES
19301 PTE HIGGINS	JAMES		TO 17/DLI DIS 392 ENL 7/9/14 DIS 11/5/16
17387 SGT HILTON	CHARLES ATKINSON	CLASS Z RES
18534 SGT HIND	CECIL HENRY		TO 19/DLI, 12/DLI, CLASS Z RES
19632 CPL HINTON	GEORGE		TO 3/DLI DIS 392 ENL 10/9/14 DIS 15/2/18
16049 PTE HIRD	RALPH BELL		ENL DURHAM 8/9/14 RES HUNWICK TO 70 /FA 28/3/16 SCABIES TO DUTY 9/5/16 WOUNDED GSW LEGS & ARMS 7/10/16 TO 2 /FA 8/10/16 DOW 10/10/16
19625 SGT HITCHIN	HAROLD EVERETT	DIS TO COMMISSION IN 18/DLI 5/1/17 MM DSO MC, RES NOTTTINGHAM
18536 PTE HOCKING	ERNEST		ENL STANLEY 8/9/14 RES ANNFIELD PLAIN IN A COMPANY TO 70 /FA SCABIES 12/10/15 TO DUTY 20/10/15 WOUNDED GSW L SHLDR RT HAND 7/10/16 1/3 NORTHUMBRIAN /FA 13 CCS 23 G HOSP H SHIP ANTWERPEN TO UK TO DEPOT 11/10/16 3/DLI 28/12/16 TO 20/DLI12/5/17 MISSING 31/7/17
15958 PTE HODGSON	ALEXANDER CLENI	TO LABOUR CORPS LAB C No 599353 DIS 27/3/19
17899 CPL HODGSON	HARRY		DIS 392
17020 PTE HODGSON	JOHN		ENL DURHAM 7/9/14 RES GILESGATE MOOR TO 100 /FA 25/4/16 23 CCS 10 G HOSP ROUEN CONV DEPOT ETAPLES 23/5/16 IPETIGO REJOOIN BN 15/9/16 WOUNDED 7/10/16 GSW LEGS TO 1 CAN G HOSP EVAC UK HOSP SHIP CAMBRIA 10/10/16 EMBARKED 1/6/17 TO 20/DLI, REPOSTED TO 10/DLI 20/6/17 MISSING 24/8/17
13854 PTE HODGSON	WILLIAM		DIS 392 ENL 6/9/14 DIS 19/6/17
18383 PTE HOGG	WILLIAM		ENL 8/9/14 CHESTER LE STREET, TO 69/FA 22/11/15, TO DUTY 24/11/15, KIA 17/7/16
13602 PTE HOLMES	HENRY		DIS 392

15897	SGT	HOLMES	RICHARD	CLASS Z RES
25467	LCPL	HOLMES	WILFRED	CLASS Z RES
18242	LCPL	HOLYOAKE	NOAH	TO 19/DLI, 1/8/DLI, CLASS Z RES
18504	CQMS	HOPE	ALEXANDER FAINE	CLASS Z RES
19601	LCPL	HORNBY	ROBERT	ENL BLACKBURN 9/9/14 RES GREAT HARWOOD TO 69/FA 12/11/15 SCABIES TO DUTY 16/11/15 LCPL 17/6/16 IN D COMPANY KIA 17/7/16
27284	PTE	HUDSPITH	ERNEST	TO ROYAL DEFENCE CORPS RDC No 81845 IN FRANCE 25/8/15 TO 15/10/16
17686	PTE	HUGHES	FREDERICK	TO LABOUR CORPS LAB C No 205016 DIS 29/11/17
22178	PTE	HUGHES	HUGH	ENL AFONWEN FLINTSHIRE 20/11/14 LCPL 8/2/18 REVERTED 30/10/18 DIED HOME 19/01/19 BURIED YSCEIFIOG ST MARY'S CHYD
19062	CSM	HUGHES	JOHN	TO 18/DLI, 12/DLI, CLASS Z RES MM
18157	SGT	HUMPAGE	JOHN	DIS 392
17449	PTE	HUNT	HENRY	ENL MIDDLESBROUGH 2/9/14 LCPL 22/8/15 CPL 2/6/16 WOUNDED & MISSING 8/7/16
19628	PTE	HUNT	WILLIAM	ENL STANLEY 7/9/14 LCPL 23/9/15 REDUCED TO PTE 12/6/16 KIA 6/7/16
18509	PTE	HUNTER	ERNEST	ENL STANLEY 8/9/14 RES STANLEY KIA 26/1/16
18507	PTE	HUNTER	VENDER	ENL STANLEY 8/9/14 RES ANNFIELD PLAIN KIA 26/1/16
21246	PTE	HUTCHINSON	ARTHUR	CLASS Z RES
21551	RSM	ILLINGWORTH	JOHN THOMAS	TO DEPOT GSW R THIGH DIS 392 ENL 31/12/14 DIS 22/5/16
22129	PTE	INGLIS	JOHN	TO LABOUR CORPS LAB C No 412532 DIS 4/3/19
22130	CPL	INGLIS	THOMAS	ENL GATESHEAD 17/11/14 RES GATESHEAD LCPL 8/5/15 CPL 25/4/16 ICT LEFT HEEL TO 4 /FA 22/5/16 No 24 AMB TRN 3 CAN G HOSP LE TREPORT 24/5/26 IBD ETAPLES 25/6/16 REJOINS BN 29/6/16 SGT 4/8/16 KIA 7/10/16
17777	PTE	INGRAM	WILLIAM	ENL GATESHEAD 6/9/14 RES GATESHEAD ATT 68/LTMB DIED 22/8/17
13970	PTE	INSKIP	JOHN	TO ARMY RES CLASS P DIS 392 ENL 4/9/14 DIS 25/6/17
17404	CPL	IRVIN	LUKE	ENL 23/8/14 W HARTLEPOOL, LCPL 14/10/14, CPL 10/5/15, SGT 14/4/16 KIA 17/7/16 PREVIOUSLY SERVED 5/DLI TERRITORIAL FORCE
19145	PTE	JACK	SAMUEL	ENL GATESHEAD 8/9/14 RES GATESHEAD MISSING 26/9/16
22179	PTE	JACKSON	GEORGE	TO ARMY RES CLASS W DIS 392 ENL 20/11/14 DIS 22/2/19 INJURY TO TOES
19171	PTE	JACKSON	HERBERT	ENL CHESTER LE STREET 10/9/14 RES GREAT LUMLEY SHELL WND LEG 11/10/17 TO 37 CCS No 28 AMB TRN 1 CAN G HOSP HOSP SHIP PIETER De COVENICK TO UK 19/10/17 TO DEPOT 20/10/17 CMD DEPOT RIPON 22/2/18 3/DLI 24/5/18 15/DLI 12/6/18 KIA 24/8/18
18891	PTE	JACKSON	JAMES THOMPSON	CLASS Z RES ACPL
16288	PTE	JACKSON	JOHN BOYD	DIS 392
21010	PTE	JAMES	FRED	TO LABOUR CORPS LAB C No 666970 CLASS Z RES 12/1/19
18016	PTE	JAMES	WALTER	TO ARMY RES CLASS P DIS 392 ENL 7/9/14 DIS 12/1/17
19673	PTE	JARRETT	JOHN GEORGE	ENL BOLDON COLLIERY 14/9/14 RES NEW HERRINGTON TO 71 /FA 6/4/16 SCABIES TO DUTY 16/4/16 KIA 20/9/17
21200	PTE	JOBES	MARK	CLASS Z RES
18250	PTE	JOBLING	JOHN W	TO 8/DLI TO R ENGINEERS RE No 255137 DIS 392
25537	LCPL	JOHNSON	FREDERICK	CLASS Z RES
19672	PTE	JOHNSON	HENRY	ENL SUNDERLAND 14/9/14 RES GRANGE TOWN SERVED A COMPANY TO 69/FA 10/1/16 IMPETIGO TO DUTY 21/1/16 KIA 17/9/16
17409	PTE	JOHNSON	JOHN WILLIAM	TO LABOUR CORPS LAB C No 237971 DIS 13/5/18
18537	PTE	JOHNSON	THOMAS	ATT XIV CORPS SCHOOL, 12/DLI, CLASS Z RES
19190	PTE	JOHNSON	WILLIAM	ENL STANLEY 12/9/14 RES WEST STANLEY TO 23 CCS - 4 STAT HOSP ST OMER 12/3/16 TONSOLITIS REJOINED 22/3/16 KIA 7/10/16
19670	PTE	JORDON	ALBERT	ENL SOUTH SHIELDS 12/9/14 RES SOUTH SHIELDS TO CCS 29/3/16 HERNIA TO 10 G HOSP ROUEN TO 3 STAT HOSP REJOIN BN 1/6/16 LCPL 22/7/16 REDUCED TO PTE 29/9/16 KIA 7/6/17
18403	PTE	KAY	JAMES WILLIAM	ENL NEWCASTLE 12/9/14 TO 70/FA INFLUENZA 4/5/16 TO DUTY 8/5/16 KIA 28/9/16
18661	LCPL	KELLY	JOHN	TO 20/DLI, 12/DLI, ATT 68/LTMB, 12/DLI, ATT 68/LTMB, CLASS Z RES
17718	PTE	KELLY	RICHARD	TO 20/DLI, DIS 392 ENL 4/9/14 DIS 23/10/19
25502	LCPL	KENNEDY	ADAM	ENL CHESTER LE STREET RES GRANGE VILLA KIA 8/7/16
21074	PTE	KENNEDY	GEORGE	CLASS Z RES
20918	PTE	KENNY	FRANK	ENL CONSETT 21/10/14 RES DIPTON TO 102//FA 25/2/16 BRONCHITIS TO DUTY 2/3/16 TO 1/NORTHUMBRIAN /FA 30/9/16 PUO TO CCS TO 28/G HOSP 7/10/16 INF BASE DEPOT ETAPLES 9/11/16 REJOINS 10/11/16 DOW 1/6/17
22166	PTE	KILBURN	GEORGE WILLIAM	ENL WAKEFIELD 17/11/14 RES CRIGGLESTONE TRIED BY FGCM SLEEPING AT POST 2/2/16 SUSPENDED TO 50 CCS 15/2/17 SCABIES REJOINED 14/3/17 9 CCS 3/7/18 TO 43 AMB TRN 29 STAT HOSP 62 G HOSP DIED MENINGITIS 13/9/18
15065	PTE	KILGALLON	THOMAS	ENL W HARTLEPOOL 22/8/14 POSTED 11/DLI TO 12/DLI 6/2/15 TO 70 /FA 7/1/16 ICT LEG 28/2/16 N MID CCS ALCHOLIC POISONING TO DUTY 1/3/16 WND 15/6/17 TO UK TO 1/5/DLI 1/12/17 MISSING 25/3/18 DOW IN GERMAN HANDS 30/3/18.
20841	PTE	KILLEEN	MATTHEW	ENL CONSETT 19/10/14 RES DIPTON DOW AT 26 /FA 8/11/15
17971	PTE	KILLEEN	WILLIAM	TO LABOUR CORPS LAB C No 636721 CLASS Z RES 2/3/19
19188	CPL	KINGSTON	LLOYD	TO 20/DLI, CLASS Z RES
21054	PTE	KIRKUP	GEORGE WILLIAM	ENL CONSETT RES BLACKHILL KIA 15/10/17
22186	PTE	KITCHEN	JOHN	ACPL CLASS Z RE
13551	PTE	KIVIL	PATRICK	TO 20/DLI, 1/6/DLI, DIS 392
16052	PTE	KNOTT	JOSEPH	CLASS Z RES
16154	PTE	LAING	ANDREW SMITH	CLASS Z RES
21248	LCPL	LAMPARD	FREDERICK NORM	DIS TO COMMISSION IN 3/NORTHND FUS 25/12/16 MC WITH 26/NF
19690	PTE	LANE	ERNEST JOHN A	ENL NEWTON ABBOTT DEVON 7/9/14 RES WOLBOROUGH TO 69/FA 27/10/15 ECZEMA TO No 2 CCS 5/11/15 SCABIES TO DUTY 18/11/15 KIA 26/1/16
13641	PTE	LANE	WILLIAM HENRY	ENL MIDDLESBROUGH 7/9/14 WND AT DUTY 24/9/16 TO 3 CAN CCS PUO 3/11/16 TO 15 AMB TRN 4/11/16 TO 9 AUS G HOSP 8/11/16 H SHIP ST DAVID TO 3/DLI TO 35IBD 4/7/17 TO 18/DLI 6/7/17, REPOSTED 14/DLI 21/7/17, KIA 6/12/17
18375	PTE	LANGDON	SIDNEY	CLASS Z RES
19702	PTE	LANGTON	THOMAS	ENL 4/9/14 SUNDERLAND RES SUNDERLAND LCPL 2/6/15 REVERTS OWN REQ 3/11/15 70 FLD AMD - 23 CCS - 1 G HOSP MAY 16 CONV DEPOT 16/6/16 ATT 1/6/WEST YORKS REGT 11/7/16 3/W RID /FA 49 DRS - TO DUTY 31/7/16, MISSING 3/9/16
15722	PTE	LARMAR	DAVID	TO LABOUR CORPS LAB C No 550197 DIS 3/12/18
13597	PTE	LATTIMER	DAVID	TO DEPOT DIS 392 ENL 3/9/14 DIS 7/12/16
18384	PTE	LAVERICK	WILLIAM	CLASS Z RES
21218	PTE	LAWINS	JOHN	TO 14/DLI, ATT 253 TUNN COY, 14/DLI, CLASS Z RES
17448	SGT	LAWSON	JAMES WILLIAM	TO LABOUR CORPS LAB C No 31806 DIS 28/6/18
14772	SGT	LEARY	JOHN WILLIAM	TO 3/DLI DIS 392 ENL 14/9/14 DIS 16/10/17
18539	PTE	LEE	JOHN JAMES	TO 10/DLI, 22/DLI, 19/DLI, 1/8/DLI, TO ARMY RES CLASS P DIS 392 ENL 13/9/14 DIS 28/4/19
18818	PTE	LEE	THOMAS	ENLISTED STANLEY 9/9/14, RES SOUTHMOOR, TO 5 /FA SCABIES 214/16 TO DUTY 29/4/16, KIA 17/07/16
17442	PTE	LEECH	ALBERT	CLASS Z RES ACPL
17055	PTE	LEWIN	HENRY	CLASS Z RES
22046	PTE	LEWINS	WILLIAM THOMAS	CLASS Z RES MM
13819	PTE	LEWIS	ALBERT THOMAS	CLASS Z RES
25504	PTE	LIDDLE	JOSEPH	TO 18/DLI DIS 392
19192	CSM	LIDDLE	WILLIAM	DIS TO COMMISSION IN 20/DLI 22/7/17, SWB 2/7/18. DCM LG 25/11/16, FROM SOUTH SHIELDS

19272 PTE	LITTLE		CLASS Z RES
20222 PTE	LOCKEY	JOHN	ENL DURHAM RES CHESTER LE ST ATT 1/AUSTRALIAN TUNN COY, ATT 35/IBD, TO 18/DLI, KIA 19/7/18
19134 SGT	LOCKEY	THOMAS GRAHAM	TO 19/DLI, 11/DLI, AWOII MM
25523 RSM	LOCKYER	HENRY WILLIAM	ATT 35 IBD EMPLOYED BASE DEPOT ATT CONV DEPOT CLASS Z RES
20618 SGT	LONG	ALFRED	ENL STANLEY 7/9/14 IN B COMPANY LCPL 27/4/16 CPL 12/7/16 SGT 22/7/16 KIA 18/5/17 MM
19130 PTE	LONG	FREDERICK	ATT 68 BDE HQ, CLASS Z RES
19137 SGT	LONGSTAFF	FRANCIS	TO 20/DL, CLASS Z RES
15920 PTE	LONGSTAFF	JOHN JOSEPH	TO DEPOT DIS 392 WOUNDS ENL 8/9/14 DIS 11/4/17
19298 SGT	LOWE	JOHN THOMAS	TO 18/DLI, 14/DLI, 18/DLI, CLASS Z RES
25538 PTE	LOWERY	JAMES BRYDEN	CLASS Z RES
25503 CPL	LOWRIE	MICHAEL	TO 13/DLI 15/DLI MM DIS 392
17437 PTE	LUBY	THOMAS	ENL W HARTLEPOOL 5/9/14 WND 6/7/16 TO UK H SHIP NEWHAVEN TO 20/DLI 25/1/17 WND 31/1/17 139 /FA GSW SHLDR 3 CAN CCS 30/1/17, TO UK 3/DLI TO 19/DLI 30/7/17 TO 12/DLI, KIA 17/10/17
14828 PTE	LYNCH	JOHN THOMAS	CLASS Z RES
16718 PTE	MacDONALD	THOMAS	CLASS Z RES ACPL
18381 LCPL	MACKAY	ROBERT	TO DEPOT DIS 392 WOUNDS ENL 8/9/14 DIS 6/4/17
18159 PTE	MADDISON	THOMAS	DIS 392
13813 PTE	MALONE	JAMES	TO LABOUR CORPS LAB C No 610478 CLASS Z RES 25/2/19
21130 CPL	MALONEY	MICHAEL	TO 3/DLI DIS 392 ENL 29/10/14 DIS 10/10/17
12024 PTE	MARSH	GEORGE	TO DEPOT DIS 392 ENL 21/8/14 DIS 21/12/17
18322 PTE	MARSHALL	ALBERT H	ENL FERRYHILL 2/9/14 RES SEAHAM TO 26//FA - 7/CCS SCABIES TO DUTY 17/3/16 MISSING 6/8/16
25544 PTE	MARSHALL	ANDREW	DIS 392
16574 PTE	MARTIN	GEORGE ALBERT	CLASS Z RES
3/10646 SGT	MARTIN	JOHN W	CLASS Z RES SERVED IN SOUTH AFRICA 1/DLI AS No 5952 QSA 2 CLASPS MSM.
19156 SGT	MARTIN	LEO	TO ARMY RES CLASS P DIS 392 ENL 9/9/14 DIS 28/4/19
20891 CSM	MARTIN	THOMAS	CLASS Z RES DCM
13850 SGT	MARTIN	WILLIAM CHRISTO	ENL CONSETT 1/9/14 CPL 13/1/15 ASGT 15/7/15 KIA 6/7/16
18474 PTE	MARTINDALE	WILLIAM ARTHUR	CLASS Z RES
19729 SGT	MATKIN	ERNEST	CLASS Z RES MM
18842 PTE	MAUDLIN	NORMAN	CLASS Z RES
15883 PTE	MAUGHAN	SAMUEL	TO LABOUR CORPS LAB C No 387589 DIS 20/3/20
18875 CPL	MAUGHAN	WILLIAM	TO DEPOT DIS 392 ENL 12/9/14 DIS 17/9/17
20998 PTE	MAWSON	ROBERT	ENL CONSETT RES LEADGATE ATT 68/MG COY KIA 7/6/17
20988 PTE	MAWSON	THOMAS	TO MACHINE GUN CORPS MGC No 72662 CLASS Z RES 28/1/19
13237 PTE	MAXTED	GEORGE	DIS 392
16143 PTE	MAXWELL	ADAM	GSW FACE 2/1/16 ADM 3 CCS EVAC 3/1/16 No 24 AMB TRN DIS 392
19756 PTE	MAXWELL	HENRY	ENL GATESHEAD 7/9/14 TO 70//FA 14/1/16 TO 1/NORTHUMBRIAN /FA ICT R ARM 1/10/16 TO DUTY HOSP S ST ANDREW 25/2/17 FRAC R LEG TO 3/DLI TO 351BD TO 19/DLI TO 12/DLI KIA 27/10/18
21271 PTE	MAYFIELD	CHRISTOPHER	TO LABOUR CORPS LAB C No 398120 CLASS Z RES 1/3/19
16164 PTE	McALLISTER	ARCHIBALD	TO 18/DLI, CLASS Z RES
25567 CPL	McAVOY	JOSEPH	BORN & ENL MIDDLESBROUGH TO 2/DLI ATT ORDNANCE WKSPS TO 2/DLI KIA 3/6/17
18311 PTE	McCABE	MICHAEL	TO LABOUR CORPS LAB C No 442629 DIS 1/2/18
25566 PTE	McCANN	LAWRENCE	BORN & ENL SOUTH SHIELDS KIA 8/7/16
15085 PTE	McCARTHY	JOHN	MM ENL STOCKTON KIA 7/10/16
19738 PTE	McCOLL	ANDREW	DIS 392
13667 SGT	McCORMICK	NEIL	TO 1/GARR BN NORTHUMBERLAND FUS NF No 25142 TO 22/NORTHBD FUS CLASS Z RES
16083 PTE	McDONOUGH	JOHN	ENL DURHAM RES DARLINGTON KIA 26/05/17
16090 PTE	McELEAVEY	THOMAS	CLASS Z RES
19746 PTE	McEWAN	JAMES	TO 1/8/DLI DESERTED 19/4/19, CLASS Z RES
17985 PTE	McFARLANE	JOHN	TO MACHINE GUN CORPS MGC No 72663 CLASS Z RES 22/2/19
15836 PTE	McGEE	ALEXANDER	TO 20/DLI, 19/DLI, CLASS Z RES.
18843 PTE	McGEE	CORNELIUS	DIS 392
16145 SGT	McGINN	JAMES FRANCIS	CLASS Z RES
19038 PTE	McGIVERN	JOHN	TT 68/LTMB, TO 3/DLI DIS 392 ENL 5/9/14 DIS 22/6/18
25468 PTE	McGOWAN	JAMES	TO DEPOT DIS 392 ENL 3/9/14 DIS 28/7/16
16725 PTE	McGRORY	MICHAEL	ENL & RES W HARTLEPOOL 17/9/14 WND & MISSING 7/10/16
25591 PTE	McGUINNESS	JOHN	TO ARMY RES CLASS P DIS 392 ENL 18/8/14 DIS 21/5/17
20910 PTE	McGURK	FRANK	TO 2/DLI DIS 392 ENL 20/10/14 DIS 20/11/18
19153 PTE	McILWRATH	JAMES	BORN HOUGHTON LE SPRING ENL CHESTER LE STREET DOW 19/07/16
15923 PTE	McKAY	MICHAEL	CLASS Z RES
18054 CPL	McKEEN	ROBERT	CLASS Z RES
15196 PTE	McKENZIE	JAMES	TO 3/DLI DIS 392 ENL 231/8/14 DIS 14/8/17
18228 PTE	McKENZIE	WILLIAM	ENL GATESHEAD 9/9/14 RES DUNSTON 7/11/15 7/CCS - 4STN HOSP 24/11/15 REJOINED BN KIA 29/5/16
21202 PTE	McKINNEY	MICHAEL	DIS 392
18111 CPL	McLEAN	HUGH ALEXANDER	ENL GATESHEAD 5/9/14 RES LOW FELL 69/FA 5/10/15 SCABIES 5//FA 20/4/16 ICT LEGS LCPL 28/6/16 CPL 12/9/16 KIA 22/9/16
17074 SGT	McMAHON	JAMES	CLASS Z RES
17941 PTE	McMAHON	ROBERT WILLIAM	CLASS Z RES MM
17072 PTE	McMANUS	JOHN	TO 3/DLI DIS 392 ENL 7/9/14 DIS 26/11/17
19735 PTE	McMULLEN	JAMES	ENL NEW SILKSWORTH 13/9/14 KIA 4/12/15
16168 PTE	McNALLY	THOMAS	CLASS Z RES
19085 PTE	McNEAL	THOMAS	CLASS Z RES MM
25469 PTE	McPEAK	JOHN	ENL GATESHEAD KIA 19/10/17
22157 PTE	McPHERSON	JOHN	TO LABOUR CORPS LAB C No 613058 CLASS Z RES 16/6/19
22187 PTE	MELLARS	JOSEPH ARNOLD	CLASS Z RES
25541 CPL	METCALFE	ALFRED	TO 14/DLI ATT 35 IBD ATT 6 D W SIG COY 14/DLI CLASS Z RES
13845 PTE	METHERINGHAM	GEORGE WILLIAM	DIS 392
18321 SGT	MIDDLETON	GEORGE CECIL	DIS TO COMMISSION IN SPECIAL RES 31/3/17
19751 CPL	MILBURN	JAMES	TO 20/DLI, ARMY RES CLASS P DIS 392 ENL14/9/14 DIS 21/3/19
17999 PTE	MILLER	ALFRED	CLASS Z RES
20624 PTE	MILLER	CHARLES	TO LABOUR CORPS LAB C No 631242 CSM CLASS Z RES 25/2/19
16726 SGT	MILLER	ERNEST	DIS 392
13927 PTE	MINIKIN	CHARLES	CLASS Z RES
17910 PTE	MITCHELL	JOHN ALEXANDER	CLASS Z RES
19752 SGT	MITCHELL	PETER	ENL 14/9/14 SUNDERLAND RES HASWELL LCPL 19/6/16 WND 6/7/16 CPL 22/7/16 SGT 26/9/16 KIA 1/1/17
18017 PTE	MOFFATT	WALTER	TO DEPOT DIS 392 ENL 8/9/14 DIS 16/6/17
20952 PTE	MONAGHAN	THOMAS	TO DEPOT DIS 392 RES LEADGATE ENL 20/10/14 DIS 24/8/16 GUN SHOT WNDS
18795 CSM	MONK	WILLIAM	CLASS Z RES
13973 PTE	MOOR	ROBERT	TO ROYAL DEFENCE CORPS RDC No 66270 IN FRANCE 25/8/15 TO 9/4/16

Number	Rank	Surname	Forename	Details
11694	PTE	MOORE	FRANCIS JOSEPH	TO LABOUR CORPS LAB C No 223072 CLASS Z RES 20/4/19
18804	PTE	MOORE	JAMES	DIS 392 ENL 8/9/14 DIS 25/2/19 MM
18968	PTE	MOORE	JAMES	TO LABOUR CORPS LAB C No 440756 CLASS Z RES 9/2/19
25543	CPL	MOORE	THOMAS	DIS 392
25539	PTE	MORGAN	WILLIAM	TO 1/6/DLI DIS 392
19776	CQMS	MORLEY	HARRY L	CLASS Z RES
23094	PTE	MORRISON	JOHN	TO LABOUR CORPS LAB C No 197040 DIS 21/1/19
19774	PTE	MOTTRAM	THOMAS	DIS 392
16698	PTE	MOULT	ALEXANDER	TO LABOUR CORPS LAB C No 219042 DIS 15/4/19
16576	PTE	MUIR	JOHN GEORGE	ENL W HARTLEPOOL 5/9/14 9/RED X HOSP 25/7/16 SHELL WND R LEG TO UK TO 20/DLI9/1/17 GSW HEAD 11/10/17 TO UK, TO 1/9/DLI 24/4/18 REPOSTED 1/7/DLI MISSING 27/5/18
18788	PTE	MURPHY	THOMAS	ENL STANLEY 8/9/14 TO 70//FA 12/10/15 IMPETIGO TO 70//FA 6/5/16 ECZEMA KIA 8/10/16
16535	PTE	MURRAY	JOHN	DIS 392 ENL 8/9/14 DIS 31/10/17
18234	PTE	MURRAY	WILLIAM	ENL FERRYHILL 9/9/14 DOW AT 26//FA 3/1/16
19757	SGT	MURTON	JOSIAH	ENL GATESHEAD 7/9/14 RES CULLERCOATES L/CPL 29/10/14 CPL 10/12/14 L/SGT 21/5/15 SGT 15/7/15 TO HOSP LEICESTER DOW 5/10/16
16178	PTE	MUSGRAVE	THOMAS	TO ARMY RES CLASS W DIS 392 ENL 7/9/14 DIS 12/10/17
13828	SGT	MUXLOW	JAMES WILLIAM	ENL MIDDLESBROUGH 4/9/14 RES GUISBROUGH 69/FA 9/10/15 SCABIES SGT 17/2/16 KiA 19/2/16
22188	PTE	NASH	JOHN HENRY	ENL SHEFFIELD 21/11/14 TO 69/FA 23/10/15 SCABIES 1/12/15 TO 8/CCS - 14/A TRN - 14/G HOSP - HOSP SHIP BRIGHTON TO UK TO 16/DLI TO 35/IBD 14/8/16 TO 15/DLI 29/8/16 WND & MISSING 16/9/16
20260	CQMS	NAYLOR	GEORGE	TO 19/DLI, 15/DLI, 19/DLI, CLASS Z RES WOII
3/11340	WO II	NEAL	JOHN W	CLASS Z RES
15359	PTE	NEVILLE	JOHN	CLASS Z RES
18639	PTE	NEWTON	ALFRED CHARLES	ENL STANLEY 8/9/14 RES BURNHOPE WND 7/10/16 GSW L ARM TO 1/3/NORTHBN /FA - 1/CAN G HOSP TO 35/IBD 16/11/16 REJOIN BN 25/11/16 LSGT 1/12/16 TO 69/FA 12/2/17 RINGWORM, TO 69/FA - 70//FA 2/5/17 KIA 20/9/17
25545	PTE	NEWTON	JOHN GEORGE	ENL BRAMSHOT RES NEWFIELD KIA 17/7/16
18788	CPL	NEWTON	JOSEPH ROBERT	ENL DURHAM RES FENCEHOUSES KIA 24/9/16
20941	PTE	NICHOL	JOHN GEORGE	TO LABOUR CORPS LAB C No 478387 TO CLASS Z RES 11/2/19
17902	PTE	NICHOL	JOHN JOSEPH	TO 19/DLI, 12/DLI, CLASS Z RES
19018	SGT	NICHOLLS	EDWARD	CLASS Z RES
13171	PTE	NICHOLSON	GEORGE WILLIAM	ENL DURHAM 3/9/14 ATT 23 DIV TUNN COY RE KIA 29/4/16
16441	PTE	NICHOLSON	RICHARD FORSYTH	ENL GATESHEAD 8/9/16 RES BENSHAM 1/CAN CCS - 22/A TRN - 26/G HOSP ABCESS SHLDRTO 6 CONV DEPOT - INF BASE DEPOT 23/4/16 REJOIN BN 18/5/16 MIA 26/9/16
20932	PTE	NIXON	ROBERT	ENL CONSETT 21/10/14 RES DIPTON WND 10/4/16 TO 21 /FA 16/8/18 KIA 28/10/18 MM
3/11881	CPL	NORTH	FREDERICK	TO 17/DLI DIS 392 ENL 7/12/14 DIS 23/5/16 SICK
15989	SGT	O'HARA	JOHN WILLIAM	ENL DURHAM 8/9/16 RES SPENNYMOOR TO 70//FA 27/3/16 SCABIES SGT COOK 21/6/16 CSM 31/3/17 MM
13354	PTE	OLIVER	ROBERT	TO DEPOT DIS 392 ENL 5/9/14 DIS 29/11/16 WOUNDS
19850	PTE	OLSEN	CHARLES	TO LABOUR CORPS LAB C No 409069
22111	PTE	OLVER	STANLEY	CLASS Z RES
20908	PTE	O'NEILL	OWEN	TO DEPOT DIS 392 ENL 20/10/14 DIS 12/3/17 SICK
19783	PTE	ORMEROD	THOMAS	TO LABOUR CORPS LAB C No 657743 CLASS Z RES 25/2/19
17680	PTE	ORMSTON	JOSEPH	TO DEPOT DIS 392 ENL 2/9/14 DIS 19/4/17 SICK
16736	PTE	OWENS	ROBERT	CLASS Z RES LCPL
16735	PTE	OWENS	THOMAS	CLASS Z RES
25506	PTE	PACE	WILLIAM HENRY	ATT REINFORCEMENT CAMP ATT 2 F DIV WING 12/DLI CLASS Z RES
19131	PTE	PALMER	GEORGE	TO DEPOT DIS 392 ENL 8/9/14 DIS 20/4/17 SICK
18642	PTE	PALMER	THOMAS	ENL STANLEY 8/9/14 RES ANNFIELD PLAIN 27-4-15 TRIED BY FGCM 42 DAYS DETENTION OFFER VIOLENCE TO SUPERIOR KFA 30/12/15 L LEG 69/FA - 8 CCS BOILS MISSING 17/7/16
13853	PTE	PARKER	FRANK	ENL MIDDLESBROUGH 5/9/14 TO 70/FA 28/4/16 TO BN 11/5/16 KIA 17/7/16
19144	PTE	PARKER	WILLIAM	ENL CHESTER LE ST 8/9/14 RES CHESTER LE ST 69/FA 29/11/15 SCABIES 6/FA - 8/MAC - 1/A TRN - 1/G HOSP 17/4/16 GSW FACE REJOINS 1/6/16 DOW 7/7/16
19797	PTE	PARKES	DANIEL	ENL NEW SILKSWORTH 14/9/14 TO 69/FA 7/16 ICT LEFT FOOT KIA 7/6/17
13901	CPL	PARKIN	SAMUEL	CLASS Z RES MM
25505	SGT	PARMLEY	JOHN	TO 4/DLI DIIS 392 ENL 7/9/14 DIS 4/9/18 MM
13909	PTE	PARMLEY	JOSEPH	ENL FELLING 4/9/14 IN A COY, KIA 17/7/16
15979	PTE	PARRY	HERBERT	ENL DURHAM 8/9/14 RES TUDHOE KIA 17/7/16
25587	PTE	PARTIS	RICHARD	TO LABOUR CORPS LAB C No 475866 DIS 5/3/19
16752	PTE	PASE	WILLIAM	DESERTER TO 19/DLI 10/DLI CLASS Z RES
19313	SGT	PATTISON	WILLIAM	CLASS Z RES MM
22132	PTE	PAYNE	JOHN	TO 15/DLI, 4/DLI DIS 392 ENL 17/11/14 DIS 8/4/18
15849	PTE	PEACOCK	WALTER HYLTON	ATT 68 INF BDE HQ, CLASS Z RES
18055	CPL	PEARCE	PHILIP	DIS 392 ASGT
18640	PTE	PEARSON	GEORGE THOMAS	ENL STANLEY 8/9/14 RES SOUTH MOOR KIA 8/7/16
17734	PTE	PEARSON	JAMES STAINTHORP	TO ROYAL DEFENCE CORPS RDC No 65446 IN FRANCE 28/5/15 TO 7/12/16
16406	CPL	PEARSON	JOSEPH	TO 18/DLI, 12/DLI, DIS 392 MM
25547	PTE	PEARSON	WILLIAM	TO LABOUR CORPS LAB C No 372526 CLASS Z RES 1/10/19
16757	PTE	PEAT	WILLIAM	ENL W HARTLEPOOL 4/9/14 LCPL 4/8/16 REVERTS 12/9/16 KIA 12/9/16 MM
13714	PTE	PEEL	JOHN	ENL HASWELL PLOUGH 8/9/14 WND 10/2/16 GSW FACE ADM 69FA TO No 2 CCS 10/2/16 EVACUATED TO No 4 G HOSP CAMIERS 22/2/16 DOW 23/3/16
18325	PTE	PEPPER	JAMES OWEN	ATT 68/LTMB, ATT 69/LTMB, ATT 68/LTMB, CLASS Z RES
23467	PTE	PERCY	JOHN	ENL 28/8/14 10/NF TRSF 12/DLI 13/8/15 KIA 7/6/17 FROM BEDLINGTON
18265	LCPL	PERRY	WILLIAM	ENL GATESHEAD 14/9/14 TO 69/FA 19/1/15 IMPETIGO TO 23/CCS - 2/A TRN -26 G HOSP 12/5/16 TO IBD 28/7/16 TO 18/DLI WND 28/3/18 TO UK GSW L ARM HOSP DEVON TO DEPOT 31/3/18 3/DLI 13/5/18 TO 15/DLI 13/6/18 LCPL 23/6/18 KIA 9/9/18
25571	PTE	PHILIPS	DAVID	TO LABOUR CORPS LAB C No 271973 DIS 26/2/19
22112	PTE	PHILLIPS	JOHN HENRY	ATT 1 AUSTRALIAN TUNNELLING COY 12/DLI CLASS Z RES
16764	PTE	PHILLIPS	WILLIAM	TO DEPOT DIS 392 ENL 1/9/10 DIS 15/5/16
16213	PTE	PICKFORD	HERBERT	TO ROYAL DEFENCE CORPS RDC No 66291 IN FRANCE 25/8/15 TO 24/6/16
17597	PTE	PIERCEY	JAMES	ENL 2/9/14, NEW BRANCEPETH, KIA 7/10/16
18644	PTE	PIPER	EDGAR	TO LABOUR CORPS LAB C No 379892 CLASS Z RES 23/1/19
22155	PTE	PLEDEGER	JOHN THOMAS	TO ARMY RES CLASS W DIS 392 ENL 18/11/14 DIS 2/4/17
13209	PTE	PORTER	WALTER HARRY	FORMERLY PTE 1/DLI REENLISTED MIDDLESBROUGH 2/9/14 LCPL 29/9/14 REDUCED 28/10/15 WND 17/7/16 GSW ABDOMEN TO No 3 CCS TO No 11 G HOSP CAMIERS DOW 29/7/16
18645	PTE	POSTLE	ROBERT	CLASS Z RES
21017	PTE	POTTS	MARK	ATT No 1 VET HOSP, ATT BASE DETAILS, CLASS Z RES
22136	PTE	PRICE	WILLIAM	CLASS Z RES
18658	PTE	PROUD	JOSEPH	TO ARMY RES CLASS W DIS 392 ENL 14/9/14 DIS 26/10/17
15771	PTE	PUNSHON	HENRY	ENLSUNDERLAND 12/9/14 RES MONKWEARMOUTH KIA 8/7/16
16774	CPL	PYE	JOHN	ENL ACCRINGTON 11/9/14 TO 69/FA - 23/CCS - 12/A TRN 3/CAN G HOSP 16/6/16 TO IBD 25/6/16 REJOINS 29/6/16 1/NORTHBN FA 3/10/16 ICT HEEL LCPL 27/9/16 KIA 16/6/17 MM
19813	PTE	QUINN	CHARLES	TO ROYAL DEFENCE CORPS RDC No 66297 IN FRANCE 25/08/15 TO 9/7/16

Number	Rank	Surname	Forename	Details
15208	PTE	QUINN	JOHN	TO LABOUR CORPS LAB C No 475370 TO CLASS Z RES 10/5/19
20898	PTE	QUINN	JOHN	CLASS Z RES
19178	PTE	QUINN	ROBERT JOHN	ENL FELLING TO 2/DLI KIA 21/03/18
17996	PTE	RATCLIFFE	MATTHEW ROBINS	DIS 392 ENL 1/9/14 DIS 10/10/17
18040	PTE	RATCLIFFE	ROBERT	ENL STANLEY 8/9/14 RES SOUTH MOOR 70/FA - 7/CCS 7/4/16 SCABIES (ISOLATION) REJOINS 25/5/16
19840	PTE	RAWCLIFFE	GEORGE	TO LABOUR CORPS LAB C No 263864 DIS 18/3/19
25589	PTE	RAWLING	ANTHONY	DIS 392 ENL 31/8/14 DIS 8/10/17
13821	PTE	READ	THOMAS HENRY	ENL MIDDLESBROUGH 4/9/14 LCPL 19/6/16 KIA 8/7/16
14053	PTE	REECE	ARTHUR	TO 13/DLI, 2/DLI, 14/DLI, 19/DLI, CLASS Z RES
20929	PTE	REILLY	GEORGE	TO LABOUR CORPS LAB C No 417494 DIS 3/3/19
17093	PTE	REYNOLDS	JOHN	ENL DURHAM DOW 28/11/18
18647	SGT	RICHARDSON	ALBERT	CLASS Z RES MM
25551	CPL	RICHARDSON	ALBERT	TO 10/DLI 20/DLI ATT 35 IBD 12/DLI CLASS Z RES
14005	PTE	RICHARDSON	PERCY	CLASS Z RES
16801	PTE	RICHARDSON	SAMUEL	CLASS Z RES
18108	PTE	RICHINGS	RICHARD	ENL GATESHEAD KIA 7/6/17
16086	PTE	RIDING	JONATHAN	ENL DURHAM 12/9/14 GSW FACE TO 44/CCS - 1/CAN G HOSP 29/7/16 TO IBD 1/8/16 REJOINS 16/8/16 KIA 7/6/17
20990	PTE	RIDLEY	WILLIAM	TO LABOUR CORPS LAB C No 619871 CLASS Z RES 26/1/19
19839	LCPL	RILEY	HARRY	ENL ACCRINGTON 12/9/14 TO DEPOT UNDERAGE 13/8/16 16/DLI 25/8/16 1/TRG RES BN 7/9/16 D COURT MARTIAL AUG 17 42 DAYS DETENTION LCPL 14/11/17 TO 19/DLI 13/2/18 REPOSTED 1/8/DLI 15/2/18 KIA 27/03/18
19075	LCPL	RILEY	JOHN	ATT BASE DEPOT ETAPLES, 12/DLI, ATT 35/IBD, 12/DLI, CLASS Z RES
19182	PTE	RILEY	MICHAEL	ENL CHESTER LE ST 11/9/14 KIA 3/1/16
18659	LCPL	RIMMER	REUBEN	ATT 68/LTMB, 12/DLI, CLASS Z RES
20989	PTE	RINGER	WALTER	ENL CONSETT 4/10/14 RES NEW BRANCEPETH 8/CCS 8/10/15 TO N MID/CCS 13/10/15 TO DUTY TO 69/FA 21/10/15 SCABIES TO 46/CCS - 12/G HOSP 24/8/16 TONSOLITIS TO REJOINS 22/9/16 KIA 7/10/16
16808	PTE	RITCHIE	ROBERT	CLASS Z RES
19483	PTE	ROBERTSON	ARTHUR	ENL SOUTH SHIELDS 12/9/14 RES SOUTH SHIELDS KIA 13/10/15
18648	PTE	ROBINSON	ALBERT	CLASS Z RES
13235	PTE	ROBINSON	ARTHUR	TO 20/DLI DIS 392 ENL 4/9/14 DIS 27/9/18
16092	PTE	ROBINSON	JOHN	TO LABOUR CORPS LAB C No 260664 DIS 10/3/19
25573	PTE	ROBINSON	JOSEPH	TO 14/DLI 12/DLI CLASS Z RES
16595	PTE	ROBINSON	ROBERT	ENL FERRYHILL RES MANCHESTER KIA 4/12/15
25550	PTE	ROBINSON	STEPHEN WHITE	ENL FELLING KIA 7/10/16
19074	PTE	ROBSON	BENJAMIN	CLASS Z RES
15773	PTE	ROBSON	EDWARD	TO DEPOT DIS 392 ENL 12/9/14 DIS 14/6/18
18506	PTE	ROBSON	GEORGE	ATT XIII CORPS SALVAGE COY, 12/DLI, CLASS Z RES
17778	CPL	ROBSON	JACOB	ENL GATESHEAD 6/9/14 TO 69/FA - 18/CCS - 11/A TRN 11/STN HOSP ICT BUTTOCKS REJOINS BN WND 8/7/16 25/G HOSP - HOSP SHIP ST DENIS TO 16/DLI 17/8/16 TO 20/DLI 24/12/16 REPOSTED TO 19/DLI KIA 13/2/18
17090	PTE	ROBSON	JAMES	CLASS Z RES
25577	PTE	ROBSON	JOHN	ATT REINFORCEMENT DEPOT CLASS Z RES
22158	PTE	ROBSON	JOSEPH WILLIAM	ENL GATESHEAD 18/11/14 RES TEAMS DOW 23/12/15
13831	PTE	ROGERS	JOHN JAMES	ENL 4/9/14 TO 18 CCS 28/4/16 IMPETIGO,7/5/16 EVAC TO 12 G HOSP ROUEN, TO BN 1/6/16, WOUNDED 7/10/16 EVACUATED TO 2 FA GSW CHEST EVACUATED 8/10/16 TO 45 CCS DOW 9/10/16
16794	PTE	ROGERS	JOSEPH	ENL W HARTLEPOOL 1/9/14 KIA 4/12/15
18318	PTE	ROONEY	JOHN	TO LABOUR CORPS LAB C No 611769 CPL CLASS Z RES 8/2/19
18226	PTE	ROSS	HARRY	CLASS Z RES
18538	SGT	ROUNSLEY	RICHARD	ENL STANLEY 12/9/14 LCPL 19/12/15 CPL 14/1/16 SGT 27/6/16 KIA 6/10/16
18633	SGT	ROWE	ARTHUR	TO 3/DLI DIS 392 ENL 8/9/14 DIS 11/2/18
3/11747	PTE	ROWE	NICHOLAS	CLASS Z RES
15777	PTE	ROWLEY	JOHN JAMES	ATT 1st FLD SURVEY COY RE, XIII CORPS HQ, 12/DLI, CLASS Z RES
18660	PTE	RUSHBROOK	ARTHUR	TO 14/DLI, 11/DLI, CLASS Z RES
3/10865	SGT	RUSHFORTH	JOSEPH	ENL SUNDERLAND 14/9/14 RES MONKWEARMOUTH EX REGULAR 2/DLI FELL FROM TRN AT GRANTHAM 7/1/15
13181	PTE	RUSSELL	GEORGE	TO 15/DLI, 12/DLI, 1/6/DLI, CLASS Z RES
18377	PTE	RUTHERFORD	ALFRED	ATT 23/DIV APM, 12/DLI, ATT 23/DIV APM CLASS Z RES
16534	PTE	RUTHERFORD	DANIEL	CLASS Z RES LCPL
25549	PTE	RUTHERFORD	THOMAS JAMES	ENL BRAMSHOTT RES HEBBURN TO 18/DLI DOW 17/2/18
15206	SGT	SAMPLE	WILLIAM BOSWELL	COMMISSIONED DLI 8/5/18
21235	PTE	SANDERSON	ALFRED ERNEST	DIS 392
13605	PTE	SAVAGE	WILLIAM	DIS 392
16135	PTE	SCHOFIELD	GEORGE HENRY	CLASS Z RES
17913	PTE	SCORER	THOMAS	CLASS Z RES
22182	PTE	SCOTT	CHARLES	TO 15/DLI CLASS Z RES
3/11741	PTE	SCOTT	DOUGLAS	ENL GATESHEAD TO 16/NORTHBLD FUS NF No 45566 KIA 6/4/17
19073	PTE	SCOTT	JOHN	ENL STANLEY 7/9/14 RES BURNOPFIELD KIA 16/4/16
25553	SGT	SCOTT	WALTER	ENL MIDDLESBROUGH RES NORTH ORMESBY KIA 26/9/16
18243	LCPL	SCOTT	WILLIAM	TO DEPOT DIS 392 ENL 11/9/14 DIS 26/1/17
18541	LCPL	SEWELL	JOHN JOSEPH	DIS 392
16188	PTE	SHANKS	SAMUEL	MM, CLASS Z RES
21110	PTE	SHARP	ALEXANDER	DIS 392 MI CARD STATES LOST AT SEA 13/4/18 POS MERCANTILE MARINE RES 926008 FIREMAN LOST ON HMS DREEL CASTLE
25556	CPL	SHARP	WILLIAM	DIS 392 ENL 3/9/14 DIS 2/10/18
19967	PTE	SHARPLES	JAMES	ENL & RES BLACKBURN LANCS KIA 4/8/16
14774	PTE	SHAW	ARTHUR	DIS 392
15887	PTE	SHEPHERD	ROBERT	TO LABOUR CORPS LAB C No 263623 DIS 14/3/18
19284	PTE	SHIELDS	ROBERT	CLASS Z RES
18812	PTE	SHIELDS	WILIAM HENRY	TO DEPOT DIS 392 ENL 8/9/14 DIS 25/10/16 SICK
19068	PTE	SHOBBROCK	RICHARD	TO 20/DLI, 14/DLI, 2/DLI, CLASS Z RES.
18019	PTE	SHORT	SYDNEY	CLASS Z RES, LCPL
13621	PTE	SHUTT	EDWARD	ENL MIDDLESBROUGH 4/9/14 ATT 68 BDE HQ, LCPL 22/9/15 REVERTED 16/1/16 KIA 23/9/16
21225	PTE	SIDNEY	THOMAS	ENL CONSETT RES LEADGATE KIA 8/7/16
3/11378	SGT	SIDLOW	WILLIAM	CQMS TO ARMY RES CLASS P DIS 392 ENL 11/9/14 DIS 22/4/18
18397	SGT	SILVERSIDES	WILLIAM HENRY	ENL & RES GATESHEAD 10/9/14 LCPL 19/10/14 CPL 8/2/15 SGT 21/5/15 KIA 31/8/16
25470	PTE	SIMM	RICHARD	CLASS Z RES
18670	PTE	SIMPSON	JAMES	CLASS Z RES
17106	PTE	SIMPSON	JOHN	ENL DURHAM 7/9/14 RES LANGLEY PARK MISSING 17/7/16
18641	LCPL	SIMPSON	JOSEPH	TO 15/DLI, CLASS Z RES DCM
15949	PTE	SINCLAIR	JOHN	ENL DURHAM 8/9/14 RES SPENNYMOOR LCPL 8/12/14 CPL 5/7/15 SGT 9/7/16 WND 30/7/16 KIA 1/1/17
22215	PTE	SINCLAIR	ROBERT COOK	TO 3/DLI DIS 392 ENL 21/11/14 DIS 10/11/17

21135	PTE	SINCLAIR	WILLIAM	TO 3/DLI DIS 392 ENL 20/10/14 DIS 22/11/17
15874	PTE	SLASOR	GEORGE	TO 1/DLI, 10/DLI, 1/8/DLI, CLASS Z RES
21904	PTE	SLEETH	THOMAS	TO 13/DLI, CLASS Z RES
13154	SGT	SMALL	GEORGE	TO 10/DLI, 22/DLI CLASS Z RES
15716	PTE	SMITH	ANDREW WOOD	ENL SUNDERLAND 12/9/14 LCPL DOW 4/8/16
16089	CPL	SMITH	GEORGE THOMAS	CLASS Z RES
25555	PTE	SMITH	HARRY	TO 14/DLI ATT 35 IBD ATT 6 D W SIG COY 19/DLI CLASS Z RES
18655	PTE	SMITH	JOHN	TO LABOUR CORPS LAB C No 442693 DIS 8/3/19
15134	PTE	SMITH	PATRICK	TO LABOUR CORPS LAB C No 379920 CLASS Z RES 25/2/19
13166	PTE	SMITH	RALPH	CLASS Z RES
18961	PTE	SNOWDON	JOHN	TO MACHINE GUN CORPS MGC No 136379 TO CLASS Z RES 18/1/19
20503	PTE	SPANTON	SAMUEL	TO ARMY RES CLASS P DIS 392 ENL 15/9/14 DIS 31/10/16
15955	CSM	SPEDDING	THOMAS	DIS 392
18662	SGT	SPEED	JAMES ARTHUR	CLASS Z RES DCM MM
13572	PTE	SPENCE	JOHN	DIS 392
21109	PTE	SPENCE	JOHN	TRF TO BEDFORDSHIRE REGT BEDFS No 46120
13974	SGT	SPENCER	WILLIAM	ATT MG SCHOOL TO 12/DLI, CLASS Z RES
16905	PTE	SPENDLEY	HERBERT	TO LABOUR CORPS LAB C No 606319 CLASS Z RES 9/3/19
25508	PTE	STANGER	JOHN HENRY	ENL W HARTLEPOOL DOW 9/10/16
16917	PTE	STANTON	W	TO TANK CORPS TC No 92269
19086	PTE	STARRS	STEPHEN	TO 20/DLI, 19/DLI, ATT 3/MBD, CLASS Z RES.
3/10564	SGT	STEARS	JAMES T	ATT FIELD DEPOT, CLASS Z RES
25507	LCPL	STEPHENS	ROBERT JAMES	CLASS Z RES
13921	PTE	STEPHENSON	ALEXANDER	ENL FELLING 4/9/14 RES USWORTH KIA 7/10/16
13904	PTE	STEPHENSON	CHARLES	TO DEPOT DIS 392 ENL 4/9/14 DIS 16/2/18
22102	PTE	STEPHENSON	RICHARD ROBINS(	CLASS Z RES
19960	LCPL	STEVENS	HAROLD EVERETT	DIS TO COMMISSION MACHINE GUN CORPS, RES BEESTON NOTTS
17861	CPL	STEWART	JAMES BRUCE	CLASS Z RES ASGT
18323	LCPL	STOCKELL	STEPHEN	ENL FERRYHILL 2/9/14 RES PICKERING LCPL 24/1/15 REVERTS 17/11/15 TO 70/FA 20/11/15 SCABIES
				TO 6/FA 27/4/16 ICT KNEE - 8/MAC- 14/A TRN - 18/G HOSP - HOSP SHIP DIEPPE TO UK TO DEPOT-
				16/DLI-1/TRG RES BN TO BEF 3/17 POSTED TO 2/DLI REPOSTED 12/DLI 11/4/17 70/FA-39/CCS 8/6/18
22167	PTE	STOREY	ROBERT LAMBERT	DIS 392
25554	PTE	STOTT	ANDREW	DIS 392
25510	PTE	STOUT	ARTHUR	DIS 392 ENL 14/9/14 3/8/18
18385	PTE	SURTEES	GEORGE	ENL 8/9/14 FERRYHILL. AWOL 13/6/15 TO 18/6/15. BORN HETTON RESIDENT EAST HOWLE
15416	PTE	SWALES	FRANK	CLASS Z RES
20416	PTE	SWEENEY	JAMES	TO LABOUR CORPS LAB C No 184764 CLASS Z RES 22/5/19
12665	PTE	TAGGART	MICHAEL	ENL SUNDERLAND 13/8/14 WND 17/7/16 REJOINED 20/7/16 MISSING 7/10/16
18629	PTE	TALLENTIRE	JOHN WILLIAM	CLASS Z RES
20923	PTE	TAYLOR	ARTHUR	TO 13/DLI, DIS 392
21075	SGT	TAYLOR	FRANCIS	TO DEPOT DIS 392 ENL 30/10/14 DIS 17/4/18 MM
22097	PTE	TAYLOR	THOMAS HENRY	CLASS Z RES
21197	PTE	TAYLOR	WILLIAM	ENL FELLING KIA 17/7/16
18400	CPL	TELFER	WALTER	CLASS Z RES
16191	PTE	THACKERAY	RICHARD	TO ROYAL DEFENCE CORPS RDC No 73239 IN FRANCE 25/8/15 TO 15/1/17
16863	PTE	THOMAS	FRED	TO LABOUR CORPS LAB C No 211003 CLASS Z RES 19/4/19
3/11722	PTE	THOMAS	THOMAS	DIS 392
3/11726	PTE	THOMPSON	CHARLES WM	CLASS Z RES
20945	PTE	THOMPSON	GEORGE	ENL & RES FELLING 22/10/14 TO 69/FA 14/1/16 SCABIES KIA 17/7/16
22121	PTE	THOMPSON	HARRY	TO 19/DLI, 12/DLI, 19/DLI, CLASS Z RES
20523	CQMS	THOMPSON	JOHN	AWOII DIS TO COMMISSION 9/NORFOLK REGT 25/12/16 STAFF LT RE RES DARLINGTON
18021	PTE	THOMPSON	JOHN EDWARD	CLASS Z RES
21113	PTE	THOMPSON	JOSEPH	TO 19/DLI, 10/DLI, 1/5/DLI, DIS 392 ENL 23/10/14 DIS 9/8/18
25557	PTE	THOMPSON	RICHARD	TO DEPOT DIS 392 ENL 14/9/14 DIS 28/3/17
19947	PTE	THOMPSON	ROBERT	ENL & RES GATESHEAD 7/9/14 KIA 29/01/16
18210	PTE	THOMPSON	THOMAS	ENL BIRTLEY 8/9/14 RES GATESHEAD TO DEPOT 19/5/16 AWOL 8/7/16 TO 26/7/16 TO 3/DLI 20/DLI
				1/9/DLI ATT 62 DIV SALVAGE COY 1/9/DLI KIA 28/3/18
16868	PTE	THOMPSON	WILLIAM	TO ROYAL DEFENCE CORPS RDC No 65451 IN FRANCE 28/5/15 TO 11/8/16
17128	CPL	TINDALL	EDWARD	CLASS Z RES
19067	PTE	TIPLADY	JOHN	ENL PELTON 7/9/14 KIA 1/1/17
25578	PTE	TODD	ALBERT	ENL NEWCASTLE RES NEW BRANCEPETH TO 18/DLI 19/DLI ATT E DEPOT TO 19/DLI KIA24/4/18
11377	CQMS	TODD	JOHN	ENL & RES MIDDLESBROUGH KIA 7/6/16
25521	LCPL	TOLLIDAY	JOHN WILLIAM	TO ARMY RES CLASS P DIS 392 ENL 20/11/14 DIS 24/6/17
22200	PTE	TROW	CLAUDE SMITH	DIS 392
15266	SGT	TURNER	ALBERT	CLASS Z RES
16177	PTE	UNSWORTH	JOHN GEORGE	CLASS Z RES ENL 12/9/14 DIS 16/6/19
15709	PTE	USHER	EDWARD	TO 20/DLI, DIS 392
3/10640	SGT	UTTING	CHARLES	CLASS Z RES
19976	PTE	VASEY	FREDERICK	CLASS Z RES
22216	LCPL	VEITCH	THOMAS HINDMAR	ENL SUNDERLAND 2/11/14 28 DAYS FP No 1 18/6/16 TO 2/FA-1/1/S MID CCS 23/G HOSP HOSP SHIP
				BRIGHTON SHELL WND HEAD 7/10/16 TO DEPOT 14/10/16 -4/DLI 22/12/16 TO BEF 22/3/17 TO 10/DLI
				REPOSTED 15/DLI 13/4/17 KIA 22/10/17
16087	PTE	VINE	BENJAMIN	CLASS Z RES
14823	PTE	WAISTELL	THOMAS	ENL NEWCASTLE 1/9/14 MM 1/9/16 WND 7/10/16 No 13 CCS TO UK 12/10/16 HOSP SHIP ST GEORGE
				TO DEPOT 13/10/16 POSTED 10/DLI CANCELLED TO, 15/DLI 18/11/17 KIA 22/4/18
13596	SGT	WALKER	FREDERICK	ATT 1st AUSTRALIAN TUNN COY, 12/DLI, CLASS Z RES
19016	LCPL	WALKER	JAMES	TO DEPOT DIS 392 ENL 7/9/14 DIS 25/8/16 WNDS
20566	PTE	WALKER	JOHN JAMES	ATT 11/R SUSSEX REGT, CLASS Z RES
18813	PTE	WALKER	PHILIP	TO 18/DLI, 20/DLI, CLASS Z RES
13283	PTE	WALKER	ROBERT	ENL MIDDLESBROUGH 3/1/16 KIA 3/1/16
19964	PTE	WALKER	THOMAS LOW	ENL ABERDEEN 9/9/14 LCPL 13/1/15 CPL 10/5/15 REVERTS PTE 31/7/15 LCPL 23/7/16 CPL 2/6/17 SGT
				16/11/17 TO 11/G HOSP DIES INFLUENZA 4/11/18
13829	PTE	WALL	PATRICK	TO ARMY RES CLASS W DIS 392 ENL 4/9/14 DIS 30/1/18
15162	PTE	WALLACE	JOHN	TO DEPOT DIS 392 ENL 25/8/14 DIS 12/5/16
16486	PTE	WALLACE	PETER	ENL NEWCASTLE 11/9/14 RES WARDLEY COLLIERY TO 7/G HOPS 28/5/16 SHELL WND HEAD & L
				ARM DOW 28/5/18
21251	PTE	WALLIS	FRANK	TO 19/DLI, 20/DLI, 19/DLI
20566	PTE	WALSHE	JOHN	TO LABOUR CORPS LAB C No 710142
16853	PTE	WALTON	JOHN WILLIE	TO LABOUR CORPS LAB C No 399724 LCPL DIS 21/1/19
3/10649	SGT	WARDLE	GEORGE	TO 3/DLI DIS 392 ENL 9/9/14 DIS 1/4/18
16880	PTE	WARNES	SAMUEL	TO LABOUR CORPS LAB C No 27457 CLASS Z RES 13/4/19
21252	PTE	WATSON	GEORGE	TO ROYAL DEFENCE CORPS RDC No 71373 IN FRANCE 25/08/15 TO 24/9/15
18238	SGT	WATSON	HARVEY	ATT 23/DIV SCHOOL , 12/DLI, CLASS Z RES
18628	SGT	WATSON	JOHN	TO 15/DLI, 12/DLI, CLASS Z RES MM

18627	CPL	WATSON	WALTER BALLANT	TO ARMY RES CLASS W DIS 392 ENL 8/9/14 DIS 3/1/17 MM
25559	PTE	WATSON	WILIAM KIPLING	CLASS Z RES MM
22113	PTE	WEALLEANS	HARRY	ENL MIDDLESBROUGH 16/11/14 DOW 2/CAN CCS 19/10/17
19013	PTE	WEBSTER	GEORGE RICHARD	ATT 68 BDE HQ, CLASS Z RES
17912	PTE	WEDDELL	THOMAS	DIS 392
18158	SGT	WEDDERBURN	NORMAN	DIS 392
20009	LCPL	WEIR	JOHN BELL	CLASS Z RES
16166	PTE	WESTGARTH	CHARLES	CLASS Z RES
25563	PTE	WHALEY	GEORGE	ENL CONSETT TO 18/DLI ATT IBD 18/DLI DIED HOME 16/5/17
18948	PTE	WHALEY	THOMAS W	ENL CONSETT 1/9/14 RES BLACKHILL KIA 8/12/15
19042	LCPL	WHARTON	JAMES	ENL GATESHEAD 6/9/14 WND AT DUTY 2/8/16 LCPL 4/8/16 KIA 7/10/16
13595	PTE	WHELAN	JOHN	DIS 392
18626	PTE	WHITFIELD	MATTHEW DICKEN	CLASS Z RES
16560	PTE	WHITFIELD	ROBERT CLARK	ENL FERRYHILL 8/9/14 LCPL 1/7/16 WND 24/9/16 TO 2/FA - 1/1/S MID CCS GSW ABDOMEN DOW 25/9/16
21016	PTE	WHITNEY	JOHN	ENL STANLEY RES DURHAM TO 2/DLI, 18/DLI, 19/DLI KIA 28/9/18
21003	PTE	WHITNEY	WILLIAM	TO 11/DLI, 12/DLI, CLASS Z RES
25520	PTE	WILDE	SETH	ENL GATESHEAD ATT HQ 23/DIV DIED 18/3/18
19080	LCPL	WILDEMAN	ARTHUR	ATT IBD ETAPLES, 12/DLI, CLASS Z RES
16525	PTE	WILDSMITH	JOHN FERGUSON	ENL GATESHEAD ATT 68/1 LTMB, TO 12/DLI, ATT CORPS SCHOOL, ATT 68 LTMB, TO 12/DLI, KIA 28/10/18 MM
17945	PTE	WILKINSON	ALBERT	ENL FERRYHILL 7/9/14 TO 70/FA 27/3/16 ICT LEGS WEST RID CCS - 19/A TRN 9/S HOSP REJOINS 5/6/16 TO 45/CCS 12/7/16 ICT FOOT 6/G HOSP CONV DEPOT 19/7/16 REJOIINS 16/8/16 KIA 7/10/16
17944	PTE	WILKINSON	THOMAS	TO ARMY RES CLASS W DIS 392 ENL 8/9/14 DIS 28/2/19
25473	PTE	WILLSHIRE	FREDERICK GEOR	ENL FELLING RES NEWCASTLE KIA 17/7/16
25561	PTE	WILSON	GEORGE	ENL B AUCKLAND KIA 14/10/15
17149	PTE	WILSON	HENRY	TO 2/DLI ARMY RES CLASS P DIS 392 ENL 15/9/14 DIS 25/4/19 MM
3/11131	SGT	WILSON	JOHN	WOII ENL 6/10/14 DIS 392 19/1/18
25562	PTE	WILSON	JOHN	TO LABOUR CORPS LAB C No 636765 CLASS Z RES 9/2/19
19103	PTE	WILSON	JOHN RICHARDSOI	ENL FELLING 7/9/14 TO 69/FA DENTAL TO 7 CCS - 4/S HOSP 10/11/15 REJOINED 5/12/15 KIA 7/10/16
13202	PTE	WILSON	RICHARD	TO 3/DLI DIS 392 ENL 1/9/14 DIS 14/8/17
16449	PTE	WILSON	ROBERT	DIS 392 LCPL
13902	PTE	WOOD	FREDERICK	TO 4/DLI DIS 392 ENL 5/9/14 DIS 11/6/18
16848	PTE	WOOD	WILLIAM HAROLD	TO 11/DLI, 1/7/DLI, CLASS Z RES
15421	CSM	WOODHEAD	WILLIAM	DIS 392 ENL 10/9/14 DIS 16/1/19 MM
18011	PTE	WOODWARD	CHRISTOPHER	CLASS Z RES MM
16851	PTE	WOODWARD	JOHN	DIS 392
15419	PTE	WRIGHT	ARTHUR	ENL CASTLEFORD 10/9/14 CPL 8/7/16 KIA 29/4/17
18352	LCPL	WRIGHT	JOHN THOMAS	TO 2/DLI, 2/7/DLI, 13/DLI, CLASS Z RES
19037	PTE	WRIGHT	JONATHAN	ATT 181 COY RE, 12/DLI, ATT CORPS REINF CAMP, ATT BASE DEPOT ETAPLES, CLASS Z RES
18625	SGT	WRIGHT	JOSEPH	DIS 392
18225	PTE	WRIGHT	NICHOLAS	TO 4/DLI DIS 392 LCPL ENL 8/9/14 DIS 11/9/17
25569	SGT	WRIGHT	THOMAS	ENL GATESHEAD ACSGT KIA 8/7/16
20909	PTE	WYNN	CHARLES	ENL CONSETT 20/10/14 TO 69/FA 29/12/15 NEURALGIA TO DUTY 6/1/16 KIA 7/10/16
25565	PTE	YARKER	EDWARD	CLASS Z RES
20298	PTE	YATES	JAMES	TO LABOUR CORPS LAB C No 602956 CLASS Z RES 27/4/19
25474	PTE	YATES	JOHN	CLASS Z RES MM
21212	PTE	YATES	ROBERT	DIS 392
17720	PTE	YEAMAN	THOMAS	TO 20/DLI LCPL CLASS Z RES
18394	PTE	YOUNG	EDWARD MALCOLI	TO ROYAL DEFENCE CORPS RDC No 65729 IN FRANCE 25/8/15 TO 28/9/16
15717	PTE	YOUNG	ERNEST	ENL SUNDERLAND 12/9/14 TO 70/FA 28/1/16 SCABIES TO 1/CAN CCS 5/2/16 ECZEMA - 14/G HOSP 6/2/16 BASE DEPOT 19/3/16 REJOINS 24/3/16 MISSING 8/7/16
15956	PTE	YOUNG	WILLIAM	ENL FERRYHILL 8/9/14 RES STOCKTON MISSING 17/7/16
18787	PTE	YOUNG	WILLIAM	TO 18/DLI, CLASS Z RES

Nominal Roll of Officers who served with the 13th (Service) Battalion Durham Light Infantry 1914–1918

Rank	Name	First Name	Dismbarked/Joined Bn	Left Battalion	REMARKS & REASON FOR LEAVING BATTALION	HOME TOWN OR ADDRESS ON MICARD
SECOND LIEUTENANT	ADAMS	H	13/04/1916	02/07/1916	TO UK SICK	BIRMINGHAM
SECOND LIEUTENANT	ADAMS	JOHN P F	28/07/1916	08/08/1916	WOUNDED TRF ROYAL FLYING CORPS 20 SQN KILLED IN ACTION 14/10/1917	EXMOUTH
SECOND LIEUTENANT	AITKENHEAD	ROBERT J	11/09/1918	08/10/1918	SERVED PTE 15224 HIGHLAND LI WOUNDED	CRAMLINGTON
SECOND LIEUTENANT	ALLAN	FRANK L	30/08/1916	29/09/1916	DIED OF WOUNDS	
SECOND LIEUTENANT	ALLCOCK	O P	16/03/1915 ?		DID NOT EMBARK WITH OR REJOIN THE BATTALION	HEATON
CAPTAIN	ARRIS	WILLIAM J	25/08/1915	02/11/1916	SERVED SGT 15223 12/DLI TO 13/DLI PRIOR TO EMBARKATION	
CAPTAIN	ARRIS	WILLIAM J	22/06/1917	08/11/1917		
CAPTAIN	ARRIS	WILLIAM J	13/11/1917	14/09/1918		
CAPTAIN	ARRIS	WILLIAM J	16/09/1918	11/11/1918		
LIEUTENAT COLONEL	ASHBY	G A	24/09/1914 ?		DID NOT EMBARK WITH OR REJOIN THE BATTALION	
LIEUTENANT	ATKINSON	ERNEST W	10/11/1915	23/10/1916	WOUNDED	NEWCASTLE
SECOND LIEUTENANT	AUDAS	FRANCIS	15/04/1918	05/10/1918	SERVED PTE 16/196 16/NORTHUMBERLAND FUSILIERS MISSING IN ACTION	HEATON
CAPTAIN	AUSTIN	ARTHUR H	25/08/1916	04/08/1916	MISSING	READING
SECOND LIEUTENANT	BAGGULEY	JAMES L	19/05/1916	06/12/1917	FROM 11/DLI KILLED IN ACTION	NEWCASTLE
SECOND LIEUTENANT	BANNERMAN	WILLIAM	08/11/1917	17/02/1919	SERVED AS PTE 2909 300497 1/8/DLI TO UK	DARLINGTON
SECOND LIEUTENANT	BAILEY	GERALD H	25/08/1915	20/10/2015	SERVED PTE 1832 5/HAMPSHIRE REGT, BN SIGNALS OFFICER DIED OF WOUNDS	BOURNEMOUTH
SECOND LIEUTENANT	BATTY	JOSEPH C	22/06/1916	19/08/1916	WOUNDED TRF ROYAL FLYING CORPS 102 SQN	WOLSINGHAM
SECOND LIEUTENANT	BEART	V L D	12/08/1916	17/09/1916	ENLISTED JOHANNESBURG KILLED IN ACTION	DURBAN
SECOND LIEUTENANT	BELL	JOHN G	25/08/1915	21/12/1915	TO UK SICK	WOKING
CAPTAIN	BELLAMY	ERNEST A	25/08/1915	09/04/2016	TO UK SICK	GOLDERS GREEN
CAPTAIN	BEWLEY	ISAAC	03/08/1917	10/10/1918	KILLED IN ACTION	WHICKHAM
LIEUTENANT COLONEL	BIDDULPH	NICHOLAS T	25/08/1915	16/05/1916	TO UK SICK	FLEET HANTS
SECOND LIEUTENANT	BISHOP	CHARLES H	05/09/1917	23/10/1918	DIED OF WOUNDS	STOKE NEWINGTON
CAPTAIN	BLAKE	HAROLD F	25/08/2015	08/01/1916		
CAPTAIN	BLAKE	HAROLD F	?	07/10/2016	WITSHIRE REGIMENT ATT 13/DLI TO UK SICK KILLED IN ACTION 7/10/1916	WIMBLEDON
LIEUTENANT	BLYTH	J B	16/10/1918	25/10/1918	TO UK SICK	
SECOND LIEUTENANT	BOLTON	THOMAS	17/12/1917	09/10/1918	WOUNDED	
MAJOR	BORROW	EDWARD	25/08/1915	07/08/1917	TO 12/DLI THEN 10/DWR	EARL'S COURT
SECOND LIEUTENANT	BRADY	JAMES	19/12/1916	26/08/1918	SERVED PS 8167 UPS BN R FUSILIERS WOUNDED 22/4/17 + 7/6/17 KILLED IN ACTION	CONSETT
LIEUTENANT	BROWN	PHILIP A	25/08/1915	04/11/1915	SERVED 6/DUKE OF CORNWALL'S LI 12351 KILLED IN ACTION	BECKENHAM
SECOND LIEUTENANT	BROWN	CHARLETON	23/06/1916		SERVED PTE 12317 NORTHUMBERLAND FUSILIERS COMM BORDER REGT ATT 13/DLI	
CAPTAIN	BUCKELL	HAROLD C	13/12/1916	20/09/1917	KILLED IN ACTION	MEDFORD MASS USA
SECOND LIEUTENANT	BURTT	J L	08/02/1915 ?		DID NOT EMBARK WITH OR REJOIN THE BATTALION	
SECOND LIEUTENANT	CALDWELL	WILLIAM T	26/07/1917	09/09/1918	SERVED AS PTE T4/173182 ARMY SERVICE CORPS TO UK TRF MACHINE GUN CORPS	NEW YORK USA
SECOND LIEUTENANT	CALLOW	ERNEST H	08/11/1917	10/10/1918	SERVED PTE UPS BN R FUS & CPL 106343 SPEC BDE R ENGINEERS WOUNDED	CAMBRIDGE
CAPTAIN	CAMPBELL	J H	18/11/1918			
CAPTAIN	CARR WEST	ARTHUR T	30/11/1918		FROM 18/8/1914 TO 1/2/1915 SERVED WITH FRENCH FOREIGN LEGION 12/DLI 1915-17 TO PARIS	PARIS
SECOND LIEUTENANT	CARROLL	JOHN P	03/03/1917	18/10/1917	WOUNDED	
SECOND LIEUTENANT	CHANDLER	A B	30/08/1916	08/01/1917	TRF ROYAL ENGINEERS	
CAPTAIN	CHAPMAN	CYRIL R	30/08/1916	05/10/1918	WOUNDED	EAST DULWICH
SECOND LIEUTENANT	CHARLTON	WILLIAM G	28/06/1916	28/07/1916	PTE INNS OF COURT OTC WOUNDED KIA 26/8/1918 WITH 15/DLI	SEATON DELAVAL
SECOND LIEUTENANT	CHILD	J M	08/03/1915 ?		DID NOT EMBARK WITH OR REJOIN THE BATTALION	
LIEUTENANT	CLARKE	DENZIL H	25/08/1915		PROMOTED CAPTAIN 4/9/16 MAJOR 16/04/18	BROMLEY KENT
LIEUTENANT COLONEL	CLARKE	DENZIL H	05/10/1918	05/10/1918	WOUNDED	
LIEUTENANT COLONEL	CLARKE	DENZIL H	18/01/1919		REJOINED	
SECOND LIEUTENANT	COFFEY	C R	30/11/1914 ?		DID NOT EMBARK WITH OR REJOIN THE BATTALION	
SECOND LIEUTENANT	COOPER	M	26/12/1914 ?		DID NOT EMBARK WITH OR REJOIN THE BATTALION	
SECOND LIEUTENANT	CROSSLAND	E A	30/01/1915 ?		DID NOT EMBARK WITH OR REJOIN THE BATTALION	
LIEUTENANT	CUTTER	E O	11/09/1918	05/10/1918	WOUNDED	

Rank	Surname	Forename	Date 1	Date 2	Details	Place
CAPTAIN	DAVENPORT	WILLIAM N	02/06/1916	20/05/1917	SERVED PRIVATE 7/CANADIAN INFANTRY BN ENLISTED VALCARTIER SICK IN UK TO 12/DLI 1! BORN LONDON	
SECOND LIEUTENANT	DAVIS	ERNEST	09/01/1917	20/05/1917	TO UK SICK	
LIEUTENANT	DAVIS	ERNEST	28/01/1918	15/04/1918	SERVED PTE 2658 16/LONDON REGT WOUNDED	FARNHAM
SECOND LIEUTENANT	DAVISON	J	14/06/1916	08/11/1917		
SECOND LIEUTENANT	DAVISON	J	08/11/1917	01/12/1918		
SECOND LIEUTENANT	DAWSON	JOHN	23/06/1916	13/09/1916	TRF TO NORTHUMBERLAND FUSILIERS	
SECOND LIEUTENANT	DEWAR	WILLIAM R	05/11/1917	06/10/1918	SERVED PTE 13771 HIGHLAND LI COMM BORDER REGIMENT ATT 13/DLI WND TRF GURKHA RIF	RUTHERGLEN
SECOND LIEUTENANT	DODDS	CECIL	03/01/1918	05/10/1918	KILLED IN ACTION	
SECOND LIEUTENANT	DODGSON	W P	18/11/1918	19/03/1919	TO UK	
CAPTAIN	DOWNEY	JOSEPH A	25/08/1915	13/03/1916	TO UK SICK	
MAJOR	DOWNEY	JOSEPH A	21/06/1916	10/12/1917		
SECOND LIEUTENANT	DUGDALE	ARTHUR G	17/05/1916	28/07/1916	WOUNDED	BOURNEMOUTH
LIEUTENANT	ESKDALE	JAMES A	25/10/1918		SERVED L/CPL 5360 ARTISTS RIFLES NORTHUMBERLAND FUSILIERS ATT 13/DLI	TYNEMOUTH
MAJOR	FABER	HENRY G	21/10/1918		FROM 1/5/DLI	NORTHALLERTON
CAPTAIN	FARRIER	ROBERT H	27/12/1917	14/02/1918	SERVED SGT 9/38 9/DLI POSTED TO 52/DLI	GATESHEAD
SECOND LIEUTENANT	FAUSSETT	NOEL E	28/06/1916	21/10/1916	TO UK	
SECOND LIEUTENANT	FORREST	EDWIN C	26/07/1917	05/10/1918	WOUNDED	
SECOND LIEUTENANT	GARDNER	HAROLD	03/10/1918		SERVED PTE S4/12804 ARMY SERVICE CORPS COMM 1/6 WEST YORKS	HORBURY Nr WAKEFIELD
SECOND LIEUTENANT	GILL	ROBERT W	31/07/1917	20/09/1917	SERVED PTE 1687 5/DLI WOUNDED	STOCKTON ON TEES
LIEUTENANT	GOLDER	WILLIAM	03/11/1917	05/10/1918	KILLED IN ACTION	BLYTH
SECOND LIEUTENANT	GRAY	JOHN W	25/08/1915	06/11/1915	TO UK SICK TO 1/DLI SERVED ON NORTH WEST FRONTIER	RYTON ON TYNE
SECOND LIEUTENANT	GRAY	GEORGE P	18/07/1916	28/07/1916	SERVED PTE 6/2195 NORTHUMBERLAND FUSILIERS WOUNDED	HEATON
MAJOR	GRAY	EDWARD	27/08/1916	02/10/1918	SERVED L/SGT 4528 20 HUSSARS F&F 16/8/1914 TO UK - TO 1/DLI	TIDWORTH BARRACKS WITH 1/DLI
SECOND LIEUTENANT	GEACH	E S	09/12/1914 ?		DID NOT EMBARK WITH OR REJOIN THE BATTALION	
SECOND LIEUTENANT	GREEN	ALFRED	28/06/1916	10/07/1916	SERVED PTE 2718 23/LONDON REGIMENT WOUNDED TO LABOUR CORPS ATT POW COMPANY 196 LAB COY ITALY	CLAPHAM COMMON
MAJOR	GREENWOOD	LEONARD M	25/08/1915	17/10/1918	DIED OF WOUNDS	STREATHAM COMMON
SECOND LIEUTENANT	GEIPEL	HENRY C	19/10/1918	26/10/1918	WOUNDED	BALHAM SW 12
LIEUTENANT	HALES	ALFRED E	04/11/1917	05/10/1918	2 Lt 11/N STAFFS TO 17/DLI WOUNDED TO 13/DLI WOUNDED	STOKE ON TRENT
LIEUTENANT	HALL	FREDERICK	29/10/1916	01/06/1917	SERVED PTE UPS BN PS/7988 21/R FUSILIERS WOUNDED	DARLINGTON
SECOND LIEUTENANT	HALL	G W	25/10/1918	04/02/1919	TRF TO 2/NORTHUMBERLAND FUSILIERS	
SECOND LIEUTENANT	HAMILTON	ARCHIBALD L	13/01/1917	10/06/1917	HIGHLAND LIGHT INFANTRY ATT 13/DLI KILLED IN ACTION	POLLOCKSHIELDS
CAPTAIN	HANDCOCK	CHARLES G	25/08/1915	11/10/1916	TRF GEN LIST STAFF CAPTAIN A/MAJOR	BOMBAY
SECOND LIEUTENANT	HANDS	CECIL	14/06/1917	12/10/1917	SERVED PTE 18/1356 18/DLI KILLED IN ACTION	SUNDERLAND
LIEUTENANT	HARMER	ALFRED S	02/03/1917	13/10/1917	SERVED LCPL 11658 2/DLI ENT F&F 8/9/1914 TO UK SICK TO 1/DLI	1/DLI BRIT SILESIA FORCE 1922
LIEUTENANT	HART	HYLU P	11/09/1918	05/10/1918	KILLED IN ACTION	WOKINGHAM
SECOND LIEUTENANT	HASTER	H J	05/03/1915 ?		DID NOT EMBARK WITH OR REJOIN THE BATTALION	
LIEUTENANT	HESELTON	GEORGE R	19/11/1916	02/06/1917	SERVED PTE UPS BN 6874 19/R FUSILIERS KILLED IN ACTION	WEST HARTLEPOOL
SECOND LIEUTENANT	HIRSCH	FRANK B	25/10/1918	01/02/1919	FROM 5/DLI TO UK POSSIBLY COMMISSIONED FROM CAMERON HIGH TO 27/DLI	
LIEUTENANT	HODGSON	WILLIAM C	12/07/1917	08/09/1918	FROM 10/DLI TO UK SICK TO 51/DLI	LOWESTOFT
LIEUTENANT	HOLDWORTH	HENRY B	09/01/1917	16/05/1917	POSTED TO 1/8/DLI KILLED IN ACTION 10/4/1918	HARROGATE
SECOND LIEUTENANT	HOLMES	ANDREW	19/10/1918	24/10/1918	SERVED 3/AIR MECH 82628 ROYAL FLYING CORPS DIED OF WOUNDS	WHITLEY BAY
CAPTAIN	HONE	PERCY F	16/10/1918	26/10/1918	Lt WELSH REGT, T/Lt COL MIDDLESEX REGT, COMDG 13/DLI WOUNDED	LONDON
SECOND LIEUTENANT	HORSLEY	W	03/12/1914 ?		DID NOT EMBARK WITH OR REJOIN THE BATTALION	
CAPTAIN	HOWARD	ADDERLEY F	25/08/1915 ?	20/03/1999	TO UK FOR DEMOB	LONDON
LIEUTENANT	HOWARD	LANGLEY W	25/10/1918		5/NORTHUMBERLAND FUSILIERS ATT 13/DLI	BARNES
SECOND LIEUTENANT	HUDSPETH	ARTHUR	01/09/1916	20/09/1916	2 Lt 10/N STAFFS, 22/DLI, 16/DLI MISSING IN ACTION	HEATON
LIEUTENANT	HUTLEY	HAROLD E	28/12/1917	30/12/1918	TO UK	
SECOND LIEUTENANT	INCHES	JOHN D	25/10/1917	18/10/1918	2Lt BORDER REGT ATT 13/DLI TO UK SICK	DUNDEE

Rank	Surname	Forename	Date	Notes	Location
SECOND LIEUTENANT	JACKSON	HAROLD K	04/08/1917	08/12/1918 SERVED SGT 12164 DUKE OF WELLINGTON'S REGT TO UK	KEIGHLEY
SECOND LIEUTENANT	JACKSON	CHARLES S	11/09/1918	06/10/1918 ENL HIGH DIV CYC COY SERVED SGT 58062 LIVERPOOL REGIMENT SEVERELY WND	ABERDEEN
SECOND LIEUTENANT	JAMES	WILLIAM A	05/06/1917	28/09/1917 TO UK SICK	
SECOND LIEUTENANT	JOHNSON	RICHARD C	25/08/1915	08/08/1916 TO UK TRF SPECIAL BRIGADE R ENGINEERS KILLED IN ACTION 31/7/1917	DARLINGTON
SECOND LIEUTENANT	JOHNSTON	SAMUEL F	14/04/1917	14/07/1918 SERVED CPL 17/HIGHLAND LI TO UK TRF MACHINE GUN CORPS	RUTHERGLEN
LIEUTENANT	KAYE-BUTTERWORTH	GEORGE S	25/08/1915	05/08/1916 SERVED PTE 6/DUKE OF CORNWALL'S LI 1914 KILLED IN ACTION	HAMPSTEAD
LIEUTENANT	KELLY	JOHN B	15/08/1916	04/10/1918 SERVED AS L/SGT 2023 WEST & CUMB YEO POSTED FROM 13/DLI TO 12/DLI BUT NEVER JOINED THAT BN TO UK SICK	DALSTON CARLISLE
SECOND LIEUTENANT	KERRIDGE	OSWALD A	22/04/1916	09/07/1916 DIED OF WOUNDS	BURY ST EDMUNDS
SECOND LIEUTENANT	KNOTTS	JOHN	28/01/1918	SERVED AS L/CPL 28334 20/DLI	
MAJOR	LINDSAY	MICHAEL E	16/08/1916	12/12/1916 7/DRAGOON GUARDS POSTED TO COMMAND 13/DLI	DAIRSIE FIFE
LIEUTENANT COLONEL	LINDSAY	MICHAEL E	11/07/1917	16/04/1918 POSTED TO COMMAND 23/MACHINE GUN CORPS	
CAPTAIN	LONG	GEORGE M	25/08/1915	12/07/1916 WOUNDED TO LABOUR CORPS 1917 ATT ROYAL FLYING CORPS 1918 FLT LT RAF POSTED TO 1/DLI	1/DLI BRIT ARMY OF THE RHINE
MAJOR	LONGDEN	JAMES M	28/08/1917	06/04/1918 FROM 12/DLI PB OFFICER	CASTLE EDEN
SECOND LIEUTENANT	MANN	CHARLES H	07/09/1916	30/09/1916 KILLED IN ACTION	CASTLE EDEN
SECOND LIEUTENANT	MANNING	REGINALD V	26/11/1918	SERVED PTE 7/1923 290407 7/NORTHUMBERLAND FUSILIERS	NEWCASTLE
LIEUTENANT	MARKHAM	HERBERT R	25/08/1915	13/04/1916 TO BDE STAFF	
LIEUTENANT	MARKHAM	HERBERT R	25/09/1916	08/10/1916 WOUNDED	
LIEUTENANT	MARKHAM	HERBERT R	03/03/1917	07/06/1917 TRF GEN LIST	
MAJOR	MARRIOTT	W	06/10/1914 ?	DID NOT EMBARK WITH OR REJOIN THE BATTALION	
SECOND LIEUTENANT	MARTYR	AUBREY	18/11/1918	20/03/1919 SERVED GS/54964 20/R FUSILIERSTO UK	OXFORD
SECOND LIEUTENANT	McBAY	WILLIAM	16/10/1918	14/02/1919 SERVED TROOPER 1254 NORTHUMBERLAND HUSSARS COMM 6/DLI WND TO 52/DLI	
CAPTAIN	MILES	WILFRED	25/08/1915	19/09/1916 TO UK SICK TO 3RD VB DEVONSHIRE REGT	MAIDA VALE
SECOND LIEUTENANT	MILLER	MOSES	13/01/1917	04/06/1917 2Lt HIGHLAND LI ATT 13/DLI TO UK SICK	GLASGOW
SECOND LIEUTENANT	MINNELL	H H	19/10/1918	14/02/1919 TO 52/DLI	
LIEUTENANT	MITCHELL	RODERICK S	30/08/1916	01/09/1921 SERVED GNR 127981 R FIELD ARTILLERY INTELLIGENCE OFFICER 13/DLI	SUNDERLAND
SECOND LIEUTENANT	MORGAN	JOHN Mc	05/09/1917	SERVED PTE M2/055054 ARMY SERVICE CORPS	LIVERPOOL
LIEUTENANT	MORRIS	R G	03/02/1915 ?	DID NOT EMBARK WITH OR REJOIN THE BATTALION	
SECOND LIEUTENANT	MORRISON	M J	18/11/1918	20/02/1919 TO UK	
SECOND LIEUTENANT	MURGATROYD	THOMAS	19/12/1916	10/06/1917 SERVED PTE 6590 UPS BN 18/R FUSILIERS WOUNDED	
CAPTAIN	NAYLOR	URMSTON S	25/08/1915	25/04/1916 TRF ROYAL IRISH REGT KIA 3/9/1916	BURY LANCS
SECOND LIEUTENANT	OAKES	WILLIAM L	23/06/1916	04/08/1916 SERVED PTE 1124 1/HONOURABLE ARTILLERY COY WOUNDED	WORTHING
CAPTAIN	O'CALLAGHAN	CYRIL T	25/08/1915	28/07/1916 WOUNDED REGULAR COMMISSION YORK LANCASTER REGT	HARTLEPOOL
CAPTAIN	OLDHAM	HUGH	20/11/1915	07/11/1916 R GUERNSEY MILITIA TO UK SICK CHIEF OF POLICE TIENTSIN CHINA	LONDON
SECOND LIEUTENANT	OLIPHANT	THOMAS A	29/05/1917	06/04/1916 TO UK SICK	TIENTSIN
SECOND LIEUTENANT	ORCHARD	GEORGE L	19/09/1916	20/09/1917 SERVED CPL S/16449 CAMERON HIGHLANDERS WOUNDED	AUCKLAND NEW ZEALAND
LIEUTENANT	OWEN	P	20/11/1915	DID NOT EMBARK WITH OR REJOIN THE BATTALION	EDINBURGH
CAPTAIN	PARKER	HUBERT J	20/11/1915	16/09/1916 SERVED PTE 1942 15/LONDON REGT TO HEADQUARTERS (BDE OR DIV??)	HEATON
CAPTAIN	PARKER	HUBERT J	15/08/1915	20/09/1917 WOUNDED	PUTNEY
SECOND LIEUTENANT	PARKER	JOHN E	30/11/1918	14/02/1919 TO UK	ACOMB YORKS
SECOND LIEUTENANT	PARR	EDWARD	03/04/1917	13/05/1917 WOUNDED TO GENERAL LIST	SUNDERLAND
SECOND LIEUTENANT	PRYSE	HERBERT W	09/01/1917	15/01/1917 TRF TO NORTHUMBERLAND FUSILIERS	STANFORD LE HOPE
SECOND LIEUTENANT	PEVERELL	B F	05/02/1915 ?	DID NOT EMBARK WITH OR REJOIN THE BATTALION	
SECOND LIEUTENANT	PULLAN	C E A	19/09/1914 ?	DID NOT EMBARK WITH OR REJOIN THE BATTALION	
SECOND LIEUTENANT	REES	FREDERICK L	20/12/1915 ?	05/08/1946 WOUNDED	LONG EATON NOTTS
SECOND LIEUTENANT	REES	FREDERICK L	21/02/1918	21/02/1918 REJOINS FROM 12/DLI WOUNDED	
CAPTAIN	REID	ALEXANDER W	25/08/1915	05/10/1918 TRF GEN LIST OC No2 MEDICAL BOARD ROUEN	MILFORD ON SEA
LIEUTENANT	REID	A W D	21/10/2014 ?	16/05/1916 DID NOT EMBARK WITH OR REJOIN THE BATTALION	
SECOND LIEUTENANT	ROBINS	CHARLES H	22/04/1916	28/07/1916 WOUNDED	AYLESBURY

Rank	Surname	First Name	Date	Details	Location
SECOND LIEUTENANT	ROBINSON	ROBERT W	08/11/1917	05/10/1918 SERVED NORTHERN CYCLIST BN 473, NORTHUMBERLAND FUS 37701 WOUNDED	CHELMSFORD
LIEUTENANT	ROLLSTON	CECIL H	19/12/1916	06/08/1918 SERVED PTE 9896 1/5/ LONDON REGT TRF GENERAL LIST TO 10/NORFOLK REGT	OXTED SURREY
SECOND LIEUTENANT	RUDLAND	HENRY	21/09/1916	01/10/1916 SERVED SOUTH AFRICAN MEDICAL CORPS GERMAN SW AFRICA 1914/15 TO UK SICK	SUNDERLAND
CAPTAIN	SAINT	THOMAS G	01/12/1915	09/02/1918 WOUNDED TO 52/DLI	
LIEUTENANT	SAUERBECK	CHARLES T	25/08/1915	20/10/1915 WOUNDED	
LIEUTENANT	SAUERBECK	CHARLES T	15/05/1916	28/07/1916 WOUNDED	
LIEUTENANT	SAUERBECK	CHARLES T	26/03/1917	11/09/1917 KILLED IN ACTION	
SECOND LIEUTENANT	SHARPE	STANLEY A	30/08/1916	23/09/1916 TO UK SICK	
SECOND LIEUTENANT	SIBAG MONTEFIORE	ERIC C	25/10/1918	28/02/1919 POSTED TO 2/DLI	LONDON
SECOND LIEUTENANT	SEBORN	ALBERT G	20/08/1917	11/10/1917 SERVED PTE 10530 G HOWARDS, L/CPL 39011 NORTHBD FUSILIERS WOUNDED	NOTTINGHAM
SECOND LIEUTENANT	SHEARDOWN	G D	12/03/1915 ?	TRF TO KRRC MC	
LIEUTENANT	SKELTON	R	05/10/1918	25/10/1918 FROM 5/DLI WOUNDED DECLARED A DESERTER FORFEITS RANK OF CAPT & MEDALS	
SECOND LIEUTENANT	SKETCHLEY	B T	12/03/1915 ?	DID NOT EMBARK WITH OR REJOIN THE BATTALION	
SECOND LIEUTENANT	SMITH	FREDERICK H	19/12/1916	20/04/1917 TRF ROYAL GARRISON ARTILLERY 52 SEIGE BTY KIA 10/12/1917	
SECOND LIEUTENANT	SMITH	FRANK E	22/08/1917	28/10/1917 SERVED ARTISTS RIFLES TO UK TRF ROYAL FIELD ARTILLERY 15/1/1918	WHITLEY BAY & LONDON
SECOND LIEUTENANT	SMITH	PHILIP G	27/02/1918	05/10/1918 WOUNDED 15/6/1918 KILLED IN ACTION 5/10/1918	HEATON
CAPTAIN & QM	SNOW	SAMUEL	25/08/1915	06/06/1918 SERVED NILE CAMPAIGN 1885 LEAVE TO UK TRF ROYAL AIR FORCE	REDCAR
SECOND LIEUTENANT	STUBBS	R H	12/09/1914 ?	DID NOT EMBARK WITH OR REJOIN THE BATTALION	
SECOND LIEUTENANT	SUTCLIFFE	R	23/02/1914 ?	DID NOT EMBARK WITH OR REJOIN THE BATTALION	
LIEUTENANT COLONEL	SOUTHEY	JOHN A	08/11/1918	04/02/1919 FROM OXFORD & BUCKS LI	WARMINSTER
SECOND LIEUTENANT	STEWART	H	09/01/1917	23/01/1917 FROM 1/7DLI POSTED BACK TO 1/7/DLI	NEWCASTLE
SECOND LIEUTENANT	STEWART	FREDERICK C	01/07/1917	10/05/1918 SERVED 2nd CPL R ENGINEERS TO UK SERVED IN IRAQ 1920	HOWDON ON TYNE
SECOND LIEUTENANT	STUBBS	ROBERT H	20/11/1915	02/01/1916 11/DLI TO 13/DLI TRF INDIAN ARMY SERVICE CORPS	
LIEUTENANT	TAIT	JAMES B	25/08/1915	04/02/1916 TRF ROYAL FLYING CORPS CAPTAIN No 2 FLYING SCHOOL	COXHOE COUNTY DURHAM
LIEUTENANT	TARGET	NOEL A	25/11/1915	04/08/1916 KILLED IN ACTION	KNIGHTSBRIDGE
LIEUTENANT	TAYLOR	GEORGE	15/07/1917	05/08/1918 TO UK SHELL SHOCK	HULL
SECOND LIEUTENANT	THOMPSON	NORMAN	23/06/1916	05/08/1916 DIED OF WOUNDS	
SECOND LIEUTENANT	THOMPSON	CECIL H	28/08/1917	07/10/1917 L/CPL 15570 COLDSTREAM GUARDS COMM KING'S LIVERPOOL REGT ATT 13/DLI POSTED TO SUNDERLAND	SUNDERLAND
SECOND LIEUTENANT	THOMPSON	S N	25/10/1918		
MAJOR	TURNER	ROBERT V	09/06/1916	31/07/1916 FROM 2/DLI TO UK SICK TO No 18 OFFICER CADET BN	BATH
LIEUTENANT	TURNER	ALFRED E	12/07/1917	06/10/1918 FROM 10/DLI TO UK SICK TO 3/DLI	SOUTH SHIELDS
SECOND LIEUTENANT	TYSSEN	SAMUEL R	19/12/1915	28/07/1916 12/DLI 16/1/15, 16/DLI 7/15, ATT 68/LTMB TRF ROYAL ENGINEERS	
SECOND LIEUTENANT	WAKEHAM	CHARLES	28/01/1918	03/02/2918 SERVED AS CSM 24258 MC, DCM, MM 10/DLI POSTED TO 12/DLI	BOURNEMOUTH
LIEUTENANT COLONEL	WALKER	CECIL E	25/08/1915	09/03/1916 TO UK SICK	ST MORITZ SWITZERLAND
SECOND LIEUTENANT	WALKER	WILLIAM E	25/10/1918	02/11/1918 SERVED AS PTE 18/900 18/DLI WOUNDED	SUNDERLAND
SECOND LIEUTENANT	WARDLE	W M	30/11/1918	14/02/2019 TO 52/DLI	
SECOND LIEUTENANT	WATERS	ALFRED G	21/10/1918	14/02/2019 SERVED PTE 73588 DLI TO 52/DLI	
SECOND LIEUTENANT	WATSON	WILLIAM B	19/12/1916	19/04/1917 SERVED UPS BN 21/R FUSILIERS TO UK SICK	EAST SHEEN
SECOND LIEUTENANT	WATSON	WILLIAM B	11/09/1917	06/11/1917 TO UK SICK	MANCHESTER
SECOND LIEUTENANT	WATSON	WILLIAM B	01/07/1918	11/11/1918 TO LABOUR CORPS 292 POW COMPANY	
SECOND LIEUTENANT	WHARTON	GEORGE	22/06/1916	10/07/1916 WOUNDED TRF TO MANCHESTER REGT 1918	CHESTERFIELD
SECOND LIEUTENANT	WHEATLEY	HAROLD R	22/06/1916	10/07/1916 ATT 6/DUKE OF CORNWALLS LI MAY 17 WOUNDED	
SECOND LIEUTENANT	WHEATLEY	HAROLD R	16/02/1917	20/09/1917 WOUNDED EMPLOYED MINISTRY OF LABOUR 1918	
MAJOR	WHITE	GEORGE	25/08/1915	01/09/1916 TO UK SICK	
CAPTAIN & QM	WILLIAMS	ARTHUR R	24/07/1918	10/10/1918 Lt R DUBLIN FUSILIERS IN RANKS 14 YEARS 164 DAYS WOUNDED R TANK CORPS 2/10/1922	UNITED SERVICES CLUB DUBLIN 2nd R TANK CORPS FARNBOROUGH
SECOND LIEUTENANT	WILLIAMS	OSWALD J	23/01/1917 `	26/02/1917 POSTED TO 1/5/DLI	
SECOND LIEUTENANT	WILLIE	J W	06/10/1918	14/02/1919 TO 52/DLI	
SECOND LIEUTENANT	WILLIS	NORMAN H	30/09/1917	04/10/1918 SERVEDCPL/12060 2/SEAFORTH HIGHLANDERS WOUNDED	
SECOND LIEUTENANT	WILLOUGHBY	E	25/10/1918	04/02/2019 TRF TO 2/NORTHUMBERLAND FUSILIERS	
SECOND LIEUTENANT	WILSON	JAMES S	25/10/1917	11/08/1918 2Lt BORDER REGT ATT 13/DLI LEAVE TO UK TERRITORIAL FORCE WAR MEDAL	

Rank	Surname	Forename	Date	Details	Place
SECOND LIEUTENANT	WILSON	JOHN L	30/11/1918	20/02/1919 TO UK	SHOTLEY BRIDGE COUNTY DURHAM
LIEUTENANT	WITHERSPOON	JOHN C	19/12/1916	11/10/1917 ENL NOV 1914 CALGARY CQMS 79690 31/CANADIAN INFANTRY BN MISSING	WEST KENSINGTON
CAPTAIN	WOOD	EDWIN A P	25/08/1915	01/06/1916 WOUNDED	BLACKHILL COUNTY DURHAM
SECOND LIEUTENANT	WOOD	GEORGE W	19/12/1916	02/06/1917 SERVED PTE 7170 UPS BN 18/R FUSILIERS WOUNDED	SHEFFIELD
CAPTAIN	WRIGHT	GEOFFREY C	20/08/1917	31/07/1920 SERVED PTE 12/275 SHEFFIELD CITY BN YORK & LANCS REGT DCM 22/9/1916	GLASGOW
CAPTAIN	WYLIE	EDWARD G	11/10/1918	18/10/1918 SERVED ASC PTE M2/113913 ENT F&F 20/9/1915 , 14/DLI ATT 11/LANCASHIRE FUSILIERS TO 13/DLI TRF GENERAL LIST STAFF CAPTAIN 75 BRIGADE HQ	

Nominal Roll of Other Ranks who landed in France 25 August 1915
with the
13th (Service) Battalion Durham Light Infantry
1914–..1918

NUMBER	RANK	NAME	FIRST NAME	REMARKS
17157	PTE	ADAMS	JOHN	ENL WARWICK RES LEAMINGTON WND NIGHT 12/13/2/16 SCALP & SHLDR TO 69/FA - 7/CCS 21/AMB TRN 9/G HOSP - IBD 29/3/16 REJOINS 14/4/16 KIA 19/7/16 B COY
16095	PTE	ADAMSON	ROBERT	TO 3/DLI DIS 392 ENL 8/9/14 DIS 15/9/17
17159	PTE	ADDISON	ROBERT	ENL W HARTLEPOOL 7/9/14 WND AT DUTY 5/6/16 WND & MISSING 4/8/16 D COY
21004	PTE	AGAR	ISAAC	WND 9/7/16 B COY TO LABOUR CORPS LAB C No 263484 DIS 10/3/19
17163	CQMS	AINSWORTH	JOHN WILLIAM	CLASS Z RES WOII
17162	PTE	AIREY	JOHN HENRY	WND 9/7/16 D COY SHELL SHOCK TO 2/DLI, DIS 392
18503	PTE	AIREY	WILLIAM	BORN & ENL GATESHEAD 8/9/14 LCPL 7/10/15 KIA NIGHT 12/13/2/16 A COY
17973	PTE	ALDERSON	GEORGE	CLASS Z RES
16928	PTE	ALDERSON	ROBERT	WND 5/10/16 DEMOBILISED
22313	PTE	ALLAN	JAMES FREDERICK	ENL GATESHEAD 8/9/14 TO 20/CCS 31/8/15 SEPTIC TOE TO 69/FA 4/11/15 TO DUTY 8/11/15 KIA AT CHARDS FARM FETCHING WATER 3/12/15 D COY
17782	PTE	ALLEN	JOSEPH	ATT 68/LTMB, CLASS Z RES
17166	PTE	ALLEN	JOSEPH WILLIAM	ENL MIDDLESBROUGH 2/9/14 KIA 20/3/16
16474	SGT	ALLISTON	JAMES	REDUCED TO PTE BY FGCM 22/11/16 B COY TO 3/DLI DIS 392 ENL 9/9/14 DIS 22/4/18
16432	PTE	ALLISTON	WILLIAM	ENL FERRYHILL 9/9/14 REJOINS EX HOSP 9/10/15 3 DAYS FP No 2 5/5/16 KIA 10/7/16
21160	LCPL	ANDERSON	JOHN	ENL CONSETT 27/10/14 LCPL 2/7/16 REVERTS 14/8/17 GSW HAND 8/17 TO DEPOT 27/9/17 CMD DEPOT RIPON 6/11/17 TRF TO MILIATRY FOOT POLICE ALDERSHOT 27/5/18 TO ARMY RES CLASS P 23/9/18 FOR EMPLOYMENT AQT CONSETT IRON WORKS MM
24803	SGT	ANDERSON	JOHN	ENL W HARTLEPOOL RES WINGATE KIA 5/10/18 DCM MM
14943	SGT	ANDERSON	WILLIAM HENRY	ENL W HARTLEPOOL 5/9/14 RES WINGATE LCPL 14/10/16 CPL 26/5/17 SGT 18/6/17 KIA
14945	PTE	ANGEL	JOHN WILLIAM	ENL W HARTLEPOOL 3/9/14 WND 19/7/16 B COY TO 12/G HOSP - UK TO DEPOT 24/7/16 3/DLI 14/10/16 ATT 1/TRG RES BN TO 2/DLI 11/11/16 3/DLI 12/1/17 TO BASE 15/5/17 18/DLI REPOSTED 14/DLI 2/6/15 TO 11/DLI 6/2/18 MISSING 24/3/18
17171	PTE	ANGEL	ROBERT	WND 14/2/16 B COY TO LABOUR CORPS LAB C No 602731 CLASS Z RES 2/4/19
13848	PTE	APPLEBY	GEORGE HENRY	TO LABOUR CORPS LAB C No 387569 TO CLASS Z RES 4/3/19
13636	PTE	APPLETON	WILLIAM FRANK	TO ARMY RES CLASS W DIS 392 5/9/14 DIS 17/12/17
17643	PTE	ARCHER	ROBERT	WND 28/12/15 D COY WND 19/9/16 B COY TO WEST RIDING REGT DWR No 24381 TO CLASS Z RES 25/2/19
18005	PTE	ARCHER	SIDNEY	CLASS Z RES
18095	CPL	ARKLESS	GEORGE EDWARD	ENL GATESHEAD 5/9/14 LCPL 20/1/15 CPL 2/7/15 L/SGT 28/6/16 KIA 16/7/16 SGT B COY
16929	PTE	ARMITAGE	FRANK ARTHUR	CLASS Z RES LCPL
13616	PTE	ARMSTRONG	CHARLES GEORGE	WND 8/7/16 WND 27/7/16 LCPL A COY to 3/DLI DIS 392 ENL 4/9/14 DIS 18/10/17 MM
21607	PTE	ARMSTRONG	DAVID	WND 4/8/16 D COY TO 19/DLI, 20/DLI, 19/DLI, 13/DLI, 18/DLI, 13/DLI, CLASS Z RES
21254	PTE	ARMSTRONG	GEORGE	ENL CONSETT 2/11/14 TO 70/FA ICT R FOOT 16/5/16 TO 69/FA ICT L FOOT 2/9/16 EVAC BASE ETAPLES TO DUTY 29/9/16 KIA 10/10/18
24795	CPL	ARMSTRONG	GEORGE NORMAN	TO 20/DLI CLASS Z RES MM
21058	PTE	ARMSTRONG	JAMES	CLASS Z RES
24794	PTE	ARMSTRONG	THOMAS	CLASS Z RES LSGT MM & BAR
19012	CPL	ARNOTT	ROBERT BELL	ENL FELLING 7/9/14 LCPL 26/3/15 CPL 9/6/16 KIA 15/6/18
15223	SGT	ARRIS	WILLIAM JOHN	FROM 12/DLI PRIOR TO EMBARKATION COMMISSIONED 13/DLI 25/4/17 MC 19/11/17
21256	PTE	ASKEW	JOSEPH	12/5/17 MM SGT TO WEST YORKSHIRE REGT W YORKS No 5/107746 POS TRG RES BN
17927	PTE	ATESS	FREDERICK WILLIAM	WND 28/5/17 D COY CLASS Z RES
21168	PTE	ATKINSON	CUTHBERT CHARLES	ENL 27/10/14 GATESHEAD 16/10/15 SCABIES TO 69/FA INFLUENZA 22/2/18 1/CAN CCS - 6/BRIT RED CROSS HOSP - HOSP SHIP DIEPPE TO DEPOT 10/3/16 17/DLI 22/4/16 TO 13/DLI 1/6/16 WND 8/7/16 TO 6/GEN HOSP - KING GEORGE'S HOSP LONDON DOW 14/7/16 A COY
21042	PTE	ATKINSON	GARDNER	ENL 26/10/14 GATESHEAD TO 70/FA 4/7/16 TO DUTY 13/7/16 TO 102/FA GSW FOOT 18/7/16 TO UNIT 24/8/16 KIA 7/10/16 C COY
24754	SGT	ATKINSON	JOHN	DIS 392
20914	PTE	ATKINSON	RALPH	WND 17/7/16 D COY TO 18/DLI, ATT 257 TUNN COY RE, ATT 13 CORPS TUNN COY, CLASS Z
21015	SGT	ATKINSON	RICHARD	WND 28/7/16 D COY ADM 3 CCS EVAC 29/7/16 No 20 AMB TRAIN TO 12/DLI, 20/DLI, ATT 238 EMP COY, 12/DLI, CLASS Z RES MM
21627	PTE	ATKINSON	WILLIAM	ENL 3/9/14 NEWCASTLE BATMAN TO LT OLIPHANT KIA 21/3/16
13264	PTE	BAGE	JOHN ROBERT	WND 11/12/15 D COY TO EAST YORKSHIRE REGT EY No 34503 DIS 392
18188	PTE	BAGGETT	JAMES REUBEN	CLASS Z RES
13311	PTE	BAINBRIDGE	THOMAS	TO MACHINE GUN CORPS MGC No 72666 CLASS Z RES 28/1/19
17211	PTE	BALL	WALTER REAY M	ENL W HARTLEPOOL KIA 9/7/16
21066	PTE	BANKS	TOM	ENL NEWCASTLE 27/10/14 KIA 8/10/18
16946	PTE	BARKER	CHARLES	ENL DURHAM 14/9/14 TO 70/FA 17/5/16 INFLUENZA TO 71/FA 18/5/16 TO DUTY KIA 7/10/16 C COY MM
22312	PTE	BARKER	THOMAS ROBSON	ACCIDENTALLY WND AT BDE MG SCHOOL 12/11/15 B COY DIS 392 ENL 31/8/14 DIS 27/8/17
13640	LCPL	BARNARD	GEORGE T T	WND SHELLSHOCK 12/4/16 TO NORTHUMBERLAND FUS NF No 6779 TO ROYAL ENGINEERS RE No WR/278772 RENUMBERED 343342
23619	LCPL	BARNETT	WILLIAM J	DIS 392 ENL 13/2/15 DIS 7/8/15
18135	SGT	BARRON	THOMAS WILLIAM	DIS 392 ENL 5/9/14 DIS 13/6/19
19112	PTE	BARTON	GEORGE MARK	ENL FELLING 7/9/14 20/11/15 2 DAYS FP No 2 WHEN ON SENTRY DUTY UNARMED, 6/4/16 TO 70/FA LARYNGITIS TO DUTY 17/4/16 KIA 5/8/16 B COY
21302	PTE	BARWISE	JOHN	WND 18/7/16 D COY TO 22/DLI ALSGT
21061	PTE	BATES	JOSEPH	TO 3/DLI DIS 392 ENL 26/10/14 DIS 27/9/18
23638	CPL	BATEY	JOHN STANLEY	CLASS Z RES
19014	PTE	BAXTER	WILLIAM	WND SELF INFLICTED 8/10/15 A COY TO DEPOT DIS 392 ENL 3/9/14 DIS 24/6/16
16532	PTE	BELL	CHARLES	DISMBODIED
15889	PTE	BELL	FRANCIS EDGELL	ENL DURHAM 8/9/14 RES LANCHESTER KIA 25/9/16 D COY
24828	PTE	BELL	GEORGE	DIS 392
13271	PTE	BELL	HARRY	ATT GHQ TO 12/DLI, CLASS Z RES
23590	PTE	BELL	JOHN WILLIAM	WND 4/8/16 B COY TO LABOUR CORPS LAB C No 441060 CLASS Z RES 27/2/19
16507	PTE	BELL	ROBERT	ATT 23/DIV TUNN COY, ATT 182 COY RE, TO 13/DLI, DISEMBODIED
24825	PTE	BELL	ROBERT	ATT 181 TUNN COY RE 13/DLI CLASS Z RES DCM
13198	PTE	BELL	WILLIAM	WND NIGHT 12/13/2/16 B COY TO 12/DLI, CLASS Z RES
19413	PTE	BELL	WILLIAM	DIS 392 FROM 13/DLI ENL 14/9/14 DIS 24/12/18
15384	SGT	BELLERBY	THOMAS	DIS 392 FROM 13/DLI ENL 5/9/14 DIS 1/4/19 MM & BAR
21169	LCPL	BENNETT	CHRISTOPHER	TO ROYAL DEFENCE CORPS RDC No 66179 IN FRANCE 25/8/15 TO 13/10/16

Number	Rank	Surname	Forename	Details
11228	PTE	BERRY	HENRY GLEW	WND 8/7/16 D COY TO ROYAL DEFENCE CORPS RDC No 65421 IN FRANCE 25/8/15 TO 10/7/16
3/11227	CPL	BERRY	ROBERT H	TO 18/DLI 2/DLI ATT 6 DIV COY, 13/DLI, SPEC RES
16954	PTE	BEWS	GEORGE	WND 10/7/16 C COY AT DUTY CLASS Z RES MM
18478	PTE	BLACK	WILLIAM NORMAN	CLASS Z RES
14855	PTE	BLACKLOCK	ROBERT WILLIAM	WND 4/8/16 B COY TO 20/DLI, 13/DLI DIS 392 ENL 01/09/14 DIS 26/2/19.
19412	PTE	BLAND	THOMAS	CLASS Z RES
17748	PTE	BLATCHFORD	FRED	CLASS Z RES
18185	PTE	BLEMINGS	ROBERT	WND 9/7/16 A COY DIS 392
17190	SGT	BOAGEY	ROBERT	CLASS Z RES MM
19190	SGT	BOAGEY	ROBERT	WND 17/7/16 C COY CLASS Z RES MM
19195	PTE	BOLGER	JAMES	STILL SERVING 1920
17198	PTE	BOND	CHARLES HENRY	STILL SERVING 1920
25476	PTE	BOWERBANK	JONATHAN W	WND 10/7/16 B COY TO 3/DLI DIS 392 ENL 1/9/14 DIS 14/8/17
24772	CPL	BOWMAN	JOSEPH	ENL DURHAM DOW 5/11/17 MM
21046	LCPL	BOWMAN	THOMAS YOUNG	ENL GATESHEAD 26/10/14 to 70/FA 4/5/16 ABCESS THIGH TO DUTY 9/5/16 LCPL 28/6/17 KIA 5/10/18 MM
21613	PTE	BOWRON	ANTHONY	WND 31/10/15 C COY TO LABOUR CORPS LAB C No 613446 CPL DIS 10/3/19
17194	LCPL	BOWRON	WILLIAM AMBROSE	WND SH SHOCK 3/6/16 WND 2/8/16 C COY SGT CLASS Z RES MM
17197	PTE	BOYD	ALEXANDER	ENL W HARTLEPOOL WND 10/7/16 B COY TO 14/DLI DOW 9/9/16
21185	PTE	BRADLEY	JAMES OLIVER	WND NIGHT 12/13/2/16 B COY TO ARMY RES CLASS P DIS 392 ENL 28/10/14 DIS 23/2/17
22431	LCPL	BRANKSTON	ALEXANDER	ENL CONSETT 8/12/14 WND SHELL SHOCK 4/8/16 C COY TO 70/FA - 23/DRS TO DUTY 9/8/16 TO BASE UNDER AGE TO Z CAMP ETAPLES TO 35/IBD 12/11/16 REJOINS 6/1/17 LCPL 5/5/18 KIA 11/10/18
15340	PTE	BRANKSTON	HENDERSON	ENL 3/9/14 DURHAM RES LANCHESTER TRIED BY FGCM 5/3/16 3MNTH FP No 1 REMITTED 6/5/16 WND 25/5/16 HELMET SAVED HIS LIFE WND 3/6/16 C COY TO 16/DLI18/7/16 1/TRG RES BN 1/9/16 3/DLI 2/12/16 13/DLI 17/1/17 MM 13/5/17 KIA 18/10/17
21610	PTE	BRANKSTON	WILLIAM	WND 7/10/16 LCPL C COY TO 18/DLI, 2/DLI, 13/DLI, 19/DLI, CLASS Z RES MM
23647	PTE	BRASS	EDMUND	ACC SHOT ON PATROL BY Lt HOWARD SERVED A COY DOW 10/10/15
18086	PTE	BRENNAN	JOHN	WND 6/1/16 D COY TO LABOUR CORPS LAB C No 9916 TO CLASS Z RES 2/2/19
23659	PTE	BRETT	JAMES WILLIAM	WND 7/10/15 A COY ENL DARLINGTON RES RICHMOND DOW 8/10/15
17749	PTE	BRIGGS	THOMAS	DIS 392 ENL 5/9/14 DIS 17/4/19
21305	PTE	BRIGHT	JOSEPH	DIS 392 ENL 3/11/14 DIS 17/4/19
21158	SGT	BRITTLE	JOHN WILLIAM	CLASS Z RES
16211	SGT	BRODRICK	STEPHEN	CLASS Z RES
24771	PTE	BROOKS	JAMES	CLASS Z RES
17750	SGT	BROUGH	MICHAEL	TO 11/DLI, 13/DLI, DIS 392 ENL 5/9/14 DIS 5/2/19 DCM, MM BAR
17221	PTE	BROWN	CHARLES ALLEN	WND 11/7/16 A COY ALIAS C SPINK TO LABOUR CORPS LAB C No 21020 CPL CLASS Z RES
16300	PTE	BROWN	GEORGE	ENL GATESHEAD WND BY RIFLE GRENADE 9/10/15 DOW
21045	PTE	BROWN	JOHN E	ENL 26/10/14 WND 10/7/16 B COY DIS 392 14/8/17 JAMES E ON SWB LIST
17187	PTE	BROWN	MICHAEL	ENL HARTLEPOOL 5/9/14 TO 70/FA 21/1/16 GSW FACE & SIDE FRAC JAW TO CCS BAILLEUL · 13/G HOSP DOW 28/1/16
18087	PTE	BROWN	W	WND 9/7/16 AT DUTY WND 28/7/16 D COY TO OXFORD & BUCKINGHAMSHIRE LI OBLI No 45423 CLASS Z RES 20/2/19
23648	PTE	BROWN	WALTER	WND 9/7/16 D COY TO LABOUR CORPS LAB C No 450854 DIS 3/3/19
18396	CSM	BROWN	WATSON WEAVER	ENL NEWCASTLE 9/9/14 RES HAMSTERLEY COLLIERY SGT 6/10/14 CSM 22/10/14 WND ACC SELF INFLICTED 6/8/16 B COY FGCM NOT GUILTY WND 7/10/16 TO 19/DLI 17/1/17 REPOSTED 13/DLI REJOINED 22/1/17 TO HOSP SHIP 16/3/17 DOW 23/9/17
19175	PTE	BROWN	WILLIAM	ENL FELLING TO 20/DLI KIA 31/01/17
20541	PTE	BROWN	HARRY	ENL W HARTLEPOOL 7/9/14 RES WILLINGTON GSW L ARM R HIP 8/8/16 TO 3/DLI, TO 2 TRG RES BN 6/10/16 3/DLI 29/11/16 TO 12/DLI, ATT 12/FLD COY R ENGINEERS 13/5/17, KIA 25/6/17
18150	PTE	BROWN	NICHOLAS	TO 14/DLI, 2/DLI, CLASS Z RES MM
13835	PTE	BROWN	PETER	WND 26/7/16 TO LABOUR CORPS LAB C No 569105 DIS 6/3/19
21029	PTE	BRUCE	THOMAS	ENL 26/10/14 RES PELAW KIA 30/5/17
17189	PTE	BRYAN	ROBERT	ENL W HARTLEPOOL 1/9/14 KIA 19/9/16 B COY
17220	CPL	BUCKLE	ALBERT EDWARD	ENL DARLINGTON 4/9/14 LCPL 6/10/14 CPL 30/1/15 TO 62/FA 10/9/15 GSW BUTTOCKS - 7/CCS MERVILLE DOW 11/9/15
16480	PTE	BURNS	DAVID	ENL 10/09/14 DIS 28/01/18 TO DEPOT DLI, DIS 392
3/11299	PTE	BURNS	FRANCIS	ENL GATESHEAD 2/9/14 SGT 6/10/14 TRIED BY FGCM 22/2/16 DISOBEYING DIRECT ORDER, DRUNKENESS RED PTE 2/3/16 WND 21/5/16 TO 6/CCS GSW BACK - 17/AMB TRN 3/CONV DEPOT 10/6/16 35/IBD 22/6/16 REJOINS BN 1/7/16 KIA 28/7/16 D COY.
17217	PTE	BUTCHER	WILLIAM	DIS 392 ENL 31/8/14 DIS 20/2/19
19442	PTE	BYFORD	SAMUEL JOHN	ENL WARWICK 7/9/14 TO 15/CCS 7/9/15 TO DUTY 9/9/15 TO 2/LONDON CCS 20/9/15 - 1/CAN CCS - 2 AMB TRN - 2/G HOSP 28/9/15 TO DUTY 22/10/15 KIA AT BREWERY POST 3/1/16 B COY
16970	SGT	CAIN	WILLIAM	CLASS Z RES
24770	PTE	CAINE	EDWARD	TO 20/DLI 19/DLI 20/DLI 15/DLI CLASS Z RES DESERTED
21062	CPL	CAIRNS	HENRY	ENL 26/10/14 WND 28/7/16 LSGT C COY TO DEPOT DIS 392 1/8/17 AGE 25
23628	PTE	CAIRNS	JAMES HENRY	ENL NEWCASTLE 18/2/15 WND & MISSING 10/7/16 B COY
15943	LCPL	CALEY	JOHN T	ENL 8/9/14 LCPL TO DEPOT DIS 392 8/11/17
18486	PTE	CALLCUTT	GEORGE	DIS 392
17277	PTE	CALVERT	ERNEST	CLASS Z RES
13245	SGT	CALVERT	WILLIAM	ENL HULL KIA 18/7/16 B COY
21621	LCPL	CAMERON	CHARLES	ENL GATESHEAD WND 10/7/16 A COY CPL TO 20/DLI, KIA 6/6/17
15963	PTE	CAMPBELL	ALEXANDER	ENL DURHAM 8/9/14 18/4/18 TRIED BY FGCM DRUNKENESS 56 DAYS F P No 1 KILLED ACCIDENTALLY 18/08/18
23595	PTE	CAMPBELL	HENRY	WND 19/9/16 B COY TO DEPOT DIS 392 ENL 11/2/15 DIS 19/4/18
21243	SGT	CAMPION	ROBERT HENRY	WND 9/7/16 LSGT A COY TO 20/DLI, CLASS Z RES
17816	PTE	CANT	THOMAS HENRY	CLASS Z RES
17250	PTE	CAREY	WILLIAM HENRY	ENL W HARTLEPOOL 4/9/14 WND 4/8/16 D COY GSW ARM & THIGH TO UK 9/8/16 HOSP ST ALBANS TO DEPOT 10/8/16 TO 3/DLI 31/10/16 TO 20/DLI 13/1/17 WND 7/6/17 GSW L SHLDR TO 140/FA - 3 CAN CCS 35 IBD 18/6/17 TO 13/DLI 22/7/17 MISSING 24/10/18
24753	SGT	CARLING	JOHN EDWIN	WND 4/8/16 D COY TO 3/DLI DIS 392 ENL 5/9/14 DIS 7/12/18
15326	PTE	CARR	JOHN	ENL GATESHEAD 2/9/14 STOPPAGE OF PAY LOSING STEEL HELMET 20/5/16 KIA 9/7/16 B COY
19467	PTE	CARR	JOHN	CLASS Z RES

21259 PTE	CARR	JOSEPH	TO LABOUR CORPS LAB C No 396921 DIS 14/3/19
16964 PTE	CARR	SAMUEL	CLASS Z RES
21013 PTE	CARRICK	JOHN	TO LABOUR CORPS LAB C No 418214 DIS 14/3/19
19047 PTE	CARSON	HENRY	ENL FELLING 7/9/14 KIA 6/11/16 A COY
21258 PTE	CARTER	RENNISON	ENL 3/11/14, DIS 392 23/4/19 TO ARMY RES CLASS P
21635 SGT	CASTLING	JOHN WILLIAM	TO 3/DLI DIS 392 ENL 29/3/15 DIS 19/10/17
17751 PTE	CAVENEY	JOHN	CLASS Z RES
13312 CPL	CAWTHORN	MARK	ENL NEWCASTLE KIA 6/12/15 BY BRITISH SHELLS
17251 PTE	CHAPMAN	EDWARD	DIS 392 ENL 4/9/14 DIS 10/2/19
13328 PTE	CHAPMAN	WILLIAM	ENL NEWCASTLE WND NIGHT 12/13/2/16 A COY DOW 4/3/16
24790 PTE	CHARLTON	JOHN	ENL SOUTH ASHFORD KIA 20/9/17
21057 PTE	CHESTERFIELD HOWLAND BURDON		CLASS Z RES
16978 PTE	CHICKEN	STANLEY	ENLHOUGHTON LE SPRING 14/9/14 WND 28/1/16 GSW LEG TO 70/FA - 2/CCS - AMB TRN - 20/G HOSP TO 23/IBD REJOINS 14/4/16 WND 28/1/16 WND 18/7/16 GSW FINGER TO 102/FA WND 7/10/16 AT DUTY KIA 20/10/17 C COY
17268 PTE	CHILESTONE	ALBERT ERNEST	ENL WARWICK 1/9/14 TO WEST RIDING CCS 22/4/16 - 25/AMB TRN - 2/CAN G HOSP - BASE DEPOT 4/6/16 REJOINED BN 4/6/16 KIA 2/8/16 D COY
23455 PTE	CHRISP	JAMES ARTHUR	WND 30/9/16 ACPL C COY DIS 392
18192 PTE	CLAIR	WILLIAM	A COY TO 12/DLI CLASS Z RES MM
21122 PTE	CLARK	ANDREW	CLASS Z RES
17240 PTE	CLARK	EDWARD	DIS 392
22000 PTE	CLARK	FREDERICK	ENLISTED SUNDERLAND WND 4/8/16 C COY TO 14/DLI, 19/DLI, 13/DLI,
24745 PTE	CLARK	JOHN	ENL ASHFORD RES GATESHEAD DESERTED 24/2/16 TO 16/NORTHBD FUS 1/7/NORTHBD FUS KIA 26/3/18
16066 PTE	CLARK	JOHN HENRY	WND SHELL SHOCK 4/8/16 C COY CLASS Z RES
20959 PTE	CLARK	JOSEPH	WND SELF INFLICTED 16/7/16 D COY CLASS Z RES MM
17236 PTE	CLARK	THOMAS	WND 9/7/16 D COY SHELL SHOCK DIS 392 ENL 2/9/14 DIS 17/1/19
16448 PTE	CLARK	W	TO TANK CORPS TC No 77182 CPL
24824 PTE	CLARKE	JAMES	DIS 392 ENL 7/9/14 DIS 28/4/19
18980 PTE	CLARKE	JAMES	ENL CONSETT FROM CATCHGATE 2/9/14 DCM 42 DAYS DETENTION STRIKING A SUPERIOR OFFICER 15/1/15 KIA 19/1/16
18357 PTE	CLIFFORD	HUGH RICE	ENL STANLEY KIA 21/10/17
21048 PTE	CLOUGH	THOMAS ANTHONY	ENLISTED GATESHEAD DOW 21/08/18
18071 PTE	COLLINGWOOD WILLIAM		TO 19/DLI, 12/DLI, CLASS Z RES
24827 PTE	COLLINS	MICHAEL	WND SHELL SHOCK 4/8/16 B COY TO LABOUR CORPS LAB C No 384859 CLASS Z RES 27/2/19
16478 PTE	COLLINSON	THOMAS	WND 27/12/15 D COY COY MG SECTION GSW L HAND ADM 69 F AMD TRF 3 CCS EVAC 27/12/15 No 16 AMB TRAIN TO MACHINE GUN CORPS MGC No 13122 CLASS Z RES 2/3/19
19174 PTE	CONWAY	EDWARD	WND 24/9/15 C COY CLASS Z RES
24787 PTE	COOK	WILLIAM	ENL SOUTH ASHFORD ATT 176 TUNN COY RE 10/DLI 11/DLI DIED 25/07/18
16963 PTE	COOPER	JAMES	TO 20/DLI, 13/DLI, CLASS Z RES
17253 PTE	COVERDALE	ROBERT	ENL WEST HARTLEPOL 2/9/14 WND 6/10/18
16101 SGT	COWELL	RALPH	WND 9/7/16 D COY AT DUTY TO 20/DLI, 13/DLI, DCM, CLASS Z RES
21171 PTE	COX	CHARLES	STILL SERVING 1920
16194 SGT	CRADDOCK	HARRY	ENL DURHAM 7/9/14 LCPL 28/6/16 CPL 13/7/16 SGT 27/8/16 TO 69/FA - 1/NORTHBN CCS ICT FOOT 20/9/16 TO DUTY 2/10/16 KIA 20/9/17 DCM MM
17239 PTE	CRAGGS	ANDREW	CLASS Z RES LCPL
24746 PTE	CRAGGS	HENRY	WND 4/8/16 C COY DIS 392 ENL 10/11/14 DIS 28/4/19
19021 PTE	CRAGGS	JOSEPH KIRTLEY	DIS 392 ENL 5/9/14 DIS 28/4/19
17747 PTE	CRAGGS	ROBERT	ENL STANLEY 3/9/14 TO 70/FA - W RID CCS GASTRITIS 7/5/16 TO DUTY 8/5/16 WND 4/8/16 A COY GSW CHEST TO 104/FA - 70/FA - 23/DRS TO DUTY 9/8/16 KIA 20/9/17
17286 PTE	CRAGGS	HAROLD	WND 5/12/16 AT DUTY D COY DIS 392
17671 PTE	CRILLEY	JAMES	WND 28/7/16 B COY TO LABOUR CORPS LAB C No 205006 DIS 15/2/19
21012 CPL	CROSSON	NORMAN	WND 28/12/15 A COY AT DUTY CLASS Z RES
17745 PTE	CROZIER	JOHN	WND 14/4/16 A COY TO 1/TRG RES BN T RES No TR/5/99715 DIS 392 ENL 5/9/14 DIS 22/11/19
17797 PTE	CULLEN	PATRICK	WND 22/1/16 WND 4/8/16 D COY TO ARMY RES CLASS W DIS 392 ENL 8/9/14 DIS 5/1/18
16979 PTE	CURRAN	JOHN	WND 19/3/16 WND 4/8/16 C COY DESERTED STILL AWOL 11/12/21
23458 PTE	DALE	THOMAS GEORGE	ENL BIRMINGHAM7/12/14 IN 10/NF NF No 10/16241 TRIED & CONVICTED BY DCM FALSE ANSWER ON ATTESTATION TRF 13/DLI 24/8/15 KIA 8/7/16 C COY
21052 PTE	DALEY	HUGH	WND 20/3/16 B COY TO 1/TRAINING RES BN TR No TR/5/1034 DIS 392
24755 PTE	DALEY	WILLIAM	WND 9/7/16 A COY SHELL SHOCK DIS 392
16144 PTE	DALKIN	FENWICK	ENL DURHAM 8/9/14 TO 23/DRS 6/2/16 NEURASTHENIA WND 2/8/16 B COY TO 2/FA - 2/1/STH MID CCS - 3CCS DOW 7/8/16
24344 PTE	DANBY	WILLIAM	TO DEPOT DIS 392 ENL 6/2/15 DIS 30/3/17
17287 PTE	DANIEL	JOHN BOYES	ENL THIRSK 8/9/14 WND 8/7/16 A COY GSW BACK HOSP SHIP ST DAVID TO UK 19/7/16 TO 3/DLI 24/10/16 26/DLI 28/2/17 3/DLI 16/2/18 20/DLI 28/3/18 REPOSTED TO 2/DLI 31/3/18 KIA
13252 PTE	DAVEY	JOHN	WND 5/8/16 A COY TO DEPOT DIS 392 ENL 6/9/14 DIS 9/8/17
13617 LCPL	DAVID	YOUNG	WND 14/2/16 A COY DIS 392
18081 PTE	DAVIDSON	MATTHEW	WND 9/7/16 C COY SHELL SHOCK TO NORTHUMBERLAND FUSILIERS NF No 202204 CLASS
13843 PTE	DAVIES	THOMAS MORGAN	DIS 392
3/11444 PTE	DAVIES	WILLIAM H	WND 4/8/16 D COY TO NORTHUMBERLAND FUSILIERS NF No 36578 CLASS Z RES 21/2/19
16046 PTE	DAVISON	JOSEPH WILLIAM	ENL 08/09/14 DURHAM, RES WILLINGTON ADM BASE HOSP ETAPLES 27/10/15 HERNIA TO DEPOT POSTED 16/DLI 10/1/16 TO 11/DLI 20/01/16 KIA 5/10/16
21027 PTE	DEAN	JOHN OLIVER	CLASS Z RES MM
13606 PTE	DEVLIN	EDWARD	CLASS Z RES
13607 PTE	DEVLIN	HENRY	WND 28/7/16 A COY AT DUTY CLASS Z RES
17805 PTE	DEWING	ARTHUR RICHARD	WND 8/10/16 A COY DIS 392 ENL 8/9/14 DIS 1/5/18
13639 PTE	DIAMOND	PATRICK	DIS 392
16476 PTE	DIAMOND	THOMAS	TO LABOUR CORPS LAB C No 444789 DIS 17/2/19
15928 PTE	DICKENSON	MARK	CLASS Z RES
21311 PTE	DIMMICK	JOSEPH	DIS 392
18353 SGT	DITCHBURN	ISAAC	ATT 23/DIV GAS SCHOOL, CLASS Z RES
19526 CPL	DIX	ALFRED	CLASS Z RES
18500 PTE	DIXON	JAMES	WND 5/8/16 A COY TO LABOUR CORPS LAB C No 442527 CLASS Z RES 1/2/19
21175 PTE	DIXON	ROBERT JAMES	WND 8/2/16 B COY TO 15/DLI, 3/DLI DIS 392 ENL 27/10/14 DIS 14/8/17

13809 PTE	DIXON	ROBERT WILLIAM	CLASS Z RES
18132 SGT	DIXON	WILLIAM K	CLASS Z RES
22386 PTE	DODDS	GEORGE T	WND 2/8/16 B COY TO ARMY ORDNANCE CORPS AOC No O38363
17905 PTE	DODDS	JOHN THOMPSON	ENL 5/9/14 WND 17/7/16 D COY TO NORTHUMBERLAND FUS NF No 40376 DIS 392 5/12/17 AGE 28 MM
17921 PTE	DODDS	WILLIAM	CLASS Z RES
17313 PTE	DODSWORTH	CHARLES	WND 8/10/16 B COY TO LABOUR CORPS LAB C No 219263 DIS 4/3/19
13278 CPL	DONAGHY	OWEN	WND 4/8/16 D COY TO 10/DLI, 22/DLI, 15/DLI, 19/DLI, CLASS Z RES CPL
16691 PTE	DONKEN	JOHN C	CLASS Z RES
17308 PTE	DONKIN	JOHN GEORGE	ENL W HARTLEPOOL 2/9/14 LCPL 6/10/14 REDUCED PTE 21/2/15 WND 28/12/15 B COY TO 69/FA BULLET WND R ARM - 2CCS - 6/G HOSP - H SHIP ST DAVID TO DEPOT 11/1/16 16/DLI 17/2/16 TO 15/DLI 7/4/16 KIA 17/7/16
15330 CPL	DONNISON	ROBERT W	WND 24/5/16 REDUCED TO PTE BY FGCM TO 16/NORTHUMBERLAND FUS NF No 40377 KIA
19119 CPL	DOUGLAS	THOMAS EDWARD	WND 4/8/16 D COY DIS 392
11379 CSM	DOW	FREDERICK	TO LABOUR CORPS LAB C No 628915 CPL CLASS Z RES 18/2/19
23587 PTE	DOWD	G	WND 7/1/16 A COY TO TANK CORPS TC No 91917
24786 PTE	DOWSON	WILLIAM	DIS 392 ENL 8/9/14 DIS 31/10/16
23472 PTE	DRINKHALL	WALTER	WND 28/1/16 D COY TO 53/DLI RENUMBERED TR/5/170240 CLASS Z RES
17316 PTE	DUCK	WILLIAM	CLASS Z RES
18061 PTE	DUNCAN	THOMAS WILLIAM	BORN B AUCKLAND ENL GATESHEAD 5/9/14 LCPL 4/12/14 DCM 6 MNTHS DETENTION 21/3/15 STEALING RE JOINED BN 5/7/15 REMISSION OF SENTENCE WND 1/8/16 B COY DOW
23674 PTE	DUNN	JOHN ALBERT	WND 10/7/16 D COY TO 18/DLI CLASS Z RES
15906 PTE	DUNN	THOMAS	ENL DURHAM 5/9/14 KIA 21/10/17
18354 LCPL	DUNNHILL	ALBERT	CLASS Z RES
17317 PTE	DYER	JOHN	CLASS Z RES MM
23468 PTE	EADINGTON	JOHN	TO 3/DLI DIS 392 ENL 31/8/14 DIS 15/5/18
17788 CPL	EALES	FRANK	WND 2/8/16 A COY COMMISSIONED 29/1/18 12/RIFLE BRIGADE FROM CONSETT
18066 CPL	EDDY	NORMAN WILKINSON	STILL SERVING 1920
18136 SGT	EDGAR	JOHN WILLIAM	CLASS Z RES
17801 PTE	EDMINSON	STEPHEN	ENL GATESHEAD 8/9/14 TO 102/FA 17/7/16 PUO TO DUTY 1/NORTHBN FA 4/10/16 CONT L HIP TO DUTY 14/11/16 71/FA 18/3/17 VOMITING TO DUTY 6?/FA SHELL WND SHOULDER 21/9/17 -17/CCS DOW 23/9/17
21615 PTE	EDMUNDS	EDWIN	WND 10/7/16 C COY TO MACHINE GUN CORPS MGC No 25321 CLASS Z RES
17893 PTE	EDWARDS	WILLIAM	TO 29/LONDON REGT LONDON No 98067 DIS 392
10157 SGT	ELGEY	WILLIAM	WND 17/9/16 SELF INFLICTED B COY CLASS Z RES
3/10157 SGT	ELGY	WILLIAM	CLASS Z RES
21626 PTE	ELLIOTT	JOSEPH	ATT 27 SAN SEC 13, DLI, ATT 35/IBD, 13/DLI, ATT REINFOR CAMP, 13/DLI, ATT GHQ REINFOR CAMP CLASS Z RES
18983 PTE	ELWOOD	THOMAS	CLASS Z RES
19535 PTE	ELWOOD	THOMAS	ATT 23/DIV TUNN COY, ATT 260 TUNN COY RE, 13/DLI, CLASS Z RES
11221 PTE	ENGLISH	EDWARD	TO LABOUR CORPS LAB C No 219244 DIS 13/2/20
16444 PTE	ERVING	JONATHAN	WND 5/1/16 A COY TO ROYAL ENGINEERS RE No WR/43001
20942 PTE	ETHERINGTON	JAMES	WND 7/10/16 C COY TO YORK AND LANCASTER REGT Y&L No 55788 CLASS Z RES 2/2/19
17320 PTE	ETHERINGTON	REGINALD	ENL DARLINGTON 2/9/14 MISSING 4/8/16 B COY
16593 PTE	EVANS	GEORGE	ENL FERRYHILL 2/9/14 TO 23/DRS GSW BACK & HEAD 9/7/16 B COY TO DUTY 12/7/16 MISSING 19/9/16
17321 PTE	EVANS	OSWALD	WND 26/7/16 B COY TO R ENGINEERS RE No WR/332622 KO YORKSHIRE LI KOYLI No 45013 DURHAM LI DLI No 79885
11222 PTE	EVERSON	THOMAS	WND 30/9/16 LCPL B COY TO R DUBLIN FUSILIERS RDF No 29650 DIS 14/12/18
16536 PTE	FAIRISH	DANIEL	TO 19/DLI, CLASS Z RES
16459 PTE	FAWCETT	GEORGE	CLASS Z RES
24813 PTE	FAWCETT	RICHARD	ENL WALLSEND REPORTED WND 26/3/16 B COY KIA SAME DAY
17564 PTE	FEETANBY	JOSEPH WILLIAM	CLASS Z RES
13626 LCPL	FENNA	WILLIAM	STILL SERVING 1920
13630 PTE	FENNY	WILLIAM	WND 10/7/16 A COY DEAD ON MIC NOT ON CWGC NO DOCUMENTS
23453 PTE	FERGUSON	WILIAM THOMAS	TO DEPOT DIS 392 ENL 29/8/14 DIS 30/1/16 DEAFNESS
16050 PTE	FERGUSON	WILLIAM	WND 9/7/16 D COY TO ARMY ORDNANCE CORPS AOC No O38360
16147 PTE	FIDDLER	HARVEY	WND 4/8/16 WND 24/9/16 AT DUTY D COY CLASS Z RES
23464 LCPL	FINLAY	PETER	WND SHELL SHOCK 4/8/16 C COY TO 11/DLI 1/6/DLI CLASS Z RES
12183 PTE	FINLEY	JAMES	D COY WND 21/5/16 TO LAB CORPS 263779, DIS 28/2/19
12183 PTE	FINLEY	JAMES	WND 22/5/16 BY SHRAPNEL D COY TO LABOUR CORPS LAB C No 263779 DIS 28/2/19
23444 PTE	FISHER	JOHN	WND 16/2/16 A COY TO DEPOT DIS 392 ENL 24/11/14 DIS 19/5/16
17711 LCPL	FITTES	ALFRED	WND 19/9/16 SGT B COY TO R ENGINEERS RE No WR/276367 RENUMBERED 308196
18170 SGT	FITZPATRICK	THOMAS	CLASS Z RES CQMS MM
24777 PTE	FLEMING	RALPH	CLASS Z RES
23454 PTE	FORREST	JOHN	ATT 178 TUNN COY RE 13/DLI ATT XIV CORPS HQ ATT DAAG XIV CORPS DETAILS BN DLI CLASS Z RES
18153 PTE	FOSTER	ALBION	CLASS Z RES
21073 PTE	FOSTER	HENRY	ATT 23/DIV DRS, ATT GHQ, TO 13/DLI, ATT XVI CORPS HQ, CLASS Z RES
16545 PTE	FOSTER	THOMAS SIDDLE	WND 8/7/16 A COY TO LABOUR CORPS LAB C No 601875 CLASS Z RES 20/1/19
15888 PTE	FRANKLIN	MARK	WND 5/1/17 C COY DIS 392 ENL 9/9/14 DIS 20/2/18
24807 PTE	FRAZER	ALEXANDER	DIS 392
19106 CSM	FREEMAN	WILLIAM WINTER	WND 17/7/16 D COY AT DUTY DIS TO COMMISSION 2/4/17, 11/DLI KIA 30/11/17 FROM FELLING
23451 PTE	FULLER	DAVID	TO LABOUR CORPS LAB C No 602719 CLASS Z RES 13/2/19
16428 PTE	GAFFNEY	PATRICK	ENL CONSETT 8/9/14 LCPL 27/9/17 KIA 19/10/17
11381 SGT	GALLAGHER	WILLIAM	TO LABOUR CORPS LAB C No 604870 CLASS Z RES 23/3/19
19041 SGT	GALLEY	WILLIAM	WND 9/7/16 C COY CLASS Z RES MM
13359 PTE	GAMWELL	JAMES	WND 19/7/16 B COY DIS 392 ENL 7/9/14 DIS 7/1/19
17358 CQMS	GANT	JAMES	CLASS Z RES
17356 PTE	GARBUTT	TOM	ENL W HARTLEPOOL WND 2/8/16 SGT WND 16/9/16 SELF INFLICTED D COY CPL REDUCED TO PTE BY FGCM, TO A COY
3/11593 PTE	GARDNER	MATTHEW THOMAS	WND 24/5/16 B COY TO ROYAL DEFENCE CORPS RDC No 66227 IN FRANCE 25/8/15 TO 9/5/17
15946 SGT	GARVEY	CHARLES GILBERT	TO 12/DLI, 13/DLI, TO DEPOT DIS 392 ENL 8/9/14 DIS 28/3/18
18721 PTE	GASKILL	ROBERT	WND 20/10/15 WND 2/8/16 SELF INFLICTED D COY TO 18/DLI, 20/DLI, CLASS Z RES

22271 CPL	GIBSON	JOSEPH	WND 18/7/16 A COY SGT CLASS Z RES
17009 PTE	GILL	EDWARD	WND 24/5/16 B COY DIS 392 ENL 5/9/14 DIS 18/3/18
17347 PTE	GILL	HAROLD	TO 2/DLI, 11/DLI/ 7/DLI, DIS 392 ENL 5/9/14 3/3/19
17011 PTE	GILL	HERBERT	ENL DURHAM 5/9/14 WND AT DUTY 8/7/16 WND & MISSING 6/10/16 B COY.
17789 PTE	GLASGOW	JOSEPH	CLASS Z RES
18782 PTE	GLASS	ROBERT	DIS 392 ENL 7/9/14 DIS 29/3/19
17657 PTE	GLENDENNING	JOHN	WND 7/10/16 B COY TO LABOUR CORPS LAB C No 382859 DIS 27/2/19
19585 PTE	GODFREY	WILLIAM	ATT 68/LTMB, DIS 392
21047 CPL	GOFTON	FRANK	WND 8/7/16 D COY TO DEPOT DIS 392 ENL 26/10/14 DIS 21/3/17 WOUNDS
21044 PTE	GOLIGHTLY	HUGH	WND 10/7/16 B COY TO ARMY ORDNANCE CORPS AOC No O38341 DIS 392
21176 PTE	GORLEY	THOMAS	ENL STANLEY 27/10/14 4 DAYS DETENTION 19/1/15 MISSING 19/9/16 B COY
23439 PTE	GOTT	ROBERT	ENL W HARTLEPOOL 24/11/14 15888 10/NORTHBD FUS TRF 13/DLI 24/8/15 A COY KIA 3 A.M 12/10/15
16491 LSGT	GOWLAND	CHARLIE	B COY MM TO ROYAL DEFENCE CORPS RDC No 66164 IN FRANCE 25/8/15 TO 13/12/16
15336 PTE	GOWLAND	THOMAS FENWICK	CLASS Z RES AWOll MM
15914 LCPL	GRAHAM	ADAM	ATT 23/DIV HQ, 13/DLI, TO 12/DLI, CLASS Z RES
21614 SGT	GRAHAM	DAVID	CLASS Z RES MM
24788 PTE	GRAHAM	JOHN GEORGE A	WND 9/7/16 C COY TO LABOUR CORPS LAB C No 654734 CLASS Z 6/2/19
17683 PTE	GRAHAM	THOMAS	TO LABOUR CORPS LAB C No 399932 CLASS Z RES 8/3/19
18368 PTE	GRANT	DAVID	WND 28/7/16 A COY TO 20/DLI 19/DLI 18/DLI CLASS Z RES
16554 PTE	GRANT	HERBERT	LCPL TO ARMY RES CLASS P DIS 392 ENL 4/9/14 DIS 31/10/16
24805 PTE	GRAY	JOSEPH	CLASS Z RES
18482 PTE	GRAYSON	F	WND 18/7/16 A COY TO TANK CORPS TC No 91932 SGT
17355 PTE	GREEN	JAMES	DIS 392
16431 CPL	GREEN	JOHN GEORGE	CLASS Z RES MM, WWII SERVED 244 COY PIONEER CORPS ENL 5/12/40 No 13037960
13609 PTE	GREENFIELD	ROBERT	WND 8/10/16 A COY CLASS Z RES
17655 PTE	GREENHOFF	MILLSON	ENL 3/9/14, WND 4/8/16 B COY HOSP SHIP ST PATRICK 7/8/16, 2 WESTERN GEN HOSP MANCHESTER SHRAP WND R ARM TO DEPOT 8/8/16, 87 TRG RES BN 13/10/16, 4/DLI 4/11/16, 10/DLI A COY 26/12/16 KIA 24/8/17 FROM WINDY KNOOK GATESHEAD
21065 PTE	GRIERSON	ROBERT HOPPER	CLASS Z RES
19168 CPL	GRIFFIN	MICHAEL	ENL FELLING 9/9/14 LCPL 2/8/15 L/SGT 19/7/16 WND 2/8/16 B COY TO 2/FA DOW 3/8/16
18472 PTE	GRIFFITHS	THOMAS	CLASS Z RES
19015 PTE	GRIMSHAW	ROBERT EDWARD	ENL BIRTLEY 3/9/14 SERVED B COY KIA 3/6/17
23650 PTE	GRUNDY	THOMAS	ENL NEWCASTLE ATT 23/DIV SANITARY SEC REJOINS 13/DLI KIA 20/9/17
21032 PTE	GUY	THOMAS	ENL FELLING 4/10/14 ACCIDENTALLY SHOT BY 22076 PTE T DAVISON 13/11/15 DOW
15034 PTE	HAIRE	ARTHUR	CLASS Z RES
16057 PTE	HALL	HERBERT	TO LABOUR CORPS LAB C No 579918 CLASS Z RES 28/1/19
18001 PTE	HALL	R	TO TANK CORPS TC No 310375
20937 PTE	HALL	TOM	JOINED FROM 35/IBD 1/7/16 EX 12/DLI WND 10/7/16 B COY TO DUTY 8/8/16 14/10/16 13/CCS - 30/A TRN- 8/G HOSP- 35/IBD TO 2/WEST RIDING REGT DWR No 24382 DOW FRACTURED SKULL 14/6/17
17393 PTE	HALL	WALTER	ENL STOCKTON 4/9/14 TO 69/FA 16/12/15 SCABIES TO DUTY 25/12/15 WND 8/7/16 D COY TO 4/G HOSP - HOSP SHIP 11/7/16 GSW RL ARM TO 3/DLI TO BEF REPOSTED TO 15/DLI 25/3/17 LCPL 30/12/17 KIA 21/3/18 ID DISC HANDED IN BY GERMAN RES INF REGT
21018 PTE	HAMER	JACK	ENL HALIFAX 26/10/14 TO 2/CAN CCS 8/6/17 GSW BACK - - 14 AMB TRN - 2/AUS G HOSP - TO UK 13/7/17 TO DEPOT 14/7/17 TO 3/DLI 1/12/17 TO 19/DL REPOSTED, 10/DLI REPOSTED 15/DLI 3/2/18 MISSING 21/3/18
18067 CSM	HAMMOND	THOMAS SEAMAN	CLASS Z RES
3/10847 SGT	HANDS	JAMES W	DIS 392
14039 PTE	HANEY	JOHN	WND 9/7/16 D COY SHELL SHOCK CLASS Z RES
18941 PTE	HANEY	ROBERT	WND 28/12/15 B COY DIS 392 ENL 1/9/14 DIS 30/8/16
15766 PTE	HANNAH	JAMES	ATT 176 TUNN COY RE, TO 1/6/DLI
24801 PTE	HANNAN	THOMAS	CLASS Z RES
11224 PTE	HARDY	GEORGE	TO LABOUR CORPS LAB C No 656312 LCPL CLASS Z RES 21/2/19
23450 PTE	HARDY	WILLIAM	TO LABOUR CORPS LAB C No 418568 CLASS Z RES 28/3/19
19610 PTE	HARGREAVES	WILLIAM	CLASS Z RES
18058 SGT	HARLAND	JAMES	TO 20/DLI, CLASS Z RES
17032 PTE	HARLE	THOMAS	TO ARMY RES CLASS P DIS 392 ENL 5/9/14 DIS 25/4/19 MM
17386 PTE	HARPER	HERBERT	WND 17/9/16 B COY TO CONNAUGHT RANGERS C RANG No 15135 LEINSTER REGT LEINSTER No 15234 CLASS Z RES FROM ALBERT ST W HARTLEPOOL
15338 PTE	HARRISON	HAROLD	ENL STANLEY 7/9/14 TO 69/FA 3/3/16 SCABIES TO NTH RID CCS 7/3/16 ICT HAND & WAIST - No 1/AMB TRN - 10/G HOSP - 24/G HOSP HERNIA 11/5/16 REJOINS BN 1/6/16 KIA 10/7/16
24762 PTE	HARRISON	JOHN STRACHAN	WND 4/8/16 C COY TO LABOUR CORPS LAB C No 196961 CLASS Z RES 19/2/19
19031 PTE	HARRISON	MATTHEW	WND 9/7/16 C COY TO NORTH STAFFORDSHIRE REGT N STAFFS No 61611 SERVED ON THE NORTH WEST FRONTIER 1919
20951 PTE	HART	WILLIAM	WND 3/6/16 C COY TO 15/DLI, ARMY RES CLASS P DIS 392 22/10/14 DIS 23/4/19 MM
16446 PTE	HASSELL	THOMAS EDWARD	TO LABOUR CORPS LAB C No 620664 CLASS Z RES 12/3/19
20931 PTE	HAUGHEY	THOMAS	BORN LEADGATE ENL CONSETT WND 4/11/16 C COY TO 12/DLI, ATT PERMANENT BASE, ATT HQ VI CORPS, ATT BASE DETAILS, ATT XIII CORPS SALVAGE COY, KIA 17/08/17.
18720 PTE	HAUXWELL	JOHN	CLASS Z RES
16547 PTE	HAW	WILLIAM	ENL STANLEY 5/9/14 LCPL 2/5/15 TO 7/CCS 11/9/15 GSW THIGH TO 30/H BARGE TO H SHIP 17/9/15 TO DEPOT 17/9/15 - 16/DLI 11/10/15 to 13/DLI 17/3/16 REVERTS TO PTE FGCM F316 AWOL 7/8/17 KIA 18/10/17
17400 PTE	HAWKIN	ERNEST WALKER	DIS 392
15908 PTE	HAYES	JOHN	WND 10/7/16 B COY DIS 392
16471 PTE	HAZELDINE	WILLIAM	WND 9/7/16 B COY TO 18/DLI, DIS 392 CPL
18359 PTE	HEATON	HERBERT	CLASS Z RES
16121 PTE	HEDLEY	ROBERT	WND 28/7/16 C COY TO DEPOT DIS 392 ENL 8/9/14 DIS 16/2/18 MM
23446 LCPL	HEDLEY	WILIAM	WND 5/1/16 A COY TO 4/DLI DIS 392 ENL 1/9/14 DIS 15/4/18
17024 PTE	HENDERSON	JOHN JAMES	ENL HOUGHTON LE SPRING 14/9/14 TO 18/CCS 18/3/16 - 2/CAN G HOSP 23/3/16 - R HERBERT HOSP WOOLWICH - 16/DLI 10/5/16 - 11/DLI 22/6/16 TO 14/DRS BOILS - 21/CCS - 35IBD TO 13/DLI KIA 21/9/17
24798 SGT	HENDERSON	ROBERT	WND 22/10/15 D COY TO ARMY RES CLASS P DIS 392 ENL 15/9/14 DIS 3/3/17
24821 PTE	HENDERSON	WILLIAM	TO LABOUR CORPS LAB C No 376178 DIS 6/3/19

Service No.	Rank	Surname	Forename	Notes
18006	PTE	HENRY	MICHAEL	ENL GATESHEAD 9/9/14 WND 28/7/16 GSW R KNEEE TO 1/S MIDLAND CCS 20/CCS 28/AMB TRAIN 15 GEN HOSP TO CONV DEPOT ETAPLES REJOINED BN 29/11/16 D COY KIA 21/9/17
18078	PTE	HERDMAN	ARTHUR	BORN & ENL CHESTER LE STREET 5/9/14 WND 23/10/18 TO 41/CCS 23/10, 50/CCS 13/11, DOW 14/12/18
17399	PTE	HEWESON	ROBERT	ENL WEST HARTLEPOOL 3/9/14 LCPL 6/10/14 REVERTS 13/12/14 TO 104/FA - 34 CCS - 6 GEN HOSP SHELL WND LEG & HEAD FRAC SKULL 29/7/16 DOW 16/8/16
16548	PTE	HEWITSON	ALBERT	TO LABOUR CORPS LAB C No 485345 DIS 6/3/19
19644	PTE	HICKSON	ROBERT	WND 4/8/16 D COY TO NORTH STAFFORDSHIRE REGT N STAFFS No 52993 CLASS Z RES
21247	PTE	HIGHFIELD	ALBERT	TO LABOUR CORPS LAB C No 263554 DIS 22/1/19
21619	SGT	HILTON	WILLIAM	WND 2/8/16 C COY CLASS Z RES
16549	PTE	HINNEGAN	MATTHEW	ENL STANLEY 5/9/14 KIA 10/6/17
17791	PTE	HOBDAY	ROBERT RICHARD	TO LABOUR CORPS LAB C No 19398 CLASS Z RES 23/3/19
16550	PTE	HODGKINS	JOHN	ENL STANLEY 5/9/14 TO 69/FA 3/5/17 KNEE - 70/FA TO DUTY 12/5/17 WND GSW SCALP 3/6/17 - 17/CCS - 26/G HOSP TO BASE DEPOT 16/6/17 REJOINS 19/6/17 WND & MISSING 20/9/17
19643	PTE	HODGSON	ALBERT WHITFIELD	ENL B AUCKLAND 7/9/14 TO 69/FA - W RID CCS - 3 AMB TRN - 20/G HOSP PYREXIA UO 23 INF BD 8/4/16 REJOINS 18/4/16 WND 4/8/16 D COY - S MID CCS - 21/AMB TRN - 13/G HOSP TO BASE DETAILS 7/9/16 TO 2/DLI KIA 26/9/16
18361	SGT	HODGSON	GEORGE WILLIAM	RES COUNDON ATT 68/LTMB, 13/DLI, 2/DLI, 13/DLI, DIS TO COMMISSION 10/9/16
18362	PTE	HODGSON	JAMES ARTHUR	RES LEASINGTHORNE DIS 392
18360	CPL	HODGSON	JOHN JOSEPH	ENL FERRYHILL SGT TRF ROYAL ENGINEERS RE No 156343 COMMISSIONED 2/Lt RE 25/12/16 KIA 184 TUNN COY 13/8/17. GRAVE RECORDS RANK AS SAPPER MIC STATES REVERTS FOR MISCONDUCT
17376	CPL	HODGSON	THOMAS WILSON	CLASS Z RES
23459	PTE	HODKINSON	JOHN	ENL NEWCASTLE 28/8/14 10/NTHBLD FUS NF No 19542 TO 13/DLI 24/8/15 TO 69/FA 26/12/15 SCABIES TO DUTY 31/12/15 TO 71/FA/2/6/17 PYREXIA TO DUTY 12/6/17 KIA 20/7/17
17391	PTE	HOGARTH	JAMES	ENL W HARTLEPOOL 31/8/14 LCPL 20/1/15 DEPRIVED 14/7/15 LCPL 16/8/16 WND 19/9/16 B COY TO 71/FA DOW 21/9/16
11594	SGT	HOLDEN	BERTRAM CHARLES	TO LABOUR CORPS LAB C No 171045 CLASS Z RES 21/3/19
23471	PTE	HOLLINGSHEAD	FRED	ENL HEDNESFORD FROM NORTHBLD FUS NF No 15932 KIA 8/7/16 D COY NO DOCS
18716	PTE	HONEY	JOHN THOMAS	ENL CONSETT DOW FROM ANNFIELD PLAIN 18/6/18
24818	SGT	HOPE	WALTER	CLASS Z RES A/CQMS
21069	PTE	HOPKINS	GEORGE	ENL 27/10/14 WND NIGHT 12/13/2/16 C COY WND 10/7/16 TO DEPOT DIS 392 20/10/16 AGE 36
17398	PTE	HORN	WILLIAM	CLASS Z RES MM
18513	CPL	HORNBY	WILLIAM	A COY DCM TO NORTHUMBERLAND FUS NF No 93957 CSM 52/NF 1920
15954	PTE	HORNER	JAMES	TO ARMY RES CLASS W DIS 392 ENL 8/9/14 DIS 4/1/17
17021	PTE	HOSIE	ALEXANDER	WND 8/7/16 D COY DIS 392 ACPL
16149	PTE	HOWE	JAMES	WND 4/8/16 A COY TO 14/DLI, 11/DLI, 20/DLI, CLASS Z RES
13326	PTE	HOWELL	THOMAS	ENL NEWCASTLE DOW 11/10/18
18209	PTE	HUDSPETH	THOMAS	CLASS Z RES
15962	CPL	HUGHES	JOHN	WND 30/1/16 D COY TO 1/TRAINING RES BN TR RES No TR/5/1018 DIS 392
18781	PTE	HUGHES	JOSEPH	ENL GATESHEAD WND 17/7/16 D COY TO 10/DLI, 11/DLI, 2/DLI KIA 23/04/18
16284	PTE	HULMES	EDWARD	TO LABOUR CORPS LAB C No 514474 CLASS Z RES 30/4/19
17388	PTE	HUMBLE	FREDERICK HERBER	DIS 392 ENL 2/9/14 DIS 12/3/19
24817	PTE	HUNT	ROBERT WILLIAM	ENL MIDDLESBROUGH WND 3/6/16 C COY DOW 3/7/16
17808	PTE	HUNTER	HARRY	WND 22/9/16 A COY TO LABOUR CORPS LAB CORPS No 576187 WORCESTERSHIRE REGT WORC REGT NO 64087 DIS 392
14933	PTE	HUNTER	JOHN	SGT TO 2/DLI ARMY RES CLASS P ENL 1/9/14 DIS 24/1/19 SWB LIST SHOWS No AS 13/14933
21606	PTE	HURWORTH	HAROLD	ATT 68/BDE HQ CLASS Z RES MM
19055	PTE	HUTCHINSON	JAMES	WND 22/5/16 BY SHRAPNEL WND 2/8/16 D COY TO LABOUR CORPS LAB C No 387536 CPL DIS 10/3/19
24775	CPL	HUTCHINSON	WILLIAM	ENL DURHAM KIA 20/09/17 MM
19647	PTE	HUTTON	WILLIAM	WND 10/7/16 D COY TO SCOTTISH RIFLES SC RIF No 31429 CLASS Z RES
17036	PTE	IBINSON	GEORGE	TO 4/DLI DIS 392 ENL 14/9/14 DIS 8/4/18
15912	PTE	INGHAM	FREDERICK	CLASS Z RES LCPL
11665	PTE	INGLEBY	ALBERT E	WND 20/3/16 B COY WND 26/3/16 BY SHRAPNEL SCALP & CHEEK TO 14/NORTHBD FUS TO 1/NORTHBD FUS NF No 46752 MM DIS 392
21612	PTE	JACKSON	ALBERT	ENL MIDDLESBROUGH WND 9/7/16 C COY KIA 18/7/16
18315	PTE	JACKSON	THOMAS	TO 12/DLI, CLASS Z RES
20950	PTE	JACKSON	WILLIAM	ENL CONSETT TO 20/DLI 19/DLI KIA 29/03/18
13993	PTE	JAGGS	WILLIAM	TO LABOUR CORPS LAB C No 441055 DIS 5/2/19
18364	PTE	JARMAN	WILLIAM	WND 18/7/16 A COY AT DUTY CLASS Z RES
17712	PTE	JEFFERS	JAMES WILLIAM	WND 4/8/16 C COY TO DEPOT DIS 392 ENL 3/9/14 DIS 10/4/18 MM
17417	CPL	JEFFERSON	CHARLES WILLIAM	CLASS Z RES
16544	SGT	JEFFERSON	JOHN	WND SHELL SHOCK 4/8/16 C COY CLASS Z RES
19367	CPL	JENKINS	ROBERT	WND 2/11/15 WND 5/8/16 A COY CLASS Z RES
20956	PTE	JENNINGS	JOSEPH	WND 3/6/16 C OY DIS 392 ENL 23/10/14 DIS 31/5/18
18324	PTE	JOBLING	ALGERNON	WND 28/7/16 D COY TO 10/DLI, 15/DLI, CLASS Z RES
21268	PTE	JOBLING	JOHN WILLIAM	DIS 392 ENL 2/11/14 DIS 8/2/17
21160	PTE	JOHN	ANDERSON	ENL 27/10/14 GSW HAND TO DEPOT 27/9/17 COMMAND DEPOT RIPON 6/11/17 3/DLI 16/3/18 MIL FOOT POLICE 27/6/18 MFP No P/15478 ARMY RES CLASS P 23/9/18 EMPLOYED AT CONSETT IRON CO DIS 14/12/18 MID JUNE 16 MM
23620	PTE	JOHNSON	FREDERICK	ENL 16/2/15 TO DEPOT DIS 392 11/1/18
17667	SGT	JOHNSON	J T	WND 8/10/15 A COY COMMISSIONED LABOUR CORPS 15/9/17 509 AGR COY CAPTAIN
15059	PTE	JOHNSON	ROBERT	WND 21/2/16 D COY TO MACHINE GUN CORPS MGC No 148240 DIS 21/8/19
18155	PTE	JOHNSON	WILLIAM	TO DEPOT DIS 392 ENL 6/9/14 DIS 1/8/18
17421	PTE	JOHNSTON	ALFRED	ENL CHESTER LE ST 4/9/14 LCPL 26/10/14 REVERTS 3/4/15 KIA 18/7/16 C COY AGE 27
21596	PTE	JOHNSTONE	ARCHIBALD	ENL FELLING 14/9/14 RES USWORTH LCPL 6/10/14 DEPRIVED OF LCPL MISSING 28/7/16 B
11592	LCPL	JOHNSTONE	DAVID	WND 8/7/16 D COY TO LABOUR CORPS LAB C No 454478 SGT TO CLASS Z RES 20/3/19
15947	PTE	JONES	CHARLES	WND 21/2/16 C COY TO YORK & LANCASTER REGT Y&L No 30037 CLASS Z RES 27/3/19
18674	PTE	JONES	GEORGE	ENL GATESHEAD 8/9/14 AWOL 12/8 - 19/8/15 WND 2/8/16 DOW AT No 2 FLD AMB 3/8/16 B COY

23646 PTE	JONES	JAMES W	WND 3/6/16 C COY TO EAST YORKSHIRE REGT E YORKS No 34473 DIS 392
24806 PTE	JONES	JOSEPH	TO DEPOT DIS 392 7/9/14 DIS 2/8/16
13268 PTE	JOYCE	PATRICK	WND 28/7/16 D COY DIS 392
20920 PTE	KEEGAN	BERNARD	WND 19/7/16 D COY TO YORK & LANCASTER REGT Y&L No 55815 CLASS Z RES 2/2/19
18491 PTE	KEENAN	JOHN	WND 9/7/16 B COY TO YORK & LANCASTER REGT Y&L No 55850 CLASS Z RES 16/4/19 MM
17044 SGT	KEENAN	PETER	ENL 3/9/14 DURHAM RES STANLEY WND 9/7/16 A COY TO 20/DLI TO 13/DLI TO 86/TRG RES BN. T RES No TR5/129409 DIS 392
17617 PTE	KELL	JOHN A	WND 10/7/16 B COY TO MACHINE GUN CORPS MGC No 58253
18942 PTE	KELLEY	PATRICK	TO ARMY RES CLASS W DIS 392 ENL 1/9/14 DIS 5/11/18
24809 PTE	KELLY	EDWARD	ENL SPENNYMOOR TO ROYAL ENGINEERS RE No 360307 CLASS Z RES 28/1/19
23460 PTE	KELLY	JAMES	TRF FROM NTHBLD FUS NF No 19544 PRIOR TO EMBARKATION WND 7/10/16 C COY TO 2/8th BN MANCHESTER REGT MAN REGT No 44916 KIA 7/10/17
17555 PTE	KELLY	RALPH ROBERT	TO LABOUR CORPS LAB C No 451056 DIS 25/2/19
13256 PTE	KEMP	JOHN W	WND SHRAPNEL 4/6/16 A COY DIS 392
21620 PTE	KENNEDY	DAVID WILSON	WND 11/5/17 D COY TO DEPOT DIS 392 ENL 30/8/14 DIS 4/9/17
17424 PTE	KENNY	THOMAS	WND /9/16 A COY CLASS Z RES, WOII, VC, WINGATE,
23657 PTE	KENNY	THOMAS	DIS 392 ENL 25/2/15 DIS 26/9/19
16542 SGT	KERR	THOMAS	TO 15/DLI, 22/DLI, CLASS Z RES
13869 PTE	KILLEEN	JOHN	RES DIPTON WND 4/8/16 C COY CLASS Z RES MM ASGT
21319 PTE	KILROY	JOSEPH HENRY T	CLASS Z RES
21634 PTE	KING	JOSEPH	WND 18/7/16 A COY TO NORTHUMBERLAND FUSILIERS NF No 5/6752 RENUMBERED 241985 DESERTED 19/6/17 KIA WITH 1/NF 20/09/18 FROM ASHFORD KENT
17989 PTE	KING	RALPH GRUNDY	ENL CHESTER LE STREET 7/9/14 TO 4/G HOSP - H SHIP DIEPPE NEPHRITIS 20/7/16 TO DEPOT 21/7/16 TRG RES BN 12/12/16 - 35/IBD TO 18/DLI 15/5/17 REPOSTED 20/DL 30/6/17 GSW SCALP & ARM 30/7/16 TO 6 G/HOSP TO 13/DLI MISSING 21/9/17
18166 PTE	KINGHORN	GEORGE	WND 4/8/16 D COY TO 14/DLI, 13/DLI, DIS 392 ENL 7/9/14 DIS 21/5/19
17422 CPL	KIRBY	ALFRED EDWARD	TO ARMY RES CLASS P DIS 392 ENL 4/9/14 DIS 13/3/19
18270 PTE	KIRKUP	TERRENCE	WND 4/8/16 D COY CLASS Z RES
23582 PTE	KIRTON	CARNABY	TO LABOUR CORPS LAB C No 517444 CLASS Z RES 12/1/19
24815 LCPL	KIRTON	ROBERT ALLEN	ATT 2nd ASC SECTION CLASS Z RES
15894 SGT	LAMB	FRANCIS O	WND 19/3/16 A COY WND 9/7/16 COMMISSIONED 8/WEST YORKSHIRE REGT 29/1/18 RESIDENT ESH HILL TOP MM 21/7/16
19095 PTE	LANE	WILLIAM	DESERTED 2/10/17 DIS 25/4/19
21128 PTE	LANGDALE	HENRY	TO ROYAL DEFENCE CORPS RDC No 71367 IN FRANCE 25/8/15 TO 13/1/16
23626 PTE	LATTIMER	THOMAS HENRY	ENL MIDDLESBROUGH 17/2/15 WND 4/8/16 B COY GSW ABDOMEN TO 2/FA - 2/1/STH MID CCS DOW 6/8/16 MM
16543 PTE	LAWS	GEORGE HENRY	ENL STANLEY 5/9/14 LCPL CPL 20/7/15 REVERTS 24/7/16 WND 5/8/16 A COY MULTIPLE GSW TO 2/FA - 38/CCS DOW 11/8/16
17052 SGT	LAWSON	JAMES	WND 3/6/16 A COY TO 12/DLI, 13/DLI, 19/DLI, 2/DLI, CLASS Z RES
17055 PTE	LAWSON	JOHN STEWART	TO ARMY RES CLASS P DIS 392 ENL 5/9/14 DIS 26/4/19
18074 PTE	LAYTON	WILLIAM	WND 18/7/16 C COY TO LABOUR CORPS LAB C No 432881 CLASS Z RES 7/3/19
17952 PTE	LEE	CHARLES	CLASS Z RES
19697 PTE	LEE	JOHN EDWARD	ENL GATESHEAD 7/9/14 TO 62/FA 15/9/15 SPRAINED ANKLE TO DUTY KIA 24/5/16 D COY
15991 PTE	LEET	ALBERT E	SNIPER IN A COY TO 3/NORTHBLD FUS NF No 26571 ENL 6/9/14 DIS 392 9/4/18
18363 CPL	LEIGH	LEONARD	WND NIGHT 12/13/2/16 SGT WND 7/10/16 C COY ATT 23/DIV TUNN COY, 13/DLI, 19/DLI, 22/DLI, 4/DLI DIS 392 ENL 5/9/14 DIS 15/4/18
21192 SGT	LEIGHTON	ROBERT	WND 4/8/16 A COY DIS 392 ENL 28/10/14 DIS 1/3/19
13767 PTE	LEVI	JAMES	ENL 25/8/14 WND 26/5/16 B COY TO 3/DLI DIS 30/3/18
21637 SGT	LIDDLE	JOSEPH WILLIAM	CLASS Z RES
17724 PTE	LIDDLE	MATTHEW	TO LABOUR CORPS LAB C No 182239 DIS 31/1/19
19192 SGT	LIDDLE	WILLIAM	ENL SOUTH SHIELDS CSM DCM DIS TO COMMISSION POSTED 20/DLI
17713 SGT	LINTON	THOMAS	WND 7/10/16 C COY TO ARMY RES CLASS P DIS 392 ENL 3/9/14 DIS 26/4/19
21020 PTE	LITTLE	EDWARD AUGUSTUS	WND 9/7/16 D COY TO LABOUR CORPS LAB C No 532860 CLASS Z RES 21/3/19
21162 PTE	LOCK	JOHN JAMES	WND 9/7/16 C COY TO ARMY RES CLASS W DIS 392 ENL 27/10/14 DIS 27/11/17
14813 SGT	LONG	CHARLES BELL	ENL NEWCASTLE LCPL 9/5/16 TO 69/FA WND SHOULDER 15/7/16 TO DUTY 22/7/16 CPL 28/7/16 LSGT 5/3/17 KIA 20/9/17
15920 PTE	LONGSTAFF	JOHN JOSEPH	WND 9/7/16 B COY TO DEPOT DIS 392 ENL 8/9/14 DIS 11/4/17
18197 PTE	LONGTHORNE	THOMSON BENSON	ENL B AUCKLAND WND 9/7/16 D COY GSW SHOULDER TO 4/DLI 18/DLI, 2/DLI KIA 14/7/18
25503 PTE	LOWRIE	MICHAEL	12/5/17 MM CPL DIS 392
19045 PTE	LUCAS	GEORGE	WND 9/7/16 A COY AT DUTY ATT BASE DEPOT ETAPLES, 13/DLI, CLASS Z RES
17054 PTE	LUKE	WILLIAM	WND 7/10/16 A COY CLASS Z RES MM
24810 PTE	LUMLEY	GEORGE	ENL 5/9/14 WEST STANLEY WND 24/5/16 GSW NOSE A COY WND 10/7/16 D COY TO 69/FA 14/7/16 REPRTED MISSING 27/7/16 TO UK GSW L ARM WAR HOSP BRADFORD 15/8/16 CONV HOSP ALNWICK TO 3/DLI 31/7/17 TO 17 BN RDC 1/9/17 TO RAMC 27/3/18 TO DEPOT RLY OP TPS RE RE No WR/282063 FROM WEST STANLEY
14878 PTE	LYONS	ARTHUR	ENL NEWCASTLE 2/9/14 LCPL 30/3/16 MISSING 6/10/16 B COY
19295 CQMS	MacGREGOR	WILLIAM	WND 24/5/16 A COY DIS TO COMMISSION 31/7/17
16585 PTE	MALLINSON	JOSEPH	ENL W HARTLEPOOL 4/9/14 TO 20/CCS - 4/S HOSP TO DUTY 21/9/15 TO 8/CCS 24/9/15 SORE FEET - NTH MID CCS 30/9/15 TO DUTY TO 7CCS - 4/S HOSP 27/1/16 DENTAL TO DUTY 6/2/16 KIA 21/9/17
16442 LCPL	MANN	JOHN	WND 8/10/16 A COY TO 20/DLI, CLASS Z RES
20620 PTE	MANNING	JOHN BRIEN	ENL SOUTH SHIELDS 14/9/14 WND 31/5/16 D COY DOW 1/6/16
17628 PTE	MARR	JOHN	WND 17/9/16 B COY TO TANK CORPS TC No 92392 KIA 10/8/18
24766 CQMS	MARSHALL	JAMES	ATT 68/LTMB TO LABOUR CORPS LAB C No 516234 CQMS CLASS Z RES 21/1/19
18743 PTE	MARTIN	JOHN WILLIAM	WND 9/7/16 B C OY TO ARMY RES CLASS P DIS 392 ENL 1/9/14 DIS 21/5/17
19729 SGT	MATKIN	ERNEST	CLASS Z RES MM
16727 PTE	MATTHEWS	THOMAS	CLASS Z RES
21348 LCPL	MATTIMORE	THOMAS	ENL BELFAST 3/11/15 LCPL 22/3/15 LSGT 11/7/16 SGT 12/8/16 SHRAP WND R SIDE 25/8/16 TO 2/CCS DOW 29/8/16
18495 PTE	MAUDE	ALBERT	WND 19/9/16 B COY TO 22/DLI, CLASS Z RES
13847 PTE	MAUGHAN	JOHN HENRY	ENL NEWCASTLE 6/9/14 DIED FROM INJURIES RECEIVED BY MEDDLING WITH AN UNEPLODED SHELL 8/4/16
24796 CQMS	MAUGHAN	WILLIAM	CLASS Z RES MM
17992 CPL	MAYLIA	JOHN	ATT 68/LTMB 13/DLI, CLASS Z RES
23448 PTE	McCABE	HUGH	WND 10/7/16 B COY TO LABOUR CORPS LAB C No 380855 DIS 7/2/19

Number	Rank	Surname	Forename	Notes
17815	PTE	McCAFFERTY	DANIEL	WND 17/7/16 D COY TO NORTHUMBERLAND FUS NF No 87144 CLASS Z RES
3/11661	PTE	McCONNELL	MATTHEW	ATT INF BASE DEPOT, 13/DLI, CLASS Z RES
13561	PTE	McCORMACK	JAMES	TO LABOUR CORPS LAB C No 517464 CLASS Z RES 3/4/19
13316	PTE	McCOY	JOHN THOMAS	REP MISSING 7/10/16 C COY REJOINED CLASS Z RES
20953	PTE	McCREARY	WILLIAM JAMES	CLASS Z RES
17071	PTE	McDERMOTT	MICHAEL	TO LABOUR CORPS LAB C No 626968 DIS 20/11/18
17610	PTE	McDERMOTT	THOMAS	TO DEPOT DIS 392 ENL 2/9/14 DIS 3/7/17
16481	PTE	McDERMOTT	WILLIAM	ENL GATESHEAD MISSING 28/7/16 B COY
15086	CPL	McDONALD	THOMAS	WND 7/10/16 B COY TO ARMY RES CLASS W DIS 392 ENL 31/8/14 DIS 22/12/17
21154	PTE	McELHATTON	JOSEPH	ENL 27/10/14 RES LANCHESTER IN D COY 6/10/15 TO10/12/15 IN HOSPITAL 22/1/16 19/5/16 IN HOSPITAL BOILS & ECZEMA KIA 29/7/16
23575	PTE	McGREAVEY	BERNARD	ENL NOTTINHAM 8/2/15 TO 20/CCS PLEURISY - 4/S HOSP 9/9/15 TO DUTY 17/9/15 ATT 176 TUNN COY RE 2/4/16 13/DLI KIA 9/10/18
16162	PTE	McGREGOR	GEORGE FREDERICH	ENL CONSETT 7/9/14 WND 19/7/16 GSW HEAD LCPL A COY TO DEPOT TO 10/DLI REPOSTED TO 22/DLI KIA 26/3/18
18207	CPL	McINTYRE	JOHN	ENL CONSETT 7/9/14 LCPL 21/7/16 CPL 27/8/16 KIA 6/10/16 B COY
24823	PTE	McKENNA	JAMES	WND 19/7/16 B COY TO LABOUR CORPS LAB C No 638274 CLASS Z RES 23/3/19
16706	PTE	McLANE	ERNEST	WND IN HEAD 4/11/15 DIED AT 69 FLD AMB 5/11/15 A COY
19744	PTE	McLEAN	ALBERT	CLASS Z RES
15911	PTE	McLOUGHLIN	ARCHIBALD	WND 9/7/16 B COY TO LABOUR CORPS LAB C No 368358 CLASS Z RES 12/2/19
21124	PTE	MICHAEL	CONNOR	WND 24/9/15 C COY TO CORPS OF HUSSARS HUS No 331063
21617	PTE	MIDDLETON	JAMES	ENL W HARTLEPOOL 5/9/14 WND 9/7/16 B COY TO 8/S HOSP GSW L HAND TO UK TO 3/DLI - 11/1/17 TO BEF TO 19/DLI REPOSTED 13/DLI 19/1/17 ATT 68/LTMB KIA 5/10/18
19770	SGT	MIDDLETON	THOMAS WILLIAM	TO 18/DLI, CLASS Z RES MM
15927	PTE	MILES	GEORGE	CLASS Z RES
13599	PTE	MILLS	ERNEST	TO MACHINE GUN CORPS MGC No 72670
16695	PTE	MILNE	NORMAN	ENL W HARTLEPOOL KIA 2/6/17
23473	PTE	MITCHELL	EDWARD	ATT 23/DIV SALVAGE COY ATT 68/LTMB CLASS Z RES
21322	PTE	MOLE	JOHN T	WND B COY 19/7/16 TO EAST LANCASHIRE REGT E LANCS No 31718 TO MANCHESTER REGT MAN REGT No 44915
18102	RQMS	MOODIE	ALBERT EDWARD	ATT 68 BDE HQ, 13/DLI, ATT 23/DIV DETAILS BN CLASS Z RES
13236	PTE	MOODY	FRANK	ENL MIDDLESBRO 4/9/14 WND NIGHT 12/13/2/16 A COY DOW 13/2/16
19368	PTE	MOODY	FRANK	WND 20/3/16 WND 18/7/16 A COY DIS 392 ENL 7/9/14 DIS 8/7/17
24751	PTE	MOODY	THOMAS	WND 12/10/15 TO DEPOT DIS 392 ENL 2/9/14 DIS 19/6/17 WNDS
23579	PTE	MOORE	WILFRED	ENL SOUTH SHIELDS 7/2/15 WND 10/7/16 D COY DOW 12/7/16
20960	PTE	MORALEE	ANDREW	DIS 392
16146	PTE	MORGAN	FREDERICK	WND 24/5/16 C COY CLASS Z RES
23577	PTE	MORGAN	JAMES	WND 9/7/16 D COY TO LABOUR CORPS LAB C No 316893 DIS 24/11/17
24783	PTE	MORGAN	W	WND 28/7/16 D COY TO ROYAL DUBLIN FUSILIERS RDF No 29663 CLASS Z RES ON MIC AS D CORNWALL'S LI.
16520	SGT	MORLAND	WILLIAM	TO 29/DLI, DISEMBODIED
17714	PTE	MORLEY	JOSEPH	TO ARMY RES CLASS W DIS 392 ENL 3/9/14 DIS 11/12/16
19268	SGT	MORNING	WILLIAM	TO 16/DLI DIS 392 ANEMIA ENL 10/9/14 DIS 5/9/16
20958	PTE	MORPETH	JOHN	ATT INF BASE DEPOT, 13/DLI, CLASS Z RES
17704	PTE	MORRISON	JOHN	WND 9/7/16 B COY TO R ENGINEERS RE No WR/42091
18387	CQMS	MORTON	MATTHEW PROCTOR	WND 4/8/14 CSM D COY TO LINCOLNSHIRE REGT LINCS No 49182 TO LABOUR CORPS LAB C No 319004 COMMISSIONED LAB CORPS
21631	PTE	MOSLEY	ROBERT	ENL SOUTH ASHFORD 29/3/15 MISSING 30/9/16 B COY
13285	PTE	MOSS	THOMAS	WND 10/7/16 D COY TO No 3 CCS 10/7/16 EVAC 13/7/16 No 6 AMB TRAIN TRF TO ROYAL AIR FORCE 12/12/17 RAF No 114105
16103	PTE	MOYLE	JOHN	WND 17/7/16 C COY TO ARMY RES CLASS P DIS 392 ENL 8/9/14 DIS 8/1/17 MM
16708	PTE	MUIR	CHARLES	CLASS Z RES, CPL
23652	PTE	MULLEN	ANDREW	TO 2/DLI 13/DLI CLASS Z RES
16713	PTE	MURPHY	FRANCIS	TO 3/DLI DIS 392 ENL 4/9/14 DIS 24/10/18
16704	PTE	MURRAY	GEORGE FREDERICH	ENL W HARTLEPOOL 4/9/14 KIA 24/5/16 D COY
21164	CPL	MURRAY	HUGH	TO ARMY RES CLASS W DIS 392 ENL 27/10/14 DIS 8/10/17
14862	PTE	MURRAY	JOHN	TO LABOUR CORPS LAB C No 119003 CLASS Z RES 13/2/19
18165	PTE	MURRAY	JOHN	WND 16/9/16 D COY ATT 23/DIV REINF CAMP, CLASS Z RES
16436	PTE	NASH	RICHARD	CLASS Z RES
16067	PTE	NATTRESS	CYRIL THOMPSON	ENL DURHAM 8/9/14 WND NIGHT 12/13/2/16 D COY DOW 13/2/16
16731	CPL	NATTRESS	HENDERSON	WND 13/5/17 D COY TO ARMY RES CLASS P DIS 392 ENL 3/9/14 DIS 25/4/19
17691	PTE	NELSON	CHARLES	TO 19/DLI, ATT 203 FLD COY RE, 19/DLI, 12/DLI, CLASS Z RES
15383	CPL	NELSON	HAROLD	TO ARMY RES CLASS P DIS 392 ENL 5/9/14 DIS 24/6/17
17079	PTE	NESBITT	THOMAS	TO ARMY RES CLASS P DIS 392 ENL 5/9/14 DIS 25/4/19
17075	SGT	NEWBY	GEORGE E	CLASS Z RES MM
21826	PTE	NEWTON	ROBERT	WND 30/9/16 C COY DIS 392 ENL 8/11/14 DIS 1/4/19
24747	WOII	NICHOL	ADAM	RES ROTHBURY WND 27/9/16 A COY CLASS Z RES AWOI
17080	PTE	NICHOL	ALBERT	ENL DURHAM 4/9/14 TO 50/NTHBN CCS 30/10/15 SEPTIC ANKLE TO 26/G HOSP 6/11/15 HAND TO 20/IBD REJOINS BN 7/12/15 KIA 12/4/16 B COY
18140	PTE	NICHOLSON	JOHN GEORGE	ACPL CLASS Z RES
21273	CPL	NIMMONS	JOHN ROBERT	WND 28/7/16 B COY DIS 392
20634	PTE	NIXON	JOSEPH	TO DEPOT DIS 392 ENL 7/9/14 DIS 6/11/17
19060	SGT	NOLAN	FREDERICK	ENL GATESHEAD 7/9/14 LSGT 6/4/16 TO A COY REVERTS CPL 20/5/16 TO D COY LSGT 25/8/16 TO C COY SGT 28/6/16 TO 71/FA 17/3/17 TO DUTY 20/3/17 KIA 20/9/17
13260	LCPL	NORMAN	CHARLES HENRY	WND 4/8/16 D COY TO ARMY RES CLASS W DIS 392 ENL 2/9/14 DIS 29/12/17
15974	PTE	O'NEILL	JOHN	ENL 08/09/14 DURHAM, SHELL SHOCKED 9/7/16 D COY TO 12 GEN HOSP EVAC ENGLAND TO DEPOT 18/7/16, COMMAND DEPOT RIPON 23/9/16, 3/DLI 23/4/17, 20/DLI 01/06/17, 10/DLI 16/06/17, KiA 17/10/17.
19782	PTE	O'ROURKE	CONSTANTINE	ENL W HARTLEPOOL 2/9/14 ACC WND 30/1/17 DOW 2 CAN CAS CLR STN 2/2/17 GSW THIGH
19785	PTE	ORR	WILLIAM	WND 10/7/16 C COY TO 12/DLI, DIS 392 MM
20884	PTE	ORWIN	EDWARD	DIS 392
16189	PTE	OXNARD	ALFRED	WND 17/7/16 C COY TO 20/DLI, CLASS Z RES
18097	PTE	OYSTON	JOHN	WND 28/12/15 C COY TO ARMY ORDNANCE CORPS AOC No 038353
13820	PTE	PAIN	ISAAC	ENL MIDDLESBROUGH 4/9/14 WND 5/12/15 D COY TO DUTY TO 4/DLI 25/11/17 TO 2/DLI 9/1/18 REPOSTED 15/DLI 13/1/18 WND & MISSING 20/5/18 MM
13226	PTE	PALLISTER	GEORGE	TO LABOUR CORPS LAB C No 451066 CLASS Z RES 5/4/19
21279	PTE	PALMER	RALPH	CLASS Z RES

Number	Rank	Surname	Forename	Details
16748	PTE	PARIAS	JAMES	WND 28/7/16 D COY TO DEPOT DIS 392 ENL 2/9/14 DIS 20/2/17
15386	PTE	PARKER	HAROLD	CLASS Z RES
16129	PTE	PARKIN	GEORGE	ENL DURHAM 8/9/14 MISSING 18/7/16 REJOINED 22/7/16 A COY EVAC HOSP SHIP ST GEORGE TO UK SHELL SHOCK 26/7/16 TO 14/DLI 25/4/17 23/7/17 18/FA - 33/CCS - 7/G HOSP SHELL WND HEAD DOW 29/7/17
18131	PTE	PATON	DENNIS	CLASS Z RES
18195	PTE	PATRICKSON	WILLIAM	WND 8/10/16 D COY DIS 392 ENL 7/9/14 DIS 28/1/19
16747	PTE	PATTERSON	DUNCAN	TO 28/DLI DIS 392 ENL 1/9/14 DIS 2/10/18 MM
18064	LCPL	PATTISON	EDWARD	WND 17/7/16 C COY TO ROYAL SCOTS R SCOTS No 202094 ACPL
24748	PTE	PEARSON	ROBERT WILLIAM	ENL SOUTH ASHFORD B COY KIA NIGHT 12/13/2/16
21326	PTE	PEART	JOHN	CLASS Z RES
21131	PTE	PEMBERTON	JOHN JAMES	WND 6/12/15 BY BRITISH SHELLS TO 12/DLI, DIS 392
19297	CPL	PENDLETON	JAMES	WND 6/1/16 C COY TO LABOUR CORPS LAB C No 606306 DIS 17/1/19
21609	PTE	PENMAN	J	WND 30/9/16 D COY TO MACHINE GUN CORPS MGC No 157495
16742	PTE	PERCIVAL	GEORGE HENRY	WND 4/8/16 C COY TO LABOUR CORPS LAB C No 181935 DIS 22/1/18
15111	PTE	PERCIVAL	ROBERT WILLIAM	TO 4/DLI DIS 392 ENL 5/9/14 DIS 13/12/17
23467	PTE	PERCY	JOHN	ENL BEDLINGTON 28/8/14 10/NORTHUMBERLAND FUS NF No 13987 TO 13/DLI 24/8/15 WND 11/517 KIA 07/06/17
18105	PTE	PEVELLER	WILLIAM	KIA 2/7/16 ATT 23 DIV TUNN COY LCPL BURIED BULLY LES MINES
17085	PTE	PHILLIPS	AARON	CLASS Z RES
18401	SGT	PHILLIPS	WILLIAM	TO R ENGINEERS 127837 TO 12/DLI ENL CHESTER LE STREET RESIDENT GATESHEAD KIA
17904	PTE	PICKARD	JAMES	ENL B AUCKLAND 7/9/14 WND SHELLSHOCK 2/8/16 D COY AT DUTY TO 2/FA 1/10/16 GSW R ARM - 45/CCS - 5/G HOSP TO HOSP CHELTENHAM TO 35/IBD 10/DLI 17/10/17 REPOSTED 15/DLI 64/FA 5/10/17 CONTUSIONS FOOT RE JOINS 9/11/17 WND & MISSING DOW IN
21625	PTE	PICKAVANCE	JAMES	TO ARMY RES CLASS W DIS 392 ENL 29/3/15 DIS 2/1/17
16213	PTE	PICKFORD	HERBERT	WND 31/5/16 B COY TO ROYAL DEFENCE CORPS RDC No 66291 IN FRANCE 25/8/15 TO 24/6/16
16768	PTE	PILCHER	FREDERICK	ENL W HARTLEPOOL 2/9/14 WND 6/10/15 B COY TO 2/CCS - 23/IBD TO DUTY 25/11/15 KIA 29/12/15
21177	LCPL	PILLING	MATTHIAS	ATT 68/LTMB, ATT MED SCHOOL, ATT BDE SCHOOL, 13/DLI, CLASS Z RES
20965	SGT	PINKNEY	JOHN PERCIVAL	DIS 392 ENL 22/10/14 DIS 11/3/19
23589	PTE	PITTILLA	JAMES	WND 3/6/16 WND 7/10/16 A COY TO 3/DLI DIS 392 ENL 10/2/15 DIS 12/12/17
19170	PTE	POTTER	ALBERT EDWARD	TO 15/DLI DIS 392 ENL 9/9/14 DIS 13/1/19
15903	PTE	POTTER	GEORGE	ENL DURHAM 5/9/14 WND 19/3/16 WND 10/7/16 WND 6/8/16 B COY LCPL ATT 250 TUNN COY R ENGINEERS 17/8/16 SHELL WND R BUTTOCK 21/9/17 6 AUS/FA - 24/CCS - 35IBD REJOINS 24/10/17 KIA 5/10/18
23469	PTE	POWELL	GEORGE	TO LABOUR CORPS LAB C No 400506 DIS 18/11/18
17089	PTE	PRICE	JOHN	WND 8/7/16 A COY TO ROYAL FLYING CORPS RFC No 147649 TO LABOUR CORPS LAB C No 263599
17635	PTE	PRIME	GEORGE	CLASS Z RES
16064	PTE	PRINGLE	JAMES	TO LABOUR CORPS LAB C No 223069 CLASS Z RES 16/3/19
23445	CPL	PRINGLE	JOHN ROBERT	CLASS Z RES
17613	CPL	PROCTOR	WILLIAM	ENL FELLING MISSING ON PATROL 22/8/16
21167	PTE	PROUD	ERNEST	DIS 392
21601	PTE	PULFORD	HARRY	ENL B AUCKLAND 7/9/14 LCPL 6/10/14 CPL 17/4/15 REVERTS 28/9/15 KIA 10/7/16
19285	PTE	PURVIS	HENRY	ENL CHESTER LE STREET 1/9/14 D COURT MARTIAL 30/1/15 STRIK A SUP OFF 42 DAYS DETENTION LCPL 14/10/15 CPL 15/4/16 LSGT 28/6/16 KIA 10/7/16
18777	PTE	PURVIS	ROBERT	WND 17/7/16 B COY CLASS Z RES MM
16769	PTE	PYLE	HENRY	WND 24/9/15 TO TRAINING RES BN TR No TR/5/4300
15918	PTE	QUINN	JOHN	ENL DURHAM TO 1/8/DLI KIA 29/3/18
13234	PTE	QUINN	THOMAS	DOW 15/2/19 BURIED NORTH ORMESBY ST JOSEPHS RC CEM
17752	CPL	RACE	HENRY BUCKLAND	ENL B AUCKLAND 5/9/14 LCPL 10/8/15 DEPRIVED 1/9/15 WND 28/7/16 D COY SH,WND R SHLDR 1/STH MID CCS - 20/A TRN 5/G HOSP TO UK TO BEF 14/12/16 TO 2/DLI LCPL 10/1/17
16776	PTE	RAILTON	CHARLES EDWARD	WND 27/7/16 A COY TO DEPOT DIS 392 ENL 4/9/14 DIS 3/3/17 WNDS
24781	PTE	RAINE	JOHN HENRY	ENL B AUCKLAND KIA 23/5/16 ATT 68/LTMB
13637	PTE	RAMAGE	THOMAS	ENL 5/9/14 MIDDLESBROUGH, WND SHRAPNEL 4/6/16 A COY, TO DEPOT DLI, 31/7/17 TO ROYAL DEFENCE CORPS, 3/11/17 TO R ENGINEERS RE No WR/278189.
15905	PTE	RAMSAY	JAMES R	WND 10/7/16 B COY TO ROYAL WEST KENT REGT RWKR No GS/31896
18189	CPL	RAMSDEN	JAMES	WND NIGHT 12/13/2/16 WND 28/7/16 D COY TO 20/DLI, CLASS Z RES MM
16780	PTE	RAYMENT	JOSEPH	WND 6/1/16 D COY TO DEPOT DIS 392 ENL 3/9/14 DIS 28/12/16 WNDS
21616	SGT	READMAN	GEORGE HOOD	TO 22/DLI, 1/7/DLI, CLASS Z RES
21628	PTE	READMAN	JOHN THOMAS	ENL FELLING 2/9/14 TO 15/CCS ICT FEET 7/9/15 TO DUTY 14/9/15 MISSING 4/8/16 B COY
17100	PTE	READMAN	ROBERT	CLASS Z RES
21285	PTE	REAY	ARTHUR	WND 5/8/16 A COY TO ARMY RES CLASS P DIS 392 ENL 2/11/14 DIS 11/6/17
21282	LCPL	REDSHAW	SIDNEY	WND 8/7/16 A COY TO LEINSTER REGT LEINSTER No 15241 DIS 392
17988	PTE	REED	JAMES	ENL CHESTER LE STREET 7/9/14 WND 19/2/16 GSW R THIGH TO 1/CCS - 13/G HOSP DOW
16080	PTE	REED	JOSEPH	TO 18/DLI, 14/DLI, 11/DLI, CLASS Z RES
13269	PTE	REID	WILLIAM	WND 7/10/16 D COY TO LABOUR CORPS LAB C No 599763 CLASS Z RES 21/3/19
13258	PTE	REILLY	JOHN	ENL DUNDEE 2/9/14 WND 4/8/16 GSW L FOOT TO 104/FA - 70/FA - 32/DRS LCPL 14/8/16 CPL 27/8/16 KIA 7/10/16 D COY
13215	PTE	RETFORD	JAMES RICHARDSON	TO 1/7/DLI, CLASS Z RES
19817	PTE	RICHARDS	PAUL M	WND 28/7/16 WND 17/9/16 SELF INFLICTED D COY TO NORTHUMBERLAND FUSILIERS NF No 58483 CLASS Z RES
13645	PTE	RICHARDS	RENEL	WND 5/8/16 D COY TO ARMY RES CLASS P DIS 392 ENL 10/9/14 DIS 31/1/17
18205	PTE	RICHARDSON	GEORGE	TO ARMY RES CLASS W DIS 392 ENL 7/9/14 DIS 29/12/17
16215	PTE	RICHARDSON	GEORGE R	WND 18/7/16 A COY TO EAST LANCASHIRE REGT E LANCS No 41324
16482	PTE	RICHARDSON	THOMAS	CLASS Z RES
21165	PTE	RIDDELL	THOMAS	WND 18/7/16 WND 28/7/16 C COY TO ARMY RESERVE CLASS P DIS 392 ENL 27/10/14 DIS
13939	CPL	RILEY	MICHEAL	WND 9/7/16 C COY TO DEPOT DIS 392 ENL 1/9/14 DIS 13/4/17 SICK
17764	CPL	ROBERTS	JOHN WILLIAM	ENL STANLEY 4/9/14 TO 69/FA 3/1/16 PUO TO DUTY 22/1/16 LSGT 24/2/16 WND 26/3/16 B COY MULTIPLE WNDS LEGS L ARM & HEAD 33/CCS - LAHORE BRIT G HOSP DANGER ILL
14890	SGT	ROBERTS	WILLIAM PATRICK	ENL 2/9/14 REDUCED TO PTE BY FGCM 13/3/16, WND 28/7/16 D COY TO ARMY RES CLASS P DIS 392 12/3/19
17766	CPL	ROBINSON	JAMES	TO LABOUR CORPS LAB C No 656408 CLASS Z RES 11/3/19
18003	PTE	ROBINSON	JAMES	CLASS Z RES
23447	SGT	ROBINSON	JAMES	WND 23/9/16 AT DUTY A COY DIS 392 ENL 22/11/14 DIS 25/4/19 MM
18112	PTE	ROBINSON	JOHN WILLIAM	CLASS Z RES

24756 PTE	ROBINSON	JOHN WILLIAM	TO 18/DLI CLASS Z RES	
21284 PTE	ROBINSON	JOSEPH	CLASS Z RES	
23457 PTE	ROBINSON	PERCY	TO 2/DLI CLASS Z RES	
23442 PTE	ROBINSON	SAMUEL	TO LABOUR CORPS LAB C No 371801 CLASS Z RES 22/3/19	
17785 CPL	ROBINSON	WILLIAM	WND 9/7/16 D COY AT DUTY CLASS Z RES	
21147 CQMS	ROBSON	JOHN	TO 15/DLI. 13/DLI. CLASS Z RES MM	
17799 RQMS	ROBSON	PERCIVAL LAIDLER	CLASS Z RES MC	
18152 PTE	ROBSON	THOMAS	WND 19/7/16 A COY TO MACHINE GUN CORPS MGC No 25324 LABOUR CORPS LAB C 603761 ROYAL FUSILIERS R FUS No 112098	
20964 SGT	ROBSON	THOMAS WILLIAM	DIS 392 ENL 26/10/14 DIS 1/8/19	
21624 PTE	ROBSON	WILLIAM	ENL STH ASHFORD ATT 181 TUNN COY RE, ATT 35/IBD, TO 13/DLI, ATT 68/LTMB DEAD DOW HOME 21/10/18	
20894 PTE	ROCHE	JOSEPH	ATT 57/BDE HQ TO 13/DLI. CLASS Z RES	
18484 PTE	ROGAN	FELIX	WND 26/3/16 B COY TO 3/DLI DIS 392 ENL 7/9/14 DIS 16/12/16	
13625 PTE	ROGERS	JOSHUA WILLIAM	WND 18/7/16 A COY TO 4/DLI DIS 392 ENL 5/9/14 DIS 12/10/17	
22144 PTE	ROGERSON	GEORGE THOMAS	ATT 68 BDE HQ TO 15/DLI CLASS Z RES	
24829 PTE	ROLLINGS	GEORGE	WND 24/9/15 C COY TO DEPOT DIS 392 ENL 25/3/15 DIS 14/4/16 SHELL WND ARM & THIGH	
13622 PTE	ROLLINGS	JAMES	DIS 392 SGT FGCM 22/6/16 REDUCED TO PTE	
21191 PTE	ROWE	GEORGE WILLIAM	WND 4/1/16 D COY TO LABOUR CORPS LAB C No 182245 DIS 14/11/17	
17769 PTE	ROWELL	HARRY	WND 29/12/15 A COY TO 19/DLI, 2/DLI, CLASS Z RES	
17091 CPL	ROWLANDS	JOHN	TO 12/DLI, 10/DLI, 15/DLI, ARMY RES CLASS P DIS 392 ENL 7/9/14 DIS 25/4/19	
18365 CPL	RUDD	MICHAEL WHITTEN	ENL B AUCKLAND 7/9/14 LCPL 7/4/15 CPL 19/10/15 TO UK EX 24/G HOSP - HOS[P LIVERPOOL 15/10/16 TO DEPOT 20/10/16 - 3/DLI TO 19/DLI REPOSTED 13/DLI REJOINS BN	
21599 CQMS	RUDD	ROY	WND 19/9/16 WND 26/1/17 D COY CLASS Z RES	
15674 PTE	SADLER	CYRIL SEMOUR	TO 20/DLI, 2/DLI, CLASS Z RES	
21611 CPL	SADLER	WILLIAM	CLASS Z RES	
21194 PTE	SAINTHOUSE	WILLIAM ROBERT	ENL NEWCASTLE 29/10/14 TO 70/FA 9/11/15 ENTERITIS TO DUTY 24/11/15 WND 5/10/18 TO 12/CCS DOW 6/10/18	
16809 SGT	SALKELD	LUKE	WND 7/10/16 B COY ATT 23/DIV RE TO 13/DLI, CLASS Z RES	
16916 LCPL	SALTMARSH	FREDERICK	ENL DARLINGTON WND 4/8/16 D COY A/WOII DOW 18/10/18 MM	
24780 LCPL	SAMPLE	JOHN WILLIAM	ENL B AUCKLAND KIA 13/05/17	
6673 PTE	SANDERSON	JACOB R	DIS 392	
15971 PTE	SANDERSON	JAMES	TO MACHINE GUN CORPS MGC No 72671 CLASS Z RES 28/1/19	
16458 PTE	SAVILLE	JAMES PERCIVAL	WND 10/7/16 B COY TO ROYAL GUERNSEY LI RGLI No 2467 DIS 392	
16812 PTE	SCALES	JOHN GEORGE	ENL W HARTLEPOOL REP MISSING 10/9/16 ACTUALLY ON LEAVE 28/9/17 1/NORTH G HOSP NEWCASTLE GSW HEAD TO 4/DLI 5/11/17 TO 2/7/DLI 18/11/17 TO 15/DLI 22/7/18 KIA 2/10/18	
17568 PTE	SCARR	JOHN THOMAS	WND 5/8/16 D COY CLASS Z RES	
13573 PTE	SCHOLES	GEORGE MASON	ENL HULL 7/9/14 TO 4/S HOSP 5/10/15 TO DUTY 25/10/15 LCPL 22/7/16 KIA 4/8/16 C COY	
20957 PTE	SCOTT	HENRY	ATT 6/WEST YORKS REJOIN 13/DLI TO DEPOT DIS 392 ENL 23/10/17 DIS 24/4/17 SICK	
24797 SGT	SCOTT	HENRY	TO 3/DLI ATT KING'S AFRICAN RIFLES CLASS Z RES	
24779 PTE	SCOTT	JAMES	ENL GATESHEAD TO 18/DLI KIA 24/9/16	
17814 PTE	SCOTT	JOHN	ENL CONSETT LCPL KIA 10/7/16	
21178 PTE	SCOTT	PETER	WND 13/5/17 D COY ATT 23/DIV TUNN COY. 13/DLI. ATT 250 TUNN COY RE. TO 18/DLI.	
16816 PTE	SHAW	JOHN ROBERT	ENL STOCKTON 2/9/16 TO 2/CCS 26/G HOSP H SHIP CAMRIA TO UK TO DEPOT 17/11/15 TO 17/DLI 6/3/16 TO 13/DLI 1/6/16 WND 2/8/16 AT DUTY GSW L HAND D COY LCPL 2/9/16 KIA	
13633 CPL	SHEARER	ALEXANDER HALDANE	WND NIGHT 12/13/2/16 A COY DIS 392 LSGT	
19270 SGT	SHEARER	SYDNEY	ENL FELLING 14/9/14 FORMER SERVICE WITH 3/DLI SPEC RES SGT 6/10/14 KIA 2/8/16 C COY	
18098 PTE	SHIELDS	JOHN	CLASS Z RES	
23630 PTE	SHILLING	JAMES	WND 19/3/16 A COY DOW AT CCS 22/3/16	
15972 PTE	SHORTT	THOMAS	TO 11/DLI 31/3/17, 1/6/DLI, ENL 08/09/14, DURHAM, KiA 14/04/18 RES CROOK,	
15900 PTE	SHUKER	FRANK	TO 20/DLI, 10/DLI, 13/DLI, CLASS Z RES	
18139 PTE	SIDDLE	MATTHEW WILLIAM	ENL CONSETT 5/9/14 AGE 19 KIA 18/7/16 C COY FROM BLACKHILL	
21170 PTE	SILVERSIDES	CHARLES	WND 5/8/16 D COY TO R ENGINEERS RE No WR/278154 RENUMBERED 323704 R DEFENCE CORPS RDC No 66308 MEDALS ISSUED BY RE	
15132 PTE	SIMPSON	JOHN	ENL W HARTLEPOOL 31/8/14 LCPL 6/10/14 REVERTS 8/10/14 WND 24/7/16 B COY TO 57/FA - 34/CCS - 21/A TRN - 12/G HOSP DOW 6/9/16 L LEG AMPUTATED.	
17116 PTE	SIMPSON	JOHN	ENL 5/9/14 WND 26/3/16 C COY SIGNALLER MENDING WIRES DIS 14/11/19 KR PARA 392	
24752 CPL	SIMPSON	ROBERT	ENL W HARTLEPOOL L/SGT KIA 11/6/17	
19126 PTE	SLACK	JAMES	TO 16/DLI DIS 392 ENL 7/9/14 DIS 23/5/16	
21161 PTE	SLANE	PETER	ENL 27/10/14 RES LEADGATE DOW AT 24 CAS CLEARING STATION 23/6/18 SERVED IN A COY	
18483 SGT	SLEDGE	ARTHUR	CLASS Z RES DCM MM	
17768 PTE	SMAILES	JOHN LOGAN	TO LABOUR CORPS LAB C No 364090 CLASS Z RES 18/2/19	
17854 PTE	SMALL	CHRISTOPHER	DIS 392 ENL 9/9/14 DIS 29/3/19	
17807 CPL	SMITH	ARTHUR CHARLES	WND 17/2/16 WND 10/7/16 AT DUTY WND 24/9/16 C COY TO 19/DLI, 20/DLI, ARMY RES CLASS P DIS 392 ENL 3/9/14 DIS 26/4/19	
24743 PTE	SMITH	CHARLES	TO LABOUR CORPS LAB C No 604418 DIS 23/11/18	
18168 PTE	SMITH	ERNEST CURRY	ATT 2/HHBD, CLASS Z RES MM	
15901 PTE	SMITH	FREDERICK	WND 7/10/16 B COY TO NORTHUMBERLAND FUSILIERS NF No 64841	
24826 LCPL	SMITH	JOHN WILLIAM	WND 24/9/15 C COY DIS 392 MM	
17120 PTE	SMITH	PATRICK	TO LABOUR CORPS LAB C No 401973 CLASS Z RES 23/2/19	
3/11273 SGT	SMITH	PETER B	ENL DURHAM 11/9/14 CPL 6/10/14 PNR CPL 10/10/14 PNR SGT 28/11/14 WND TO 103/FA DOW 20/7/16 B COY	
19057 PTE	SMITH	RICHARD GARBUTT	ENL FELLING TRF FROM D COY TO C COY AS OFFICERS SERVANT ATT 3/ECHELON AS SERVANT TO SICK OFF 19/6/16 REJOINS 27/6/16 KIA 7/10/16 C COY	
24785 SGT	SMITH	THOMAS	ENL DURHAM KIA 5/8/16 B COY	
20017 PTE	SMITH	WILFRED	ENL SUNDERLAND 14/9/14 ATT 68/LTMB 26/12/15 TO 70/FA 11/2/16 BRONCHIAL CATARH TO DUTY 14/2/16 KIA 17/7/16	
24778 PTE	SMITH	WILLIAM	CLASS Z RES	
22611 SGT	SMITH	WILLIAM HENRY L	WND 23/9/16 A COY MM TO MACHINE GUN CORPS MGC No 172369 CLASS Z RES 23/2/19	
23663 PTE	SNAITH	GIBSON	ENL NEWCASTLE WND 28/7/16 ADM 3 CCS D COY DOW 4/8/16	
18519 PTE	SNAITH	WILLIAM	ENL GATESHEAD WND 28/7/17 KIA 7/10/16 C COY	

No.	Rank	Surname	Forename(s)	Notes
10577	SGT	SNELGAR	ARTHUR	REDUCED TO PTE BY FGCM 14/2/16 WND 28/7/16 SGT C COY TO NORTHUMBERLAND FUSILIERS A/CSM NF No 94503
17111	PTE	SNOWBALL	JOHN	ENL DURHAM 7/9/14 LCPL 31/7/16 KIA 30/9/16
23465	PTE	SNOWDON	PERCY G H	WND 3/12/15 ADM 3 CCS 5/12/15 GSW R THIGH EVAC 6/12/15 No 14 AMB TRAIN C COY TO 1/7/DLI CLASS Z RES
17744	PTE	SOWERBY	ARTHUR	ENL 5/9/14, KIA 11/11/15 BORN APPLEBY SERVED IN B COY
18198	SGT	SPOORS	JOSEPH PERCIVAL	WND 10/7/16 D COY DIS 392 ENL 7/9/14 DIS 28/4/19
15191	CPL	SPURGEON	HENRY HERBERT	WND 10/7/16 C COY TO 18/DLI, 12/DLI, 13/DLI, LSGT CLASS Z RES
16817	SGT	STABLER	JOHN	CLASS Z RES AWOII
18367	PTE	STAINBANK	ROBERT NORMAN	TO 18/DLI 2/DLI CLASS Z RES
17113	SGT	STAINSBY	CHARLES	ENL DURHAM 14/9/14 SGT 6/10/14 TO BASE DEPOT 6/2/16 HOSP SHIP DIEPPE 27/7/16 TO HOSP IN DEVON TO DEPOT 28/7/15 TO 17/DLI 24/8/16 DIED AUTORISM OF THE HEART 28/01/17
23461	PTE	STANNARD	FREDERICK	ENL 28/8/14 WND 9/7/16 C COY TO LAB CORPS LAB C No 563372 TO SOUTH LANCASHIRE REGT S LANCS No 37698 TO NORTHUMBERLAND FUSILIERS NF No 89897 DIS 392 5/11/19
16451	PTE	STEEL	JAMES	ENL GATESHEAD 8/9/14 DIED OF ASPHYXIA DUE TO BLOCKING OF THE PRIMA GLOTTIDIS 21/2/18
23463	PTE	STEEN	ADAM	ENL NEWCASTLE 29/8/14 TO 13/DLI 24/8/15 TO DEPOT 24/11/15 TO 14/DLI 30/3/16 KIA 18/9/16 FORMERLY 6823 10/NF TRF AT OWN REQUEST
16894	PTE	STENSON	THOMAS HENRY	CLASS Z RES
16902	PTE	STEPHENS	WILLIAM	ENL W HARTLEPOOL 1/9/14 KIA 28/7/16
21618	SGT	STIRLING	CHARLES ALBERT	CQMS MM, CLASS Z RES
18024	SGT	STODDART	WILLIAM	TO ROYAL DEFENCE CORPS RDC No 66156 IN FRANCE 25/8/15 TO 23/12/16
21030	LSGT	STOKOE	WILLIAM	WND 9/2/16 B COY TO LINCOLNSHIRE REGT LINCOLNS No 38504 DIS 392 11/10/17
15379	PTE	STOREY	JAMES	TO ARMY RES CLASS W DIS 392 ENL 2/9/14 DIS 22/1/17
21151	PTE	STOREY	WILLIAM	ENL CONSETT 27/10/14 LCPL 18/8./15 CPL 14/3/16 KIA 6/4/16 C COY DIRECT HIT ON DUGOUT
17118	PTE	STOREY	WILLIAM ERNEST	TO ROYAL DEFENCE CORPS RDC No 66907 IN FRANCE 25/08/15 TO 20/7/16, WND TO UK IN FRANCE DLI BASE DEPOT 24/1/17 TO 20/2/17 TO 12/DLI 21/2/17 TO 7/5/17
18358	PTE	STOTT	JOSEPH	WND 8/7/16 A COY TO 19/DLI, CLASS Z RES
16151	CPL	STOUT	GEORGE	DIS 392 ENL 8/9/14 DIS 12/11/16
17773	PTE	STRAKER	GEORGE	CLASS Z RES
17115	PTE	STRINGER	HENRY	ENL DURHAM C COY KIA 19/10/15
20525	PTE	STRONG	GEORGE	ATT 23/DIV APM, CLASS Z RES
20595	PTE	STRONG	GEORGE	WND 20/10/15 A COY CLASS Z RES
16915	SGT	STUBBINGS	HARRY	ENL DARLINGTON 15/9/14 LCPL 6/10/14 CPL 22/1/15 SGT 8/33/16 REVERTS 20/5/16 LSGT 1/6/16 SGT 4/6/16 KIA 2/8/16 A COY
17107	PTE	SUDDER	WILLIAM R	CLASS Z RES
17108	PTE	SUDDES	THOMAS	CLASS Z RES MM 21/7/16
20913	PTE	SULLIVAN	JOHN WILLIAM	TO LABOUR CORPS LAB C No 376588 CLASS Z RES 10/3/19
18319	PTE	SUMMERSON	ROBERT	WND SHELLSHOCK 12/4/16 B COY TO LABOUR CORPS LAB C No 542226 DIS 25/10/19
14072	PTE	SWAN	PETER JOSEPH	WND 3/6/16 C COY TO DEPOT DIS 392 ENL 15/9/14 DIS 16/9/16
13222	PTE	SWORD	FREDERICK	ENL DURHAM 3/9/14 LCPL 6/10/14 CPL 8/3/15 REVERTS PTE 2/7/15 GSW BACK 20/7/16 C COY 70/FA- 2/CCS - 13/G HOSP H SHIP UK TO DEPOT 10/10/16 TO 18/DLI 2/3/17 LCPL 19/5/17 KIA 29/6/17
19100	PTE	TAGUE	JOHN WILLIAM	WND 6/7/16 A COY TO 20/DLI,19/DLI, ATT IBD, 19/DLI, 22/DLI, 1/7/DLI, CLASS Z RES
21602	LCPL	TATTERS	JAMES	ENL GATESHEAD 8/9/14 WND 8/7/16 A COY TO 23/DRS GSW SHLDR REJOINS 12/7/16 TO DEPOT 28/11/16 SICK ON LEAVE UK 11/5/18 9/CCS - 31/A TRN REJOINS 12/9/18 DIS 5/10/18
21622	CQMS	TAYLOR	EDWARD SAMUEL	DIS TO COMMISSION 15/8/18 FROM STOCKTON ON TEES
19939	PTE	TAYLOR	HENRY	WND 4/6/16 SELF INFLICTED A COY TO LABOUR CORPS LAB C No 553471 DIS 19/3/19
19061	SGT	TAYLOR	ROBERT WILLIAM	ENL GATESHEAD 7/9/14 LCPL 4/5/16 TO 71/FA - 18/CCS - 10/A TRN - 16-G HOSP 9/5/16 REJOINS 7/6/16 CPL 24/7/16 SGT 27/8/16 KIA 2/6/17
21598	PTE	TAYLOR	THOMAS WILLIAM	WND 13/5/17 B COY TO DEPOT DIS 392 ENL 4/9/14 DIS 2/3/18
19948	PTE	TAYLORSON	DAVID	WND 28/5/17 D COY TO DEPOT DIS 392 ENL 7/9/14 DIS 15/10/17
17631	PTE	TEASDALE	THOMAS	TO DEPOT DIS 392 ENL 2/9/14 DIS 9/10/16 SICK
21146	PTE	TEMPLE	WILLIAM	TO ROYAL DEFENCE CORPS RDC No 66332 IN FRANCE 25/8/15 TO 9/7/16
20934	PTE	THIRLWELL	WILLIAM	WND 18/7/16 D COY TO RIFLE BRIGADE RIF BDE No 45289 MIDDLESEX REGT MDSX No G/44767
15915	PTE	THOMAS	SCOTT	WND 28/12/15 A COY COMMISSIONED 3/DLI 25/9/17 MISSING 27/5/18 FROM LANCHESTER
17935	PTE	THOMPSON	ALEXANDER	WND 4/8/16 C COY DESERTED DIS 392 ENL 6/9/14 DIS 29/3/19
23462	PTE	THOMPSON	DAVID	TO LABOUR CORPS LAB C No 406330 DIS 11/11/18
24800	PTE	THOMPSON	JAMES	TO 14/DLI TO DEPOT DIS 392 ENL 15/4/15 DIS 26/10/17
17125	PTE	THOMPSON	JAMES A U	TO MACHINE GUN CORPS MGC No 72672 CLASS Z RES 28/1/19
19303	PTE	THOMPSON	JOHN	WND 5/8/16 D COY CLASS Z RES
19303	PTE	THOMPSON	JOHN	CLASS Z RES ACPL
16470	PTE	THOMPSON	THOMAS HENRY	ENL GATESHEAD 6/9/14 GSW R HAND 10/7/16 34/CCS - A TRN - 8/S HOSP ATT 2/AUS G HOSP FOR DUTY 24/7/16 TO 10/DLI 28/8/16 TO 43/FA - 38/CCS - 9/G HOSP TO UK H SHIP ASTURIAS TO DEPOT 28/9/16 2 TRG RES BN TO 19/DLI REPOSTED 12/DLI, 24/1/17 LCPL 25/5/17 WND & MISSING 7/6/17
18124	SGT	THOMPSON	WILLIAM HENRY	CLASS Z RES MM
24792	PTE	THOMSON	WILLIAM	ENL SOUTH ASHFORD WND 24/9/15 C COY DOW HOME 6/10/15
13864	PTE	TILLEY	WILLIAM ALFRED	CLASS Z RES
15893	SGT	TILLOTT	ALEXANDER	ENL DURHAM 5/9/14 LCPL 6/10/14 CPL 22/1/15 L/SGT 15/6/15 SGT 14/3/16 GSW L ARM TO 12/G HOSP H SHIP ST ANDREW TO UK 13/7/16 TO 20/DLI 9/1/17 REPOSTED 13/DLI 10/1/17 ATT 23/DIV REINF CAMP, 13/DLI KIA 5/10/18
17124	CPL	TINDALE	ROBERT W	WND 9/7/16 D COY SHELL SHOCK TO 1/TRAINING RES BN TRG RES No TR/5/976 DIS 392 ENL 5/9/14 DIS 1/1/17
23578	PTE	TODD	GEORGE WILLIAM	ENL SOUTH SHIELDS 6/2/15 KIA 10/7/16
18125	CPL	TOMANEY	JAMES	TO LABOUR CORPS LAB C No 566215 CLASS Z RES 24/1/19
13304	CPL	TONKIN	JAMES	CLASS Z RES MM CPL
18572	SGT	TOWERS	ALEC	DIS 392 ENL 31/8/14 DIS 17/12/18
21035	PTE	TRAINOR	HUGH	TO 1/9/DLI, DIS 392 ENL 26/10/14 DIS 29/3/19
20013	PTE	TREES	JOHN HENRY	CLASS Z RES
23438	PTE	TREWITT	THOMAS HENRY	TO DEPOT DIS 392 ENL 31/8/14 DIS 27/8/16 GSW WND R ELBOW

Number	Rank	Surname	Forename	Details
20425	PTE	TROTT	ALFRED	TO ARMY RES CLASS W DIS 392 ENL 6/10/14 DIS 22/1/17
18707	LCPL	TROTTER	JOHN	ENL CHESTER LE STREET 2/9/14 LCPL 6/9/16 KIA 19/9/16 B COY
19133	PTE	TROTTER	WILLIAM	WND 5/8/16 A COY TO 20/DLI, 2/DLI, DIS 392 ENL 8/9/14 DIS 24/1/19
19065	PTE	TRUEMAN	MATTHEW	ENL FELLING 7/9/14 LCPL 14/8/16 CPL 4/9/16 L/SGT 17/10/16 REVERTS PTE 24/11/16 GSW BUTTOCKS 5/10/18 TO 55/CCS DOW & DOUBLE PNEUMONIA 19/10/18
20565	PTE	TUNNICLIFFE	WILLIAM TRAVES	ENL HULL 1/9/14 WND GSW HEAD 19/9/16 TO 36 CCS - AMB TRAIN 11 GEN HOSP CAMIERS TO No 6 CONV DEPOT 28/10/16 TO 35 IBD 30/10/16 TO 13/DLI 11/10/16 KIA 13/5/17 B COY
19949	PTE	TURNBULL	WILLIAM JOHN	DIS 392 ENL 7/9/14 DIS 26/5/16
17126	PTE	TURNER	GEORGE	CLASS Z RES
18059	PTE	TURRELL	FREDERICK	WND 27/11/15 GSW L THIGH ADM 3 CCS 28/11/15 EVAC 29/11/15 No 1 AMB TRAIN D COY ENL 4/9/14, DIS 392 3/4/16 TO DEPOT
17132	PTE	TWEDDLE	GEORGE	WND 24/9/16 CCOY TO MANCHESTER REGT MANC REGT No 44923
13331	PTE	TYSON	JOHN WILLIAM	ENL NEWCASTLE 5/9/14 WND NIGHT 12/13/2/16 A COY SHRPN WND FACE TO 26/FA -DRS REJOINED GSW CHEST 3/6/16 - TO 2/CAN G HOSP H SHIP ST ANDREW TO UK 13/6/16 TO 4/DLI 7/2/17 TO 35/IBD 17/5/17 TO 22/DLI REPOSTED 14/DLI KIA 19/10/17
13634	PTE	UMPLEBY	JOHN ROBERT	WND 7/10/16 C COY TO 18/DLI, 14/DLI, CLASS Z RES
19957	PTE	URWIN	RALPH	TO ARMY RES CLASS W DIS 392 ENL 5/9/14 DIS 31/10/16
13492	PTE	URWIN	THOMAS	DIS 392 ENL 4/9/14 DIS 13/9/16
19046	PTE	USHER	WILLIAM	ATT 176 TUNN COY RE, CLASS Z RES
18128	PTE	VAYRO	HARRY	CLASS Z RES LCPL
18489	PTE	VIPOND	HENRY	WND 18/7/16 A COY CLASS Z RES
16429	PTE	VIPOND	JOHN ELLIOTT	ENL CONSETT 8/9/14 TO 69/FA ICT BOTH FEET WND 7/10/16 C COY TO 2/FA SHELL WND CHEST FACE & L HAND TO 45/CCS EDGEHILL DOW 14/10/16 MM
19945	SGT	WALDRAM	LEONARD JAMES	CLASS Z RES MM
24776	PTE	WALKER	HENRY	ENL CROOK REP MISSING 16/7/16 D COY TO 12/DLI 15/DLI KIA 3/5/17
17707	SGT	WALKER	HUGH	CLASS Z RES
17717	PTE	WALKER	JESSE	ENL 4/9/14, KIA 30/12/15 . FROM BIRTLEY
23576	PTE	WALKER	ROBERT	ENL SOUTH SHIELDS 5/2/15 IN MULTIPLE FA & CCS BETWEEN 11/10/15 & 10/3/16 UNTIL EVAC ON H SHIP ST DENNIS ON 24/3/16 DIED IN VAD HOSP EXETER 8/4/16
23651	PTE	WALTERS	FRANCIS	WND 9/7/16 C COY TO 3/DLI DIS 392 ENL 23/2/15 DID 14/8/17
14783	PTE	WALTON	ERNEST	ENL MIDDLESBROUGH KIA 9/7/16 B COY
23440	PTE	WALTON	JOHN	TO 18/DLI ATT IBD CLASS Z RES
24749	PTE	WALTON	JOHN W	WND 9/7/16 B COY TO NORTHUMBERLAND FUSILIERS NF No 5/6778 RENUMBERED 242009 DIS 392
15163	SGT	WANLEY	THOMAS	CLASS Z RES
16167	PTE	WARBURTON	JONAS	TO 12/DLI, ATT 2/YORK & LANCS, CLASS Z RES
15166	PTE	WARD	HAROLD	TO DEPOT DIS 392 ENL 31/8/14 DIS 18/3/18
21137	PTE	WARDLE	JAMES	WND 19/9/16 B COY TO ARMY RES CLASS P DIS 392 ENL 27/10/14 DIS 25/5/17
18130	PTE	WARNER	GEORGE HENRY W	ENL BISHOP AUCKLAND LCPL DOW 8/10/18
21118	CPL	WATSON	EDWARD	WND 4/8/16 D COY TO ARMY RESERVE CLASS P DIS 392 ENL 5/9/14 DIS 10/4/17
13267	CPL	WATSON	JAMES	ENL MIDDLESBROUGH WND 30/9/16 LSGT B COY DOW 2/10/16
13632	PTE	WATSON	JOHN EDWARD	ENL SUNDERLAND LSGT KIA 25/08/17
16874	PTE	WATT	ROBERT	ENL W HARTLEPOOL KIA 4/11/15 B COY
18477	PTE	WEARMOUTH	GEORGE	ENL CROOK 7/9/14 7/9/15 TO 15/CCS ICT FEET TO DUTY 12/9/15 ATT 68/MG COY 14/3/16 MISSING 10/7/16
13261	PTE	WEATHERLEY	ARTHUR	WND 5/1/16 A COY REPORTED AS 18261 DIS 392 ENL 2/9/14 DIS 31/3/19
17943	CPL	WEATHERLEY	MATTHEW	ENL FELLING 7/9/14 LCPL 20/12/15 CPL 11/7/16 KIA 4/8/16 A COY
14854	PTE	WEATHERSPOON	G	WND 18/7/16 B COY TO TANK CORPS TC No 302119
17137	PTE	WEBSTER	WADDINGTON	CLASS Z RES MM
15935	PTE	WELFORD	ANTHONY	CLASS Z RES
20940	PTE	WEST	RALPH	CLASS Z RES
21335	PTE	WHALEY	ALBERT HEWITSON	ENL CONSETT 3/11/14 KIA 22/9/17
19023	PTE	WHARTON	JOSEPH ROBERT	ENL 5/9/14 FERRYHILL LCPL 6/10/14 CPL 10/8/15 REVERTS AT OWN REQUEST 6/10/15 KIA 12/10/17
20579	PTE	WHEATLEY	JOHN JAMES	TO LABOUR CORPS LAB C No 29264 CLASS Z RES 17/5/19
23449	PTE	WHEATLEY	JOSEPH	MIC IDICATES DEAD NOT IB=N SDGW OR CWGC DEAD
18386	CPL	WHEELER	JOHN EDWARD	TO LABOUR CORPS LAB C No 182365 DIS 17/2/19
20774	PTE	WHITE	FRANK	WND 8/10/16 D COY TO WORCESTERSHIRE REGT WORC REGT No 62800 TO LABOUR CORPS LAB CORPS No 44689 DIS
21630	PTE	WHITE	JAMES	WND 4/8/16 C COY TO LABOUR CORPS LAB C No 327409 CLASS Z RES 20/1/19
19988	PTE	WHITELOCK	WILLIAM	WND 31/1/17 C COY TO DEPOT DIS 392 ENL 13/9/14 DIS 12/1/19
16592	PTE	WHITFIELD	GEORGE	TO 1/7/DLI, 19/DLI, CLASS Z RES
21336	PTE	WHITFIELD	SAMSON	CLASS Z RES
19986	PTE	WIDDRINGTON	WILLIAM	SEC B A RES
13296	PTE	WILFORD	LANCELOT	WND 9/7/16 D COY TO LABOUR CORPS LAB C No 167374 TO ROYAL FUSILIERS R FUS No 144181
18050	PTE	WILKINSON	EDWARD	DIS 392 ENL 2/9/14 DIS 2/12/19 MM
17809	PTE	WILKINSON	JOHN JOSEPH	ENL CONSETT 8/9/14 LCPL 15/3/15 REVERTS 27/11/15 WND 18/7/16 C COY TO 10/DLI 24/8/16 18/DLI REPOSTED 13/DLI 18/4/17 KIA 20/9/17 MM
18068	PTE	WILKINSON	JOSEPH	WND 20/7/16 C COY TO NORTHUMBERLAND FUSILIERS NF No 40439 DIS 392 26/3/19
18499	PTE	WILKINSON	WILLIAM	ENL GATESHEAD 8/9/14 WND 17/9/16 A COY SHRPN WND SHLDR TO 1/3/NTHBN FA - 13/CCS - 1/STH MID CCS - A TRN TO 4/G HOSP TO 6/CONV DEPOT TO DUTY 23/9/16 KIA 5/10/18
17148	PTE	WILLIAMS	SAMUEL	WND 9/7/16 C COY TO ROYAL DEFENCE CORPS RDC No 82000 IN FRANCE 25/8/15 TO
17649	PTE	WILLIAMS	WILLIAM HENRY	CLASS Z RES
21152	PTE	WILLIAMSON	GEORGE	WND 25/12/15 BY ENEMY SHELL ON BILLETS B COY DOW 26/12/15 AT 26 FLD AMB RAMC
16847	SGT	WILLIS	FRANK	ENL NOTTINGHAM 7/9/14 LCPL 6/10/14 CPL 1/12/14 LSGT 15/6/15 SGT 13/1/16 KIA 8/10/16 D COY
15873	PTE	WILSON	ALFRED	ENL GATESHEAD 3/9/14 TO 69/FA ARTHRITIS 16/12/15 TO DUTY 31/12/15 23/DRS 8/7/16 - 33CCS -12/G HOSP DAH REJOINS 17/9/16 ADMT 1/NORTHN G HOSP NEWCASTLE 10/12/16 REJOINS 25/5/17 KIA 3/6/17
15296	PTE	WILSON	FRANCIS JAMES	ENL W HARTLEPOOL 4/9/14 TO 71/FA 21/9/17 TO DUTY TO 9/CCS 27/4/18 - 21/A TRN 71/FA - 23DRS ?/5/18 WND & MISSING 10/10/18
13965	PTE	WILSON	GEORGE	TO ARMY RES CLASS P DIS 392 ENL 3/9/14 DIS 24/4/19

20569	PTE	WILSON	JOHN	WND 4/8/16 C COY TO SOUTH STAFFORDSHIRE REGT S STAFFS No 34111
25293	PTE	WILSON	THOMAS	TO 3/DLI DIS 392 ENL 5/9/14 DIS 17/12/18
16514	PTE	WILSON	WILFRED	TO 18/DLI, 1/5/DLI, 1/7/DLI, DISEMBODIED
18096	PTE	WILSON	WILLIAM	ATT 68 BDE HQ, 13/DLI, CLASS Z RES
17141	PTE	WIND	SINCLAIR	WND 10/7/16 A COY TO 3/TRAINING RES BN TRG RES No TR/5/8660 DIS 392 ENL 5/9/14 DIS 6/1/17 WNDS
21036	PTE	WOOD	ANDREW	ENL FELLING TO 69/FA 18/15 - 23/DRS TO DUTY KIA 6/1/16 D COY
15192	SGT	WOOD	AUSTIN EVART	ATT GHQ, CLASS Z RES
21063	PTE	WOOD	GEORGE	ENL FELLING DOW 8/10/18
22295	SGT	WOOD	SAMUEL	CLASS Z RES
15965	PTE	WOOD	JAMES	ENL DURHAM 8/9/14 WND 4/8/16 C COY GSW FACE TO 11/S HOSP - H SHIP ST GEORGE TO UK TO DEPOT 7/8/16 CMD DEPOT RIPON 4/10/16 - 3/DLI 3/11/16 TO 20/DLI 9/1/17 KIA 24/2/17
18094	PTE	WOODHEAD	HERBERT	WND 9/7/16 C COY TO NORTHUMBERLAND FUSILIERS NF No 40356 SGT CLASS Z RES
21605	CPL	WOODWARD	WILLIAM	ENL B AUCKLAND 8/9/14 LCPL 26/3/15 CPL 30/10/15 LSGT 27/8/16 A SGT 4/9/16 WND & MISSING 7/10/16 A COY
21603	LCPL	WORTON	JOSEPH CHARLES	WND 17/7/16 A COY DIS 392 DCM
17140	PTE	WRAY	JOHN	CLASS Z RES
21138	PTE	WRAY	MATTHEW	TO 19/DLI, 18/DLI, CLASS Z RES
18101	SGT	WRIGHT	ALFRED	CLASS Z RES
16857	PTE	YARDLEY	HERBERT	TO LABOUR CORPS LAB C No 610192 CLASS Z RES 24/2/19
15334	PTE	YOUNG	GEORGE	CLASS Z RES
24808	PTE	YOUNG	GEORGE WILLIAM	WND SHELL SHOCK 1/7/16 D COY TO 14/DLI 20/DLI 15/DLI CLASS Z RES

96030 Private Jasper Tewart, from West Cornforth, County Durham, joined 13/DLI in France in late 1918 and was transferred to Class Z Reserve having survived the war.